GROUND WARFARE

An International Encyclopedia

INTERNATIONAL WARFARE ENCYCLOPEDIAS FROM ABC-CLIO

Spencer C. Tucker, General Editor

Air Warfare: An International Encyclopedia, Walter J. Boyne, Editor

Naval Warfare: An International Encyclopedia, Spencer C. Tucker, Editor

Ground Warfare: An International Encyclopedia, Stanley Sandler, Editor

GROUND WARFARE

An International Encyclopedia

VOLUME TWO, H–Q

EDITED BY
Stanley Sandler

ASSOCIATE EDITORS
Michael Ashkenazi
Paul D. Buell

FOREWORD BY
General Henry H. Shelton, USA (R)

ABC CLIO

Santa Barbara, California Denver, Colorado Oxford, England

Library of Congress Cataloging-in-Publication Data
Sandler, Stanley, 1937–
Ground warfare : an international encyclopedia / Stanley Sandler ; foreword by Henry H. Shelton.
p. cm
Includes bibliographical references and index.
ISBN 1-57607-344-0 (Hardcover: alk. paper) — Ebook ISBN 1-57607-733-0
1. Battles—Encyclopedias. 2. Military history—Encyclopedias. 3. Military biography—Encyclopedias. I. Title.
D25.A2 S26 2002
355'.003—dc21

2002004568

07 06 05 04 03 02 10 9 8 7 6 5 4 3 2 1

This book is also available on the World Wide Web as an e-book. Visit abc-clio.com for details.

ABC-CLIO, Inc.
130 Cremona Drive, P.O. Box 1911
Santa Barbara, California 93116-1911

This book is printed on acid-free paper.
Manufactured in the United States of America

EDITORIAL BOARD

CONTENTS

A-TO-Z LIST OF ENTRIES

Ferdinand, Karl Wilhelm, Duke of Brunswick (1735–1806)
Film and War
Finances, Military
Finnish Civil War (1918)
Firearms
Fleurus, Battle of (26 June 1794)
Flipper, Henry Ossian (21 March 1856–3 May 1940)
Flodden, Battle of (9 September 1513)
Foch, Ferdinand (1851–1929)
Fontenoy (1745)
Fontenoy en Puisaye, Battle of (France, 25 June 841)
Forrest, Nathan Bedford (1821–1877)
Fort Donelson (11–16 February 1862)
Fort Duquesne, Seizure of (1758)
Fort Sumter (12–14 April 1861)
Fort Ticonderoga
France (1940)
France and the American Revolution
Franco, Francisco (1892–1975)
Franco-German War (978–980)
Franco-Prussian War (1870–1871)
Franco-Spanish War (1648–1659)
Frankish Civil Wars (670–719)
Frankish-Moorish Wars (718–759)
Franklin, Battle of (30 November 1864)
Franks
Frederick I Barbarossa (1152–1190)
Frederick II (1194–1250)
Frederick the Great, King of Prussia (1712–1786)
Frederick William, Elector of Brandenburg (1620–1688)
Frederick William I, King of Prussia (1688–1740)
Fredericksburg (11–15 December 1862)
French, John Denton Pinkstone, First Earl of Ypres (1852–1925)
French and Indian War (1759–1763)
French Army
French Colonial Wars (1800–1939)
French Foreign Legion
French Revolutionary Wars (1792–1802)
French Wars of Religion (1562–1598)
Friedland (14 June 1807)
Fronde, Wars of the (1648–1653)
Frunze, Mikhail Vasil'evich (1885–1925)
Fuller, John Frederick Charles (1878–1966)

Gage, Thomas (1721–1787)
Gallic Wars (58–51 B.C.E.)
Galliéni, Joseph Simon (1849–1916)
Gallipoli (1915–1916)
Gamelin, Maurice (1872–1958)
Garibaldi, Giuseppe (1807–1882)
Gates, Horatio (1728–1806)
Gaugamela, Battle of (1 October 331 B.C.E.)
de Gaulle, General Charles (1890–1970)
Gempei War (1180–1185)
General Order No. 100 (24 April 1863)
Geneva Conventions (1864–1949)
Genghis Khan (c. 1162–1227)
German Army
German Colonial Wars (1884–1919)
German Wars of Unification (1864–1871)
Germantown (1777)
Geronimo (c. 1827–1909)
Gettysburg (American Civil War, 1–3 July 1863)
Ghaznavid Empire (977–1180)
Gibraltar, Siege of (1779–1783)
Gierczak, Emilia (1925–1945)
Glendower's Revolt (1400–1413)
Gneisenau, August Neidhart von (1760–1831)
Goethals, George Washington (1858–1928)
Goose Green, Battle for (28–29 May 1982)
Gordon, Charles George ("Chinese" Gordon) (1833–1885)
Goring, Hermann Wilhelm (1893–1946)
Gorlice/Tarnow (May 1915)
Gothic War (534–554)
Goths
Gotthard Abbey (1664)
Grand Alliance, War of the (1688–1697)
Grandson and Morat, Battles of (Switzerland, 2 March and 22 June 1476)
Granicus, Battle of the (May/June 334 B.C.E.)
Grant, Ulysses Simpson (1822–1885)
Great Wall of China (16th Century)
Greco-Turkish War (1920–1922)
Greek Civil War (1944–1949)
Greek War of Independence (1821–1832)
Greek-Persian Wars (499–448 B.C.E.)
Greene, Nathanael (1742–1786)
Grenada (October 1983)
Gribeauval, Jean Baptiste Vaquette de (1715–1789)
Grotius, Hugo (1583–1645)
Guadalajara (8–18 March 1937)
Guadalcanal (August 1942–February 1943)
Guatemalan Civil War (1954)
Guderian, Heinz (17 June 1888–14 May 1954)
Guernica, Bombing of (April 1937)
Guerrilla/Partisan/Irregular Warfare
Guevara de la Serna, Ernesto "Che" (1928–1967)
Guilford Court House (15 March 1781)
Guinea-Bissauan War of Independence (1961–1975)
Guiscard, Robert (1016–1085)
Guise, François de Lorraine, Second Duke of (1519–1563)

Meuse-Argonne (26 September–11 November 1918)
Mexican Revolution (1810–1821)
Mexican Unrest and Civil War (1911–1929)
Mexican-American War (1846–1848)
Mexico, U.S. Punitive Expedition in (1916–1917)
Mexico City, Battles for (20 August–14 September 1847)
Miles, Nelson Appleton (1839–1925)
Military and Society
Military Justice
Military-Industrial Complex
Milne Bay (1942)
Milvian Bridge, Battle of (28 October 312)
Minamoto, Yoshitsune (1159–1189)
Minden (1 August 1759)
Minié Ball
Mithradatic Wars (88–63 B.C.E.)
Mogul-Persian Wars (1622–1653)
Mohács, Battles of (29 August 1526, 12 August 1687)
Mohi or Sajo River, Battle of (April 1241)
Moltke, Graf Helmuth Johannes Ludwig von (1848–1916)
Moltke, Graf Helmuth Karl Bernhard von (1800–1891)
Mongol Empire (1206–1259)
Mongol-Song Wars (1267–1279)
Monmouth (27–28 June 1778)
Mons Graupius, Battle of (September 83)
Montcalm-Gozon, Louis-Joseph de, Marquis de Montcalm de Saint-Véran (1712–1759)
Montecuccoli, Raimondo, Prince (1609–1680)
Monterrey (20–24 September 1846)
Montgomery, Bernard Law (1887–1976)
Montmorency, Anne, Duc de (1493–1567)
Montrose, James Graham, Marquis of (1612–1650)
Mormon War (1838–1839)
Mortars
Mosby, John Singleton (1833–1916)
Moscow (30 September 1941–April 1942)
Moscow, Retreat from (19–23 October 1812)
Mount Badon, Battle of (c. 490–516)
Mountbatten of Burma, Louis Francis Albert Victor Nicholas (1900–1979)
Mountjoy, Charles Blount, Lord (1562–1606)
Mozambican War of Independence (1963–1974)
Muhammad Ahmad (al-Mahdi, Muhammad Ahmad Ibn As-Sayyid' Abd Allah) (1844–1885)
Muhammad Ali (c. 1770–1849)
Muhammad of Ghur, Conquests of (1175–1206)
Muhlberg, Battle of (24 April 1547)
Mukden, Battle of (21 February–10 March 1905)
Murat, Joachim, Grand Duke of Cleves-Berg, King of Naples (1767–1815)
Murfreesboro (31 December 1862–2 January 1863)
Musa ibn Nusayr (c. 640–714)
Music, Military
Muslim Civil War (656–661)
Muslim Civil War (861–870)
Muslim Conquests (624–982)
Mutaguchi, Renya (1888–1966)
Mysore Wars (1767–1799)

Nadir Shah (a.k.a. Tahmasp Qoli Khan) (1688–1747)
Nagashino, Battle of (1575)
Napalm
Napier, Sir Charles James (1782–1853)
Napoleon I (1769–1821)
Napoleonic Wars (1803–1815)
Narses (c. 478–c. 574)
Naseby (14 June 1645)
Nashville, Battle of (2–15 December 1864)
National Security Agency/Central Security Service
Navarro, Pedro, Count of Olivetto (c. 1460–1528)
Ndlela kaSompisi Ntuli (?–1840)
Německý Brod (Deutschbrod) (1422)
Neville's Cross, Battle of (17 October 1346)
New Orleans, Battle of (8 January 1815)
Ney, Michel, Duc d'Elchingen, Prince de La Moskova (1769–1815)
Nez Percé (June–October 1877)
Nicaragua, Walker's Invasion of (1855–1857)
Nicaraguan Civil War (1925–1933)
Nicaraguan Civil War (1979)
Nicephorus II Phocas (r. 963–969)
Nicholas, Grand Duke (1856–1929)
Nieuport (1600)
Nigerian Civil War (1967–1970)
Nightingale, Florence (1820–1910)
Nine Years' War (1595–1604)
Nivelle, Robert (1856–1924)
Nogi, Maresuke (1843–1912)
Nongovernmental (Extranational) Organizations: Their Role in War and in the Wake of War
Nordlingen (1634)
Norman Conquest (1066–1072)
Norman-Byzantine Wars (1081–1108)
Normandy Landings (1944)
North Atlantic Treaty Organization (founded 4 April 1949)
Northern Ireland, Civil War in (1969–present)
Northern War, Great (January 1700–August 1721)
Northern War, Second (1655–1660)
Norway and Denmark, Invasion of (9 April–10 June 1940)
Novgorod, Muscovite Conquest of (1471–1479)
Nuclear and Atomic Weapons

Sedan (1–2 September 1870)
Sedgemoor (5–6 July 1685)
Seeckt, Hans von (1866–1936)
Sekigahara (1600)
Seljuqs
Sempach, Battle of (9 July, 1386)
Sennacherib (r. 705–681 B.C.E.)
Septimius Severus (Lucius Septimius Severus Pius Pertinax) (146–211)
Sevastopol, Siege of (October 1854–11 September 1855)
Seven Days' Battles (25 June–1 July 1862)
Seven Years' War (1756–1763)
Shaka kaSenzangakhona (c. 1787–1828)
Shapur I (r. 240–272)
Shapur II (309–379)
Shays's "Rebellion" (1786–1787)
Sheridan, Philip Henry (1831–1888)
Sherman, William Tecumseh (1820–1891)
Sherman's March to the Sea (mid-November–December 21, 1864)
Shiloh (6–7 April 1862)
Shimabara Revolt (1637–1638)
Short, Walter Campbell (1880–1949)
Siamese (Thai)–Burmese Wars (1548–1792)
Sicilian-Byzantine Wars (1147–1185)
Sidi Barrani (1940)
Sikorski, Wladyslaw Eugeniusz (1881–1943)
Silla Kingdom
Sinai-Suez Offensive (1956–1957)
Singapore (1942)
Sino-Japanese War (1894–1895)
Sino-Japanese War (1937–1945)
Sino-Korean Wars and the Wars of Korean Unification (598–676)
Sioux Wars (1862–1891)
Sitting Bull (1831–1890)
Six-Day War (5–10 June 1967)
Slim, William Joseph, First Viscount (1891–1970)
Smolensk (1941)
Smuts, Jan Christian (1870–1950)
Soccer War (1969)
Solferino (24 June 1859)
Somalia, U.S. Military Operations in (1987–2000)
The Somme (1916)
Songhay Empire (15th–16th Centuries)
Song-Jin Wars (1125–1141)
Sonni 'Ali (d. 1492)
Sosabowski, Stanislaw Franciszek (1892–1967)
Soult, Nicolas-Jean de Dieu (1769–1851)
South Africa/Namibia (1960–2000)
South American Wars of Independence (1810–1824)
Soviet-Afghan War (1979–1989)
Spanish Civil War (1936–1939)
Spanish Colonial Wars (1492–1898)
Spanish Succession, War of the (1701–1714)
Spanish-American War (1898)
Spanish-Portuguese Wars (1580–1763)
Special Operations Executive (SOE)
Special Operations Forces
Spotsylvania Court House (12–20 May 1864)
Sri Lankan Civil War (1983–)
SS
St. Clair's Defeat (4 November 1791)
St. Gotthard Abbey (1664)
St. Mihiel (12–16 September 1918)
St. Quentin (10 August 1557)
Stalin (Iosif Vissarionovich Dzhugashvili) (1878 or 1879–1953)
Stalingrad (17 July 1942–2 February 1943)
Stamford Bridge, Battle of (25 September 1066)
Steuben, Friedrich Wilhelm Augustin, Freiherr von (1730–1794)
Stilicho, Flavius (365–408)
Stilwell, Joseph Warren (1883–1946)
Stimson, Henry Lewis (1867–1950)
Stirling Bridge (11 September 1297)
Stuart, James Ewell Brown ("Jeb") (1833–1864)
Student, Kurt (1890–1978)
Sudanese Civil War (1955–)
Süleyman I (c. 1495–1566)
Sulla, Lucius Cornelius (138–78 B.C.E.)
Sumter, Thomas (1734–1832)
Sundjata (c. 1215–c. 1255)
Sun-tzu (Sunzi) (fl. 500 B.C.E.)
Suvorov, Aleksandr Vasilyevich (1729–18 May 1800)
Swinton, Sir Ernest Dunlop (1868–1951)
Swiss Neutrality, Defense of
Syracuse, Siege of (415–413 B.C.E.)
Syrian-Egyptian Wars (274–168 B.C.E.)

Tactics
Taginae, Battle of (552)
Taiping Rebellion (1850–1864)
Takeda, Shingen (1521–1573)
Talas River, Battle of (July 751)
Tamerlane (Temürlenk, 1336–1405)
Tannenberg, Battle of (15 July 1410)
Tannenberg and the Masurian Lakes (25–30 August, 9–13 September 1914)
Tarawa (20–23 November 1943)
Tariq ibn Ziyad (fl. 711–712)
Taylor, Zachary (1784–1850)

Waterloo (18 June 1815)
Wavell, Archibald Percival, First Earl (1883–1950)
Wayne, Anthony (1745–1796)
Wellington, Arthur Wellesley, Duke of (1769–1852)
Westmoreland, William (1914–)
Weyler y Nicolau, Valeriano, Marquis of Tenerife (1838–1930)
Whiskey Rebellion (1794)
White Mountain, Battle of (Weißer Berg, 8 November 1620)
White Plains (28 October 1776)
Whitney, Eli (1765–1825)
Wilderness (5–7 May 1864)
William II (Friedrich Wilhelm Viktor Albert) (1859–1941)
William the Conqueror (c. 1028–1087)
Wingate, Orde (1903–1944)
Wolfe, James (1727–1759)
Wolseley, Garnet Joseph, Viscount (1833–1913)
Women in the World's Militaries
Wood, Leonard (1860–1927)
Worcester, Battle of (3 September 1651)
World War I (1914–1918)
World War II (1939–1945)
Wounded Knee, Battle of (28 December 1890)
Wrangel', Peter Nikolaevich (1878–1928)

Xenophon (c. 431–c. 354 B.C.E.)
Xerxes I (c. 519–465 B.C.E.)

Yalu River (1 May 1904)
Yamagata, Aritomo (1838–1922)
Yamashita, Tomoyuki (1885–1946)
Yang Jian (Yang Chien) (541–604)
Yang Xiuqing (c. 1817–1856)
Yangzhou (Yang-chou), Siege of (1645)
Yarmuk, Battle of (20 August 636)
Yellow Ford (1597)
Yemenite Civil Wars (1961–1967, 1994)
Yonglo (1360–1424)
Yorktown (1781)
Ypres, Battles of (1914–1918)
Yuan Shikai (1859–1916)
Yue Fei (1103–1141)
Yugoslavian Civil Wars (1990–2000)

Zama, Battle of (October 202 B.C.E.)
Zapata, Emiliano (c. 1879–1919)
Zapatista Rebellion (1994–)
Zenta (1697)
Zhukov, Georgy Konstantinovich (1896–1974)
Zibhebhu kaMaphitha Zulu (c. 1841–1904)
Zimbabwe Independence Struggle (1967–1980)
Žižka, Ján (c. 1360–1424)
Zulu Civil Wars and Rebellion (1879–1888)
Zulu Kingdom (c. 1820–1879)
Zuo Zongtang (Tso Tsung-tang) (1812–1885)

MAPS

ACRONYMS

ABM Antiballistic Missile Treaty
ACP automatic cartridge pistol
AEW Airborne Early Warning
AFVs armored fighting vehicles
AIF Australian Imperial Force
ALB Air Land Battle Doctrine
ANZAC Australian and New Zealand Army Corps
ARVN Army of the Republic of Vietnam
ASDIC Anti-Submarine Detection Investigation Committee
ASW antisubmarine warfare
ATC American Tobacco Company
AWACS airborne warning and control system
BEF British Expeditionary Force
C2 Command and Control system
C3I command, control, communications, and intelligence
Cheka Chrezvychainaya Komissariat po bor'be s kontrarevoliutsiei i sabotazhem (All-Russian Commission for Struggle against Counterrevolution and Sabotage)
CI counterintelligence
CIA Central Intelligence Agency
CIGS chief of the Imperial General Staff
CORDS American Office of Civil Operations of Rural Development Support
CPB Communist Party of Burma
CTBT Comprehensive Test Ban Treaty
DIA Defense Intelligence Agency
DK Democratic Kampuchea
DPRK Democratic People's Republic of Korea
DSM Distinguished Service Medal
EAM-ELAS National Liberation Front–National Popular Liberation Army
EDES Greek Democratic National Army
ELN Ejercito de Liberación Nacional (Army of National Liberation)
EOKA National Organization of Greek Fighters
EPL Ejercito Popular de Liberaci (Army of Popular Liberation)
EVA Ever Victorious Army
FARC Fuerzas Armadas Revolucionarias de Colombia (Colombian Revolutionary Armed Forces)
FLEC Front for the Liberation of Cabinda
FLN National Liberation Front
FNLA National Front for the Liberation of Angola
GCNG Greek Cypriot National Guard
GDP gross domestic product
GDR German Democratic Republic
GPU Gosudarstvennoe Politicheskoe Upravlenie (State Political Administration)
GULAG Glavnoe Upravlenie Ispravitel'no-trudovykh Lagerei (Chief Administration of Corrective Labor Camps)
HUMINT human intelligence
I&W Indicators and Warnings
IDF Israeli Defense Forces
IFF Identification Friend-or-Foe transponders
IMINT (aerial and satellite photo and radar) imagery intelligence
INA Indian National Army (Azad Hind Fauj)
INF intermediate-range nuclear forces
IR infrared (radar)
IRA Irish Republican Army
IRB Irish Republican Brotherhood
JDA Japanese Defense Academy
JTF Joint Task Force
KGB Komitet Gosudarstvennoi Bezopastnosti (Committee of State Security)
KNU Karen National Union

KPA	Korean Peoples Army
KUFNS	Khmer United Front for National Salvation
M-19	Movimento 19 de Abril (19th of April Movement)
MACV	U.S. Military Assistance Command
MAUD	Military Application of Uranium Detonation
MED	Manhattan Engineer District
MFA	armed forces movement
MID	Military Intelligence Division of the Army General Staff
MLRS	Multiple Launch Rocket System
MPLA	Popular Movement for the Liberation of Angola
MVD	Ministerstvo Vnutrennikh Del (Ministry of Internal Affairs)
NATO	North Atlantic Treaty Organization
NF	Intermediate Nuclear Forces Treaty
NKGB	Narodnaya Komissariat Gosudarstvennoi Bezopastnosti (People's Commissariat for State Security)
NKVD	Narodnaya Komissariat Vnutrennikh Del
NSA	National Security Agency
NSC	National Security Council
NVA	North Vietnamese Army
OAS	Secret Army Organization
OECS	Organization of Eastern Caribbean States
OFS	Orange Free State
OGPU	Unified State Political Administration
OKW	Wehrmacht High Command
OPEC	Organization of Petroleum Exporting Countries
ORBAT	Order of Battle information
OSRD	Office of Scientific Research and Development
OSS	Office of Strategic Services
PAIGC	African Party for the Independence of Guinea and Cape Verde
PG	Provisional Government
PLO	Palestinian Liberation Organization
PNI	Partai Nasional Indonesia (Indonesian Nationalist Party)
PPA	Planters Protective Association
PRA	People's Revolutionary Army
PRD	Dominican Revolutionary Party
PRK	People's Republic of Kampuchea
RADAR	Radio Detecting and Ranging
RAR	Royal Australian Regiment
RDF	Radio Direction Finding
RKKA	Workers and Peasants Red Army
ROK	Republic of Korea
RPF	Assembly of the French People Party
SALT	Strategic Arms Limitation I Interim Agreement
SAMS	surface-to-air missile defenses
SAS	Special Air Service
SBS	Special Boat Service
SEAL	sea, air, and land team
SIGINT	signals intelligence
SLORC	State Law and Order Restoration Council
SONAR	Sound Navigation and Ranging
START	Strategic Arms Reduction Talks I and II
TECHINT	technical intelligence
TOW	target on wire
UN	United Nations
UNC	United Nations Command
UNEF	United Nations Emergency Force
UNITA	National Union for the Total Independence of Angola
VOC	Vereenigde Oost-Indische Compagnie (Dutch East India Company)

GLOSSARY

(Recurring topics. Each listing in this glossary has its own article in the text.)

Airborne Operations The insertion of troops and equipment on the battlefield by means of parachute, helicopter, or glider.

Armor Body protection for soldiers.

Armored Fighting Vehicles Protected vehicles used on the battlefield.

Arms Control Limits, usually set by treaty, on the number and types of weapons; usually refers to nuclear weapons.

Artillery Basically, a heavy metal tube from which a missile is discharged violently by explosive force.

Awards and Honors Recognition granted by authorities for meritorious service by soldiers.

Ballistics The science of projectiles, divided into interior and exterior ballistics. Its aim is to improve the design of shells/projectiles so that increased accuracy and predictability are the result. It deals also with rockets and ballistic missiles.

Bayonet Metal blade or spike that, when fixed to a musket or rifle, facilitates its use in hand-to-hand combat. In recent decades, more likely to be used for opening ration tins.

Bazooka Shaped-charge, smoothbore, man-portable, antitank, and pillbox weapon.

Buffalo Soldiers African-American troops of the late-nineteenth-century U.S. regular army.

Catapult Engine for throwing a heavy weight, using an arm released from tension; the artillery of the ancient world.

Cavalry The noble, mobile arm of battle; the traditional horse-borne arm of mobility; can now refer to a motor vehicle–mounted unit.

Chaplains Military officers who tend to the spiritual, moral, and physical needs of troops in the field and in camp; pastors in uniform.

Chemical and Biological Warfare The deliberate use of chemical or biological agents against an enemy.

Civil Affairs/Military Government Those activities of a commander that embrace the relationship between the military forces and civil authorities and people in a friendly country or area (Civil Affairs) or occupied country or area (Military Government).

Coastal Defense The defense of a nation's coast from an enemy sea invasion or blockade, accomplished with heavy artillery, mines, small warships, and nets.

Cold War (1946–1989) Period of tension between the Soviet Union and the People's Republic of China and their allies, representing communism (the East); and the United States and its allies, representing capitalism and democratic socialism (the West); punctuated with several "hot" wars, the most significant being the Korean War (1950–1953) and the Vietnam War (c. 1955–1975). The Cold War ended unexpectedly with the fall of the Berlin Wall and the bloodless victory of the West.

Communications, Military The application of technology to the transmission of military orders and intelligence.

Conscription The selection of persons for involuntary military service.

Death Squads Clandestine and usually irregular organizations, often paramilitary in nature, that carry out extrajudicial executions and other violent acts against clearly defined individuals or groups of people.

Disarmament The removal or drastic reduction by nation-states of major weapons.

Economic Warfare Compelling an enemy to submit either by direct action against its economic basis or indirectly through blockade or boycott.

Electronic Warfare The use of the electromagnetic

spectrum to gain knowledge of the presence and movement of an opposing force and also to deny any opposing force the use of that spectrum.

Engineering, Military The application of science and technology for military purposes, primarily through the use of civil engineering.

Ethics of War Rules, principles, or virtues applied to warfare.

Firearm A tube, closed at one end, that has in it an explosive with a projectile above it, nearer to the open end of the tube. An ignition system fires the explosive charge, which forces the projectile along the tube by means of the gases from the explosion; can include both artillery and small arms.

History, Military History dealing with the use of organized armed force, either on behalf of some form of recognized state authority or against it.

Infantry Lightly armed ground troops; the backbone of any army; not only the most numerous of the fighting arms but the only one that can actually take and hold ground.

Intelligence, Military Military specialty that provides a commander and staff with the knowledge of the enemy and of weather and terrain required for the planning and conduct of operations. (There is no truth to the assertion that "military intelligence" is an oxymoron.)

Laws of War International laws, enforced sometimes by nations after war and sometimes by commanders in battle, governing both the decision to engage in war and the manner of its conduct, particularly the forms of violence used, the definition of combatants, the treatment of prisoners, and the treatment of neutrals and noncombatants.

Logistics Largely an American usage, encompassing military supply, transportation, medical service, and construction-maintenance.

Machine Gun Rapid-firing small arm that can maintain a high rate of fire without the requirement of reloading after each round, which today means a fully automatic weapon; either man-portable ("machine pistol") or heavier.

Maps and Cartography The result of the utilization of cartography and topographical reproduction for military strategy and operations.

Medals and Decorations Tangible recognition of faithful military service or success awarded to individual soldiers.

Medicine, Military The medical and surgical specialty concerned with the ailments of soldiers and sailors.

Mercenaries Hired professional soldiers who fight for a state or entity without regard to political interests or issues.

Military-Industrial Complex The institutions and people that plan, procure, and fight a war and that supposedly shape the economy, the political realm, and the wider society, even in peacetime. Term first used by outgoing U.S. President Dwight D. Eisenhower in 1961.

Mortar Muzzle-loaded weapon firing its bomb at a high angle to attack protected positions and trenches.

Pacifism/War Resistance The organized opposition to war, killing, or violence; usually divided into two segments: religious (e.g., Quakers, Mennonites) and secular.

Paramilitary Organizations Unofficial groups organized along military lines yet lacking the traditional role or legitimization of conventional or "genuine" military organizations.

Propellants Compounds used to move a projectile from the firing device to the target.

Psychological Operations The use of psychology and propaganda by military units to persuade target audiences to adopt at least some of their views and possibly to modify their behavior.

Rank, Military Official indication of a soldier's length and quality of service in organized militaries.

Rifles Firearms designed with barrel grooves to impart a spin and thus far greater accuracy; either small arms or artillery.

Tactics The theory and practice of using military forces in combat.

Terrorism Acts of violence intended for a wide audience in order to create an environment of fear for political reasons.

Theory, Military That body of knowledge usually published in books and journals that examines the nature of wars and the art of war on an abstract level.

Unarmored Fighting Vehicles Unprotected military vehicles, either specially built for the military or adapted from commercial models and used in combat-support roles (e.g., Jeeps, trucks, ambulances).

Uniforms Military clothing worn by organized bodies of troops to distinguish them from the uniformed personnel of other armed forces and to strengthen morale.

War Crimes Actions in wartime that violate the laws or usages of war.

H

Hadrian (Publius Aelius Hadrianus) (76–138)

Military reformer, Roman emperor from 117 to 138. Before becoming emperor, Hadrian had a long military career, serving in Spain, Pannonia, Moesia, Germany (with the XXII Legion, the Primigenia Pia Fidelis), and Parthia. During the First and Second Dacian Wars (102–103 and 105–106), Hadrian served variously as quaestor, legate, praetor, and commander of a legion. He became governor of Pannonia in 107, consul in 108, and governor of Syria in 114. Hadrian was in line to receive a second consulship in 118 when, upon hearing of the death of Emperor Trajan (d. 8 August 117), the armies of Syria proclaimed Hadrian to be emperor of Rome. Deeming Trajan's wars of expansion a waste of blood and treasure, Hadrian pursued a policy of imperial consolidation. In 122, preferring peace to war, Hadrian negotiated an armistice with the Parthians. Touring the empire and inspecting the provinces in order to make reforms, Hadrian established large-scale border fortifications, which not only protected the frontiers from Barbarian attacks, but also served as checkpoints for trade. The most famous of these fortifications, Hadrian's Wall, was erected between Tyne and the Solway Firth in Britain. Although he demanded rigid discipline, Hadrian's military reforms and personal inspection tours throughout the empire won the intense loyalty of his legions. Perhaps one of Hadrian's most significant reforms was the elimination of distinctions between the legions and the auxiliary corps, which meant that Roman citizens and noncitizens now served in the same units. Hadrian also reintroduced the tactical modification of the Macedonian phalanx, in which auxiliary troops led an attack followed later by a reserve of legionnaires. Hadrian's reign was generally marked by peace and sensible policies, except in Judea, where Hadrian's insensitivity provoked the Second Jewish Revolt (132–135).

Eric D. Pullin

See also: Jewish Revolts

References and further reading:

Birley, Anthony R. *Hadrian: The Restless Emperor.* London: Routledge, 1997.

Goldsworthy, Adrian Keith. *The Roman Army at War, 100 B.C.–A.D. 200.* New York: Oxford University Press, 1996.

Webster, Graham. *The Roman Imperial Army of the First and Second Centuries C.E.* Norman: University of Oklahoma Press, 1998.

Haig, Douglas (1861–1926)

British field commander in World War I. Haig was born into the famous family of distillers in Edinburgh, Scotland, on 19 June 1861. Educated at Oxford and graduating first in his class at Sandhurst in 1885, Haig was commissioned in the 7th Hussars and saw service in India, Africa, and on the home front. In the Nile Valley during the Mahdist War, he fought at Atbara and Omdurman. In the Second Boer War, with his superior officer, John French, and ambulance volunteer Mohandas K. Gandhi, Haig escaped Ladysmith by train just before the Boers surrounded it. In 1901–1902 he fought Jan Smuts's guerrillas in the Cape Province. He was promoted to major general in 1905 and to lieutenant general in 1910.

Again under French in 1914, he commanded the I Corps of the British Expeditionary Force at Mons and the Marne and in Picardy and Artois. He became commander of the First Army in February 1915. The Germans stopped him at Neuve-Chapelle from 10 to 13 March, at Festubert from 9 to 26 May, and at Loos from 26 September to 14 October. Haig replaced French in December and began to plan the great offensive of the Somme. After this offensive succeeded (at enormous cost), late in 1916, in reducing threats to the poilus at Verdun, Haig was promoted to field marshal.

Operating under Robert Nivelle, Haig made gains at Arras from 9 to 15 April 1917. After Henri Pétain replaced Nivelle on 15 May, Haig improved the French position by attacking at Passchendaele from 31 July to 10 November. He contained Erich Ludendorff's offensives at the Somme and the Lys in March and April 1918, then counterattacked at Amiens on 8 August. He commanded the Flanders operation in Ferdinand Foch's final offensive from 26 September to 11 November. Created earl in 1919, he died in London on 29 January 1926.

Haig has come to symbolize the unimaginative head-on tactics on the western front that nearly destroyed a British generation in World War I.

Eric v. d. Luft

See also: Amiens; Boer Wars; Foch, Ferdinand; French, John Denton Pinkstone, First Earl of Ypres; Ladysmith, Siege of; Ludendorff, Erich Friedrich Wilheim; Marne, Battle of the; Nivelle, Robert; Omdurman; Pétain, Henri-Philippe; The Somme; Verdun; World War I

References and further reading:

Bond, Brian, and Nigel Cave, eds. *Haig: A Reappraisal 70 Years On.* London: Leo Cooper, 1999.

Terraine, John. *Douglas Haig: The Educated Soldier.* London: Leo Cooper, 1990.

Warner, Philip. *Field Marshal Earl Haig.* London: Bodley Head, 1991.

Winter, Denis. *Haig's Command: A Reassessment.* London: Viking, 1991.

Haitian Civil War (1806)

After independence Haiti was ruled by the despotic Jean-Jacques Dessalines, who proclaimed himself emperor. Dessalines, who had been born in Africa, discriminated against the mulattoes. Moreover, his regime was corrupt and stole most of the national treasury. In 1806 Dessalines was murdered and Haiti plunged into civil war. The civil war centered around two strongmen who vied to be master of Haiti. The first was Henri Christophe, a black man who had been one of Tousaint L'Overture's lieutenants in the war for independence from France. The other was Alexandre Pétion, a prominent mulatto who had led that segment of Haitian society in battles with the French and Haitian slaves. An assembly attempted to establish a national government with Christophe as president and Pétion as head of the legislature. Under this arrangement the mulattoes would dominate and Christophe would be a mere figurehead.

Christophe rejected the plan and attempted to seize power by marching on Port-au-Prince, but he was thwarted by Pétion's superior army, which was equipped with artillery. Christophe retreated and established a state in the northern portion of Haiti with the capital at Cap-Haitien. In 1811 he proclaimed himself King Henry I and built a magnificent palace. In order to maintain his personal power, Christophe brought African warriors who formed his palace guard and were called Royal Dahomets.

Pétion established a republic in the southern portion of Haiti with himself as president for life. The division of Haiti into two distinct states resulted in clashes, but for many years neither section had the strength to defeat the other. Pétion pursued economic policies that rewarded the mulatto elite, but his racial policies were less discriminatory than those in Christophe's kingdom. Both states showed a marked contrast between the small wealthy ruling class and the balance of the population, which was impoverished.

When Pétion died in 1818 Christophe sought to unify the country under his leadership, a move that was rejected by the southern elite, who did not want a black leader. Instead, General Jean-Pierre Boyer was selected by the republican senate to be president. In 1820 Christophe suffered a severe stroke and later took his own life. Boyer then united the country and ruled until 1843.

George M. Lauderbaugh

See also: Toussaint L'Overture, Wars of

References and further reading:

Heinl, Robert Debs, Jr., and Nancy Gordon Heinl. *Written in Blood: The Story of the Haitian People, 1492–1971.* Boston: Houghton Mifflin, 1978.

Moran, Charles. *Black Triumvirate: A Study of Louverture, Dessalines, Christophe—The Men Who Made Haiti.* New York: Exposition Press, 1957.

Nicholls, David. *From Dessalines to Duvalier: Race, Colour, and National Independence in Haiti.* London: Cambridge University Press, 1979.

Halleck, Henry Wager (1815–1872)

Union field commander and administrative officer in the American Civil War, known (and not with affection) as "Old Brains." Halleck was born in Westernville, New York, on 16 January 1815. Assigned to the engineers after graduating from West Point in 1839, he studied fortifications in Europe and wrote a book on military science, published in 1846. As brevet captain in the Mexican-American War, he saw little battle action but excelled at engineering. He resigned his commission in 1854 and became a lawyer in San Francisco.

Recalled to active duty upon the recommendation of Winfield Scott, Halleck was commissioned major general on 19 August 1861. He replaced John C. Frémont in command of the Department of Missouri on 19 November and straightened out the administrative mess that Frémont had made. After Ulysses S. Grant captured Forts Henry and Donelson in February 1862, Halleck, as Grant's commanding officer, was rewarded on 13 March with command of all Union forces in the western theater.

Halleck's only field campaign was the march on the Confederate supply base at Corinth, Mississippi, in May and June. He was severely criticized for his creeping, mile-a-day advance, which allowed P. T. Beauregard and Braxton Bragg to escape and regroup after Shiloh. Abraham Lincoln relieved him of field command on 19 September and brought him to Washington, D.C. As general in chief from 11 July 1862 to 12 March 1864, and as chief of staff until 16 April 1865, he performed much better as an administrator than he had as a field commander.

After the Civil War, Halleck held commands in Virginia, the Pacific, and Kentucky. He died in Louisville, Kentucky, on 9 January 1872.

Eric v. d. Luft

See also: American Civil War; Beauregard, Pierre Gustave Toutant; Bragg, Braxton; Engineering, Military; Fort Donelson; Grant, Ulysses Simpson; Mexican-American War; Scott, Winfield; Shiloh

References and further reading:

Ambrose, Stephen E. *Halleck: Lincoln's Chief of Staff.* Baton Rouge: Louisiana State University Press, 1962.

Simon, John Y. *Grant and Halleck: Contrasts in Command.* Milwaukee: Marquette University Press, 1996.

Hamilcar Barca (c. 270–228 or 229 B.C.E.)

Carthaginian general during and after the First Punic War, and father of Hannibal and Hasdrubal. In 247 B.C.E. Hamilcar was sent to Sicily to take over command of the fleet. He raided the coast of Italy, hoping both to bring the Italian population to revolt against the Romans and to keep Roman forces occupied. When this remained ineffective he landed in Sicily with a force of mercenaries and started a guerrilla war. After he had captured the town of Eryx (244 B.C.E.) he succeeded in prolonging the war in Sicily until 241 B.C.E. The Carthaginians were defeated at sea near the Aegeates islands. Hamilcar was given full authority to negotiate a peace treaty.

Due to the cost of the war effort Carthage was not able to pay its mercenaries, which were the bulk of its army. They revolted and besieged Carthage. Hamilcar assumed command of the Carthaginian army. As in Sicily he preferred a war of mobility and small-scale action rather than one of large battles. By cutting off the supply lines of the insurgents he forced them to raise the siege. The war was brought to an end in 237 B.C.E. by Hamilcar, sharing command with his political rival Hanno, in a battle near Leptis Minor.

After the revolt Hamilcar went to southern Spain to recover the territories Carthage had lost during the war with Rome. He campaigned in the peninsula until he drowned during the siege of Helice (near Alicante) on the east coast of Spain, where he was treacherously defeated by a local king. By that time he had reestablished Carthage's Iberian empire. As a result the city regained its position as a major power in the western Mediterranean. Hamilcar became the effective ruler of the province, a power base that he passed on to his house. With its resources his son Hannibal almost brought Rome to its knees.

M. R. van der Werf

See also: Hannibal Barca; Punic Wars

References and further reading:

Bagnall, Nigel. *The Punic Wars. Rome, Carthage and the Struggle for the Mediterranean.* London: Pimlico, 1999.

Caven, Brian. *The Punic Wars.* London: Weidenfeld & Nicolson, 1980.

Lazenby, J. F. *The First Punic War.* London: University College London Press, 1996.

Hamilton, General Ian Standish Monteith (1853–1947)

British soldier and author. Ian Hamilton was first noticed by Lord Roberts during the Second Anglo-Afghan War (1878–1880) and became his aide-de-camp in 1882. He saw action in South Africa during the Transvaal War of Independence (1880–1881) and was severely wounded and captured during the fateful battle at Amajuba (27 February 1881). He then took part in the Gordon Relief Expedition in the Sudan (1884–1885). At the time of the outbreak of the Anglo-Boer War (1899–1902) he was General George White's assistant adjutant general in Natal and was besieged with White in Ladysmith, playing a pivotal role in several battles, including Platrand (Wagon Hill and Caesar's Camp, 6 January 1900). After the relief of Ladysmith, Hamilton commanded Roberts's Mounted Infantry Division. He took part in Roberts's advance from Bloemfontein to Pretoria, saw action at Donkerhoek (Diamond Hill, 11–12 June 1900), but was unable to corner General Christiaan De Wet (August 1900). At the end of 1900, Hamilton accompanied Roberts back to England and became his military secretary at the War Office. He returned to South Africa in November 1901 to become Lord Kitchener's chief of staff but was soon ordered to command mobile columns in the western Transvaal during the final weeks of the antiguerrilla campaign. He defeated the Boers at Roodewal (11 April 1902) and was one of the few British commanders who emerged from the war with an enhanced military reputation.

During the Russo-Japanese War (1904–1905), Hamilton was a British observer in the field. He was adjutant general, 1909–1910, and became commander in chief of the Mediterranean Command in 1910.

When World War I broke out, he was given command of the Central Force for the defense of the United Kingdom and in March 1915 he was placed in command of the Dardanelles operation. However, lack of success (and heavy casualties) led to his recall in October 1915. He was not given another command.

Hamilton was the gifted author of several books, including *The Fighting of the Future* (1885), *A Staff Officer's Scrap Book* (2 volumes, 1905–1907), *Gallipoli Diary* (2 volumes, 1920), *Anti-Commando* (with A. Wools-Sampson, 1931), *When I Was a Boy* (1939), and *Listening for the Drums* (1944). He also published novels and poems. Hamilton was a confident and resourceful officer, but "The Happy Warrior" lacked the ruthless drive and single-mindedness that are prerequisites for a truly great commander. Nevertheless he was a rare phenomenon, an intellectual professional soldier with a keen interest in all the arts.

André Wessels

See also: Boer Wars; De Wet, Christiaan Rudolph; Gallipoli; Kitchener, Horatio Herbert; Roberts, Frederick Sleigh, First Earl, Viscount St. Pierre of Kandahar; World War I

References and further reading:

Aspinall-Oglander, C. F. "Hamilton, Ian Standish Monteith." In *The Dictionary of National Biography 1941–1950.* Eds. L. G. Wickham Legg and E. T. Williams. London: Oxford University Press, 1959.

Churchill, W. S. *Ian Hamilton's March.* London: Longmans, Green, 1900.

Hamilton, I. S. M. *The Happy Warrior: A Life of General Sir Ian Hamilton.* London: Cassell, 1900.

Spies, S. B. "Hamilton, Ian Standish Monteith." In *Dictionary of South African Biography,* vol. 2, eds. W. J. de Kock and D. W. Krüger. Pretoria: Human Sciences Research Council, 1972.

Han Wudi (r. 141–87 B.C.E.)

Chinese emperor of the Han Dynasty who maintained strong, forward positions against the Xiongnu Rising in the north. More or less contemporaneous with the unified Chinese empires of Qin and Han was the steppe state of the Xiongnu (possibly the ancestors of the Huns), which not only seriously threatened Chinese rule in north China but also prevented direct Chinese contacts with the wealthy Greek world of the distant west. Han rulers responded to the Xiongnu threat in various ways, but under Wudi a "modernist" school of administration insisted upon direct confrontation with their steppe enemies and the maintenance of a forward position of military bases and border colonies to keep the Xiongnu as far away from China as possible.

Wudi's policy was a concerted attempt to "use the barbarians to control the barbarians." This involved the encouragement of subversion within the Xiongnu, above all through substantial bribes to the right parties, a carefully controlled marriage policy, and a search for allies to support the Han cause. It was in support of this latter goal that the courtier Zhang Qian was sent west to establish contact with the Yuezhi, "moon clan," traditional enemies of the Xiongnu. After harrowing adventures that brought the Chinese explorer as far as Sogdia and Bactria, whence the Yuezhi had moved, he returned with no alliance but with abundant information about the west and the roads leading there. Armed with this intelligence, Wudi's armies, which had already begun an advance into what is now Chinese Turkistan, quickly conquered the entire area as far as Ferghana in what is now western Turkistan. This advance not only outflanked the Xiongnu but brought China, for the first time, into direct contact with the west. This was the real beginning of the famous Silk Route.

Paul D. Buell

See also: Ban Chao; Huns

References and further reading:

Barfield, Thomas J. *The Perilous Frontier, Nomadic Empires and China.* Cambridge, MA, and Oxford, UK: Basil Blackwell, 1989.

Loewe, Michael. "The Campaigns of Han Wu-ti." In *Chinese Ways in Warfare,* eds. Frank A. Kierman and John K. Fairbank, 67–122. Cambridge, MA: Harvard University Press, 1974.

Hancock, Winfield Scott (1824–1886)

Impeccable Union field commander in the American Civil War. Hancock was born in Montgomery Square, Pennsylvania, on 14 February 1824. After graduating from the U.S. Military Academy at West Point in 1844, he served under his namesake in the Mexican-American War and was brevetted first lieutenant at Churubusco. In the 1850s, he fought the Seminoles in Florida, the factions in Kansas, and the Mormons in Utah.

Stationed in California when the Civil War broke out, he returned east and was promoted to brigadier general of volunteers on 23 September 1861. After leading a masterful flank attack at Williamsburg, Virginia, on 5 May 1862, he was called "Hancock the Superb." He fought at Seven Pines and Fair Oaks from 31 May to 1 June, at Frayser's Farm on 30 June, commanded a division at Antietam, and became major general of volunteers on 29 November. He attacked Marye's Heights at Fredericksburg and performed expert rearguard maneuvers at Chancellorsville.

On the first day at Gettysburg, Confederates under Henry Heth and A. P. Hill pushed him southeast to defensive positions on Cemetery Ridge. He held the Federal center left on the second day and the center the third day but was critically wounded on Cemetery Ridge as his forces brought George Pickett's famous charge to a halt. Returning to action six months later, he distinguished himself at the Wilderness and was brevetted major general in the regular army for his service at Spotsylvania. He failed at Cold Harbor only because of Ulysses S. Grant's error. Troubled by his Gettysburg wound, he deferred command at Petersburg and went on furlough. Hill and Wade Hampton dealt him an embarrassing defeat at Reams' Station, Virginia, on 25 August. Relieved of field command on 27 November, he finished the war commanding garrisons around Washington, D.C.

Hancock was the Democratic candidate for president in 1880. After losing to James A. Garfield, he returned to active military duty and died at his headquarters on Governor's Island, New York, on 9 February 1886.

Eric v. d. Luft

See also: American Civil War; Antietam/Sharpsburg; Chancellorsville, Battle of; Cold Harbor, Battle of ; Fredericksburg; Gettysburg; Grant, Ulysses Simpson; Hill, Ambrose Powell; McClellan, George Brinton; Meade, George Gordon; Mexican-American War; Mexico City, Battles for; Mormon War; Petersburg, Siege of; Pickett, George Edward; Seven Days' Battles; Sioux Wars; Spotsylvania Court House; Utah War; Wilderness

References and further reading:

Coates, Isaac Taylor. *On the Plains with Custer and Hancock: The Journal of Isaac Coates, Army Surgeon.* Boulder, CO: Johnson, 1997.

Gambone, A. M. *Hancock at Gettysburg and Beyond.* Baltimore: Butternut and Blue, 1997.

Jordan, David M. *Winfield Scott Hancock: A Soldier's Life.* Bloomington: Indiana University Press, 1988.

Tucker, Glenn. *Hancock the Superb.* Indianapolis, IN: Bobbs-Merrill, 1960.

Hannibal Barca (247–188 B.C.E.)

The greatest Carthaginian general during the Second Punic War. Hannibal was the son of the famous general Hamilcar Barca, who took him to Spain in 237 B.C.E. According to Roman tradition Hannibal was raised to hate Rome, swearing an oath forever to be its enemy. Although Hannibal became an implacable enemy of Rome, his reputation for cruelty, malice, and greed, attributed to him by biased Roman writers, is not backed by evidence.

In 220 B.C.E. Hannibal became commander of the Carthaginian army in Spain. After subduing the north of the peninsula he attacked the city of Saguntum (Sagunto) in 219 B.C.E. The Romans protested, claiming that the city was an ally, and declared war. Hannibal immediately prepared for an invasion of Italy. His plan was based upon the assumption that if he attacked the Romans in Italy, many of Rome's allies would change sides. Having set out with an army of 50,000 foot, 9,000 horse, and some 40 elephants, Hannibal marched through the Pyrenees and southern Gaul. After a difficult march through the Alps he reached the Po valley and defeated the Romans at the Trebia (218 B.C.E.).

The following year Hannibal marched over the Apennines into Etruria (Tuscany), where he destroyed a Roman army at Lake Trasimene (217 B.C.E.). Again a Roman force marched to fight Hannibal. At Cannae (216 B.C.E.) two Roman armies were totally destroyed. Hannibal showed superior generalship and complete control over his troops.

Although Hannibal had won three major victories, things did not turn out as he expected. The Romans showed remarkable tenacity. Following the advice of Fabius Maximus, they dogged Hannibal's footsteps, denying him battle but undoing his successes behind his back. The delaying tactics wore Hannibal down, denying him the opportunity to win the war decisively.

Rome's allies also proved far more loyal than Hannibal had expected. Few of Rome's major allies came over to him. Moreover, as abandoning his newfound allies would negate any chances of more Italians joining him, Hannibal was forced to protect them. As the Romans set in on pushing renegade allies into line, Hannibal had to march regularly to their relief and had to use up valuable manpower on garrisons.

Despite Hannibal's initial successes, he received few reinforcements from Carthage partly because of significant political opposition. Moreover the Carthaginians deemed the protection of their empire in Spain more important than the war in Italy. An attempt by Hannibal's brother Hasdrubal to reinforce him with an army from Spain was foiled at the Metaurus in northern Italy (207 B.C.E.).

Hannibal campaigned in Italy until he was recalled to Africa in 202 B.C.E., when Carthage itself was threatened by Scipio Africanus. At Zama (202 B.C.E.), Hannibal was defeated decisively. Knowing that Carthage had lost the war, he advocated peace. For a while Hannibal was allowed to follow a political career in Carthage, but eventually he was forced to flee to King Prusias of Bythinia in Asia Minor by Roman machinations. To avoid being extradited to the Romans, Hannibal committed suicide.

M. R. van der Werf

See also: Animals in War; Cannae, Battle of; Fabius Maximus Verrucosus "Cunctator"; Hamilcar Barca; Marcellus, Marcus Claudius; Punic Wars; Scipio Africanus Major, Publius Cornelius; Trebia, Battle of the; Zama, Battle of

References and further reading:

Bagnall, Nigel. *The Punic Wars: Rome, Carthage and the Struggle for the Mediterranean.* London: Pimlico, 1999.

Carthaginian General Hannibal crossing the Alps into Italy with elephants during the Second Punic War between Carthage and Rome 218-202 B.C.E. (Hulton/Archive)

Beer, Sir Gavin. *Hannibal. The Struggle for Power in the Mediterranean.* London: Thames & Hudson, 1969.
Bradford, Ernle. *Hannibal.* London: Macmillan, 1981.
Lazenby, J. F. *Hannibal's War. A Military History of the Second Punic War.* London: Aris & Phillips, 1978.

Harpers Ferry (American Civil War, 12–15 September 1862)

One of the greatest capitulations in American military history. After the Battle of Second Bull Run/Manassas Junction, Robert E. Lee and the Army of Northern Virginia "invaded" Maryland with plans to move into Pennsylvania. Using cavalry along the fall line of the mountains, Lee screened his movements from George McClellan, who moved cautiously.

When Lee learned that the Union garrison at Harpers Ferry, (West) Virginia, had not abandoned the munitions and supply depot there, he ordered General Thomas J. "Stonewall" Jackson and three of Lee's four columns to surround the town and compel its surrender.

The Union garrison under Colonel Dixon Miles held out until the Confederates placed artillery on the heights overlooking the town, which was in the valley at the confluence of three rivers. Miles surrendered his garrison of more than 12,000 men and the vital supplies to Jackson, who meanwhile sent his columns hurrying to join Lee at Antietam, where Lee had decided to make a stand against McClellan. The last of Jackson's columns, under General A. P. Hill, was the last to leave and therefore the last to arrive at Antietam, blunting Burnside's late afternoon assault.

Charles M. Dobbs

See also: American Civil War; Antietam/Sharpsburg; Jackson, Thomas "Stonewall"

References and further reading:

Farwell, Byron. *Stonewall: A Biography of General Thomas J. Jackson.* New York: W. W. Norton, 1993.

Gallagher, Gary W., ed. *The Antietam Campaign.* Chapel Hill: University of North Carolina Press, 1999.
Robertson, James I., Jr. *Stonewall Jackson: The Man, the Soldier, the Legend.* New York: Macmillan, 1997.

Harrison, William Henry (1773–1841)

American frontiersman, field commander, politician, and president. Born on his father's plantation, Berkeley, in Charles City County, Virginia, on 9 February 1773, Harrison graduated from Hampden-Sidney College in 1790. His father, Benjamin Harrison, a signer of the Declaration of Independence and the governor of Virginia from 1782 to 1784, sent him to Philadelphia to study medicine under Benjamin Rush. When his father died in 1791, Harrison immediately abandoned medicine and received an ensign's commission in the 1st Infantry, which was stationed in Ohio with standing orders to patrol the Northwest Territory.

As lieutenant and aide-de-camp to "Mad Anthony" Wayne, Harrison fought with distinction at Fallen Timbers on 20 August 1794. Promoted to captain in 1797, he commanded Fort Washington, near Cincinnati, until he resigned in 1798 to become territorial secretary for the Northwest. He was territorial delegate to Congress in 1799 and governor of the newly created Indiana Territory from 1800 to 1812. A significant part of his duties was to maintain good relations with the natives of the territory and thus ensure safety for white settlers. He undercut his own efforts at peace by forcing a series of land-grabbing treaties on the Shawnee and other indigenous nations. Tecumseh and his brother, Tenskwatawa, organized native resistance against Harrison's policies.

On 7 November 1811, at the confluence of Tippecanoe Creek and the Wabash River, Harrison defeated Tenskwatawa and burned his village, losing about 180 of the 950 regulars and militia under his command. This battle destroyed the fragile coalition of natives in Indiana and made Harrison a national military hero with the nickname "Tippecanoe." Tecumseh led the remnants of the tribes into Canada, where they became staunch allies of the British during the War of 1812.

Appointed major general of the Kentucky militia in August 1812, Harrison relieved Fort Wayne and was commissioned brigadier general of regulars in September. Seeking to recoup the losses suffered by James Winchester in the west, Harrison built Fort Meigs and Fort Stephenson in Ohio and waited for reinforcements. Promoted to major general of regulars in March 1813, he marched north that autumn, recapturing Detroit on 29 September and decisively defeating the British and Indians at the Thames on 5 October. His nemesis, Tecumseh, was killed in that battle. He resigned his commission in May 1814 and returned to Ohio.

Harrison represented Ohio in Congress from 1816 to 1819 and in the Senate from 1825 to 1828. He lost a four-way election for president to Martin Van Buren in 1836, but won the White House as a Whig in 1840. He died on 4 April 1841 from the pneumonia he caught while delivering his inaugural address a month earlier, the first American president to die in office.

Eric v. d. Luft

See also: American Indian Wars; Fallen Timbers; Taylor, Zachary; Tecumseh; Thames; Tippecanoe, Battle of ; War of 1812; Wayne, Anthony

References and further reading:

Cleaves, Freeman. *Old Tippecanoe: William Henry Harrison and His Time.* Newtown, CT. American Political Biography Press, 1990.
Goebel, Dorothy Burne. *William Henry Harrison: A Political Biography.* Philadelphia, PA: Porcupine, 1974.
Green, James A. *William Henry Harrison: His Life and Times.* Richmond, VA: Garrett & Massie, 1941.
Todd, Charles Stewart, and Benjamin Drake. *Sketches of the Civil and Military Services of William Henry Harrison.* New York: Arno, 1975.
Young, Stanley. *Tippecanoe and Tyler Too!* New York: Random House, 1957.

General William H. Harrison at the Battle of Tippecanoe in 1811. (Library of Congress)

Harsha (c. 590–c. 647)

Starting as the teenage ruler of a small Indian state, Harsha came close to recreating the mighty Gupta Empire. In 606, Harsha Vardhana became ruler of Thaneswar, a small state located in the Punjab between the northern Indus and northwestern Ganges Valley. He married into the neighboring Maukhar kingdom and relocated to the capital at Kanauj. In 618, Harsha invaded the Gauda kingdom with 50,000 troops, 20,000 horsemen, and 5,000 elephants. Centered in modern Bangladesh, Gauda was responsible for the death of Harsha's older brother. "The elephants were never unharnessed and the soldiers never unhelmeted" until Harsha made Gauda his tributary.

Generally, however, Harsha preferred to negotiate his neighbors into his empire as allies rather than use force. These tactics made the rulers of Sindh, Ghujarat, and Valabhi become vassals (Samantas), placing much of the Indus Valley and the Arabian Sea coast under his sway. However, Pulakeshin II, ruler of the Decca plains south of the Narmada River, spurned Harsha's diplomacy. In 633, when Harsha attempted to march into Pulakeshin's territory, the Deccans forced him back across the Narmada. Three years later, he expanded his empire to the east, moving down from Gauda to annex more of Bengali coast.

Later foreign sources comment on the extent of Harsha's cavalry (100,000 horse and 60,000 elephants). Despite this great host, Harsha preferred a feudal-confederal decentralism over militaristic despotism. Patron of arts, culture, public charities, and scholarship, historical sources are kind to his memory. Nonetheless, Harsha was assassinated in 647 and his empire disintegrated almost immediately.

Weston F. Cook Jr.

References and further reading:

Devaluti, D. *Harsha: A Political Study.* London: Oxford University Press, 1970.

Smith, Vincent A. *The Oxford History of India.* 4th ed. Oxford, UK: Oxford University Press, 1981.

Harun al-Raschid (766–809)

Sultan of the Abbasid Empire. Member of the dynasty that had overthrown the Umayyads, and established themselves as the successors of Muhammad and rulers of a rich empire centered on Baghdad, Harun al-Raschid is primarily known as a patron of the arts and sciences. With extraordinary revenues from trade, Harun al-Raschid supported a spectacular court that inspired the *Thousand and One Nights* and perfected the pursuits of falconry, polo, and chess. He was one of the first sultans to make diplomatic contact with western Europe, sending Charlemagne an elephant as a gift and establishing himself as the protector of Christian pilgrims to the holy land.

Nonetheless, Harun al-Raschid's rule was far from peaceful. Constantly on the alert against internal threats, he maintained an elaborate secret police network. His system of regional emirs contributed to constant revolts of Berbers, and Egyptians, as well as Khazars, who collaborated with the Byzantines. Public works projects such as hospitals and universities were offset by large-scale military fortress building on the borders, garrisoned by fanatical ghazis. The Byzantines were Harun al-Raschid's greatest enemy, although despite the use of Greek fire, there were few permanent gains for either side because of prisoner exchanges and truces. Unfortunately, the excesses of his court and the internal dynamics of his family guaranteed that the empire was plunged into destructive rounds of fratricide and civil war when Harun al-Rashid died.

Margaret Sankey

See also: Abbasid Revolution

References and further reading:

Audisio, Gabriel. *Harun al-Raschid, Caliph of Baghdad.* New York: McBride & Company, 1931.

Bekrine, Mustapha. *Haroun al-Raschid.* Algir: SNED, 1971.

Hasegawa, Yoshimichi (1850–1924)

Japanese field marshal who earned worldwide attention with his accomplishments during the Russo-Japanese War. Hasegawa was born in the Iwakuni subfief of the Choshu clan's territory, now the prefecture of Yamaguchi. When the Choshu joined with the Satsuma clan to overthrow the shogun and restore the emperor to power in 1868, Hasegawa participated in the fighting. When the new government established an army to replace the old clan armies, he joined as a captain in 1871. By the time of the Satsuma Rebellion in February 1877, he was a major and commanded a regiment. Hasegawa's regiment was among those sent to relieve Kumamoto Castle in April 1877, and he distinguished himself in the fighting. After the war, Hasegawa was sent to France during 1885–1886, to review military developments in that nation. When he returned, the army promoted him to major general.

Hasegawa's next war was the first Sino-Japanese War of 1894–1895. He commanded a brigade during the fighting in Korea. At the battle of Pyongyang on 15 September 1894, Hasegawa won distinction for his valor and for the performance of his brigade. During the fighting at Haicheng in December 1894 and January 1895, his unit once again was recognized. As a reward, Hasegawa was promoted to command of the Guards Division in General Kuroki's First Army during the Russo-Japanese War of 1904–1905. He led his division from its landing in Korea to the Yalu River. During the Battle of the Yalu (30 April–May 1904) Hasegawa was recognized for his aggressive drive against the Russian defenders; crossing the river, he forced them to retreat. In June 1904, he was promoted to general.

Hasegawa served as commander of the Korean Garrison Army from September 1904 to December 1908. He tried to exclude civilian authorities from his area of responsibility as much as possible. In 1912, he was promoted to chief of staff of the army and served until 1915. His disdain for civilians was made obvious in 1913, when he protested directly to the emperor regarding a plan to allow reserve officers to hold positions as service ministers in the government. Hasegawa was promoted to field general when his term as chief of staff ended.

Tim J. Watts

See also: Kuropatkin, Aleksey Nikolaevich; Mukden, Battle of; Nogi, Maresuke; Russo-Japanese War; Sino-Japanese War (1894–1895); Yalu River

References and further reading:

Connaughton, R. M. *The War of the Rising Sun and Tumbling Bear: A Military History of the Russo-Japanese War, 1904–5.* New York: Routledge, 1988.

Walder, David. *The Short Victorious War: The Russo-Japanese Conflict, 1904–5.* London: Hutchinson, 1973.

Warner, Denis Ashton. *The Tide at Sunrise: A History of the Russo-Japanese War, 1904–1905.* New York: Charterhouse, 1974.

Hastings, Battle of (14 October 1066)

Decisive battle between William of Normandy and Harald II Godwinsson. Hastings provided the final resolution to the Danish Wars of Succession and marked the end of the Anglo-Saxon kingdoms. It resulted in the administrative, legal, and social restructuring of England by William I, the Conqueror.

The events leading to the battle were the death of Edward the Confessor with no clear heir to the throne; election by the Witan of one of the claimants, Harald II Godwinsson, brother-in-law to Edward; and the battle of Stamford Bridge between two of the claimants, Harald Sigurdsson of Norway and Harald II Godwinsson of England. Immediately after Harald II Godwinsson's victory at Stamford Bridge (25 September 1066), word came of the landing of William's invasion force at Pevensey on 29 September 1066. Hoping to duplicate the tactics that had worked so well at Stamford Bridge—a surprise attack cutting the enemy off from his ships—Harald quickly returned to the south.

The speed of his forced march coupled with losses at Stamford Bridge meant that Harald arrived with depleted resources. Many of Harald's foot troops and archers were left behind. That, coupled with insufficient time to regroup and call up fresh reinforcements, played a significant role in Harald's subsequent loss of the battle to the Normans.

The opponents were positioned on two hills with an intervening valley. At 9 A.M. William's attack surprised Harald, forcing him to fight a defensive battle with largely unseasoned levies. Harald's housecarls took the front and flank positions of the tightly grouped Anglo-Saxon army. This was a good defensive stand. It also blocked the road to London.

William deployed his army into three main groups: Breton auxiliaries on the left, the bulk of Normans in the center, and a mixed group on the right. The van was comprised of light foot soldiers and archers, who were followed by more heavily armed infantry, and finally, squadrons of mounted knights. Initially, William's battle strategy was an uncoordinated series of attacks by infantry and cavalry. After the first waves were repulsed by Harald, William altered his strategy to combined attacks. Archers shot high to disable and occupy the defenders while the knights attacked to break the defense line. William was successful. Harald died in the blizzard of arrows, and the Anglo-Saxon line broke.

Tamsin Hekala

See also: Norman Conquest; Stamford Bridge, Battle of; William the Conqueror

References and further reading:

Brown, R. A. "The Battle of Hastings." In *Proceedings of the Battle Conference on Anglo-Norman Studies III 1980,* ed. R. A. Brown, 1–21. Woodbridge, UK: Boydell Press, 1981.

Douglas, David C. *William the Conqueror: The Norman Impact upon England.* Berkeley: University of California Press, 1964.

Walker, Ian W. *Harold: The Last Anglo-Saxon King.* Thrupp Stroud, Glouchestershire, UK: Sutton Publishing, 1997.

Hattin, Battle of (4 July 1187)

A severe defeat of the crusaders by the Muslims under Saladin. Sultan Saladin (Salah al-Din) organized forces to retake the Holy Land from the Christian kingdoms established in the Levant after the First Crusade. To counter this, King Guy of Lusignan organized an army of 15,000 at Sepphoris, near Nazareth. Against the advice of his advisers, Guy's army began their march into the arid region of the eastern Galilee on 3 July 1187 to relieve the Muslim siege of Tiberias.

The Christian army consisted of about 1,500 knights and 4,000 cavalry, the remainder being infantry. The march proceeded slowly as Muslim cavalry harassed the advanced units. By the afternoon the Christians were out of water and growing weary. Guy decided to turn toward the springs at Hattin, overlooking the sea of Galilee. Two rocky outcrops, known as the Horns of Hattin, dominated the barren plain. As the Christian army camped that night Saladin encircled their position.

At dawn on 4 July the Christians resumed the march. Saladin's infantry lit brush fires that blew smoke toward the Christians. With the two armies arrayed, the Christian knights charged, driving back the Muslims. The Christians were unable to drive them off, however, and became more fatigued from lack of water, heavy mail, and the smoke. Some of the Christian cavalry broke through and escaped, the remainder of the army was mired near the rocky horns.

Saladin's forces attacked on all sides, and the exhausted Christians surrendered, with a remnant of the True Cross falling into Saladin's hands. The numerous bishops and noblemen captured along with King Guy were ransomed, while the foot soldiers were sold into slavery. Saladin took the rest of the region, eventually capturing Jerusalem.

Robert Dunkerly

See also: Crusades; Saladin

References and further reading:

Nicolle, David. *Hattin: Saladin's Greatest Victory.* London: Osprey Publishing Co., 1993.

Hawaiian Wars (1782–1810)

The three decades from about 1780 to 1810 that saw the Hawaiian Islands brought together into a unified kingdom for the first time by King Kamehameha "the Great" (c. 1752–1819). As in other parts of the world, this consolidation was made possible in the Hawaiian Islands in great part through the introduction of firearms.

When Captain James Cook was killed on the Big Island of Hawaii in 1778 by armed warriors of that island's primary chief, Kalaniopuu, the islands of Hawaii were far from a unified polity. Political power and control varied from island to island, with even the Big Island divided among rival chieftains. Yet within a generation the armaments and technology that Cook and other Western traders and explorers introduced would become decisive in that archipelago's unification. Soon after Chief Kalaniopuu's death in 1782 a rivalry ensued between Kalaniopuu's relations, including his sons Kiwalao and Keoua and his nephew Kamehameha, for control of the Big Island. But the rival chieftains and their bands of warriors were of relatively equal strength, and as a result their struggle persisted throughout the 1780s without conclusive results.

In 1790 an American trading vessel, the *Fair American,* along with its guns and two English crewmen, fell into the hands of Kamehameha after it was attacked and seized as retaliation for losses suffered in an encounter with an earlier Western ship. Such trading vessels had begun to appear with increasing frequency in the islands, a convenient watering hole between China and the West Coast of the Americas. Kamehameha would use the two foreigners to manufacture Western handguns and train his men in Western fighting tactics.

Even before establishing his power on the Big Island, Kamehameha decided to attack the neighboring island of Maui, then under the control of the most powerful chief in the islands, Kahekili. In the narrow valley of Iao on Maui, Kamehameha, employing his two Englishmen and newly acquired guns, inflicted a decisive defeat upon an army led by Kahekili's son. Despite this victory Kamehameha returned to the Big Island, where fighting had erupted again in his absence. The renewed struggle on the Big Island was again indecisive until Kamehameha ambushed and killed his chief rival, Keoua, along with his retinue of warriors, after inviting him to meet at a newly constructed *heiau* (temple), dedicated tellingly to the god of war. With this death Kamehameha established himself as master of the Big Island of Hawaii.

Soon thereafter Kahekili sent a fleet of native canoes and special bands of warriors, along with his own Western vessel, to harass Kamehameha on his own turf. A sea battle was fought off the Big Island between the two rival chieftains' vessels, which proved sanguinary but indecisive. Kahekili died on his home island of Oahu soon afterward, his domains, like those of Kalaniopuu previously, falling into dispute between his various heirs. Only in late 1794 did Kahekili's son Kalanikupule emerge as victor, following the defeat on Oahu of his half brother, and primary foe, with the help of guns supplied by an English merchant. In January 1795 the victorious Kalanikupule decided to take his campaigns to the Big Island of Hawaii, hoping to defeat his father's rival Kamehameha. Now equipped with a plentiful supply of firearms and several Western vessels, his hopes of bringing the Big Island under his control were not farfetched. His luck did not hold, however, and the foreign crews of his ships, pressed into his service, mutinied and succeeded in driving Kalanikupule and his warriors overboard and back to Oahu in humiliation.

Kamehameha meanwhile had been colluding with the English. In 1794 he agreed to "cede" the Big Island of Hawaii to Great Britain and in return received English help in building a fighting ship. Eyeing his strategic opportunity, Kamehameha decided to move and in early 1795 seized Maui and the narrow island of Molokai, which lay just to its north. Despite the defection of one of his primary chiefs to Kalanikupule, Kamehameha proceeded with plans to attack Oahu and landed on that island's southern coast near modern Waikiki. Kamehameha scattered his foe, driving many over the high cliffs of the pass, and with his victory, and the death of Kalanikupule, secured his control over Oahu.

The only island remaining outside Kamehameha's control was the far western island of Kauai. On Oahu Kamehameha received further British help in building a 40-ton ship with which to attack Kauai. Kamehameha and his forces set sail for Kauai in summer 1796, only to have his plans postponed at the last moment by an uprising on the Big Island. Perhaps the delay was fortunate. The uprising was soon subdued but plans for the invasion of Kauai were put on hold. The interval allowed Kamehameha time to consolidate his newly won domains and to set up efficient means of administration and communication. He set up governors on each of the islands, and like resourceful rulers before him, such as France's Louis XIV or Toyotomi Hideyoshi in Japan, he invited potential rivals to dwell with him in his capital. He also set about building a stronger navy, switching to innovative twin-hulled canoes rather than the traditional and less stable single-hulled ones. From the foreigners arriving in increasing numbers and with increasing frequency in the islands Kamehameha procured yet more armaments and foreign vessels.

In 1802 Kamehameha finally sailed again for Kauai, then ruled by the chief Kaumualii, with a fleet of nearly 800 vessels and an armed force of thousands. Kamehameha and his fleet tarried for some time on Maui, hoping unsuccessfully to threaten Kaumualii into submission, before continuing westward to Oahu. On Oahu in 1804 Kamehameha's efforts were struck an almost fatal blow, in the form of an epidemic that wiped out many of his troops, though it spared him. For several more years Kamehameha stayed on in Oahu, which was yearly growing in population and prosperity. At this point Kamehameha let it be known that he would be satisfied with the outward submission of his rival on Kauai, and gaining it would allow him to rule on there as his governor. The two rival chieftains were finally brought together in Honolulu in early 1810. The result was the formal inclusion of Kauai as a tributary island to Kamehameha with Kaumualii as its leader. It was a diplomatic terminus to almost two decades of conflict, and with it Kamehameha secured his control over all of Hawaii and effected the first unification of the islands in their history.

Daniel Kane

References and further reading:

Cahill, Emmett. *The Life and Times of John Young: Confidant and Advisor to Kamehameha the Great.* Honolulu: Island Heritage Publishers, 1999.

Daws, Gavan. *Shoal of Time: A History of the Hawaiian Islands.* Honolulu: University of Hawaii Press, 1968.

Kuykendall, Ralph S. *The Hawaiian Kingdom.* 3 vols. Honolulu: University of Hawaii Press, 1967.

Hawkwood, John, Sir (c. 1321–1394)

English soldier and mercenary captain-general in Italy. The son of Gilbert Hawkwood of Essex, he fought under King Edward III in the Hundred Years War at the battles of Crécy (1346) and Poitiers (1356). Knighted after Poitiers, and unemployed after the Treaty of Bretigny (1360), he joined the mercenary White Company, so named for their brilliantly polished armor. While serving the Italian city-state of Pisa, Hawkwood was elected captain-general of the White Company in January 1354. He led the Pisan forces against Florence (1364), before committing his company to the service of Bernabo Visconti of Milan against Emperor Charles IV. Hawkwood was captured near Arezzo and held until ransomed in 1369. Entering the service of Pope Gregory XI in 1372, he fought in an indecisive war against Milan in 1374 and led papal forces during the War of the Eight Saints (1375). Leaving papal service, Hawkwood joined the antipapal alliances and served as captain-general of Florence from 1378 to 1381. He led Padua, an ally of Florence, to a decisive victory over Verona in the Battle of Castagnaro (11 March 1387). Hawkwood led the Florentine army in his last campaign during an inconclusive war against Milan in 1390–1392.

Hawkwood utilized the English longbow and tactics developed in the French war during his Italian service. He was renowned for his infantry tactics, unit discipline, and utilization of lighter armor and equipment to improve the rapidity of troop movements.

Hawkwood died on 16 March 1394 in Florence. King Richard II later had his body returned and reinterred in Hawkwood's native village.

Brigitte F. Cole

References and further reading:

Temple-Leader, John, and Guiseppe Marcotti. *Sir John Hawkwood.* London: T. F. Unwin, 1849.

Trease, Geoffrey. *The Condottieri.* New York: Holt, 1971.

Henry II, King of England (1133–1189)

Henry Plantagenet, king of England, conqueror, reformer. Henry was duke of Normandy from perhaps 1149, count of Anjou from 1151, and duke of Aquitaine through his marriage to Eleanor in 1152. He is best remembered for his quarrel with Archbishop Becket, for his troubled relations with his wife and sons, among them the future kings Richard I and John, and for his sweeping constitutional reforms in England. His contemporaries recognized him as a military leader without peer. On behalf of his mother, Mathilda, he organized the forces against Stephen of Blois in the civil war for the crown that followed the death of Mathilda's father, Henry I. On the Continent, he regularly subdued rebellious vassals, later including those supporting his sons, and established dominance over virtually all of the princes of northern France, as well as a cowed King Louis VII. While he marshaled the full feudal resources of his realms for major campaigns in Toulouse (1159), Wales (1165), and Ireland (1171), most of his career was spent besieging castles. Castles were both a symbol and a consequence of baronial power at the expense of overlords in the twelfth century.

Henry first besieged and leveled the castles of those refusing to accept his lordship, then strengthened and rebuilt his own castles to preserve order in his realms. His successful castle strategy avoided the necessity of expensive pitched battles. To accomplish this strategy, he increasingly relied on mercenary footmen trained and equipped for castle siege and defense, and not on his feudal levies.

Despite this, Henry was still a feudal king and his administrative reforms in England were marked by two significant initiatives in this capacity: the 1166 Cartae Baronum (Baronial Charters) and the 1181 Assize of Arms. The Baronial Charters were written statements from all of Henry's tenants-in-chief identifying feudal obligations to knight service, thus allowing the king to discover the full extent of his feudal military resources. The Assize of Arms identified and classified each vassal's obligation according to wealth, establishing a hierarchy of military obligation based on a single recruitment system. It would be the first of a series of such attempts that continued into the thirteenth century.

Robert Babcock

See also: Philip II Augustus; Richard I

References and further reading:

Keefe, Thomas K. *Feudal Assessments and the Political Community under Henry II and His Sons.* Berkeley: University of California Press, 1983.

Warren, W. L. *Henry II.* 2d ed. New Haven, CT: Yale University Press, 2000.

Henry V, King of England (1387–1422)

English king, victor at Agincourt. Henry V was born 16 September 1387, at Monmouth, Monmouthshire, Wales, and died 31 August 1422 at Bois de Vincennes, France, as Prince of Wales, duke of Cornwall, earl of Chester, prince of Aquitaine, duke of Aquitaine, and duke of Lancaster. Henry was the eldest son of Henry IV, and he first fought alongside his father during the Welsh (against Owain Glyn Dwr) and English (against Henry Hotspur Percy and Edmund Mortimer) rebellions. Like his father, Henry wished to expand English influence in French territories, and his most famous victory at Agincourt on 25 October 1415 confirmed his place in British history. This battle, which resulted in the destruction of many of the most powerful French nobles, saw the loss of some 6,000 Frenchmen, but only 400 English. Not a decisive victory, Henry was forced to continue to push his way inland, finally capturing Normandy in the spring of 1419. Eventually, Henry signed the Treaty of Troyes with the Burgundians in May 1420, and this solidified his claim to the French throne.

Henry married Katherine, the daughter of the French king, and after a brief tour of the English countryside with his new bride, he returned to France and defeated the stronghold at Meaux in May 1422. It was during this time that Henry's health began to fail him, and he died prematurely of dysentery on 31 August 1422, at the young age of 34. His death was a major blow to the English, who had become quite loyal to him, and while he never saw his goal of conquering France come to fruition, he did leave his kingdom to a nine-month-old successor, Henry VI.

David J. Tietge

See also: Agincourt, Battle of

References and further reading:

Allmand, C. T. *Lancastrian Normandy, 1415–1450: The History of Medieval Occupation.* Oxford, UK: Oxford University Press, 1983.

Jacob, Ernest Fraser. *Henry V and the Invasion of France.* London: English Universities Press, 1947.

Wylie, James Hamilton. *The Reign of Henry the Fifth.* Westport, CT: Greenwood Press, 1968.

Heraclius (c. 575–641)

Byzantine emperor (r. 610–641) who managed to save the empire from defeat at the hands of the Persians and Avars. During the eight-year reign of Phocas I, responsible for a rule of mindless cruelty and terror, the eastern empire all but ceased to exist. Its position in the Haemus collapsed and Persian armies reached the Bosphorus in 608. With the empire in extremis, the exarch of Africa, Heraclius the Elder, raised the standard of revolt and a fleet commanded by his son made its way to Constantinople. There Heraclius the Younger overthrew Phocas and was installed as emperor.

The change of emperor brought no immediate improvement of the empire's position. Damascus fell in 613, Jerusalem in 614, Chalcedon, on the Marmara, in 616. The loss of Egypt (616–619) followed. With Avar raids reaching the walls of Constantinople (617–619), Heraclius determined to abandon Constantinople in favor of the African provinces but was prevented by popular protests and a pledge by Church and people to defend the empire (619). From this time dated the militarization of the state: It underwent fundamental reform, which, over decades, gave rise to the creation of an Anatolian peasantry that held land in return for military service.

With these various changes in hand, in 622 Heraclius left Constantinople with an army to begin operations in Cilicia and Syria. The war was taken into Armenia and thence into Media and Mesopotamia: In 624 Istfahan was occupied. By 625 the Persian Empire, under obvious threat, allied itself with the Avars. Heraclius, returning to Constantinople, resorted to alliance with the Khazars in an attempt to divide Persian attention. Then, leaving Constantinople under the command of the patriarch, Heraclius returned to Armenia and the Caucasus.

Another Persian invasion of Anatolia reached the Bosphorus on 29 June 626 at the same time as an Avar army, of about 80,000 men, reached Constantinople's walls. There followed a climactic 10-day battle on land and at sea as the Avars sought to land forces inside the Golden Horn. The shattering of this attempt forced the Avars to abandon their effort: The Persians were left in Anatolia with a double threat in the mountains and Mesopotamia. Over the next two years the war was carried into the Persian heartland once more. In 628 a peace agreement restored all the eastern empire's lost possessions.

To have been responsible for such a feat of survival would have assured Heraclius of a place in history, but in the 13 years after his return to Constantinople in May 628 the eastern empire lost one-third of its territory. Between 634 and 640 Palestine and Syria were overrun once again; Egypt was lost for good between 639 and 640. Within 25 years of the death of Heraclius the empire had lost half of its territory and faced threats as grave as those that it had faced in 626.

H. P. Willmott

See also: Byzantine-Persian Wars

References and further reading:

Haldon, John. *Warfare, State and Society in the Byzantine World, 565–1204.* London: University College London Press, 1999.

Norwich, John Julius. *Byzantium: The Early Years.* London: Viking, 1988.

Hideyoshi, Toyotomi (1537–1598)

Hideyoshi began his career as a peasant's son in Nakamura, Japan, but rose through the ranks of Oda Nobunaga's army until he became a general. When Akechi Mitsuhide assassinated Nobunaga, Hideyoshi halted his attacks, returned to Kyoto, and executed Akechi. Hideyoshi then served as one of four regents to the grandson of Nobunaga in 1582. By 1585, Hideyoshi had established himself as the successor to Nobunaga's legacy and concluded several alliances, including one with Tokugawa Ieyasu. He then proceeded to unify Japan. Hideyoshi amassed an army of 200,000 men and invaded Chosokase in 1585. Then, in 1587, he assembled an even larger army of 280,000 men and took Kyushu.

Portrait of Hideyoshi, "the Napoleon of Japan." (Bettmann/Corbis)

By 1590, Hideyoshi, after the battle of Odawara, had successfully unified Japan. The key to his success was due more to his political acumen in arranging alliances than to military force. He did, however, possess the military might to enforce his alliances. Furthermore, in order to prevent rebellion, he arranged national sword hunts and disarmed all but the bushi, or samurai class.

Hideyoshi was not satisfied with the conquest of all of Japan but envisioned the conquest of China. He intended to march through Korea and then invade China from the north. After the kingdom of Korea refused him free passage, he invaded it in 1592. His army of 200,000 overran most of Korea but encountered the Ming Chinese army at Pyongyang. Negotiations began, but they eventually broke down. So another invasion occurred in 1597–1598 with another massive army but in the process Hideyoshi died.

Hideyoshi's greatest contribution was the unification of Japan. Furthermore, he was able to harness its nascent military ability and focus it away from deleterious civil war and into foreign ventures. The sheer size of his armies are testaments to Hideyoshi's organizational and logistical abilities.

Timothy May

See also: Japanese Invasion of Korea; Japanese Wars of Unification; Oda, Nobunaga; Samurai; Sekigahara; Tokugawa, Ieyasu

References and further reading:
Berry, Mary Elizabeth. *Hideyoshi.* Cambridge, MA: Harvard University Press, 1982.
Dening, Walter. *The Life of Toyotomi Hideyoshi.* New York: AMS Press, 1971.
Toyotomi Hideyoshi. *101 Letters of Hideyoshi: The Private Correspondence of Toyotomi Hideyoshi.* Ed. Adriana Boscaro. Tokyo: Sophia University Press, 1975.

Hill, Ambrose Powell (1825–1865)

Confederate general, tenacious fighter, and one of Robert E. Lee's most valued subordinates. A. P. Hill was born in Culpeper, Virginia, on 9 November 1825. At the U.S. Military Academy at West Point, he was a member of the class of 1847 and the roommate of future Union commander George B. McClellan. He fought as an artilleryman in the Mexican-American War and against the Seminoles. On 31 March 1861, he resigned from the U.S. Army as first lieutenant.

Commissioned colonel of the 13th Virginia Regiment in May, Hill was in reserve at First Bull Run. Promoted to brigadier general on 26 February 1862, he distinguished himself at Yorktown, Williamsburg, and Hanover Court House, Virginia, in May. He was made major general on 26 May and quickly assembled the famous Hill's Light Division, which became a key element in the peninsular campaign. Hill's setbacks during the Seven Days Battles were not through lack of either courage or tactical skill, but from the absence of the support he expected from Stonewall Jackson.

Hill and Jackson subsequently worked better together. At Cedar Mountain on 9 August they combined to rout Nathaniel Banks. Their cooperation helped the Confederates at Second Bull Run, Harpers Ferry, Antietam, and Fredericksburg. Hill accompanied Jackson around the Union right flank at Chancellorsville and took over command when Jackson was hit. Robert E. Lee promoted Hill to lieutenant general on 24 May 1863, hoping to replace Jackson.

Hill proved inadequate for corps command. His accomplishments after Chancellorsville never matched his earlier work. His III Corps was the first to attack at Gettysburg, but it did not perform well. His hasty attack on a superior Union force under Gouverneur Kemble Warren at Bristoe Station, Virginia, on 14 October without first gathering the necessary reconnaissance devastated his troops and thwarted Lee's offensive. He likewise failed to meet Lee's expectations at the Wilderness, North Anna, and Cold Harbor. He was killed in action at Petersburg on 2 April 1865.

Eric v. d. Luft

See also: American Civil War; Antietam/Sharpsburg; Bull Run, First/Manassas; Bull Run, Second/Manassas Junction; Chancellorsville, Battle of; Cold Harbor, Battle of; Fredericksburg; Gettysburg; Harpers Ferry; Jackson, Thomas "Stonewall"; Lee, Robert Edward; Longstreet, James; McClellan, George Brinton; Petersburg, Siege of; Seven Days Battles; Wilderness

References and further reading:
Hassler, William Woods. *A. P. Hill, Lee's Forgotten General.* Richmond: Garrett & Massie, 1962.
Schenck, Martin. *Up Came Hill: The Story of the Light Division and Its Leaders.* Harrisburg, PA: Stackpole, 1958.

Hindenburg, Paul von Beneckendorf und von (1847–1934)

World War I commander and president of the Weimar Republic. Hindenburg was born on 2 October 1847 in Posen. He entered the Prussian army in 1866 and fought in the last two wars of German Unification, the Austro-Prussian War (1866) and the Franco-Prussian War (1870–1871). From 1873 to 1876 he studied at the Prussian War Academy before entering the Prussian General Staff with the rank of captain. A solid officer, Hindenburg steadily rose through the ranks of the Prussian army and was even considered for the posts of chief of the general staff and Prussian war minister. Hindenburg commanded an army corps from 1903 to 1911, when, having achieved the rank of lieutenant general, he retired after a successful if not brilliant military career. World War I changed that.

On 22 August 1914, Hindenburg was recalled to active duty and given command of the Eighth Army in East Prussia. His chief of staff was Erich von Ludendorff. The careers and fortunes of both men would henceforth be inexorably linked. Sent to East Prussia to deal with the Russian threat, Hindenburg and Ludendorff inflicted two major defeats on the Russians at the battles of Tannenberg and the Masurian Lakes (August–September 1914). As a result of these spectacular victories, Hindenburg became the most famous and most popular general in Germany, a status that he was to keep for the remainder of his long life. In the wake of Tannenberg and the Masurian Lakes, Hindenburg was promoted to the rank of field marshal and appointed commander in chief on the eastern front in November 1914. In this position Hindenburg and his chief of staff Ludendorff came into increasing conflict with the commander in chief of the general staff, Erich von Falkenhayn, over the question of German military strategy. Moreover, Falkenhayn's inability to break the military stalemate redounded to Hindenburg's benefit, as many ordinary Germans now looked to the hero of the eastern front as Germany's savior. On 28 August 1916, Hindenburg replaced Falkenhayn as chief of the general staff, with Ludendorff serving as first quartermaster general. In addition to their responsibilities for German military strategy, Hindenburg and Ludendorff were increasingly in charge of German domestic policy as well, which led to the creation of a "silent dictatorship."

Domestically, Hindenburg and Ludendorff sought to place the German economy on a total war footing by enacting a massive munitions program, accompanied by an Auxiliary Service Law aimed at mobilizing German manpower. Yet they could do little about the food situation, brought about by the Allied naval blockade, and for several winters, turnips seemed to be about the only food available. This near famine is all the more remarkable considering that after 1917, Germany had control of the Ukraine, one of the world's greatest food producers, as well as one of Europe's most efficient railway systems to transport the wealth of the Ukraine to the Reich. Germany did exact huge reparations in specie from the defeated Russians, but the German people could not eat gold.

Hindenburg and Ludendorff were also instrumental in the downfall of Chancellor Theobald von Bethmann-Hollweg in July 1917 and his replacement by a string of weak chancellors who could be bent to the military's will. In terms of military strategy Hindenburg and Ludendorff were responsible for the reintroduction of unrestricted submarine warfare in April 1917, which brought the Americans into the war; the annexationist peace treaties imposed on Rumania and Russia in 1918; and the final German effort on the western front in 1918. As grand strategists both left much to be desired.

Hindenburg retired from the army for the second time in 1919 but remained a popular figure in a postwar Germany bitterly resentful of the Versailles diktat. (Of course, the terms imposed by Germany on her defeated enemies were certainly diktats by any definition of the word.) In 1925 Hindenburg again emerged from retirement and was elected president of the Weimar Republic. Although a monarchist at heart, he was initially loyal to the republic. However with the onset of the Depression in 1929, the rise of Nazism after 1930, and his advancing age, he became increasingly dependent on a rightist camarilla determined to destroy German democracy. Under the influence of this rather unsavory circle, Hindenburg appointed Adolph Hitler chancellor on 30 January 1933. Relegated to the sidelines as a senile figurehead, Hindenburg died on 2 August 1934, at his estate in Neudeck, East Prussia. It was an ill day for Germany when Hindenburg was translated from his field command to political power.

J. David Cameron

See also: Falkenhayn, Eric von; Ludendorff, Erich Friedrich Wilheim; William II

References and further reading:

von Hindenburg, Paul. *Aus meinem Leben.* Leipzig: S. Hirzel, 1920.

Kitchen, Martin. *The Silent Dictatorship: The Politics of the German High Command under Hindenburg and Ludendorff, 1916–1918.* New York: Holmes & Meier, 1967.

Wheeler-Bennett, John W. *Hindenburg: The Wooden Titan.* New York: Macmillan, 1967.

Hiroshima and Nagasaki, Atomic Bombings of (1945)

Ended World War II and began the nuclear age. The Japanese cities of Hiroshima and Nagasaki were devastated by atomic bombs in August 1945. Their destruction culminated years of intensive research and the investment of $2 billion into the Manhattan Project, the top-secret American effort to develop atomic weapons.

By 1944, American scientists believed they could produce an atomic chain reaction sufficient to generate an unprecedented explosion, and army leaders created the 509th Composite Bomb Group to develop tactics for utilizing the new weapon as a bomb. Colonel Paul Tibbets's 393d Bombardment Squadron pioneered these tactics in the 509th, using modified B-29 Superfortresses to drop single bombs accurately from high altitudes and then climb, turn, and dive away at high speed to escape the shockwave generated at detonation. After training in Utah, Tibbets and his men flew to the Pacific island of Tinian and awaited delivery of atomic bombs for use against Japan.

Their delivery came closer on 15 July 1945, when scientists detonated the first atomic device at the Trinity test site, near Alamogordo, New Mexico. With an estimated yield of 15,000–20,000 tons of TNT, the explosion exceeded even the wildest expectations of Manhattan Project scientists, and President Harry Truman quickly approved the use of atomic weapons against Japanese cities. Hiroshima, Kokura, Niigata, and Nagasaki were the possible targets, chosen for their military value and because they had been relatively undamaged by previous raids.

Tibbets and crew began their mission to Hiroshima by boarding the *Enola Gay,* a B-29 named for Tibbets's mother, on 6 August 1945. They carried a bomb nicknamed Little Boy, in honor of Franklin Roosevelt, which utilized a uranium 235 core to generate an atomic explosion. Tibbets dropped the device at 8:15 A.M. and it detonated 1,900 feet above Hiroshima with a force of 15,000 tons of TNT. It destroyed five square miles of the city, along with 140,000 people, who died from the initial explosion or from radiation and blast burns over the next several months.

On 9 August, the United States launched a second atomic strike, sending a B-29 named *Bock's Car* commanded by Ma-

The atomic bombing of Nagasaki, Japan. (Library of Congress)

jor Charles Sweeney to attack the city of Kokura. When clouds obscured the city, Sweeney switched targets and bombed Nagasaki at 11:02 A.M. with a plutonium bomb named Fat Man (after Winston Churchill). Though more powerful than Little Boy, Fat Man caused less damage because hills around Nagasaki contained the explosion. The bomb killed 73,884 people outright, injured 74,909, and destroyed 2.6 square miles of the city.

Historians and many concerned citizens still vehemently debate the wisdom and morality of dropping the atomic bombs and their role in compelling the Japanese surrender on 14 August 1945. The surrender came five days after the destruction of Nagasaki, but Japanese leaders were influenced by the entry of the Soviet Union into the war against them perhaps as much as by the power of atomic bombs. Their surrender made the invasion of Japan, the greatest planned military operation in history, completely unnecessary.

Lance Janda

See also: Atomic Bomb, Development of; World War II

References and further reading:

Alperovitz, Gar. *The Decision to Use the Atomic Bomb.* New York: Vintage Books, 1995.

Rhodes, Richard. *The Making of the Atomic Bomb.* New York: Touchstone Books, 1995.

History, Military

The study of the planning for and the use of organized armed force, either on behalf of some form of recognized state authority or against it. It differs from other branches of history insofar as it calls upon knowledge of certain specialized areas, such as strategy and tactics.

Military history can be said to have existed since men began to write about armed conflict: The Hebrew Scriptures contain many accounts of battles and can be considered a military historical source. The Athenian Thucydides, whose history of the Peloponnesian War is often cited as an early example of military history, provided accounts of sea operations, clashes between armies, and the strategies of the opposing sides and did not demonize the opposing forces. But he also examined the nature of state power, the effects of war, and offers of peace, so much so that one of the first translators of the work, Thomas Hobbes, described its author as "the most Politick Historiographer that ever writ," thereby highlighting a perennial problem of military history: deciding the point at which it overlaps so much with other areas that it becomes political or general history.

Nevertheless, throughout its development, military history has been marked by certain recurring characteristics. In particular, the motivation of authors and the functions that it has served can be identified as follows: to provide a record of heroic or sacrificial deeds for coming generations; to pay tribute to the achievements of those who fought soon after the conflict; to assist in the discovery of lessons for future wars; to satisfy the demand of the public for accounts of battles; to cover up mistakes by commanders or leaders by falsifying, omitting, or distorting events; to provide inspiration to soldiers and future soldiers; to act as a teaching tool for military instructors; to encourage feelings of identification within a group, community, or state; and to satisfy scholarly interest. Trends in military historiography have been largely defined by the interplay of these motivations.

While in many early accounts enjoyment in the destruction and slaughter can be clearly detected, before and during the early modern period the *genius* of the warlord played a central role in the writing of military history. Although the organization, equipment, and movement of armies were described, the commander was usually the monarch or nobleman and hence was honored through accounts of his campaigns. The function of this military history, though, was not simply to generate propaganda on behalf of the ruler: It was assumed that the performance of the commander was normally the factor that decided the outcome. It should also not be forgotten that in times of high illiteracy rates military history should also be considered to have included visual records, such as the Bayeux Tapestry, or the woodcut illustrations of the sixteenth and seventeenth centuries.

Two parallel developments at the beginning of the nineteenth century, however, ushered in important changes: the professionalization of historical research and writing at universities and of armies through the establishment of military academies and general staffs.

Even before the Franco-Prussian War, military history began to be systematized, with the use of battles to illustrate certain points of military operations and tactics. In Britain the first example was probably Major General Patrick MacDougall's *Theory of War Illustrated by Numerous Examples from Military History,* published in 1856, followed by the more influential work by General Sir Edward Hamley, *The Operations of War Explained and Illustrated,* first published in 1866 and continually republished until 1922. Hamley's work is interesting for the way in which it shows the blurred dividing line between military theory and military history. Hamley's starting point was to complain that military history was written very much like novels, with the reader accepting uncritically the opinions of the writer. In fact, in the nineteenth century mainstream military history was dominated by the assumption that turning points in history were epitomized by decisive battles, an approach enshrined in Sir Edward Creasy's *The Fifteen Decisive Battles of the World* (1851).

After the conclusion of the Franco-Prussian War, military history enjoyed a new period of popularity in Europe, with numerous illustrated and well-documented histories of that war appearing. The most significant development was arguably the emergence of official histories, the American Civil War being most memorably commemorated by the *War of the Rebellion: A Compilation of the Official Records of the Union and Confederate Armies,* consisting of an astonishing 128 volumes, published between 1881 and 1901. But most professional of the official military histories was the more manageable eight-volume history of *The German-French War of 1870–71,* undertaken by the Military History Section of the German General Staff; the first volume was published in 1874, the last in 1881. This work was the first official military history to be researched and written in conformity with the standards of the emerging history profession and was characterized by detail and analysis down to company level and up to panoramic descriptions of all the engagements. The first volumes won the prize for German History awarded by the Prussian Academy of Science in 1878, and their publication opened the era of professionally respectable military history.

With the expansion of staff work, so began an increase in the volume of documents left behind by wars; and as the official archives grew, so did the desire of armed forces to keep them under their own control. One of the few historians in Germany to challenge this monopoly was Hans Delbrück, an academic at Berlin University, who argued that the subject needed to broaden its focus, taking into account the political intentions of national leaders. His view that military history ought to be conducted outside the general staff provoked bitter opposition.

The writing of the history of World War I saw the apogee of the dominance of official military history. Although the Red Army did not produce an official history of Russian operations 1914–1917, and the Americans contented themselves with the publication of documents, the voluminous British, German, and French historical undertakings were severely hampered by the determination of the military establishments to prevent damage to the reputation of commanders and their armies. The German official history, although published by the state archives, was written mainly by former officers who had not been accepted by the Reichswehr, the intention being to counteract the defamation of the military that followed the defeat in 1918. The British official history demonstrated a further problem: With the first volume appearing in 1922, and the final one in 1947, the slow progress put into question the value of such works for instructional purposes.

In Britain, a reaction occurred against self-serving military history in the 1930s, Basil Liddell Hart and J. F. C. Fuller in particular making influential contributions. Although their works on the American Civil War and World War I did not meet the standards of later academic monographs, they encouraged a more critical attitude to the use of sources and the official version of events.

As it turned out, the official British history of World War II far exceeded the quality of its predecessor. The U.S. histories were likewise of a high standard, the range of publications being particularly noteworthy. Only the Russian official histories of the "Great Patriotic War" can be criticized for omitting significant facts and for its propaganda. The history the Wehrmacht remains, however, the most problematic case study in the writing of the history of World War II. Many of the surviving German records were captured by the Western Allies, and the U.S. Army established an Operational History (German) Section in January 1946, employing 328 ex-Wehrmacht officers by June 1946. Its successor, the Control Group, survived in skeleton form until 1961. The studies conducted under American auspices assessed the war only within the narrow framework of "lessons learned," yet they were not only the basis for many later published works, the results flowed into official U.S. military thinking. Mistakes and atrocities were almost always blamed on Hitler. No doubt as a reaction to this traditional concept, the first volumes of the Federal German official history of World War II (volume 1 was published in 1979) undertaken by the armed forces Military History Research Office adopted a wider and more critical approach. But by the close of the twentieth century the work was still uncompleted, illustrating that some of the problems of official history have remained.

Despite the dominance of World War II as the main subject for military historians throughout the 1950s and 1960s, the postwar period has seen a revolution in the writing of military history. The increasing numbers of military officers who take doctorates before assuming posts as historians has led to a remarkable improvement in research standards. The U.S. Army Command and General Staff College at Fort Leavenworth has been influential in promoting an expansion in the scope of combat studies, geographically and thematically. Equally important is the emergence of a new concern with the experience of battle, a trend confirmed by John Keegan's innovative *The Face of Battle* (1973). Keegan's book inspired many more studies of this kind, marking a decisive break with the operational narrative tradition, which usually excluded the horrors of battle. The new concern for the "ordinary soldier" (undoubtedly a reflection of the prevailing interest in the academic history establishment of "history from the bottom up") expressed itself particularly effectively in studies of war in the trenches, such as Tony Ashworth's *Trench Warfare 1914–1918: The Live and Let Live System* (1980). These works opened up new possibilities for historians to use microstudies to put official accounts to the test, showing how *the system* actually worked.

Beyond the experience of combat, other types of military history have been developing, most notably studies of armies in peacetime. Building on insights from sociology and organization theory and pioneering sociological studies of various officer corps, major studies have been published on military reform, military debates, and the dynamics of the introduction of new weapons. Well-researched monographs on the development of armored forces, 1919–1939, for instance, have not simply added to gaps in knowledge, they have improved awareness of the fact that poor battlefield performance can have doctrinal causes that stem from decisions taken during peacetime. They have also contributed to the development of methodologically pioneering works on military effectiveness, innovation, doctrine, and culture, a recent example being *Military Innovation in the Interwar Period* (1996), edited by Williamson Murray and Allan Millett.

The organizational approach in studies of armies has likewise led to significant improvements in understanding such subjects as war planning, mobilization, surprise attack, and failures in intelligence assessment. Indeed, the role of intelligence in both peacetime and wartime has emerged of late as a subject in its own right.

Perhaps the most important postwar trend in the writing of military history has been the body of literature that falls under the rubric of "war and society." This school of thought, which became popular in the 1970s, seeks to examine the effects of warfare on political institutions, economies, popular culture, and postwar societies. It has assisted, for example, in encouraging study of the home fronts during both world wars and militarism in Wilhelmine Germany. The problem with this approach is that it lacks any clear theoretical or methodological underpinning, leading often to imprecise generalizations. Perhaps more stimulating have been those works that have examined specific aspects of warfare over several centuries, original studies such as Martin Van Creveld's path-breaking *Supplying War* (1977), which examined logistics since Gustav Adolphus, or William McNeill's *The Pursuit of Power* (1983), discussing the interaction of war, technology, finance, and society. One criticism that can be leveled against such works is that they tend to be bloodless accounts of a very bloody process: men with lice crawling over their testicles dying and being mutilated in very unpleasant ways.

In short, since 1945 the thematic and methodological scope of military history has widened dramatically, producing a concomitant trend of specialization within an increasing number of subdisciplines. The use of military history for instructional purposes has continued, but it has become more subject to academic scholarly standards than ever before, suggesting perhaps the fulfillment of Hans Delbrück's original demands.

Alaric Searle

See also: Theory, Military

References and further reading:

Fortescue, J. W. *Military History.* Cambridge, UK: Cambridge University Press, 1914.

French, David. "Sir James Edmonds and the Official History of the Great War." *RUSI Journal* 131 (March 1986).

Liddell Hart, Basil: *Why Don't We Learn from History?* London: Allen & Unwin, 1944.

Kühne, Thomas, and Benjamin Ziemann, eds. *Was ist Militärgeschichte?* Paderborn: Schöningh, 1999.

Hitler, Adolf (1889–1945)

Austro-German statesman, classic and supreme symbol of evil for the twentieth century. Hitler was born on 20 April 1889 to Alois, a focused, able civil servant of the multiethnic Austro-Hungarian Empire, and his much younger wife, Klara. Alois died in January 1903, after years of often-violent conflict with Adolf that apparently only taught the son to defy the father by rejecting everything that Alois stood for: thrift, discipline, work, a family life, and a measure of political tolerance. Hitler fully justified his father's fears when his mother allowed him to lead an idle life in the family home in Linz.

In September 1907, Hitler went to Vienna, seeking admittance to the Academy of Fine Arts. Rejected for inadequate preparation, he returned to Linz to care for his mother during her long, painful death from breast cancer, moving to Vienna in February 1908. There, he wasted his mother's inheritance in lazy fantasy at the opera and reading a gutter press that intensified the pan-German nationalism and anti-Semitism he had absorbed as a child. By the winter of 1909–1910, he was homeless, seeking shelter in a men's hostel. Only then did he paint hack work routinely. In May 1913, Hitler received his father's inheritance and moved to Munich immediately afterwards. He refused service in the multiethnic Austro-Hungarian army during the Balkan War only to volunteer for service in August 1914 in the Bavarian army, eventually serving as a dispatch runner in the 16th Reserve Infantry Regiment.

Hitler with Nazi troops. (Library of Congress)

A committed soldier, he was highly decorated, respected, and very odd: He seems to have had no lovers nor close friends even though his regiment may have been his first home since his mother's death. He vehemently disapproved of humanitarian considerations influencing military policy and reacted violently to defeatist comments. The mass killing of World War I apparently deadened Hitler's already numb emotions. In an era tainted by a pseudo-Darwinian emphasis upon combat as the ultimate test of nations, as well as of men, he thought that the Jews had grown rich upon German suffering and defeat. Selected for army propagandist training in 1919, he created a theoretical framework for his obsessions; in September of that year, he first wrote of annihilating the Jews.

Hitler considered himself the drummer of Germany's *völkisch* right when he led an almost comical putsch in Munich on 8 November 1923. His trial for high treason transformed him into the right's national leader. Sentenced to five years' fortress confinement in Landsberg prison, he served only nine months, during which time he dictated *Mein Kampf* to his epigone, Rudolph Hess.

Like his father, Hitler preferred young, dependent women who could be manipulated and controlled. In 1929, he took as his lover his niece Geli Raubal, 19 years his junior. His insecurity permitted her no independence: the evidence points to her suicide, rather than murder, on 18 September 1931. Hitler claimed to be married to Germany and to every German woman. In reality, he simply could not permit a woman any standing of her own, even in the domestic sphere national socialism prescribed for women. Nevertheless, it is a mistake to stress Hitler's very real misogyny too much: However dim his view of German womanhood, he was also a catastrophe for German manhood.

Hitler and the Nazi Party did not seize power but received a majority of the votes cast in the Reichstag elections of July 1932. Despite defeat in the November 1932 elections, Hitler had mobilized the masses and so he was brokered into the chancellorship in January 1933 by conservative allies. However antidemocratic and authoritarian they were, they were also deeply divided amongst themselves about how to control him. On 23 March 1933, the Reichstag granted Hitler an Enabling Act, figuratively voting itself out of existence; on 30 June 1934, the Night of the Long Knives, Hitler crushed any internal Nazi opposition with the blessing of the German army.

By 1939, Hitler had stamped Germany with his personal insecurity and pseudo-Darwinian preference for conflict, often duplicating, even triplicating, traditional institutions with competing Nazi ones. The result was that even quite trivial decisions were referred to Hitler, which may have salved his ego but as policy was folly in peacetime and calamity in wartime. This subversion of bureaucratic power bases ensured confidants who would tell Hitler what he wanted to hear. Many Germans shared his racial views of Nordic superiority, Slavic inferiority, the necessity of exterminating the Jews, and cleansing the Germanic race. However, the increasing violence of Nazi rule was an extremely powerful motivation for *all* Germans to "work toward the Führer," on these matters. It was thus unnecessary for Hitler personally to direct the extermination of Europe's Jews, the Final Solution, chosen during the Wannsee Conference in January 1942.

By nature a gambler, Hitler actively pursued war with Britain and France during the Polish crisis of August 1939. An unhealthy hypochondriac, he was convinced he would die young. He thought no one else could lead Germany down his path of annihilatory racism, endemic though racism and anti-Semitism were in German society. He was probably right: Hitler was a revolutionary, not a reactionary.

Insecure and undisciplined, Hitler surrounded himself with advisers who craved his favor, shared his racism, and could not contradict his flood of facts, half-truths, and outright lies masquerading as knowledge. Hitler deliberately created an environment for himself that made it impossible for him accurately to assess risks, strengths, and weaknesses in any given situation. His successes before 1941 made him utterly resistant to criticism. The pivotal events of World War II show this clearly.

Despite the advice of his armor experts, Hitler regarded the area around Dunkirk as unsuited to armored operations, and so he entrusted the destruction of Britain's only field army to the Luftwaffe in May and June 1940. Wary of the British navy until he had a blue-water fleet capable of defeating it, Hitler postponed the invasion of Britain, leaving it an unreduced fortress in his rear while he turned east.

Supported this time by his military staff, Hitler insisted that Germany could invade the Soviet Union on 21 June 1941 and defeat the Red Army in six weeks, a tacit admission that German victory depended upon defeating the Soviet Union within that time frame. On 10 December 1941, as German troops retreated from Moscow, Hitler, in an act of supreme folly, declared war upon the United States of America in the aftermath of Pearl Harbor. Once the Soviet Union was defeated, Hitler intended to turn upon Britain and crush its resistance. The Reich would then fight and defeat the U.S., which Hitler despised for its racial "impurity" and "weaknesses," despite its immense industrial resources.

As the war progressed, Hitler intervened at increasingly lower levels of military decision making. He had always mistrusted the army leadership, which accepted his bribes and decorations to keep faith with him during the war, only to blame him for their mistakes as well as his own afterwards. From the army's middle ranks came a series of assassination attempts motivated by compassion toward the conquered, a horror of retribution for German crimes, especially against the Soviets, and shame for what Germany had become. Rather than await the end of the war in relative safety, these men made a final attempt to kill Hitler and overthrow his regime on 20 July 1944. Few survived. Their gesture of atonement only strengthened Hitler's belief that he was appointed by Providence to lead Germany to victory or doom. He would not countenance surrender.

Despite looming catastrophe, the German people greeted Hitler's survival with public expressions of relief. Although his personal popularity declined with approaching defeat, Hitler retained an amazing degree of loyalty from the common German, civilian or soldier, who often attributed misdeeds to party functionaries. To a great extent, Hitler was never a tyrant. It is true that the mechanisms of repression, selective breeding, and genocide were created for and first practiced upon the German people. However, many Germans supported Hitler's most extreme plans not only for the conquered, but also for Germany, including scorching German earth before the Allied onslaught.

On 29 April 1945, Adolf Hitler married his longtime mistress, Eva Braun, in Berlin. Although for many years the greatest desire of this unsophisticated young woman had been to become Frau Hitler, her lover obliged her only when it no longer mattered. They committed suicide the next day, rather than face their people and the enemy or assume responsibility by fighting to the death in the ruins of what had once been an imperial capital. Hitler left Germany utterly defeated, ground like grain between the Soviets and the Western Allies, in moral and physical ruins, soon to be partitioned, its rich cultural heritage almost effaced by twelve years of Nazism.

The profound cruelty Hitler inflicted on the world is not reducible to his anti-Semitism. The destruction of the Sixth Army at Stalingrad, the militarily useless sacrifice of poorly armed and trained troops, and the execution of thousands of German soldiers by their comrades are not comparable to the Holocaust, the vicious antipartisan warfare in Serbia, or the destruction of Warsaw. But all of these German crimes were part of a whole, rooted in German history and culture, as indeed any nation's actions must be, just as all serious German resistance to Hitler was fiercely reactionary, based on older, more humane values that were also authentically German. Hitler brilliantly understood his adopted country, and he shared its hopes and fears to an extraordinary degree, tremendously exaggerating them in his slaughterhouse heart.

Erin E. Solaro

See also: Bolshevik Revolution; Churchill, Sir Winston; Ethics of Warfare; German Wars of Unification; Guderian, Heinz; Rommel, Erwin Johannes Eugen; Roosevelt, Franklin D.; Stalin; World War I; World War II; Ypres, Battles of

References and further reading:

Bullock, Alan. *Hitler and Stalin: Parallel Lives.* New York: Alfred A. Knopf, 1992.

Burleigh, Michael. *The Third Reich: A New History.* 4th ed. New York: Hill & Wang, 2001.

Fest, Joachim. *Hitler.* New York: Harcourt, Brace, Jovanovich, 1974.

Kershaw, Ian. *Hitler, 1889–1936: Hubris.* New York: W. W. Norton & Co., 1999.

———. *Hitler, 1936–1945: Nemesis.* New York: W. W. Norton & Co., 2000.

Lukacs, John. *The Hitler of History.* New York: Alfred A. Knopf, 1998.

Weinberg, Gerhard L. *A World at Arms: A Global History of World War II.* London: Cambridge University Press, 1994.

Hittites (c. 2000–1100 B.C.E.)

A major Anatolian state during the late Bronze Age, rivaling New Kingdom Egypt in power. Hittite political and military history is known from the thousands of cuneiform texts from Anatolia in the late Bronze Age. Beginning with Hattushili I, approximately 15 kings are known to have ruled from Hattusha in the Old Kingdom (c. 1750–1600 B.C.E.). During the reign of Hattushili I (c. 1700 B.C.E.), the Hittites expanded into northern Syria and west into the land of Arzawa. Mursili I (c. 1600 B.C.E.) raided the city of Babylon (c. 1595 B.C.E.) and ended the First Dynasty of Babylon. However, the Hittites were unable to permanently expand into Mesopotamia, and Hittite control of eastern territories seems to have collapsed soon thereafter.

Hittite influence in western Asia Minor and northern Syria was reasserted by Tudhaliya II (c. 1420–1370 B.C.E.). The greatest expansion took place during the reign of Shuppiliuiluma I and his immediate successors (c. 1350–1250 B.C.E.). The Hittites conquered the powerful Hurrian state of Mitanni, controlled all of Syria north of Damascus, and fought with the Egyptians in Syro-Canaan. Hattushili III (c. 1250 B.C.E.) made a treaty with Rameses II following Kadesh and gave him a Hittite princess in marriage. This treaty stayed in effect until the fall of Hittite power in 1180 B.C.E. Due to a number of factors, Hittite power began to decline during the reigns of the three monarchs following Hattushili III: Tudahiyah IV, Arnuwanda III, and Shuppiluiluma II. The rising power of Assyria in northern Iraq severely truncated Hittite power in Syria. Ahhiyawa (possibly the Hittite term for the Achaeans), a powerful kingdom to the west, threatened Hittite power in western Anatolia. The Hittites also had serious troubles with the rival Hittite kingdom of Tarhuntassha in the south.

What is not certain, however, is what brought about the fall of the Hittite capital, Hattusha. Invaders from the west, usually identified with the Sea Peoples in Egyptian sources, may have been the catalyst. Contrary to popular scholarly tradition, Hittite power did not end with the fall of Hattusha; successor dynasties continued at Tarhuntassha and southeast at Carchemish on the Upper Euphrates. Smaller Neo-Hittite states continued in southeast Anatolia and Syria for at least the next 500 years (to c. 700 B.C.E.). These states were often in conflict with rival Aramean dynasties. Both Aramean and Neo-Hittite states were absorbed into the Assyrian world state. Passages from 1 Samuel and 1 and 2 Kings that mention the Hittites most likely refer to the Neo-Hittite states of Syria.

The Hittite king was the supreme war commander, and the Hittite annals imply that all kings were required to campaign on a regular basis. Their wars were a major source of tribute income and manpower that was used to maintain the agricultural base of the Hittite state. A Hittite king successful in war signaled the favor of the gods. The Hittites were also known to have performed purification and scapegoat rituals directed toward the enemy army before important pitched battles such as the Battle of Kadesh.

Mark W. Chavalas

See also: Kadesh, Battle of

References and further reading:

Beal, R. *The Organization of the Hittite Military.* Heidelberg: Carl Winter Universitätsverlag, 1992.

Bryce, T. *The Kingdom of the Hittites.* Oxford, UK: Clarendon Press, 1998.

Goetze, A. "Warfare in Asia Minor." *Iraq* 25 (1963), 124–130.

Howinckten Cate, P. "The History of Warfare according to Hittite Sources: The Annals of Hattusilis I." *Anatolica* 11 (1984), 147–183.

Ho Chi Minh (1890–1969)

Ho Chi Minh, who used at least 20 pseudonyms during his long and adventurous career (adopting his final most famous name only in 1944), drew upon Vietnam's millennia-old tradition of nationalist resistance to foreign rule and combined it with Marxist-Leninist doctrine to lead successful resistance against the Japanese, French, and Americans during the Pacific War and the two Indochina Wars. Originally named Nguyen Sinh Cung, he was born into a mandarin family in Nghe An Province in north central Vietnam, traditionally a center of rural unrest. His father and siblings were bitterly opposed to French colonial rule. After studying at the elite Quoc Hoc Secondary School in Hue, he began a career overseas, working first as a sailor aboard a French liner and not returning to his own country until 1941. From 1917 to 1923 he lived in France and became one of the founding members of the French Communist Party, established in December 1920.

In 1923, Ho journeyed to Moscow and the following year attended the Fifth Congress of the Communist International (Comintern). Thus began his Bolshevik phase from 1924 to 1941, when he lived and worked in Soviet Russia, Europe, China, and Thailand. He organized revolutionary groups among overseas Vietnamese, of which the most important were the Revolutionary Youth League (1925) and the Indochina Communist Party (1930).

After the Japanese military occupation of French Indochina in late 1940, Ho Chi Minh's career took a fundamentally new turn, the "people's war" phase. In May 1941, he established the Vietnam Doc Lap Dong Minh Hoi (League for the Independence of Vietnam), or Vietminh, which made village-based guerrilla warfare an extension of revolutionary politics, abandoning urban-based Bolshevik methods, which were of limited relevance in a largely rural society. Influenced by Mao Zedong's military doctrines, the Vietminh operated in the mountainous China-Vietnam border region.

Ho and his comrades, including Vo Nguyen Giap, commander of the Vietminh's armed forces, established village-level networks of National Salvation Associations and Vietminh Committees, which assumed local governmental

Portrait of Ho Chi Minh with two young girls, 1954. (Library of Congress)

functions and served as the "infrastructure" for guerrilla resistance. Ho's united front tactics, his emphasis on peasant mobilization, diplomatic skills in winning Chinese and American support, and highly popular appeals to nationalism and anti-imperialism at a time when Vietnam suffered greatly from the Japanese occupation (including a famine that killed between 1 and 2 million people in the north) contributed to the rapid expansion of Vietminh "liberated areas" north of the Red River. On 19 August 1945, the revolutionaries entered Hanoi, and on 2 September Ho Chi Minh declared Vietnam's independence. The Vietminh had to fight the American-backed French for nine more years before the independence of the North, following the brilliant victory at Dien Bien Phu, became a fact. Following the 1954 Geneva Conference, Ho became leader of the Democratic Republic of Vietnam (North Vietnam).

By 1955 Ho had embarked upon guerrilla warfare against the American-backed government of the Republic of (South) Vietnam. Again, it would be a long struggle, not ending for another two decades with the complete surrender of the South in 1975. The two Indochina Wars, against France (1946–1954) and against South Vietnam and its American backers (1959–1975), validated the "people's war" strategy. Ho did not live to see the reunification of Vietnam in 1975. North Vietnamese regulars rather than guerrillas won the final victory in the South. It can be argued that the United States and the Republic of Vietnam had indeed won the war against the North after the disastrous Tet Offensive in early 1968, but by then Americans were sick of the war and gradually withdrew. The forces of the South, with some exceptions, could not match the discipline, organization, and dedication of Ho's armies.

Donald M. Seekins

See also: Vietnam Conflict; Vo Nguyen Giap

References and further reading:

Harrison, James P. *The Endless War: Vietnam's Struggle for Independence.* New York: Columbia University Press, 1989.

Lacoutre, Jean. *Ho Chi Minh: A Political Biography.* New York: Random House, 1968.

Tin, Bui. *From Cadre to Exile: The Memoirs of a North Vietnamese Journalist.* Chiang Mai, Thailand: Silkworm Books, 1995.

Hochkirch, Battle of (14 October 1758)

Rare defeat of Frederick the Great by the Austrians. Frederick the Great marched from East Prussia to defend Saxony from an Austrian advance. Weakened by the battle of Zorndorff (25 August), he could muster only 36,000 men compared to 80,000 Austrians under Field Marshal Leopold Daun, which stood east of Dresden in broken country suitable for the defense. He hoped Frederick would attack his larger force. Frederick decided to maneuver Daun's army from its position. On 9 October, after nearly a month of maneuver, Frederick encamped near the village of Hochkirch to resupply. His forces stretched from north to south with the center and right fortified by redoubts around Hochkirch and its prominent walled church.

Frederick assumed incorrectly that Daun would remain inactive. Instead, Daun, urged by his chief of staff Franz Moritz Lacy, attacked Frederick's camp. At 5:00 A.M. on 14 October their army advanced in columns and completely surprised the Prussian right flank, overrunning tents with still-sleeping soldiers. As his army disintegrated at first Frederick dismissed the shouts of his men. Although Prussian cavalry attacks failed to stem the Austrian advance, it was halted by the walled churchyard. This delay allowed James Keith and Prince Moritz of Dessau to reform the Prussian center and counterattack. Both Keith and Moritz died as their desperate charge collapsed under the weight of Austrian numerical superiority. Frederick arrived on the scene, rallied his men, but knew the battle was lost when the his left flank collapsed. By 10:00 A.M. he had withdrawn his army toward the northwest.

Hochkirch resulted from Frederick's underestimation of his enemy. It had little impact on the war. Nearly 9,000 Prussians were killed or wounded while Austria lost 7,000 dead and wounded, but Daun failed to derive any strategic advantage from his victory due to Frederick's skillful retreat.

Patrick J. Speelman

See also: Frederick the Great, King of Prussia; Seven Years' War

References and further reading:

Duffy, Christopher. *Frederick the Great: A Military Life.* London: Routledge & Kegan Paul, 1985.

Showalter, Dennis. *The Wars of Frederick the Great.* London and New York: Longman, 1996.

Weigley, Russell F. *The Age of Battles: The Quest for Decisive Warfare from Breitenfeld to Waterloo.* Bloomington and Indianapolis: Indiana University Press, 1991.

Holy Roman Empire (800–1806)

Greatest power in central Europe until the eighteenth century. Though unified under a single emperor, the empire was composed of lesser powers. As a result, aside from defense and an initial period of expansion, warfare served chiefly as a means for resolving frequent conflicts over territory and authority among them, and between them and the emperors.

Charlemagne's empire (800–814) required annual campaigns to provide land and wealth to secure the allegiance of lesser lords whose forces made up his army. This concentration of military strength in the hands of powerful subjects contributed to the fragmentation of the empire but provided a basis for the development of localized feudal hierarchies. These later proved effective against Viking and Magyar incursions of the ninth and tenth centuries.

The empire's initial avenue of military expansion was southwards into Italy. The papacy initially welcomed the imperial presence as a safeguard, but papal attitudes changed as the popes sought to establish their own authority against the emperors. The ensuing conflict contributed to the dissolution of central authority within the empire between the tenth and thirteenth centuries. Both lesser princes and rival emperors could justify their opposition to an excommunicated emperor.

The greatest expansion occurred in the east between the twelfth and fourteenth centuries into areas inhabited by Slavic peoples. This expansion included the conquest of Prussia and the Baltic provinces by the Teutonic Knights, but these territories did not come under imperial jurisdiction. By the end of the fourteenth century the empire had reached the limits of its growth.

Although the medieval empire had engaged in frequent wars with France over claims to territories lying between them, the most serious rivalry between the two came with the accession of Charles V (1516–1556). Charles was not only emperor, but also king of Spain, and France was now surrounded by Habsburg territories. French kings from Francis I (1515–1547) onward sought to undermine Habsburg power to prevent the encirclement of France.

Conflict with France further complicated the struggle for authority within the empire, particularly after the Protestant Reformation. Many territorial princes adopted Lutheranism and denied the authority of the Catholic Charles. Tensions culminated in the Schmalkaldic War between the Protestant princes (supported by France) and the emperor. Unable to confront both internal and external enemies simultaneously, Charles was forced to concede the existence of a rival Protestant religious power within the empire in the Peace of Augsburg (1555).

The tensions continued and later erupted into the Thirty Years' War (1618–1648). Attempts to consolidate imperial authority were finally defeated due to the support of resisting princes by Denmark, Sweden, and France. The Peace of Westphalia (1648) not only granted the princes autonomy and the ability to conclude military allegiances with foreign powers, but foreign intervention within the empire was constitutionally recognized. France and Sweden became guarantors of the peace and of religious equality.

From the end of the seventeenth century until the middle of the eighteenth, the empire had to confront the Ottoman Empire as well as the France of Louis XIV. The Ottomans had controlled a large part of Hungary since the sixteenth century, but the high-water mark of Ottoman expansion into the empire was reached in the Siege of Vienna in 1683. A successful war of reconquest followed under the emperor Leopold I (1658–1705), leading the Holy League. This army combined imperial forces with those of other European nations in a new crusade declared by the pope, but tension between the emperor and the princes resurfaced. The latter resented the use of the imperial army to regain purely Habsburg territory (Hungary, like Prussia, was beyond imperial jurisdiction). When the French attacked the Rhineland in 1688, most of the princes withdrew to defend Germany. Further conflict in the east became a purely Habsburg affair.

Some of the larger territories, including Prussia, succeeded in establishing themselves as rivals to the Habsburg emperors. Frederick the Great's (1740–1788) victories in the War of Austrian Succession (1740–1748) and in the Seven Years' War (1756–1762) turned Prussia into a great power and a chief rival of the Austrian Habsburgs. The empire's final half century was marked by Austro-Prussian dualism as each sought to consolidate the allegiance of the lesser princes or gain control over them. Despite this, the princes resisted assimilation and clung to imperial traditions to defend their autonomy. As a consequence, it was only the conquest and consolidation of Germany by Napoleon that finally spelled the end of the empire.

Christopher C. W. Bauermeister

See also: Austrian Succession, War of the; Austro-Swiss Wars; Austro-Turk Wars; Charlemagne; Charlemagne's Wars; Franco-German War; Frederick I Barbarossa; Frederick II; Frederick William, Elector of Brandenburg; French Revolutionary Wars; Grand Alliance, War of the; Holy Roman Empire–Papacy Wars; Hungarian War with the Holy Roman Empire; Hussite Wars; Magyars; Napoleonic Wars; Otto I, the "Great"; Schmalkaldic War; Seven Years' War; Spanish Succession, War of the; Teutonic Knights; Thirty Years' War; Valois-Habsburg Wars; Vienna, Sieges of; Viking Raids

References and further reading:

Arnold, Benjamin. *Princes and Territories in Medieval Germany.* Cambridge, UK, and New York: Cambridge University Press, 1991.

Barraclough, Geoffrey. *The Origins of Modern Germany.* New York and London: W. W. Norton and Company, 1984.

Gagliardo, John. *Germany under the Old Regime.* London and New York: Longman, 1991.

Wilson, Peter H. *German Armies: War and German Politics 1648–1806.* London: University College London Press, 1998.

Holy Roman Empire–Papacy Wars (1077–1250)

The conflicts between the Holy Roman Empire and the papacy were defining events during the eleventh through thirteenth centuries as the papacy became a formidable power in Europe. As part of these conflicts, Holy Roman emperors and popes, and their respective supporters, wrote countless documents debating such topics as the source of the emperor's power: Was it from election by the German princes or from the pope who crowned him? This war of words carried over into physical altercation. The emperors wished to consolidate power in northern Italy and, later, attain the kingdom of Sicily. The papacy, as the authority in central Italy, did all it could to repel this incursion.

The conflict began in the ambitions of Emperor Henry IV (1071–1106) and Pope Gregory VII (1073–1085). Gregory had continued the reforms of Pope Leo IX, influenced by monastic movements, which focused on such corruptions as lay investiture. Henry invested—that is, appointed—his own bishops in Germany, and Gregory excommunicated him. Henry begged for and received reconciliation from Gregory at Canossa in January 1077, but in March a number of German dukes rebelled against the emperor and elected another king. Henry, with military victories at Mellrichstedt, Flarcheim, and the river Elster, reasserted his claim to the throne.

Gregory excommunicated Henry a second time, only to be deposed himself by Henry in 1080. Henry placed his own pope in power, but neither that antipope nor his successors posed any major threat to the cardinal-elected popes. Between 1090 and 1092, Henry fought Matilda of Tuscany and Duke Welf of Bavaria, allies of Pope Urban II. On 31 December 1105, Henry's son, Henry V, forced his father to abdicate the throne. In 1122, Henry V and Pope Clement II reached an agreement concerning lay investiture at the Concordat of Worms, nominally ending lay investiture but allowing the emperor to veto the election of a bishop by refusing to accept feudal homage from him.

The larger papal-imperial conflict escalated with Frederick I (Barbarossa, 1152–1190). In 1159, Frederick tried to consolidate his power in northern Italy and to place his own pope in power. The cardinal-elected pope, Alexander III (1159–1181), the Norman king of Sicily, the Byzantine emperor, and the northern Italian resistance formed the Lombard League to keep Frederick at bay.

After six separate campaigns in Italy, Frederick finally withdrew, maintaining some influence in Lombardy. Frederick's son, Henry VI, succeeded him and conquered the whole of Italy, including Sicily and the Papal States. When Henry died in 1197, he failed to make the empire hereditary as the German princes reclaimed the right to elect the German king. Pope Innocent III (1198–1216) took advantage of the situation and chose another man as successor. Henry's son Frederick was too young; and when the German-elected king died in 1208, Otto IV, supported by the papacy, became Holy Roman Emperor.

Otto defied Innocent and revived imperial authority in northern Italy. Innocent gained support from King Philip Augustus of France, accepted Henry's son, Frederick II (1215–1250), whom he had earlier bypassed as emperor, and, ultimately, stopped Otto. As emperor and as king of Sicily, Frederick II also turned against the papacy and continued the policy of invading northern Italy. He was excommunicated, first by Pope Gregory IX and then by Innocent IV as the conflict reached new heights; but he could not vanquish the papacy. After Frederick's death in 1250, subsequent Holy Roman emperors could not gain enough power to threaten the papacy, and the papal-imperial conflict faded away.

Christopher P. Goedert

See also: Frederick I Barbarossa; Frederick II

References and further reading:

Jedin, Hubert, and John Dolan, eds. *Handbook of Church History.* Vols. 3 and 4. Trans. Anslem Biggs. New York: Herder & Herder, 1969.

Morris, Colin. *The Papal Monarchy: The Western Church from 1050 to 1250.* Oxford, UK: Clarendon Press, 1989.

Tierney, Brian. *The Crisis of Church and State, 1050–1300.* Englewood, NJ: Prentice-Hall, 1964.

Tout, T. F. *The Empire and the Papacy, 918–1273.* London: Rivingtons, 1965.

Honduran-Nicaraguan War (1907)

Honduras invaded Nicaragua in January 1907 on the pretext that Nicaragua was aiding Honduran rebels who were trying to overthrow President Policarpo Bonilla. Nicaraguan dictator Jose S. Zelaya denied involvement in the affair and offered to submit the dispute to an international tribunal. Negotiations were unsuccessful and both sides continued fighting until the Nicaraguan army defeated the invaders. El Salvador and Guatemala threatened to intervene and place former Honduran president, Terencio Sierra, in office. Mexico and the United States persuaded all five Central American nations to meet in Washington to resolve their differences.

The conference met from 14 November until 20 December and was noteworthy for the establishment of the Central America Court of Justice to resolve disputes between the five member states. In the summer of 1908, Nicaragua charged that Guatemala and El Salvador were supporting another attempt from Honduras to overthrow Zelaya and presented its case to the court. After an investigation, the court ordered all four nations to cut the size of their armies and to agree not to intervene in each other's internal affairs. All parties agreed and peace was restored, making this one of the first successful resolutions of war by an international tribunal.

George M. Lauderbaugh

References and further reading:

Woodward, Ralph Lee, Jr. *Central America: A Nation Divided.* New York: Oxford University Press, 1976.

Hong Xiuquan (1814–1864)

Charismatic founder of the Taiping movement and leader of the Taiping Rebellion. Hong was born as Hong Fuoxiu in Huaxian, Guangdong Province, on 1 January 1814, of a Hakka farming family.

At fifteen Hong passed the preliminary level of imperial examinations; he taught school from 1830 to 1843 but in four tries did not manage to pass the advanced civil-service examination. He received Christian pamphlets and, after falling dangerously ill, dreamt that he had been approached by God and by Elder Brother Jesus and exhorted to fight evil. After a brief period of Bible study in 1847, Hong joined Feng Yünshan, founder of the Society of God Worshippers, at Thistle Mountain in Guangxi Province and declared himself the Second Son of God. By 1850 he had about 20,000 militant anti-Manchu followers, mostly Hakkas and local miners. They rebelled in summer 1850. On 11 January 1851 Hong declared the new dynasty of Taiping Tianguo, with himself as the Heavenly King (Tian Wang). He achieved initial successes, but after 1856, mostly reverses. The military ineptitude of his own leadership was exceeded only by the fragmentation and unpreparedness of the imperial forces.

Increasingly debauched, withdrawn, and irrational, Hong continued to lead the revolution until April 1864 when he mysteriously fell ill. Trusting in divine providence rather than sound military policy as the Qing army besieged the Taiping capital, Nanjing, he died in his palace on 1 June 1864, possibly by suicide but more likely from disease.

Eric v. d. Luft and Sarah Luft

See also: Chinese Imperial Wars; Gordon, Charles George; Li Hongzhang; Religion and War; Taiping Rebellion; Wolseley, Garnet Joseph, Viscount; Yang Xiuqing; Zuo Zongtang

References and further reading:

Anderson, Flavia Giffard. *The Rebel Emperor.* Garden City, NY: Doubleday, 1959.

Boardman, Eugene Powers. *Christian Influence upon the Ideology of the Taiping Rebellion, 1851–1864.* New York: Octagon, 1972.

Hamberg, Theodore. *The Visions of Hung-Siu-tshuen, and Origin of the Kwang-si Insurrection.* New York: Praeger, 1969.

Spence, Jonathan D. *God's Chinese Son: The Taiping Heavenly Kingdom of Hong Xiuquan.* New York: W. W. Norton, 1996.

Honors and Awards, Military

From earliest times honors have been bestowed on victorious warriors. Many of the earliest known pictographs illustrate the exploits of men in battle. Ancient grave sites reveal ritually buried warriors complete with their weapons and armor. Successful military leaders were showered with lands, riches, and the spoils of war. Even simple soldiers shared in the treasure of conquest. There are stunning examples of Greek, Roman, Chinese, Egyptian, and Persian art displaying returning armies bearing captured arms and slaves from their vanquished enemies.

The ancient Greeks awarded arms and armor to victorious commanders. The Romans, who also crowned their successful generals with laurel wreaths of silver and gold, adopted this practice. Later they awarded large circular medallions, or phalerae, that were mounted on the breastplate of the recipient. These medallions were also awarded to entire Roman legions that distinguished themselves in battle. The phalerae, mounted on the legion flagstaff, served as a public symbol of distinction and a symbol of honor to the legion.

In time, medals, orders, and decorations were authorized to honor the heroism of individual soldiers. For military formations the banner or flag displayed the unit's collective honors. Flags served an important purpose in early warfare, providing the soldier with a point to rally in the confusion of battle. The first flags bore heraldic devices of the leaders for whom the soldiers fought. With the advent of body and horse armor in the Middle Ages, soldiers themselves wore these devices.

The armies of Spain under the royal flag and the banners of the church carried out the conquest of the Americas. The armies of Pizarro and Cortes had their own standards, as did the native armies they faced. At the Battle of Otumba (1520) the Aztec standard, known as Quetzalteopamil, composed of a dazzling representation of the sun surrounded by quetzal plumes, was lashed to the back of the Aztec general. The capture of this standard by a young conquistador, Juan de Salamanca, demoralized the Aztec troops and led to an overwhelming Spanish victory. The Aztec banner was incorporated into Salamanca's coat of arms.

The creation of modern, state-organized and supported European armies in the sixteenth and seventeenth centuries saw the size and function of military units stabilize. King Gustavus II Adolphus of Sweden recognized the value of experienced and cohesive military formation. His administrative and tactical innovations led to the establishment of the modern regiment. One of the key elements in creating a collective identity for a regiment was the regimental standard.

In England, the regimental system was introduced with the restoration of the monarchy in 1660. The years that followed were filled with both domestic and international strife. Between 1660 and 1747, British noblemen received royal warrants to raise and maintain regiments for use by the monarch. Some distinguishing badge was allowed on the regimental standard acknowledging the sponsor. In 1747, the crown forbade the use of these private badges on the standard. Regulations also stipulated that two flags would be used by the regiment, the King's (or Queen's) First Colour, or the Great Union, and the regimental color. The regimental flag had as its background the same hue as the facings (collars, cuffs, and piping) on the regimental uniform.

King William III granted the 18th Regiment of Foot (the Royal Irish) the right to have the Lion of Nassau and the motto VIRTUTIS NAMURCENSIS PROEMIUM emblazoned on its regimental color in recognition of its valor at the Battle of Namur in 1695. This was the first battle honor granted by an English monarch.

In Britain, battle honors are the gift of the sovereign to particular regiments for distinguished service in a specific engagement. Honors may take the form of a badge, a motto, or, more often, a name embroidered on a ribbon sewn on the field of the regimental color. Only battles that are deemed victories are eligible as honors. Battles fought in civil wars, like the English Civil War and the American War of Independence, are not carried on the color. With well over 100 battle honors authorized for World War I, honors on a regimental color were limited to 10 from any single war. Army units that participate in almost every engagement, like the Royal Artillery, do not have individual battle honors. However, the badge and colors of the Royal Artillery both bear witness to its wide service through its motto, UBIQUE (Everywhere).

In the United States, militia regiments had their own standards or color before the establishment of the United States Army in 1775. After the revolution, two flags were authorized for each infantry regiment, a regimental standard of a blue field with the seal of the United States in the center, below which was a riband bearing the regiment's designation and a national color, the Stars and Stripes. Cavalry regiments had regimental color but did not carry the national color. They used a smaller flag, a guidon, similar to the national color, with 13 stripes and a blue field and no set pattern for the stars but cut like a swallowtail.

Shortly after the opening of the American Civil War, the War Department authorized the inscribing on its national color the names of engagements in which a regiment distinguished itself. It was hoped that units would regard their colors as representing the regiment's honor and rally to protect the colors in battle. To underscore the importance of the colors, the War Department also encouraged the award of the Medal of Honor to flag bearers who saved a regiment's flags from capture.

As battle followed battle, there was little room left on most regimental national colors for additional honors. The War Department authorized silver rings engraved with battle honors affixed to the staff bearing the regimental color.

Initially, the regiments themselves chose battles commemorated by honors. An inventory of honors was undertaken by the army in 1878 to verify and standardize the criteria for their use. This process was not completed until 1919, when 76 battles were deemed suitable for recognition. The next year a new method of displaying honors was introduced: ribbon streamers in the colors of the appropriate campaign medal, embroidered with the name of the engagement and suspended from the finial of the staff bearing the regimental color. Today, the United States Army recognizes more than 172 battle honors.

A regiment's participation in a particular battle can also be incorporated into its regimental badge. The British Army's Royal Regiment of Wales was created through the amalgamation of several regiments, one of which was the South Wales Borderers. In 1879, that regiment, then known as the 24th Regiment of Foot, lost 599 officers and men in the Battle of Isandhlwana to Zulu regiments. Queen Victoria placed a wreath of immortelles on the regimental Queen's Colour and commanded that a silver replica of the wreath be carried on the flagstaff thereafter. The cap badge of the South Wales Borderers, and later the collar badge of the Royal Regiment of Wales, is surrounded by an unbroken wreath of immortelles to commemorate the queen's gesture.

It is interesting to note that two of the three Victoria Crosses awarded for Isandhlwana went to Lieutenants Melville and Coghill of the 24th Regiment, ordered to take the Queen's Colour to safety when it was obvious the column was doomed. Their bodies were later found in a nearby river alongside the Colour.

The distinctive insignia used by the regiments of the United States Army may also incorporate elements of a regiment's history and battle honors into their design. For example, the distinctive insignia of the 19th Infantry is a shield of azure with an infantry bugle of 1861 enclosing the numeral 19 with three white stars above the bugle. Below the shield is a riband bearing the unit motto. The bugle with the number is a reproduction of the 19th Infantry's Civil War insignia when it received the nickname "The Rock of Chickamauga," which also serves as its motto. The three stars represent service in the Civil War, the war with Spain, and the Philippine Insurrection.

In many of the world's armies, units may be awarded decorations for particularly meritorious service. The United States, the Philippines, and the Republic of Korea each have a Presidential Unit Citation, designed to honor entire units. Several regiments of the United States Army were awarded the French Croix de Guerre and Medaille Militaire in recognition of their service in the first and second world wars. The Soviet government often awarded orders and decorations to outstanding regiments during World War II.

Honors and awards are intended to recognize exceptional service and build loyalty. This is true of medals and decorations awarded to individual soldiers as well as battle honors, flags, and heraldic devices bestowed upon military units. They bind the recipient to the government that grants the honor. In the case of military units, awards and honors create a bond between the soldiers in those units by paying tribute their common history, sacrifice, and spirit.

The greatest threat to the value of such devices and emblems is their occasional wholesale awarding and subsequent cheapening, as was the case when the U.S. Army after the Grenada incursion awarded more medals than there were troops involved! There is also the danger that they may be awarded to the unworthy, as in one-party states, where commanders can cover their chests with medals that bear little correlation with their actual battlefield experience. Wise government avoids this cheapening of their military awards and honors, and even the Soviet Union and Nazi Germany reserved special recognition devices that, at least in wartime, had nothing to do with a soldier's politics.

The physical cost of producing these bits of cloth and metal is infinitesimal. But such awards and honors repay their cost many times over in troop and unit efficiency, motivation, and morale.

Eric Smylie

See also: British Military; Cortes, Hernando; German Army; Gustavus II Adolphus; Pizarro, Francisco; U.S. Army

References and further reading:

Baker, Anthony. *Battle Honours of the British and Commonwealth Armies.* London: Ian Allen, 1986.

Edwards, T. J. *Regimental Badges.* London: Charles Knight & Co., 1974.

Farwell, Byron. *Mr. Kipling's Army.* New York: Norton, 1981.

Joslin, E. C., A. R. Litherland, and B. T. Simpkin. *British Battles and Medals.* London: Spink & Son, 1988.

Lemonofides, Dino. *British Infantry Colours.* Edgeware, Middlesex, UK: Altmark Publishing, 1971.

Mahon, John K., and Romana Danysh. *Army Lineage Series, Infantry.* Part I, *Regular Army.* Washington, DC: Office of the Chief of Military History, United States Army, 1972.

Taylor, Arthur. *Discovering Military Traditions.* Tring, Hertsfordshire, UK: Shire Publications, 1969.

Wilson, John B. *Campaign Streamers of the United States Army.* Arlington, VA: Association of the United States Army, 1995.

Hood, John Bell (1831–1879)

Confederate general, capable at the brigade or division level, but unqualified to command larger forces. Hood was born in Owingsville, Kentucky, on 1 June 1831. After graduating from the U.S. Military Academy at West Point in 1853, he served with the infantry in Missouri and California until assigned to the Second Cavalry in Texas in 1855. He took a Comanche arrow in the left hand at Devils River, Texas, on 20 July 1857.

Hood resigned as first lieutenant from the U.S. Army on 16 April 1861 and was immediately commissioned captain in the Confederate cavalry. On 30 September he was named colonel of the 4th Texas Infantry and on 2 March 1862 brigadier general of the Texas Brigade, which soon became one of the Confederacy's toughest fighting forces. It excelled during the Seven Days' Battles, especially at Gaines's Mill on 27 June. Hood commanded a division of the Army of Northern Virginia, including his Texas Brigade, at Second Bull Run, Antietam, and Fredericksburg. His stellar performances earned his promotion to major general on 10 October.

His left arm was crippled near Little Round Top on the second day at Gettysburg, and he lost his right leg at Chickamauga. While recovering from the amputation, he was promoted to lieutenant general on 1 February 1864.

Hood served under Joseph Johnston trying to stop William T. Sherman's march to the sea. Jefferson Davis, dissatisfied with Johnston in this campaign, brevetted Hood full general on 18 July and placed him in command. Hood's immediate and reckless attacks on Sherman showed that Davis was mistaken. Beaten by Sherman, Hood retreated into Tennessee to disrupt Union supply lines. Crushed by John McAllister Schofield at Franklin, Tennessee, on 30 November and almost annihilated by George H. Thomas at Nashville on 15–16 December, he was relieved of command at his own request on 23 January 1865. Fleeing toward Texas, he surrendered in Natchez, Mississippi, on 31 May. He died in New Orleans on 30 August 1879.

Eric v. d. Luft

See also: American Civil War; Antietam/Sharpsburg; Atlanta, Battles Around; Bull Run, Second/Manassas Junction; Chickamauga, Battle of; Fredericksburg; Gettysburg; Johnston, Joseph Eggleston; Lee, Robert Edward; Longstreet, James; Nashville, Battle of; Seven Days' Battles; Sherman, William Tecumseh; Thomas, George Henry

References and further reading:

Bailey, Anne J. *The Chessboard of War: Sherman and Hood in the Autumn Campaigns of 1864.* Lincoln: University of Nebraska Press, 2000.

Dyer, John Percy. *The Gallant Hood.* Indianapolis, IN: Bobbs-Merrill, 1950.

Hay, Thomas Robson. *Hood's Tennessee Campaign.* Dayton, OH: Morningside, 1976.

McMurry, Richard M. *John Bell Hood and the War for Southern Independence.* Lincoln: University of Nebraska Press, 1992.

Hooker, Joseph (1814–1879)

Aggressive, popular, and sometimes reckless Union field commander in the American Civil War. Hooker was born in Hadley, Massachusetts, on 13 November 1814. Assigned to artillery after graduating from the U.S. Military Academy at West Point in 1837, he fought in the Seminole Wars and, under both Zachary Taylor and Winfield Scott, in the Mexican-American War. When the Civil War began he was colonel of the California militia.

After witnessing the Union loss at First Bull Run as a civilian and thinking that he could do better, he raised a brigade of volunteers and commanded a division at Williamsburg, Virginia, on 5 May 1862. Promoted to major general of volunteers, he fought well at Seven Pines, in the Seven Days' Battles, and at Second Bull Run and South Mountain. Wounded at Antietam, he was promoted to regular brigadier general on 20 September, led a corps at Fredericksburg, and replaced Ambrose Burnside as commander of the Army of the Potomac on 26 January 1863.

Uncharacteristic hesitancy made "Fighting Joe" the loser at Chancellorsville. His usual cockiness might have beaten Robert E. Lee, whom he outnumbered about 75,000 to 50,000. Abraham Lincoln replaced Hooker with George G. Meade three days before Gettysburg.

Serving under William S. Rosecrans and Ulysses S. Grant, Hooker achieved an important victory with the capture of Lookout Mountain, Tennessee, on 24 November. For this he was brevetted major general. Reassigned under William T. Sherman, he distinguished himself during the siege of Atlanta. Disgruntled when passed over for command of the Army of the Tennessee after James Birdseye McPherson's death on 24 July 1864, he asked to be relieved of field service and spent the rest of the war behind a desk.

Hooker was a man of intemperate morals and routinely allowed prostitutes to follow his camp. There is no truth to the prevalent notion that the slang term *hooker* for prostitute derives from his name, but the coincidence of his name with the preexistent word certainly helped to popularize it.

Hooker retired in 1868 when he suffered a stroke. He died in Garden City, New York, on 31 October 1879.

Eric v. d. Luft

See also: American Civil War; Antietam/Sharpsburg; Atlanta, Battles Around; Bull Run, First/Manassas; Bull Run, Second/Manassas Junction; Burnside, Ambrose Everett; Chancellorsville, Battle of; Chattanooga, Battle of; Fredericksburg; Gettysburg; Grant, Ulysses Simpson; Jackson, Thomas "Stonewall"; Lee, Robert Edward; Lincoln, Abraham; McClellan, George Brinton; Meade, George Gordon; Mexican-American War; Pope, John; Rosecrans, William Starke; Scott, Winfield; Seven Days' Battles; Sherman, William Tecumseh; Thomas, George Henry

References and further reading:

Hebert, Walter H. *Fighting Joe Hooker.* Lincoln: University of Nebraska Press, 1999.

Horseshoe Bend, Battle of (27 March 1814)

Decisive battle in the Creek War. Andrew Jackson marched about 4,000 regulars, volunteers, and Cherokees south from Fort Strother, Alabama, in March 1814 to seek and destroy the renegade "Red Stick" Creeks and their Spanish allies. Under Chief Red Eagle, alias William Weatherford, about 1,200 Creeks had fortified a small peninsula formed by a "horseshoe bend" in the Tallapoosa River northeast of Montgomery, Alabama. With earthworks across the neck of the thickly wooded peninsula, the Creeks were well equipped to withstand bombardment, assault, or siege.

The morning of 27 March, Jackson surrounded the Creek position and dispatched the Cherokees to swim the river and steal the Creek canoes. That done, he fired his only gun, a six-pounder, at the earthworks to signal attack. First, John Coffee's Tennessee militia attacked amphibiously on three sides in the stolen canoes while the six-pounder provided covering fire as rapidly as possible, then Jackson led about 600 regulars in a frontal assault against the earthworks. Because Coffee had already engaged the barricade's defenders from the rear, Jackson's infantry met little resistance.

About 700 Creek warriors died. Jackson's casualties were 111 wounded, including Sam Houston, and 26 killed. Red Eagle was not present. Jackson marched downstream toward the Creek "Holy Ground" near the confluence of the Coosa and Tallapoosa Rivers. When Red Eagle saw that his headquarters were doomed, he offered unconditional surrender and Jackson gave him a generous settlement. Living thereafter as Weatherford, Red Eagle became a peaceful Alabama planter.

Eric v. d. Luft

See also: Creek War; Houston, Samuel; Jackson, Andrew; War of 1812

References and further reading:

Brantley, William Henderson. *Battle of Horseshoe Bend in Tallapoosa County, Alabama, March 27, 1814.* Birmingham, AL: Southern University Press, 1969.

Holland, James Wendell. *Andrew Jackson and the Creek War: Victory at the Horseshoe.* Tuscaloosa: University of Alabama Press, 1968.

Mackenzie, George C. *The Indian Breastwork in the Battle of Horseshoe Bend: Its Size, Location, and Construction.* Washington, DC: Division of History, U.S. Office of Archeology and Historic Preservation, 1969.

Houston, Samuel (1793–1863)

American and Texan field commander and politician. Born near Lexington, Virginia, on 2 March 1793, Houston grew up in Blount County, Tennessee, and lived with the Cherokees from 1808 to 1811. Commissioned ensign in the regular army in 1813, he served under Andrew Jackson in the Creek War and was wounded in the left thigh and right shoulder during the assault on the earthworks at Horseshoe Bend. From 1815 until he resigned in May 1818, he was a military agent to the Cherokees, usually dressing like them and tak-

Photograph of Samuel Houston, c. 1860. (Library of Congress)

ing their side on almost all issues. He began practicing law in Nashville in 1818, became major general of the Tennessee militia in 1821, a member of Congress from Tennessee in 1823, and governor of Tennessee in 1827, but suddenly resigned in 1829, despondent when his wife, Eliza Allen, fled back to her father.

Houston went west and returned to the Cherokees, who called him "Big Drunk." He lived in despair for three years, but in 1832, with his sense of purpose restored, he traveled to Washington to lobby for the Cherokees with the Jackson administration. He impressed Jackson by beating up an anti-Jackson congressman. Jackson pardoned him immediately after his conviction and sent him on a fact-finding mission to Texas late in 1832. Houston settled there and soon became an activist for Texan rights and separate statehood within the nation of Mexico.

In November 1835 Houston became commander in chief of the Texan army and on 2 March 1836 he cosigned the Texas Declaration of Independence. His battle plans and tactics crushed the Mexicans at San Jacinto and won independence for Texas. He was president of the Republic of Texas from 1836 to 1838 and from 1841 to 1844. After the United States annexed Texas in 1845, Houston represented Texas as a senator from 1846 to 1858 and served as governor from 1859 until he was overthrown in March 1861 for refusing to support secession. He died in Huntsville, Texas, on 26 July 1863.

Eric v. d. Luft

See also: Alamo; Creek War; Horseshoe Bend, Battle of; Jackson, Andrew; San Jacinto; Santa Anna, Antonio López de; Texas War of Independence; War of 1812

References and further reading:

Braider, Donald. *Solitary Star: A Biography of Sam Houston.* New York: Putnam, 1974.

De Bruhl, Marshall. *Sword of San Jacinto: A Life of Sam Houston.* New York: Random House, 1993.

James, Marquis. *The Raven: A Biography of Sam Houston.* Norwalk, CT: Easton, 1988.

Williams, John Hoyt. *Sam Houston: A Biography of the Father of Texas.* New York: Simon & Schuster, 1993.

Hue, Battle of (31 January–2 March 1968)

Major battle of the Tet Offensive during the Vietnam conflict. As part of the Tet Offensive, North Vietnamese and Vietcong main force units attacked the old imperial capital of Hue in northern South Vietnam. The effort to retake the city soon became the longest and bloodiest of all of the Tet Offensive fighting. To appease Vietnamese sensibilities, the old imperial citadel was off-limits to U.S. combat units, and the enemy quickly seized control. During the period of Communist control, cadres rounded up various "enemies of the people," apparently conducted "people's trials," and murdered them in a bloodbath.

South Vietnamese and American forces quickly responded. The South Vietnamese 1st Division immediately counterattacked and requested U.S. support. Elements of the U.S. 1st Cavalry Division and 101st Airborne Division blocked off the city on the west to prevent possible enemy reinforcements. Still, General William Westmoreland limited reinforcements, believing that the siege at Khe Sanh potentially was a more critical situation and wanting to preserve his strategic reserve in the region. Meanwhile Army of the Republic of Vietnam (ARVN) troops and U.S. Marines engaged in block by block, house by house fighting to regain the old capital. The U.S. Marines took one casualty for every yard gained, and one combat reporter, Don Oberdorfer of the *Washington Post,* called it "quite possibly, the longest and bloodiest single action of the Second Indochina War."

On 2 March, the Military Assistance Command, Vietnam declared the battle officially over. More than half of the city had been destroyed in the fighting to retake it; Communist military units had suffered more than 5,000 casualties, while

A U.S. Marine carries a Vietnamese woman to safety during the Battle of Hue, the longest and bloodiest of all the Tet Offensive battles. (National Archives)

Vietnamese, U.S. Marine, and U.S. Army casualties combined exceeded 3,500 killed and wounded.

Charles Dobbs

See also: Tet Offensive; Vietnam Conflict; Westmoreland, William

References and further reading:

Hammel, Eric M. *Fire in the Streets: The Battle for Hue, Tet 1968.* Chicago, IL: Contemporary Books, 1991.

Nolan, Keith William. *Battle for Hue: Tet 1968.* Novato, CA: Presidio Press, 1983.

Smith, George. *The Siege at Hue.* Boulder, CO: Lynne Rienner, 1999.

Hukbalahap Revolt (1945–1959)

One of the Philippines' periodic agrarian rebellions. The Hukbalahap revolt's roots were in the conditions of peasant distress before World War II, though the Hukbalahap (the term essentially meaning People's Army) came into being in 1942, when fragments of left-wing guerrilla units fighting the Japanese came together under Luis Taruc as their military commander. Centered in Luzon, these remnants grew into an army of 15,000 by the end of the war, despite competition with partisan forces organized by the U.S. Army.

Seen as little more than bandits by the newly established government of the Philippines, the Huks reformed their political organization and established plans to create a people's republic. This course of action was greatly assisted by the distressed state of the country in the wake of World War II and further abetted by the counterproductive fashion in which Manila fought. Against the backdrop of a kleptocratic government, occasional infantry sweeps of battalion strength were conducted with indiscriminate violence and looting, driving the population into the arms of the rebels. By 1949, 37,000 government soldiers faced a movement with a population base of a million supporters dominating half of Luzon. Very little held the Huks back except their own material weaknesses, and the occasional overreaching atrocity, such as the assassination of the revered widow of wartime president Manuel Quezon in a convoy ambush near Manila.

In 1950, the ascension of Ramón Magsaysay to the post of defense chief and the outbreak of the Korean War led to a change of fortune. It became possible to finance an expansion of the war while the necessary leadership was available to reform the Filipino military.

By increasing troops levels from 10 to 26 battalions, and providing adequate logistical and air support, enough forces were available to cover the affected region. These troops mounted continuous patrols so as to give the guerrillas no sanctuary, while specialized units mounted deep-penetration missions to further add to the disruption. This went hand-in-hand with a civic action program designed to provide training and land for those in the areas most dominated by the Huks, beginning the process of winning the population back to Manila. Sophisticated psychological warfare also alienated the population from the Huks and made the rebels themselves doubt their cause. By 1953, the Huks had been reduced to 2,300 active fighters in uncoordinated bands, while Luis Taruc himself surrendered in 1954—and became a born-again Christian.

The suppression of the Huks was seen as a model of war in the postcolonial world. The essential problem was that the course of this campaign depended on the existence of exemplary leadership—Magsaysay and U.S. intelligence adviser Edward Lansdale were lionized; Magsaysay's death in a 1957 airplane crash was a near-catastrophe for the Philippines—a condition that did not obtain in the Vietnam conflict or in future Filipino insurgencies.

George R. Shaner

See also: Cold War; Guerrilla/Partisan/Irregular Warfare; Indochina Wars; Magsaysay, Ramón; Malayan Emergency

References and further reading:

Currey, Cecil B. *Edward Lansdale: The Unquiet American.* Boston: Houghton Mifflin, 1988.

Greenberg, Lawrence M. *The Hukbalahap Insurrection: A Case Study of a Successful Anti-Insurgency Operation in the Philippines, 1946–1955.* Washington, DC: U.S. Army Center of Military History, 1987.

Kerkvliet, Benedict J. *The Huk Rebellion: A Study of Peasant Revolt in the Philippines.* Berkeley: University of California Press, 1977.

Hundred Years War (1337–1453)

Most important Anglo-French conflict of the Middle Ages. The war had complex roots. It was the last and more violent stage of an old conflict arising due to the fact that the English king was, at the same time that he was king of England, a vassal of the French king for Guyenne. By the early fourteenth century, there were many new areas of confrontation as well: who was to control Flanders (vital for the English wool market); the succession war of Brittany; the revival of the "Auld Alliance" between the Scots and the French that caught the English in a vise; who was to control the Channel and North Sea; and, from 1328, the French dynastic conflict.

The last son of King Philippe IV ("the Fair") had died without heir. The closest male in a collateral line was Edward III of England, Philippe's grandson through Philippe's daughter (Isabelle of France, who had married King Edward II of England). Edward III thus had a valid claim on the French crown, but French lords were unwilling to accept the idea that Edward might become their king. In order to reject his claim, French lawyers drew on old Frankish law (Salic law), which stated that property could not descend through a female.

Philippe VI de Valois, Philippe's IV nephew, was consequently chosen as king. Despite the disparity in power (France was the most populous and wealthiest country in western Europe), England was ready to support the claim of its popular king. In 1337, Philippe VI seized Edward's fiefs in France, marking the beginning of the war. The conflict can be divided in four phases.

During the first phase, 1337–1360, France suffered repeated military disaster (Sluys in 1340, Crécy in 1346, Poitiers in 1356). The 1360 Treaty of Brétigny gave England a third of French territory.

During phase two, 1360–1415, French armies gradually recovered lost territory. As a consequence, at the end of Charles V's reign (1380), England had lost most of its holdings in the French interior, ending up controlling only a few ports. Neither France nor England was able to prosecute the war to its end due to internal difficulties. In France, the intermittent insanity of Charles VI ("the Mad," 1380–1422) prompted a power struggle between the dukedoms of Orleans and Burgundy. This grew into a full-scale civil war, considerably weakening the kingdom. England also had to face internal instability, including the Wat Tyler uprising in 1381, but central authority was reestablished under Kings Henry IV (1399–1413), and Henry V (1413–1422).

During phase three, 1415–1429, Henry V seized the opportunity presented by French anarchy. Henry crushed the French royal army at Agincourt (1415). He conquered Normandy and used diplomacy (an alliance with the Burgundian party) to force Charles VI to sign the Treaty of Troyes (1420), which disinherited Charles's son. Henry then married Charles's daughter. His infant Henry VI was declared king of England, as well as of France (1422). But most of southern France remained loyal to Charles VII, the Dauphin, nicknamed "King of Bourges" (his tiny capital). England controlled northern France and had nearly rid itself of Charles VII when Jeanne d'Arc raised France's spirits again.

During the years 1430–1453, the final stage of the Hundred Years War, English troops were regularly defeated by French armies (Orleans and Patay, 1429; Formigny, 1450; Castillon, 1453). In 1435, Charles VII signed the Peace of Arras with Burgundy, destroying the Burgundian-English alliance. France had rallied around the idea that it was a united nation and that the *goddons* (English) were foreigners to be swept away. Between 1449 and 1453, England lost all his territories save for the tiny foothold of Calais. The Hundred Years War had definitively come to an end by 1475, when Louis XI of France prevented an invasion by bribing Edward IV into returning to England.

This Hundred Years War was a chaotic conflict between princes, with no definitive peace at its end. It led to political unrest (War of the Roses in England, War of the Public Good in France) but also gave birth to a protonationalism. Fewer than 20 major battles occurred. The real war was comprised of innumerable skirmishes. Towns were more often taken by surprise, or treason, than by sieges. English raids (five between 1339 and 1360) often had a greater psychological than physical impact. The employment of a scorched earth policy by French kings proved a useful deterrent.

The conflict had a disastrous impact on French wealth. The defeats of the fourteenth century, combined with the Black Death, paralyzed the economy. It was the middle of the fifteenth century before trade returned to the levels of 1300.

The war proved to be too costly for England's 3 million inhabitants as well. As long as the booty was flowing from France, English kings enjoyed the support of Parliament, but any setback could provoke a change of dynasty (Lancaster, in 1400; then York, in 1455). England failed to foresee the military vicissitudes of the fifteenth century.

During the entire war, the English relied on mobility and a powerful archery, but English mobility was checked by the hundreds of fortified places that a wealthy France could afford to build. Archery won battles as long as French knights looked for glory and fame, but the emergence of professional soldiers (1445), in a standing French royal army, resulted in tactical and technical superiority for the French.

French armies of the late war could choose when to give battle (Formigny or Castillon). The French standing army was paid by the first modern tax system. The French king no longer had to live from the proceeds of his estates. A permanent tax gave him the power to make policy. The idea of the nation and of a modern, centralized monarchy is the principal legacy of the Hundred Years War.

Gilles Boué

See also: Agincourt, Battle of; Crécy, Battle of; Edward, the Black Prince; Edward III; Henry V, King of England; Joan of Arc; Orleans, Siege of; Poitiers, Battle of

References and further reading:

Allmand, Christopher. *The Hundred Years War.* Cambridge, UK: Cambridge University Press, 1988.

Contamine, Philippe. *War in the Middle Ages.* Trans. Michael Jones. New York: Blackwell, 1984.

———. *La Guerre de Cent Ans.* 7th ed. Paris: PUF, 1992.

Sumption, Jonathan. *The Hundred Years War.* 2 vols. Philadelphia: University of Pennsylvania Press, 1990–1999.

Hungarian Civil Wars (1526–1547)

Wars between rival claimants of the Hungarian throne, ending in the division of the country between the Habsburg and Ottoman empires and the dependent Principality of Transylvania. The death of Louis II at the Battle of Mohács (1526) left the Hungarian throne vacant. A majority of the nobles elected the Transylvanian Vajda János Zápolyai king in October 1526; a smaller number, joined by the chancellor, supported Austrian Archduke Ferdinand Habsburg, brother of Emperor Charles V. Reinforced by German mercenaries after Charles's conquest of Rome (1527), Ferdinand quickly drove Zápolyai out of the country.

Rather than abdicate, Zápolyai appealed to Sultan Süleyman I for aid. Süleyman recognized Zápolyai as the legitimate king and led an army into Hungary to reestablish his position. The Ottoman army easily pushed Ferdinand's forces out of central Hungary but failed to capture Vienna (1529). A second campaign by Süleyman against Ferdinand's capital in 1532 was stopped by the determined resistance of the town of Köszeg (Gün).

In the following years, while the two kings' armies competed for control of the country, the Ottomans expanded their base in Hungary by occupying Slavonia and placing a garrison near Buda. As it became evident that the Ottomans alone stood to profit from the continued division of the kingdom, Ferdinand and Zápolyai worked to negotiate a settlement. By the Treaty of Várad (1538), Ferdinand recognized Zápolyai's claim and pledged to support him with imperial forces; in return, Zápolyai named Ferdinand his heir to the throne. At Zápolyai's death in 1540, however, his treasurer György Martinuzzi, bishop of Várad, refused to honor the agreement and had Zápolyai's infant son elected King János II. Ferdinand's forces were too small to occupy the kingdom and failed in two attempts to capture Buda.

In August 1541 Süleyman marched to the capital, declared himself János's guardian, and occupied the castle. He made Buda the administrative center of a new Ottoman pashalik and gave Transylvania and the lands east of the Tisza River to János to hold as a dependent principality.

After a failed attempt by Ferdinand to recapture Buda in 1542, Süleyman carried out another campaign in Hungary, conquering Siklós, Székesfehérvár, Esztergom, and Szeged (1543). Unable to break Süleyman's hold on the country, Ferdinand and Charles V, in the Treaty of Edirne (1547), finally extended de facto recognition of the Ottoman conquest of Hungary by agreeing to pay Süleyman an annual gift of 30,000 gold florins for possession of the northern and western portions of Hungary still in Habsburg control.

Brian Hodson

See also: Austro-Turk Wars; Mohács, Battles of; Vienna, Sieges of

References and further reading:

Perjes, Géza. *The Fall of the Medieval Kingdom of Hungary: Mohács 1526-Buda 1541.* Ed. Mario Fenyö. Boulder, CO: East European Monographs, 1989.

Hungarian Revolt (1956)

Popular uprising against the Soviet-backed Communist regime. Following the harsh imposition of Communist rule after World War II, the New Course of de-Stalinization, beginning in 1953, split the Hungarian Communist Party between conservatives and reformers and led to a loosening of political controls over public discourse. In the summer of 1956, conservatives attempted to placate the reformers by removing the unpopular party secretary, Mátyás Rákosi, and rehabilitating a number of victims of Stalinist-era purges.

Encouraged by this and the success of similar reform efforts in Poland, Budapest University students, joined by thousands of workers, marched to the Parliament building on 23 October with a list of demands for further change. Reform leader Imre Nagy addressed the crowd, which dispersed, but later in the evening protestors toppled the Stalin monument in the city park and seized the radio station. In response, the party appointed Nagy prime minister on 24 October, simultaneously announcing that it had requested Soviet military assistance to maintain order. The announcement provoked a general strike, followed by armed clashes between the Soviet troops and freedom fighters, who seized key positions in the capital.

Relative peace was restored after 28 October, when Nagy announced a cease-fire, amnesty, reorganization of the party, and the withdrawal of Soviet forces. Though willing to cooperate with the new government, the freedom fighters hesitated to disarm. A confrontation with security troops on 30 October led to a siege of the Communist Party headquarters and the lynching of a number of security personnel. The following day the Soviet army began to reoccupy strategic points. After receiving evasive replies from the Soviet government about their intentions, Nagy declared Hungarian neutrality and its withdrawal from the Warsaw Pact. To ward off a Soviet attack, the Nagy government attempted to quiet the revolutionary situation in the country, arranging the end of the general strike on 3 November.

On the night of 3–4 November, 16 Soviet divisions invaded Hungary and installed a new government under János Kádár. The Hungarian army was quickly disarmed and most of the country occupied within days. Fighting continued in Budapest until 11 November, while 200,000 refugees fled the country. As many as 25,000 Hungarians were killed in the fighting between 23 October and 11 November; officially, Soviet losses were 700.

The blatant suppression by the Red Army of the relatively modest Hungarian demands led to worldwide condemnation, and communists left their national parties in numbers not seen since the Hitler-Stalin pact of 1939; many fellow travelers also were alienated. The Kádár government embarked on a program of economic reform but also brutally hanged Nagy and Hungarian army general Paul Maleter in 1958.

Brian Hodson

References and further reading:

Hodson, Brian. *The Hungarian Revolution of 1956: Reform, Revolt and Repression 1953–1963.* Ed. György Litván. Trans. János Bak and Lyman Legters. London and New York: Longman, 1996.

Zinner, Paul. *Revolution in Hungary.* New York: Columbia University Press, 1962.

Hungarian War with the Holy Roman Empire (1477–1485)

War fought between Hungarian king Matthias Corvinus, and Holy Roman Emperor Frederick III, over possession of Lower Austria. In the early spring of 1477, Matthias sent his light cavalry on raids to distract and occupy Frederick's army, while his main force operated against the towns. Though he failed to capture Vienna, by the end of the year Matthias had gained possession of Styria and most of Lower Austria without fighting a single major battle, forcing Frederick to sue for peace. For the next four years, Matthias's Hungarian forces were occupied by the Hungarian-Turkish Wars, allowing Frederick to recover most of his losses.

After securing peace with Mehmed II of Turkey, Matthias again declared war against Frederick in 1482. To break Frederick's hold on Lower Austria, Matthias conducted a systematic campaign against the towns surrounding Vienna and Wiener Neustadt, capturing Hainburg (1482), Klosterneuburg (1483), and Bruck an der Leitha (1484), using light cavalry as before to harass Frederick's less mobile forces. Frederick's attempt to raise the siege of Kornenburg resulted in a disastrous defeat at Leitzersdorf (November 1484), destroying his field army and leaving the rest of his forces isolated in the towns without a chance for relief. The subsequent capture of Kornenburg by Matthias closed the ring around Vienna, which surrendered in May 1485.

The following year, Matthias completed his conquest of Lower Austria by taking Wiener Neustadt and forcing Frederick to recognize his claims. Matthias's success left him isolated. He was unable to prevent the election of Frederick's son Maximilian I as Holy Roman Emperor (1486), nor was he able to consolidate his hold on Austria, which reverted to Maximilian at Matthias's death in 1490.

Brian Hodson

See also: Bohemian Civil Wars; Matthias I

References and further reading:

Rázsö, Gyula. *Die Feldzüge des Königs Mathias Corvinus in Niederösterreich, 1477–1490.* Militärhistorische Schriftenreihe 24. Vienna: Heeresgeschichtliches Museum, Militärwissenschaftliches Institut, 1981.

Hungarian-Turkish Wars (1437–1526)

Series of wars between the Kingdom of Hungary and the Ottoman Empire, beginning with the Ottoman occupation of Serbia (1438–1439) and ending with the collapse of Hungary in the Hungarian Civil Wars (1526–1547). The failure of Hungarian king Albrecht's crusade in 1437 introduced a new phase of the Ottoman wars of European expansion in the Balkans, which were now waged up to and across the borders of Hungary. To support deposed Serbian despot George Brankoviæ, Hungarian general János Hunyadi counterattacked into Wallachia in 1442. In the winter of 1443–1444 Hunyadi invaded Bulgaria, forcing Sultan Murad II to agree to the restoration of Serbia to Brankoviæ. Assured by the pope that promises made to infidels need not be honored, Hungarian King Ulászlo I broke the peace and launched another crusade in 1444. The crusading army was cut off and destroyed by Murad at Varna, where Ulászlo was killed. Hunyadi escaped but was defeated again at Kosovo Polje in 1448. A continuing succession crisis left Hungary too weak to intervene in the Ottoman conquest of Constantinople (1453). Hunyadi gathered sufficient forces to break the siege of Belgrade (1456), but the Hungarians were unable after his death to prevent the Ottoman conquest of Serbia (1457–1458).

Though Hunyadi's campaigns against the Ottomans ultimately failed to recover any territory, they did revitalize and provide leadership for the resistance of the Balkan peoples fighting against the Turks, encouraging Skander Beg (George Kastriota) to renounce Ottoman suzerainty and launch the Albanian-Turkish wars for independence.

In 1463 Mehmed II invaded and occupied Bosnia, prompting a winter counterattack by Hunyadi's son, Matthias Corvinus, who recaptured the strategic fortress of Jajce. From 1464–1466 the Hungarians and Ottomans fought ineffectually in Bosnia, eventually dividing the kingdom between themselves.

Subsequently, Matthias focused on strengthening the line of fortresses established by King Sigismund along the southern borders of Transylvania and Slavonia through Bosnia to the Adriatic while the Ottomans consolidated their Balkan conquests. The following 50 years were marked by repeated border incursions and raids from both sides, over time weakening the fortress system. A large raid by Ali Beg of Smederevo in 1479 was followed by a campaign by Matthias into Wallachia, Serbia, and eastern Bosnia in 1480, capturing Srebrenica and briefly restoring the frontier defenses.

After Matthias's death, the Hungarians successfully repulsed an attack on Belgrade in 1494, but by the first decades of the sixteenth century Ottoman raiders were penetrating deeper into the frontier zone and inflicting defeats on Hungarian counterattacks inside Croatia and Hungary, notably at Sinj (1508), Knin (1511), and Dubica (1520). The recurrent raids devastated the frontier regions, leaving the fortresses isolated and unsupported in the deserted land. Srebrenica was recaptured by the Ottomans in 1512, completing the Turkish conquest of Bosnia. The border defenses were fatally breached with the capture of Belgrade by Süleyman I in 1521 and the fall of Orsova and Knin the following year.

With the lower Danube firmly in his control, Süleyman invaded Hungary in force, defeating the Hungarian army in the Battle of Mohács (1526), at which King Louis II was killed. Louis's death marked the end of the medieval Hungarian kingdom, which was subsequently divided among the Ottomans, Austrian Habsburgs, and the dependent principality of Transylvania.

Brian Hodson

See also: Matthias I; Hunyadi, János; Mohács, Battles of; Süleyman I; Turkish Wars of European Expansion

References and further reading:

Sugar, Peter. *Southeastern Europe under Ottoman Rule: 1389–1814.* Seattle: University of Washington Press, 1977.

Szakály, Ferenc. "Phases of Turco-Hungarian Warfare before the Battle of Mohács." *Acta Orientalia Academiae Scientiarum Hungaricae* 33 (1979): 65–111.

Hungarian-Venetian Wars (1345–1381)

Three wars between Hungary and Venice that took place during the reign of Hungarian king Louis I ("The Great," 1342–1382). At that time both the Hungarian kingdom and the Venetian republic were prosperous and major powers in southern Europe. Dalmatia was the major flash point between them. Louis sought to extend Hungarian power into the Balkans and, on the basis of dynastic right, to secure the throne of Naples. Louis's aspirations in Italy were unacceptable to Venice and to the papacy.

The first war was fought during 1345–1348, with Genoa on Louis's side. Doge of Venice Andrew Dandolo ordered the siege of Zara, under Hungarian rule, and a rival trading city to Venice on the Adriatic. The city was well fortified and resisted. In July 1348 Louis attacked the Venetian siege positions but was defeated. His army, which was principally of mounted knights, was unable to achieve any significant success against the Venetian fortified positions, and Louis decided to return home. The decision was also forced by the situation in Naples, where the king, Louis's younger brother, had been murdered. Zara continued to resist the Venetians but finally had to surrender in December. The first war ended with a cease-fire concluded on 5 August 1348, under the terms of which Hungary accepted Venetian rule in Dalmatia in return for which the trade and logistics routes between Hungary and Naples would remain open.

The second war occurred during 1356–1358. Peace talks started in Buda in 1349, but no agreement was possible because both parties wanted to rule Dalmatia. Louis began this second war in 1356. He divided his forces near Zagreb and sent the viceroy of Croatia to besiege Zara, while he led the main forces against the Venetian continental territories known as Terra Ferma. Following a few successful minor battles and sieges, in July Louis initiated a siege of Treviso. The city was close to capitulation when in November papal mediation brought about a cease-fire.

Louis's plan to attack Venice's mainland territories, where it could not use its formidable fleet, was brilliant, but the Hungarian forces lacked adequate siege equipment. Treviso pinned down the stronger Hungarian land forces, and they were unable to engage the Venetians in open battle.

Peace talks were again unsuccessful, and Louis changed his strategy. Instead of a large heavy force, he sent smaller cavalry units to raid the Venetian hinterland. He also ordered the viceroy of Croatia John Csuzi to carry out the same tactics in Dalmatia. These were successful, as the exhausted Dalmatian cities changed sides. The war ended with a peace agreement on 18 February 1358, with Venice giving up its claims to Dalmatia; Louis's forces departed Terra Ferma and freedom of the trade on the Adriatic was established.

In 1370 Louis acquired Poland from his uncle. The third war with Venice occurred during 1372–1381. Venice attacked Louis's ally Prince Francis Carrara of Padua in 1371, and the Hungarians came to his rescue in 1372. Carrara and the Hungarians defeated the Venetian forces at the Battle of Piave di Sacco but failed to take Treviso. This led to a disadvantageous peace for Padua.

Hungary, Genoa, and Padua formed a new alliance against Venice in 1378, but after a Venetian victory at sea, the allies turned to the old strategy of raiding the Venetian land-supply lines. The year 1379 brought successes to the allies. They defeated the Venetian fleet at Pola, and Charles of Durazzo, the new Hungarian commander in chief, besieged Treviso. Finally, the allied forces occupied Choggia, the "gateway to Venice." An exhausted Venice sued for peace, but the alliance broke up and Venice was able to retake Choggia.

The wars between Hungary and Venice ended by the peace of Turin on 8 August 1381. Its terms were advantageous to Hungary. Venice had to pay an annual tribute to Hungary and lost Dalmatia. But it had survived the war and maintained a leading role in Adriatic trade.

Ákos Tajti

References and further reading:

Bánlaki, József, of Doberdo. *A magyar nemzet hadtörténelme* (The Military History of the Hungarian Nation). Vol. 8. Budapest: Grill, 1934.

Kristó, Gyula. *Az Anjou kor háborúi* (The Wars of the Anjou Era). Budapest: Zrínyi, 1988.

Molnár, Erik, ed. *Magyarország története* (History of Hungary). Vol. 1. 2d ed. Budapest: Gondolat, 1967.

Ráth, Károly. *Magyar királyok hadjáratai utazásai és tartózkodási helyei* (Campaigns, Travels, and Residences of the Hungarian Kings). Gyor, Hungary: Sauervein, 1861.

Huns

Pastoral nomads of uncertain origin threatening the Roman world. Appearing unexpectedly in the steppes north of the Black Sea around 370, the Huns pushed the Goths west, across the Danube into Thrace. In 395, the Huns themselves crossed the Danube, thereby coming into direct conflict with the Roman world.

Superb horsemen—Ammianus Marcellinus and Zosimus describe them eating, sleeping, and even performing bodily functions while on horseback—they rode the ill-shaped but hardy steppe breed of horse. Thus mounted the Huns fought with a reflex composite bow—with which they were highly skilled even when drawn from a galloping or wheeling horse—a small shield, and a spear. The stave of the composite bow was constructed of laminated materials, usually wood (core), sinew (back), and horn (front). When strung, the bow was opened back against its natural curve, and held that way by the bowstring. More powerful than the longbow, it could penetrate armor at 100 meters.

A Hunnic army is described by Ammianus as forming up, with much disorderly movement and savage noise, into wedge-shaped masses. Some of these would break up into scattered bands, which would rush around with surprising speed and apparent chaos, inflicting casualties with their shooting. Other bands would relieve the first to maintain an incessant barrage, until the enemy was sufficiently weakened or demoralized. Each warrior would then charge at the gallop, regardless of risk to his own safety, to fight at close quarters with sword and spear. A Hun charge was executed with such speed and suddenness that it usually overwhelmed everyone and everything in its path. Huns terrified people by their outlandish appearance, but it was their very name that soon came to symbolize the epitome of swift, merciless destruction.

Nic Fields

See also: Attila the Hun; Châlons, Battle of; Goths
References and further reading:

Lindner, R. P. "Nomadism, Horses and Huns." *Past and Present* 92 (1981), 1–19.
Maenchen-Helfen, O. J. *The World of the Huns.* Berkeley: University of California Press, 1973.

Hunyadi, János (c. 1407–1456)

Hungarian general and regent. The son of a Romanian noble granted the estate of Hunyad (Hunedoara) in Transylvania by King Sigismund, Hunyadi began his military career serving the king in Italy and in the Hussite Wars in Bohemia. Originally a supporter of Albert of Habsburg following Sigismund's death, Hunyadi later opposed the succession of Albert's infant son, Ladislas Posthumus. In 1441, Hunyadi led the army of Polish king Wladyslaw II Jagiellon to victory over Ladislas's guardian, Frederick III at Bátaszék, winning the throne for Wladyslaw, crowned Ulászló I of Hungary.

In 1443 Hunyadi led Ulászló's Hungarian-Polish crusade against the Ottomans, driving the Turks out of Serbia, Bosnia, and Bulgaria in a winter campaign. A second crusade in 1444 ended in disaster at Varna on the Black Sea coast, where Sultan Murad II surprised and destroyed the Christian army and Ulászló was killed. Hunyadi escaped to Hungary and headed a regency council that opened negotiations with Frederick for the return of Ladislas. From 1446 to 1453, Hunyadi served as governor of Hungary in the name of the still-absent king. His third crusade against the Ottomans resulted in another defeat at the Second Battle of Kosovo Polje (1448).

After Ladislas's return to the throne, Hunyadi continued to serve the king as chief captain and administrator of royal revenues. In 1456, Hunyadi and the Minorite monk Giovanni di Capestrano organized a popular crusade in Austria and Hungary for the relief of Belgrade, besieged by Ottoman sultan Mehmed II. Hunyadi's small army, consisting largely of peasants and townsfolk, cut the Ottoman supply lines, repelled a Turkish assault, and impetuously attacked and broke the Ottoman army. On 11 August 1456, two weeks after his greatest victory, Hunyadi died in an epidemic that broke out in the Christian camp.

Brian Hodson

See also: Hungarian-Turkish Wars
References and further reading:

Bak, János. "The Late Medieval Period, 1382–1526." In *A History of Hungary,* ed. Peter Sugar. Bloomington: University of Indiana Press, 1990.
Held, Joseph. *Hunyadi: Legend and Reality.* Boulder, CO: East European Monographs, 1985.

Hurrians (c. 2300–1100 B.C.E.)

An Upper Mesopotamian people who were the dominant ethnic group of the Mitanni state (c. 1600–1100 B.C.E.) that ruled much of the ancient Near East in the late first millennium B.C.E. The earliest attestation of the Hurrians are in Sumero-Akkadian sources from the reign of Naram-Sin in the late third millennium B.C.E. They are described as inhabiting the land of Subartu—the Upper Mesopotamian regions of the Khabur and Balikh river basins in Syria, as well as the Tigris River basin in northern Iraq. By the end of the third millennium B.C.E., north Mesopotamia was thoroughly Hurrianized, with well-established Hurrian states that continued until the rise of a powerful Hurrian-based kingdom of Mitanni (c. 1600 B.C.E.).

The kingdom of Mitanni was a confederation of Hurrian states in Upper Mesopotamia in the late second millennium B.C.E. Its capital, Washukanni, has not been located for certain; it may have been Tell Fakhariyah, a mound located near the headwaters of the Khabur River in Syria. By 1450 B.C.E., Mitanni was the most powerful state in the Tigris-Euphrates region, composed of confederate and vassal city-states, each with its own king. Although the state of Mitanni was dominated by Hurrians, there was a significant percentage of Indo-European West Semitic–speaking peoples, Hittites, and Assyrians.

Because of our fragmented sources, the military history of the Mitanni state can only be partially reconstructed. It appears that by 1500 B.C.E. Mitanni had expanded into most of Syria under the reigns of Paratarna and Saustatar. This newly formed confederation was likely in conflict with the expansionist policies of Thutmose III of Egypt (c. 1504–1450 B.C.E.). Later Mitanni kings are known primarily through the Amarna letters from Egypt (c. 1411–1350 B.C.E.), where the Mitanni kings engaged in diplomatic relations with the kings of Egypt. The marriage alliances between the two states may have been due to the rise of Assyria in northern Iraq and the Hittites in Anatolia, which severely threatened the Mitanni state. Under Tushratta Mittani became somewhat fragmented and suffered defeat at the hands of the Hittite king Shuppiliuiluma. Thus, after c. 1350 B.C.E., the Hurrian state ceased to be a major role player in ancient Near Eastern politics. Mitanni continued to be a buffer between the Hittites and Assyria for at least the next two centuries, until the area was absorbed into the Assyrian Empire.

Mark W. Chavalas

See also: Assyria; Babylonian Empire; Hittites

References and further reading:

Gelb, I. *Hurrians and Subarians.* Chicago: Oriental Institute, 1944.

Morrison, M. A., and D. I. Owen, et al. *Studies on the Civilization and Culture of Nuzi and the Hurrians.* 9 vols. Winona Lake, WI: Eisenbrauns, 1981.

Wilhelm, G. *The Hurrians.* Westminster, UK: Aris & Phillips, 1989.

Wiseman, D. *The Alalakh Tablets.* London: British School of Archaeology in Iraq, 1953.

Hussein, Saddam al-Tikriti (1937–)

Iraqi dictator. Born 28 April 1937 near Tikrit, Saddam Hussein never knew his father and has spent his life seeking to become the father of a new empire centered on Baghdad. He became involved with the Ba'athist Party and participated in a failed coup attempt in 1959 against Abdul-Karim Qassem. He fled to Egypt, where he was educated until he returned to Iraq. Following a coup in 1968, his cousin Ahmad Hassam al-Bakr became president. Saddam Hussein became the vice president of the Revolutionary Command Council, commanding internal security. Replacing his cousin, he took over Iraq in 1979.

Aiming to reestablish the dominance of Baghdad in the Arab world, Saddam Hussein studied and patterned himself after Joseph Stalin. Indeed, his regime continues to exist in large measure due to repeated purges of any whom Saddam Hussein suspects of harboring even thoughts of rebellion.

Iraq is an oil-producing country, but Saddam Hussein sought greatness through military adventures. He pursued the acquisition of nuclear, biological, and chemical weapons but was thwarted in developing a nuclear capacity initially by an Israeli air strike in 1981. His eight-year war with Iran failed to achieve its goals. Iraq emerged heavily in debt from that war with the fourth largest military in the world, numbering 1 million.

Saddam wasted little time before embarking on his sec-

Iraqi propaganda art glorifying Saddam Hussein's supposed military prowess. (National Archives)

ond war, the invasion of Kuwait. His defeat, in one of the most one-sided conflicts of modern times, resulted in the decimation of Iraq's military, economy, and infrastructure. One of the world's most unsuccessful military leaders, he remains the president of Iraq.

John R. Popiden

See also: Gulf War; Iran-Iraq War

References and further reading:

Makiya, Kanan. *Republic of Fear: The Politics of Modern Iraq.* Los Angeles and Berkeley: University of California Press, 1989, 1998.

Miller, Judith, and Laurie Mylroie. *Saddam Hussein and the Crisis in the Gulf.* New York: Times Books/Random House, 1990.

Hussite Wars (1419–1436)

Religious wars and revolt of Bohemia against the Holy Roman Emperor. The Hussite revolt began as a religious reform movement with strong popular support. In 1415, the movement's doctrine was declared heretical and its leader, Ján Hus, was burned at the stake at the Council of Constance. King Václav (Wenceslas) IV failed to control the resulting unrest in Bohemia, which spread along both national and class lines.

The Hussites were predominantly Czech and included both a moderate, mostly bourgeoisie, and noble Utraquist party and the more radical Taborites, largely peasants and villagers. Their opponents drew support from the German-speaking inhabitants of the kingdom and the upper nobility.

When Václav died in 1419, his brother, Holy Roman Emperor Sigismund, claimed the throne over the objection of the Hussites, who held him responsible for Hus's death. With the support of Pope Martin V, Sigismund entered Bohemia with an army of German and Hungarian crusaders in 1420 but was defeated by the Taborite general Ján Žižka outside Prague and forced to retire. A Second Crusade by German princes in 1421 ended in the failed siege of Zatec. Separately, Sigismund reentered Bohemia from Hungary and captured Kutna Hora but failed to trap Žižka's army.

Žižka returned to attack Sigismund's forces in their winter quarters, destroying his army in a running battle from Nebovidy to Německý Brod (6–10 January 1422). After defeating a Third Crusade led by Frederick I of Brandenburg, the Hussites were split by tensions between the Utraquists, who sought a settlement with the Catholic Church, and the Taborites, who pressed for continued reform and resistance. Taborite victories under Žižka's command over the Utraquists at Strachov (August 1423) and at Malešov (June 1424) shortly before his death ensured the continuation of the war.

Under Žižka's successor, the Taborite priest Prokop the Bald, the Hussites defeated a German army at Usti and launched raids into Silesia and Austria, burning Landshut (October 1426) and defeating an Austrian army near Linz (March 1427). A Fourth Crusade against the Hussites ended with the aborted siege of Støíbro and Prokop's victory over the crusaders at Tachau (1427).

In the following years, Hussite armies continued their raids into Germany and Hungary and briefly aided the Poles in their war with the Teutonic Knights. The defeat of a Fifth Crusade at Domazlice (1431) led the Council of Basel to open negotiations with the Hussites, resulting in a settlement with the Utraquists (1433), which the Taborites rejected. Allied now with the Catholics and barons, the Utraquists defeated the Taborites at the Battle of Lipany (1434), in which Prokop was killed. A final agreement between the two sides was reached in the Compacts of Jihlava (1436), which permitted the Hussites the use of their own communion rite in return for recognition of the authority of the Catholic Church and Sigismund's kingship.

Brian Hodson

See also: Německý Brod, Battle of; Prague, Siege of; Žižka, Ján

References and further reading:

Bartoš, František. *The Hussite Revolution, 1424–1437.* Trans. John Klassen. Boulder, CO, and New York: East European Monographs, 1986.

Heymann, Frederick. *John Zizka and the Hussite Revolution.* Princeton, NJ: Princeton University Press, 1955.

Hydaspes, Battle of the (May 326 B.C.E.)

Alexander's final major victory in Asia, in the Indus River valley. After the Macedonian king Alexander III the Great had conquered the Persian Empire, he crossed the Hindu Kush into India. A local king called Poros opposed him, holding the far bank of the river Hydaspes (Jhelum).

Poros's army consisted of 30,000 foot, 3,600 horse, 200 elephants, and 180 chariots. The elephants were deployed in a line in the center, with the infantry positioned behind them, opposing Alexander's cavalry, whose horses were terrified of the elephants. Poros's flanks were covered by cavalry and chariots. Alexander's force consisted of 5,000 cavalry and 10,000 infantry. The infantry were deployed in line, with the right flank covered by the majority of the cavalry. The remainder of the cavalry were deployed on the left, possibly shielded behind the infantry line.

Alexander left a holding force to keep Poros's army in place, while Alexander with the rest of his forces forded the river upstream and attacked the Indian king. Alexander initiated the battle by attacking the enemy cavalry with his own cavalry force on the right. As the numerically inferior Indian horse were under severe pressure, Poros ordered the cavalry on the other flank to reinforce them. Thereupon the Macedonian cavalry detachment on the left crossed the battlefield and attacked the Indian horse in the flank. The Indian horse were surrounded and destroyed.

Meanwhile the infantry lines had clashed. At first the Macedonians had a hard time with the elephants, but soon they opened gaps to let the panicked beasts through or turned them with their pikes, driving them back into the Indian line, then charged the disordered Indians. Twelve thousand Indians were killed, 9,000 captured. Their king fought heroically until he was persuaded to surrender. The Macedonians lost 1,000 men, a heavy toll for Alexander's depleted and weary troops.

Maarten van der Werf

See also: Alexander the Great; Alexander's Wars of Conquest

References and further reading:

Fuller, J. F. C. *The Generalship of Alexander the Great.* London: Eyre & Spottiswoode, 1958.

Green, Peter. *Alexander of Macedon, 356–323 B.C.E. A Historical Biography.* Harmondsworth, UK: Penguin, 1974. Reprinted Berkeley and Los Angeles: University of California Press, 1991.

Hammond, N. G. L. *The Genius of Alexander the Great.* London: Duckworth, 1997.

Tarn, W. W. *Alexander the Great.* Cambridge, UK: Cambridge University Press, 1948.

Hydrogen Bomb, Development of (1942–1952)

The United States detonated the world's first hydrogen, or thermonuclear, bomb on 31 October 1952. This bomb, codenamed Mike, stood three stories high and exploded with a force of 10.4 megatons, or over 10 million tons of TNT. The mushroom cloud from the explosion rose to a height of more than 100,000 feet and could be seen from a distance of 50 miles. A new era in nuclear weaponry began as the destructive power of such weapons increased from thousands of tons to millions of tons of TNT equivalence.

Nuclear weapons are of two basic types. Atomic bombs, such as those used in World War II combat against Hiroshima and Nagasaki, split atoms of the elements uranium or plutonium. Hydrogen bombs fuse atoms of the hydrogen isotopes deuterium and tritium. In both types of weapons, large amounts of energy are released in the form of blast waves and radiation. The very sudden release of this energy causes the enormous destructive power of nuclear weapons.

Edward Teller and Enrico Fermi first studied the possibility of a hydrogen bomb in 1942. Based on the research of Hans Bethe, who pioneered studies of thermonuclear reactions in stars, Teller and Fermi believed that atoms of deuterium, an isotope of hydrogen, could be fused into helium with a simultaneous release of energy. Because such a process required stellar temperatures, then unobtainable on earth, Teller originally doubted that a hydrogen bomb could be built.

Despite his original doubts, Teller continued to study thermonuclear reactions and became convinced that a hydrogen bomb was possible. By this time, however, it had been decided that the United States would concentrate its World War II nuclear efforts on building a fission device at the Los Alamos Laboratory in New Mexico. A thermonuclear weapon would be too difficult to develop in time to assist the war effort. Despite the wartime concentration on the fission weapons, Fat Man and Little Boy, Teller and a small group of scientists did conduct some elementary research on the hydrogen bomb. In particular, Teller and his colleagues found that much less deuterium and tritium would be required than originally thought, thereby making a hydrogen bomb more realistic.

With the end of World War II, the United States demobilized. The wartime weapons laboratories, including Los Alamos, faced severe shortages of manpower as senior scientists returned to their prewar university positions and younger staff left to enter graduate school. As a result, very little research and development of the hydrogen bomb took place. Between 1946 through 1949, for instance, fewer than 12 theoretical physicists worked full time on the hydrogen bomb. Despite the shortage of scientist staff, work continued at Los Alamos during the late 1940s on the hydrogen bomb. Among the technical accomplishments during the late 1940s was the improvement of fission devices, the use of computers and computational modeling, and the development of cryogenic technology to produce the liquid deuterium required to make a hydrogen bomb.

The ultimate success of the United States' thermonuclear program rested on five accomplishments. First was the discovery of how to make such a device work. This discovery had to overcome a fundamental problem uncovered during early thermonuclear research. Thermonuclear systems lose as much energy as they create. Second, Los Alamos had to increase the size of its scientific staff significantly. The hydrogen bomb problem required complex interactions among the entire range of physicists, chemists, and metallurgists and their respective skills. Third, smaller and more efficient fission bombs were needed to start a thermonuclear fire. Fourth, computational ability had to be greatly enhanced. Fifth, the political will had to exist to marshal the resources necessary to accomplish the task in a complex technical and political environment.

The design adopted for the first hydrogen bomb did not come easily or quickly. Unlike fission weapons that are one of two types, scientists did not have a clear idea of the range of physical constraints governing thermonuclear weapon design. Extensive mathematical modeling and simulation were required before any kind of scientific judgment could be made. It took five years to discover the ultimate design.

The shortage of scientific staff, particularly theoretical and experimental physicists, also took five years to overcome. In the short term, the Los Alamos Laboratory used consultants such as university professors on leave. Many of these consultants had worked at Los Alamos during World War II and knew the nature of problems facing thermonuclear development. Eventually the pool of scientists grew as postwar university graduation rates increased. However, not enough can be said for the small cadre of scientists who stayed at Los Alamos after the war and advanced thermonuclear work under less than ideal conditions.

Because a hydrogen bomb requires extremely high temperatures to ignite the thermonuclear fuel, temperatures found only in stars, the only possible way to ignite a hydrogen bomb was by using an atomic bomb. For the development of the hydrogen bomb to go forward, fission weapons had to be improved. The two wartime fission devices, Fat Man and Little Boy, were crude prototypes and not capable of being adapted for use in a hydrogen bomb. A new class of fission bombs had to be designed, built, and tested. This process took years. The first testing of new fission devices did not take place until 1948, with more design improvements following in 1950.

Because all of the design work on a hydrogen bomb involved complex mathematical modeling and simulation, the need for better and better computers was compelling. During World War II, all computing at Los Alamos was done with desktop calculators and a variety of IBM business machines. Such machines were not capable of handling the complex modeling required for developing the hydrogen bomb. Beginning shortly after the war, true computers started to become available, beginning with the ENIAC, IBM's SSEC, and the National Bureau of Standards' SEAC. Because these machines were on the East Coast, many of the thermonuclear calculations actually took place far from Los Alamos. Although the first hydrogen bomb could have been developed without modern computers, such development would have been substantially delayed.

Finally, a political mandate was necessary to concentrate and focus the final development of the hydrogen bomb. By the late 1940s the Cold War had begun in earnest, and in 1949 the Soviet Union detonated its first atomic bomb. Concern arose in the national security establishment that the United States could be overtaken militarily by the USSR if the U.S. did not develop thermonuclear devices. Fission bombs have a natural upper limit to the explosive power they could produce. Hydrogen bombs do not. By adding more fuel, thermonuclear bombs can be made ever larger. A Soviet Union with unchallenged thermonuclear capability was a sobering thought. Taking all of this into account, President Harry Truman directed an accelerated effort to develop the hydrogen bomb in January 1950.

Shortly after Truman's directive, hydrogen-bomb research began to bear fruit. Edward Teller and Stanislaw Ulam came up with a promising design, radiation implosion, which was translated by Richard Garwin into a working design. Once the design concept was reviewed and approved, work began on constructing the Mike device and planning for a full-scale test at the Pacific Proving Ground in the Marshall Islands. Every atmospheric nuclear test was a major undertaking. The first hydrogen bomb test was even more so, involving thousands of people, millions of dollars, and countless pieces of equipment and conducted in the remote reaches of the Pacific Ocean.

Mike was not a bomb in the combat sense of the word. Weighing more than 1 million pounds, standing three stories high, and using a cryogenic fuel, it was a stationary device. Work began immediately to make hydrogen bombs deliverable, first by aircraft and later by missiles. It took some two years after the Mike shot to reach this goal. This work involved moving away from the constraints of cryogenic to dry fuel and building devices based on the demands of air force and navy aircraft and the nose cones of ballistic missiles.

Atomic bombs ended World War II. As destructive as Fat Man and Little Boy proved to be, some governments thought a nuclear war might be won—albeit at great cost. Thermonuclear weapons destroyed this concept of survivability. In 1954, the United States tested its largest ever hydrogen bomb, Bravo, which exploded with the energy of 15 megatons. The Soviet Union, in the early 1960s, exploded a device of 50 megatons—the world's largest explosion. Capable of theoretically unlimited destruction, thermonuclear weapons could destroy not only entire cities, but civilizations as well. The testing of thermonuclear devices brought the United States and the Soviet Union to the bargaining table and a test moratorium. The consequences of a thermonuclear war were too terrible to ignore.

Roger A. Meade

See also: Cold War

References and further reading:

Hewlett, Richard G., and Francis Duncan. *Atomic Shield: A History of the United States Atomic Energy Commission,* Vol. 2, *1947–1952.* Berkeley: University of California Press, 1990.

Rhodes, Richard. *Dark Sun: The Making of the Atomic Bomb.* New York: Simon & Schuster, 1995.

I

Ia Drang Valley (October–November 1965)

The first real test of North Vietnamese and U.S. regular armed forces in the deepening conflict in Vietnam. Although the Americans won, both sides drew important conclusions about strategy and tactics that would influence the course of the war.

In early 1964, the government in Hanoi had begun sending regular North Vietnamese Army main force units to augment Vietcong guerrillas in South Vietnam; a year later, the United States also began committing regular army and Marine Corps forces.

In October 1965, the North Vietnamese began attacking a U.S. Army Special Forces camp at Plei Me in the central highlands of South Vietnam. They were planning to destroy an expected South Vietnamese Army relief column. However, the U.S. Army's 1st Cavalry Division had arrived at Pleiku and was ready to test a new type of warfare, using helicopters to fly over enemy positions to deliver troops and firepower where needed. On 14 November, U.S. troops landed at a site some 14 miles east of Plei Me, which to their surprise was in the middle of a North Vietnamese Army (NVA) regiment, and a major two-day battle began. The Americans were supported by massive artillery and air strikes, including the first use of B-52 bombers in Vietnam, flying from Guam, each with payloads of 200 tons of 500-pound bombs.

The North Vietnamese eventually broke off contact and retreated across the Cambodian border. They had lost 2,000 killed and wounded; the Americans, 79 killed and 121 wounded. The NVA leadership concluded they could not fight another such battle; either they would have to select situations where they could overwhelm smaller and more isolated American units or else they would have to "hug" American forces, getting so close that the U.S. troops would not call in air strikes and artillery for fear of being hit themselves. General William Westmoreland concluded that the so-called airmobile concept and his seizing of the tactical initiative (while conceding the strategic initiative) would work, and so the American phase of the protracted conflict proceeded.

Charles M. Dobbs

See also: Vietnam Conflict; Vo Nguyen Giap; Westmoreland, William

References and further reading:

Moore, Harold G., and Joseph L. Galloway. *We Were Soldiers Once and Young: Ia Drang, the Battle that Changed the War in Vietnam.* New York: Random House, 1992.

Pimlott, John. *Vietnam: The Decisive Battles.* New York: Macmillan, 1990.

Turley, William S. *The Second Indochina War: A Short Political and Military History, 1954–1975.* Boulder, CO: Westview Press, 1986.

Illyrian Wars (229–219 B.C.E.)

Two wars fought between Rome and the coastal kingdom of the Illyrians (modern Croatia). In the First Illyrian War (229–228 B.C.E.) the expanding Roman Republic clashed with Queen Teuta and her Illyrian pirates. The Illyrians had raided Greco-Roman shipping lanes, besieged the Greek port of Corcyra (Corfu), and killed Roman ambassadors in an ambush after attempts to negotiate with the aggressive Illyrians had failed. The Roman senate, seeking revenge, sent a Roman land and sea expedition to relieve the siege at Corcyra. Queen Teuta capitulated and agreed to give up land claims and pay reparations. Macedonia allied with Rome to form an additional counter to Illyrian aggression.

In the Second Illyrian War (219 B.C.E.) Demetrius of Pharos succeeded Queen Teuta as the Illyrian leader and renewed land intrusions into Roman protectorates and piracy against Roman shipping. The Romans acted quickly, perhaps because war with Carthage was imminent. Two Roman

Men from the 25th Infantry Division take cover during the bitter fight at the Imjin River on April 23, 1951. (National Archives)

armies besieged the fortified Illyrian cities of Dinale and Pharos, with the former falling in seven days and the latter in one day. Demetrius fled and the conditions of the first war were reimposed on the Illyrians.

Christopher Howell

See also: Macedonian Wars; Punic Wars; Roman Republic, Wars of the

References and further reading:

Adcock, Frank E. *The Roman Art of War under the Republic.* Revised edition. New York: Barnes & Noble, 1963.

Harris, W. V. *War and Imperialism in Republican Rome.* Oxford: Clarendon, 1979.

Sherwin-White, A. N. *Roman Foreign Policy in the East.* Norman: University of Oklahoma Press, 1984.

Imjin River (April 1951)

Prominent river in Korea, scene of heavy fighting numerous times during the Korean War (1950–1953), most notably in the spring of 1951 during the Communist Fifth Phase Offensive. The offensive, primarily carried out by the Chinese People's Volunteers, was designed to capture Seoul, the South Korean capital, which had already changed hands several times since the commencement of hostilities in June 1950. The Chinese commanding general, Teh-huai Peng, hoped to present Seoul to Premier Mao Zedong as a gift for the 1 May communist holiday.

Beginning on 22 April 1951, the Communists pushed southward across the entire expanse of Korea. Particularly hard hit were the positions of the British 29th brigade, especially the Gloucestershire Battalion, usually referred to as the Glosters. The Glosters held positions immediately south of the river. Troops from the Chinese Sixty-third Army fought desperately and repeatedly to ford the river in the area defended by the Glosters. Finding it impossible to breach the river in the face of the Glosters' deadly firepower, the Chinese pressed across in weaker, adjacent sectors. By 25 April, the Glosters were threatened with encirclement. Efforts to relieve them failed in the face of strong Chinese resistance. By the end of the month, almost all of the battalion had been killed, wounded, or captured. These were the kind of losses the hard-pressed British could ill afford.

The annihilation of the Glosters had political, not just military, consequences. Striving to hold together its diverse coalition of United Nations forces, the United States sought to maintain the continued support of its British ally. General Mathew Ridgway, commander of all UN forces, even demanded a formal report on the loss of the Glosters. Although the destruction of the unit was blamed primarily on the size and ferocity of Chinese opposition, Ridgway took great care from that point forward to make sure that no similarly disastrous situations confronted British forces in Korea. The Communist offensive put a major dent in allied lines but came nowhere near capturing Seoul. This campaign was the last Communist offensive against non-ROK (Republic of Korea) United Nations Command (UNC) forces. The Communists had suffered terrible losses and were not willing to try matters again against the Americans, the Commonwealth Division, and so on, on a large scale. The Americans, for their part, were unwilling to invest the resources needed for victory in Korea while Europe, where in their eyes the main threat lay, remained basically unprepared for defense against Communist designs. Two months later, the Communist side called for negotiations and an armistice.

John C. McManus

See also: Korean War; Ridgway, Mathew B.; Van Fleet, James A.

References and further reading:

Alexander, Bevin. *Korea: The First War We Lost.* New York: Hippocrene, 1993.

Appleman, Roy E. *Ridgway Duels for Korea.* University Station: Texas A&M Press, 1990.

Sandler, Stanley. *The Korean War: No Victors, No Vanquished.* Lexington: University of Kentucky Press; and London: Baker & Taylor, 1999.

Whelan, Richard. *Drawing the Line: The Korean War, 1950–1953.* Boston: Little, Brown, 1993.

Imphal and Kohima (8 March–22 June 1944)

Critical World War II battles in the China-Burma-India theater, arguably the worst defeat suffered by Japanese ground forces in the war. Located in northeast India, Imphal and Kohima became focal points of one of World War II's most desperate campaigns when Japan's Fifteenth Army, commanded by General Mutaguchi Renya, invaded India (Operation U-GO) in late winter 1944. Mutaguchi's objectives included preempting a British invasion of Burma, establishing a foothold for the collaborationist Indian National Army (INA) in hopes of provoking an India-wide revolt against British rule, and capturing large portions of Manipour and Assam provinces, both essential for the Allies' hump air route to China.

During the campaign's opening month, Mutaguchi's forces—three Japanese divisions and 7,000 troops from the INA—besieged both Imphal and Kohima, key supply bases for General William Slim's British Fourteenth Army. Bitter, attritional fighting occurred at both towns, the British demonstrating a resolve and skill not evident during their ignominious retreat from Burma just two years earlier or their aborted Assam offensive the year earlier. Ultimately a combination of combat skill, determination, quantitative superiority in men and equipment, air power, and Slim's command decisions proved decisive. The Fourteenth Army relieved both Imphal and Kohima in June and then drove the Japanese back into Burma in July.

At a cost of 17,000 casualties, British Fourteenth Army inflicted more than 50,000 casualties, destroying Japan's Fifteenth Army, eliminating the Japanese threat to India, and paving the way for the reconquest of Burma that followed between August 1944 and May 1945.

Bruce J. DeHart

See also: Chindits; Merrill's Marauders; Slim, William Joseph, First Viscount

References and further reading:

Allen, Louis. *Burma: The Longest War, 1941–1945.* London: J. M. Dent, 1984.

Grant, Ian Lyall. *Burma: The Turning Point.* Chichester: Zampi, 1993.

Rooney, David. *Burma Victory: Imphal and Kohima, March 1944 to May 1945.* New York: Continuum, 2000.

Inca Civilization

The Andean valleys of northern and western South America were populated from approximately 1200 B.C.E. by a succession of societies. The Chavin culture, first of the great civilizations in the region, was noted for its pottery, architecture, and sculpture, especially bas relief, and for their introduction of maize as a major food crop prior to the end of the eighth century C.E. Later societies added their own distinct contributions, many of which were later utilized by the Incas. The Nazca people were noted for their colorful ceramics and for developing irrigation systems for agriculture. The Mochica, a theocratic people, built temples, pyramids, and roads, engaged in metal work, and made ceramic portraiture, which explicated their life activities. The Tiahuanaco and Huari peoples developed a military state. Under the Chimu, urbanization increased. For several millennia, the llama was the principal beast of burden for all peoples. The polygamous Quechua-speaking Incas, originally humble mountain people, arose near present-day Cuzco and borrowed heavily from the cultural, administrative, and military precedents set by their predecessors. They eliminated many elements of earlier civilizations and developed myths demonstrating the divinity of the Inca, their ruler, from which their society took its name. The *coya* (queen) was chief wife of the Inca ruler. The Inca (ruler) owned all land, and individual citizens through their local communes, the *ayllu,* merely had the use of it. Major Inca expansion began under Pachacuti Inca Yupanqui (r. 1438–1471), and their centralized feudal society, with its administrative districts and advanced social welfare system, exercised effective control over a widely dispersed population. Public buildings were constructed of stone, carefully cut and fitted so as to preclude any need for mortar. Wide, well-maintained roads, facilitating wars of conquest, stretched from Peru south to the town of Constitucion in modern central Chile. The Inca were almost unique in being a civilization that had no written language, but government runners, carrying *quipu,* a message system employing knotted strings, communicated essential intelligence throughout their far-flung empire. Their army operated as a form of agricultural militia. The government provided needed arms and armament. Tightly disciplined, Inca warriors fought en masse in battle. Principal weapons included slings, a six-foot-long spear and spear throwers, stone or metal-headed clubs, war axes, and double-edged wooden swords. Helmets were made of cane or wood, and their square shields were made of wood and animal hides. Body armor consisted of quilted cotton jackets. Under Pachacuti's successors, Topa Inca Yupanqui (1471–1493) and Huayna Capac (1493–1527), Inca power was consolidated. In 1527, the Inca leader Huascar succeeded, but during much of his six-year tenure, he was engaged in civil war with his illegitimate half brother Atahualpa. Huascar's forces were ultimately defeated by Atahualpa in 1532. Spanish conquistadors under Francisco Pizarro arrived shortly thereafter. Atahualpa met Pizarro at Cajamarca on 16 November 1532. His unarmed troops were slaughtered and Atahualpa captured. Despite having met Spanish demands for a substantial ransom, in return for which he had been promised his freedom, Atahualpa was publicly garroted at Pizarro's order on 29 August 1533. The Spanish conquest was completed by 1535.

Keir B. Sterling

See also: Pizarro, Francisco

References and further reading:

Garcilaso de la Vega. *El Inca. Obras Completas.* Madrid: 1960.

Hemming, John. *The Conquest of the Incas.* London: Macmillan, 1970.

Prescott, William H. *The History of the Conquest of Mexico and the History of the Conquest of Peru.* New York: Modern Library, n.d.

Stern, Steve J. *Peru's Indian Peoples and the Challenge of Spanish Conquest.* Madison: University of Wisconsin Press, 1982.

Inca Empire Imperial Wars (1438–1540)

Wars that led to the Inca Empire becoming the largest of its day. The Inca Empire eventually dominated much of western South America, including the highland and coastal Andes areas. At the heart of this empire was its ability to use grand strategy to wage imperial wars against less organized, though often militarily superior, opponents. Although Spanish and native sources differ with archaeological data on exact dates, it is clear that Pachacutec Yupanqui deserves much of the credit. He ruled from 1438 to 1471 and developed a permanent military system and imperial grand strategy.

Significant wars were mounted against highland Andes chiefdoms like the Chanca and Lupaca after the Battle of Cuzco in 1438. Highland strategies involved the use of alliances, a complicated road network and supply system, fortifications, and llamas as backpack animals. Inca logistics was far superior and the empire infrastructure, based on labor taxes and movement of people, became the rival of any in the world. Considering the lack of draft animals, wheels, and iron metallurgy, the gain and consolidation of territory are even more astounding.

Coastal lowland wars were fought using rotating 20,000-men armies based on decimal units. During the war with the Chimu state, bronze weaponry became more common. Military schools trained ethnic Inca to lead loyal allied troops into battle. The Sapa Inca, or emperor, often appointed kin to command the rotating armies and eventually stayed in Cuzco to oversee all operations. By the time of Spanish invasions in 1531, the Inca had permanent standing armies, excellent logistics, and a tested grand strategy based both on military might and on management of human and natural resources that could be used to wage economic warfare.

After Pachacutec had established the empire, his son Topa Yupanqui continued conquests in the late fifteenth century and passed on the title of Sapa Inca to his son Hauna Capac, who conquered much of Ecuador and Columbia in the early sixteenth century.

Capac died of smallpox along with many other Andean Indians, and his sons Atahualpa and Hauscar fought a civil war in the early 1530s that devastated the empire further. At this point conquistador Francisco Pizarro and about 150 fellow Castillians had boldly invaded and taken control of the Inca Empire, executing Atahualpa, taking the Inca capital of Cuzco, and establishing a Spanish port capital at Lima. The royal Inca Paullu was established as a puppet ruler at Cuzco while his brother Manco carried on against the Spanish from the highland jungle fortifications of Vitcos and Vilcambamba, the legendary lost city of the Inca.

Between 1535–1540, Mancos, who studied and employed Spanish battle tactics—even riding a captured horse himself—organized huge rebellions that killed hundreds of

Spanish, mainly by ambushes in battles, and threatened to push the Spanish back into the Pacific. In 1536, he gathered a 100,000-man force to besiege Cuzco but failed to kill the brothers of Francisco Pizarro and his forces there. The battle centered around the monstrous Inca fort of Sacsahuaman, which was eventually retaken by the Spanish.

Although Manco's son, Tito Cusi, carried on the defense against the Spanish into the 1560s from Vilcambamba, the chance for regaining the empire had passed. A devastating epidemic in the 1570s killed millions more Andean Indians and ended all hope of future empire-wide rebellions.

Christopher Howell

See also: Chan Chan, Battle of; Cuzco, Battles of; Pachacutec Yupanqui

References and further reading:

Bram, Joseph. *An Analysis of Inca Militarism.* New York: Augustin Publisher, 1941.

D'Altroy, Terrence, ed. *Provincial Power in the Inca Empire.* Washington, DC: Smithsonian Institution Press, 1992.

Garcilaso de la Vega, El Inka. *The Incas: Royal Commentaries.* 3d ed. Ed. Alain Gheerbrant. New York: Avon Books, 1971.

Hemming, John. *The Conquest of the Incas.* New York: Harvest-Harcourt Brace Jovanovich, 1970.

Inchon Landings (15 September 1950)

The U.S. landings that changed the course of the Korean War, temporarily. For several weeks, Eighth U.S. Army and Republic of Korea forces had stubbornly held a perimeter around Pusan in extreme southeastern Korea. The Korean People's Army of North Korea had committed the bulk of its forces there and allied air attacks had limited supplies to the front. The North Koreans were stretched dangerously thin.

MacArthur overrode concerns by U.S. Navy and Marine Corps strategists about the dangers of assaulting Inchon by sea—Operation CHROMITE. High tides, a narrow shipping channel, and a very tall sea wall worried virtually every senior officer who reviewed the plans. MacArthur believed that the advantages, especially an attack along a line of least expectation, outweighed the concerns. And he ordered decoy attacks farther south along both coasts to distract the North Korean command.

The attack at Inchon went spectacularly well. U.S. Marines landed first and secured the port; U.S. Army units provided added punching power. After securing the port, the invasion force moved the short distance to Seoul by September 29. Meanwhile, United Nations (UN) forces in the Pusan perimeter scheduled a simultaneous breakout that linked up with the Inchon invading force on September 26 near Osan, site of the first American resistance to and defeat by the North Koreans. The North Koreans were cut off and, by September's end, that army largely had ceased to exist as an organized force south of the thirty-eighth parallel. The Inchon landings have been held up through the subsequent decades as a near-perfect example of amphibious operations. Inchon was not the "desperate gamble" of legend, however; American forces had complete control of the air and seas and a substantial superiority in numbers. Still it was MacArthur's last victory and a most impressive operation.

Charles M. Dobbs

See also: Korean War; MacArthur, Douglas

References and further reading:

Heinl, Robert Debs, Jr. *Victory at High Tide: The Inchon-Seoul Campaign.* Annapolis: Nautical and Aviation Publishing Company of America, 1980.

Langley, Michael. *The Inchon Landing: MacArthur's Last Triumph.* New York: Times Books, 1979.

Sandler, Stanley. *The Korean War: No Victors, No Vanquished.* Lexington: University of Kentucky Press; London: Routledge, 1999.

Sheldon, Walt. *Hell or High Water. MacArthur's Landing at Inchon.* New York: Macmillan, 1968.

Indian Border Conflicts (1962–1971)

The granting of Indian independence in August 1947 occasioned a series of long-standing border disputes with neighboring countries. Foremost of these was the Indian annexation of Kashmir to the north, despite its predominately Muslim population. Beyond Kashmir was the Jammu region adjacent to Tibet, then jointly claimed by both India and China. Prime Minister Jawaharal Nehru was intent upon maintaining friendly relations with the People's Republic, but as early as August 1958 he complained of Chinese border violations in the Longju and Ladakh regions. Troops were rushed in to enforce Indian claims, but in October 1962, the government of Chairman Mao Zedong launched a massive surprise attack to evict them. Through a series of lightning thrusts, Indian forces were handily repulsed from the disputed territories, at which point China declared a unilateral cease-fire. India, soundly trounced, had no recourse but to accept a truce.

In the spring of 1965 violence sprang up along the border with Muslim Pakistan over the issue of Kashmir, which also spilled over into the Indian state of Punjab. In August 1965 India commenced formal hostilities with a large-scale raid into Kashmir, which was followed by a major Pakistani thrust into the same region. The fighting was particularly intense and featured widespread use of aircraft against cities and large-scale tank battles. The result, however, was a bloody stalemate and by September 1965 a United Nations–brokered cease-fire was enacted. Further border tensions with China also induced the Indian government to enter a 20-year Treaty of Friendship with the Soviet Union in exchange for large shipments of modern weapons. The Indian governments resolved to be fully prepared for the next round of fighting, when it occurred.

In December 1971, civil war erupted in the nominally Muslim state of East Pakistan, which was separated from West Pakistan by 1,000 miles of Indian territory. Rebels in East Pakistan were seeking autonomy and readily turned to Hindu India for help. The result was an increase of border tensions with West Pakistan, which goaded that country into launching a preemptive air strike against India on 3 December 1971. The Indians, however, were ready and easily parried the blow. Moreover, enjoying a threefold manpower advantage, their forces rolled into East Pakistan. The West Pakistani garrison there was hard-pressed, so as a diversion Pakistani forces also launched an unsuccessful diversionary attack into Kashmir. However, Indian numbers prevailed, and on 16 December 1971 they captured the East Pakistani capital of Dacca, which signaled the general collapse of resistance. Pakistan had been badly defeated, with losses of 4,000 dead and 10,000 wounded; Indian losses were half that. Moreover, a new state, Bangladesh, was created from the former East Pakistan, which effectively reduced West Pakistan's influence throughout the region. The Kashmir issue remains unresolved, and Indian and Chinese forces still dispute some of the most remote and elevated regions on earth.

John C. Fredriksen

References and further reading:

Ganguly, Sumit. *The Origin of War in South Asia: Indo-Pakistani Conflicts since 1947.* Boulder, CO: Westview Press, 1986.

Palit, D. K. *War in High Himalaya: The Indian Army in Crisis, 1962.* New York: St. Martin's Press, 1991.

Indian Mutiny (1857)

Violent uprising of the Indian Bengal Army, hailed by many Indians as a nearly successful revolution. The Indian army of the time was a mixture of 39,750 British officers and troops supervising 226,400 trained Indian soldiers. During the 1850s the British Indian Officer Corps had declined in numbers, quality, and experience and had begun to cause bitter resentment among Indian troops by widespread disrespect for their religious and ethnic beliefs.

In 1856 an Indian revolutionary movement began targeting Indian troops with stories of religious persecutions and blasphemies planned by the British. Although the movement was not highly organized, the situation was aggravated by continued British acts of ignorance, and by 1857 an uprising was inevitable.

Rumors had been spread that cartridges for the new Enfield rifle, which required handling during loading, contained pig and beef fat, which was highly offensive to both Muslims and Hindus. On 8 May 1857, the mutiny was triggered when some Indian troops of the 3d Light Cavalry stationed in Meerut were forced to declare their individual position regarding the new cartridges; those renouncing use of them were court-martialed and jailed. The Indian garrison in Meerut mutinied and freed the prisoners on Sunday, 9 May, and with a growing civilian mob took over the town, which led to a massacre of local Europeans.

The mutineers then moved to Delhi, 40 miles distant. Delhi had symbolic importance as the former center of the Mogul Empire and was also the focus of British administration for the whole of northern India. The 54th Native Infantry Regiment in Delhi turned on its English officers and joined the 3d Light Cavalry in capturing the city, and most resident Europeans were slaughtered. Bahadur Shar, last of the line of Mogul rulers, was proclaimed head of a new Mogul Empire. Unfortunately for the rebels, he was ineffectual; a strong leader might have driven the British out of India entirely. (The Indians had a saying, "If we would all only spit together, the British would drown!")

British garrisons and civilian enclaves throughout central and northern India were aware of the danger but could only await events during May 1857. Regiments disarmed their Indian troops or retreated into semifortified positions. However, word of events in Delhi spread among the Indians and many local revolts occurred rapidly. Cawnpore was captured after a three-week battle, and Lucknow besieged. In most smaller towns Europeans were massacred before rebel troops moved on to join larger actions.

It took a series of campaigns lasting until March 1858 (when Lucknow was finally recaptured) to end the mutiny. Sir Henry Havelock led the first relief column from Allahabad to Lucknow via Cawnpore but was besieged in turn, and not until November were the surviving Europeans evacuated. Delhi was recaptured in September 1857 by British troops with help from Sikhs under John Lawrence. Sir Hugh Rose suppressed the mutiny in the central districts of India in a series of operations. As the details of the Cawnpore massacre became widely known, British treatment of rebels was brutal, and executions were indiscriminate—many captured rebels being blown from cannons.

After the mutiny, the British army replaced East India Company garrisons throughout India, and native troops were not trained in artillery specialities.

Michael Hyde

See also: British-Indian Army

References and further reading:

Forbes-Mitchell W. *Reminiscences of the Great Mutiny 1857–59.* London: Macmillan and Co., 1893.

Haq, S. Moinul. *The Great Revolution of 1857.* Karachi: Pakistan Historical Society, 1968.

Harris, J. *The Indian Mutiny.* London: Hart-Davis MacGibbon, 1973.

Holmes, T. R. E. *A History of the Indian Mutiny, and the Disturbances which Accompanied It among the Civil Population.* London: W. H. Allen and Co., 1883.

Indian National Army (1943–1945)

An "independent" Indian army established under Japanese tutelage in 1943 to overthrow British rule in India. Started by the Japanese, it came into its own with Subhas Chandra Bose as its leader. Bose had been elected president of the Indian National Congress in 1938 and was a political and ideological rival to Gandhi. He resigned when he was unable to gain Gandhi's support after a bitter reelection. Arrested by the British in 1940, he went on a hunger strike that secured his release from prison. He evaded the British and fled in January 1941 to Berlin, via Moscow, to work for the Nazi's Special Bureau for India in 1942. A year later, after Japanese advances into Southeast Asia, he traveled to Tokyo and proclaimed a provisional Indian government. He became leader of the Indian Independence Movement and set about building up a Indian National Army (INA, also known as the Azad Hind Fauj), many of whose troops were disaffected Indian POWs from the ignominious fall of Singapore to the Japanese.

In 1944, his army took to the field with Japanese troops, advancing through Rangoon, and then into India, across the national frontier on 18 March 1944. In rough fighting, the Indian National Army was unable to occupy Kohima and advance toward Imphal. The British under General William Slim were able to resist and the joint Indian National/Japanese Army force was driven back, due in large part to a lack of air support. The INA was able to maintain some semblance of legitimacy, of carrying the banner of Indian liberation, but waned as the Japanese were driven back by the Allies, and many troops deserted back to the British-Indian forces. When Japan surrendered, so did the Indian National Army. Bose died in a mysterious aircraft crash sometime in August 1945.

Drew Philip Halévy

See also: Slim, William Joseph, First Viscount; World War II

References and further reading:

Calvocoressi, Peter, and Guym Pritchard. *Total War: Causes and Courses of the Second World War.* New York: Pantheon Books (1989).

Indochina Wars (1945–1954)

When the Pacific War ended suddenly in September 1945, Great Britain arranged for the return of the French to their colonies in Indochina. During the war, the Japanese had taken advantage of the regime in Vichy to occupy Indochina, and later, in March 1945, to disarm and imprison French troops. When Chiang Kai-chek's Nationalist forces left northern Indochina, it appeared the French had successfully reestablished that part of their empire.

It was not to be. During the long years of war a Vietnamese independence movement, dominated and led by Communist cadres, had arisen. Led by Ho Chi Minh, a charismatic leader, the so-called Vietminh had proclaimed Vietnamese independence in fall 1945 (the French had divided Vietnam into three units—Annam, Tonkin, and Cochin China—and thus Indochina into five states). Nonetheless, the French had little difficulty in reestablishing control. They drove Ho and his colleagues out of Hanoi and established a nominally independent regime under the emperor Bao Dai, although all real power remained in French hands.

Until the Communists conquered southern China in late 1949, the French were able to maintain control. But with the Communists on Vietnam's border, Ho's guerrillas would benefit from more secure access to supplies and advice, and the tide of war began to turn slowly but increasingly against France. Within a couple of years the French largely controlled only the two major river deltas, the Red River in the north (centering on the port of Haiphong and the capital city of Hanoi) and the Mekong River in the south (centering on the one-time fishing village of Saigon), as well as a coastal strip connecting the two. Control over much of the countryside and, at night, even major transportation routes was ceded to the Vietminh.

By 1953, the Vietminh had the upper hand. The French commander, Henri Navarre, decided to reverse policy and establish a strong base in northwestern Vietnam at Dien Bien Phu, about 180 miles from French bases around Hanoi, to interdict Vietminh forces moving onto the strategic Plaine des Jarres in Laos. Dien Bien Phu is an isolated plateau, surrounded by mountains; the French gambled that they could bring in a large garrison, occupy the surrounding hills, and destroy the Vietminh when they came out onto the plains to attack the entrenched French.

The French had seriously miscalculated. The Vietminh commander, Nguyen Vo Giap, decided to concentrate against the French garrison. He moved at least 50,000 men into the surrounding hills; using gang labor, he brought up artillery and weapons the French believed they could not transport. Soon the French were caught in a trap of their own making. The siege began in December 1953. On 13 March, after an intense artillery barrage, the Vietminh sent two battalions each against French outposts, and thereafter Vietminh artillery closed the airfield. Air dropping of supplies was haphazard and only added to the desperation of the French defenders. In late March, Giap's forces overran the other French outposts, and then a month of siege tactics ensued, followed by an attack on 1 May that led to the garrison's surrender on 7 May 1954. When the garrison surrendered, it seemed to mark an end to the French effort; the Geneva Conference on Indochina had begun, and the French withdrew. It would be America's turn next.

Charles M. Dobbs

See also: Chinese Civil War; Dien Bien Phu; Indonesian War of Independence; Vietnam Conflict

References and further reading:

Devillers, Philippe, and Jean Lacouture. *End of a War: Indochina, 1954.* Trans. Alexander Lieven and Adam Roberts. New York: Praeger, 1969.

Fall, Bernard. *Street without Joy: Indochina at War, 1946–1954.* Harrisburg, PA: Schoken Books, 1961.

Hammer, Ellen J. *The Struggle for Indochina, 1940–1955.* Stanford, CA: Stanford University Press, 1966.

Pike, Douglas. *History of Vietnamese Communism, 1925–1976.* Stanford, CA: Hoover Institution Press, 1978.

Indonesian War of Independence (1945–1949)

An internal conflict, that, with United Nations and United States aid, brought about the independence of Indonesia. As the Japanese were surrendering in World War II, Indonesian nationalists developed the Jakarta Charter, a plan for an independent, secular Indonesian state, which was proclaimed on 17 August 1945. Before Allied forces could intervene, Indonesian armed forces were formed and put to work crushing Muslim and Marxist revolutions in the north. British Indian troops finally arrived at Jakarta on 30 September. Violence erupted at Surabaya in East Java on 28 October. Hundreds of Indian troops were killed and thousands of Indonesians perished in British reprisals and Indonesian counterattacks. Convinced that they could not manage a military solution, the British urged talks between the Indonesians and Dutch. The Linggajati Agreement of 25 May 1947 provided for a Netherlands-Indonesian union, to which neither side was truly committed. Dutch forces, now numbering about 92,000, launched what they termed a "police action" on 21 July 1947, extending Dutch control to all of Java and Sumatra except the area around Jakarta. On 17 January 1948, the Renville Agreement recognized Dutch control of these areas but mandated plebiscites. Despite this, all Dutch-held areas were organized into a system of federated republics. Outrage at the situation sparked a communist uprising in September, whose speedy suppression by loyal Indonesian forces led the United States to view a prospective Indonesian republic as a bulwark against communism. The U.S. could exert enormous pressure on the Netherlands because of the Dutch need for American economic aid in the wake of World War II. But the fact that the communist uprising had happened at all led the Dutch to think that the republican movement was about to fracture, and on 19 December they occupied Jakarta and imprisoned the republican leaders. Guerrilla activity intensified, and the United Nations Security Council demanded restoration of the republican leadership and a complete transfer of authority. On 27 December 1949 full sovereignty was transferred to the Indonesian Republic and the 15 Dutch-established states. By November 1950 the 15 had been absorbed by the republic, and Indonesian sovereignty was complete.

Joseph M. McCarthy

See also: Dutch Colonial Wars

References and further reading:

Cribb, Robert E. *Gangsters and Revolutionaries: The Jakarta People's Militia and the Indonesian Revolution, 1945–1949.* Honolulu: University of Hawaii Press, 1991.

Frederick, William H. *Visions and Heat: The Making of the Indonesian Revolution.* Athens: Ohio University Press, 1989.

Wild, Colin, and Peter R. B. Cary, eds. *Born in Fire: The Indonesian Struggle for Independence, an Anthology.* Athens: Ohio University Press, 1988.

Infantry

Lightly armed ground troops. The backbone of any army is the infantry. Not only the most numerous of the fighting arms, but the only fighting arm that can take and hold ground. It has long been recognized that well-trained infantry would always beat mere masses of men. Further, if the well-trained men were also well armed, well led, and well equipped, they would be second to none.

The armies of Greece boasted the men of the phalanx; of Rome, the men of the legions. When led by great generals such as Philip of Macedon and Marius, Caesar, and Pompey, these infantry were capable of great feats of arms and endurance, achieved almost always by maneuver rather than face-to-face slogging. These were the forebears of all the infantry who have come onto the battlefield since, and their tradition of fighting with honor is perpetuated today.

Traditionally the infantryman has always been regarded as the "footslogger," the soldier who gets about on foot, and this has been true until the twentieth century. The rate of advance of the Greek phalanx and the German army of 1914 were virtually identical. The need for mobility and maneuver was foreseen by Napoleon, and his troops were able to move quickly by forced march, but little could be done to bring true mobility to the infantry until the advent of the internal combustion engine. During the wars of the nineteenth and early twentieth centuries, just as before, the infantry had the task of advancing toward the enemy until contact was established. Once that had occurred, with or without support from artillery, and later armor, it was the infantry's task to bring the enemy to battle and to kill him. The great generals, of course, were those who outmaneuvered the enemy in these advances, catching the enemy in the flank or the rear rather than head-on.

World War I saw more massed infantry involvement than in any previous conflict. In the east, German infantry fought and beat Russian infantry after three years of war. In the west the so-called war of attrition lasted for more than four years. Despite every indication that frontal attack was not viable against barbed wire, entrenched defenders, machine guns, artillery, and gas, both sides continued to make frontal assaults at a cost in men that presents a sickening picture of classic military ineptitude at command and staff level.

The arrival of effective armor and air support, heralded by the German blitzkriegs of 1939 and 1940, preempted the expected stalemate, in both the west and the east. Hitler's highly mobile Panzer formations, supported in the main by infantry on foot, defeated the forces of Poland, France (and the static Maginot line), Great Britain, Belgium, Holland, Norway, Yugoslavia, and Greece.

Hitler then sent his army into Soviet Russia. Initially successful, the German infantry got to the gates of Moscow. Then, however, the Hitlerian exhortations to hold at all costs, avoid retreat, and fight to the last man and bullet led to ultimate defeat. Despite the many tanks and aircraft at their disposal, it was infantry who formed the heart of both the German and Russian armies.

Masses of infantry moving on foot were standard until motorization. Aside from the American and British forces, armies have only truly become motorized since World War II. The German army between 1939 and 1945 was still heavily dependent upon the horse, in both offense and defense. However, at the end of the twentieth century, most developed nations have equipped their infantry with armored transport, either wheeled or tracked, the aim of which is to deliver them as far forward in the battle zone as possible under protection and unfatigued. Infantry, it has finally been recognized, need to be fresh and unharmed when they go into battle.

Modern infantry still have the prime role in land warfare—taking and holding ground. However, the modern infantryman has become a specialist. Regular infantry must be expert in small arms, antitank weapons, signals, and field engineering, as well as able to cope with threats from nuclear, chemical, and biological weapons.

In the last decade of the twentieth century many infantrymen have become peace keepers, especially in the former Yugoslavia, as well as in some areas of Africa.

Today all entrants to land forces are trained initially as infantrymen. Infantry skills are indispensable to all soldiers, and every soldier, whether truck driver, cook, bandsman, artilleryman, and so on, must be prepared to fight as an infantry soldier. Skills taught include group training, such as drill, battle PT, and first aid. Further infantry skills are added and exercised throughout every man's career. Expertise in using rifles, machine guns, mortars, and antitank and antiaircraft weapons; practice in field craft, battle craft, river crossing, mountain and arctic warfare, and warfare in wooded and built-up areas; and signals communications, infantry-tank, infantry-air, and infantry-artillery cooperation are all taught, practiced, and used. No longer is the infantryman just a body on the battlefield; he is, today, as skilled as any other specialist, and furthermore he is always at the sharp end.

Further infantry specialization has led to the formation of airborne troops (both parachute and air-mobile) and special forces. Airborne forces are projected behind enemy lines to capture and hold strategic points, where they hold on until relieved by troops advancing to relieve them. Special operations forces, such as Rangers or Special Forces, perform specialized tasks, often in aid of other governmental authorities. In war they destroy headquarters and other strategic targets by coup de main, raise insurgency warfare against unfriendly powers, or train friendly forces in counterinsurgency.

Infantry have benefited greatly from modern concepts and are rarely committed without armor, artillery, air, and logistic support. The infantry may still march on its stomach, but it fights as a combined team. The use of infantry is now part of the maneuverist approach, whether by land, sea, or air. Every modern generation has its experts predicting their war of tomorrow, push-button warfare, and so on, but almost all wars tend, finally, to come down to the infantryman in the mud.

David Westwood

See also: Airborne Operations; Armor, Ancient and Medieval; Artillery

References and further reading:

Eady, Major H. G. *Historical Illustrations to Field Service Regulations.* Vol 2. London: Sifton Praed and Co, 1927.

Chandler, David, ed. *The Oxford History of the British Army.* Oxford and New York: Oxford University Press, 1994.

Dupur, R. Ernest, and Trevor N. Dupuy. *The Collins Encyclopedia of Military History.* London: BCA, 1993.

Inkerman, Battle of the (5 November 1854)

Allied victory over Russia, regarded by Britain as a moment of glorious triumph in the Sebastopol campaign of the Crimean War. The British 2d Division under General Sir George De Lacy Evans, 3,000 strong, defended 18 field pieces on the rugged plateau east of Sevastopol between the Tchernaya River and Careening Ravine. It was a weak point in the allied lines because the position allowed concealed approaches through Careening Ravine to the west, Volovia Ravine to the north-northwest, Quarry Ravine to the north, St. Clements' Ravine to the north-northeast, and several adjoining gullies. Also, many of its key defenders, including General Sir Colin Campbell's 93d Highlanders, had been transferred south to defend Balaklava. The Light Division, 1,200 under General Sir George Brown, and the Guards, 1,300 under General H. J. Bentinck, were camped about a mile south. French and Turkish reserves, 23,000 under General Pierre Jean François Bosquet, were camped a few miles east and southeast.

On 5 November 1854 Prince Alexandr Sergeevich Menshikov ordered 19,000 men with 38 guns under Lieutenant General F. I. Soimonov to split the British army from the west, 16,000 men with 96 guns under Lieutenant General P. I. Paulov to attack from the north, 22,000 men with 88 guns under Prince Mikhail Dmitriyevich Gorchakov to prevent Bosquet from providing reinforcements, and 20,000 men under General P. A. Dannenberg to wait in reserve to the northwest. The Russians had to attack uphill and the British Minié rifles had twice the range of the Russian muskets, but the main reason that the British defense succeeded was because the Russian generals did not communicate effectively. British reinforcements broke through early in the day. Bosquet joined the battle much later.

In total, about 22,000 British and 20,000 French and Turks took part in the engagement. After eight hours of fighting, Russian casualties were more than 12,000, British about 2,500, and French and Turkish about 1,700. Inkerman was the last serious Russian attempt to destroy the allies in the Crimea. From then on, attrition and logistics decided the Sebastopol campaign.

Eric v. d. Luft

See also: Alma; Balaklava; Campbell, Colin; Crimean War; Light Brigade, Charge of the; Sevastopol, Siege of

References and further reading:

Barker, A. J. *The War Against Russia, 1854–1856.* New York: Holt, Rinehart & Winston, 1971.

Barthorp, Michael. *Heroes of the Crimea: The Battles of Balaclava and Inkerman.* London: Blandford, 1991.

Royle, Trevor. *Crimea: The Great Crimean War, 1854–1856.* New York: St. Martin's, 2000.

Seaton, Albert. *The Crimean War: A Russian Chronicle.* London: Batsford, 1977.

Intelligence, Military

Military speciality that provides a commander and staff with the knowledge of enemy weather and terrain required for the planning and conduct of operations.

The requirement for information on an opponent has existed throughout recorded history. The Hebrew Scriptures and Sun Tzu's *Art of War* (c. 500 B.C.E.) refer repeatedly to aspects of intelligence, reconnaissance, counterintelligence, and awareness of weather and terrain. Although military espionage existed in the intervening period, it was not until the twentieth century that the importance of military intelligence was firmly established, with increased efforts made to formalize its processes. This change began during the industrialized stalemate of World War I. Sheer weight of arms often proved inadequate to force a military decision, thus providing impetus to fight more wisely. World War II's technological improvements, such as the interception and analysis of strategic communications, brought international consensus on the growing significance of intelligence. The threat of nuclear warfare by the five declared atomic powers, coupled with development programs in other countries, keeps postwar intelligence efforts robust. The main focus has been on acquiring information on weapons characteristics and seeking warnings of potential nuclear attacks.

The emphasis on military intelligence operations continued beyond the end of the Cold War as targeting shifted to other concerns, such as terrorism and narcotics. Concurrently, traditional war fighting interests of military intelligence have been expanded by the concept of *information operations,* which envisages attacking an adversary through electronic and information systems technology. The span of options include traditional psychological operations or tactical radio jamming as well as attacking an electronic banking system or those computers that control the dams that keep an enemy's country from flooding. In all of these, intelligence provides the knowledge of the adversary's vulnerabilities and a follow-on assessment of the operation's success. There is naturally a concomitant requirement to defend one's own exposed infrastructure.

Intelligence will often occupy a separate appointment among the headquarters staff. Within Western armies the four key appointments are G1-Personnel Administration, G2-Intelligence, G3-Operations, and G4-Logistics, although the letter may vary; for example, J2 for Joint Staff Intelligence or A2 for Air Staff Intelligence. The Prussian General Staff popularized this practice of separate staff appointments in the nineteenth century; hence, G for General Staff. Specific appointments occurred as the functions became sufficiently specialized that the tasks required dedicated expert personnel. An additional benefit is that the division between operations and intelligence reduces the likelihood that the intelligence product will be skewed to fit a preconceived operational plan. During Operation MARKET GARDEN in 1944 Holland, repeated cancellations of airborne operations due to the rapid Allied advances proved frustrating to the senior paratroop officers. Thus significant indications of German tank formations in the vicinity of the farthest objective, Arnhem, were ignored in order to ensure that the operation was approved.

The general focus on enemy, weather, and terrain provides awareness sufficient to conduct most war-fighting operations. The elements of strategic intelligence are generally accepted as collection, analysis, counterintelligence, and covert action. However, in a military context the latter is a Special Operations Forces responsibility, notwithstanding their distinct military intelligence requirements.

Collection refers to the gathering of information for intelligence staff assessment. Information sources can be divided roughly between technical and human means. The former will include signals intelligence (SIGINT), gained from intercepting radio and radar emissions; aerial and satellite photo and radar imagery (IMINT); and capabilities and weaknesses determined from examining captured equipment or intercepted telemetry (TECHINT). Human intelligence (HUMINT) traditionally meant spies. Within a military intelligence context, however, reconnaissance troops and questioning prisoners of war or refugees provide HUMINT. Humanitarian operations with the attendant nongovernmental organizations throughout a theater of operations are further potential information sources. Finally, open source information from readily accessible publications and broadcasts provides much data.

Analysis is the process of turning information into intelligence. Interpreting often fragmentary or ambiguous information requires reasoned assessment through comparison with other details, either known facts or previous assessments of how an adversary traditionally operates. This process generates three types of intelligence: basic intelligence, such as the enemy force strength and composition (order of battle, or ORBAT, information); current intelligence, providing awareness of an adversary's current activities and specific indicators and warnings (I&W); and estimates or forecasts of the enemy's future activity. Military intelligence estimates are often prepared with a view toward the enemy's most likely and most dangerous courses of action. These intelligence types are interrelated. For example, IMINT and national-level ORBATs indicate that the enemy has a tank division on the far side of a river (basic intelligence). A captured soldier and intercepted radio communications indicate that the enemy division is preparing to attack (current intelligence). The intelligence staff assesses that the enemy will likely attack where the river is narrowest, but could attack downstream where the terrain would provide the defenders with difficulty counterattacking. The commander may then choose to reinforce the downstream site before the attack, but concentrate on defending at the river's narrowest point.

The focus of counterintelligence (CI) is different from, but complementary to, traditional intelligence. CI protects information and a military's intelligence system rather than aiming to collect and analyze information, thus providing similarities with a police function. The two subsets of CI are security and counterespionage. Because security aims to keep information from those not authorized access, coverage often falls upon physical security: locks, fences, and security sweeps. In a tactical situation, field security would be concerned with keeping soldiers from carrying unit identifiers or operational plans into battle. Counterespionage previously emphasized apprehension or neutralization of an enemy's information-collection agents. However, in a technical environment, human spies are no longer an overarching counterespionage concern. Much information previously acquired through spying can now be gathered through technical means, such as monitoring the electronic emanations from computers rather than stealing their documentary product. Additionally, neutralizing an enemy's collection efforts can be accomplished through deception operations. These aim to provide an enemy intelligence service, and hence their commander, with false or misleading information. Deception operations will be more effective if they are fed through multiple channels, thus appearing to provide confirmation, and if these messages reinforce an enemy's preconceived notions. This was the case during the World War II Normandy invasion when false radio traffic, mock-up vehicles, and the physical isolation of the southeast coast of England from German espionage all indicated that a First U.S. Army under General Patton was poised to strike at Calais, a point already believed by Hitler to be the assault objective.

A number of factors make intelligence failure or surprise practically inevitable. In the previous example an attack is expected, but because of active deception and inclement weather, the intelligence picture indicated a different location and time. A more damaging surprise occurs when intelligence provides no warning of enemy assault, as seen with the Japanese naval attack at Pearl Harbor. Surprise may also result from having adequate information misinterpreted through faulty understanding of an adversary's doctrine. During the Korean War (1950–1953), Chinese light infantry dispersed away from the main highways, unlike North Korea's mechanized army. This differing doctrine negated the American air superiority, allowing the Chinese initially to rout the allied forces. Intelligence failures are therefore a problem of active deception (Normandy), information not being available in a clear and timely manner (Pearl Harbor), or mirror-imaging (blinding) analysts to the significance of different enemy doctrine (North Korea).

The breadth and depth of information requirements will vary with the strategic versus tactical level of operations. For example, in a conventional war, knowing an enemy's strategic oil reserves is of little interest to a platoon commander holding a ridgeline against enemy attack. Conversely, the difference between that attacking enemy possessing three tanks or twenty is of little interest to the National Command Authority. However, nontraditional conflicts falling outside of conventional war, such as humanitarian relief operations or those missions conducted by Special Operations Forces, pose different demands upon military intelligence. An on-scene commander may need intelligence on the religious beliefs of a particular village or cleared routes to a neonatal care facility rather than the range of a particular antitank weapon system. In these operations, political and economic concerns, previously the purview of strategic-level staffs, are required at the tactical level.

Military intelligence will remain focused upon the basics of enemy, weather, and terrain for the foreseeable future. However, changes in technology, doctrine, and forms of conflict will continue to force military intelligence evolution.

Robert Martyn

See also: Psychological Operations; Special Operations Forces

References and further reading:

Gudgin, Peter. *Military Intelligence: A History.* New York: Sutton Publishing, 2000.

Handel, Michael. *Intelligence and Military Operations.* London: Frank Cass, 1990.

Shulsky, Abram. *Silent Warfare: Understanding the World of Intelligence.* 2d ed. Washington: Brassey, 1993.

Interventions in Civil Unrest, Strikes, Military

Around the world, there remain many regimes in power only by the intervention of the military within that country. In China, the picture of the man and the tank from Tiananmen Square speaks volumes. The demise of the Soviet Empire and the Warsaw Pact began when Prime Minister Mikhail Gorbachev refused to use troops in the Baltic countries or to support regimes such as East Germany.

In the United States, military intervention in civil unrest is the exception, not the rule. However, the drawing up of the Constitution of the United States drew impetus from the failure of the national government under the Articles of Confederation to aid Massachusetts in suppressing Shays's Rebellion in 1786. Thus the nation ratified a constitution that authorized the federal government to use military force in civil disorders, first to enforce federal authority, and second to assist states when they were unable to restore domestic tranquility.

The first use of military intervention under the Constitution occurred in response to the Whiskey Rebellion of 1794. President George Washington called out militia from four states to march on western Pennsylvania to suppress the tax revolt. President Washington set a precedent for presidents acting with great restraint in matters regarding military intervention into civilian life.

For the next 80 years, slavery and abolition provided most of the occasions for military intervention. Federal troops were sent to Boston in the 1850s to quell demonstrations against the enforcement of the Fugitive Slave Law. Similarly they were dispatched to "Bloody Kansas" in the late 1850s. Of course, federal troops quelled the "rebellion" in the southern states, 1861–1865.

One exceptional case in 1857–1858 saw the use of 2,500 regulars under the command of A. S. Johnson to enforce federal law and court orders in Utah Territory regarding the Mormon Church.

After the Civil War, the main use of U.S. troops in domestic affairs was in the widespread activities of the Freedmen's Bureau, established to aid the newly freed blacks in the South, headed by an army general whose policies were carried out throughout the South by regular troops and black state militias. Although the Freedmen's Bureau carried out many good works (providing the South with its first tax-supported public school system, for example), it was detested by white southerners, who liked military government no more than Americans from any other section of the nation.

The U.S. military was also involved in industrial strikes and disturbances in the postwar decades, and often reserve or state militia troops were involved, rather than regulars. Five times in 1877, President Hayes sent in troops to assist states, although he denied four other requests. In 1894 President Grover Cleveland sent regular troops to Chicago during the railroad strike. At the beginning of the twentieth century, President Theodore Roosevelt exercised greater reticence in responding to similar requests. However, both Presidents Woodrow Wilson and Warren Harding sent in troops in 1914 and 1921, respectively.

In most of these cases, when federal troops arrived, calm was restored quickly with no loss of life. Aside from the Civil War, one of the worst incidents was the Ludlow Massacre, in which 13 women and children died in 1914.

Since World War II, urban and racial disturbances have occasioned most military interventions. Detroit (1943, 1967), Los Angeles (1965, 1997), and the numerous riots that occurred upon the assassination of Martin Luther King Jr. (1968) were the most prominent. Regular troops and National Guardsmen were also deployed to enforce federal court desegregation orders in the 1950s and 1960s.

In general, the United States military has had little desire or preparation for military inventions in civil disorder. During most of the history of the United States, the military operated only under direct orders of the commander in chief. The one exceptional period occurred during 1917–1920, when the newly created Military Intelligence Division (MID) of the Army General Staff engaged in its own domestic surveillance and even arrest of various labor radicals deemed Bolsheviks.

At present, guided by their oath "to support and defend the Constitution of the United States against all enemies, foreign and domestic," the military is much more interested in confronting foreign enemies. It is glad to leave the decision to intervene militarily in any civilian turmoil in the hands of the civilian leaders. The marked American distaste for the military, despite the nation's propensity for individual firearm violence, has made military intervention in civil life all the more rare.

A few other democratic states have had to use the military in a far more direct role than was the case in the United States. Canadian military forces deployed into the streets of Quebec's cities in 1970, arresting and holding citizens without warrant in the wake of Separatist violence, and British troops have policed Northern Ireland since the early 1970s. The German, Japanese, Italian, French, and Scandinavian governments have, on the other hand, refrained since the end of World War II from using their militaries to intervene in civil disturbances.

John R. Popiden

See also: Civil Affairs/Military Government; Military and Society

References and further reading:

Coakley, Robert W. *The Role of Federal Military Forces in Domestic Disorders, 1789–1878.* Washington, DC: Government Printing Office, 1988.

Cooper, Jerry M. "Federal Military Intervention in Domestic Disorders." In *The United States Military under the Constitution of the United States, 1789–1989,* ed. Richard H. Kohn, 120–150. New York: New York University Press, 1991.

Engdahl, David E. "Soldiers, Riots and Revolution." *Iowa Law Review* 57 (October 1971), 35–42.

Sandler, Stanley. *Glad to See Them Come and Sorry to See Them Go: A History of U.S. Army Tactical Civil Affairs/Military Government, 1775–1991.* Fort Bragg, NC: U.S. Army Special Operations Command, 1998.

Iran Hostage Rescue Attempt (24–26 April 1980)

Failed attempt by the U.S. Armed Forces to rescue American hostages being held in the American embassy in Teheran. The rescue attempt was made after Iranian "students" seized the embassy on 4 November 1979 and seized most of its staff. Shortly after the seizure a joint task force (JTF) was established to begin planning a rescue. The JTF's plan was complex, involving members of all of the armed services and calling for several C-130s to land at a site in the Iranian desert code-named Desert One. The aircraft would transport the highly secret special operations unit, Delta Force, and other support troops to the site and refuel the RH-53 helicopters that would transport the commandos to Teheran to rescue the hostages. Almost immediately after landing at the site, trouble occurred when a bus full of Iranians was detained on what was supposed to be a remote road. The helicopters encountered the weather phenomenon known as a *haboob,* a dust cloud, which delayed their arrival at Desert One. During refueling at the site one of the helicopters suffered a hydraulic failure, leaving the mission with five helicopters when six had been determined as the mission minimum. The decision had already been made to abort the mission when one of the helicopters collided into a C-130. The ensuing explosion killed eight flight crew members.

The failure of this mission led to the establishment of the Special Operations Command and the U.S. 160th Special Operations Aviation Regiment and to an upgrading of all American special operations assets by the incoming Reagan administration.

Michael Mulligan

See also: Entebbe Rescue Raid; Special Operations Forces

References and further reading:

Beckwith, Charlie A. *Delta Force.* New York: Harcourt Brace Jovanovich, 1983.

Kyle, James H. *The Guts to Try.* New York: Orion Books, 1990.

Iran-Iraq War (1980–1988)

The longest war between Third World countries since the end of World War II, and Saddam Hussein's first war. On 22 September 1980, Iraqi divisions crossed the Iranian border. In eight days Iraqi troops reached six to twenty-five miles deep into Iran, including the outskirts of the oil port cities Khorramshahr and Abadan on the Shatt al Arab.

The causes of this war were political, economic, and religious. In 1975 Iran and Iraq agreed over their border along the Shatt al Arab. In 1980, now ruling Iraq, Saddam Hussein claimed complete control of the Shatt al Arab to gain clear access to the Persian Gulf for oil export. Similarly, Iran, now under the rule of the Ayatollah Khomeini, had sought to undermine the Iraqi regime by instigating rebellion by both the Shiites in the south and the Kurds in the north. Also random Iranian artillery fire and air strikes struck towns and oil facilities in Iraq.

The initial success led Saddam Hussein to call for negotiations, which Khomeini rebuffed. In November 1980, Iraqi troops took Khorramshahr.

However, from then on, Iran gained the military advantage. Iranian volunteers, many of them teenagers, formed the Revolutionary Guards Corps. Also, Iran had the better air force, striking Iraqi air bases and oil facilities with impunity. By the end of the first year, losses were estimated to be 38,000 Iranians and 22,000 Iraqis.

Military tactics stressed entrenchments and the husbanding of valuable equipment. Iranian tactics relied on World War I–style frontal assaults. Iraq introduced chemical weapons on occasion against Iranian troop concentrations, Iranian cities, and Kurd civilians. Both sides used surface-to-surface missiles (SAMs) to attack each other's cities. Eventually, Iran regained its lost territory and entered Iraq, threatening Basra.

In early 1984, both sides escalated the war into the Persian Gulf (the Tanker War). Iraq's best weapon was the Super-Etendard jet using Exocet missiles against tankers carrying Iranian oil. As the flow of oil became hampered, the United States sent its naval forces to protect shipping. In 1987 the United States reflagged Kuwaiti tankers to provide direct protection. Although U.S. activities tended to favor Iraq, the U.S. surreptitiously sold 4,000 target on wire (TOW) and additional spare parts to Iran (Iran-Contra Affair).

In 1987 two Iraqi Exocet missiles struck USS *Stark,* killing 37 U.S. sailors. In 1988, USS *Vincennes* inadvertently shot down an Iranian airliner, killing 290 civilians.

An Iraqi offensive with the greatly expanded Republican Guard recaptured lost territory, returning the frontlines to nearly the original borders. Both sides then agreed to a cease-fire 20 August 1988, after some 262,000 Iranians and 105,000 Iraqis had died. As the interminable war finally ended, Iraq was militarily strong but economically crippled and in massive debt to Kuwait and Saudi Arabia.

John R. Popiden

See also: Hussein, Saddam al-Tikriti

References and further reading:

El-Shazly, Nadia El-Sayed. *The Gulf Tanker War.* New York: St. Martin's, 1998.

Hiro, Dilip. *The Longest War.* New York: Routledge, 1991.

Rajaee, Farhang, ed. *The Iran-Iraq War.* Gainesville: University Press of Florida, 1993.

Irish Easter Uprising, War for Independence, and Civil War; The Easter Rebellion (1916–1923)

The first of a series of events that culminated in the independence of 26 of Ireland's 32 counties. The Irish Republican Brotherhood (IRB) had patiently waited for a chance to stage a rebellion against British rule, and World War I provided an opportunity to achieve their stated goal of an independent Irish republic. Confused by the contradictory orders emanating from the leadership, most of the rural volunteers failed to rise and only 1,600 republicans were engaged in the fighting in the capital, Dublin, throughout Easter week. Without the expected German arms what little hopes the conspirators may have entertained of victory evaporated: 550 were killed, 2,000 wounded, and £2.5 million of damage caused. Initially, the Irish response to the rising was hostile, but the mindless executions of 15 leaders fundamentally altered the political landscape.

The War for Independence

The conflict with Great Britain that won the independence of the 26 counties in the south of Ireland. Sinn Fein, the political arm of the Irish Republican Army (IRA), won the vast majority of seats in Ireland during the British general election of November 1918 and proceeded to establish an independent parliament in Dublin, which Britain refused to recognize. At the same time the IRA began a guerrilla war against British forces. According to IRA leader Michael Collins, the organization's effective fighting strength never exceeded 3,000. The British, however, used enough force to alienate Irish and international (particularly American) opinion, but never enough to suppress the IRA. On 11 July a truce between British forces and the IRA came into force, the terms of which allowed both sides to retain their arms. Negotiations followed, during which the British delegation, led by Prime Minister David Lloyd George, employed the threat of war to ensure that the Sinn Fein delegation accepted a treaty that fell well short of its demands.

Civil War

The treaty, which left the issue of Northern Ireland unresolved, led directly to civil war. An oath of fidelity to the British monarch, the constitutional status of the new Irish Free State, and the partition of the country were among the

Soldiers and civilians shoot at each other on a narrow, smoke-filled street as an overturned cart burns in the foreground; Dublin, April 1916. (Hulton/Archive)

issues that brought erstwhile comrades into mutual armed conflict. Large-scale engagements were confined to the early stages of the war. The assassination of pro-treaty IRA leader Michael Collins on 22 August 1922 strengthened the hand of those who sought a more rigorous campaign. Seventy-seven republicans were executed and 12,000 were interned. By April 1923, most of the IRA's original leadership was either dead or in prison, and during the following month it announced that it was dumping its arms. As a result, Northern Ireland (Ulster) remained an integral part of the British Isles, and the Irish Free State (Erie) an independent nation.

Donnacha Óbeachdáin

See also: Boyne; Irish Uprising; Northern Ireland, Civil War

References and further reading:

Augusteijn, Joos., *From Public Defence to Guerrilla War.* Dublin: Irish Academic Press, 1996.

Neeson, Eoin. *The Civil War 1922–23.* Dublin: Poolbeg, 1989.

O'Malley, Ernie. *The Singing Flame.* Dublin: Anvil, 1979.

Irish Rebellion, Great (1641–1649)

A free-for-all between disunited factions of Scots Protestants, Old English Catholics, Irish Catholics, English Protestants, and the forces of Charles II. Under the "thorough" and ruthless administration of Thomas Wentworth, Earl of Stafford, the Old England and Old Irish were increasingly alienated from the English Crown. After Stafford was executed in London at the wishes of Parliament in 1641, the Ulster Irish exploded in rebellion, attacking English and Scottish Protestant settlers. This attack, beginning October 1641, was chaotic and bloody and quickly focused on the Protestant towns such as Dundalk, Dungannon, and Newry, which fell to the Irish one by one. Because Wentworth's army had been disbanded at his death, the Protestant Earl of Ormond raised a defense force and waited for reinforcement from England, while the Old English, angry at being blamed for the rising alongside the Irish, confederated themselves at Kilkenny and declared their loyalty to the king and to the rebellion.

In the spring of 1642, a Scottish Covenanter army arrived and began to retake Antrim and Down. Faced with a complex and bizarre civil war, the beleaguered King Charles I demanded that Ormonde reach a truce with the rebels in 1642 so that Irish troops could be used in England against Parliament. Although Ormonde offered generous terms in 1646, the papal nuncio threatened to excommunicate Catholics who accepted, so the fighting continued. At Benburn, on the River Blackwater, Owen Roe O'Neill, a professional soldier who had served in Spain, led the Catholics to defeat Ormonde, but then retreated to Kilkenny and did not move on Dublin. To confuse matters further, Parliament sent a Roundhead army under Colonel Michael Jones later that year, while O'Neill campaigned in Munster and Ormonde briefly resurfaced as the leader of royalists in Cork and was defeated by parliamentarians in August 1649 at Rathmines.

With Charles I dead at the hands of Parliament, Oliver Cromwell turned his attention to the chaotic situation in Ireland and arrived with an army. At Drogheda, he set a pattern for the conquest of Ireland: surrender or be brutally sacked. Unlike the 1641 atrocities, which were disorganized and the result of personal animosity, Cromwell's were object lessons in the futility of defiance, and the major fortresses capitulated, including Wexford, Dundalk, and Trim. O'Neill, who escaped from Kilkenny before it surrendered to Cromwell, died in November 1648 trying to hold the Old English and Irish together, while Ormonde, who had failed to hold Drogheda, joined Charles II in Scotland. Satisfied that Ireland was under control, Cromwell returned to England, leaving behind his son-in-law, Henry Ireton, who oversaw the surrender of Limerick in 1651.

Cromwell's triumph over his enemies on behalf of Parliament led to the annexation of Ireland by the Protectorate and a harsh program of repression and land redistribution.

Margaret Sankey

See also: Cromwell, Oliver; English Civil War; English Wars in Ireland

References and further reading:

Bennett, Martin. *Civil Wars Experienced.* New York: Routledge, 2000.

O'Siochan, Michael. *Confederate Ireland 1642–49.* Dublin: Four Courts Press, 1999.

Irish Uprising (1798)

One of the very few Irish Protestant resistance movements. Heavily influenced by the ideals proclaimed in the American and French Revolutions, the United Irishmen was founded in 1791 by Irish Protestants who sought to ally themselves with the native Catholic majority in an effort to establish an Irish republic, independent of Britain, which had ruled the country with varying degrees of success since 1169. The United Irishmen was a secret oath-bound organization with a peak membership of about 300,000.

Bedeviled by informers, its leadership arrested or in exile, and bereft of expected French military assistance, the United Irishmen rebellion of 1798 ("The '98") was largely a collection of isolated battles. Though large in numbers, the Irish mainly fought with pikes against smaller contingents of well-trained British professional soldiers backed with heavy artillery. A tiny French force of 1,100 arrived on 22 August and with Irish peasant support enjoyed some initial victories before being defeated by a much larger British force at Ballinamuck. Approximately 30,000 died during the rebellion. Reflecting the marked imbalance in military might, only 3,000 of these were killed by Irish insurgents.

Having destroyed the most serious military threat to emerge in Ireland for more than a century, British rule was consolidated and institutionalized by the Act of Union (1801), which established the United Kingdom of Great Britain and Ireland.

Donnacha Óbeacháin

See also: Irish Easter Uprising, War for Independence, and Civil War; The Easter Rebellion

References and further reading:

Cullen, Mary, ed. *1798: 200 Years of Resonance.* Dublin: Irish Reporter, 1998.

Pakenham, Thomas. *The Year of Liberty.* London: Abacus, 2000.

Keogh, Daire, and Nicholas Furlong. *The Women of 1798.* Dublin: Four Courts Press, 1999.

Iroquois-French Wars (1609–1697)

A war over control of the fur trade by aboriginal tribes in North America, which soon led to a war between the Iroquois League and the French. Some historians trace its roots to when a Huron band of warriors led by Samuel de Champlain in July 1609 killed two Iroquois chiefs, but more likely it was an outgrowth of the ancient hostility between the tribe of the Iroquois League (Mohawk, Oneida, Onondaga, Cayuga, and Seneca) and the Algonquin tribe allied with the French. As the beaver trade flourished, the Iroquois depleted the populations in their area. The Iroquois in all likelihood did not want to fight the French but rather to displace tribes such as the Illini and Hurons as middlemen in the pelt trade and take over more plentiful lands. They were given the resources to do this when the Dutch traders in the Hudson Valley of New York in 1610 began to trade steel knives, tomahawks, powder, guns, and ammunition for pelts. While the French were not their primary target, they continued raids and engaged in hit-and-run warfare against them in the St. Lawrence Valley and southern Ohio.

The Iroquois began to expand their area to take over lands controlled by the Neutrals and Erie Indians south of the Great Lakes. By 1655, they had also defeated the Nipissings and Hurons, but they could not overcome the Ottawa, located in the western Great Lakes. They were also defeated the next year in warfare with the Chippewas and Illini. Not giving up, a war party of 500 Iroquois and 100 of their allies prepared to attack an Illini village of Kaskaskia, near what is today Peoria, in September 1680. While most of the Illini warriors and Chief Chassagoac were at Cahokia attending a religious ceremony, the remaining Illini warriors attempted to ambush the advancing Iroquois between the Illinois and Vermillion Rivers before they reached the village. They met with some success, and French representative Henri de Tonti tried to negotiate a peace treaty with them. Iroquois warriors stabbed him, causing him to retreat to Lac du Illinois. After eight days of fighting, the Iroquois laid siege to the village. Surviving Illini fled down the Illinois River while captives were killed and mutilated. The Kaskaskia, Cahokia, Chinkoa, Omouahoa, Coiracoentanon, Moingwena, Chepoussa, and Peoria all left the area, while the Iroquois killed or captured 700 members of the tribes remaining at the mouth of the Illinois.

The main body of Illini tribesmen came back to Kaskaskia but were soon confronted by the news that the Iroquois were about to return. They turned to the French Fort St. Louis, located near present-day La Salle, Illinois, under the command of de Tonti. Informed that the fort was too small to protect them, the Illini fled. The Iroquois, finding their enemy gone, attacked Fort St. Louis. After firing on the fort for several days, the Iroquois tried to assault the walls but were beaten back by cannon and musket fire, leading them to retreat. Shortly after this, Tonti and 200 warriors joined a large contingent of Canadian soldiers in an invasion of what is now upper New York, destroying several Iroquois villages along the Mohawk River. By 1696, the Iroquois, with the exception of northern Pennsylvania and eastern Ohio, had retreated to their traditional homelands. In 1687 the French attacked Seneca and Onodaga villages on Iroquois land, and in August 1689 a massive warrior party of 1,200 Iroquois attacked Lachine, near Montreal, killing 200 French settlers. The next year, the French and their Indian allies attacked Schenectady and in retaliation the Mohawk attacked the Sokoki at St. François in 1690 and 1692. The French then launched three campaigns under Louis Frontenac from Quebec between 1693 and 1696 on Iroquois villages. Yet it was smallpox that brought the Iroquois to the peace table. Although they were unable to work out a peace, the Treaty of Ryswick in 1697, which ended the war between England and France, also placed the Iroquois under British protection. Worrying that any conflict with the league would bring another conflict with the British, the French agreed to mediate any disputes between the Iroquois and the Algonquin.

T. Jason Soderstrum

See also: American Indian Wars; French and Indian War

References and further reading:

Eckert, Allan W. *The Wilderness War: A Narrative.* Boston: Little Brown, 1978.

Hunt, George T. *The Wars of the Iroquois.* Madison: University of Wisconsin Press, 1960.

Stewart, Alexander McGinn. *French Pioneers in North America.* 3 vols. Millwood, NY: Kraus Reprint Company, 1976.

Isandlwana (South Africa, 22 January 1879)

The greatest Zulu victory of the nineteenth century over the forces of colonialism and one of the heaviest defeats ever suffered by British troops during the small wars of the Victorian era. Paradoxically, Isandlwana sealed the fate of the independent Zulu kingdom, for in order to reassert their paramountcy in southern Africa, it became imperative for the British to avenge their defeat, crush the Zulu army in battle, and impose a peace settlement entirely on their own terms.

On 20 January 1879 the British Number 3 Column under Lieutenant General Lord Chelmsford encamped at the eastern base of Isandlwana hill. The next day Chelmsford despatched a reconnaissance-in-force under Major J. G. Dartnell toward the southeast to seek out the Zulu army and to establish the column's next campsite. During the night, Chelmsford strongly reinforced Dartnell, leaving the depleted garrison at Isandlwana under the command of Colonel H. B. Pulleine. For the whole of 22 January Chelmsford skirmished with Zulu irregulars, who, in accordance with Zulu strategy, steadily drew him away from his camp.

Colonel A. W. Durnford reinforced the camp midmorning of 22 January with men from Number 2 Column and immediately moved out northeastwards to intercept Zulu reportedly threatening Chelmsford's rear. One of his mounted pa-

Cetshwayo's Zulu warriors defeat the invading British forces at the Battle of Isandlwana in 1879. (Library of Congress)

trols stumbled upon the Zulu army concealed in the Ngwebeni valley only nine miles from the camp.

Undetected by the British, the Zulu army under Chief Ntshingwayo kaMahole Khoza and Chief Mavumengwana kaNdlela Ntuli had reached their bivouac by the early hours of 22 January. Their plan to divide the British forces had succeeded, and they were preparing to fall on the British camp held by 67 officers and 1,707 men, about half of whom were African auxiliaries.

At about 12:15 P.M. the British formed an extended skirmishing line about half a mile in advance of the camp, both to command the dead ground and to support Durnford's horsemen and other detached units as they fell back before nearly 20,000 Zulu. The Zulu center was pinned down by British fire, but the horns extended to outflank the British line and raced around to enter the rear of the camp. (Without their realizing it, the Zulu leaders had achieved every European commander's dream: a "Cannae," an encirclement of an enemy.) Realizing they were being enveloped, at 1:00 P.M. the British precipitately fell back on their camp, losing all cohesion in hand-to-hand fighting with the Zulu. Though harried, a few mounted men broke southwestwards through the Zulu encirclement to escape over the Mzinyathi (Buffalo) River at the aptly named Fugitives' Drift. Many of the infantry conducted a fighting retreat in the same direction but were all cut off and killed before they reached the Manzimyama stream one and a half miles away. The Zulu pillaged the camp and retired at nightfall when Chelmsford and his force finally marched back in battle order.

No less than 1,000 Zulu died in the encounter. The British lost 52 officers and 739 white troops, 67 white NCOs, and close to 500 of the Natal Native Contingent.

John Laband

See also: Anglo-Zulu War; Khambula; Rorke's Drift

References and further reading:

Knight, Ian. "The Battle of Isandlwana, 22 January 1879." In *Great Zulu Battles.* London: Arms & Armour Press, 1998.

Laband, John, ed. *Lord Chelmsford's Zululand Campaign 1878–1879.* Stroud, UK: Alan Sutton Publishing for the Army Records Society, 1994.

———. *The Rise and Fall of the Zulu Nation.* London: Arms & Armour Press, 1997.

Laband, John, and Paul Thompson. *The Illustrated Guide to the Anglo-Zulu War.* Pietermaritzburg: University of Natal Press, 2000.

Isonzo, Battles of the (1915–1917)

Series of no less than 12 battles fought between the Austro-Hungarians and the Italians along the Isonzo River. On 23 June 1915 the Italians attacked Austria across the Isonzo with superior numbers. The Italian generals failed to supply forward units with enough arms, ammunition, and artillery. As the Austrians rushed troops to defend the inadequately held frontier, the Italians made three more bids to break through. The second (July–August), third (October–September), and fourth (November–December) battles of the Isonzo were as inconclusive as the first, and the customary trench warfare ground into an even more bitter contest along the frozen Alpine mountain tops.

Here the soldiers of both sides endured the horrors of fighting in the trenches; however, dizzying heights, the constant cold, flash floods in the valleys, poor supplies, rudimentary medical attention and sanitation, and poor shelter compounded the suffering troops endured. The fifth bid by the Italians to break through began on 11 March 1916, but an Austrian offensive in the Trentino sector offset the small gains the Italians made. A sixth bid to break the river barrier began in August 1916; this time the Italians managed to seize the town of Gorizia but failed to achieve a breakthrough. The seventh, eighth, and ninth battles, September–November 1916, developed along the same patterns as the first six battles. In May 1917 the tenth Isonzo began as the Italians joined the overall allied spring and summer offensive. In particularly brutal fighting, 125,000 casualties achieved scant gains. The Italians followed this with the eleventh battle in August and at last achieved a limited breakthrough at Bainsizza, once again at a heavy price. The Battle of Caporetto (twelfth Isonzo), where the Germans led their Austrian allies in a major drive against Italy, offset all the summer gains, forcing the Italians off the frontier and back to the Piave River.

Stephen Chenault

See also: Caporetto; World War I

References and further reading:

Herwing, Holger H. *The First World War, Germany and Austria-Hungary, 1914–1918.* London: Arnold, 1997.

May, Arthur J. *The Passing of the Habsburg Monarchy, 1914–1918.* Philadelphia: University of Pennsylvania Press, 1966.

Israeli Military

Israel's armed forces have evolved from prestate vigilante bands to the paramount strike force in the Middle East. In 1908 Jewish settlers formed an ad hoc society of armed sentinels, called Ha-Shomer, or Guardsmen, to replace mercenary, untrustworthy hired Arab watchmen in thwarting robbery, cattle-rustling, and poaching. The Jewish farm laborers on the settlements (the Shomrim would not protect farms with an Arab or mixed workforce) comprised a reserve to assist the patrol cadres, who were equipped with a motley collection of obsolescent firearms. Another armed band, the Jaffa Group, provided security for the Jews of that community and Tel Aviv.

These organizations kept a low profile during World War I, as the Turks (and Palestine) were formally allied with Germany, and Jewish loyalties were suspect. Nevertheless, the Palestine-based spy ring NILI—an acronym for the Hebrew verse Netzah Yisrael Lo Yeshaker (The strength of Israel will not lie [1 Sam. 15:29]), which served as its password—comprised of a former Zionist youth corps, worked for British interests, while other Palestinian Jewish adolescents were conscripted into the Turkish army. Zionists expelled from Palestine by the Turks formed the Zionist Mule Corps, providing logistic support in the Gallipoli Campaign. Veterans of the Mule Corps created the nucleus of new all-Zionist battalions, the British 38th and 39th King's Fusiliers, which met the test of fire in Allenby's Palestine Campaign, 1917–1918.

All of these ventures provided valuable military experience for a proficient cadre, which returned to postwar Palestine, now under the British Mandate, whereby a Jewish homeland was to be established alongside an Arab nation. The British high commissioner encouraged the Zionist administration in Palestine to set up an executive framework under the auspices of the formally sanctioned Jewish Agency for Palestine. Independent of but allied to these was the Histadrut, nominally a populist labor society, but in reality the linchpin of Zionist industrialization and agricultural expansion in Palestine.

Established by the labor mainstream, Histadrut, after the murderous Arab riots in 1920, set up the Hagganah (self-defense force), which rapidly became a country-wide Jewish army as Jewish immigration swelled to a flood upon the rise of Hitler, and Palestinian Arab resistance hardened in response. Armed defense organizations were illegal under the mandate, so Hagganah had to organize, train, and procure weapons covertly. The organization even managed to establish a backyard armaments industry producing bullets and crude submachine guns and mortars.

After the Arab riots of 1929, Hagganah was transferred from the authority of Histadrut to the quasi-governmental Jewish Agency, which had formerly spurned any connection with outlawed clandestine groups. This progression entailed splitting Hagganah high command into left and right political factions. Although illegal, every Jewish town and neighborhood in Palestine was affiliated with a district command of Hagganah. Elements of the conservative wing split from the labor-left mainstream and allied themselves with Zeev Jabotinsky's Revisionist Party, the foundation of today's Likud, thereby forming the renegade National Military Party, or Etzel (alternately, Irgun). The latter, at most consisting of 250 firebrands, were ruthless in their attacks on Arabs, while Hagganah counseled restraint so as to forestall unwelcome British attention.

The Palestinian Arab Revolt of 1936–1939, largely directed at the British Mandatory government, brought a measure of unusual cooperation between the colonial counterterrorism effort and specially constituted Jewish Supernumerary Police, developing commando expertise under the able direction of the New Testament Zionist Orde Wingate. In 1938 and 1939, Hagganah benefited by the appointment of a nonpartisan nationwide commander and the establishment of a professional military general staff to coordinate the formerly diversified elements.

During World War II, Hagganah and segments of the Irgun collaborated with the British authorities in fighting the Nazi menace; however, a renegade sector of the Irgun, Lehi, informally the Stern Gang, rashly attacked British and Arab civilians. (The British high commissioner for Egypt was assassinated by Jewish terrorists in 1944.) Also during the war, the left wing of the Hagganah formed an elite strike force, or Palmach, sanctioned because it would embody a potential guerrilla resistance to Rommel's advancing Afrika Corps. In addition, 30,000 Palestinian Jews gained invaluable experience serving with the British armed forces, including a Jewish Brigade Group. Hagganah meanwhile developed a field corps, a medical service, a signals corps, an arms industry, and an intelligence section, the last assisting illegal immigration of Holocaust refugees. Intelligence became paramount in the postwar years when Hagganah conducted an effective insurgency campaign against British military and police logistics, while the Irgun and Stern groups focused on terrorizing British individuals.

During the 1948 Israeli War of Independence, Israeli political leader David Ben-Gurion remodeled Hagganah as the national defense force of the newborn state. Early in the war, Irgun was forcefully integrated into the Israeli Defense Forces (IDF), the new designation for the armed forces of Israel. In the course of desperate fighting, the patchwork geographical structure of company-sized lots amalgamated into battalions, then regiments, which nonetheless retained their regional identification. Makeshift aviation and naval assets were likewise "born in battle" and integrated into the whole. The IDF would win every one of its subsequent conflicts against its hostile Arab neighbors, and such success would be studied in some detail by military academies around the world (with the conspicuous exception of Arab military academies). But the reason for the IDF success, aside from the numerous Arab military deficiencies (lack of coordination, unprofessional officers, untrained troops, etc.), came down to a simple point: Israel had no alternative to victory. Defeat meant literal death.

Jim Bloom

See also: Gallipoli; Israeli-Arab Wars; Megiddo (September–October 1918); October War; Sinai-Suez Offensive; Six-Day War

References and further reading:

Allon, Yigal. *The Making of Israel's Army.* New York: Universe Books, 1971.

Dupuy, Trevor N. *Elusive Victory: The Arab-Israeli Wars, 1947–1974.* New York: Harper & Row, 1978.

Morris, Benny. *Righteous Victims: A History of the Zionist-Arab Conflict, 1881–1999.* New York: Alfred A. Knopf, 1999.

Schiff, Zeev. *A History of the Israeli Army (1870–1974).* San Francisco: Straight Arrow Books, 1974.

Van Creveld, Martin. *The Sword and the Olive: A Critical History of the Israeli Defense Force.* New York: Public Affairs, 1998.

Israeli-Arab Wars (1948–1999)

A series of wars between Israel and its Arab neighbors that saw the establishment of the Jewish state.

1948, War of Independence

After Britain announced it would withdraw from its mandate in Palestine, the United Nations (UN) passed a partition plan on 29 November 1947 that divided Palestine along existing settlement lines between the Arab and Jewish populations, which the Jewish authorities accepted and the Arab leaders rejected. Civil war soon broke out between the Arabs and Jews. The Jewish leadership declared the independent state of Israel on 14 May 1948, an announcement followed immediately by a declaration of war by the Arab states of Egypt, Iraq, Lebanon, Syria, and Transjordan. Coop-

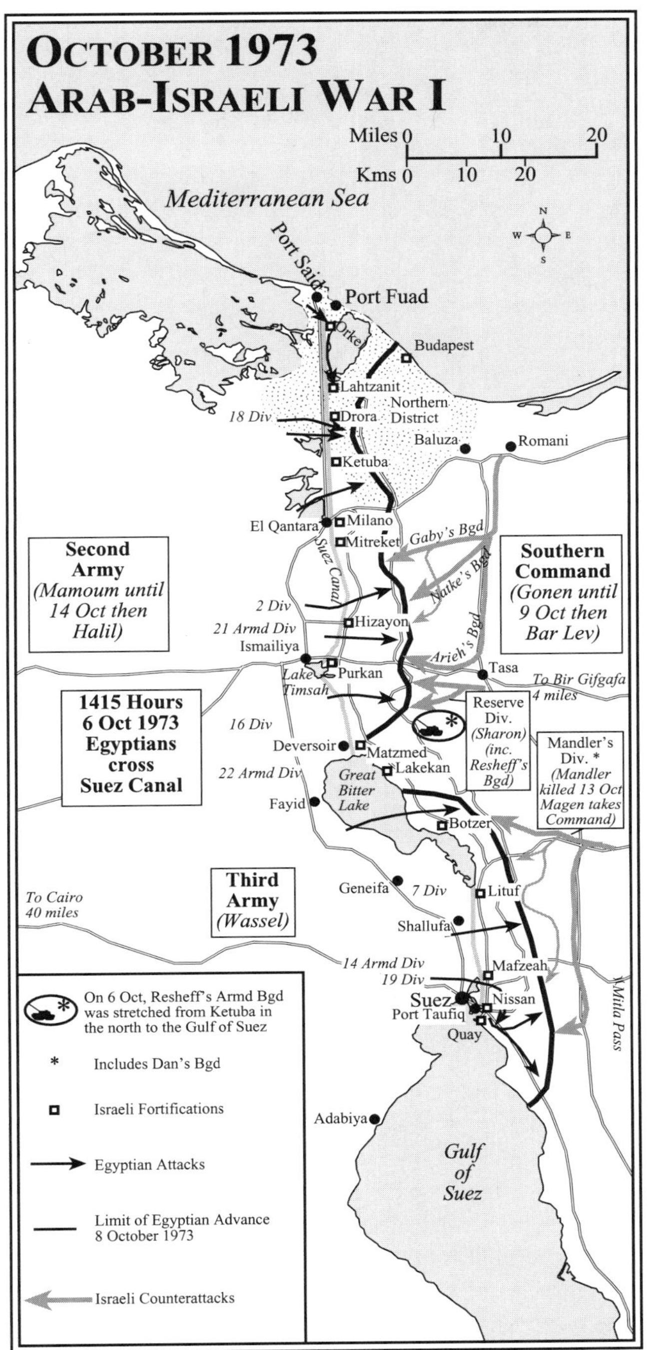

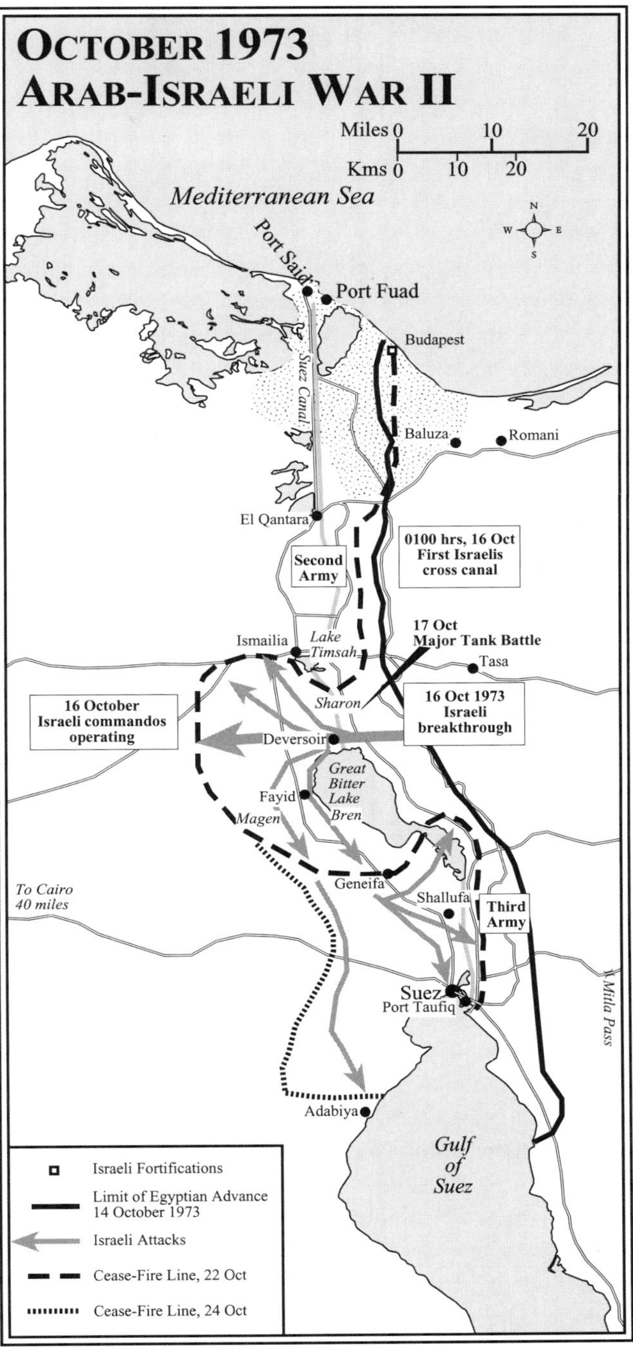

erating with local Arab militia, the invading Arab states enjoyed early success, choking the supply roads to Jewish population centers and driving Israelis from the Old City of Jerusalem. These successes were short-lived. The Arab states claimed they were liberating Palestine from the Jews but failed to coordinate military operations and often pursued conflicting territorial goals. Moreover, the Arab forces were poorly supplied, received inadequate training, and suffered from poor morale. The Israeli Defense Forces (IDF) did not fare much better during the first month of the war. The tide began to shift in Israel's favor after the IDF obtained weapons and supplies despite a UN embargo. Between June 1948 and January 1949, the IDF counterattacked and captured significantly more territory than it had been allotted by the UN partition plan, including the Negev and the Galilee. Four thousand Israeli soldiers and 2,000 civilians were killed during the war; the number of Arabs killed is unknown. Between 550,000–750,000 Arab refugees (estimates vary) fled Israel as a result of the war. Their fetid camps became a breeding ground for generations of young Arab fighters against the "Jewish entity."

1956, Sinai-Suez

During 1955–1956, Gaza and the Sinai Peninsula served as bases for numerous terrorist attacks against Israel. In September 1955, Egyptian prime minister Gammal Abdel Nasser ordered the closure of the Straits of Tiran, an international waterway, effectively blockading Israel's port at Eilat. Israel regarded the blockade as an act of war. At the same time, Britain and France had grown increasingly frustrated with Nasser. The French resented Nasser's support of Algerian nationalists, who were engaged in a war of independence from France, and the British opposed his nationalization of the Suez Canal on 26 July 1956. Thus Israeli, British, and French interests converged in the Suez-Sinai campaign. Their joint plan was divided into two distinct military operations, one led by the Israelis and the other by the British and French, and had the primary goal of deposing Nasser. Israel, ostensibly acting alone, launched its invasion of the Sinai on October 29. The Israelis, led by General Moshe Dayan, combined airborne and armored assaults to seize the Suez Canal by 31 October and to gain control of most of the Sinai by 3 November. As planned, the British and French then demanded that both Israel and Egypt pull back from the Suez Canal. When Nasser, as predicted, refused to withdraw, the British and French began a three-day air assault on 31 October, destroying the Egyptian air force on the ground. Within two days, British and French airborne troops had secured the canal. Militarily, the campaign was a success; politically, it was a disaster. U.S. president Dwight D. Eisenhower, preoccupied with the upcoming presidential election and Soviet repression in Hungary, opposed the Israeli-British-French collusion. On 2 November, the United Nations passed a U.S.-sponsored resolution calling for the immediate cessation of hostilities and the withdrawal of all foreign forces from Egyptian territory. France and Britain withdrew in humiliation, but Israel remained in the Sinai until March 1957. Nasser regained control of the Suez Canal and convinced the UN to dispatch a United Nations Emergency Force (UNEF) to the Sinai as a buffer between Israel and Egypt. The UNEF also prevented any further blockade of the Straits of Tiran. The Suez-Sinai campaign bolstered Israel's military reputation, enhanced Egypt's political influence in the Third World, and demonstrated that Britain and France were no longer world powers.

1967, Six-Day War

Tensions between Israel and its Arab neighbors significantly increased during 1966–1967. Israel's borders saw repeated Arab terrorist attacks and Syrian military activity. Throughout May, Nasser called for the destruction of Israel, and on 16 May demanded the withdrawal from the Sinai of the UNEF, which cravenly left three days later. On 22 May, Egypt closed the Straits of Tiran to Israeli shipping. Three days later, Egypt, Iraq, Jordan, Kuwait, Lebanon, Saudi Arabia, and Syria mobilized 547,000 troops, 2,504 tanks, and 957 aircraft along the Israeli border. Threatened by terrorist attacks, anti-Israel rhetoric, the closure of the Straits, and hostile troops on its borders, the Israelis launched their preemptive attack on 5 June 1967. On the first day, the Israeli Air Force, flying French Mirage fighter-bombers, attacked Arab airfields, destroyed the bulk of its enemies' aircraft on the ground. The IDF then struck into the West Bank and the Sinai. Lacking air cover, the Jordanian and Egyptian armies quickly retreated. On 7 June, the IDF seized the West Bank (Judea and Samaria), previously controlled by Jordan, and captured east Jerusalem. Suffering 5,000 casualties, King Hussein of Jordan agreed to a cease-fire that same day. In the Sinai, the IDF quickly raced across the Sinai and inflicted perhaps as many as 12,000 casualties upon the Egyptians. Nasser agreed to a cease-fire on 9 June. With Jordan and Egypt defeated, Israel turned its armor and aircraft against Syria. The Israelis, after only 27 hours, entered Kuneitra and captured the Golan Heights, inflicting more than 1,000 Syrian casualties.

The UN negotiated a cease-fire between Syria and Israel on 10 June. Israeli air power was crucial to the destruction of the Arab armies in the war. Israel gained control of the Sinai Peninsula, the West Bank with all of Jerusalem, and the Golan Heights. Israel suffered the loss of 766 soldiers, compared with over 18,000 Arab casualties during the war.

1973, Yom Kippur War

In an attempt to regain the territories lost in 1967, Egypt and Syria launched a surprise attack against Israel, on 6 October 1973, the Jewish Day of Atonement (Yom Kippur). Poor political and military intelligence and an easy contempt for Arab military ability caused Israel to discount Arab frustration with the results of the Six-Day War and also misinterpreted Arab mobilization for the attack as annual military maneuvers. The Israelis finally realized the threat eight hours before the attack, but Israeli prime minister Golda Meir ruled out a preemptive strike for fear of being perceived as the aggressor. When fighting began at 2:00 P.M., the Israelis had not yet fully mobilized and were outnumbered 12 to 1. Backed by $3.5 billion worth of aid from the Soviet Union, the Egyptians opened with an air and artillery assault into the Sinai, and the Syrians followed soon after with a thrust into the Golan Heights, taking Mount Hermon. Initial Arab gains were impressive, but the Israelis stopped the

Egyptians by 8 June, the Syrians by 11 June, and captured the Suez Canal on 18 October. Initially reluctant to offer assistance, the U.S. then funded Israel with $2.2 billion worth of aid, which proved vital to Israel's war effort. The Organization of Petroleum Exporting Countries (OPEC), because of U.S. support for Israel, imposed an oil embargo upon the U.S. that lasted until 1974. Despite the active involvement of the U.S. and the USSR, the risk of superpower confrontation was never a serious possibility, and both powers brokered a cease-fire between the Israelis and the Syrians and Egyptians. Israel's military reputation declined as a result of the war; the nation had suffered 3,000 killed and 8,000 wounded, compared with 8,500 Egyptians and Syrians killed and 20,000 Syrians wounded.

But this conflict yielded two positive consequences. Egyptian president Anwar as-Sadat could now treat with the Israelis as a military equal for peace and recognition of the state of Israel. American president Jimmy Carter brokered the agreements in 1977, and both shared Nobel Peace Prizes for their work. But Sadat was assassinated by Muslim extremists five years later. The end of the war also saw the emergence of the Israeli peace movement.

1982, Lebanon and Beyond

Between 1978 and 1982, the Palestinian Liberation Organization (PLO), using Lebanon as a base for terrorist attacks, created instability along Israel's border. In early 1982, Maronite Christians in Lebanon and the Israelis began discussing a joint punitive war against PLO targets in Lebanon. Using the attempted assassination of the Israeli ambassador to the United Kingdom as a pretext, Israeli defense minister Ariel Sharon devised an invasion plan of Lebanon with three goals: the elimination of the PLO in Lebanon; the creation of a stable Maronite government in Lebanon; and the expelling of Syria from Lebanon. On 6 June 1982, IDF armor struck into Lebanon, attacking the PLO along the coast toward Beirut and Syrian forces near the Bekaa Valley. The IDF linked up with Maronite Christian forces outside Beirut on 8 June, but the Maronites were unwilling to attack the PLO in west Beirut. Fighting alone, the Israelis besieged west Beirut on 1 July. The Israelis led air, artillery, and naval bombardments against PLO positions in west Beirut until 6 August, when the PLO agreed to a U.S.-sponsored withdrawal agreement. Fighting elsewhere in Lebanon continued until 21 August. On 16 September, members of the Lebanese Christian Kataib militia massacred between 700 and 2,000 Palestinians at the Sabra and Shatila refugee camps. The IDF claimed to be unaware of the massacre going on about them. On 28 September, the IDF pulled out of west Beirut. Although a military success, the Israelis achieved only one of their three goals, the elimination of the PLO in Lebanon. The Syrian military remained in Lebanon and the Maronites were unable to maintain a stable government friendly to Israel. The IDF withdrew from Lebanon altogether in 1985 but left a buffer zone maintained by Lebanese-Christian police north of its border until May 1999. Although this was the last overt Arab-Israeli conflict to date, cross-border raids, Israeli air strikes, and nearly continuous unrest between Palestinians and Israelis have kept the area in turmoil.

The Israelis were victorious in their Arab wars because they knew that, for them, defeat was not an option. (More than one Arab leader of the time criticized Adolf Hitler for not killing more Jews.) The Arabs knew, conversely, that they could be defeated in a particular war and come back to fight another day. Israeli society, with its many highly educated and technically skilled citizens and, usually, facing annihilation, fostered innovation and careers open to all talents, just what was needed in the fast-moving, combined-arms Middle East conflicts. The impoverished, authoritarian, underdeveloped Arab societies, with their formulaic, hierarchical militaries, at least until 1973, could hardly compete.

Eric D. Pullin

See also: Israeli Military; Refugees and Victims of Ethnic Cleansing; Sinai-Suez Offensive; Six-Day War; United Nations and Conflict Resolution

References and further reading:

Gilbert, Martin. *Atlas of the Arab-Israeli Conflict.* 6th ed. New York: Oxford, 1993.
Lacquer, Walter. *Confrontation: The Middle East and World Politics.* New York: New York Times Books, 1974.
Ovendale, Ritchie. *The Origins of the Arab-Israeli Wars.* 3d ed. London and New York: Longman, 1999.
Schiff, Ze'ev. *A History of the Israeli Army.* London: Sidgewick & Jackson, 1987.
Schulze, Kirsten E. *The Arab-Israeli Conflict.* London and New York: Longman, 1999.

Issus, Battle of (November 333 B.C.E.)

The second victory of the Macedonian king Alexander III the Great over the Persian king Darius III that took place on the eastern coastline of the gulf of Iskanderun in southern Turkey. The battlefield was divided by a river called the Pinarus.

After Alexander had marched through Asia Minor, he followed the Syrian coastline southwards. The Persian army occupied a position north of the Macedonian army, blocking the road to the rear. Alexander immediately turned to meet Darius in battle, the Macedonians deploying south of the Pinarus, the Persians to the north.

Alexander's army consisted of 26,000 infantry and 5,300 cavalry. He positioned his heavy infantry in the center, with a small force of cavalry on the left. The right wing consisted of the guard infantry and the bulk of the cavalry, including Alexander at the head of his guard-heavy cavalry, and light troops.

We know that the Persian army greatly outnumbered Alexander's, but it is impossible to assess its exact numbers. It contained a sizable cavalry force, a large contingent of Greek mercenaries, probably some 30,000 strong, and a large number of Asiatic infantry. Having reinforced the riverbank with battlements, the Persians took position on the riverbank with the Greeks in the center, some 30,000 Persian infantry on each wing, and an unknown number of local troops in the rear. The cavalry formed the right wing, closing the gap between the main battle line and the sea.

Alexander opened the battle by crossing the river and charging the Persian left, routing the Persian infantry. The Persian king fled immediately, though the Greek mercenaries had put severe pressure upon the Macedonian center, which was driven back into the river. However, as Alexander turned with his guard troops upon the Greek mercenaries from rear and flank, the Persian army was routed and broke, suffering heavy losses. The Macedonian losses numbered 450 dead and 4,500 wounded.

Maarten van der Werf

See also: Alexander the Great; Alexander's Wars of Conquest

References and further reading:

Fuller, J. F. C. *The Generalship of Alexander the Great.* London: Eyre & Spottiswoode, 1958.

Green, Peter. *Alexander of Macedon, 356–323 B.C.E. A Historical Biography.* Harmondsworth, UK: Penguin, 1974. Reprinted Berkeley and Los Angeles: University of California Press, 1991.

Hammond, N. G. L. *The Genius of Alexander the Great.* London: Duckworth, 1997.

Tarn, W. W. *Alexander the Great.* Cambridge, UK: Cambridge University Press, 1948.

Italian Colonial Wars (1882–1936)

The Italian quest for prestige. Though it would seem that the pursuit of an overseas empire would be a low priority for the newly unified Italian state, with its lack of internal integration, serious border disputes with Austria, and a general paucity of resources, Rome still sought this objective in competition with the other major powers of the nineteenth century. The objectives being international prestige, potential markets, and an outlet for Italy's excess population that would still be under Rome's political control. A particular impetus for Italian expansion was the resonance of the very name Rome with *empire.*

While allowed by the British government to gain a foothold in what is now Somalia, Italian efforts to create a protectorate over the Ethiopian Empire failed. Despite losing to feudal levies at Dogali in 1887, Rome signed the treaty of Wichale with Emperor Menelik II in 1889. The emperor believed he had signed a treaty recognizing his sovereignty. The Italian government felt they had cleverly bound the Ethiopians with an admission of overlordship. When Menelik came to understand the true meaning of the treaty, he repudiated the document in 1893 and went to war.

The climax of this campaign was the disastrous Battle of Adowa in 1896, though the Italians were also fought to a standstill at Amba Alagi (1895) and Macalle (1896). Essentially, the Italo-Ethiopian conflict had become a proxy fight between London and Paris over control of the Sudan, with the result that the Ethiopian military, while essentially a feudal horde, had access to modern French and Russian weapons. When added to the raw numbers and traditional warrior ferocity of Menelik's army, the result was a crushing Italian defeat. Rome was unable even to mount a retaliatory campaign to exact revenge for the worst humiliation ever visited by a traditional state on a modern Western army.

The second major effort by the Italians came in North Africa, as the Agadir Incident encouraged Rome to try to turn its area of influence in Cyrenica and Tripolitania (modern Libya) into a formal colony, mostly from fear of French aggrandizement. This move led to the Italo-Turco War (1910–1911), which, although a war between organized armies, was mostly about securing colonial possessions in compensation for other governments' gains.

Once the Turks had stepped back from their confrontation with the Italians, mostly to deal with the Balkan War, Rome found itself locked into a long-running guerrilla war with the Senussi, a culture of desert nomads with no intention of compromising their traditions for the sake of Rome's economic and political aspirations. With encouragement from Turkey and Germany, the Senussi (under their emir Idris) were able to fight the Italians to a standstill; by 1919 Rome was forced to grant the nomads autonomy.

These were circumstances that Benito Mussolini was not prepared to tolerate upon his accession to power, though it was not obvious that he would be interested in pursuing a formal empire. As a former socialist, Mussolini was nominally an anti-imperialist. There was also the more cynical consideration of whether adopting such a pose would better serve the ends of the new regime. In the end, Mussolini was further concerned with achieving victories for his regime so as to solidify his domestic power, in addition to the usual Italian colonial goals.

Mussolini assigned Emilio De Bono the task of bringing the Senussi to heel, thus beginning a campaign that lasted into the early 1930s. De Bono was chosen because he was the most eminent soldier to join the Fascist cause, and his success would reflect glory on the Blackshirt movement, but his lack of progress led to his replacement by the regular army generals Pietro Badoglio and Rodolfo Graziani.

Their strategy was the traditional anti-insurrection method of concentrating the noncombatant population in secured camps so as to separate them from the active fighters, there being no more than 1,000 active guerrillas at any one time. The anti-insurgency campaign was carried out with all of the expected Fascist brutality and much of the social and economic infrastructure of Libya's traditional peoples was destroyed; it was estimated that by 1932 some 100,000 persons had died in Cyrenica alone, roughly half the population of that region.

It was probably inevitable that Mussolini would revisit the question of exacting revenge from Ethiopia for the debacle of 1896, the rationale given to the Italian population. Though Rome had been able to exert more influence over Addis Ababa, Haile Selassi had continued to try to play off the major European powers against each other so as to maintain the sovereignty of his state. Believing himself to have a free hand from London and Paris, Mussolini began his second colonial war much as he had his campaign in North Africa, by dispatching De Bono with a large force of Blackshirt militia to march on the Ethiopian capital so as to monopolize all the glory for his regime.

As before, a larger than expected force (some 800,000 men were mobilized) under professional officers was required to bring the formal campaign to a conclusion, a campaign that nauseated the democracies with its use of chemical weapons, indiscriminately spread by air. Much of the war became desultory after the Ethiopian regular army was defeated.

However, formal military conquest did not lead to a pacified region and the Italians found themselves contending with a constant level of insurrection, a matter not helped by the fragmentary control that the Ethiopian central government had exerted over the country. Neither sanguinary violence nor relative benevolence was able to solidify the Italian position before the country's defeat at the hands of the British in 1941 and the total loss of empire. The entire Italian adventure in imperialism brings to mind the supposed quotation of Chancellor Otto von Bismarck, "The Italians have strong appetites but weak teeth."

George R. Shaner

See also: Adowa; Italo-Turkish War

References and further reading:

Gooch, John. *Army, State and Society in Italy, 1870–1915.* London: Macmillan, 1989.

Mack Smith, Denis. *Mussolini's Italian Empire.* New York: Viking Press, 1976.

Mockler, Anthony. *Haile Selassi's War: The Italian-Ethiopian Campaign, 1935–1941.* New York: Random House, 1984.

Tripodi, Paola. *The Colonial Legacy in Somalia: Rome and Mogadishu from Colonial Administration to Operation Restore Hope.* New York: St. Martin's Press, 1999.

Italian Wars of Unification (1848–1870)

Series of wars that resulted in the unification of Italy. The unification of Italy, or Risorgimento, was achieved in several wars fought between 1848 and 1870 by the various states that comprised the Italian peninsula. With French support these states fought against Austria and the pope. By 1870 Italian patriotism created a unified Italy under the Royal House of Savoy.

The unification wars stemmed from the inadequate 1814–1815 Congress of Vienna settlements that restored the status quo of the pre-Napoleonic era. The various states had different monarchs who aimed to increase their power. Unification also was spurred by the liberal ideas of Guiseppi Mazzini (1805–1872), Vincenzo Gioberti (1801–1852), Massimo d'Aseglio (1798–1866), and Giuseppe Garibaldi (1807–1882), who had stirred revolutionary agitation throughout Italy since the 1830s. Revolts in Parma, Romagna, Umbria, and the Marches were harshly put down by the Austrians.

Yet Camillo Benso di Cavour (1810–1861), Piedmont's prime minister from 1852 to 1859, was the chief architect of Italian unification. Piedmont king Charles Albert (1798–1849) had agreed to a constitutional monarchy in February 1848, but the first battle for unification occurred at Custozza on 23–25 July 1848. There the Austrians, under their master tactician Field Marshal Joseph Radetsky, defeated the Italians. The Austrians also outmaneuvered them at the 23 March 1849 Battle of Novara. These humiliating defeats led King Charles Albert to abdicate in favor of his son Victor Emmanuel II (1820–1878).

Pope Pius IX (1792–1878), elected in 1846, exacerbated the situation. He had initially seemed liberal with his welcome refreshing reforms. However, his proclamation on 20 April 1848 that Italians should not fight another Catholic country earned him great enmity from his compatriots and resulted in rioting. The pope's temporal powers were abolished on 9 February 1849; he fled from Rome on 29 November 1849. He was returned to Rome under French protection on 12 April 1850. French troops occupied Rome as a protective force until 1870.

Cavour cleverly persuaded French emperor Napoleon III to join Piedmont and Sardinia in July 1858. Success finally came when the combined French-Piedmontese army attacked the Austrian army on 20 May at Montebello. The Piedmontese won again on 30–31 May at Palestro. Then this combined army of 59,100 soldiers and 91 artillery pieces defeated the 58,000 troops and 176 pieces of the Austrians at the Battle of Magenta on 4 July 1859, where some 6,000 died.

The same forces defeated the Austrians at the Battle of Solferino on 24 June 1859, which resulted in 14,000 Austrians either killed or wounded with 8,000 missing or prisoners. The victors lost 15,000 killed or wounded and 2,000 missing or prisoners. The victory led to most of Lombardy being annexed to Sardinia-Piedmont. The horrific slaughter and bloodshed severely stretched the medical capabilities of both camps. Henry Dunant (1828–1910) succored the wounded for three days and nights and subsequently established the International Red Cross. Napoleon then signed an armistice with Emperor Franz-Joseph at Villafranca, allowing Austria to retain Venice, which annoyed Cavour, who resigned.

Cavour returned to power in January 1860 and secretly agreed to turn Nice and Savoy over to Napoleon. The remnants of the Papal States, except for Rome itself, were occupied. The Piedmontese Parliament proclaimed Victor Emanuel II king of Italy. Rome was to be the future capital of the Italian nation.

Although Cavour was forced to cede Nice and Savoy to France, a plebiscite held on 15 April 1860 resulted in Parma, Tuscany, Romagna, and Modena voting to join Piedmont.

On 6 February 1860, Victor Emmanuel annexed Umbria and the Marches. In 1860, Garibaldi invaded Sicily and defeated the Neapolitans at Calatafimi on 15 May 1860. He seized Palermo and Naples in a plebiscite, again resulting in a decision to join Italy. Victor Emmanuel not only defeated the pope's army at Castelfidardo on 18 September and Ancona on 30 September, but he also confiscated all of the papal possessions outside Rome. Although Italy lost several battles (including a second loss at Custozza), it was rewarded with Venetia in 1866 as a reward for Italian aid to Prussia against Austria. Finally, on 20 September 1870, with the guardian French troops being withdrawn to fight the Prussians in the Franco-Prussian War, Victor Emmanuel seized Rome and made it Italy's capital city, thereby ending the Italian wars of unification.

Annette Richardson

See also: Garibaldi, Giuseppi

References and further reading:

Coppa, Frank J. *Camillo di Cavour.* New York: Twayne Publishers, 1973.

———. *The Origins of the Italian Wars of Independence.* London and New York: Longman, 1992.

Garibaldi, Giuseppe. *Autobiography.* Trans. A. Werner. New York: Howard Fertig, 1971.

Katz, Robert. *The Fall of the House of Savoy.* New York: Macmillan, 1971.

Mack Smith, Denis. *Cavour.* New York: Knopf, 1985.

———. *Mazzini.* New Haven: Yale University Press, 1994.

Reader, Harry. *Italy in the Age of the Risorgimento.* New York: Longman, 1983.

Ridley, Joseph. *Garibaldi.* New York: Viking, 1976.

Italo-Turkish War (1911–1912)

Italy's preoccupation with national unification in the mid- to late nineteenth century meant that it invariably fell behind other European countries in the quest for overseas colonies. Imperial aspirations thus became inextricably linked with national pride, and the government focused upon nearby North Africa for territorial gains. Italian immigrants and merchants began arriving in Libya in 1880 and within two decades constituted the most numerous foreigners in that Turkish colony. The Ottoman Empire being in decline, on 29 September 1911 Italy suddenly declared war on the Turks, alleging mistreatment of its nationals in Libya. A force of 50,000 men was then dispatched overseas, which caught the Ottoman garrison completely unprepared. By October Italian forces under General Carlo Caneva were in complete control of Tripoli and Tobruk and had carved out several enclaves along the coast. Turkish resistance was either weak or ineffective. However, strong resentment and resistance from the Muslim population culminated in the Battle of Tripoli, 23–26 October 1911, where Turkish-leaning Senussi tribesman tried and failed to recapture the capital after heavy casualties. Italian losses had also been considerable and they were dissuaded from pushing further inland. Despite the Italians' enjoying every advantage in terms of modern weaponry, an embarrassing stalemate ensued.

As events in Libya unfolded, the Italians also dispatched naval forces to harass the Ottoman coast. In April 1912 Italian warships bombarded the Dardanelles while other forces seized the Dodecanese Islands and Rhodes. It was not until July 1912 that Caneva led his forces away from the coast, and several pitched encounters were waged, but the Italians finally emerged victorious. Furthermore, because events in the Balkans began spinning rapidly out of control, the Sublime Porte entered negotiations to cease hostilities altogether. The Italo-Turkish War was finally concluded by the Treaty of Ouchy, signed 15 October 1912, whereby Italy gained Libya, Rhodes, and the Dodecanese Islands. Ottoman losses amounted to 14,000 men, while the Italians, better armed and equipped, lost half that tally. It was hardly a glorious triumph for the Italians, and the conflict may prove of interest more for the fact that it was the first to employ aerial reconnaissance, aerial bombardment, and armored vehicles.

John C. Fredriksen

See also: Balkan War, First; Italian Colonial Wars

References and further reading:

Childs, Timothy W. *Italo-Turkish Diplomacy and the War over Libya, 1911–1912.* New York: E. J. Brill, 1990.

Simon, Rachel. *Libya between Ottomanism and Nationalism: The Ottoman Involvement in Libya during the War with Italy (1911–1919).* Berlin: K. Schwarz, 1987.

Ivan III (1440–1505)

Ruler who laid the foundation of the modern Russian state, expanded and recovered much of Russia's western "historical lands," and shook off Mongol, or Tartar, rule. Ivan was born in Moscow on 22 January 1440. During his long reign, he gathered, absorbed, and incorporated into the Muscovite state most of the Russian independent principalities and free cities through conquest, diplomacy, annexation, or voluntary surrender. He transformed the small and often contested role of the principality of Moscow into the political center of a unified Russian state.

Ivan's most important achievement was the ending of Mongol rule over the Russian people. Friction between Moscow and the Mongol khans of the Golden Horde came to a head when the Russian and Mongol armies met on the opposite banks of the Ugra River in 1480. For more than two months neither army attacked the other. The Mongols suddenly withdrew their troops without a battle. In this rather inglorious manner Ivan ended Mongol domination.

Ivan's next major objective was the recovery of the ancient territories of Kievan Russia from Lithuania. In 1500, Ivan's army invaded Lithuania, and during the next three years, his forces captured much of Russia's western lands and saved Kiev and Smolensk.

Ivan's successes and victories over Lithuania brought Russia into direct contact with Europe, whose sovereigns viewed him now as a powerful and independent ruler. To augment his authority, he added the title of Sovereign of All Russia to that of czar.

Ivan died in Moscow on 27 October 1505, leaving a much expanded and more powerful country than when he had ascended to power.

James J. Farsoals

See also: Ivan IV, ("the Terrible"); Novgorod, Muscovite Conquest of

References and further reading:

Fennel, J. L. *Ivan the Great of Moscow.* New York: St. Martin's, 1962.

Grey, Ian. *Ivan III and the Unification of Russia.* New York: Collier Books, 1964.

Soloviev, S. M. *The Reign of Ivan III.* Gulf Breeze, FL: Academic International Press, 1978.

Ivan IV ("the Terrible") (1530–1584)

Complex and violent monarch who strove to create a powerful national monarchy and to expand Muscovite territory beyond the Ural Mountains. Ivan was born in Moscow on 25 August 1530. He was orphaned at the age of eight and a group of aristocrats (boyars) assumed controlled of the regency. His childhood was marred by acts of violence and murders, often in his presence, leaving a deep psychological trauma on his personal life and character. It was perhaps this violent experience that contributed to his vindictive and brutal conduct, earning him the epithet "the Terrible."

Ivan was crowned Czar of Moscow and All Russia in 1547. During the first years of his reign he introduced a series of administrative reforms. He organized a new force of infantrymen (*streltsy*), the first Russian soldiers to carry firearms. With this new army, he invaded the Mongol, or Tartar, khanates of Kazan and Astrakhan to the east and southeast of Russia and annexed them to the Muscovite state in the 1550s.

But the most important military event during Ivan's reign was the Livonian War—an abortive attempt to gain an outlet to the Baltic. In 1558, Ivan opened hostilities against the Livonian Knights, who had ruled Livonia (Estonia) since the thirteenth century, and captured much of its territory. But in 1561, Sweden, Lithuania, and Poland entered the war, defeated the Russian army, and forced Ivan to give up all of his gains along the Baltic.

In 1581 the exploration of western Siberia began. By 1583, the entire region came under Russian control, thus opening the road to further expansion into Siberia.

On 18 March 1584, in the midst of a chess game, Ivan suddenly collapsed and died in Moscow.

James J. Farsolas

See also: Livonian War

References and further reading:

Bobrick, Benson. *Fearful Majesty: The Life and Reign of Ivan the Terrible.* New York: Putman, 1987.

Carr, Francis. *Ivan the Terrible.* New York: Barnes & Noble, 1980.

Troyat, Henri. *Ivan the Terrible.* New York: Dutton, 1984.

Ivry, Battle of (14 March 1590)

The decisive battle that ended the Wars of Religion in France. Henry de Navarre became king after the murder of Henry III in 1589; only the Catholic League supported by Spain dared to challenge him. Henry tried to take Paris but was repulsed by the rebels led by the Duc de Mayenne. He decided then to besiege the town of Dreux, 40 miles west of Paris. Mayenne, with the help of Spanish veteran troops, attacked the royal/Huguenot army.

The king's army was made of French loyal subjects but also of German *reiters* and Protestant Swiss. His 11,000 soldiers had to face more than 15,000 Catholics, including elite cavalry from Spanish Flanders and German Protestant mercenaries.

After some skirmishing, the two armies faced each other on a plain without any terrain features. They deployed like pawns on a chessboard. The royal army had its left wing slightly forward and the right wing some way back as a reserve. Mayenne, confident in his superior number, disposed his troops in a crescent around the royals. Henry IV gave his troops a rallying point: three pear trees he could see behind Mayenne's lines. At 12 P.M., the royal artillery fired nine volleys into the crowding Catholics before Mayenne ordered his German cavalry to charge. The Protestants advanced but refused to fire on their coreligionists and instead they rode at full speed through the waiting Catholic infantry. The infuriated Spanish cavalry charged home on the royal artillery. Henry, leading his gendarmes, stopped this dangerous move; the fight was now a tangle of intermingled cavalry. The royal reserve took the opportunity to charge into the fray, after seeing that all the Catholics had fired their pistols and had no more powder. The Spanish survivors left the battlefield around 1 P.M. The king, following them, led the pursuit to the pear trees and then turned his cavalry toward the three large blocks of Catholic infantry. After a few volleys of artillery, he offered them to surrender. As Mayenne fled the battlefield, they asked for mercy. More than 4,000 were taken prisoners; all the German *landsknechts* were slaughtered by the royal Swiss.

The battle was over by 2 P.M. The Catholics had lost their field army and had to rely more than ever on the Spanish troops. It would take four more years before Mayenne and the Catholic League chose to rally Henry IV.

Gilles Boué

See also: French Wars of Religion

References and further reading:

Bayrou, François. *Henry IV.* Paris: Fayard, 1996.
Cornette, Joel. *Le XVIème Siècle.* Paris: SEDES, 1995.
Hardy, Etienne. *Batailles Françaises.* Paris: Dumaine, 1881.

Marines raising the American flag on Mount Suribachi, Iwo Jima, 1945. (Library of Congress)

Iwo Jima, Battle of (19 February–15 March 1945)

One of the bloodiest battles of World War II in the Pacific. In order to provide American warplanes with an airfield only 600 miles from Japan and to shorten the attack route toward the Japanese home islands, the United States planned an invasion of Iwo Jima for February 1945. Iwo Jima, only 8 square miles in area, was defended by 21,000 soldiers who were literally dug into the island. The Japanese commander, General Kuribayashi, was determined to inflict maximum casualties on the American forces by fighting to the last man. His soldiers used Iwo's soft volcanic ash and extensive caves to build an effective network of underground tunnels, fortifications, and concrete pillboxes, and from these well-entrenched positions the Japanese prolonged the battle and exacted high American losses.

After a three-day naval bombardment rather than the 10 days originally requested by the marines, the main American assault led by the 4th and 5th Marine Divisions started on 19 February 1945. Although 30,000 U.S. soldiers were ashore by the end of the first day, the volcanic sand made mobility difficult. With the beach crowded with marines and equipment, the Japanese opened fire and inflicted heavy losses, and even marine veterans commented on the ferocity and violence of the first days. Moving to the south, one regiment of marines captured Mount Suribachi in the face of withering Japanese fire and decided to raise the American flag in order to increase the morale of the marines below and naval vessels offshore. The image of the flag raising, captured by war photographer Joe Rosenthal, provided one of the most famous images of World War II. Despite this symbolic victory, the battle raged for 30 more days, with reinforcements from the 3d Marines joining the 4th and 5th divisions driving north against difficult terrain and the Japanese tunnels throughout the island. The United States employed heavy firepower from the air and from artillery, grenades, mortars, and tanks with flame throwers and slowly began to move northward across the island. The carnage on both sides can be seen in the nickname the "Meat Grinder" for Japanese defensive positions in the reinforced hills. Finally the Japanese defenders were isolated in the northern corner and destroyed.

While nearly the entire Japanese force of 21,000 was killed, the Americans suffered 26,000 casualties, including more than 6,000 killed, an average of more than 700 dead for every square mile on the island and the first time that American casualties exceeded those of the Japanese. In the end, 27 marines were awarded the Medal of Honor. General Holland Smith praised General Kuribayashi's toughness and tenacity, while Admiral Chester Nimitz proclaimed: "Among the Americans who served on Iwo Island, uncommon valor was a common virtue."

Harold J. Goldberg

See also: U.S. Marines

References and further reading:

Bradley, James. *Flags of Our Fathers: Heroes of Iwo Jima.* New York: Delacourt Press, 2001.

Garand, George W., and Truman R. Strobridge. *Western Pacific Operations: History of the U.S. Marine Corps Operations in World War II.* Washington, DC: United States Marine Corps, 1971.

King, Ernest J. *U.S. Navy at War, 1941–1945. Official Reports to the Secretary of the Navy.* Washington, DC: United States Navy Department, 1946.

Spector, Ronald H. *Eagle against the Sun.* Norwalk, CT: Free Press, 1985.

J

Jackson, Andrew (1767–1845)

American field commander, politician, and seventh president, the first to be elected from the frontier. Jackson was born on 15 March 1767 in Waxhaw, South Carolina, the youngest of three sons of recent Scots-Irish immigrants. Because his father and namesake died before his birth, his mother, Elizabeth, moved the family into the home of her brother-in-law, James Crawford. Jackson received only rudimentary schooling.

When the British invaded the Carolinas in 1780, Jackson's eldest brother, Hugh, volunteered for the militia and was soon killed. After Colonel Banastre Tarleton defeated the militia near Waxhaw in May, Elizabeth, Andrew, and his brother Robert helped care for the American wounded. The brothers volunteered for the mounted militia and fought at Hanging Rock, South Carolina, on 1 August. After several months as guerrillas in the backwoods, they were captured early in 1781. Both received saber cuts for refusing to polish a British officer's boots. As prisoners of war in Camden, South Carolina, they contracted smallpox. Elizabeth negotiated their exchange but Robert died on the way home. After she nursed Andrew back to health, she nursed American prisoners on British ships in Charleston harbor, where she died of typhus. These incidents prompted Jackson's lifelong hatred of the British.

In 1786 Jackson began to practice law in Martinsville, North Carolina. Eager for the rough life, he moved to Tennessee in 1788 and became a prosecuting attorney for Nashville in 1789. He married Rachel Donelson Robards in 1791, both of whom believed in good faith that her divorce from Lewis Robards was final. Discovering later that she was not legally divorced until 1793, they remarried in 1794. These circumstances dogged Jackson the rest of his life and led to his fighting many duels to defend his wife's honor. In a duel with Charles Dickinson on 30 May 1806, he took a bullet in the chest, then deliberately aimed and "killed his man." Jackson carried his bullet to the grave.

Through Rachel's family's money and his own shrewd land deals, Jackson quickly became a wealthy man with a large plantation. He served in the U.S. House of Representatives from 1796 to 1797, in the U.S. Senate from 1797 to 1798, and on the Tennessee Supreme Court from 1798 to 1804. After 1802 he was a major general of the Tennessee State Militia. He volunteered his troops for service as soon as the War of 1812 began. Ordered to Natchez, Mississippi, to prepare to invade Florida, he earned the nickname "Old Hickory" by being tough enough to maintain discipline after Congress canceled the invasion. He did not see action until after the Fort Mims massacre on 30 August 1813. His victories at Talladega, Alabama, on 9 November and Horseshoe Bend on 27 March 1814 won him a commission as a major general in the regular army on 28 May.

Using Mobile, Alabama, as a base, he captured Pensacola, Florida, on 7 November and thoroughly defeated the British at New Orleans on 8 January 1815. Now a national hero, he commanded the Southern Division, headquartered in Nashville. From 1817 to 1819 he fought the Seminoles in Spanish Florida, hanging two British subjects as spies in April 1818 and capturing Pensacola again in May, nearly provoking war with both Britain and Spain. He resigned his commission and served briefly as the first governor of Florida Territory in 1821, then was a U.S. Senator from 1823 to 1825. After losing a controversial four-way presidential election in 1824, he won by landslides in 1828 and 1832. Throughout his presidency, he vigorously supported westward expansion and the forcible appropriation of Indian lands. It would be difficult to imagine anyone at the time who more exemplified the virtues and vices of mid-nineteenth-century Americans.

Eric v. d. Luft

See also: American Indian Wars; American Revolution; Creek War; Horseshoe Bend, Battle of; Houston, Samuel; New Orleans, Battle of; War of 1812

References and further reading:

Bassett, John Spencer. *The Life of Andrew Jackson.* Hamden, CT: Archon Books, 1967.

Davis, Burke. *Old Hickory: A Life of Andrew Jackson.* New York: Dial, 1977.

Heidler, David Stephen, and Heidler, Jeanne T. *Old Hickory's War: Andrew Jackson and the Quest for Empire.* Mechanicsburg, PA: Stackpole, 1996.

James, Marquis. *The Life of Andrew Jackson.* Indianapolis: Bobbs-Merrill, 1938.

Remini, Robert Vincent. *Andrew Jackson.* New York: HarperPerennial, 1999.

Jackson, Thomas "Stonewall" (1824–1863)

Confederate commander-hero and General Robert E. Lee's irreplaceable "right arm." Born on 21 January 1824 in Clarksburg, Virginia, and orphaned at seven, he was raised by an uncle. Despite a poor formal education, he was appointed to the U.S. Military Academy. Through determination, he improved his academic standing steadily, graduating in 1846 in the upper third of his class.

In the Mexican War Jackson served with distinction as an artillerist during General Winfield Scott's campaign to Mexico City. Jackson saw action at Veracruz, Cerro Gordo, Churubusco, and Chapultepec, twice earning brevet promotions. In 1851, Jackson resigned his commission for a position as a professor of artillery and natural philosophy at the Virginia Military Institute.

At the outbreak of the American Civil War, Jackson was commissioned a brigadier under General Joseph E. Johnston in the Confederate States Army. At First Bull Run, his steadiness anchored the Confederate line at the crucial moment, buying time for the tide of battle to turn. The nickname "Stonewall" was thereafter applied to both Jackson and his heroic brigade. Jackson was subsequently promoted to major general.

Commanding his own small army, Jackson received the task of preventing several Union armies from converging on Richmond. His subsequent "Valley Campaign" was masterful and is still studied today in war colleges around the world. Striking at first one then another of the disjointed Union formations, Jackson tied down superior forces under generals Nathaniel Banks, Irvin McDowell, and John C. Frémont, while General Lee dealt with the main Union advance on Richmond.

After a string of minor but timely victories, Jackson's troops made a key contribution to Confederate victory at Second Bull Run. Though Antietam was a strategic loss, Jackson's role in the invasion of Maryland had been laudable, earning him a promotion to lieutenant general and corps command in Lee's Army of Northern Virginia. In late 1862, at Fredericksburg, Jackson held down the vulnerable flank before executing an explosive counterattack. During Chancellorsville in May 1863, Jackson received a mortal wound from the fire of his own troops, died from his wounds on 10 May 1863 at Guiney's Station, and was buried in Lexington. Jackson's loss left an almost inconsolable General Lee without his most trusted and reliable lieutenant. It would be difficult to imagine a worse blow to the Confederacy.

Michael S. Casey

See also: American Civil War; Antietam/Sharpsburg; Chancellorsville, Battle of; Bull Run, First/Manassas; Bull Run, Second/Manassas Junction; Lee, Robert Edward

References and further reading:

Farwell, Byron. *Stonewall: A Biography of General Thomas J. Jackson.* New York: W.W. Norton, 1992.

Robertson, James I., Jr. *Stonewall Jackson: The Man, The Soldier, The Legend.* New York: Simon & Schuster, 1999.

Selby, John. *Jackson as Military Commander.* Princeton: Van Nostrand, 1968.

Tanner, Robert G. *Stonewall in the Valley: Thomas J. "Stonewall" Jackson's Shenandoah Valley Campaign, Spring, 1862.* Garden City, NY: Doubleday, 1976.

Jacobite Rebellions (1689–1746)

Uprisings that attempted to restore the Stuart Dynasty, and the last land battles on English and Scottish soil. Following the Revolution of 1688—which had been sparked by the birth of a son and potentially Catholic heir to James II of Great Britain, and the successful invasion of William of Orange, the king's Protestant son-in-law, who assumed the throne with his wife, Mary—James fled to France with his wife and son. For the next 57 years, Jacobitism, the support for the exiled branch of the Stuart family, would be a major tool of European foreign policy and spark four armed uprisings and numerous plots in England, Scotland, and Ireland.

Returning to Ireland in March 1689 with a contingent of French officers sent by Louis XIV, James began to muster an Irish army. Meanwhile, in Scotland, John Graham, Viscount Dundee, had also raised a Jacobite army and, after a successful series of raids, had defeated government forces at Killiecrankie. Although defeated at Dunkeld, Dundee's army, gaining support among the Highland Scots, fought on. In Scotland, the government was forced to an expensive policy of fort building and slow harassment of the clans, while in Ireland, the government fought using mercenaries hired

Charles Edward Stuart (also known as Bonnie Prince Charlie) departs Scotland in 1746, five months after the disastrous Jacobite defeat at the Battle of Culloden. (Library of Congress)

from Europe to augment English forces. William of Orange defeated James on 1 July 1690 at the Battle of the Boyne, although French naval support allowed the Jacobites to continue fighting until government reinforcement arrived and captured Limerick and Galway. With the Jacobites defeated, William turned his resources to fighting France until the treaty of Ryswick in 1697.

The next Jacobite rising occurred in 1715, following an abortive invasion scare in 1708. The Earl of Mar, unhappy with his prospects under the new king, George I, raised the banner of James II's son, James ("the Old Pretender"), in the highlands, expecting significant French assistance. A corresponding English rising, centered on northern Catholics, failed to accomplish much and was defeated and captured at Preston in November 1715. Mar, meanwhile, fought an indecisive battle at Sheriffmuir on 13 November against the Duke of Argyll. When James Stuart arrived in December, without French aid, the rebellion was fading, and most of the leaders had fled to France by February 1716.

In 1719, with Britain and Spain on hostile terms because of Spain's invasion of Sicily, Cardinal Alberoni, prime minister to Philip V of Spain, lent his support to a Jacobite invasion of Scotland. Again mustering highlanders to augment 250 Spanish regulars, the Jacobites, under the command of the earl Marischal and marquis of Tullibardine, quarreled among themselves and were caught at the pass of Glenshiel by government forces. The Scots fled, leaving the Spanish as prisoners of war until ransomed by their own government.

The final Jacobite campaign, "The '45," was first sponsored as a French diversion meant to draw British troops out of the War of the Austrian Succession. A 1744 invasion, to be led by the Marshal de Saxe, fell through after a great storm not only destroyed stockpiled supplies but disrupted the French fleet sent to gain control of the English Channel. Not to be dissuaded, the Stuart claimant, Charles Edward Stuart ("the Young Pretender" or "Bonnie Prince Charlie"), prepared an invasion on his own, borrowing money and counting on a mass uprising upon his arrival in Scotland. Again due to poor weather, the Jacobites arrived with only half the planned men and supplies. (Many began to mutter that "God is a Protestant!") The Jacobites did muster a number of highlanders, captured Edinburgh Castle, and defeated the local government forces at Prestonpans, before marching south into England with an army of about 4,500. The Jacobite army turned back at Derby, now convinced that there was no support in England or substantial French aid on the way, abandoning a strike at London in favor of a retreat back to Scotland.

Pursued by two Hanoverian armies under the Duke of Cumberland and George Wade, they collected a trickle of smuggled French supplies and, after successfully holding off the government troops at Falkirk, went to ground over the winter of 1745/6. Charles Edward Stuart, emerging from a fit of petulance over the retreat from Derby, insisted on a conventional action rather than continued evasion and in April 1746 met Cumberland at Culloden, where the Jacobites were decisively defeated.

Fleeing, Charles Edward Stuart dismissed the survivors of his army who had rallied after the battle and made his way in secret through the Highlands before reaching France. Ruthlessly punished by the government for their participation, the Scots, disenchanted by Jacobitism, abandoned the Stuarts to romantic nostalgia and the Jacobite threat ceased to exist.

Margaret Sankey

References and further reading:

Jarvis, R. C. *Collected Papers on the Jacobite Risings.* 2 vols. Manchester, UK: Manchester University Press, 1972.

Reid, Stuart. *1745: A Military History of the Last Jacobite Rising.* New York: Sarpedon, 1996.

Szechi, Daniel. *The Jacobites: Britain and Europe.* Manchester, UK: Manchester University Press, 1994.

Jan III Sobieski (1629–1696)

Polish military commander, savior of Vienna. Heir to three of Poland's wealthiest landowning families, Jan Sobieski received a cosmopolitan education and as a young man traveled western Europe on the Grand Tour. In 1648, he joined the Polish army, beginning his career with the suppression of the rebellion of Hetman Chmielnicki and his Cossacks. In protest against King John Casimir, Sobieski briefly served under Charles X of Sweden in his 1655 invasion of Poland but changed sides the following year to drive out the invader. With court patronage, Sobieski rose quickly to field hetman, then grand hetman of the Polish forces while conducting successful campaigns against the Tartars and Cossacks in the Ukraine.

In 1672, the Ottoman Empire, whose border was only 40 miles from Crakow, invaded Polish territory and Sobieski took the field against the invaders, annihilating an entire Ottoman army at the Battle of Chocim, on the Dnieper River, in 1673, only days after the death of King Michael Piast.

This victory, and Sobieski's reputation, won him the elective monarchy of Poland. Still at war with the Ottomans, he defended the fortresses of Lwow and Trembowla and reached a truce with the sultan in September 1676. This truce gave him breathing space to improve the army, increase the mobility of artillery, enlarge the dragoons, and reduce reliance on pikemen. However, still operating within the semifeudal politics of Poland, he was unable to centralize fiscal planning or logistical supply.

Sobieski's planned pro-French foreign policy crumbled against the realities of Poland's relationship with the Habsburg emperor and their mutual enmity to the Ottomans; and he willingly answered the appeal of Leopold II for troops to relieve Vienna from Ottoman siege. Acting as commander in chief of a 75,000-man relief force of Lithuanians, Poles, and Germans, Sobieski, particularly skillful in his transport of artillery into the Vienna Woods and the construction of a pontoon bridge across the Danube, defeated Kara Mustafa at Khalenberg and saved Vienna. Unfortunately, attempts to follow this victory with repeated campaigns in Moldavia between 1687 and 1691 failed and drained Polish resources. Suffering repeated heart attacks after 1691 and forced to deal with the rising power of Prussia and the increasing intransigence of Lithuania, Sobieski died in 1696.

Margaret Sankey

See also: Vienna, Sieges of; Turkish Wars of European Expansion

References and further reading:

Davies, Norman. *God's Playground: A History of Poland.* New York: Columbia University Press, 1982.

———. *Sobieski's Legacy.* London: Orbis, 1985.

Morton, J. B. *Sobieski, King of Poland.* London: Eyre & Spottiswoode, 1932.

Janissaries

An elite corps of the Ottoman Empire and perhaps the first standing army in Europe. It helped conquer the Byzantine Empire, Egypt, and much of the Balkans, eventually becoming the praetorian element in Ottoman palace intrigues until brutally suppressed in 1826.

The Janissaries, from the Turkish *yeni cheri* (new troops), were formed in 1330 as a bodyguard under the personal command of Sultan Orkhan. They were reformed as a military corps by Sultan Murad I in 1365, using captives from the Byzantine city of Adrianople (Eridne, Turkey). Originally recruits consisted of 1,000 men drawn from the fifth part (*besinci*) of the human booty, which, according to Ottoman law, belonged to the sultan. Replacements of Christian prisoners of war forced to accept Islam or Christian volunteers who later converted to Islam proved insufficient for meeting the demands of the growing corps, and captive Christian

Engraving of Janissaries and Spahis, 17th century. (Chris Hellier/Corbis)

children were recruited beginning in the second half of the fourteenth century. This too proved insufficient and Sultan Selim I imposed the *devsirme,* or forced levy of children, on subject Christian populations in the Balkans. The Janissaries numbered 16,000 by 1520 and 37,000 by 1609. Christians were recruited because Janissaries became slaves of the sultan, and the enslavement of Muslims is forbidden by the Koran. However, once recruited and enslaved, a Janissary was converted to Islam.

The Janissary corps consisted of cavalry, infantry, artillery, and sailors. They often were armed with firearms, taking part in all the major battles and wars of the Ottoman Empire for more than half a millennium, including the capture of Constantinople in 1453, the conquest of Egypt in 1517, the Battle of Mohács in 1526, and the siege of Vienna in 1683. The Janissaries' failure to suppress the Greek revolt in 1820, and their own numerous mutinies and stiff resistance to military reforms led Sultan Mahmud II ruthlessly to suppress the corps after its attempted revolt on 14–15 June 1826.

Michael C. Paul

See also: Byzantine-Ottoman Wars; Constantinople, Siege of (1453); Mamluks; Turkish Wars of European Expansion

References and further reading:

Goodwin, Godfrey. *The Janissaries.* London: Saqi, 1997.

Japanese Civil Wars (1450–1550)

The period from 1450 to 1550 in Japan known as the Epoch of the Warring Country, or Sengoku Period, that marked a time of continual civil war and unrest. It also marked the decline of central power and the rise of samurai and daimyo (who as great provincial lords were also samurai). Daimyo and their loyal retainers, samurai, battled other daimyo to take advantage of perceived weaknesses or to gain control over economically important areas. The older order, the powerful families in Kyoto, the land stewards, and so on, began to disappear and power diffused throughout the country to the new class of daimyo.

For many years, Japan was controlled by a series of families operating at the capital, Kyoto, who employed stewards throughout the country. While the emperor was weak, power was centralized among these families. The Onin War and the ensuing century of civil wars ended their control outside Kyoto and ushered in a new era that eventually would lead to the consolidation of power behind a new elite.

In addition to the level of destruction, there was the beginning of a new order, or a reorder. Daimyo sought to control their holdings and tried to categorize the quality of agricultural land and manufacturing production in towns. They engaged in *sword hunts* to disarm the peasantry and also sought to elevate the status of samurai, the only warriors allowed to wear the two swords, one long and one short. Samurai were encouraged to settle in fortified castle towns and leave the countryside, and thus the daimyo sought to increase economic production to expand their sources of wealth.

There were other issues, to be sure. The daimyo to the south and west benefited from trade with China and, toward the end of the Sengoku Period, contact with the West; daimyo received valuable goods from China for trade and received more accurate calendars, improved medical knowledge, and guns and gunpowder from the Portuguese, Spanish, and later Dutch traders. The fighting of samurai to samurai with swords, reflecting many years of training and fierce discipline, began to give way to fighting with muskets and cannon and favored those daimyo with greater economic resources or the good fortune to consider converting to Christianity. The samurai perfected the tea ceremony and looked to Buddhism to balance the carnage of continual fighting.

Toward the end of the period (for which there really is no exact date), several groupings of daimyo began to emerge who gathered great power. In time, three great daimyo arose—Oda Nobunaga, Toyotomi Hideyoshi, and Tokugawa Ieyasu—who eventually unified the country, made peace among the contending factions, tried to close the country to foreign influences, and took Japan into a period of 250-plus years of isolation and yet great change.

Charles M. Dobbs

References and further reading:

Elison, George, and Bardwell L. Smith, eds. *Warlords, Artists & Commoners: Japan in the Sixteenth Century.* Honolulu: University of Hawaii Press, 1981.

Hall, John Whitney, ed. *Japan before Tokugawa: Political Consolidation and Economic Growth, 1500–1650.* Princeton, NJ: Princeton University Press, 1981.

Totman, Conrad D. *Early Modern Japan.* Berkeley: University of California Press, 1993.

Japanese Colonial Wars (1874–1945)

Japan's 60-year period of seeking to establish a colonial empire for economic exploitation and to gain equality of a sort with the major European powers. The Meiji Restoration oligarchs had their differences, and one was over an early invasion of Korea as a prelude to expansion on the Asian continent. Realizing that Japan was still too weak, the leaders instead decided to bring the Ryukyu Islands firmly under Japanese control. The people of the Ryukyus were related to the Japanese and were controlled by the former daimyo of Satsuma but had long-established tributary relations with China. In 1872, the new government in Tokyo claimed control and, acting on behalf of the islanders, sent a punitive expedition to Taiwan to avenge the murder of some islanders by Taiwanese aborigines. This campaign took until 1874. The Chinese government in Beijing paid an indemnity, implying a recognition of Tokyo's new territory in the Ryukyus.

The next target, not unnaturally, was Korea. In 1875, the Japanese demonstrated several of the Western-built ships in their new navy off Korean waters and in 1876 gained the Treaty of Kanghwa, opening the former Hermit Kingdom to Japanese trade and claiming Korean independence (from China). Japanese interest in Korea eventually led to the Sino-Japanese War of 1894–1895, pitting the small modern army and navy of Japan against the larger but seriously outdated military forces of China; the Japanese won easily but saw the fruits of their victory—a leasehold over the Kwantung Peninsula—taken away in the Triple Intervention. But Japan did gain control over Taiwan and the nearby Pescadores Islands, reflecting Japan's increasing economic interest along China's coast. In 1902, the Anglo-Japanese Alliance brought British recognition of Japan's interest in Korea "in a peculiar degree politically as well as commercially and industrially."

Japan faced few difficulties in its occupation of Taiwan. The effort to develop Taiwan economically and to bring it within the emerging Japanese system really began in 1898. Japanese authorities suppressed bandits and established order; they also raised health standards, improved diets, and provided widespread basic education for all Taiwanese. However, to advance beyond basic education required Japanese language ability and a willingness to accept Japanese cultural norms. While the Japanese did tighten controls in the mid-1930s, they never faced any real threats of rebellion until the end of the Pacific War.

The stage was set for the Russo-Japanese War of 1904–1905. When the exhausted combatants agreed to the invitation by U.S. president Theodore Roosevelt for peace negotiations, the resulting Treaty of Portsmouth recognized Japan's "paramount interest" in Korea, implied that the Russians would vacate Manchuria (thereby leaving it available for Japanese exploitation), and turned over to Japan the Russian leasehold on the Kwantung Peninsula, ownership of the South Manchurian Railway, and the southern half of Sakhalin Island.

The Koreans did not accept the end to independence easily. Korea had a long history, perhaps longer than Japan's, and Koreans were proud of their past; they did not move easily into Japan's Inner Empire and give up their sense of nationhood. When Japan declared Korea a protectorate in 1907 the Koreans responded with more than 1,400 armed attacks and outbreaks of violence between 1908 and 1910, and a Korean patriot in late 1909 assassinated a key Japanese oligarch, Ito Hirobumi, who had appointed himself resident general in Korea. Japan exploited Korea's economy more than Taiwan's, and the result was a declining standard of living for many Koreans; the lack of political freedoms, omnipresent Japanese control, and economic deprivations combined to spark the great Mansei revolt in March 1919; more than a million demonstrators protested for Korean independence as the world was negotiating the Versailles Peace Treaty in France. In turn, the Japanese moved to convert the well-ordered system of Korean schooling into Japanese-intensive education and to control Korean life ever more tightly. But between a strongly developed sense of Korean nationalism, the continuing influence of American Christian missionaries, and the growing influence of Marxism, especially of the Chinese Communist variety, Koreans were most uneasy subjects in the Japanese empire.

World War I increased the growing Japanese colonial empire. In addition to Korea, the Ryukyus, the Pescadores, Taiwan, and also interests in southern Manchuria, Japan sided with the Allies (based on its treaty with Great Britain) and as a consequence gained at the Versailles peace negotiations. Japan received German concessions in the Pacific—a series of island chains—and German holdings in China, especially Kiaozhou Bay and the port of Qingtao in Shandong. (No one inquired of the Chinese as to these transferrals of what was originally their territory.)

The East Asian world was somewhat fluid during the 1920s, but in September 1931 the Japanese Kwantung Army used the Mukden Incident as an excuse to seize control over Manchuria the next year and then gradually to expand, first into that part of China outside the Great Wall and then by the mid-1930s to significant parts of North China inside the Great Wall. In December 1941 the Pacific War began in earnest and within months the Japanese had acquired a large colonial empire for its Greater East Asia Co-Prosperity Sphere; many Asian nationalists admired Japan's early victories over European nations and the United States. In fact, Japan declared the "independence" of a number of former Asian colonies that they had conquered, including Malaya, Burma, and the Philippines. But nationalists increasingly resented the substitution of Japanese colonial administration for that of Europe or the United States. In August 1945, Japan's surrender to the Allies ended World War II and Japan's overseas empire.

Charles M. Dobbs

See also: World War II

References and further reading:

Beasley, W. G. *Japanese Imperialism: 1894–1945.* Oxford and New York: Clarendon, 1987.

Giffard, Sydney. *Japan among the Powers, 1890–1990.* New Haven, CT: Yale University Press, 1994.

Montgomery, Michael. *Imperialist Japan: The Yen to Dominate.* New York: St. Martin's Press, 1987.

Nish, Ian Hill. *Japanese Foreign Policy, 1869–1942.* London and Boston: Routledge & Kegan Paul, 1977.

Japanese Invasion of Korea (1592–1598)

The Japanese invasions of Korea describe two campaigns launched against Korea by Toyotomi Hideyoshi (1537–1598), the warlord and hegemon of Japan. Though the Japanese enjoyed initial success on land, Japan's inability to maintain control of the seas, continuous harassment by Korean guerrilla forces, the intervention of Ming Chinese forces, and ultimately, the death of Hideyoshi doomed the invasion to failure.

After gaining control over Japan in the last quarter of the sixteenth century, Hideyoshi turned his sights toward the conquest of China. This had as much to do with a need to occupy Japan's warrior class as with Hideyoshi's own grandiose visions. Such a continental invasion (just as with the Mongol invasions of Japan in the thirteenth century) necessitated the active cooperation of Korea, the closest mainland coast to the Japanese archipelago. Korea refused to collude with Hideyoshi, for geopolitical reality as well as Confucian principles required Korea's loyalty to China. In 1591 Hideyoshi ordered the invasion of Korea as a preliminary to the proposed China conquest.

Hideyoshi delegated leadership to a handful of loyal generals under the command of the Christian Konishi Yukinaga. In spring 1592 a vanguard Japanese force of over 50,000 embarked for the Korean city of Pusan. Though the Korean court had made some preparations for the attack, having received alarming reports of Japanese preparations, the Korean armies were eminently ill prepared to deal with the invasion. After landing with overwhelming force at Pusan the Japanese forces advanced in three prongs northward, making quick progress toward the Korean capital of Seoul. King Sonjo (r. 1567–1608) fled with his royal entourage to the more northern city of Pyongyang. In late spring 1592 Japanese forces captured and burned Seoul. Soon thereafter reinforcements arrived from China via Manchuria, and the land conflict was pushed to stalemate, with Chinese and Korean troops holding around Pyongyang and the Japanese barricaded in and around Seoul.

Meanwhile, Korean guerrilla armies and the navy under admiral Yi Sun-shin (1545–1598) harried Japanese troops and supply lines. Yi defeated the Japanese fleet at Pusan in late 1592, seriously hampering Japan's ability to procure reinforcements and supplies. Konishi agreed to armistice talks, and by 1594 the Japanese had completed their withdrawal from Korea.

Hideyoshi ordered a second invasion in 1597. Once again Hideyoshi chose Konishi to lead the attack. As before, the Japanese armies, numbering almost 150,000, met with initial success, defeating a Chinese army near Ulsan in early 1598. In late 1597, however, the Korean Admiral Yi Sun-shin had again inflicted a heavy blow on the Japanese fleet in the Battle of Myongnyang Straits. The sudden death of Hideyoshi in late 1598 brought the second invasion to an abrupt conclusion.

The invasion inflicted serious damage to the Korean landscape, and the famines and epidemics that resulted were harbingers of popular unrest to come. The cultural damage inflicted by the invaders on temples, official structures, and artifacts was also severe. The expenses and losses suffered during the invasions by China's Ming Dynasty (1368–1644) contributed to that dynasty's overthrow by the Qing (1644–1911) less than 50 years later.

Daniel Kane

See also: Japanese Wars of Unification; Hideyoshi, Toyotomi

References and further reading:

Lum, Peter. *Six Centuries in East Asia: Japan and Korea from the 14th Century to 1912.* New York: S. G. Phillips, 1973.

Turnbull, S. R. "Hideyoshi's Korean War." In S. R. Turnbull, *The Samurai: A Military History.* New York: Macmillan, 1977.

———. *The Samurai: A Military History.* New York: Macmillan, 1977.

Japanese Military, Twentieth Century

The first modern Asian military power. Combining Prussian military theory and traditional warrior values, the Imperial Japanese military had two prime missions: defense of the home islands against Western powers and the unification of the local polities under the new central government. The first campaign of the new Japanese military was the suppression of the Satsuma revolt (1877–1878).

Having defeated the traditional horde fielded by China (1894–1895) and a Russian military in decline (1904–1905), the roots of ultimate Japanese military failure were nonetheless planted during World War I. Lacking direct experience of the fighting in Europe, there was no experience of the traumatic challenges of these campaigns to force the reassessment of received wisdom, the exception being Germany's vulnerability to economic blockade. The ultimate response was conversion of the informal zone of influence in China into a formal empire, leading to the Manchurian Incident (1931) and Japan's political isolation from the liberal West.

Besides deteriorating economic and geopolitical circumstances, the failings of the Meiji constitution were a factor. Active-duty officers held the positions of army and navy ministers and had open access to the emperor. Being a free agent under this system, the military could pull down any given cabinet and arrogated increasing political influence for themselves, culminating with General Hideki Tojo becoming prime minister in October 1941.

Another factor leading to the drive for military political supremacy were political cliques in the army itself, as the so-called Imperial Way and Control factions strove for predominance. The Imperial Way desired the demise of the liberal order of the 1920s and the imposition of direct imperial rule. Meanwhile, the Control faction sought to suppress the political extremists and build up the modern capabilities of the army, in expectation of a coming war with the Soviet Union. By the end of 1936, the Control faction had brought to heel its rival, but the unifying factor for the army remained the drive for a secure economic base on the Asian mainland, particularly as massive resources were poured into the Manchurian and northern Korean industrial base.

As all-out war with China opened in 1937, Japan finally had to face its limitations. Despite the imperial forces' many advantages, the Chinese were still able to muster superior numbers and inflict sobering losses. Further, the Japanese defeat by the Soviet army at Nomonhan taught a direct lesson as to how war had changed in the wake of World War I.

As a result, Tokyo signed a nonaggression pact with Moscow and cultivated a new interest in the Western colonial interests in Southeast Asia, a course of action that brought strategic congruence with the imperial navy.

In choosing war with the West rather than the USSR, Prime Minister Tojo and the army general staff allowed themselves few doubts, in that they believed it was better to lose than not to try. They also hoped that victory would buy the time to create the resources needed to fight the larger war.

Their belief had always been that a well-led and motivated force would be able to overcome either the mass army of a traditional state or the small constabulary armies of the Western colonial powers. In reality, the Japanese military lacked the resources to go up against the modern mass army of a determined state for any length of time, a lesson that could have been learned as early as 1905.

By 1943, every Japanese liability was being ruthlessly exposed. The veneer of modernity created by aircraft and light arms disguised that many structural basics were lacking in the composition of the force. Relative poverty had put an emphasis on doing more with less, but it also inculcated an indifference to questions of intelligence, logistics, and signals.

There were also basic failures to adjust to modern circumstances at the psychological level, as officers continued to consider themselves a social caste and cultivated a theatrical style of leadership. Failing to master the skills of modern military professionals, Japanese staff schools taught advanced infantry tactics instead of preparing Japanese officers to think in operational-level terms. The final result would be an empty force reduced to claiming that superior spirit would defeat the Allies in 1945.

The demise of a Japanese military system was a short-lived development, though. In spite of the new Japanese constitution forswearing war, the North Korean invasion of 1950 forced the creation of the Japanese "Self-Defense" Force.

Starting with the so-called National Police Reserve—created at the direction of General MacArthur's headquarters to replace the American occupation troops deployed to fight in Korea—American officers and Japanese enlisted personnel were formed into new units. Besides the steady infusion of Japanese company and field-grade officers from the former imperial army, the sign that the new force was more than an

Japanese soldiers in action, 1942. (Library of Congress)

emergency extemporization was the creation of the Japanese Defense Academy in 1953. The JDA was an all-services institution designed both to overcome the factionalism of the prewar military and to inculcate a respect for civilian authority and the rule of law in the new officers.

Despite frequent domestic criticism as to its role, the Japanese Self-Defense Force has functioned as a component of the Japanese-American security agreement. Mostly existing to deny an enemy an easy target, it represented a return to the original function of the first modern Japanese military.

George R. Shaner

See also: Hasegawa, Yoshimichi; Japanese Colonial Wars; Khalkin-Gol; Russo-Japanese War; Sino-Japanese War; Terauchi Hisaichi; Yamagata, Aritomo; Yamashita, Tomoyuki; World War II

References and further reading:

Drea, Edward J. *In the Service of the Emperor: Essays on the Imperial Japanese Army.* Lincoln: University of Nebraska Press, 1998.

Humphreys, Leonard A. *The Way of the Heavenly Sword: The Japanese Army in the 1920s.* Stanford, CA: Stanford University Press, 1995.

Maeda, Tetsuo. *The Hidden Army: The Untold Story of Japan's Military Forces.* Chicago: Edition Q, 1995.

Millett, Allan R., and Williamson Murray. *Military Effectiveness.* 3 vols. Boston: Allen & Unwin, 1988.

Japanese Wars of Unification (1550–1615)

The years from about 1550, with the introduction into Japan of Western firearms, to the siege of Osaka Castle in 1615 by the forces of the shogun Ieyasu Tokugawa, were the final act in an extended period of armed struggle in Japan, going back to the early fifteenth century. It was during these approximately 75 years that three military leaders would emerge to forge a unified Japan: Nobunaga Oda (1534–1582), Toyotomi Hideyoshi (1536–1598), and Ieyasu Tokugawa (1542–1616). It would end with the victory of Ieyasu and the unchallenged hegemony of the Tokugawa Shogunate he established and usher in a period of unprecedented centralized power in Japan.

The year 1549 saw the beginning of regular contact between foreign, which is to say Catholic, missionaries and the Japanese. The Japanese reaction to Western Christianity aside, it was the Western introduction of firearms, in the form of the arquebus and cannon, that was to prove revolutionary and instrumental in reshaping the Japanese political landscape. By 1560 they were being used in battle, and it was the richer and more powerful local lords, or daimyo, who could afford them who would benefit most.

The Ashikaga Shogunate (1338–1573) had from its establishment proved lacking in central authority. Its founder Ashikaga Takauji was but one among a group of powerful military leaders vying for control. Indeed, the Ashikaga government ruled through a system of delegating authority in the provinces to constabularies, usually powerful military leaders loyal to the Ashikaga, who in return for their formal recognition of Ashikaga supremacy were granted almost total control over provincial domains. The central authority of the Ashikaga house, already delicate, was further weakened in the fifteenth century by civil wars between varying claimants to the shogunate. The Onin War (1467–1477) ushered in a period of more vigorous and ruthless warfare between local military leaders, who with Ashikaga weakness had begun to consolidate their individual power and private loyalties and to expand territorially. These local military leaders were for the most part no longer related to the officially sanctioned constabulary of the earlier Ashikaga. They were local military men who had risen to the top by dint of their ruthlessness, cunning, and military abilities. By the late fifteenth century the Ashikaga shoguns were reduced to insignificant bystanders in a contest between these powerful and autonomous local military lords, or daimyo. This so-called Period of Warring States (Sengoku jidai), from approximately 1467 to 1568, may have been fought into a stalemate, but the introduction of Western firearms proved decisive.

In 1568 a young man named Nobunaga Oda, then the heir to a daimyo around Kyoto, seized Kyoto, the capital of the Ashikaga, eventually overthrowing the last Ashikaga shogun in 1573 (an act in itself that garnished little attention, such had the Ashikaga fortunes fallen). In a close working alliance with another regional daimyo, Ieyasu Tokugawa, Oda set about consolidating the central region of Japan under his control. This meant eliminating many of the powerful Buddhist sects that had come to play prominent political roles through their alliances with rival families. In a battle with the Takeda clan of central Honshu in 1575 (Nagashino), Oda became the first military leader to rely primarily on muskets in battle, soundly defeating his foe. Oda's assassination at the hands of one of his own vassals in 1582 put a premature end to his efforts at reunification.

Oda typifies the type of man who could rise to prominence in the chaos of the Warring States period. He owed much of his success to the sheer will of his ambition and the ruthless means he was prepared to employ to augment and preserve his power. Such were the characteristics of his successor as well.

One of Oda's most able generals was Toyotomi Hideyoshi, a man who had risen from the most humble origins as a peasant's son. It was while fighting the forces of the Mori family in western Honshu for Oda that he heard of his master's assassination. Hurrying back to Kyoto, Hideyoshi quickly eliminated his rivals (including Oda's own son) to establish himself as successor. Gaining recognition as Oda's successor within Oda's coalition of daimyo, Hideyoshi then set about expanding his territorial control. His most powerful rival was perhaps Ieyasu Tokugawa, established in central Honshu. But in 1584, after an indecisive battle, Tokugawa had opted to swear fealty to Hideyoshi. Through marriages the Hideyoshi and Tokugawa clans were brought closer together and in 1590 Tokugawa aided Hideyoshi in his campaigns against the Hojo clan in the Kanto region around Edo (modern Tokyo). In return for his support, with the defeat of the Hojo Tokugawa was granted an immense swath of their former domains, transferring Tokugawa's power base north to Edo.

By 1590 Hideyoshi had succeeded in subduing, through battle or otherwise, all the rival daimyo. Though he was now in the position to name himself shogun, Hideyoshi deferred, perhaps recognizing the aristocratic pedigree that position had customarily held. Rather, he satisfied himself with the titles of regent *(kampaku)* in 1585 and then chancellor *(dajo daijin)* in 1586. Hideyoshi's domestic policies went far in establishing central authority. To quell disturbances in the countryside, he issued orders forbidding peasants from leaving the land, and he had their weapons confiscated. To eliminate daimyo rivalry, he forbade alliances between them without his approval, whether marital, military, or political. Seeing Western Christianity as a potential threat to central authority, in 1587 he ordered all foreign missionaries out of Japan. Though only sporadically enforced under Hideyoshi, this would later become strict policy under Tokugawa.

When Hideyoshi died in 1598 he left only an infant son, Hideyori, as heir. To govern, Hideyoshi had arranged for a coregency of five powerful daimyo to rule during Hideyori's minority. The most powerful of these daimyo-regents was Tokugawa. When it became clear that Tokugawa was acting as nominal ruler above the other coregents a coalition soon rose up against him, led by one of Hideyoshi's former vassals Ishida Mitsunari (1560–1600). Gathering a coalition of other daimyo around him, primarily from the western regions of Japan, Mitsunari eventually met the forces of Tokugawa at the battle of Sekigahara in central Honshu in 1600. Tokugawa's victory secured his position as hegemon. In 1603 Tokugawa named himself shogun, establishing the Tokugawa Shogunate (1603–1868) based at the Tokugawa capital of Edo. A final rally by the forces still loyal to Hideyoshi, who had lost at Sekigahara, occurred in 1614, briefly threatening the young Tokugawa government. When thousands of masterless samurai rallied to the side of the young Hideyori, now ensconced in the family castle at Osaka, Tokugawa sent a large force against them, eventually overcoming the castle defenses in 1615, putting an end to the Hideyori threat.

The establishment of the Tokugawa government was to usher in a period of unprecedented peace and central authority that would last until well into the nineteenth century. Tokugawa went to great lengths to further the power of the Tokugawa government by expanding and augmenting the domestic policies of Hideyoshi. The Tokugawa systematically eliminated those daimyo who were thought untrustworthy by confiscating their holdings. An "alternate attendance system" (*sankinkotai*), whereby the daimyo were forced to reside part of the year at Edo and to leave family members there permanently as hostages, further ensured daimyo loyalty. Oaths of loyalty were also administered to all daimyo, in which they pledged to aid the shogun in times of trouble. As before, the daimyo were forbidden from concluding alliances, or even from building castles or bridges, without the express consent of the shogunal government. And the threat from abroad, which in many ways had ushered in the unification of Japan, was eliminated when Japan began to seal itself off from the outside from 1635. All foreign contact was soon reduced to the small island of Deshima in Nagasaki harbor.

Daniel Kane

See also: Hideyoshi, Toyotomi; Nagashino, Battle of; Oda, Nobunaga; Osaka Castle, Siege of; Samurai; Sekigahara; Tokugawa, Ieyasu

References and further reading:

Hall, John Whitney, et al., eds. *Cambridge History of Japan*. Volume 4: *Early Modern Japan*. Cambridge, UK: Cambridge University Press, 1988.

Jansen, Marius B. *The Making of Modern Japan*. Cambridge, MA: Harvard University Press, 2000.

Sadler, A. L. *The Maker of Modern Japan: The Life of Tokugawa Ieyasu*. Tokyo: Charles E. Tuttle, Co. 1937.

Java War (1825–1830)

The last instance of armed resistance to the Dutch colonial regime by the aristocrats of Java and an inspiration to future generations of Indonesian nationalists who celebrated it as a patriotic struggle uniting noble and commoner alike. Essentially a guerrilla conflict, villagers of central Java accounted for most of the 200,000 casualties due to combat, disease, and starvation (the island's total population in 1830 was around 7 million).

The British occupation of Java during 1811–1816 caused great unrest, particularly in the old, semiautonomous kingdoms of central Java, Yogyakarta, and Surakarta. Conditions were not improved by Dutch attempts to reassert their weakened authority after the British returned the East Indies to them in 1816. Their governor-general passed a decree, highly unpopular with the nobles, that prohibited them from leasing their land to European and Chinese planters. Rebellion broke out in July 1825. Its leader was the charismatic Pangeran Dipanagara (1785–1855), eldest son of the Yogyakarta sultan who had been promised, then denied, the throne.

Dipanagara united in himself diverse strands of Javanese culture: Islam (the theme of holy war against the Dutch infidels), Javanese mysticism (he meditated in sacred caves and claimed the Goddess of the Southern Ocean came to him in a vision), and the royal traditions of the Mataram Dynasty, which had fought against, then been subjugated by, the Dutch in the seventeenth and eighteenth centuries. Common people as well as nobles were attracted to these appeals, and the Dutch found themselves hard-pressed to reimpose control, especially in Yogyakarta.

By implementing the *bentengstelsel* (fortress system), the Dutch matched the speed and flexibility of Dipanagara's guerrillas through the construction of a network of fortified points linked by roads, where they posted mobile columns. These could strike quickly, before local resistance organized. By 1827–1828, the course of the war turned against Dipanagara. He was imprisoned by the Dutch while conducting negotiations with them in March 1830 and exiled to the eastern island of Sulawesi.

The Java War taught the Dutch the need for brutal, grassroots policing of the villages and the wisdom of co-opting the old nobility. Many central Java aristocrats, including the ruler of Surakarta, chose to back the Dutch against the rebels. After 1830, they evolved into a parasitic class who prospered while Javanese farmers were ground down by Holland's increasingly harsh policies of economic exploitation.

Donald M. Seekins

See also: Dutch Colonial Wars

Javanese Wars of Succession (1685–1755)

Three wars that increased the dominance of the Dutch East India Company. The Dutch, through the power of the Vereenigde Oost-Indische (VOC, Dutch East India Company), intruded on the affairs of Javanese rulers in the East Indies.

The first war began in 1685 with the organization of a rebellion against the Dutch by a former VOC soldier, Surapati (or Untung), a former slave and outlaw. His followers killed officials who had rebelled against the authority of the central Javanese kingdom of Mataram. The grateful king of Mataram, Susuhunan Amangkurat II (1677–1703), granted Surapati refuge. Upon Amangkurat II's death in 1703 the Dutch supported a rival claimant to the throne, Amangkurat's uncle Pakubuwono (1704–1719). Surapati eventually claimed kingship over the northeastern part of Java. War continued until Surapati died in 1706 of battle wounds. Susuhunan Amangkurat III (1703–1708) surrendered all of his possessions, became a prisoner of war, and was exiled to Ceylon.

The second war erupted when Susuhunan Pakubuwono I died in 1719. The claims of numerous princes instigated war. The Dutch again intervened and gave support to whoever upheld their endeavors. Four years of fighting led to all the rival claimants and Surapati's descendants being captured by VOC forces and sent into exile. The Dutch extended their control in Java.

During the third war Mataram became a vassal of the Dutch East India Company. Susuhunan Pakubuwono III (1749–1788) received Dutch military support against two challengers. In 1751 the Dutch were seriously defeated and lost their commander. The 13 February 1755 Gianti Agreement, agreed upon by one challenger, split Mataram in two. The eastern region of Pakubuwono had its capital at Surakarta with Susuhunan Pakubuwono III as king. The western region made Yogyakarta its capital with Sultan Hamengkubuwono I (1749–1792) as its ruler. The VOC retained control over the northern provinces. Ultimately, the VOC militarily expanded its power to gain commercial supremacy over the region.

Annette Richardson

References and further reading:

Boxer, C. R. *The Dutch Seaborne Empire, 1600–1800.* Harmondsworth, Middlesex, UK: Penguin Books, 1990.

Greig, Doreen. *The Reluctant Colonists. Netherlanders Abroad in the 17th and 18th Centuries.* Assen, Netherlands: Van Gorcum, 1987.

Israel, J. *The Dutch Primacy in the World Trade 1585–1740.* Oxford, UK: Clarendon Press, 1989.

Jayavarman VII (r. 1181–c. 1220)

One of the greatest kings of Cambodia's Angkor period (802–1431). Jayavarman VII is best known today for his construction of the temple city of Angkor Thom, the mysterious Bayon temple decorated with huge, enigmatic faces of the Bodhisattva Avalokitesvara, and the temple-monastery of Ta Prohm, dedicated to his mother. He is also remembered as a fervent patron of Mahayana Buddhism who broke with Angkor's Hindu traditions of aloof, godlike kingship and devoted himself to good works in order to relieve the suffering of his subjects. For their benefit, he built hundreds of hospitals, rest houses, and roads.

To his contemporaries, however, Jayavarman VII was probably best known as a military leader. In the late twelfth century, the Angkor empire was one of the strongest states in mainland Southeast Asia but was vulnerable to the aggression of its eastern neighbor, the coastal state of Champa (located in what is now central Vietnam). In 1177, a Cham naval expedition sailing up the Mekong and Tonle Sap Rivers to the Tonle Sap (Great Lake) captured the Cambodian capital (near the modern town of Siem Reap), putting the Cambodian king to death and carrying away huge amounts of booty and slaves. During 1178–1181, Jayavarman drove the Chams out of his homeland, becoming king in 1181, and invaded Champa in 1190, making it a province of the Angkor Empire in 1203–1220. His realm also encompassed much of modern Laos, the northern Malay Peninsula, and the Menam Valley in Thailand.

Bas-reliefs in the Bayon temple depict Cambodian and Cham armies fighting on land and water and grim vignettes such as Cambodian soldiers displaying the severed heads of their enemies, artistic testimony to the savagery of war.

Donald M. Seekins

References and further reading:

Chandler, David P. *A History of Cambodia.* 2d ed. Boulder, CO: Westview Press, 1992.

Coedes, G. *The Making of South East Asia.* Berkeley: University of California Press, 1969.

Freeman, Michael, and Claude Jacques. *Ancient Angkor.* Bangkok: Asia Books, 1999.

Jena and Auerstädt (13–14 October 1806)

Decisive simultaneous French victories that cleared Napoleon's way to Berlin. After Napoleon created the Confederation of the Rhine on 12 July 1806 to bring the German states under French control, and after Emperor Francis II dissolved the Holy Roman Empire on 6 August, only Prussia, some Saxon states, and Russia continued to resist Napoleon. In October Napoleon deployed 148,500 French against 111,500 Prussians and Saxons under King Frederick William III in the Saale Valley, Thuringia, Germany.

On 13 October François Joseph Lefebvre's 15,000 Imperial Guard infantry occupied Jena and Napoleon inspected the town. Jean Baptiste Jules Bernadotte's I Corps, with 20,000 men, was just south of Naumburg. Louis-Nicolas Davout's III Corps, with 26,000, was at Kösen, between Naumburg and Auerstädt. Nicolas-Jean de Dieu Soult's 18,000 in IV Corps were evenly divided between Jena and Eisenberg. Jean Lannes's V Corps had 20,500 a mile north of Jena. Michel Ney, southeast of Jena, sent 4,500 of his VI Corps to Jena and the remaining 15,000 to Roda. Pierre François Charles Augereau, southeast of Jena with 16,500, separated his VII Corps into thirds, northwest toward Jena, east-southeast toward the Saale, and west toward Magdala. Joachim Murat split his cavalry reserves, 6,000 east of Bernadotte, 7,000 southeast of Ney.

Karl William Ferdinand, Duke of Brunswick, led 63,500 Prussians east toward Auerstädt. Friedrich Ludwig Hohenlohe, commanding 35,000 Saxons and Prussians northwest of Jena, just beyond Lannes, deployed southwest and northeast. Ernst Friedrich Wilhelm Philipp von Rüchel kept 13,000 infantry in reserve at Weimar.

In the midmorning of 14 October, Brunswick and Davout engaged frontally halfway between Auerstädt and Kösen. Brunswick failed to exploit his superior numbers. Davout used artillery, then seized an opportunity to sweep one division around to crush Brunswick's right. Brunswick was mortally wounded. Soon the French were able to create the classic pincer attack, routing the Prussians back through Auerstädt and southwest.

Meanwhile, Bernadotte and his portion of Murat's cavalry hurried southwest to check Hohenlohe's left flank. Lannes held the center while Soult attacked Hohenlohe's left and Augereau his right. Murat made random assaults. Napoleon took full advantage of the various skills of his generals to deploy his troops in diverse, flexible formations to confuse and entrap the Germans. Hohenlohe's conservative tactics could not counter these swift maneuvers. Soult and Lannes had routed their enemy by midafternoon. Augereau mastered first Hohenlohe's Saxons, then Rüchel's reinforcements.

The French lost 6,000 at Jena and 7,100 at Auerstädt. German casualties were 12,000 killed or wounded and 15,000 taken prisoner at Jena, 10,000 killed or wounded and 3,000 taken prisoner at Auerstädt, plus 20,000 more taken prisoner within the week.

Eric v. d. Luft

See also: Bernadotte, Jean Baptiste Jules; Blücher, Gebhard Leberecht von; Brunswick, Frederick William, Duke of; Clausewitz, Karl Maria von; Davout, Louis-Nicolas, Duke of Auerstädt, Prince of Eckmühl; Lannes, Jean, Duke of Montebello; Murat, Joachim, Grand Duke of Cleves-Berg, King of Naples; Napoleon I; Napoleonic Wars; Ney, Michel, Duc d'Elchingen, Prince de La Moskova; Scharnhorst, Gerhard Johann von; Soult, Nicolas-Jean de Dieu

References and further reading:

Chandler, David G. *Jena 1806: Napoleon Destroys Prussia.* London: Osprey Military, 1993.

Hourtoulle, F. G. *Jena-Auerstaedt: The Triumph of the Eagle.* Trans. Alan McKay. Paris: Histoire & Collections, 1998.

Maude, F. N. *The Jena Campaign, 1806.* London: Greenhill, 1998.

Petre, F. Loraine. *Napoleon's Conquest of Prussia, 1806.* London: Greenhill, 1993.

Jericho, Siege of (1400? B.C.E.)

One of the oldest cities, and probably the most ancient walled settlement on earth, made famous by the biblical account of its siege and destruction. Emerging from their years of wandering in the Sinai, the tribes of Israel needed to establish a beachhead west of the Jordan River to facilitate their invasion and conquest of Canaanite territory. The most obvious site was Jericho. From this oasis, they could advance into the Judean hills. Men sent ahead to gather intelligence and reconnoiter the city stopped at the inn run by Rahab "the harlot" and learned that the people of Jericho were demoralized by the news of the Israelites' defeat of two Amorite kings.

Joshua, given supreme command by the leaders of the tribes, crossed the Jordan River with the help of a minor earthquake, which temporarily dammed the river, a phenomenon seen as recently as 1927. Although the biblical story attributes the fall of Jericho to the walls actually falling because of the blasts from Joshua's trumpet, the real story may be far simpler and militarily plausible. Encamped around the city, whose walls may have been damaged in the earthquake or in poor repair, the Israelite army in full battle dress marched around the city every day for six days, parading the Ark of the Covenant before their troops. This provoked the response of the city's defenders, who, by the seventh day, tired of the false alarms and relaxed their vigilant defense. Joshua led the troops in assaulting the walls, leading to the surrender of the city. Immediately settling the area with trustworthy tribesmen and their families, Joshua had secured a base for supply and further operations as he moved into the second stage of his conquest.

Margaret Sankey

See also: Ancient Warfare

References and further reading:
Herzog, Chaim, and Mordechai Gichon. *Battles of the Bible.* New York: Random House, 1978.
Kenyon, Kathleen Mary. *Digging Up Jericho.* New York: Praeger, 1957.

Jerusalem, Siege of (Palestine) (1099)

On 7 June 1099, the members of the First Crusade encamped before the walls of Jerusalem, the future capital of the Latin Kingdom of Jerusalem. After years of hardship they had reached their goal, although to enter the city the crusaders had to defeat the Fatamid governor, Iftikhar al-Dawla, and his garrison of Arab and Sudanese troops. To prevent treachery, Iftikhar al-Dawla sent the Christian population outside the city.

Due to Jerusalem's immense size, the crusaders could not invest it completely. They also faced a shortage of water and food. The Fatamid garrison, on the other hand, though numerous and well armed, could not man the entire wall. They hoped for the arrival of a relief army from Egypt.

On 13 June 1099, the crusaders attempted an assault. This quickly overran the outer walls, but due to insufficient siege weapons and ladders to continue the assault, they retreated. In order to build siege engines the crusaders endured skirmishes while securing lumber from as far away as Lebanon. Morale also declined as news of the approach of a Fatamid army circulated in their camp.

Raymond of Toulouse and the other leaders realized that time was short. With approximately 14,000 soldiers, they assaulted Jerusalem in the middle of the night on 13 July 1099. On 15 July 1099, the crusaders seized a portion of the wall. The crusaders stormed the city through this breach. Iftikhar al-Dawla realized he had lost Jerusalem and surrendered to Raymond. The rest of the Muslim and Jewish population was massacred, even those who took refuge in mosques and synagogues.

Despite petty jealousies throughout the leadership of the crusade, the capture of Jerusalem culminated in the establishment of the Kingdom of Jerusalem, which lasted as a Latin presence in the Holy Land for almost 200 years.

Timothy May

See also: Crusades; Religion and War

References and further reading:
Holt, P. M. *The Age of the Crusades.* London: Longman Group, 1990.
Mayer, Hans Eberhard. *The Crusades.* Oxford, UK: Oxford University Press, 1988.
Runciman, Steven. *A History of the Crusades.* Vol 1. Cambridge, UK: Cambridge University Press, 1951.
Riley-Smith, Jonathan. *The Crusades: A Short History.* New Haven, CT: Yale University Press, 1987.

Jewish Revolts (66–135)

Two major Jewish rebellions against the Romans.

66–73 Revolt (the Zealots Revolt)

Upon arriving as Roman procurator of Judea in 64, Gessius Florus immediately encountered political crises. In Caesarea Maritima, the major Roman seaport of Judea, Florus angered Jews by siding with Greeks during intercommunal rioting. In Jerusalem, he angered Jews by seizing the payment of a large fine from the Temple treasury because Jewish payment of taxes was in arrears. When rioting erupted there, Florus's reprisals were brutal. In order to defuse talk of rebellion, King Agrippa II, the Jewish puppet ruler of Judea, argued that subordination to Rome was no shame and warned that no foreign power, particularly Parthia, would intervene on behalf of the Jews. Indeed, King Vologases I of Parthia agreed to a pact of friendship with Rome in 66. And, despite widespread opposition to Roman rule, the Jews were not united.

Eleazar ben Ananias, guardian of the Temple, prohibited sacrifices by foreigners. This was, in effect, an act of rebellion because it rudely ended the daily sacrifices on behalf of Rome and the emperor. Eleazar then seized control of the Temple, the Lower City, and the Upper City. Soon Jewish forces led by Menachem ben Judas captured the Dead Sea fortress of Masada from a small Roman garrison. By September 66, the Romans had been pushed from most areas of Judea. Cestius Gallus, the Syrian governor, marched a legion and 6,000 auxiliaries into Judea and pacified the Galilee in October. He then marched on Jerusalem but was repulsed and harassed into a humiliating retreat through the area of Beit-Horon around Jerusalem. The Jews' early successes were impressive but short-lived. The Jewish rebels in Jerusalem soon became overconfident and divisive. Eleazar sanctioned the murder of Menachem, and Eleazar himself was soon deposed and sent to command a small force in Idumaea.

In the spring of 67, Emperor Nero dispatched Titus Flavius Vespasianus (Vespasian) to Judea with two legions. Joined by a third legion commanded by his son, Titus, Vespasian now commanded a force of 60,000 and laid siege to Jotapata in the Galilee. After 47 days, the Jewish commander Yosef ben Mattitias (Josephus) surrendered, becoming the Romans' official historian. Instead of advancing directly upon Jerusalem, Vespasian cautiously spent the next three years suppressing revolt in cities like Tiberias, Gischala, and Gamala. Vespasian could afford delay, because violent disunity was destroying Jews in Jerusalem as effectively as Rome's legions. Vespasian returned to Italy in order to become emperor, following Nero's assassination, and left Titus in command of the Judean legions. Titus marched on

Jerusalem in the spring of 70 and captured the Temple in early August. (The Jewish fast day on the Ninth of Av laments this catastrophe.) Roman victory was inevitable despite the resistance of Eleazar ben Ya'ir at the fortress of Masada. Flavius Silva led a siege of three years, which finally captured the fortress in 73, whereupon the defenders committed suicide. In June 71, Titus held a triumph in Rome, where the Arch of Titus was erected next to the Forum to commemorate his victory.

The 132–135 Revolt (Bar Kochba's Revolt)

After the Roman Emperor Hadrian (Publius Aelius Hadrianus) banned circumcision and changed the name of Jerusalem to Aelia Capitolina (named after Hadrian himself), Judea rebelled against Roman rule. The Second Jewish Revolt was well planned in secret and ably led by a messianic figure named Shimon bar Kosiva (later bar Kochba). In the fall of 132, bar Kochba seized Jerusalem from its small garrison, expelled Tineius Rufus, Judea's consular governor, and struck coins in commemoration of the victory. Although the exact course of the rebellion is obscure, it appears that bar Kochba's forces used guerrilla tactics rather than engage the Romans in open field combat. The Jews enjoyed a number of early successes. In 133, Hadrian sent eight legions, commanded by the able Sextus Julius Severus, who employed a strategy of attrition against the Jews. Unable to draw bar Kochba into open combat, Severus surrounded strongholds and starved out the rebels. Despite this strategy, the Romans suffered significant losses. For example, almost an entire legion was killed with poisoned wine, and many thousands more were killed by the Jews' guerrilla attacks. In the spring of 135, after a two-year-long siege, the Romans captured the fortress of Betar, the last refuge of bar Kochba, who was killed in the battle. As punishment for the rebellion, the Romans changed the name of Judea to Palestine and expelled most of the Jews into the diaspora, into what amounted to an exile of over 1,800 years.

Eric D. Pullin

See also: Hadrian; Josephus, Flavius; Masada, Siege of; Parthian Empire; Vespasian

References and further reading:

Grant, Michael. *The Jews in the Roman World.* New York: Scribner, 1973.

Josephus, Flavius. *The Jewish War.* New York: Penguin, 1981.

Tacitus, Cornelius. *The Complete Works of Tacitus.* New York: Modern Library, 1942.

Portrait of Joan of Arc. (Library of Congress)

Joan of Arc (Jeanne d'Arc) (1412–1430)

Patron saint of soldiers and probably most famous female military commander in history. Jeanne d'Arc was probably born on 6 January 1412 in Domremy, Champagne, France. At age 12, she claimed to hear voices and have visions informing her of her mission to restore the dauphin, Charles Valois, later Charles VII, to the French throne and rid the country of English occupation and their Burgundian allies. In February 1429, she met with the dauphin and his commander, Robert de Baudricourt, and somehow convinced them of her mandate.

Dressed in male garb and examined by clergy, Joan was awarded the rank of captain and given command of a small army at Blois. She led her army to the besieged city of Orleans in May. A few days after her arrival, while her army marched to the city by a northern route, citizens armed themselves and took the weakest of 10 Norman/English blockhouses by coup de main. On 7–8 May 1429, she led her troops on a series of successful sorties against the enemy, causing them to retreat. While other advisers wanted to attack Normandy, she made the decision to march upon Rheims.

In the Loire campaign, beginning with the fall of Jargeau on 10 June, she mastered the use and placement of artillery.

At the Battle of Patay, on 18 June, the French defeated the Norman/English under Sir John Fastolfe and Lord Talbot, with 1,800 English soldiers lost. Retreating to Paris, French forces had a clear road to Rheims. On 16 July, Charles entered the city and was crowned king the next day.

In the spring of 1430, Joan was captured by Burgundians at Compiegne, near Paris, in a failed sortie. Sold to the English, she was put on trial by the ecclesiastical court at Rouen. On 30 May 1431, she was burned at the stake in the marketplace after being convicted of heresy and witchcraft. Canonized in 1920, her moral importance to the French during the Hundred Years War has been stressed by historians, but her abilities as a military commander have often been overlooked. Nonetheless, Joan of Arc became almost immediately after her death a symbol, a veritable icon, of the spirit of France.

T. Jason Soderstrum

See also: Hundred Years War
References and further reading:

DeVries, Kelly. *Joan of Arc: A Military Leader.* Stroud, UK: Sutton, 1999.
Giles, France. *Joan of Arc: The Legend and the Reality.* New York: Harper & Row, 1981.
Smith, John Holland. *Joan of Arc.* London: Sidgewick & Jackson, 1973.

Jodl, Alfred (1890–1946)

Hitler's most important military adviser during World War II. Born 10 May 1890 at Würzburg (Bavaria), Jodl married Irma von Bullion (d. 1943) in 1913 and Luise von Benda in 1944 but had no children. He entered military service at the age of 13 and was promoted to lieutenant in 1912. He took part in World War I and joined Reichswehr in 1919, held several commands, and was promoted to general major in 1939.

Called back to Berlin he took over Wehrmachtführungsstab, the operation staff within Wehrmacht High Command (OKW). Nominally subordinated to Wilhelm Keitel as chief of OKW, he worked largely on his own, having permanent access to Hitler. After the invasion of Russia (June 1941) Jodl's staff was responsible for every theater of war except the eastern front. His duty was to prepare reports on strategic questions, to participate in the daily briefings (more than 5,000 during the war), and to transmit Hitler's directives. Working very hard, he hardly left the führer's headquarters to visit the front. Frictions with Hitler culminated in autumn 1942, but Jodl held his job. No successor was at hand and Hitler valued Jodl's competence, diligence, and admiration for him. He was promoted to general colonel in January 1944.

On 22 April 1945 Jodl left Berlin and joined Grand Admiral Karl Dönitz's staff in northern Germany. His final duty was to sign the German surrender at Reims, 7 May 1945.

Soviet demands led to his arraignment at the Nuremberg trial of the major German/Nazi leaders. Confronted with numerous criminal orders bearing his signature, he argued that as a German officer he had to obey Hitler's directives. The court did not believe that he, staying in daily contact with the dictator, could have failed to notice events and orders bearing on war crimes. Found guilty, he was hanged on 16 October 1946.

Questions as to whether Jodl deserved the death penalty arose among the Nuremberg judges and are still current among historians.

Martin Moll

See also: Hitler, Adolf; Keitel, Wilhelm; World War II
References and further reading:

Scheurig, Bodo. *Alfred Jodl. Gehorsam und Verhängnis.* Schnellbach: Bublies, 1999.

Joffre, Joseph Jacques Césaire (1852–1931)

French marshal. Born on 12 January 1852, at Rivesaltes, Joseph Joffre interrupted his studies at the École Polytechnique to serve in the 1870–1871 Franco-Prussian War. He resumed his studies after the war and on graduation was stationed in the Far East and Madagascar. He led an expedition to Timbuktu (Africa) in 1893 and served as a fortifications specialist in Madagascar during 1900–1905. He joined the Supreme War Council in 1910 and became chief of the general staff and commander in chief designate the next year.

At the outbreak of World War I, Joffre's War Plan XVII, intended to secure Alsace-Lorraine, failed to anticipate the main German deployment through Belgium because he was convinced the Germans would not use their reserves on the front lines. Following the defeat of the French offensive and the development of the German threat to the north, he skillfully redeployed his assets and conducted a fighting retreat to the Marne.

Joffre orchestrated the Battle of the Marne, 5–11 September 1914. It ended in a German withdrawal and was the high point of his career. Joffre's major offensives of 1915 and 1916, including Champagne, Somme, and Artois, were failures. He justified these as serving to convince Italy to join the Entente and to take pressure off Russia.

Joffre fell under severe criticism, especially when the February 1916 German offensive at Verdun caught him by surprise and with French defenses unready. He was also blamed for the Romanian disaster later that year. Removed as commander of French forces on the western front in December 1916, he was made marshal of France and named technical adviser to the government. Joffre then headed the French military mission to the United States in 1917, retiring after the war. He died in Paris on 3 January 1931.

Spencer C. Tucker

See also: Foch, Ferdinand; French Army; Pétain, Henri-Philippe; World War I

References and further reading:

Porch, Douglas. *The March to the Marne. The French Army, 1871–1914.* Cambridge, UK: Cambridge University Press, 1981.
Varillon, Pierre. *Joffre.* Paris: Arthème Fayard, 1956.
Williamson, Samuel R., Jr. *The Politics of Grand Strategy; Britain and France Prepare for War, 1904–1914.* Cambridge, MA: Harvard University Press, 1969.

John I Tzimisces (924–976)

Byzantine general and emperor. Tzimisces began his career as an officer in the Byzantine forces commanded by his uncle, Nicephorus Phocas. In 956, he served as strategus of Mesopotamia, with little success. In 958, he led a raid into southern Armenia, and in 962 he accompanied his uncle in a very successful invasion of Syria. In 963, he encouraged Phocas to stage a coup against Joseph Bringas, an official in the court of the recently deceased Romanus II Porphyrogenitus. As a result of this coup, Nicephorus married the empress Theophano, widow of Romanus, and became coemperor with her two minor children.

Tzimisces was rewarded with the title Domestic of the Scholae, essentially commander of the Byzantine army in Anatolia. He held this position for less than two years before being dismissed and replaced with another nephew of the emperor, Peter Phocas the Eunuch, who was deemed to pose no danger to the regime.

In December 969 Tzimisces entered into a conspiracy to murder Nicephorus, having been encouraged in this by the empress Theophano. The conspiracy succeeded, and Tzimisces took part personally in the murder of his uncle. Crowned coemperor, Tzimisces exiled all of the members of the Phocas clan, except for Peter the Eunuch, whose services he retained. Tzimisces also sent the empress Theophano to a convent.

Shortly thereafter, Rus forces under Svyatoslav, Prince of Kiev, invaded Bulgaria, took Preslav, and captured the Bulgarian royal family. A further Rus advance, into Byzantine territory, was defeated by imperial troops sent by Tzimisces and commanded by Bardas Sclerus. It is possible that some sort of treaty was agreed to at this time between the empire and the Rus. Although Tzimisces was preparing a further expedition against the Rus in 970, he was diverted from his purpose by a further revolt of the Phocas clan, which he suppressed.

In spring 971, Tzimisces was finally ready to attack the Rus. He found the passes into Bulgaria unguarded. The Byzantine forces moved quickly to Preslav, where they destroyed most of the Rus army. A siege of Preslav allowed Tzimisces to capture the Bulgar royal family, whom he imprisoned in Constantinople. The Byzantines then discovered that Svyatolav had gone to Dristra, which the Byzantines besieged until 24 June, when the remaining Rus were captured after an attempt to break out of the town. Svyatoslav and his followers were released and, for the most part, were massacred by the Petchenegs while attempting to return home.

Tzimisces was thus free to turn his attention back to the Arab frontier. An expedition to Baghdad was contemplated in 972 or 973 but never launched. In 974, Byzantine forces marched through Armenia, securing that kingdom as a client state and a recruiting ground. In 975, the emperor marched into Syria, Lebanon, and Palestine, taking Homs, Damascus, Beirut, Sidon, Tiberias, and Nazareth. Pockets of opposition forced Tzimisces to turn back and prevented him from capturing Jerusalem. At the end of the campaign, the emperor fell ill and returned to Constantinople, dying on 10 January 976, shortly after his arrival.

Tzimisces recovered territory lost to the Byzantines and revitalized the army. At the same time, his failure to leave an heir, his suppression of the Phocas family, and his promotion of other families to supplant the Phocas clan created factions within the army, which would shortly cause a civil war over the succession.

Joseph M. Isenberg

See also: Byzantine-Muslim Wars; Nicephorus II Phocas

References and further reading:

Fine, John V. A. *The Early Medieval Balkans.* Ann Arbor: University of Michigan Press, 1991.
Norwich, John Julius. *Byzantium: The Apogee.* New York: Knopf, 1991.
Wittrow, Mark. *The Making of Byzantium, 600–1025.* Berkeley: University of California Press, 1996.

John II Comnenus (1088–1143)

Byzantine emperor, son of Alexius I Comnenus. John II succeeded to the throne upon the death of his father in 1118. He was initially forced to deal with efforts by his mother, sister, and brother-in-law to overthrow him, but by 1119 he felt secure enough to cancel the trading privileges of Venice in Byzantium, which provoked a war, and to attack Turkish strongholds in the Meander valley.

John II's campaigns against the Turks in 1119 and 1120 proved successful. He recaptured Laodicea and Sozopolis and separated the Turkish sultanate of Iconium from the Turkish settlements in Caria. A Pecheneg and Cuman invasion in 1121 forced John to divert his attention from the Anatolian Turks. He negotiated with the invaders in 1121 and in 1122 launched a surprise attack upon the nomads. He defeated the Petchenegs and Cumans, enlisting some, while enslaving others. The war with Venice proved less fortunate, as the Venetians quickly overran several Aegean islands. John, having disbanded the Byzantine navy as a cost-saving measure, settled the dispute with the restoration of Venetian trading privileges.

In the autumn of 1127, the Hungarian king, Istvan II, attacked the Byzantine Empire, which had given refuge to a rival claimant to the Hungarian throne. The Hungarians sacked Belgrade, Nish, Sardica, and Philippopolis (Plovdiv) before being forced to withdraw. In 1128, John attacked the Hungarians and defeated them at Sirmium. Nevertheless, the Hungarians reinvaded Byzantine territory and incited a rebellion among the Serbians of Raska. John defeated the Serb rebellion and was able to negotiate a peace with the Hungarians upon the death of the offending claimant.

In 1130, John began a series of campaigns against the Turks. The first campaign ended suddenly, when John's brother, Issac, defected to the Turks. A campaign in 1132 was more successful, with the Byzantine forces ravaging considerable territory. In 1135, John captured the fortresses of Castamon and Gangra. John then turned his attention to forcing the crusader principality of Antioch into vassalage, which he accomplished in 1137. An attempt to seize Aleppo in 1138 failed.

From 1139 to 1141, John recovered the Black Sea coast of Anatolia, from Sinope to Trebizond, for the empire but made little progress in reconquering the interior of Anatolia. In 1142, the emperor forced the count of Edessa to swear homage to him and made further demands upon the principality of Antioch. Before John could settle affairs with Antioch in 1143, though, he died, allegedly from cutting himself with a poisoned arrow while hunting.

John Comnenus continued the policy of his father in improving the army. He also developed a stronghold at Lopadium, to better defend Anatolia. At the same time, he demobilized the Byzantine navy, leaving the empire dependent upon the goodwill of the Genoese and Venetian governments. John also failed to evict the Turks from Central Anatolia, which, though poor, was a region crucial for the defense of the Anatolian frontier. This failure left the borders of the empire nearly impossible to defend.

Joseph M. Isenberg

See also: Alexius I Comnenus; Antioch, Battle of; Crusades; Seljuqs

References and further reading:

Comnena, Anna. *The Alexiad of Anna Comnena.* Trans. E. R. A. Sewter. New York: Penguin Books, 1969.

Norwich, John Julius. *Byzantium: The Apogee.* New York: Alfred A. Knopf, 1991.

Ostrogorsky, George. *History of the Byzantine State.* Trans. Joan Hussey. Rev. ed. New Brunwick, NJ: Rutgers University Press, 1969.

Johnston, Albert Sidney (1803–1862)

Confederate field commander whose death in battle on 6 April 1862 was a devastating loss to the Confederacy. A. S. Johnston was born in Washington, Kentucky, on 2 February 1803. After graduating from the U.S. Military Academy at West Point in 1826, he fought in the Black Hawk War of 1832. He resigned from the U.S. Army in 1834, moved to Texas, and enlisted as a private in Sam Houston's army in 1836. By January 1837 he was commander in chief of the Texas army, and from 1838 to 1840 he served as secretary of war for the Republic of Texas.

As brevet colonel of the 1st Texas Volunteer Rifles, he fought under Zachary Taylor in the Mexican-American War, distinguishing himself at Monterrey. He became a U.S. Army paymaster with the regular rank of major in 1849 and regular colonel of the Second Cavalry in 1855. As brevet brigadier general, he led a successful expedition against the Mormons in 1857 and was named commander of the Department of the Pacific in 1860.

Johnston resigned his commission in April 1861 and traveled by way of Texas to Richmond, Virginia, where Jefferson Davis made him a full general on 30 August and gave him command of all Confederate forces in the west. He ranked second among the five original Confederate generals, behind only Samuel Cooper, and first among field commanders, ahead of Robert E. Lee, Joseph Johnston, and P. T. Beauregard.

Outnumbered from the start, he raised the Army of the Mississippi to face Ulysses S. Grant in Kentucky and Tennessee. He retreated from Kentucky after George B. Crittenden lost to Don Carlos Buell and George H. Thomas at Mill Springs on 19 January 1862 and deeper into Tennessee after the fall of Fort Henry on 6 February and Fort Donelson on 16 February. With forces and supplies gathered at Corinth, Mississippi, and reinforced by Beauregard, he took the offensive against Grant in April. Hit in the hip the afternoon of the first day at Shiloh, he bled to death before surgeons could reach him.

Eric v. d. Luft

See also: American Civil War; Beauregard, Pierre Gustave Toutant; Bragg, Braxton; Fort Donelson; Grant, Ulysses Simpson; Houston, Samuel; Johnston, Joseph Eggleston; Lee, Robert Edward; Mexican-American War, Mormon War; Shiloh; Texas War of Independence; Thomas, George Henry

References and further reading:

Johnston, William Preston. *The Life of Gen. Albert Sidney Johnston, Embracing His Services in the Armies of the United States, the Republic of Texas, and the Confederate States.* New York: Da Capo, 1997.

Moore, Avery C. *Destiny's Soldier.* San Francisco: Fearon, 1958.

Roland, Charles Pierce. *Albert Sidney Johnston: Soldier of Three Republics.* Lexington: University Press of Kentucky, 2000.

———. *Jefferson Davis's Greatest General: Albert Sidney Johnston.* Abilene, TX: McWhiney Foundation, 2000.

Johnston, Joseph Eggleston (1807–1891)

Extraordinarily skillful Confederate field commander whose effectiveness was limited throughout the Civil War by his quarrels with President Jefferson Davis. Johnston was born in Prince Edward County, Virginia, on 3 February 1807. Assigned to artillery after graduating from the United Sates Military Academy at West Point in 1829, he fought in the Seminole Wars, the Mexican-American War under Winfield Scott, and the Utah War. Brevetted colonel and wounded at Cerro Gordo, he earned an excellent reputation. He was a brigadier general and U.S. Army quartermaster when he resigned to join the Confederacy on 22 April 1861. With Stonewall Jackson at Harpers Ferry, he organized Virginia volunteers into the Army of the Shenandoah.

The five original Confederate generals were, in order of seniority, Samuel Cooper, A. S. Johnston, Robert E. Lee, J. E. Johnston, and P. T. Beauregard. At First Bull Run, Beauregard served under J. E. Johnston, but they commanded as equals to defeat Irvin McDowell. Johnston was wounded at Fair Oaks on 31 May 1862. Commanding the Department of the West after 4 December, he opposed Ulysses S. Grant around Vicksburg in May 1863, losing his base at Jackson, Mississippi, on 14 May.

In a brilliant defensive campaign, Johnston defeated William Tecumseh Sherman at Kenesaw Mountain on 27 June 1864 but could not prevent Sherman's larger and better equipped force from entering Atlanta. Davis, unreasonably disappointed that Johnston could not hold Sherman, replaced Johnston with John Bell Hood on 18 July. Hood's command was a complete disaster, and Lee had Davis recall Johnston on 25 February 1865. Severely outnumbered but undaunted, he lost to Sherman at Bentonville, North Carolina, on 19–21 March and surrendered to him at Durham Station, North Carolina, on 26 April.

After the war, Johnston was a paragon of reconciliation with the North. A Democrat, he represented Virginia in Congress from 1879 to 1881 and was President Grover Cleveland's railroad commissioner from 1887 to 1891. He died on 21 March 1891 of pneumonia, caught while acting as pallbearer at Sherman's funeral in Washington, D.C.

Eric v. d. Luft

See also: American Civil War; Atlanta, Battles Around; Beauregard, Pierre Gustave Toutant; Bragg, Braxton; Bull Run, First/Manassas; Bull Run, Second/Manassas Junction; Cerro Gordo, Battle of; Chattanooga, Battle of; Grant, Ulysses Simpson; Harpers Ferry; Hood, John Bell; Johnston, Albert Sidney; Jackson, Thomas "Stonewall"; Lee, Robert Edward; McClellan, George Brinton; McDowell, Irvin; Mexican-American War; Mormon War; Scott, Winfield; Sherman, William Tecumseh; Utah War; Vicksburg, Siege of

References and further reading:

Davis, Stephen. *Atlanta Will Fall: Sherman, Joe Johnston, and the Yankee Heavy Battalions.* Wilmington, DE: Scholarly Resources, 2001.

Johnston, Joseph Eggleston. *Narrative of Military Operations during the Civil War.* New York: Da Capo, 1990.

Lash, Jeffrey Norman. *Destroyer of the Iron Horse: General Joseph E. Johnston and Confederate Rail Transport, 1861–1865.* Kent, OH: Kent State University Press, 1991.

Symonds, Craig L. *Joseph E. Johnston: A Civil War Biography.* New York: Norton, 1992.

Jomini, Antoine Henri, Baron de (1779–1869)

Military thinker and writer. Born Payerne, Swiss canton of Vaud, Jomini, son of town mayor. Banker in Basle (1796) and Paris (1798, 1801), becoming major in French-sponsored Swiss army in the Swiss Revolution (1800). Obtaining a French army staff position under Marshal Michel Ney (1800–1802) and serving as an aide-de-camp to Ney (1803), he wrote the first of his renowned works, *Traités des grandes operations militaires* (1801–1804), published in 1805. On Ney's staff during the Austerlitz campaign (1805) he served at Ulm (October) and Austerlitz (December). Napoleon (who had read Jomini's book) appointed him a colonel on his staff for the Auerstädt campaign (1806–1807). Jomini then served at Jena (October 1806) and Eylau (February 1807). He was created a baron (1807) and was appointed chief of staff in Ney's corps in the Peninsular War (1808–1811), becoming brigadier general (1810) and director of the pioneering French General Staff's historical section (1811). In the Russian campaign (1812) he was governor of

Vilno and Smolensk but rejoined Ney for the battles of Lützen and Bautzen (1813).

Jomini failed to achieve further promotion, possibly because of his disconcerting tendency to resign posts on impulse, but also likely because he was jealously disliked by Berthier, Napoleon's imperial chief of staff, who had him arrested for a minor misdemeanor in 1813.

Jomini responded by defecting to the Russian army, gaining the rank of lieutenant general, and serving as an aide-de-camp to Czar Aleksandr I (1813–1814) during the War of Liberation, although he refused to enter Paris with allies in 1814.

Living between Russia and Brussels, Jomini wrote more books, serving as military tutor to the Russian Grand Dukes Michael and Nicholas (1816–1826), becoming the latter's aide-de-camp and general in chief on his ascension as Czar Nicholas I (1825), and fighting at the Siege of Varna during the Turkish War (1828–1829). He then played a major role in establishing the Russian Nikolaevskii General Staff Academy in 1832. Four years later he published his most influential work, *Précis de l'art de guerre.* He remained an adviser to Nicholas I, fulfilling this role in the Crimean War (1853–1856). He then retired to Passy, near Chamonix in 1859, dying there 10 years later.

Although Jomini lacked a formal military education and never commanded in battle, his theories, along with those of Karl von Clausewitz, formed the basis of modern military thought. His contributions were more quickly utilized than those of Clausewitz, strongly influencing European and American military leaders alike. Jomini's conclusions rested on his knowledge of the wars of Frederick the Great, French Revolutionary Wars, eighteenth-century military theoretical study, and his personal Napoleonic Wars experience.

Far from proclaiming Napoleon an original commander, Jomini explained his rise and fall through his adherence to or straying from historic military principles, which Jomini reduced to several simple codified laws, which supposedly explained the "art" of warfare.

His greatest contribution was his identifying of the fundamental principle of war as the concentration of the mass of troops against an enemy's weak point, thus allowing breakthrough and victory. Maneuver was vital, positioning the attacking force in the most advantageous position; concealment, surprise, and intelligence—gathering essential information to determine the best point to strike and when. Jomini stressed enveloping one or both enemy flanks (if numbers allowed) and recommended cutting enemy supply lines and communications. Fronts should be kept small, allowing swift maneuver to any weak point, with feints used to break up enemy forces. Commanders must strike decisively to forestall enemy countermaneuvers. Internal operational lines were preferable, as these allow swift movement and concentration of troops, whereas external lines split the force, creating the potential for defeat. These principles allow coordination of offensive actions, leading to total victory. Viewing the battlefield as a mathematical square, territory was the important factor for victory, not destruction of the enemy army. Jomini abhorred total war on the Napoleonic scale; eighteenth-century warfare was his ideal.

Limiting his writings to commanding armies in the field, always recommending limited wars along pre-Napoleonic dimensions, preventing large-scale endless bloodshed to retain status quo, Jomini was a prisoner of his times and experiences. Much of his writing was overtaken by industrialization and technology, but his basic principles remain valid.

Neil Croll

See also: Austerlitz, Battle of; Berthier, Louis-Alexandre, Prince of Neuchatel and Valangin, Prince of Wagram; Clausewitz, Karl Maria von; Crimean War; Friedland; Jena and Auerstädt; Napoleon I; Napoleonic Wars; Ney, Michel

References and further reading:

Brinton, C., G. A. Craig, and F. Gilbert. "Jomini." In *Makers of Modern Strategy.* Princeton, NJ: Princeton University Press, 1943.

Jomini, Baron A. H. de. *Précis de l'art de guerre. [Summary of the Art of War].* Reprint of 1862 translation, with introduction by C. Messenger. Philadelphia: Greenhill Books, 1992; London: Stackpole Books, 1996.

Shy, J. "Jomini." In *Makers of Modern Strategy from Machiavelli to the Nuclear Age,* ed. P. Paret. Oxford, UK: Clarendon Press, 1986.

Strachan, H. *European Armies and the Conduct of War.* London: Routledge, 1991.

Joseph the Younger, Chief (Hinmaton Yalatkit, Heinmot) (1840–1900)

Aboriginal American chief and military leader. Joseph was born Hin-mah-too-yah-lat-kekht, or Thunder Rolling Down the Mountain, in the Wallowa Valley in northeast Oregon in 1840. His father, who also had the Christian name Joseph, was leader of the Nez Percé, a tribe that had peaceably coexisted with the United States and had willingly settled on a reservation in Idaho. In 1863, the federal government renegotiated its treaty with the tribe and reduced the size of the reservation by 90 percent, seizing 6 million acres. The Nez Percé refused to honor this agreement because the new location of the reservation was difficult to survive in and they wanted to stay on their traditional homelands. Thunder Rolling Down the Mountain became chief in 1871 when his father died and took up the name Joseph. In 1877, Joseph was given an ultimatum by General Oliver Otis Howard to return to the boundaries of the new reservation or risk military consequences. Resisting, Joseph moved his followers

Painted portrait of Chief Joseph, Nez Percé chief. (Library of Congress)

slowly to their new home. Before reaching their destination, a small band of young warriors killed some settlers in anger.

Joseph and 700 of his followers decided to flee to the safety of Canada. He was able to elude and foil the army on several occasions for more than three months and cover more than 1,600 miles using rearguard tactics, skirmish lines, and field fortifications. But while camping near the Chinook on September 30, the army surprised the Nez Percé. After five days of fierce fighting and the loss of three chiefs, more than 30 warriors and a number of women, children, and horses, Joseph decided to surrender. The government dispersed the remaining Nez Percé to several different reservations. Joseph died on the Colville Reservation in Washington State in 1900.

T. Jason Soderstrum

See also: American Indian Wars

References and further reading:

Beal, Merrill D. *I Will Fight No More Forever: Chief Joseph and the Nez Perce War.* Seattle: University of Washington Press, 1996.

Josephy, Alvin M. *The Nez Perce Indians and the Opening of the Northwest.* New Haven and London: Yale University Press, 1965.

Lavender, David. *Let Me Be Free: The Nez Perce Tragedy.* New York: HarperCollins Publishers, 1992.

Josephus, Flavius (c. 37–c. 100)

Jewish historian and military leader who chronicled the fall of Jerusalem during the First Jewish Revolt. Born the child of aristocrats in Jerusalem circa 37, as a young man he was a member of the Pharisees, a sect that wanted religious freedom but did not necessarily desire independence from Roman rule. In 64, Josephus traveled to Rome on a diplomatic mission and was awed by the seemingly invincible strength of the empire. In 66 Judea revolted against Rome, and despite his misgivings, Josephus became a military leader in the Galilee. Though sometimes portrayed as a collaborator, he withstood a Roman army led by future emperor Vespasian for 47 days at the fortress of Jotapata before being forced to surrender. As a prisoner, he curried favor with Vespasian and regained his freedom in 69. Convinced the Romans were too powerful to be resisted, he served with the Roman army during the siege of Jerusalem in 70 and thus was seen as a traitor by the Judeans. His attempts to act as a neutral arbiter failed. After Jerusalem fell and the revolt was put down, Josephus retired to Rome to write. He is remembered mainly for his histories of the revolts entitled *History of the Jewish War,* and for a history of the Jewish people, *The Antiquities of the Jews.*

Harold Wise

See also: Jewish Revolts; Masada, Siege of; Vespasian

References and further reading:

Schwartz, Seth. *Josephus and Judean Politics.* Boston: Brill Academic Publishers, 1997.

Thackery, Henry. *Josephus, the Man and the Historian.* Hoboken, NJ: Ktav Publishing House, 1968.

Joubert, Petrus Jacobus ("Piet") (1831–1900)

Charismatic Boer leader against the British. Joubert was born on the family farm near Prince Albert, South Africa, on 20 January 1831. His parents took him on the Great Trek to Natal when he was six. Settling later in Transvaal, he was always a farmer at heart, with a kindly, diplomatic nature, but was also successful in law, business, and politics. He was a popular civilian leader with almost no military experience when he was elected commandant general at the start of the First Boer War in December 1880. He defeated General Sir George Pomeroy Colley at Laing's Nek on 28 January 1881, Ingogo on 8 February, and Majuba Hill on 27 February, thus liberating Transvaal and becoming a national military hero. He nonetheless lost four presidential elections to Paul Kruger in the 1880s and 1890s but at the same time remained in power to enlarge and improve the Boer army, especially the artillery. He brought in the famous 155 mm

"Long Tom" siege gun from Schneider-Creusot and the 120 mm rapid-fire howitzer from Krupp.

When the Second Boer War erupted in October 1899, Joubert defeated the British again at Laing's Nek on 12 October, at Talana on 15 October, Elandslaagte on 21 October, and Nicholson's Nek and Modderspruit on 30 October. Having forced the British to retreat into Ladysmith, he began the siege of that town on 2 November. Joubert's victories were mostly due to British mistakes, which offset Joubert's shortsighted preparations, overly defensive tactics, and natural aversion to violence.

The gentle Joubert was especially ineffective while besieging Ladysmith; his main concern was to make peace. Disabled on 23 November by a fall from his horse, he resigned his commission and was replaced as commandant general by Louis Botha on 25 November. He fell ill and died on 27 March 1900 in Pretoria.

Eric v. d. Luft

See also: Boer Wars; Botha, Louis; Buller, Sir Redvers Henry; French, John Denton Pinkstone, First Earl of Ypres; Haig, Douglas; Kruger, Paul-Stephanus Johannes Paulus; Ladysmith, Siege of; Smuts, Jan Christiaan

References and further reading:

Bateman, Philip. *Generals of the Anglo-Boer War.* Cape Town: South African Historical Mint, 1977.

Coetzer, Owen. *The Anglo-Boer War: The Road to Infamy, 1899–1900.* London: Arms & Armour, 1996.

Meintjes, Johannes. *The Commandant-General: The Life and Times of Petrus Jacobus Joubert of the South African Republic, 1831–1900.* Cape Town: Tafelberg-Uitgewers, 1971.

Ransford, Oliver. *The Battle of Majuba Hill: The First Boer War.* New York: Crowell, 1968.

Julian (Flavius Claudius Julianus "The Apostate") (332–363)

An outstanding military leader of the later Roman Empire. Flavius Claudius Julianus was born at Constantinople in 332, a relative of Emperor Constantine the Great. He survived a massacre of his family by political rivals and spent most of his early youth in exile. At the age of 20 he secretly renounced Christianity and embraced both paganism and Hellenic philosophies. In 356 Julian was regarded as safe enough for public service, so his cousin, Emperor Constantius II, appointed him caesar of Gaul.

Gaul was then besieged by German tribes, who swarmed across the Rhine River in large numbers. Despite his lack of formal military training, Julian rebuffed the Alamanni in several small encounters, and in August 357 his 13,000 Romans soundly defeated 30,000 warriors at Strasbourg and subsequently drove the Franks from Gaul. For the first time in many years, Roman military authority was reasserted along the Rhine frontier. Julian also effectively overhauled provincial administration, lowered taxes, and won the affection of his troops.

Constantius II, fearing a potential rival, ordered Julian to transfer the best parts of his army to the east for a war against Persia. The troops refused and proclaimed Julian emperor. Constantius II died of a fever as both men's armies advanced toward Constantinople, and Julian was proclaimed emperor in December 361. He was nicknamed "the Apostate" by later Church historians for officially embracing paganism and shunning Christianity, although he never initiated any persecution.

Over the next year, the Romans made feverish preparations for a showdown against the Persian Empire under Shapur II. Julian led 65,000 well-trained men through Mesopotamia and across the Tigris River. Supplied by a large fleet of warships accompanying him downstream, Julian easily defeated Shapur II in several sharp engagements and at length stood before the winter capital at Ctesiphon. He then waited for reinforcements from Armenia that were not forthcoming. Julian commenced a fighting withdrawal northward, defeating the Persians in several battles. In a minor skirmish on 26 June 363, he was mortally wounded. His successor, Jovian, concluded a peace accord by ceding considerable Roman territory to Persia.

John C. Fredriksen

See also: Shapur II

References and further reading:

Bowersock, Glen W. *Julian the Apostate.* Cambridge, MA: Harvard University Press, 1997.

Browning, Robert. *The Emperor Julian.* Berkeley: University of California Press, 1976.

Nicasie, Martinus J. *Twilight of Empire: The Roman Army from the Reign of Diocletian until the Battle of Adrianople.* Amsterdam: J. C. Gieben, 1998.

Justinian I (482–565)

Ruler of the eastern Roman Empire, sought to restore the unity of the Roman Mediterranean through military, diplomatic, religious, economic, and cultural initiatives that instead created Byzantium. When Justinian became emperor in 527, he inherited a strategic orientation founded on four principles: (1) keeping Constantinople, the capital, impregnable; (2) guarding against the Persian Empire to the east, Byzantium's primary military threat; (3) managing the ill-organized German kingdoms of western Europe, and the Maghrib as a "second front"; and (4) supervising the north-

A mosaic from San Vitale, Ravenna, depicting "Justinian the Great." (Library of Congress)

ern frontier created by the Danube River and the Balkans, that unstable territory between Constantinople and the river. Instead, he resolved to alter this approach permanently by reclaiming the lost provinces of the west.

A diplomatic quarrel led Justinian into an unwanted war with Persia in 530, but a new shah, Khusrauw, ended the hostilities in 532. Justinian used peace with Persia to launch an invasion of the Vandal kingdom of Carthage. Belisarius, the Byzantine general, made unexpectedly quick work of the Vandals, and in 533 the lands of Libya and Tunisia became Byzantine provinces. Consolidating his hold in Africa, a crisis in the Ostrogothic state of Italy offered Justinian another opportunity. In 535, backed by the navy, Belisarius invaded Sicily, crossed into Italy, and entered Rome in December 536. Although the Ostrogoth king Vitigis besieged Rome for over a year, the eternal city held, and he withdrew to his capital of Ravenna. Three years later, Vitigis surrendered the city to Belisarius.

Despite these successes, Justinian's fortunes reversed dramatically in the 540s. Shah Khusrauw, prompted by Arab and Armenian allies and fearing that the balance of power was tipping against Persia, stormed through Syria and sacked Antioch. Five years of inconclusive invasion and counter-invasion followed. While Persia preoccupied Justinian, wandering Slavic, Bulgarian, and Germanic peoples began to infiltrate the Balkans. In addition, Totila, a new Goth ruler, recaptured most of Italy and in 549 took Rome.

In 552, Justinian dispatched General Narses to Italy with 30,000 men, including Lombard mercenaries. Narses crushed Totila at Busta Gallorum, occupied Rome, and permanently ended Gothic power in Italy. He also sent his general Solomon to seize a slice of coastal Spain as a weight against the Visigothic kings there. In the Balkans, the crisis continued unabated as Zabregan, chief of the Kutrigurs, raided with virtual impunity, and even threatened Constantinople in 557. Lacking local resources, Justinian simply bribed Zabregan to leave, and then bribed another barbarian king to make war on the Kutrigur. Byzantium adopted this bribe and divide tactic repeatedly to manage barbarian threats in the Balkans. It could backfire. In 562, for example, impervious to payoffs, the Huns sacked the city of Anastasiopolis.

Justinian's successors soon lost Spain and, within a few centuries, Italy and most of his other acquisitions. Historians continue to debate whether his military legacy to Byzantium was one of short-lived grandeur or debilitating overextension.

Weston F. Cook, Jr.

See also: Belisarius; Byzantine-Persian Wars; Gothic War; Huns; Narses

References and further reading:

Moorhead, John. *Justinian.* London and New York: Longman Press, 1994.

Norwich, John J. *Byzantium: The Early Centuries.* New York: Alfred A. Knopf, 1994.

K

Kadesh, Battle of (1274 B.C.E.)

The Hittite and Egyptian empires clashed for control of the Levant at Kadesh in the largest, best-documented Bronze Age battle. In 1275–1274 B.C.E. Egyptian pharaoh Rameses II ("the Great") invaded the Levant, sending his Na'arm division along the coast while he led the Amun, Ra, Ptah, and Seth divisions inland. Egyptian forces included 20,000 Nubian and Egyptian infantry, Libyan mercenaries, and Egyptian chariots. The Hittite king, Muwatallis, responded with 35,000 allies and 2,500 chariots. Egyptian forces utilized bows and light chariots while Hittites were known for iron weapons and heavy chariots.

At Kadesh, Muwatallis set a trap, using spies to suggest that the Hittite army was still far to the north. Rameses fell for the ruse and raced ahead with the Amun division to seize Kadesh. At this time, the Hittites emerged from behind Kadesh, crossed the Orontes River and hit the Ra division squarely on its right flank. The Ra division broke and fled toward the Amun division. Fortunately, the Egyptian Na'arm division arrived just in time to stop a rout.

Rameses rallied the fast-moving Egyptian forces and rolled back the Hittites with swift chariot attacks. The Hittites were in danger of being crushed between the northerly Na'arm, Amun, and Ra divisions and the southerly Ptah and Seth divisions. Muwatallis decided to withdraw east across the Orontes River and occupy Kadesh. With no siege equipment Rameses could not take Kadesh. Both sides eventually agreed to a peace treaty (each loudly proclaiming victory), with Rameses marrying a Hittite princess.

Christopher Howell

See also: Ancient Warfare; Hittites

References and further reading:

Newby, P. *Warrior Pharaohs: The Rise and Fall of the Egyptian Empire.* New York: Faber Press, 1980.

Shaw, Ian. *Egyptian Warfare and Weapons.* Buckinghamshire, UK: Shire Egyptology Publications, 1991.

Yadin, Y. *The Art of Warfare in Biblical Lands.* New York: McGraw-Hill, 1963.

Kamenev, Sergei Sergeevich (1881–1936)

Czarist officer, Red Army commander in chief, military theoretician. Born in Kiev, son of a military engineer, Kamenev graduated from the Aleksandrovskii Military Academy (1900), joining the 165th Lutskii Regiment; he graduated from the General Staff Academy in 1907.

In World War I, Kamenev was a semi-adjutant in the Operational Department, First Army, 30th Poltavskii Infantry Regiment; a commander of a rifle corps; and a chief of staff. He emerged a colonel.

After the October Revolution, he sided with the Bolsheviks, was elected chief of staff, XV Rifle Corps, then Third Army, before demobilization.

During the Russian Civil War, Kamenev was a Red Army volunteer; a military head of the Nevel'skii District, western screens (April 1918); and Smolensk District military commander (August).

From September 1918 to July 1919, he was eastern front commander and oversaw the counteroffensive against Kolchak (April–July), taking the north and central Urals. But he was stripped of command in July by Trotsky after strategic disagreements with Vacietis, who wished the eastern front to dig in, allowing troop transfers southward to face Denikin. Eastern front commanders' complaints persuaded Lenin to reinstate Kamenev.

Sponsored by Stalin, Kamenev replaced Vacietis (Trotsky's candidate) as Red Army commander in chief (July 1919–April 1924). He oversaw the Red Army campaigns that defeated Kolchak (July–December 1919), Denikin (August 1919–April 1920), and Wrangel (April–November 1920), but was partially to blame for the defeat in Soviet-Polish War (April–October 1920). He failed to coordinate or control the western (Tukhachevskii) and southwestern (Egorov) fronts' advances into Poland, allowing the Polish counteroffensive at Warsaw (August 1920). He then oversaw the clearing of anti-Soviet forces in Ukraine, Belorussia (Makhno, Bulak-Balakhovich), and Turkestan (Basmachi).

Kamenev supported Frunze's military doctrinal ideas and became the principal tactics lecturer at the Red Army Military Academy; inspector, Red Army (April 1924); chief of staff (March 1925); head, Main Administration (November 1925), CEC member.

As deputy peoples commissar, Naval, Military Affairs, deputy chairman RVS USSR (May 1927), Kamenev finally joined the Communist Party in 1930. He was appointed head of administration, Red Army antiair defense, then a member of the Military Soviet Under-Defense Commissariat (June 1934). He also found time to lead Arctic exploration efforts. Kamenev wrote military works assessing civil war operations, changing conditions, and modern warfare developments.

Kamenev died, supposedly of heart failure, in Moscow when Stalin's purges of the military had gathered strength. He was branded a conspirator in the Tukhachevskii Plot (1937) but was later rehabilitated in the post-Stalin era. (Note: S. S. Kamenev should not be confused with L. Kamenev, the party leader executed by Stalin in the same year that S. S. Kamenev supposedly died of a heart attack.)

Neil Harvey Croll

See also: Russian Civil War (1918–1921); Russo-Polish War; Stalin; World War I

References and further reading:

Bubnov, A., S. S. Kamenev, R. Eidemanis, and M. N. Tukhachevsky. *Grazhdanskaia voina, 1918–1921* (Civil War, 1918–1921). Moscow: Izdat. Voennye vestnik, 1928, 1930, 1972, 1974, and 1978.

Bystrov, V. E. *Sovetskie polkovodtsy i voenachal'niki. Sbornik* (Soviet Leaders and Military Chiefs Collection). Moscow: Molodaia gvardiia, 1988.

Kamenev, S. S., L. M. Spirin, and P. P. Chernushkov. *Zapiski o grazhdanskoi voine i voennom stroitel'stve. Izbrannye stat'i.* (Notes about the Civil War and Military Construction. Selected Essays). Moscow: Voenizdat, 1963.

Kameneva, N. S., *Put' polkovodtsa: vospominaniia ob ottse.* (The Path of a Leader: Recollections about My Father). Kiev: Politizdat Ukrainy, 1982.

Kandahar (31 August–1 September 1880)

Final battle of the Second Anglo-Afghan War (1878–1880), the decisive British victory that made a hero of Frederick Sleigh Roberts. In the context of the so-called Great Game or Tournament of Shadows between Russia and Great Britain throughout most of the nineteenth century for control of southern Asia, Britain kept close watch on the northwest Indian frontier. Afghanistan was an important buffer state, and Britain sought to extend its influence there, despite the Afghans' dangerously intense and implacable hatred of all foreigners.

Roberts won the battle at Charasiah on 6 October 1879; occupied the capital, Kabul, on 12 October; deposed Amir Yaqub Khan; and ruled Afghanistan by strict martial law for the next eight months. In June 1880 Yaqub Khan's younger brother, Ayub Khan, began a jihad, or holy war, against the British occupation. At Maiwand on 27 July, 10,000 Afghans under Ayub Khan ambushed a British and Indian brigade of 2,500 under George Reynolds Scott Burrows, inflicting 40 percent casualties while suffering only 25 percent of their own. Ayub Khan then besieged the garrison of 4,000 under James Primrose at Kandahar.

Roberts immediately mobilized 10,000 men, mostly Indians, and marched them across 313 miles of treacherous mountain paths and burning deserts in just 23 days to relieve Primrose. Roberts's logistical and psychological genius ensured the success of this march and earned him an honored place in military history. Arriving north of Kandahar on 31 August, he attacked Ayub Khan's camp near Baba Wali Pass the next day and overwhelmed him, thus ending the war. The British and Indians lost 40 killed, but more than 600 Afghans died.

Satisfied with both the military and political outcome, the British withdrew from Afghanistan in April 1881. The new emir, Abdul Rahman Khan, Yaqub Khan's nephew, then ruled Afghanistan as a neutral state.

Eric v. d. Luft

See also: Roberts, Frederick Sleigh, First Earl, Viscount St. Pierre of Kandahar

References and further reading:

Hannah, W. H. *Bobs: Kipling's General: The Life of Field-Marshal Roberts of Kandahar, VC.* Hamden, CT: Archon, 1972.

O'Ballance, Edgar. *Afghan Wars, 1839–1992: What Britain Gave Up and the Soviet Union Lost.* New York: Brassey's, 1993.

Roberts, Frederick Sleigh. *Roberts in India: The Military Papers of Field Marshal Lord Roberts, 1876–1893.* Ed. Brian Robson. Dover, NH: Alan Sutton for the Army Records Society, 1993.

Robson, Brian. *The Road to Kabul: The Second Afghan War, 1878–1881.* London: Arms & Armour, 1986.

Kangxi (K'ang-his) (1662–1722)

Reign name of a Chinese Manchu emperor born with the name Hsüan-yeh. He survived smallpox as a youth and ruled the Manchu Empire for 60 years. His reign flourished in all respects, but in the realm of military affairs, Kangxi demonstrated particular acumen.

The completion of the conquest of China marked Kangxi's greatest accomplishment. Several Chinese generals had assisted the Manchu in their conquest of China; three of these renegade generals had established quasi-independent states known as the Three Feudatories. From 1673 to 1681, Kangxi's armies battled the Three Feudatories until he achieved victory. The complete domination of China came when Kangxi's army finally seized Taiwan from the heirs of Koxinga (Zheng Chenggong) in 1683.

Kangxi also expanded the empire into inner Asia. Freed from the threat of civil war and rebellion with the defeat of the Three Feudatories, Kangxi turned to meet the threat of the Russians and the Oirat Mongols. Russian Cossacks had made inroads on the Manchu northern frontier and even exacted tribute from his subjects. After destroying the Russian outpost of Albazin, Kangxi offered a peace treaty to the Russians at Nerchinsk in 1689. Thus, Kangxi could now bring the full weight of his military against the Oirats, without fear that the Czar would ally with them. The Oirats threatened to control all of Mongolia, Xinjiang, and part of Kazakhstan. The Khalkha Mongols, of modern Mongolia, turned to Kangxi and offered their submission in return for protection from the Oirats. Kangxi consented at the treaty of Dolon Nur in 1696. At the battle of Jao Modo, Kangxi defeated Galdan Khan, ruler of the Oirats. With this victory, Kangxi secured Mongolia and extended his influence into Xinjiang.

Timothy May

See also: Koxinga; Manchu Expansion, Wars of; Qianlong

References and further reading:

Crossley, Pamela Kyle. *The Manchus.* Cambridge, UK: Blackwell Publishers, 1997.

———. *A Translucent Mirror: History and Ideology in Qing Imperial Ideology.* Berkeley: University of California Press, 1999.

Kessler, Lawrence D. *K'ang-Hsi and the Consolidation of Ch'ing Rule, 1661–1684.* Chicago: University of Chicago Press, 1976.

Rossabi, Morris. *China and Inner Asia.* New York: Pica Press, 1975.

Kars, Battle of (16 November 1877)

One of the battles of the Russo-Turkish War (1877–1878), resulting in a Russian victory and the aggrandizement of Russian territory in the Caucasus. In support of Balkan rebellions against Ottoman rule, Russian czar Alexander II declared war on 24 April 1877. Russian forces were divided into two main armies: Danube and Caucasus.

The Russian army of the Caucasus was commanded by Grand Duke Michael and numbered 60,000, with a reserve force of approximately 50,000. It was divided into four operational groups: Kobulety, Akhaltsykh, Aleksandropol, Erevan. Their mission was to overcome the Turkish fortresses of Batumi, Arduhan, Kars, Bayazid, and Erzerum. Opposing Turkish forces were divided into two groups: 60,000 commanded by Mukhtiar Pasha and an army of 40,000 near Erzerum.

By the end of April, Michael's forces had occupied Bayazid. By mid-May, Russian forces had seized Ardahan and were besieging Kars. However, by the end of August, Turkish counterattacks lifted the siege of Kars.

Kars was a stone citadel upon a gorge, composed of 12 detached forts for a defensive line of 17 kilometers. Mukhtiar Pasha's army was encircled and destroyed by a two-prong Russian pincer in October. However, Khalil Pasha refused to surrender Kars and his force of 25,000 men.

The Russians divided their 50,000 troops into seven detachments, two of which were diversionary. Kars was captured on 16 November. The main fort (Kamli) was seized by three Russian detachments. The Turks lost 70,000 men and 17,805 were taken prisoner. The number of Russians killed and wounded was 2,270.

Adrianople/Edirne was captured on 20 January 1878, and the war was concluded by armistice on 31 January, with Russian forces outside Constantinople.

Kars remained part of the Russian Empire until the Treaty of Brest-Litovsk in March 1918 returned it to Turkey.

Neville G. Panthaki

See also: Balkan War, First; Poltava; Russo-Turkish Wars (1676–1878)

References and further reading:

Anderson, M. S. *The Eastern Question.* London: Macmillan, 1970.

Menning, Bruce. *Bayonets before Bullets: The Imperial Russian Army, 1861–1914.* Bloomington: Indiana University Press, 1992.

Rupp, George. *A Wavering Friendship: Russia and Austria, 1876–1878.* Philadelphia, PA: Porcupine Press, 1976.

Seaton-Watson, Hugh. *The Decline of Imperial Russia.* London: Methuen, 1966.

Kasserine Pass (14–23 February 1943)

A gap in Tunisia's western Dorsal mountains where American troops met defeat in their first major engagement with the Germans in World War II. The two-mile-wide pass, situated between two 4,000-foot mountains, was considered the gateway to Tunis, a city the Allies hoped to capture in early 1943. To prevent the capture of Tunis, and with the hope of splitting Allied forces in two and reaching the north coast of Tunisia, German commander Erwin Rommel launched an armored offensive against thinly held Allied lines near the pass. Because they misinterpreted ULTRA intelligence, the

Allies had made the mistake of placing most of their reserves too far north, leaving the troops guarding the pass extremely vulnerable to the German attack.

On 19 February Rommel's 10th Panzer Division, along with Italian armor and infantry, attacked northwestward and forced a breakthrough in the American lines. The inexperienced American troops gave way too easily, leaving behind many of their weapons and much of their heavy equipment. More than 1,000 were killed and many hundreds taken prisoner. The American commander on the scene, the blowhard General Lloyd Fredendall, proved inadequate to the crisis created by Rommel's attack. After the battle he would be relieved in favor of Lieutenant George S. Patton.

Instead of continuing westward to exploit his breakthrough, Rommel was ordered to turn north toward the port of Le Kef. In so doing his spearheads ran into the teeth of the Allied reserves, who fought the Germans to a standstill amid heavy rains. In the process the tide of battle turned and the pass was recaptured on 24 February. Kasserine Pass served as a hard-learned lesson to the United States Army as to the kind of training, toughness, command, and coordination necessary to defeat the Germans in World War II. Rommel himself warned the German military against making too much of their easy victory; the Americans would learn, he asserted, and more quickly than their allies.

John C. McManus

See also: Eisenhower, Dwight David; Montgomery, Bernard Law; Rommel, Erwin Johannes Eugen; World War II

References and further reading:

Blumenson, Martin. *Kasserine Pass.* New York: Tower Books, 1966.

Eisenhower, Dwight D. *Crusade in Europe.* Garden City, NY: Doubleday, 1948.

Howe, George F. *North Africa: Seizing the Initiative in the West.* Washington: U.S. Army Office of the Chief of Military History, 1957.

Kearny, Philip (1814–1862)

Internationally renowned cavalry officer and Union general. Philip Kearny was born into a wealthy family in New York City on 1 June 1814. His uncle was the famous soldier Stephen Watts Kearny. Philip attended Columbia University in 1833, graduating in 1837 with a law degree. He soon accepted a commission in the 1st Dragoons. In 1839 he was sent to Europe to study cavalry tactics. After attending the French cavalry academy, he served as a volunteer in Algiers with the Chasseurs d'Afrique, seeing action across North Africa and building a wide reputation as a fearless tactician.

Returning to the United States in 1840, he served in administrative billets until he secured a position on the staff of General Winfield Scott. Kearny commanded a cavalry company during the Mexican-American War. In engagements at Contreras, Churubusco, and Mexico City, he increased his reputation but lost his left arm. In 1851 he resigned his commission and traveled widely and in 1859 rejoined the chasseurs to participate in the Italian war. At Solferino, his charge essentially won the day and earned him the cross of the French Legion of Honor, the first American so honored.

Upon the outbreak of the American Civil War, Kearny offered his services to the Union. As a brigadier with the New Jersey Volunteers in the Army of the Potomac, he saw action at Williamsburg and Seven Pines during the Peninsular campaign. In May 1862, at Second Bull Run, his troops turned back the assault by General Thomas "Stonewall" Jackson's troops. Nearby, at Chantilly, on 1 September, he mistakenly rode into rebel lines and was shot down. The Confederates graciously returned his body for burial. At the time of his death, Kearny was considered perhaps the bravest man in an era of brave soldiers.

Michael S. Casey

See also: American Civil War; Mexican-American War

References and further reading:

Kearny, Thomas. *General Philip Kearny.* New York: G. P. Putnam's Sons, 1937.

Werstein, Irving. *Kearny the Magnificent: The Story of General Philip Kearny, 1815–1862.* New York: John Day, 1962.

Kearny, Stephen Watts (1794–1848)

American commander. Kearny was born on 30 August 1794 in Newark, New Jersey, into a wealthy family. He served as an ensign in the New York State Militia while he attended Columbia College in New York City. At the outbreak of the War of 1812 Kearny entered the United States Army and was commissioned a second lieutenant. At the Battle of Queenston Heights Kearny was wounded and captured.

Kearny spent most of the next 35 years serving in the American West, where he took part in many exploration expeditions. In 1836 Colonel Kearny succeeded to the command of a dragoon regiment. In 1837 he wrote a manual for the dragoons, earning him the nickname "Father of the Cavalry." Upon the declaration of war against Mexico in May 1846 he was appointed commander of the Army of the West and given orders to secure New Mexico and California. He entered Santa Fe in August and, acting as military governor, established a government. In September Kearny marched on California. Having received word that Commodore Richard Stockton had pacified California, Kearny brought only 110 dragoons. Upon arrival, however, he discovered that the Cali-

Field Marshal Wilhelm Keitel (right) standing in an open car in a victory parade in Bucharest, upon the return of the Romanian troops from Odessa, 1941. (Library of Congress)

fornians had reestablished themselves. Kearny led his weary men into action and obtained a costly victory at the Battle at San Pascual on 6 December 1846. By January he had secured California for the United States. A dispute between Kearny and Stockton developed over who should govern California. When the authorities in Washington, D.C., sustained Kearny, he had Stockton's choice of governor, Lieutenant Colonel John C. Frémont, arrested for insubordination.

In the spring of 1848 Kearny was ordered to Mexico, where he served as military governor of Veracruz, and later Mexico City, where he contracted yellow fever and took ill. He died 31 October 1848 in St. Louis, Missouri.

Gregory Dehler

See also: Cavalry; Mexican-American War; Queenston Heights; Scott, Winfield; War of 1812

References and further reading:

Clarke, Dwight L. *Stephen Watts Kearny: Soldier of the West.* Norman: University of Oklahoma Press, 1961.

Goetzmann, William H. *Army Exploration in the American West, 1803–1863.* New Haven, CT: Yale University Press, 1959.

Harlow, Neal. *California Conquered: The Annexation of an American Province.* Berkeley: University of California Press, 1982.

Keitel, Wilhelm (1882–1946)

Hitler's chief of Wehrmacht High Command (OKW). Keitel was born 22 September 1882 at Helmscherode near Hannover and joined the Prussian army in 1901, becoming a lieutenant the following year. He married Lisa Fontaine in 1909 and had six children.

Keitel fought during World War I and entered the postwar Reichswehr as a captain in 1919. From 1925 on he held administrative positions within the then-camouflaged general staff responsible for organizational matters and plans for rebuilding a strong army. As a general major he led the armed forces department within the War Ministry from 1935.

After the dismissal of War Minister Werner von Blomberg and Army Commander Werner von Fritsch in February 1938, Hitler made himself Wehrmacht's supreme commander and created OKW under Keitel as his personal staff. Keitel was without executive power toward the army, navy, or air force because Hitler kept command authority to himself, using Keitel as a high-ranking secretary. Because of his weak position and submissiveness toward Hitler, Keitel, promoted to field marshal on 19 July 1940, was called Lakeitel (lackey) by those who knew him. He occasionally disputed matters with the dictator, but Hitler kept the busy and experienced field marshal in office and Keitel progressively abandoned any critical attitude. Without prestige among the officer corps but backed by Hitler, Keitel was allowed to sign orders in Hitler's name ("Der Führer—by authority Keitel"), among them the infamous commissar order and many other criminal directives.

Little research exists about his activities in wartime industry and domestic activities as member of the Reich Defense Council. Leaving operational matters to Jodl he participated in many conferences on coordinating warfare, negotiated with German allies, and held important administrative functions, which indicates that his position as near–war minister is still underestimated.

Keitel left Berlin a week before Hitler's suicide but returned to sign the surrender to the Soviets, 9 May 1945. He was found guilty of war crimes at Nuremberg and hanged 16 October 1946.

Martin Moll

See also: Hitler, Adolf; Jodl, Alfred; World War II

References and further reading:

Görlitz, Walter, ed. *Generalfeldmarschall Keitel.* Verbrecher oder Offizier. Göttingen-Berlin-Frankfurt/Main: Musterschmidt, 1961.

Kellogg-Briand Pact (27 August 1928)

A multinational treaty actually outlawing war. The Kellogg-Briand Pact grew out of two trends that dominated diplomacy in the 1920s. First, the French search for security, and second, the intense desire in the United States for peace in isolation after World War I.

Aristide Briand, the French foreign minister, sought to protect France through a series of treaties known as the Locarno agreements. After solidifying alliances with potential enemies of Germany, he looked to secure improved Franco-American relations, chilled by America's insistence on collecting war debts for World War I. But Briand hoped at least to sign a pact with the United States that proposed to ban war as an instrument of national policy. United States secretary of state Frank Kellogg feared that France was attempting to draw the United States into a negative alliance and preventing the United States from ever declaring war against France, no matter the circumstances. War with France seemed highly unlikely, but such a treaty might prevent the United States from retaliating against French interference with American flagships trading with Germany during a time of war.

Briand communicated his plan directly to the American people in April 1927, ignoring the usual diplomatic channels and infuriating President Calvin Coolidge. Moreover, the wily Frenchman met with leaders of the peace movement in the United States in an effort to encourage them to spur on their reluctant government. The trans-Atlantic flight of Charles Lindbergh in May 1927 seemed to draw the two nations closer.

Throughout the fall of 1927 Kellogg stalled negotiations as he considered options to outmaneuver Briand. In November he proposed that the treaty should be multilateral, with an invitation extended to all nations to sign the agreement. Although Kellogg at first hoped this would scuttle talk of a concept he considered foolish, he later became convinced of its practicality and its rewards (a possible Nobel Prize) for himself. Unable to counter Kellogg's move, Briand assented. On 27 August 1928, 15 nations signed the agreement. Within five years, a total of 64 countries signed the treaty to renounce war as an instrument of national policy.

The treaty failed to include any enforcement mechanisms or even of any method to judge if a nation did in fact use war as an instrument of foreign policy. There was no mention of such issues as defense or alliances. Despite these shortcomings, the Kellogg-Briand Pact was, in fact, the legal basis for bringing Germany to account at the Nuremberg tribunal following the end of World War II.

Gregory Dehler

See also Disarmament; Laws of War; Pacifism/War Resistance

References and further reading:

Ellis, L. Ethan. *Frank B. Kellogg and American Foreign Policy, 1925–1929.* New Brunswick, NJ: Rutgers University Press, 1961.

Ferrell, Robert H. *Peace in Their Time: The Origins of the Kellogg-Briand Pact.* New Haven, CT: Yale University Press, 1952.

Kesselring, Albert (1885–1960)

German field marshal most famous for his defense of Italy, 1943–1944. Born at Marktsteft, near Bayreuth, 30 November 1885, Kesselring enlisted in the 2nd Bavarian Foot Artillery in 1904. During World War I he served in artillery staff positions on the western front, becoming a general staff officer in late 1917, then was assigned to a division on the eastern front. Promoted to colonel in 1930, and having already proved his ability as an administrator, he was transferred to the Air Ministry in 1933, promoted to general major in 1936, and became the air force chief of staff in the same year.

During the Polish campaign, Kesselring commanded the First Air Fleet and succeeded in breaking the defenses in Warsaw. He also played an important role in the French campaign in 1940 as the commander of the Second Air Fleet, supporting the actions of Army Group B. In the first three months of Operation BARBAROSSA (invasion of the Soviet Union) Kesselring commanded the air fleet assigned to Army Group Center but was transferred to Italy in November 1941, becoming commander in chief south, nominally the direct superior of Rommel. On 21 November 1943 he became commander in chief of Army Group C, the commander of German forces in Italy. He conducted defensive operations against the Allies skillfully until he suffered a severe road accident in October 1944. After returning to Italy for a few weeks, Kesselring became commander in chief west on 9 March 1945.

In February 1947 Kesselring was charged with the shooting of civilians in Italy in March 1944 and sentenced to death, subsequently reprieved, then released on 23 October 1952 on the grounds of ill health. Kesselring died on 16 July 1960 at Bad Nauheim.

Alaric Searle

See also: Anzio, Battle of; Salerno

References and further reading:

Kesselring, Albert: *Memoirs.* London: Kimber, 1953.
———. *Gedanken zum Zweiten Weltkrieg.* Bonn: Athenäum 1955.
Macksey, Kenneth: *Kesselring.* New York: David MacKay, 1978

Kett's Rebellion (1549)

In 1548, agrarian disturbances, spurred by rising inflation, enclosure of common lands, and debasement of the coinage, began to break out all over England. Most were handled firmly but leniently by the local authorities, urged by Protector Somerset, regent for Edward VI, to address grievances and disperse the rebels without using force, especially because English troops were involved in fighting Scotland. Unfortunately, by 1549, Norfolk was involved in a serious uprising that no threats of forfeitures or martial law could stop. Norfolk was without a great noble family the people respected and obeyed after the purges of the Tudors' Plantagenet relatives, and its citizens had little respect for their unpopular bishop, William Rugge. The ensuing rebellion centered on Robert Kett, a 57-year-old gentleman landowner, who assumed leadership of the angry mob of yeomen that had come to tear down his own fences and kill his sheep.

Kett led the increasingly large group to march on Norwich, where it camped outside the city, on Mousehead Heath, en route tearing down fences and destroying the hated dovecotes of landlords, whom they took as hostages and used as a human shield as they marched. On July 22, the rebels attacked the walled city with help from disaffected city dwellers and broke in through one of the gates, seizing all of the arsenal before retreating back to the heath, where Kett had set up an elaborate administration, with clerks, legal courts, and a provisioning system. Kett and his men issued a declaration to the crown, "Twenty-Nine Demands," most of which called for the preservation of traditional, conservative rights against recently corrupt practices of enclosure and economic repression.

The government first sent William Parr, Marquis of Northampton, who allowed himself to be trapped inside the city of Norwich, attacked, and forced to retreat, then John Dudley, Duke of Northumberland, who arrived on 24 August and took possession of the city. Dudley declared that he would stay there to the last man in his army, which included Italian mercenaries. Kett, who had sent out agents to try to enlarge the rebellion by contacting other agrarian rebels engaged in minor revolts nearby, failed to rally more men, and also failed to repeat his previous success of attacking Norwich, once Dudley was inside. Street fighting quickly fizzled, and Kett was forced to engage the Crown's army in an open field battle northeast of the city, where the professional soldiers decimated the rebels, killing perhaps 3,000 of them in battle and executing a number of men identified as ringleaders, before offering a pardon to those who surrendered.

Kett himself, and his brother, William, were captured and taken to the Tower, where they were tried for treason. Returned to Norwich for execution, they died on 9 December 1550. Ironically, the rebellion brought about the collapse of the government of Protector Somerset, who was sympathetic to the grievances of the rebels, and led to the rise of Robert Dudley, the Duke of Northumberland.

Margaret Sankey

References and further reading:

Clayton, Joseph. *Robert Kett and the Norfolk Rising.* London: M. Seker, 1912.
Cornwall, Julian. *Revolt of the Peasantry 1549.* London: Routledge & Kegan Paul, 1977.
Land, Stephen K. *Kett's Rebellion: The Norfolk Rising of 1549.* Totowa, NJ: Rowman & Littlefield, 1977.

Khalid ibn al-Walid (d. 642)

Primary Arab general during the first phase of the Arab conquests. Khalid fought against the Prophet Muhammad at the Battle of Uhud but later converted to Islam in 627 (or 629; historians are unsure). Khalid took part in the conquest of Mecca in 629, and then led several other expeditions.

After the death of the Prophet in 632, Abu Bakr sent Khalid on several missions to quell rebellion. As Khalid demonstrated exceptional prowess, he was placed in charge of an army to invade Iraq. In Iraq, Khalid conquered several locations before leading his army into Syria, by crossing the desert, although there is disagreement in sources as to whether Khalid went first to Syria, and then marched to Iraq to take the strategic location of Dumat al-Djandal before returning to Syria. Once in Syria, Khalid assisted the Arab armies already fighting the Byzantines there.

Eventually, Khalid's army returned to Iraq to resume its duties there, but Khalid himself remained in Syria. Khalid's success by this time was enormous and he eventually gained the sobriquet of Sayf Allah, or the Sword of God, although later sources refer to him with the less prestigious title of Sayf Rasul Allah, or the Sword of the Messenger of God (that is, of Muhammad).

Khalid rose to be the commander of the armies in Syria, but after the death of Caliph Abu Bakr in 634, his fortunes declined momentarily. Caliph 'Umar ibn al-Khattab demoted Khalid from his position, although he was not removed from Syria. He continued to lead troops in northern Syria as a lieutenant of Abu 'Ubayda. Khalid led numerous raids on the Byzantine border until his death in 642. There is some speculation that Khalid was assassinated by the future Caliph Mu'awiya, who envied Khalid's status.

Timothy May

See also: 'Amr ibn al-'As; Byzantine-Muslim Wars; Charles Martel; Heraclius; Musa ibn Nusayr; Muslim Civil War; Muslim Conquests; Religion and War; Sassanid Empire; Tariq ibn Ziyad; Yarmuk, Battle of

References and further reading:

Belyaev, E. A. *Arabs, Islam, and the Arab Caliphate in the Early Middle Ages.* London: Pall Mall Press, 1969.

Donner, Fred M. *The Early Islamic Conquests.* Princeton, NJ: Princeton University Press, 1981.

Shaban, M. A. *Islamic History: A New Interpretation.* London: Cambridge University Press, 1971.

Khalkin-Gol (Battle of Nomonhan, May–September 1939)

A series of border battles between Soviet and Japanese forces, resulting in Japan's defeat. In the summer of 1939, the Japanese Kwantung Army in Manchuria fought several battles against Soviet forces in Siberia over the exact border along the Khalkin-Gol River at a town named Nomonhan. There were several stages to the fighting.

First, Soviet troops occupied the disputed territory to a depth of about 12 miles to the east in May 1939.

Second, the Japanese attacked with a reinforced division and were initially successful. They had expected to fight Mongolian troops and were surprised at the appearance of regular Soviet Red Army forces. After the initial success in driving the Soviets out of disputed territory, Japanese troops crossed into Mongolia, where despite reinforcements of artillery and tanks, they were stopped.

Third, Soviet forces, now commanded by General Georgy K. Zhukov, drove back the badly outnumbered Japanese across the border and back to Nomonhan. Zhukov threw 65,000 troops against 28,000 Japanese and soon pushed them 20 miles into Manchuria.

Finally, before the Japanese Kwantung Army commander could employ the three divisions he had concentrated for a counterattack, the Japanese high command took control from the nearly autonomous Kwantung Army and called a halt to the fighting in mid-September 1939.

The Japanese learned little from the Soviet attack. Supposedly, the Japanese experience in fighting the Soviets and the situation of the European empires in Southeast Asia after the German victories in the West in the spring of 1940 caused the Japanese to look south to expand into the resource-rich southern Asia-Pacific region and hence to consider a preemptive strike against the American Pacific Fleet in its anchorage at Pearl Harbor, Honolulu, Hawaii.

Charles M. Dobbs

See also: Zhukov, Georgy Konstantinovich

References and further reading:

Coox, Alvin D. *Nomonhan. Japan against Russia, 1939.* Stanford, CA: Stanford University Press, 1985.

Drea, Edward J. *Nomonhan: Japanese-Soviet Tactical Combat, 1939.* Ft. Leavenworth, TX: United States Army Command and General Staff College, Combat Studies Institute, 1981.

Zhukov, Georgi K. *Marshal Zhukov's Greatest Battles.* Trans. Theodore Shabad. New York: Harper & Row, 1969.

Khambula (29 March 1879)

The turning point of the Anglo-Zulu War, breaking the morale of the Zulu army. Colonel Evelyn Wood's number 4 (left) column of 2,086 officers and men maintained an active presence in northwestern Zululand after the other invading British columns were thrown onto the defensive by defeat at Isandlwana. Wood's fortified position at Khambula consisted of a wagon laager, connected to an earthwork redoubt and a smaller cattle laager. At midday on 29 March the Zulu army of about 20,000 men, under the command of Chief Mnyamana kaNgqengelele, halted four miles southeast of the camp. Aware of the danger of attacking entrenched positions, King Cetshwayo had instructed Mnyamana to draw the British into the open by threatening their line of supply. But Mnyamana was overborne by the younger warriors, who insisted on a direct assault.

The Zulu army deployed with the intention of enveloping Khambula, but at 1:30 P.M. the right horn began an unsupported advance from the north, drawn on by mounted troops sent forward by Wood, and was repulsed. The Zulu were consequently unable to complete their envelopment of the camp, whose northern and western salients remained unthreatened, thus enabling the British to concentrate against the main Zulu attack, which unfolded at 2:15 P.M. from the south.

The Zulu drove the British from the cattle laager and threatened the main laager. Several British companies then sortied and drove the Zulu back at bayonet point, and by 3:00 P.M. the Zulu had abandoned their assault from the south. Over the next two hours they renewed the attack, first from the east, and then from the northeast. At about 5:00 P.M., when the Zulu attack slackened off, British infantry sortied once more, supported by the mounted troops. The exhausted Zulu were unable to rally, and their retirement turned into a rout. The mounted troops relentlessly pursued them eastwards until night fell.

The British lost 29 killed, the Zulu more than 1,000. The fighting spirit of the Zulu army never recovered from this crushing defeat, and the Zulu had lost the initiative in the war.

John Laband

See also: Anglo-Zulu War; Isandlwana; Rorke's Drift

References and further reading:

Jones, Huw M. "Why Khambula?" *Soldiers of the Queen* (September 1993).

Laband, John. "The Battle of Khambula, 29 March 1879: A Reexamination from the Zulu Perspective." In *Kingdom and Colony at War: Sixteen Studies on the Anglo-Zulu War of 1879,* John Laband and P. Thompson. Pietermaritzburg and Cape Town: University of Natal Press and N & S Press, 1990.

———. *Kingdom in Crisis: The Zulu Response to the British Invasion of 1879.* Manchester and New York: Manchester University Press and St. Martin's Press, 1992.

Laband, John, and P. Thompson. *The Illustrated Guide to the Anglo-Zulu War.* Pietermaritzburg: University of Natal Press, 2000.

Kharkov (12–28 May 1942)

World War II battle on eastern front, catastrophic defeat for Red Army. The second largest city in Ukraine, Kharkov fell to German forces 24 October 1941, four months into Hitler's invasion of the Soviet Union. Seven months later, in May 1942, Kharkov became the site of a major defeat for the Red Army.

The so-called Second Battle of Kharkov (12–28 May 1942) developed when Marshal S. K. Timoshenko's Southwestern Front, supported by Marshal R. Ia. Malinovsky's Southern Front, undertook an offensive to recapture the city and destroy the German forced deployed in its defense. Attempting a pincer operation, Soviet Twenty-eighth, Twenty-first, and Thirty-eighth Armies attacked from Volchansk in the northeast, while Soviet Sixth and Bobkin Army Group struck from the Izyum Bulge in the southeast.

Both arms of the Soviet pincer made substantial advances until 16 May. However, Timoshenko's failure to commit armored forces fast enough allowed the Germans to blunt the Soviet drives and mount a counterstrike. Codenamed Operation FREDERICUS, the German counteroffensive of 17–18 May saw the southern prong of the Soviet offensive encircled by General Friedrich Paulus's Sixth Army, attacking from the north, and General Ewald von Kleist's Army Group (Fourth Panzer and Seventeenth Army), attacking from the south.

Although a few Soviet units managed to escape, the Second Battle of Kharkov cost the Red Army an estimated 277,000 men, 4,900 guns and mortars, and 652 tanks.

Bruce J. DeHart

See also: Timoshenko, Semen Konstantinovich; World War II

References and further reading:

Erickson, John. *The Road to Stalingrad: Stalin's War with Germany.* New Haven, CT: Yale University Press, 1999.

Glantz, David, and Jonathan House. *When Titans Clashed: How the Red Army Stopped Hitler.* Lawrence: University of Kansas Press, 1995.

Ziemke, Earl, and Magna E. Bauer. *Moscow to Stalingrad: Decision in the East.* Washington, DC: U.S. Army Center of Military History, 1987.

Khartoum, Siege of (13 March 1884–26 January 1885)

Evacuation, defense, and massacre in the First Mahdist War. In the early 1880s the Sudan was ruled by Egypt, which was itself a puppet state of Great Britain and nominally part of the Ottoman Empire. Native Sudanese resented foreign domination and grumbled for home rule. Sudanese nationalist/theocratic uprisings led by the Mahdi, a charismatic Nubian Sufi fundamentalist mystic, began in 1881. British prime minister William Gladstone tried to remain aloof from what he perceived as an internal Egyptian affair, but the British became embarrassed by their inability to safeguard Egypt's control of the Sudan. The khedive of Egypt pleaded unsuccessfully for British support.

Finally bowing to public pressure in January 1884, Gladstone reluctantly sent a popular hero, Charles George "Chinese" Gordon, to the Sudan with orders first to evacuate Egyptian troops from Khartoum, then, if possible, regroup and retaliate against the Mahdi. Gordon left London on 18 January, arrived in Khartoum on 18 February, judged immediately that transport was insufficient for a well-managed withdrawal of troops, and set about to evacuate women, children, the sick, and the disabled. Gordon had evacuated only about 2,000 of these civilians when the Mahdi besieged Khartoum on 13 March. Gordon's garrison was about 8,000 men. Besides an unknown number of Mahdist troops, Gordon estimated that two-thirds of Khartoum's native population of 40,000 was against him.

Gladstone, annoyed at Gordon's apparent insubordination, did not authorize relief until October, then sent a rescue force under Garnet Joseph Wolseley. Advance British gunboats under Lord Charles Beresford arrived on 28 January 1885, two days too late, as Mahdists had already breached the walls and killed the entire garrison. Wolseley withdrew, leaving the Mahdi free to govern. The Mahdi proclaimed an Islamic state from the Red Sea to central Africa with its capital at Omdurman but died of natural causes in June. Gladstone's weak handling of the Sudan crisis contributed to his replacement as prime minister by the marquis of Salisbury on 23 June; many Britons blamed him personally for Gordon's death and Khartoum's fall.

Eric v. d. Luft

See also: Buller, Sir Redvers Henry; Gordon, Charles George; Kitchener, Horatio Herbert; Muhammad Ahmad; Wolseley, Garnet Joseph, Viscount

References and further reading:

Compton, Piers. *The Last Days of General Gordon.* London: Hale, 1974.

Hake, Alfred Egmont. *Gordon in China and the Soudan.* London: Darf, 1987.

Neillands, Robin. *The Dervish Wars: Gordon and Kitchener in the Sudan, 1880–1898.* London: Murray, 1996.

Nushi, Muhammad. *General Report on the Siege and Fall of Khartum by Mohammed Nushi Pasha and Several Native Officers Who Were in Khartum or Its Vicinity at the Time of the Siege and Assault.* Khartoum, Sudan: 1970.

Khe Sanh, Siege of (21 January–8 April 1968)

A major siege operation against a U.S. Marine combat base. At the time the siege of Khe Sanh, an isolated marine base along Route 9 in extreme northern South Vietnam, caused some to recall the French debacle at Dien Bien Phu in 1954. President Lyndon Johnson emphasized to the chairman of the Joint Chiefs of Staff, Earle Wheeler, "I don't want any damn Dinbinfoo," and Johnson received assurances that, unlike the French, the United States could sustain the marines.

Unlike the French, the marines held the hills surrounding their base camp and prepared for the attack. The North Vietnamese set up positions around the marines' perimeter, moved in thousands of troops, and engaged in classic siege measures. To upset North Vietnamese plans, U.S. air power saturated the area: B-52 bombers, marine and naval aviators, and army long-range artillery dropped more than 100,000 tons of bombs and shells on suspected enemy positions. Finally, in early April, the U.S. 1st Cavalry Division moved up Route 9 and linked up with the marines on 8 April, ending the siege. Later, to some bitter reaction, Khe Sanh was abandoned.

However, there will always be a question as to the goals of the North Vietnamese. Was this a decoy, to draw U.S. attention away from the cities and the coast immediately prior to the Tet Offensive? Was it simply a probe to test American resolve? Or was it preparation for a cross-parallel invasion to follow up a supposedly successful Tet Offensive and popular, antigovernment uprising in the South? The answers remain, to this day, unclear.

Charles M. Dobbs

See also: Tet Offensive; Vietnam Conflict; Vo Nguyen Giap; Westmoreland, William

References and further reading:

Pimlott, John. *Vietnam: The Decisive Battles.* New York: Macmillan, 1990.

Pisor, Robert. *The End of the Line: The Siege of Khe Sanh.* New York: W. W. Norton, 1982.

Prados, John. *Valley of Decision: The Siege of Khe Sanh.* Boston: Houghton Mifflin Co., 1991.

Khmer-Cham Wars (1050–1203)

A series of wars between the Khmer Empire and a resurgent Champa state for control of Indochina. In Southeast Asia, Hindu and Buddhist kingdoms from India and China had developed into independent polities centered around ethnic groups such as the Annam in north Vietnam, the Cham in central Vietnam, the Khmer in Cambodia, and the Tai in Siam. These polities had thrown off the yoke of Chinese and Indian overlordship and then turned on each other. The Khmer-Cham Wars, Khmer-Thai Wars, Vietnamese-Cham Wars, and the Vietnamese-Khmer Wars all stemmed from this struggle to control Southeast Asia and the rich trade that flowed between China and India.

The first Khmer-Cham War (1050–1051) involved revolts in Khmer territories. The Cham king Jaya Paramesvarman and his son Yavuraja then invaded the northern Khmer territory of Sambhupura while supporting a revolt in the Khmer south. Khmer generals suppressed the revolt and crushed Cham forces in the north.

The second Khmer-Cham War (1144–1150) followed the Vietnamese-Khmer War of 1123–1136. The Khmer king Suryavarman II controlled modern Cambodia and Laos but sought all of Vietnam by allying with Champa and invading Annam. Instead, a Cham-Annam alliance formed and opposed the Khmers. Khmer armies invaded Cham and captured its capital of Vijaya. Cham forces still held out under Harivarman I at Chaklyang and destroyed Khmer and Vijayan armies in two Phanrang Valley battles. Champa troops then marched north, captured Vijaya, and defeated the Khmer forces at Mahisa. A final Khmer force sent by Suryavarman II was also crushed.

The third Khmer-Cham War of 1167–1190 saw the Cham king Jaya Indravarman IV invade the weakened Khmer Empire using cavalry and naval forces, instead of the traditionally slow elephants and water buffalo. These concepts, learned from the Chinese, led to startling initial victories over the Khmers. In 1177 Cham naval forces sailed up the Tonle Sap (great lake) of the Khmer and destroyed the Khmer capital at Angkor (Yasodharupura).

Cham now threatened to overrun Southeast Asia but a wealthy Thai-Khmer alliance under the Khmer Jayavarman VII arose against it. Both sides became dependent on China for naval aid and horses, with most going to the wealthy Khmer Empire. An 1181 sea victory over Champa allowed the rebuilding of Angkor Thom, north of the original Khmer capital. Champa was invaded in 1190 and its capital at Vijayana sacked.

The fourth Khmer-Cham War of 1191–1203 saw Champa rebel against Khmer rule. Two Khmer armies were defeated, but the Khmer king Jayavarman VII used Cham traitors to regain control of the Champa throne. The renewed Khmer Empire remained dominant in Southeast Asia until Thai-Cham forces sacked Angkor-Thom after a seven-month siege in 1430 and destroyed vital irrigation systems in 1444, signaling the end of the mighty Khmer Empire.

Christopher Howell

See also: Jayavarman VII

References and further reading:

Briggs, Lawrence. *The Ancient Khmer Empire.* New York: White Lotus, 1999.

Embrick, A., and C. Gluck. *Asia in Western and World History.* London: M. E. Sharpe, 1997.

Kiev (16–26 September 1941)

The greatest single military victory in modern history, and the worst defeat in Soviet military history. On 16 September 1941, 680,000 Soviet troops of General M. P. Kirpanov's Southwestern Front suffered encirclement in the Kiev pocket (130 miles in width and depth) when the German Second Panzer Group, commanded by General Heinz Guderian, advancing from Smolensk in the north, linked up with the German First Panzer Group, commanded by General Ewald von Kleist, advancing from Kremenchug in the south at Lokhvitsa (125 miles east of Kiev). For the next 10 days, six trapped Soviet armies, the entire strength of the southwestern front, struggled to break out, while German forces, their movements coordinated by Field Marshal Gerd von Rundstedt, commander of Army Group South, fought to reduce the pocket.

Although 15,000 Soviet troops ultimately escaped, Kirpanov's armies lacked sufficient power to achieve a large-scale breakout against a numerically superior enemy who also enjoyed command of the skies. Kiev itself fell 20 September, and six days later the last Soviet resistance inside the pocket ended. Four entire Soviet armies were destroyed, and two others severely emasculated. German statistics revealed that the Battle of Kiev cost the Soviets 665,000 prisoners, 3,018 guns, and 418 antitank guns. General Kirpanos himself was killed attempting to break out of the pocket.

The annihilation of the Soviet Southwestern Front opened the door for Army Group South to capture central and eastern Ukraine and most of the Crimea in the last months of 1941.

And yet Hitler's diversion of additional German forces to the Kiev encirclement delayed the drive on what should have been the ultimate goal of the German invasion—Moscow. By the time German forces finally approached the Soviet capital in early December, it was winter and too late. Germany had won a great operational victory at Kiev but had lost any chance of destroying the Soviet union.

Bruce J. DeHart

See also Guderian, Heinz; World War II

References and further reading:

Boog, Horst, et.al. *Germany and the Second World War.* Vol. 4, *The Attack on the Soviet Union.* Oxford, UK: Clarendon Press, 1998.

Erickson, John. *The Road to Stalingrad: Stalin's War with Germany.* New Haven, CT: Yale University Press, 1999.

Glantz, David, and Jonathan House. *When Titans Clashed: How the Red Army Stopped Hitler.* Lawrence: University of Kansas Press, 1995.

Killiecrankie (27 July 1689)

A major defeat of the British at the hands of the Highland Scots, and the last true Scottish battle. The overthrow of James II by the English Parliament and the subsequent ascension to the throne by William III and Mary II led to an uprising by Scottish clans supporting the Stuart claim. In 1689, John Graham of Claverhouse, Viscount Dundee, unfurled the Stuart standard in the Highlands. He quickly raised an army of 1,800 soldiers, including men from the various clans, along with 500 Irish mercenaries. Dundee marched his force to secure Blair Castle (Atholl), an important strategic site in the Grampian Highlands near Perth.

To suppress this revolt, General Hugh Mackay marched north with a force of approximately 3,500 royalist troops. Mackay's force consisted mostly of Lowland Scots, many of whom were recent recruits. The most direct route to Blair Castle was to traverse the Pass of Killiecrankie, a narrow rugged area that was easily defensible. Furthermore, Dundee knew this was the likely avenue of march and moved his army to defend the pass. On 27 July, the advance guard of the royalist army entered the pass and found it undefended. Here Mackay made a critical error. Instead of quickly moving his entire force through the pass, he ordered his men to take up positions in the nearby grain fields to allow the artillery and baggage train to traverse the steep hills. This allowed Dundee to consolidate his forces on the battlefield. Mackay could have ordered an assault on the enemy, but lacking intelligence about the size of his opponent, he organized his units in defensive positions. He divided each battalion into two units, three men deep with intervals between each group. Mackay unlimbered his three artillery pieces and began a harassing fire on the Jacobites.

Dundee arranged his smaller army by clans with large intervals between units. He also shifted his line toward the enemy's right flank to prevent his own flank from being enveloped. At 7 P.M., the weight of the royalist cannon fire prompted Dundee to order an assault. The Highlanders launched a fierce charge, with each man bent forward to provide a smaller target, using his shields to protect the upper body. Mackay's troops fired three volleys at the advancing Jacobites, with little effect because each unit fired by platoon, instead of withholding fire for a concentrated volley. Some units did not fire at all. This allowed the Highlanders to fall upon Mackay's unnerved troops with broadswords and pole-axes before they could insert their socket bayonets. Hundreds were hacked down and the royalist infantry broke into rout. The entire force would have been destroyed had Dundee not been killed at the moment of victory and the Jacobites stopped to plunder the royalist baggage train. After suffering nearly 2,000 casualties, the remnants of Mackay's army retreated to Perth. Jacobite losses were approximately 500 men.

Killiecrankie is touted as the last of the true Scottish battles, as most of the participants were Scots. It was a tactical masterpiece by Dundee, but his death prevented the Jacobites from exploiting the victory. Colonel Cannon, Dundee's successor, was repulsed by the royalists at Dunkeld and the uprising soon lost momentum.

Barry P. Neville

See also: Anglo-Scots Wars (1513–1560)

References and further reading:

Brown, Peter H. *History of Scotland.* Vol. 3. New York: Octagon Books, 1971.

Reese, Peter. *The Scottish Commander: Scotland's Greatest Military Leaders from Wallace to World War II.* Edinburgh: Canongate Books, 1999.

Kim Il-sung (1912–1994)

Founding leader of the Democratic People's Republic of (North) Korea. Kim Il-sung was born in 1912 near Pyongyang in Japanese-occupied Korea and began his revolutionary career in 1929 when he was jailed for student activism. The next year he received the nom de guerre of Kim Il-sung—a famous former revolutionary—and for the next decade probably fought with Chinese guerrillas in Manchuria. In 1939, he likely reentered Korea to fight the Japanese occupiers and two years later he retreated into the Soviet Union. Little is known of his time in the USSR; there is no firm evidence to support the rumor that he fought at Stalingrad.

At the end of World War II, in September 1945, Soviet authorities brought Kim back to Korea and later presented him as the leader of the Soviet-imposed regime north of the thirty-eighth parallel. There probably was a struggle for power between Kim, an expatriate, and local Korean communists. In 1948 the Soviets established the Democratic People's Republic of Korea with Kim as its leader and set up the Korean People's Army. By the next year, American intelligence experts were expecting warfare across the parallel in the near future.

That attack began on 25 June 1950, and North Korean troops seemingly overwhelmed the South Korean defenders. Eventually, U.S. air power inhibited North Korean supply lines and General Walton Walker held the Pusan perimeter; on 15 September General Douglas MacArthur launched the Inchon offensive and North Korea nearly collapsed. Had the Chinese not intervened, Kim would have lost everything; presumably in the aftermath of Chinese intervention, he owed the Chinese a huge debt of gratitude, which probably was difficult for a committed though Communist Korean nationalist.

Kim retained power after the armistice with the United Nations forces defending South Korea and served as general secretary of the party as well as chairman of the party's military commission and president of the Democratic People's Republic of Korea (DPRK). He increasingly almost deified himself in a cult of personality that seemed to out-Stalin Stalin. To the consternation of the more credulous DPRK citizens, he died on 8 July 1994.

Charles M. Dobbs

See also: Chosin/Changjin Reservoir; Korean War; MacArthur, Douglas; Pusan Perimeter; Ridgway, Mathew B.

References and further reading:

Kim, Doug Joong, ed. *Foreign Relations of North Korea during Kim Il Sung's Last Days.* Seoul: Sejong Institute, 1994.

Sandler, Stanley. *The Korean War: No Victors, No Vanquished.* Lexington: University of Kentucky Press, 1999.

Scalapino, Robert, and C. Lee. *Communism in Korea.* Berkeley: University of California Press, 1972.

Suh, Dae-sook. *Kim Il-sung: The North Korean Leader.* New York: Columbia University Press, 1988.

Kim Yu-sin (595–673)

General and statesman of the Silla Kingdom (c. 200–905), one of the primary architects of Silla's unification of the Korean peninsula in 668. Kim Yu-sin was born in an aristocratic family in 595, at a time of increasing rivalry between Korea's three dominant kingdoms—Paekche in the southwest, Koguryo in the north, and Silla in the southeast—and was brought up in the strict military and Buddhist discipline common to the youths of the Silla nobility. Later legends relate how he was visited by a mountain spirit that predicted his eventual defeat of Silla's rivals.

For almost two centuries before Kim's birth, the three Korean kingdoms had fought an ever-shifting, three-way struggle for territorial expansion. By the early seventh century, the issue had become one of peninsular hegemony. After Silla secured an alliance with the Tang Dynasty (618–907) to overcome both Koguryo and Paekche, Kim Yu-sin led Silla forces in 661 in a combined Silla-Tang attack upon Paekche that culminated in that kingdom's utter defeat. The defeat of Koguryo, again through a Silla-Tang alliance, soon followed in 668, but Kim Yu-sin would die before witnessing the final Silla unification. This came in 676 with Silla's defeat of its erstwhile ally and would-be overlord, Tang China. Regardless, Kim Yu-sin is viewed as the father of Korean unification, and legends have continued to be built around him since his death. His tomb can still be seen in the historic city of Kyongju, the former capital of the Silla Kingdom.

Daniel Kane

See also: Chinese Imperial Wars; Koguryo; Paekche; Silla Kingdom; Sino-Korean Wars and the Wars of Korean Unification

References and further reading:

Adams, Edward B. *Korea's Golden Age: Cultural Spirit of Silla in Kyongju.* Revised edition. Seoul: Seoul International Publishing House, 1991.

Chu, Yo-sop. *Kim Yusin :The Romances of a Korean Warrior of the 7th Century.* Seoul: Mutual Publishers, 1947.

Yi, Ki-baek. *A New History of Korea.* Trans. Edward W. Wagner with Edward J. Shultz. Seoul: Ilchokak Publishers, 1984.

Kimberley, Siege of (14 October 1899–15 February 1900)

Unsuccessful siege in the Second Boer War. The diamond-mining frontier town of Kimberley was a key British outpost in the Cape Colony of South Africa in the late nineteenth century. Just days after the onset of hostilities, 4,000 Boers under Cornelius J. Weasels invested 600 British regulars and 4,000 local police and militia inside the town on 14–15 October 1899. The British command was uneasily divided between Lieutenant Colonel Robert G. Kekewich and a domineering civilian, Cecil John Rhodes, the founder of De Beers Consolidated Mines and a former prime minister of the Cape Colony, who usurped Kekewich's authority at every turn and generally harassed his efforts to run an efficient military operation. The Boers never attacked Kimberley, but surrounded it, cut communication, and tried to starve the garrison and inhabitants into submission. There was sporadic artillery fire from both sides. On 4 November Weasels issued a written ultimatum to surrender, which Kekewich immediately rejected.

In mid-November British commander in chief Redvers Buller ordered Lord Paul Sanford Methuen to reopen the railroad to Kimberley and rescue the garrison. Boer leaders Jacobus Hercules De La Rey and Jacobus Prinsloo were more than a match for Methuen's unimaginative tactics at Belmont on 23 November, Graspan on 25 November, and the Modder River on 28 November. Methuen's frontal assault withered against small arms fire from Piet Cronjé's skillfully entrenched Boer positions at Magersfontein on 11 December. Thus the first significant British effort to break the siege failed.

In January 1900 the new British commander in chief, Frederick Sleigh Roberts, demoted Methuen and ordered John French to relieve Kimberley. French led an exhausted division of cavalry into the town on 15 February. Only 21 inside the town had died from enemy action, but more than 1,500 had expired from disease. With the siege of Kimberley lifted, Roberts was able to defeat Cronjé at nearby Paardeberg on 27 February.

Eric v. d. Luft

See also: Boer Wars; Buller, Sir Redvers Henry; French, John Denton Pinkstone, First Earl of Ypres; Roberts, Frederick Sleigh, First Earl, Viscount St. Pierre of Kandahar

References and further reading:

Ashe, Evelyn Oliver. *Besieged by the Boers: A Diary of Life and Events in Kimberley during the Siege.* New York: Doubleday, Page & Co., 1900.

Duminy, Kokkie. *Summer of 1899: The Siege of Kimberley, 14 October 1899 to 15 February 1900.* Ed. Steve Lunderstedt. Kimberley: Kimberley Africana Library, 1999.

Gardner, Brian. *The Lion's Cage.* London: Barker, 1969.

Roberts, Brian. *Kimberley: Turbulent City.* Cape Town: D. Philip in Association with the Historical Society of Kimberley and the Northern Cape, 1976.

King Philip's War (1675–1676)

Proportionally in terms of population, both aboriginal and settler, the most devastating war in American history. The conflict basically erupted over differing concepts of land ownership. Indians viewed land as a shared environment; however, the English perspective was based on boundaries and exclusive ownership. The Plymouth settlement had expanded rapidly to almost 50,000 colonists by the mid-1670s. This development combined with religious zeal to threaten the stability of Indian culture, leading to resentment and eventually violence.

In the midst of this tension Philip assumed leadership as sachem of the Wampanoag in 1662. Philip sought to demonstrate leadership through shows of force. However he was coerced into surrendering all weapons and recognizing English sovereignty.

When Christian Indian John Sassamon was found murdered, the colonists accused and executed three Wampanoags. Philip's perceived weakness led stronger and younger warriors to seek direct conflict with the colonists. The Wampanoag began to ambush settlers in outlying areas while using the swamps for protection. They destroyed 12 towns, including Deerfield, Massachusetts, and killed thousands of settlers. Other tribes, such as the Narraganset and Nipmuc, joined with the Wampanoag to attack settlements across New England.

The colonists soon raised armies adapted to wilderness warfare that destroyed Indian crops, captured their families, and offered protection for those who rejected Philip's leadership.

The Narraganset Indians were decisively defeated during the Great Swamp Fight of December 1675, in which colonists overran a defensive stockade and killed more than 600 Indian warriors and their families. The colonists' superior

English troops taking King Philip's fort at South Kingston, Rhode Island, December 1675. (Library of Congress)

numbers and firepower, combined with Indian allies from the Iroquois tribes, spelled doom for Philip's efforts. Philip was killed during an ambush in August 1676 and his head put on display in Plymouth.

The war effectively ended with Philip's death, but not the violence as the colonists sought to exterminate or enslave the Indians. The death of almost 5,000 Indians from war, starvation, and disease destroyed the tribal societies of New England and removed barriers to further white settlement. The English paid a heavy price as well, with half their towns damaged and thousands of colonists killed during the merciless and brutal struggle. Most significantly, King Philip's War reflected a pattern of cultural conflict that would repeat itself over the next 200 years.

Steven J. Rauch

References and further reading:

Ferling, John. *Struggle for a Continent: The Wars of Early America.* Arlington Heights, IL: Harlan Davidson, 1993.

Lepore, Jill. *The Name of War: King Philip's War and the Origins of American Identity.* New York: Alfred A. Knopf, 1998.

Leach, Douglas Edward. *Flintlock and Tomahawk: New England in King Philip's War.* 2d ed. East Orleans, MA: Parnassus Imprints, 1995.

King's Mountain (7 October 1780)

A small but sanguinary conflict between civilians on both sides of the American Revolution. British Major Patrick Ferguson commanded approximately 1,000 loyalist troops moving through the western Carolinas guarding the left flank of Charles Lord Cornwallis's advance. On 7 October 1780, along the South Carolina/North Carolina border, Ferguson and his men occupied heavily wooded King's Mountain, about 60 feet above the surrounding plain. The plateau was about 600 yards long and varied in width from 70 feet to 120 feet; Major Ferguson assumed it was too steep to be scaled. In fact, he felt sufficiently safe to ask Lord Cornwallis for reinforcements to reach out and secure the backcountry.

Patriot forces from the surrounding Appalachian Mountains, aroused by Ferguson's threats against them if they did not submit to the Crown, arrived at the mountain, tied up their horses, and moved through the woods. These militiamen also sought revenge for an earlier battle (and massacre) at Waxhaws Creek.

At this point, the weakness of the loyalist position became clear. The thick woods prevented the kind of advance by column and deployment into line that was the basis of late-eighteenth-century European warfare; meanwhile, to defeat the patriots, the loyalists had to attack them. Loyalist units sought to descend the plateau and come down the hillsides to attack the patriots. Exposed to sharpshooters hiding in the trees and brush, the loyalists suffered many casualties; Ferguson, easily recognizable in a red hunting shirt, was wounded several times and died.

Soon thereafter the British surrendered, and several of the worst offenders in the hanging of captured patriot militiamen were themselves hanged after brief courts-martial. Fearing that Cornwallis would seek revenge, most of the patriot militia went home, never really to appear again in the conflict, but they did set the stage for the ensuing victory at the Cowpens, the skillful retreat to the Dan River, the key battle at Guilford Court House, and Cornwallis's decision to abandon the Carolinas and retreat to Virginia—and Yorktown.

Charles M. Dobbs

See also: American Revolution; Greene, Nathanael

References and further reading:

Lumpkin, Henry. *From Savannah to Yorktown: The American Revolution in the South.* New York: Paragon Publishers, 1987.

Messick, Hank. *King's Mountain.* Boston: Little, Brown, 1976.

Weigley, Russell. *The Partisan War: The South Carolina Campaign of 1780–1782.* Columbia: University of South Carolina Press, 1970.

Kinsale, Siege of (1601)

The climactic action of the Nine Years' War in Ireland. Hugh O'Neill, Earl of Tyrone, who had been in rebellion since 1595, had long awaited Spanish aid, but the arrival of Don Juan Aguila's 3,500 men at Kinsale on 22 September 1601 presented problems for both sides. Kinsale was in southwestern Ireland, while O'Neill's main forces were in Ulster, so joining the Spanish required a march across the island. Meanwhile, Charles Blount, Lord Mountjoy, the English lord deputy, faced the logistical problem of moving his own forces, including his siege train, from Dublin. Mountjoy successfully concentrated 7,000 men outside Kinsale, and English control of the sea allowed delivery of heavy guns and supplies needed to initiate a siege. However, Mountjoy's troops were poorly supplied, and as the siege continued through November, sickness began to reduce his numbers.

O'Neill also experienced difficulty moving his army in that season. His advanced guard, commanded by Hugh O'Donnell, arrived near Kinsale in November, but O'Neill did not arrive until December. With 6,000 men, his plan was to blockade Mountjoy's besieging forces until disease and hunger forced their withdrawal. O'Donnell and Spanish representatives, however, insisted on a relief attempt. This operation was mounted on 24 December. The English had the advantage in the ensuing set piece battle, and their cavalry routed O'Neill's advanced guard as it passed through a bog. Its retreat threw the army into disorder, and a charge by Mountjoy's reserves drove the Irish from the field with more than 1,200 casualties. During the action Aguila made no move to break out of Kinsale, and O'Neill's defeat left him with no hope of relief. The Spanish surrendered on 2 January 1602.

John S. Nolan

See also: Mountjoy, Charles Blount, Lord; Nine Years' War

References and further reading:

Falls, Cyril. *Elizabeth's Irish Wars.* Syracuse, NY: Syracuse University Press, 1997.

Silke, John J. *Kinsale: The Spanish Intervention in Ireland.* Liverpool: Liverpool University Press, 1970.

Wernham, R. B. *The Return of the Armadas: The Last Years of the Elizabethan War against Spain.* New York, Oxford: Clarendon, 1994.

Kitchener, Horatio Herbert (1850–1916)

British field commander, staff officer, and politician. The son of a career army officer, Kitchener was born in County Kerry, Ireland, on 24 June 1850. After graduating from the Royal Military Academy in Woolwich, he was commissioned in the Royal Engineers in January 1871 and saw action as a volunteer on the French side in the Franco-Prussian War. After extensive service as a British military surveyor and intelligence officer around the eastern Mediterranean, he was assigned to cavalry in Cairo, Egypt, in 1882, and was Sir Garnet Wolseley's intelligence officer from October 1884 to March 1885 during the futile expedition to rescue "Chinese" Gordon.

Horatio Herbert Kitchener. (Library of Congress)

As governor of British Red Sea Territories after 1886, Kitchener faced significant Mahdist resistance. He was wounded and defeated by Mahdist leader Osman Digna at Suakin on 17 January 1888. While still a colonel in the British army, he became sirdar, or commander in chief, of the Egyptian army in 1892. After training this army in modern methods for four years, he invaded the Sudan to avenge Gordon, winning at Dongola on 21 September 1896, Abu Hamed on 7 August 1897, Atbara River on 7 April 1898, and Omdurman on 2 September. He drove Jean-Baptiste Marchand's French army from Fashoda, Sudan, on 18 September 1898.

In the Second Boer War, Kitchener was assigned to Frederick Sleigh Roberts as chief of staff on 18 December 1899. His tactics defeated Piet Cronjé at Paardeberg on 18–27 February 1900, frustrated Boer guerrillas, and resulted in the capture of Bloemfontein on 13 March, Johannesburg on 31 May, and Pretoria on 5 June. He replaced Roberts as commander in chief of British forces in South Africa on 29 November. Continuing his offensive against guerrillas, he invented the concentration camp, in which he imprisoned guerrillas, their families, and their supporters.

Appointed secretary of war in July 1914, Kitchener, almost uniquely, foresaw a long war against Germany and urged massive British mobilization. But he was among those lost when HMS *Hampshire* struck a German mine near the Orkneys and sank on 5 June 1916.

Eric v. d. Luft

See also: Boer Wars; Botha, Louis; Gordon, Charles George; Khartoum, Siege of; Omdurman; Roberts, Frederick Sleigh, First Earl, Viscount St. Pierre, of Kandahar; Wolseley, Garnet Joseph, Viscount; World War I

References and further reading:

Cassar, George H. *Kitchener: Architect of Victory.* London: Kimber, 1977.

Royle, Trevor. *The Kitchener Enigma.* London: Joseph, 1985.

Smithers, A. J. *The Fighting Nation: Lord Kitchener and His Armies.* London: Cooper, 1994.

Warner, Philip. *Kitchener: The Man Behind the Legend.* New York: Atheneum, 1986.

Kléber, Jean-Baptiste (1753–1800)

One of the most capable field commanders of the French Revolutionary and early Napoleonic wars. Kléber was born in Strasbourg on 9 March 1753. He served in the imperial army (1777–1785). Influenced by French revolutionary ideas, he joined the national guard at Belfort and rose to lieutenant colonel in a volunteer battalion. His aggressive defense of Mainz earned him a promotion to brigadier general (17 August 1793). He fought the Vendean rebels, and his achievements, especially at Cholet, earned him a battlefield promotion to division general (17 October). He captured Le Mans in December.

As a division commander Kléber played a crucial role at Charleroi (25 June 1794). At Fleurus (26 June) his left wing drove the Austrians into retreat. He captured Maestricht (4 November) and participated in the invasion of the Rhineland. But in spite of a series of victories Kléber, perhaps feeling inadequately rewarded, resigned all active field command on 21 December 1796.

Kléber by now had earned a reputation for great concern for his men's welfare. He was known for great tactical flexibility. He employed both line and column formations but preferred columns for attack.

Kléber returned to active service in 1798. Seriously wounded leading an attack at Alexandria, Egypt (21 July 1798), he also fought in Syria, distinguishing himself in the capture of El Arish (20 February 1799) and at Gaza, Jaffa, and Acre. At Mount Tabor (16 April) his troops held off the main Turkish army until relief arrived. He commanded the rear guard on the retreat into Egypt. Kléber, who had opposed the Egyptian campaign, now advocated a French evacuation. Ironically Napoleon appointed him to command the French forces left in Egypt.

On 24 January 1800 Kléber signed the Armistice of El Arish, providing for a French evacuation. The British disavowed it. With growing enemy opposition, Kléber audaciously resumed hostilities. He defeated the Turks at Heliopolis (20 March) and reconquered Cairo (25 April) and lower Egypt. On 14 June 1800 a Muslim nationalist assassinated Kléber in Cairo. His remains were returned to France in 1801.

James K. Kieswetter

See also: Aboukir; Fleurus, Battle of; French Revolutionary Wars; Napoleon I; Pyramids

References and further reading:

Chandler, David G. *The Campaigns of Napoleon.* New York: Macmillan, 1966.

Lynn, John A. *The Bayonets of the Republic Motivation and Tactics in the Army of Revolutionary France, 1791–1794.* Chicago: University of Illinois Press, 1984.

Herold, Jean Christopher. *Bonaparte in Egypt.* New York: Harper & Row, 1962.

Lucas-Dubreton, Jean. *Kléber 1753–1800.* Paris: Paul Hartmann, 1937.

Knox, Henry (1750–1806)

Continental army officer and secretary of war. At the beginning of the American Revolution, Knox constructed American defenses near Boston. Impressed by Knox's work and his knowledge of artillery, General George Washington commissioned him colonel of the Continental Artillery Regiment. Knox remained a trusted adviser to Washington throughout the war.

During the winter of 1775–1776, Knox directed the transfer of British ordnance captured at Fort Ticonderoga to Boston, which compelled the British to abandon the city. He participated in almost every major battle of the northern campaigns and Yorktown, rising in rank to major general. In 1783, Knox founded the Society of Cincinnati.

As secretary of war (1785–1794), he battled persistent distrust of standing armies yet organized Anthony Wayne's successful Indian campaign, reestablished the U.S. Navy, and secured congressional support for the Uniform Militia Act of 1792. In 1798, Knox was appointed major general in the Provisional Army in anticipation of war with France but refused to serve under Alexander Hamilton, his subordinate during the American Revolution.

Dean Fafoutis

See also: American Revolution; Brandywine; Fallen Timbers; Germantown; Monmouth; Princeton, Battle of; Trenton; Wayne, Anthony; Washington, George; Yorktown

References and further reading:

Callahan, North. *Henry Knox: General Washington's General.* New York: Rinehart, 1958.

Ward, Harry M. *The Department of War, 1781–1795.* Pittsburgh, PA: University of Pittsburgh Press, 1962.

Koguryo (attributed 37 B.C.E.–668 C.E.)

Northernmost of three kingdoms dominating the Korean peninsula. Although the oldest extant in Korean history, the *Samguk sagi* (*History of the Three Kingdoms,* 1145), dates the foundation of Koguryo to 37 B.C.E., there is no evidence for its existence prior to the first century C.E. At that time it emerged in the mountainous region now separating North Korea from China, expanding at the expense of lowland groups.

Following the fall of the Han (206 B.C.E.–220 C.E.), the various small states of northeast China entered a period of intensive competition. Koguryo's power was briefly eclipsed by that of the state of Wei (225–265), which overran its capital in 244, but it soon recovered. In the late fourth century, primarily under the inspired leadership of young king Kwanggaet'o (r. 391–413), a series of successful military campaigns brought Koguryo hegemony over a good part of Manchuria and northern Korea. Early in the fifth century, Koguryo moved its capital south to modern Pyongyang in North Korea, leaving it better positioned for competition with other Korean states.

The next 250 years were ones of growing competition between Koguryo and the other two major states on the peninsula, Paekche and Silla. In 668, Koguryo was conquered by the southern state of Silla, then in alliance with Tang (618–906) China. Although Silla was able to incorporate Koguryo territories as far as the Yalu River (separating modern North Korea from China), Koguryo possessions beyond permanently passed from Korean control with Koguryo's defeat.

Because of its positioning, Koguryo faced frequent and formidable military threats from nomadic tribes and other groups living in Manchuria, and from more centralized Chinese dynasties, Sui (587–618) and Tang in particular. For this reason it gained a reputation for martial spirit and strength of arms. Koguryo is often lauded by modern Koreans for its heroic defense of the peninsula from would-be foreign conquerors.

Daniel Kane

See also: Paekche; Silla Kingdom; Sino-Korean Wars and the Wars of Korean Unification

References and further reading:

Gardiner, K. H. J. *The Early History of Korea: The Historical Development of the Peninsula Up to the Introduction of Buddhism in the Fourth Century A.D.* Honolulu: University of Hawaii Press, 1969.

Iryon. *Samguk Yusa: Legends and History of the Three Kingdoms of Ancient Korea.* Trans. Tae-Hung Ha and Grafton K. Mintz. Seoul: Yonsei University Press, 1972.

Lee, Ki-baik. *A New History of Korea.* Trans. Edward W. Wagner with Edward J. Shultz. Cambridge, MA: Harvard University Press, 1984.

Kokoda Trail (1942)

The first substantial land defeat of Japanese forces in World War II. In early 1942 the Japanese were consolidating the southern boundaries of their Southern Economic Zone along a line through Timor, western New Guinea, Rabaul, and Micronesia, when Australian and U.S. air forces commenced an aggressive bombing campaign from Australia and Port Moresby in New Guinea. In response, the Japanese commenced operations to capture the whole of New Guinea. The first attempt was turned back during the Battle of the Coral Sea in May 1942.

On 22 July 1942 the Japanese landed a 2,000-man advance unit of General Horii's South Seas Force at Buna on the north coast of New Guinea with orders to commence an overland assault on Port Moresby. Their route was to be a walking track leading over 10,000-foot-high passes in the Owen Stanley Mountains—the Kokoda Trail.

A component of the Australian 39th Militia Battalion made an orderly fighting withdrawal without slowing the Japanese. By 21 August, 13,500 Japanese troops had been committed and had captured the town of Kokoda near the summit of the Owen Stanley Mountains. The Australian 53d battalion was ordered northwards up the Kokoda Trail to reinforce the 39th and was followed by the 21st brigade, which reached Isuvura at the southern side of the summit on 23 August.

Conditions were horrific. All supplies, including dismantled artillery and mortars, had to be carried by hand. The muddy, narrow trail crossed a series of very steep valleys, up to 3,000 feet deep, as it climbed either side of the mountains. The Japanese were now two full brigades in strength and continued to push the Australians, who had been reinforced by elements of the 25th brigade, back in fierce and continuous fighting. By 16 September they reached Imita Ridge, only 26 miles from Port Moresby. However, because of the situation at Guadalcanal, Japanese Imperial Army Headquarters ordered a withdrawal on 20 September, and with all supplies exhausted, the retreat commenced. It rapidly degenerated into a rout for the Japanese, and starvation, total breakdown in discipline, killing of sick and wounded, and cannibalism were evident. However, savage firefights did still occur frequently. Of 14,500 Japanese troops committed, only 5,000 survived to reach Buna by mid-November 1942.

Michael Hyde

See also: Guadalcanal; Milne Bay; World War II

References and further reading:

Japanese Monograph No. 37. "South-east Asian Operations Record: 18th Army Operations on New Guinea and Rabaul (January 1942–June 1943), The Southern Area (Part II)." In *War in Asia and the Pacific,* Vol. 7, ed. D. Detwiler. New York: Garland Publishing Co., 1980.

McCarthy, D. *Australia in the War of 1939–1945.* Series One, *Army.* Vol. 5, *South West Pacific Area—First Year Kokoda to Wau.* Canberra: Australian War Memorial, 1959.

Odgers, George. *Army Australia—An Illustrated History.* New South Wales: Child and Associates, 1988.

"Aleksandr Vasilyevich Kolchak, supreme ruler of all Russian government." Poster, 1918. (Library of Congress)

Kolchak, Aleksandr Vasil'evich (1874–1920)

Russian admiral, polar explorer, White Civil War leader. Born in St. Petersburg, son of a naval officer, Kolchak graduated from St. Petersburg Naval Academy (1894) and served in the Pacific and Indian Oceans, becoming a naval lieutenant in 1899. A specialist in oceanography and hydrology, he completed two Arctic exploratory trips (1900–1904) and was prestigiously awarded for his published results (1909).

With the outbreak of the Russo-Japanese War (1904–1905) he rejoined the navy, commanding a destroyer, and was decorated for mine-laying work and sinking an enemy cruiser. Forced ashore by ill health, he commanded a naval battery during the siege of Port Arthur, was captured, but repatriated in 1906.

A founder of the Naval General Staff, he served in this, becoming chief of the organization section for the Baltic Fleet, pressing for naval modernization and reforms. Between postings, he organized and planned another Arctic expedition to chart the northern Siberian coast.

During World War I he enjoyed a distinguished active service: Baltic Fleet (1914–1916) and commander of the Black Sea Fleet (July 1916–July 1917). Becoming vice admiral in August 1916, he won further decorations for mine-laying and naval defense work.

After the February Revolution, he supported the provisional government but resigned in June 1917 with his command disintegrating. Traveling to America via London, he made links with the American and British navies, joining the latter in December 1917 after the Bolshevik Revolution. In Japan December 1917–April 1918 and July–September 1918, he also served General Horvath in Harbin. Coveted as an anti-Bolshevik figurehead after his impressive military career and foreign connections, he was summoned back to Russia and installed as supreme ruler of Russia after the Omsk coup in November 1918.

During the Russian Civil War, Kolchak established a military dictatorship, but his initial support deteriorated amidst political corruption, repression, and misuse of Allied aid to create vast discontented partisan networks in his rear, which came to favor the Red Army. Kolchak launched an initially successful offensive, taking Perm (December 1918), but was pushed back by Red eastern front counteroffensives (April–December 1919). His capital, Omsk, fell on 14 November; he resigned on 4 January 1920 as supreme ruler of Russia, naming Denikin as his successor.

Fleeing eastwards, he was captured by Czechs and handed over to social revolutionaries in Irkutsk. Tried by a hastily assembled Communist revolutionary tribunal, he was executed on 7 February.

Neil Harvey Croll

See also: Denikin, Anton Ivanovich; Russian Civil War (1918–1921); Tukhachevsky, Mikhail Nikolayevich; World War I

References and further reading:

Collins, D., and J. Smele. *Kolckak i Sibir': Issledovaniia* (Kolchak and Siberia: Documents and Studies), *1919–1926.* Vols. 1 and 2. New York: Kraus International Publishers, 1988.

Krasnov, V. *Kolchak i zhizn', i smert' za Rossiiu, knigi I & II.* Moscow: Olma-Press, 2000.

Smele, J. *Civil War in Siberia: The Anti-Bolshevik Government of Admiral Kolchak, 1918–1920.* Cambridge, UK: Cambridge University Press, 1996.

Varneck, E., and H. H. Fisher, eds. *The Testimony of Kolchak and Other Siberian Materials.* Stanford, CA: Stanford University Press, 1935.

Konev, Ivan Stepanovich (1897–1973)

Soviet military commander marshal of the Soviet Union (1944). Of peasant origins, from northern Dvina Province,

Konev joined the Russian army (1916), saw little action, but emerged an NCO. A Bolshevik supporter, he returned home after the October Revolution, becoming Nikol'sk District military commissar. He ended the Russian Civil War as an armored-train political commissar, serving in the east against Kolchak, Semenov, and Japanese forces until 1922, and in suppression of the Kronstadt Revolt (March 1921).

He graduated from Frunze Military Academy staff training courses (1926, 1934) and somehow survived Stalin's purges to gain rapid promotion. He commanded 57th Special Corps in Mongolia (1937) and Second Separate Red Banner Army in the Far Eastern, Transbaikal, and Northern Caucasus Military Districts.

After mixed fortunes, Konev emerged as one of the most original, capable Soviet World War II commanders. As Nineteenth Army commander, he counterattacked at Smolensk to delay the Germans, but as Western Front commander in September 1941, he was partly responsible for the Viazma-Briiansk encirclement, wherein 500,000 Russians were taken prisoner. Escaping trial for this, he was given the Kalinin Front, counterattacking with Zhukov in December to halt Operation BARBAROSSA before Moscow.

He commanded the Western Front from August 1942, Northwestern Front from March 1943, the Steppe (later 2d Ukrainian) Front from June 1943, and the 1st Ukrainian Front (May 1944–May 1945), playing a leading role in Soviet Operations at Kursk, Korsun'-Cherkassy, Vistula-Oder, Berlin, and Prague.

Postwar, Konev served as Soviet commander in Austria (1945–1946), chief inspector of the Soviet Army (1950–1951), commander in chief of Soviet Land Forces and deputy minister for war (1946–1950, 1955–1956), and Carpathian Military District commander (1951–1955). Benefiting under Khrushchev at Zhukov's expense, Konev became first deputy minister for defense and commander in chief of Warsaw Pact forces (1956–1960). He commanded Soviet forces in suppressing the 1956 Hungarian uprising and in Germany during the construction of the Berlin Wall, all actions which Stalin would have approved.

Konev remained an adviser in retirement, wrote his memoirs, and died of cancer in Moscow.

Neil Harvey Croll

See also: Hungarian Revolt; Kursk, Battle of; Moscow; Stalin; World War II; Zhukov, Georgy Konstantinovich

References and further reading:

Bystrov, V. E. *Sovetskie polkovodtsy I voenachal'niki. Sbornik* (Soviet Leaders and Military Chiefs. Collection). Moscow: Molodaia gvardiia, 1988.

Kolesnikov, A. A. *Marshaly Rossii* (Marshals of Russia). Iaroslavl': Izdat. Niuans, 1999.

Konev, I. S. *Zapiski komanduiushchego frontom 1943–45* (Notes of a Front Commander, 1943–45). Moscow: Voenizdat, 1982 and 1991.

Shukman, H., ed. *Stalin's Generals.* London: Weidenfeld & Nicolson, 1993.

Kongo, Kingdom of the (14th–17th Centuries)

An ally of Portugal, adopting European military technology, but eventually undone by internal conflict, marauding neighbors, and the intrigues of foreign slave traders. The Kingdom of the Kongo arose in the 1300s along the mouth of the Congo River in western central Africa. The ruler, the Mani-Kongo, functioned as an absolute monarch, supervisor of an intricate administrative organization, and a semidivine religious authority in an intricate system that extended from the capital through all cities, provinces, and villages. An agrarian people, the Bakongo people were also active in mining, smelting, and in woven raffia products. Advised by a council of landed nobles, the king used trade, tribute, and occasional demonstrations of force to ensure peace with neighboring peoples.

In 1483, a Portuguese vessel arrived at the mouth of the Congo River and began a long and complex relationship with Kongo. By 1506, the Mani-Kongo, many nobles, and ordinary people had converted to Catholicism. King Afonso I (1509–1543) used the church, Portuguese mercenaries and advisers, and trade revenues to centralize his power. He mixed traditional Kongolese light infantry, shield-bearing "heavy" infantry, and Portuguese mercenaries armed with pikes and arquebus rifles. He campaigned against his neighbors, the kingdoms of the Angola, Banguela, and Nziki as well as more rustic peoples like the Mbundu, the Teke, and the Jaga. To support these efforts, Afonso engaged in slave trading with Portuguese merchants, operating out of São Tomé and other offshore islands. The demand for slaves generated a pervasive, pernicious, and hugely profitable commerce that neither the Portuguese authorities nor Afonso could control. Slavers relentlessly thwarted all Afonso's work by allying with other kingdoms, funding slaver gangs and rebellious nobles, and draining resources from the monarchy.

Future kings had to balance their dependency on Portugal for arms, assistance, and trade with the intrigues of Portuguese merchants, slave dealers, and mercenaries to promote rivalries, wars, and instability throughout the region. In 1569, for example, King Alvaro confronted a massive invasion by the Jaga. The Jaga sacked the capital at São Salvador, nearly drove Alvaro to the coast, and sent thousands of captives to the eager slavers at São Tomé. Lisbon came to Alvaro's rescue in 1571 and drove the Jaga out. Shortly thereafter, Portugal established another great enslavement center south of Kongo at Luanda in Angola territory. Thus, relations between Kongo and Portugal would remain active, but the slave trade also ensured that these relations would be brittle and unstable.

In the 1640s, Dutch efforts to seize Angola encouraged the Kongo kings to reduce Portugal's influence. In 1665, a boundary dispute led to war between the Kongo and Portuguese forces protecting Angola. At the Battle of Mbwila, the Kongo army shattered on the Portuguese formations and King Antonio died of a bullet wound. The Kongo fragmented into warring components.

In 1670, another Portuguese force from Luanda tried to place a candidate on Kongo's throne, only to be annihilated at the Battle of Colombo by troops from Nsoyo Province. São Salvador was destroyed and abandoned in 1678. The Kongo knew no peace until 1709, when Pedro IV finally emerged as the victor.

Pedro's Kongo was not the Kongo envisioned by Afonso 200 years before. Decentralized, unstable, plagued by rebel nobles and outside incursions, the proliferation of firearms in the eighteenth century only sharpened the turbulence. The Kongo had, in effect, imploded.

Weston F. Cook, Jr.

References and further reading:

Thornton, John K. *The Kingdom of Kongo.* Madison: University of Wisconsin, 1983.

———. *Warfare in Atlantic Africa, 1500–1800.* London: University College Press, 1999.

Königgrätz, Battle of (1866)

Battle that secured Prussian dominance of central Europe for Otto von Bismarck. The battle began in the morning of 3 July 1866 with a Prussian enveloping attempt, but the maneuver failed when two Prussian armies failed to connect and a third failed to advance because of ground fog. Prussia was forced to engage all its reserves, while Austria did not even have to commit its cavalry. When the Prussian Second Army finally arrived on the Austro-Saxon flank in the late afternoon, they forced an Austrian retreat. Some 250,000 Prussians had defeated a comparable number of Austrians and Saxons, ending the Seven Weeks' War. The Austrians had lost 45,000 casualties and 20,000 captured, while Prussian forces sustained only 10,000 casualties. Vienna lay open to Prussian attack, forcing Austria to sue for peace.

Prussian soldiers had several important advantages in the battle. First, their breech-loading needle-guns (so-called because of their long firing pins) were far superior rifles to the Austrian muzzle-loaders. The Austrian rifle had better range and accuracy, but men lying down and presenting a smaller target could use the Prussian gun.

Second, the superior organization and planning of the Prussian army, led by the general staff under Helmuth Karl von Moltke, quickly recovered from the mistakes of the morning and saved the day.

Finally, the Prussians moved large numbers of forces rapidly using the extensive Prussian railroad system. In contrast, Austrian movements were clumsy and slow. The Prussians saved their troops for battle rather than losing them to fatigue on march and earned an element of surprise.

The battle, which took place near the Czech town of Sadowa, was the largest European battle until 1914.

David C. Arnold

See also: Bismarck, Otto von; Custozza, Second Battle of

References and further reading:

Blackbourn, David. *The Long Nineteenth Century: A History of Germany, 1780–1918.* Oxford, UK: Oxford University Press, 1998.

Goerlitz, Walter. *History of the German General Staff, 1657–1945.* Trans. Briand Battershaw. New York: Praeger, 1962.

Showalter, Dennis E. *Railroads and Rifles: Soldiers, Technology and the Unification of Germany.* Hamden, CT: Archon Books, 1975.

Korean War (1950–1953)

Korea had been a part of Japan's Inner Empire until Japan surrendered to end World War II in the Pacific. At the Yalta Conference, Soviet leader Joseph Stalin promised Soviet intervention in the war against Japan soon after the war in Europe ended. Meanwhile, on the night of 10–11 August 1945, two American army colonels, Dean Rusk and Charles Bonesteel, sat down with a map to determine an American zone of occupation to accept the Japanese surrender in Korea; they chose a temporary demarcation line at the thirty-eighth parallel. Thus, the most homogeneous nation on earth was divided as an administrative convenience.

By 1950, the situation had worsened for the U.S. government. The Soviets had isolated their sector and had set about almost immediately to organize life in the north along People's Republic lines. Meanwhile, the southern zone needed continuing American economic assistance, which was difficult in those days of limited foreign aid budgets and many more deserving or perhaps more important countries.

In a notorious speech in January 1950, Secretary of State Dean Acheson outlined the U.S. defense perimeter in the western Pacific and Asia—and explicitly excluded southern Korea. Perhaps the North Korean invasion was inevitable; perhaps the government in Pyongyang assumed American noninterference given Acheson's remarks and America's

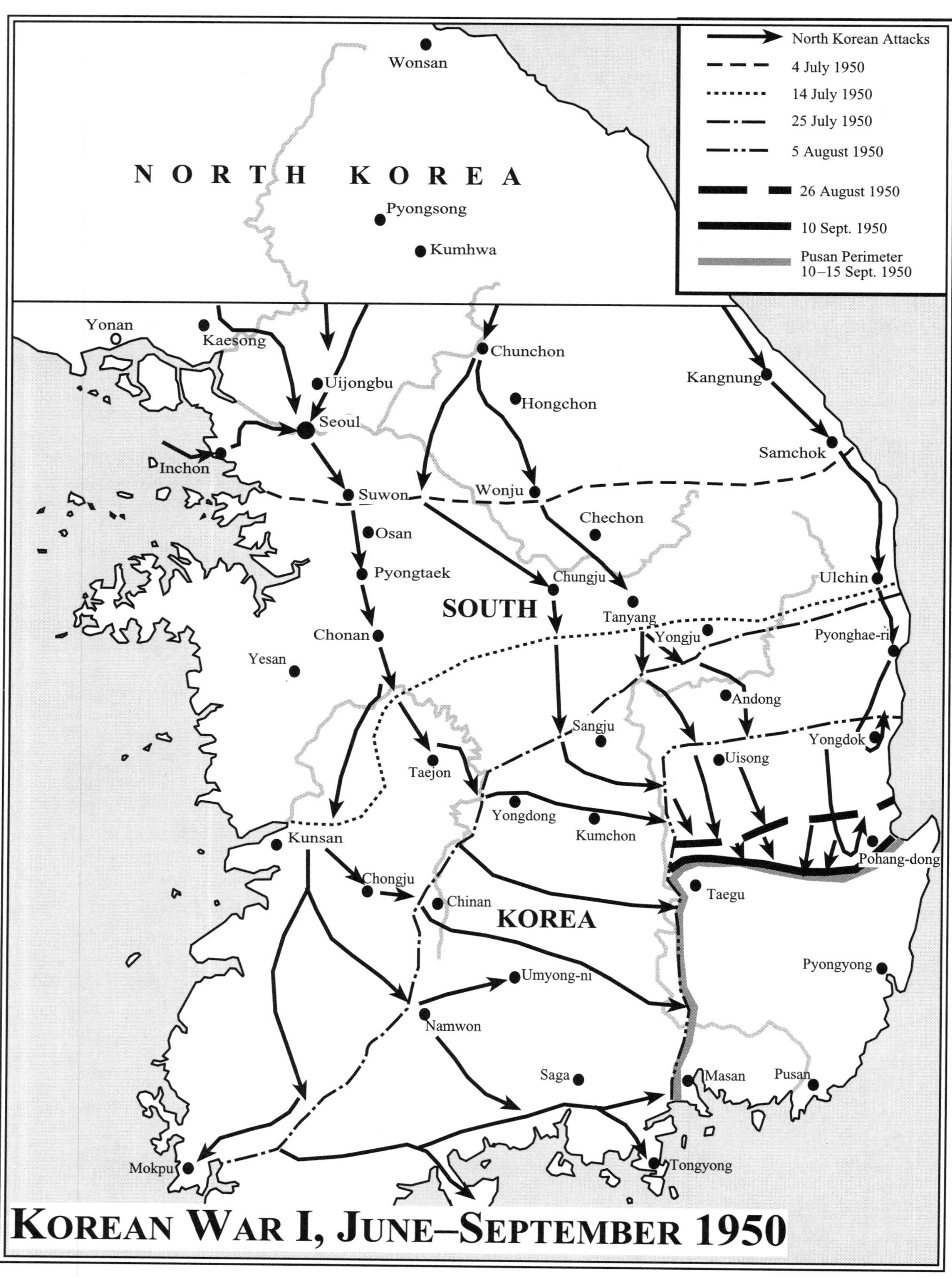

Korean War I, June–September 1950

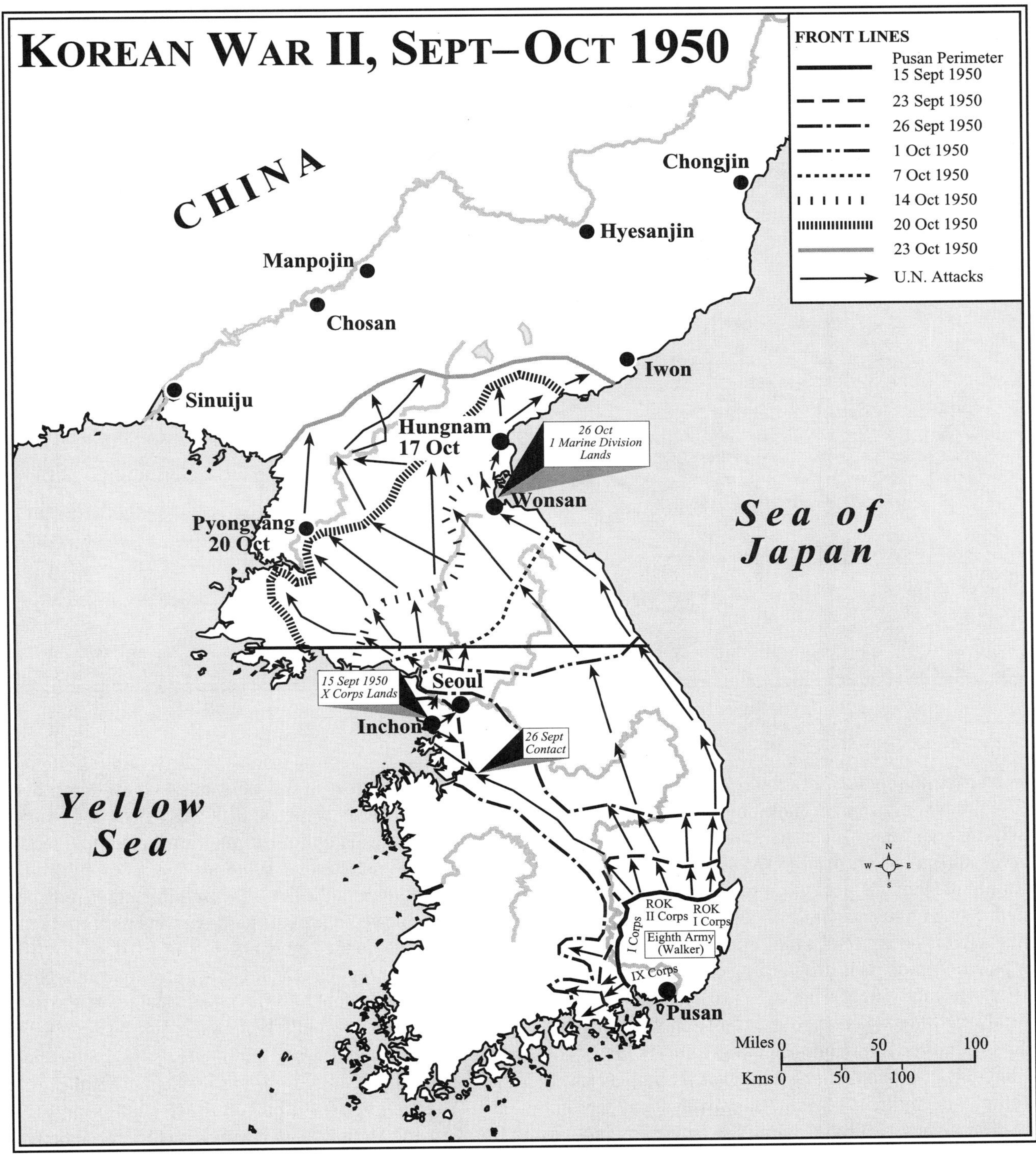

KOREAN WAR II, SEPT–OCT 1950
FRONT LINES
Pusan Perimeter 15 Sept 1950
23 Sept 1950
26 Sept 1950
1 Oct 1950
7 Oct 1950
14 Oct 1950
20 Oct 1950
23 Oct 1950
U.N. Attacks
CHINA
Chongjin
Hyesanjin
Manpojin
Chosan
Iwon
Sinuiju
Hungnam 17 Oct
26 Oct 1 Marine Division Lands
Wonsan
Sea of Japan
Pyongyang 20 Oct
Seoul
15 Sept 1950 X Corps Lands
Inchon
26 Sept Contact
Yellow Sea
ROK II Corps
ROK I Corps
I Corps
Eighth Army (Walker)
IX Corps
Pusan
Miles 0 50 100
Kms 0 50 100

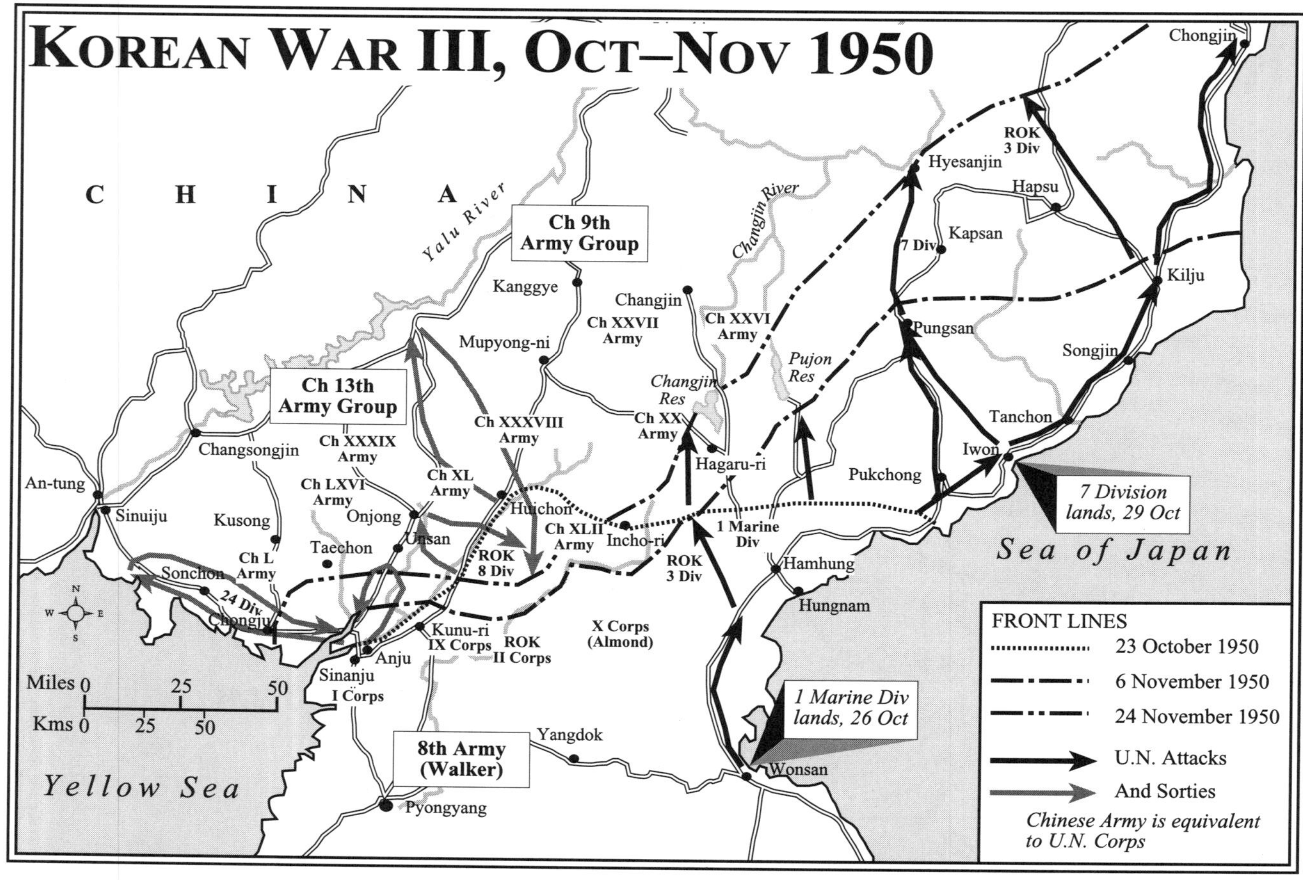

nonreaction to the "loss" of China. Regardless, on 25 June 1950, North Korea launched a major invasion of the south.

The Korean War can be seen in five stages. Initially, North Korea's Korean People's Army (KPA) unleashed a surprise attack against the lightly armed South on 25 June 1950. The South Korean army was really a constabulary with mostly antiguerrilla warfare, few heavy weapons, and practically no air power. Some of its higher-ranking officers did have military experience—fighting in the Japanese army in World War II. Many North Korean soldiers had experience fighting with the Chinese Communists in World War II or in the long Chinese civil war; more tellingly, they had Soviet T-34 tanks, artillery, and antitank weapons. They easily broke through the defenses at the thirty-eighth parallel and, after pausing for several days to cross the Han River before Seoul, they poured southwards. President Harry Truman committed U.S. forces to resist this aggression, and available infantry units sought to delay the Communist drive down the west side of the peninsula. But the Americans, pulled from their easy Japanese occupation duties, were too few in number, had too little artillery and tanks, and were kept off-balance by the North Koreans, who were able to move faster and punch harder. By early August the Communists had pinned the South Koreans and their American allies to a small perimeter around Pusan in southeast Korea. But they had a long supply line and the U.S. was committing more ground, sea, and air power to hold the perimeter and to interdict the flow of supplies to the aggressors.

Then came the American counterattack—the second stage. On 15 September 1950 General Douglas MacArthur mounted a surprise amphibious assault deep behind enemy lines at Inchon on the west coast near the capital, Seoul, and UN forces in the Pusan perimeter soon linked with the invasion force, cutting off the bulk of the North Korean army. U.S. Navy and Marine Corps commanders had great doubts about the wisdom of invading Inchon, but events proved that MacArthur was correct to follow the line of least expectation. Within a few weeks, the North Korean army in the south ceased to exist as an organized fighting unit, although many North Korean soldiers escaped north of the thirty-eighth parallel but without their equipment and armaments. After considering the alternatives, including a halt to the

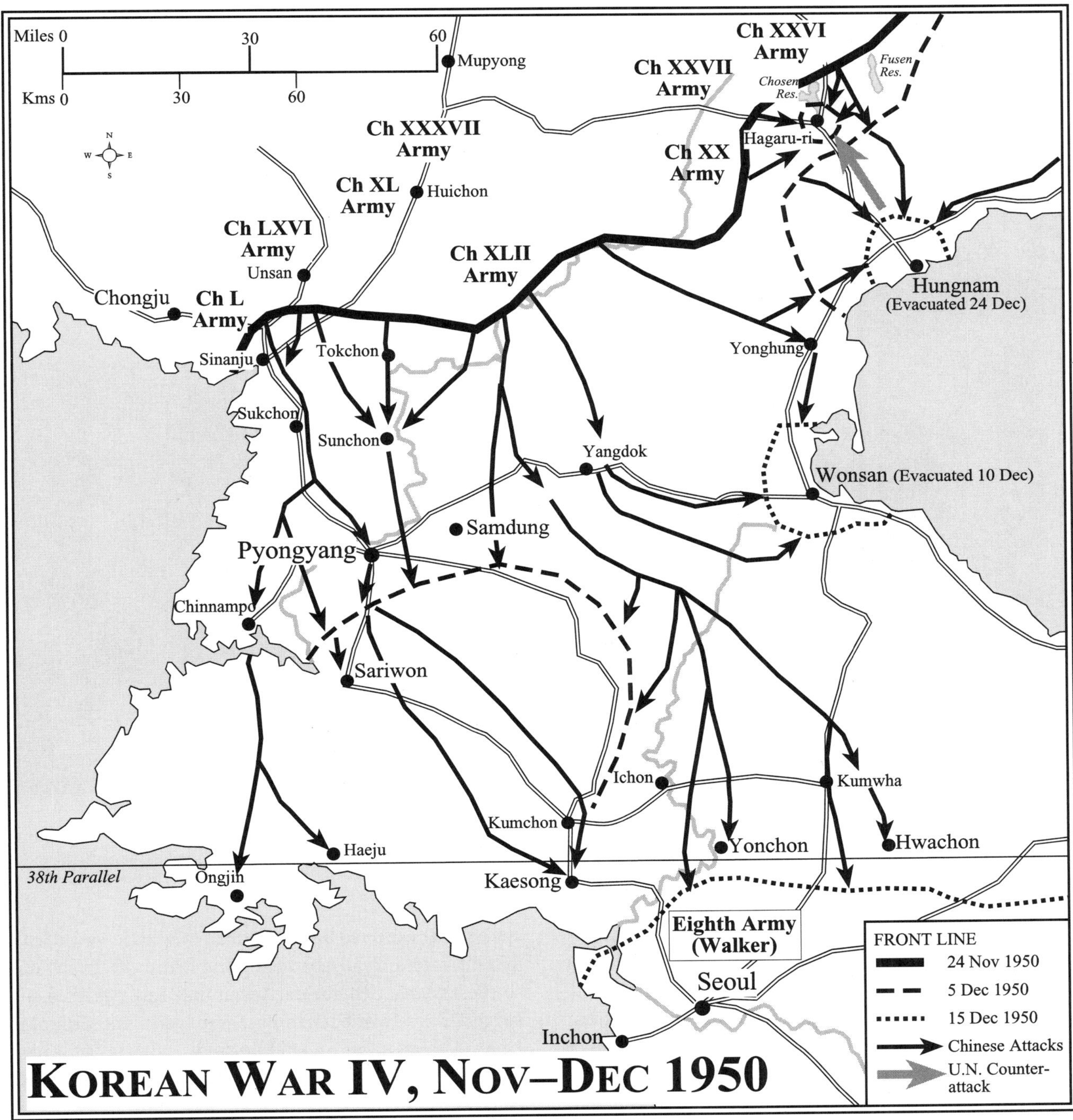

KOREAN WAR IV, NOV–DEC 1950

fighting at the thirty-eighth parallel, President Truman gave permission for MacArthur to cross the thirty-eighth parallel and to proceed north to "free" the entire peninsula from Communist control unless UN forces ran into Chinese or Soviet troops operating in Korea. Only South Korean units were to approach the sensitive borders with China and the Soviet Union. But MacArthur in Tokyo and many American officials in Washington, D.C., discounted warnings from the Chinese Communist leaders in Beijing, relayed through the Indian government, that the Chinese would intervene unless the drive northwards was halted; similarly, U.S. intelligence discounted evidence of hundreds of thousands of Chinese soldiers moving north to Manchuria from the provinces opposite Taiwan and in south China. (Recent evidence suggests

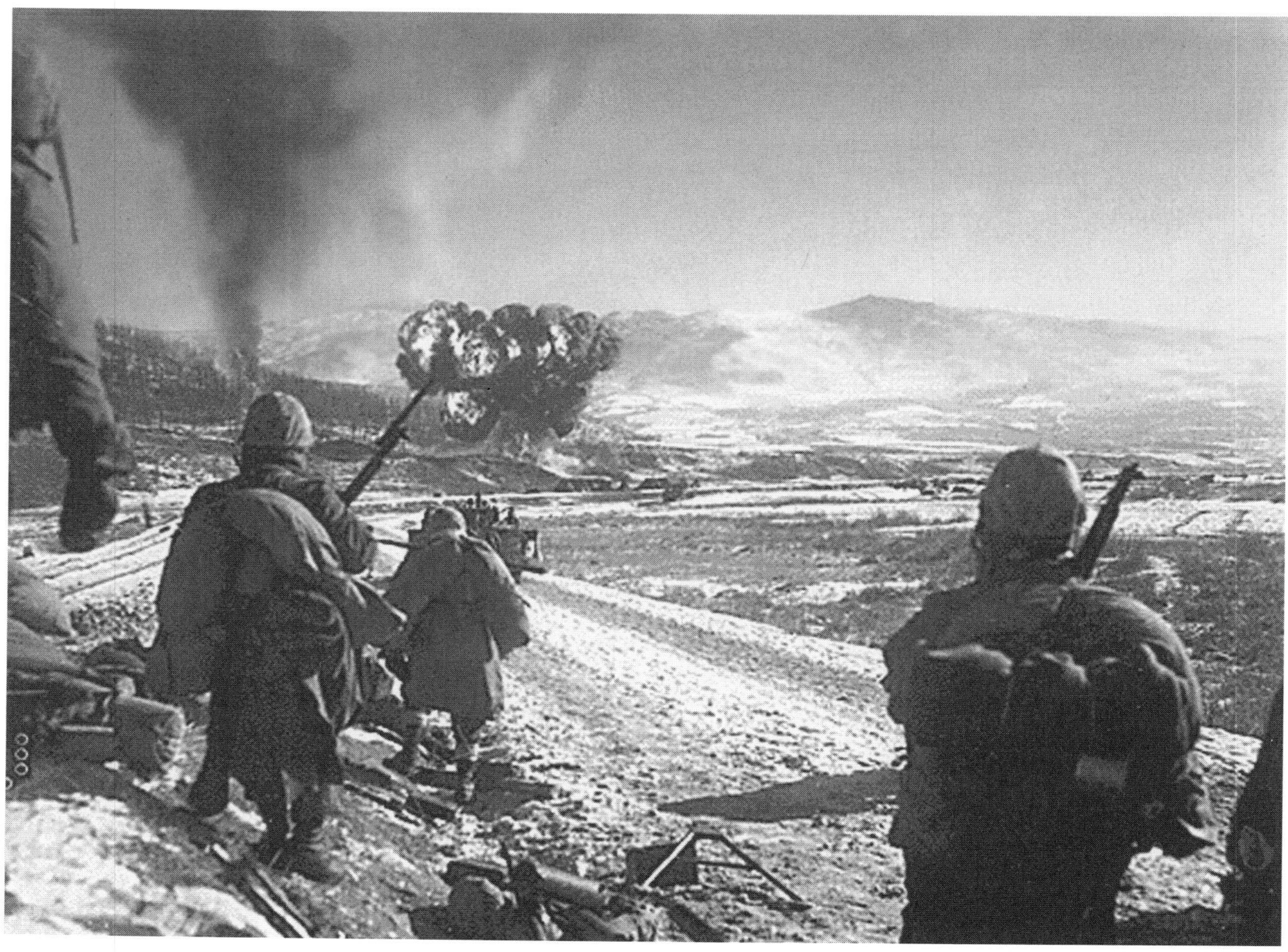

U.S. Marines move forward after effective close-air support flushed out the enemy from their hillside entrenchments on December 26, 1950. (National Archives)

that the Chinese Communist leadership seriously considered intervention in the Korean War from as early as late July 1950.)

Once again, there was a surprise attack—the third stage. In late October, Chinese Communist "volunteers" struck at Republic of Korea (ROK) units that had neared the Yalu River. They bloodied the South Koreans and then seemingly disappeared. MacArthur stubbornly continued to discount the possibility of a major Chinese Communist intervention. Then, in November, the Chinese Communists, who had infiltrated more than 300,000 men, struck hard and suddenly, and broke the United Nations Command (UNC) drive to the Yalu River. As MacArthur noted, "It was an entirely different war." Within a few weeks, American and ROK troops were retreating south of the thirty-eighth parallel and abandoning Seoul for the second time. The Chinese recognized their limitations in terms of firepower and logistics, and sought to set up positions behind the Americans and South Koreans, and cut off their expected lines of retreat; this tactic was, at least initially, incredibly disconcerting and hence effective. It was so effective that General MacArthur may have panicked and suggested a retreat back to Pusan or even a withdrawal to Japan. Although there would be media reports of Chinese hordes, the truth was that both sides had approximately equal numbers of troops, and UN forces clearly had more artillery, logistical support, and air power than the Chinese and North Koreans. The Communists were more willing to fight close up and were clearly less reliant on motorized transport and tank and artillery support, and it would take the American infantry time to relearn how to fight hard.

After General Walton Walker was killed in a jeep accident, General Mathew Ridgway was appointed to command the U.S. Eighth Army and later to overall command; he managed to stabilize the lines near the original border marking northern and southern Korea. He understood the limitations of the enemy and designed his strategy to take advantage of their weaknesses in logistics. He realized that American morale was low, and troops had become too accustomed to motorized transport, artillery support, and air power. He raised their fighting spirit, prepared them better for the changed nature of the conflict, and took advantage of the Chinese dependence on porters carrying supplies from Manchuria to the front lines. He realized the Chinese could not sustain an offensive for more than two weeks without running short of supplies. Operation RIPPER (called Operation KILLER by the press) accepted the initial Communist attack and then, as Communist supplies of ammunition decreased, prepared for a powerful counterattack. By summer 1951, the lines had largely stabilized along the thirty-eighth parallel, a little to the south (on the west)—Line Kansas—and a little more to the north (on the eastern side of the peninsula)—Line Wyoming.

Then came the final phase—not peace, not war—for another two years, during which Dwight Eisenhower became U.S. president and Soviet leader Joseph Stalin died. Suddenly the armistice talks, basically deadlocked for almost two years over the question of the forced repatriation of POWs, moved to closure and the guns fell silent in late July 1953, although the Chinese did threaten along the mostly American sector to the west and engaged in several serious efforts to destroy South Korean army units, perhaps to indicate they were still capable of fighting.

To the rest of the world, Korea was an example of a kind of limited war, fought after 1950 for limited goals. For the troops who fought in Korea, it was an intense conflict, with bloody hand-to-hand combat and incredible artillery duels reminiscent of World War I. And certainly the troops had to be motivated, prepared, supplied, and led as in any previous intense conflict—which was not easy to do, given the limited goals of the fighting.

But the conflict was limited because the major power combatants had other obligations and tasks that prevented them from investing the manpower and logistics of a major war in the Korean peninsula. The United States had to retain enough strength to meet an imagined Soviet threat to Western Europe; the Chinese Communists wanted to remake a society and rebuild a country devastated by years of political decline and corruption, external invasion and exploitation, and war. The Soviet Union was still rebuilding from the devastation of World War II. Thus neither side would invest what it would take to achieve victory in the sense of destroying one's enemy; instead, each side became content to demonstrate that it could resist and make the cost of an advance too great to be worth the expense.

Equally important, neither the United States nor the Soviet Union turned to nuclear weapons to force a decision. Although such weapons appeared to be the ultimate weapon, fortunately for the world the bombs remained safely away from the front, although there have been unsubstantiated claims that Dwight Eisenhower threatened their use to force the Chinese to hold real negotiations for an armistice after he became president in January 1953.

Charles M. Dobbs

See also: MacArthur, Douglas; Peng Dehuai; Ridgway, Mathew B.; Van Fleet, James A.; Walker, Walton

References and further reading:

Alexander, Bevin. *Korea: The First War We Lost.* New York: Hippocrene Books, 1997.

Rees, David. *Korea: The Limited War.* London: Macmillan; New York: St. Martin's Press, 1964.

Ridgway, Matthew B. *The Korean War.* New York: Da Capo, 1988.

Sandler, Stanley. *The Korean War: An Encyclopedia.* New York, London: Garland Publishing, 1995.

———. *The Korean War: No Victors, No Vanquished,* London: Routledge; Lexington: University of Kentucky Press, 1999.

Whelan, Richard. *Drawing the Line: The Korean War, 1950–1953.* New York: Little, Brown, 1990.

Kosciuszko, Tadeusz Andrezj Bonawentura (1746–1817)

Polish officer who fought against the British in the American Revolution. Born on 4 February 1746, in Mereczowszczyzna (in present-day Belarus), Kosciuszko was educated in military engineering in Warsaw and in military and civil architecture in Paris. Influenced by French ideas of liberalism, he went to America in 1776 to serve alongside the colonists in the American Revolution. Appointed a colonel of engineers under Major General Horatio Gates, Kosciuszko selected the defensive position that contributed to the American victory at the Battle of Saratoga in 1777. After spending two years directing the construction of fortifications at West Point, New York, he served under Major General Nathanael Greene in South Carolina. In 1783, as a reward for his services, Kosciuszko was granted U.S. citizenship and promoted to brigadier general.

In 1784, Kosciuszko returned to Poland and became a major general in the Polish army. Following the second partition of Poland in 1793, he led a rebellion against Russia and Prussian rule. Proclaimed supreme commander and given dictatorial powers, Kosciuszko defeated the Russians at Raclawice in April 1794 but was defeated in June by a combined Russian and Prussian force. After successfully defending Warsaw against both the Russians and Prussians (July–September 1794), he was defeated and wounded at the Battle of Maciejowice in October, which marked the end of the Polish nation. Kosciuszko was held prisoner in Russia

Engraved portrait of Thaddeus Kosciuszko. (Library of Congress)

until 1796, when he was released on the promise that he never again take up arms against Russia. In 1797 he visited America, where he was awarded a $15,000 pension and a grant of 500 acres of land in Ohio. After 1798, Kosciuszko lived in France and Switzerland, where he unsuccessfully sought Polish independence, while refusing to break his promise by joining Napoleon's invasion of Russia. He died 15 October 1817, in Solothurn, Switzerland. Kosciuszko's remains were carried to Krakow and were buried among the Polish kings in the Royal crypt of Wawel Cathedral. In accordance with his will, his Ohio property was sold and the money used to establish a school to educate freed African Americans at Newark, New Jersey.

Alexander Bielakowski

See also: American Revolution

References and further reading:

Haiman, Miecislaus. *Kosciuszko in the American Revolution.* New York: Kosciuszko Foundation, 1975.

Kajencki, Francis C. *Thaddeus Kosciuszko: Military Engineer of the American Revolution.* El Paso, TX: Southwest Polonia Press, 1998.

Pula, James S. *Thaddeus Kosciuszko: The Purest Son of Liberty.* New York: Hippocrene Books, 1999.

Kosovo, Battles of (20 June 1389, 17 October 1448)

Ottoman Turkish victories in the Balkans. The First Battle of Kosovo was fought on 20 June 1389 as part of the Ottoman Wars of Expansion. King Lazar of Serbia had taken advantage of issues of succession to the sultanate throne caused by the death of Süleyman the Magnificent and by Byzantine intrigues. Lazar formed a Christian coalition army that defeated the Turks at the River Topolica in 1387. In response the Turks, led by Murad I, advanced into Bulgaria, crushing the rebellion there. Murad I then turned his 60,000 Turks to face Lazar's 100,000-man league of Serbs, Bosnians, Bulgars, Poles, and Albanians on the plain of Kosovo (plain of Blackbirds), 60 miles north of Uskub.

Murad's army was composed of Janissaries and *sipahis.* The Janissaries—the name comes from the Turkish for new army (*yeniçeri*)—was an army raised from Christian slave recruits from all over Europe, most of whom were raised by the Turks themselves as foster children. The *sipahis,* developed by Süleyman, were heavy cavalry and proved effective in the battle to come.

The Turks won a hard-fought key victory, but Murad was mortally wounded by a Serbian aristocrat posing as a deserter. Murad's brother, Bayazid, led the Turks to victory by encouraging the 12,000 men under Vuk Brancovic to switch to the Turkish side late in the day when it appeared Lazar's forces had the upper hand. Lazar was captured and beheaded.

The Turks then turned their attention to a siege of Constantinople, having taken almost all other Byzantine territory. Only the arrival of mercenaries looking for payment from the last vestiges of the Byzantine treasury saved the city, albeit temporarily. After the first Battle of Kosovo, the Byzantines had no allies within territories nominally controlled by them. Instead they had to rely upon tenuous tricks to survive, including encouraging pretenders to the sultan's throne.

The Second Battle of Kosovo, 17 October 1448, was much more closely fought than the first. Eighty thousand Hungarians and Wallachians under John Hunyadi constructed trenchworks against a much larger Turkish army. On the 17th, the Christian forces, attempting to relieve Constantinople, surprised the Turks by leaving their trenches and attacking and holding them at bay for the entire day. On the 18th, the Turks, wily as always, enticed the Wallachians to switch sides, causing the Hungarians to retire from the field.

The Hungarians lost at least 17,000, while the Turks lost perhaps 40,000. The Turks, led by Sultan Muhammed II, "the Conqueror," could now turn their attentions entirely to the siege and capture of Constantinople, which they finally took in 1453.

Christopher Howell

See also: Byzantine-Ottoman Wars; Constantinople, Siege of (1453); Hunyadi, János; Ottoman Empire; Turkish Wars of European Expansion

References and further reading:

Turfan, Naim. *Rise of the Young Turks: Politics, the Military and Ottoman Collapse.* Istanbul, London: I. B. Tauris & Co. Ltd., 2000.

Vaughan, Dorothy. *Europe and the Turk: A Pattern of Alliances, 1350–1700.* Liverpool, UK: Liverpool University Press, 1954.

Koxinga (Zheng Chenggong) (1662–1722)

Leader of the last effective Ming resistance against the Manchus. Zheng Chenggong, who was half Japanese, is best known by the nickname given him by the Portuguese, Koxinga. This was based upon his honorary title, Guoxing Ye (Gentleman with the Dynastic Surname), which he acquired after being granted the imperial surname, Zhu, by the Ming pretender, the prince of Tang, as a reward for his loyalty.

Koxinga's military career began soon after the Manchus, founders of the Qing Dynasty (1644–1911), invaded China. As the son of a Ming admiral, Koxinga was quickly thrust into service. At first Ming loyalist forces, who had lost the north and the capital of Beijing to the rapidly advancing Manchus, hoped to make a stand along the Yangtse, but further Manchu advances, and confusion within loyalist ranks, soon made this impossible.

Hoping to repeat the success of the founders Southern Song, who when faced with an invasion by the Jurchen, the ancestors of the Manchus, in the mid–twelfth century adopted a flexible maritime strategy based on the Chinese southeast, Koxinga took to the seas. He and a band of men rallied on Nanao island, in eastern Guangdong. His forces steadily grew, and in 1647 Koxinga led an army unsuccessfully against the city of Quanzhou in Fujian. Although repulsed, Koxinga continued to raid the coast of China with growing success.

In 1650, Koxinga annexed the trading port of Amoy in Fujian and Quemoy, an island guarding its approaches. From these bases, Koxinga became involved in Chinese overseas trade to finance his operations. During this period, although Koxinga enjoyed success against the Qing armies on land, it was not universal; however he did control the sea, and the entire coastline of China was fair game for his operations.

In 1659, Koxinga attempted a major invasion into the lower Yangtze River valley. He sailed directly to Nanking, sweeping opposition before him, but his army was routed at the gates of the former Ming capital. Koxinga's overconfidence and lack of military strategy had undermined his efforts. This invasion effectively ended Koxinga's ability to restore the Ming and reclaim China, although he remained a thorn in the side of the Qing Dynasty.

By 1660, Koxinga was the sole remaining resistance to the Qing armies. In need of a secure food supply, he invaded Taiwan in 1661. Despite stiff resistance from the Dutch, who held the island with Qing consent, Koxinga eventually succeeded. Thereafter, Koxinga established an administration and governed the island, but this was his last adventure, although he did threaten the Spanish governor of the Philippines with invasion. In 1662, Koxinga died of illness. His successors continued to hold Taiwan until 1683, when the island was surrendered to the invading Qing.

Timothy May

See also: Chinese Imperial Wars; Kangxi; Manchu Expansion, Wars of; Yangzhou, Siege of

References and further reading:

Crozier, Ralph. *Koxinga and Chinese Nationalism: History, Myth, and the Hero.* Cambridge, MA: Harvard University, East Asian Research Center, 1977.

Hsu, Immanuel. *The Rise of Modern China.* New York: Oxford University Press, 1970.

Kruger, Paul-Stephanus Johannes Paulus (1825–1904)

South African statesman and military leader. Bush-trained trekboer, soldier, pioneer, farmer, politician, and South African statesman, Kruger took part with his family in the Great Trek from Cape Colony to Transvaal. Strictly reared in Dutch Calvinism, with scant formal education, he was profoundly affected by tribal opposition and his lifelong struggle for independence from the despised British, which he countered with fearlessness and cunning. While a teenager Kruger simultaneously farmed and held military and civil posts. In 1864 he became Transvaal commandant general and worked toward establishing constitutional authority. Lucrative minerals were found in 1868, leading the British to annex Transvaal in 1877.

In 1880 he traveled to England for talks to regain independence but was thwarted, leading Kruger, Piet Joubert, and Martinius Pretorius to oppose a British-inspired federation.

The Transvaal War saw numerous Kruger-led victories, climaxed by the Battle of Majuba Hill (27 February 1881), which restored independence to the Afrikaners at the Pretoria Convention of 1881. Once president in 1883, a position to which he was reelected in 1888, 1893, and 1898, Kruger stringently opposed political equality for *uitlanders* (mostly British and German foreigners) who arrived with the gold rush of Witwatersrand in 1886 and doubly outnumbered Afrikaners.

The Cecil Rhodes–inspired 1895 Jameson Raid to overthrow Kruger's government failed. Kaiser Wilhelm II's telegram congratulating Kruger for the victory was widely interpreted as German support. This struggle led to the Boer War of 1899–1902, which resulted in the 31 May 1902 Peace of Vereeniging, making Transvaal a British crown colony.

During the Second Boer War Kruger did not take to the field, but traveled to Europe to obtain aid. He was unsuccessful and never returned to Transvaal. The "old lion of Transvaal" died in Switzerland in 1904.

Annette Richardson

See also: Boer Wars; Buller, Sir Redvers Henry; Joubert, Petrus Jacobus; Kimberly; Ladysmith, Siege of

References and further reading:

Fisher, John. *Paul Kruger.* London: Secker & Warburg, 1969.

Gordon, C. T. *The Growth of Boer Opposition to Kruger, 1890–1895.* Cape Town and New York: Oxford University Press, 1970.

Marais, J. S. *The Fall of Kruger's Republic.* Oxford, UK: Clarendon Press, 1962.

Nathan, Manfred. *Paul Kruger: His Life and Times.* Durban: Knox Publishing Company, 1941.

Kublai Khan (1215–1294)

Founder of the Mongol-Chinese Yuan Dynasty. Kublai Khan, or in Mongolian, Qubilai-qan, was the second of four sons of Tolui-noyan (c. 1190–1231/32), who was the youngest son of Cinggis-qan (Genghis Khan). Kublai was at first just one of many Mongolian princes holding appanages near China. This changed with the events of 1251 that brought his elder brother, Möngke (Mongke), to the throne. Kublai became his viceroy in northern China and went on to build up an independent power base there that stood him in good stead after Möngke's death in 1259 and the end of a unified Mongolian empire.

Kublai rushed back to north China from Yunnan, where he had been campaigning, convened a *quriltai* of supporters, and had himself elected *qan.* He then set about establishing a regime largely using savvy local advisers he had acquired as Möngke's viceroy.

Kublai's claim as Möngke's successor was challenged by his younger brother, Arigh Böke (d. 1266). The latter enjoyed wide support and controlled Qaraqorum, the capital. Also an opponent of Kublai and his house from domains in Siberia was Qaidu, representing the line of *qan* Ögödei (Ogadei), excluded from the succession in 1251.

The war with Arigh Böke lasted until 1264 and ended with his rival's defeat, thanks to Kublai's superior resources. The war with Qaidu continued until 1303. At one point it seriously threatened the survival of Kublai's *qanate* (after 1271, Yuan Dynasty). Such central Asian concerns remained critical for Kublai and his house until the end.

Once relatively secure in Mongol China, that is, the north and parts of the southwest, Kublai set about expanding his power. His most important line of advance was due south, into Southern Song domains, definitively conquered by the Mongolian general Bayan in 1276, although the mop-up continued until 1279. Other campaigns were two failed invasions of Japan (1274 and 1281) and successful campaigns in Vietnam, Burma, and across the sea to Java, as, under Kublai, China became a base for a most aggressive sea power for the first time in its history.

Kublai died in 1294, nearly 80. No other ruler of Mongol China ever rose to his stature. Thanks to Marco Polo, Kublai has remained the very symbol of the Oriental potentate. It was his world, by then long lost, that the Portuguese and others went looking for in the fifteenth and sixteenth centuries, marking the beginning of our own era.

Paul D. Buell

See also: Genghis Khan; Mongol Empire; Ögödei

References and further reading:

Allsen, Thomas T., *Mongol Imperialism.* Berkeley: University of California Press, 1987.

Rossabi, Morris. *Khubilai Khan: His Life and Times.* Berkeley: University of California Press, 1988.

Kuropatkin, Aleksey Nikolaevich (1848–1925)

Disastrous Russian commander. Of noble origins, Kuropatkin was born in Pskov Province, graduated from Pskov Military Academy (1866), General Staff Academy (1874), and served in Turkestan (1866–1871, 1875–1877, 1879–1883). He participated in the capture of Samarkand (1868) and Kokand (1876) and was an infantry division chief of staff under General Skobelev in the Russo-Turkish War of 1877–1878. He fought at the third Battle of Plevna (1877) and Senova (1878), participated in the attack on Geok Tepe (1880–1881), and became a major general (1882), serving on the general staff (1883–90). He also published *Deistvia otriadov generala Skobeleva* (1885), on the Balkan and

Russo-Turkish War campaigns, and became head of the Transbaikal District (1890–1898).

His impressive military record and diplomatic experience in the Far East saw him appointed minister for war from 1898 to 1904. Kuropatkin supported expansion into the Far East but failed to negotiate the corruption of czarist court politics to modernize and professionalize the army or keep pace with technological developments. His failure was brutally exposed in the Russo-Japanese War (1904–1905). Kuropatkin's underestimation of Japan, his indecisiveness in planning and in battle as Russian Land Forces commander in chief were similarly revealed. Pressured to relieve Port Arthur, he suffered reverses at Laioyang, Sha-Ho River, and Sandepu before defeat at Muckden saw him demoted to First Army commander.

While a State Duma member Kuropatkin wrote "The Russian Army in the Japanese War" (1909), an attempt to justify his performance.

Kuropatkin's shortcomings in the Russo-Japanese War did not preclude him from commanding a corps and the Fifth Army (1915), and on the northern front (February–July 1916). He also seemed not to have learned much, compiling a similarly poor command in this most disastrous of czarist wars. He initially doubted the possibility of the Brusilov Breakthrough, then failed to support it, contributing to its loss of impetus.

He was finally removed from military command and appointed Turkestan governor-general, until February 1917. He was arrested in April by the Tashkent Soviet, transferred to Petrograd, but freed by the provisional government. Kuropatkin rejected White overtures to fight in the Civil War. French offers to emigrate probably enabled him to live out his life back in Pskov Province, teaching at a middle school and an agricultural school that he founded.

Neil Harvey Croll

See also: Russo-Japanese War

References and further reading:

Jones, N. F. *The First and Last Man of the War: The Far Eastern Crisis and the Career of General Kuropatkin, 1895–1905.* M.A. diss., University of North Carolina at Greensboro, 1991.

Kuropatkin, A. N., A. B. Lindsay, and E. D. Swinton. *The Russian Army and the Japanese War: Being Historical and Critical Comments on the Military Policy and Power of Russia and on the Campaign in the Far East by General Kuropatkin.* London: J. Murray, 1909.

———. *Russko-iaponskaia voina* (The Russo-Japanese War). Leningrad: Gosizdat, 1925.

Story, Douglas. *The Campaign with Kuropatkin.* London: T. W. Laine, 1904; Philadelphia: J. B. Lippincott Co., 1905.

Aleksey Nikolaevich Kuropatkin. (Library of Congress)

Kursk, Battle of (1943)

The greatest tank battle in history. After the disastrous loss at Stalingrad in World War II, German army commanders, with Adolf Hitler's enthusiastic approval, planned a massive offensive in 1943. In March, German field marshal Fritz von Manstein had achieved a great victory at Kharkov for Army Group South, leaving a bulge of 100 miles north and south and 75 westward into the German lines of Army Group Central at Kursk. Bad weather and German indecision interfered with von Manstein's plans for a pincer movement to encircle the Soviet army in the salient, allowing the Red Army under General Nikolai Vatutin in the south and General Konstantin Rokossovski in the north time to build defenses and prepare for a large counterattack.

On 10 May, Hitler consented to the plan called Operation ZITADELL. Colonel General Model's Ninth Army, with seven Panzer, two Panazergrenadier, and nine infantry divisions, were to attack from the north and Colonel General Hoth's Fourth Panzer Army, with 10 Panzer, one Panzergrenadier, and seven infantry, would advance from the south—roughly 570,000 men.

Delayed until 4 July, the Germans found themselves confronted by 11 Russian armies (alerted by Allied ULTRA intelligence) of 977,000 men. Soviet defenses in the north corner of the salient were particularly dense with 2,200 antitank and 2,500,000 antipersonnel mines and 20,000 guns of various kinds.

For the next eight days, the Germans tried to advance in the face of bitter fighting but Soviet artillery knocked out 40 percent of German armor. On 12 July, at the battle of Prokhorovka, 600 German tanks clashed with 850 Soviet tanks. The battle became a war of attrition with both sides calling for reinforcements.

On 13 July, due to the American invasion of Sicily and fears of a landing in Italy, Hitler ordered German units to disengage. Retreating on 17 July, the Nazis left 70,000 dead and 2,950 tanks on the battlefield. The Soviets following the German retreat ordered an immediate counteroffensive. The lack of victory at Kursk by the German army spelled an end to any more major offenses on the Russian front to the end of the war.

T. Jason Soderstrum

See also: Armored Fighting Vehicles; World War II

References and further reading:

Dunn, Walter S. *Kursk: Hitler's Gamble.* Westport, CT: Praeger, 1997.

Glantz, David M. *The Battle of Kursk.* Lawrence: University Press of Kansas, 1999.

Solov'ev, Boris G. *The Battle of Kursk, 1943.* Moscow: Novsti Press Agency Publishing House, 1988.

Kut-al-Amara (1915–1916)

One of the very few capitulations in British military history. In December 1915, after an unexpected defeat at Ctesiphon on the drive to capture Baghdad from the Turks, British troops fell back to the town of Kut-al-Amara, located on the Tigris River. Lacking the troops to relieve them immediately, the British High Command ordered them to retire further south. The order came too late, as the British force of about 16,000 was now surrounded by the Turks. When General Charles Townsend, in command of the British forces, suggested a breakout, he was told to stay in Kut-al-Amara in order to tie down as many Turkish troops as possible. The Turks immediately ordered a number of failed assaults on the town, with heavy losses on both sides. While the troops in Kut-al-Amara held out, a relief expedition was formed in order to try to break through the British lines. It failed, with the British suffering 23,000 casualties, and the Turks about 10,000. Attempts to resupply by river boat failed, and in April 1916, with food supplies dwindling and threats of epidemics looming, General Townsend asked the Turks for a six-day armistice in order to discuss surrender. The Turks, wanting to add to the British humiliation at Gallipoli, replied that they would only accept unconditional surrender. On 29 April 1916, British forces surrendered to the Turks. It was one of the largest capitulations for the British army up to that time.

For the British troops who had endured the siege, the worst came after the surrender. The surviving troops, weakened by disease and near starvation, were taken to POW camps under a brutal forced march by the Turks. More than 3,000 perished on the way, or about 2 percent of all those who surrendered. Conditions in the POW camps were little better, and those who survived the inhuman conditions came out of the camps in 1918 as little more than skeletons.

Drew Philip Halévy

See also: Gallipoli

References and further reading:

Braddon, Russell. *The Siege: The Forgotten Siege of Kut El Amarah, Mesopotamia, 1916.* Viking: New York, 1970.

Miller, Ronald. *Death of an Army: The Siege of Kut, 1915–1916.* Boston: Houghton Mifflin Company, 1970.

Kutuzov, Prince Mikhail Illarionovich Golenishchev (1745–1813)

Credited for defeating Napoleon's Grande Armée in the Russian campaign. Kutuzov was born in St. Petersburg and enrolled in a military engineering school at age 12. A corporal at age 14, he lost the sight in one eye during the Russo-Turkish War (1768–1774). Kutuzov served six years under the command of Aleksandr Suvorov in the Crimea and was promoted to colonel in 1777 and major general in 1784.

During the War of the Third Coalition, Kutuzov was appointed commander of Austro-Russian forces at Vienna and attempted to link up with General Mack at Ulm. However, the latter was defeated by Napoleon on 19 October 1805, before Kutuzov arrived. Kutuzov avoided Napoleon's pursuit, but Czar Alexander I demanded Kutuzov engage the French. At Austerlitz on 2 December, 90,000 Austro-Russian troops were defeated.

Kutuzov was retired and reappointed as supreme commander in 1811 during the Russo-Turkish War (1806–1812).

After Napoleon's 600,000 Grande Armée invaded Russia and reached Smolensk, Kutuzov was made a prince and appointed supreme commander on 20 August 1812. Kutuzov withdrew Russian forces, ordering the destruction of all unevacuated supplies and lodgings. To further weaken the

French, Kutuzov fought minor engagements. However, Alexander ordered Kutuzov to stand at Borodino on 7 September, where Kutuzov lost 42,000 of his 112,000 troops and withdrew southeast, allowing the remaining 58,000 of 130,000 French forces to enter Moscow. Failing to defeat the Russians and unwilling to winter in a Moscow that had been burned out, Napoleon retreated.

By giving battle at Maloiaroslavets on 24 October, Kutuzov forced Napoleon to retrace the path of the French advance. Kutuzov's troops continuously molested the retreating French, engaging them at Viazma and Krasnoie. The remnants of Napoleon's army narrowly escaped annihilation during the crossing of the Berezina River on 27–28 November. Kutuzov died while in pursuit of the French, at Bunzlau in Silesia.

Neville G. Panthaki

See also: Austerlitz, Battle of; Berezina River, Battle of; Borodino; Moscow, Retreat from; Napoleon I; Napoleonic Wars; Russo-Turkish Wars

References and further reading:

Austin, Paul Britten. *1812 Napoleon's Invasion of Russia.* London: Greenhill Books, 2000.

Cate, Curtis. *The War of the Two Emperors.* New York: Random House, 1985.

Nafziger, George F. *Napoleon's Invasion of Russia.* Novato, CA: Presidio Press, 1988.

Nicolson, Nigel. *Napoleon 1812.* New York: Harper & Row, 1985.

L

Ladysmith, Siege of (1899–1900)

Major siege of the second Boer War. The Boer independence movement conflicted with British governance in Natal colony, located on the route around Africa. Ladysmith was strategically sited where the main rail line from coastal Durban divided, providing communications with Transvaal and the Orange Free State. General Piet Cronjé's Boers surrounded Ladysmith, severing the rail line on 2 November 1900. Lieutenant General Sir George White, Victoria Cross, commanded 12,500 British soldiers in this town of 21,300 persons.

Similar to the French at Dien Bien Phu in Vietnam (1953–1954), the British garrison was situated in low ground and dominated by enemy observation and artillery fire from surrounding hills. The Boer's rapid-firing German and French artillery was superior to that of the British, with the exception of the two 4.7-inch naval guns and four long-range 12-pounder guns from the *Powerful.* Although the naval guns were more effective, the navy provided merely 500 rounds of ammunition. The Boer advantage was negated by poor gunnery. Thus, the battle reverted to the centuries-old siege technique of starvation and disease.

Ladysmith, unlike the other major sieges at Kimberly and Mafiking, was noteworthy for the level of sickness and disease. The garrison held sufficient rations for two months, with the perimeter holding one month's forage for the horses and pack animals. Fever cases peaked at 1,314 on 27 January 1900, when eight deaths per day became the average.

Field Marshal Lord Roberts commanded a relief column of 30,000 troops, having replaced General Sir Redvers Bullers, Victoria Cross, following his defeat at Colenso. The lead elements under Lord Dundonald arrived on 28 February 1900, ending the four-month siege.

Robert Martyn

See also: Boer Wars

References and further reading:

Sharp, Gerald. *The Siege of Ladysmith.* London: MacDonald and Janes, 1976.

Lafayette, Marie Joseph Paul Yves Roch Gilbert du Motier, Marquis de (1757–1834)

French field commander and politician and hero of the American Revolution. Lafayette was born to wealth in Chavaniac, Auvergne, France, on 6 September 1757. He joined the infantry in 1771 and the dragoons in 1773 and was promoted to captain in 1774. Inspired by the American cause and intending a jab at Britain for the sake of France, Lafayette arrived in America in 1777 with Baron Johann de Kalb and offered his services to the Continental Congress. He was commissioned a major general in the Continental army on 31 July.

Lafayette distinguished himself at Brandywine, where he was wounded, spent the winter at Valley Forge, and excelled at Barren Hill on 18 May 1778, Monmouth on 28 June, and in the Rhode Island campaign of July and August. He returned to France in 1779 to secure more French help for the Americans, was promoted to colonel in the French army, and returned to his command in Virginia in April 1780. He sat as a member of the court-martial that convicted Major John André in September, engaged Benedict Arnold's British forces several times in Virginia in 1781, supported Anthony Wayne at Green Spring, and was an important factor in the defeat of Charles Cornwallis at Yorktown. Upon his return to France in December, he became a major general in the French army.

Lafayette entered French politics in 1787, represented Auvergne in the Estates General in 1789, assumed command of the National Guard on 26 July, and tried to mediate among the various revolutionary factions and the crown. Promoted to lieutenant general and briefly in command of the Army of the Center, he was persecuted by the Jacobins and fled to Belgium in 1792. Captured, he was held as a prisoner of war, first by Austria and then by Prussia. After his release on 23 September 1797, he returned to France, avoided Napoleon, and kept a low profile, but he reentered politics during the Hundred Days, helping to ensure Napoleon's second abdication. Thereafter, he served liberalism in France until his death in Paris on 20 May 1834. Lafayette was lionized in the United States, with numerous towns and cities (e.g., Fayetteville, North Carolina and Arkansas; Lafayette, Indiana) and counties named in his honor.

Eric v. d. Luft

See also: American Revolution; Arnold, Benedict; Brandywine; Cornwallis, Sir Charles; France and the American Revolution; French Revolutionary Wars; Monmouth; Napoleon I; Napoleonic Wars; Revolutions of 1830; Valley Forge; Washington, George; Wayne, Anthony; Yorktown

References and further reading:

Bernier, Olivier. *Lafayette: Hero of Two Worlds.* New York: Dutton, 1983.

Buckman, Peter. *Lafayette: A Biography.* New York: Paddington, 1977.

Criss, Mildred. *La Fayette: On the Heights of Freedom.* New York: Dodd, Mead, 1954.

Gerson, Noel Bertram. *Statue in Search of a Pedestal: A Biography of the Marquis de Lafayette.* New York: Dodd, Mead, 1976.

Lake Trasimene, Battle of (2 June 217 B.C.E.)

The second of three disastrous defeats the Romans suffered at the hands of the Carthaginian general Hannibal. The year after his victory at the Trebia River, Hannibal crossed the Apennines into Etruria (Tuscany) with an army of 55,000 men. A Roman army under the command of the consul Flaminius tried to intercept him.

Hannibal directed his army to the northern shore of Lake Trasimene (Lago di Trasimeno), a perfect place for an ambush. The road passed through a narrow valley that was bordered by the lake to the south and by hills to the north. There was only a narrow path westward. An easily defensible hill blocked the eastern side. Because the Romans would come from the west, Hannibal positioned his Spanish troops and his light infantry in the east, on the hill at the end of the valley. Both Hannibal's cavalry and his Celtic troops took a position in hiding along the hills to the north. A large force of Celts was positioned near the western passage.

The Roman force, 30,000 strong, entered the valley in marching order. A dense mist obscured the hills, and the Romans failed to send out reconnaissance parties. When the entire Roman column had marched into the valley, the Celts attacked the rear end of the column, blocking the retreat. The cavalry charged downhill upon the Roman troops. The Romans were totally surprised.

What followed was more a slaughter than a battle. Thousands were killed on the shore or driven into the lake. Only the Roman vanguard, 6,000 men, succeeded in fighting through the Carthaginian line, though they too were captured the following day. The Roman army was crushed, with 15,000 troops taken prisoner and 15,000 killed, among them the consul himself. Hannibal lost only 1,500 men.

M. R. van der Werf

See also: Cannae, Battle of; Hannibal Barca; Punic Wars; Trebia, Battle of the

References and further reading:

Bagnall, Nigel. *The Punic Wars. Rome, Carthage and the Struggle for the Mediterranean.* London: Pimlico, 1999.

Conolly, Peter. *Greece and Rome at War.* London: Greenhill Books; Harrisburg, PA: Stackpole Books, 1998.

Lazenby, J. F. *Hannibal's War. A Military History of the Second Punic War.* London: Aris & Phillips, 1978.

Land Mines

Explosive charges that are usually concealed by their small size or by being buried just under the surface of land; pressure sensors detonate land mines when they are passed over by troops or vehicles. Their primary objective was originally to slow down large-scale troop advancement, but as they evolved, they came to be used in all phases of war, for purposes ranging from tactical defense to strategic offense.

Land mines were first used in World War I, when Germans troops buried live artillery shells and left only their fuses exposed. They were meant to act as a defense against advancing French and British tanks, but these land mines could easily be dug up, removed, and stolen by enemy troops on foot. This practice gave rise to the development of smaller mines, which were placed alongside the bigger mines to prevent them from being moved. Since World War I, technology has made land mines smaller and more destructive.

The two main classes of mines are antitank (AT) and antipersonnel (AP) mines. Antitank mines employ a large amount of explosives, weigh more than 5 kilograms, are detonated by a pressure of more than 120 kilograms, and are used primarily to immobilize tanks. It can be done by either a blast explosion that cuts the vehicle's tracks or a killer explosion that sends a plate through the tank and destroys both the tank and crew. Antipersonnel mines employ a smaller explosive charge and are detonated by pressure of more than 5 kilograms. Antipersonnel mines are intended to disable or kill personnel. Blast mines cause injury by shattering extremities or otherwise disabling personnel. Fragmentation mines are designed to kill personnel by exploding into the air and producing fragments. Offensively, land mines are used for protection along flanks and to cut off an enemy's withdrawal. Defensively, they are used to slow the advance of an enemy.

Since the end of World War II, antipersonnel land mines have become a lingering threat in many areas of the world, mainly to civilians. The United Nation estimates that there are more than 110 million buried mines left from the numerous wars of the twentieth century in more than 62 countries. Some 20,000 antipersonnel land mines detonate a year, taking with them a limb or the life of a civilian adult or child. The difficulty in avoiding them is that many minefields are uncharted because an accurate track of their location has not been kept. To add to the problem, land mines are mainly used by Third World nations because they are cheap and can be easily dispersed over a large area. Although easy to deploy, the recovery cost of land mines can be upwards of U.S.$1,000 per mine. There is some hope for the future in mines than can be remotely exploded when no longer required. But these weapons are expensive and so far are mainly used by wealthy nations.

It is only recently that nations have come to acknowledge that the strategic and tactical value of land mines does not outweigh humanitarian concerns. In May 1997, a U.S.-led United Nations resolution won the support of more than 150 counties in calling for a global ban on land mines. The United States was following a different path from that taken in Canada. On 3 December 1997, the Convention on the Prohibition of the Use, Stockpiling, Production, and Transfer of Anti-Personnel Mines and on Their Destruction (informally known as the Ottawa Convention), a Canadian-led initiative, was signed by 122 nations (11 nations subsequently added their signatures) and came into legal force in March 1999. However, two of the top producers and sellers of land mines, Russia and China, have not signed the Ottawa Convention; nor has the United States.

Matthieu J.-C. Moss

References and further reading:

Croll, Mike. *The History of Landmines.* Barnsley, UK: Leo Cooper, 1998.

Lannes, Jean, Duke of Montebello (1769–1809)

One of the most audacious field commanders of the French Revolutionary and Napoleonic Wars. Born on 10 April 1769 at Lectours (Gers), Lannes was commissioned on 10 June 1792, earning rapid promotion and the reputation of leading from up front. As a colonel he was the first across the Po River at Piacenza (7 May 1796) and was the first to reach the Austrian positions at Lodi (10 May) in Napoleon's audacious and decisive Italian campaign. This campaign brought him Napoleon's attention and a promotion to brigadier general.

Lannes participated in the capture of Alexandria, Egypt (2 July 1798). He distinguished himself at El-Arish (8–19 February 1799) and at Acre (8 May). Appointed a division general (10 May), Lannes left Egypt with Napoleon (22 August). He provided vital support for Napoleon at the coup of 18 Brumaire, which made Napoleon first consul of France.

Lannes led the advance guard through the Great Saint Bernard Pass (16–21 May 1800) and defeated the Austrians at Montebello (9 June). At Marengo (14 June), his badly outnumbered troops held the Austrians until Louis Desaix arrived. Appointed a marshal (19 May 1804), Lannes helped trap Karl Mack at Ulm (20 October 1805). At Austerlitz (2 December), he blocked Austro-Russian attempts to outflank the French left. Lannes drove the Prussians and Saxons back at Jena (14 October 1806). His decisive command of the center at Friedland brought victory and rewards, including the title Duke of Montebello (15 June 1808).

Sent to Spain, Lannes was victorious at Tudela (23 November 1808) and captured Saragossa (21 February 1809). Napoleon, however, recalled him for the 1809 campaign against Austria. At Ratisbon, when his troops balked at assaulting the walls, Lannes himself shouldered a scaling ladder. His troops took the city (23 April 1809). On 21 May Lannes and André Masséna spearheaded the ill-fated attempt to cross the Danube River. Then Lannes seized and held Essling against overwhelming numbers while the French evacuated. On 22 May, a cannonball shattered his legs, necessitating the amputation of the right leg. Gangrene developed, and Lannes died on 31 May at Ebersdorff, Austria. The first marshal of France to die of battle wounds, Lannes was Napoleon's friend among the marshals and one of his most aggressive commanders.

James K. Kieswetter

See also: Aboukir; Austerlitz, Battle of; French Revolutionary Wars; Friedland; Lodi; Marengo, Battle of; Masséna, André, Duc de Rivoli, Prince d'Essling; Murat, Joachim, Grand Duke of Cleves-Berg, King of Naples; Napoleonic Wars; Rivoli

References and further reading:

Chrisawn, Margaret Scot. *The Emperor's Friend: Marshal Jean Lannes.* Westport, CT: Greenwood Press, 2000.

Damamme, Jean-Claude. *Lannes: Maréchal d'empire.* Paris: Payot, 1987.

Laffargue, André. *Jean Lannes, maréchal de France.* Paris: Bouquet, 1975.

Macdonnell, Archibald Gordon. *Napoleon and His Marshals.* New York: Macmillan, 1934.

Laotian Civil War (1954–1973)

Laos declared its independence from France in July 1949 and was finally recognized in 1954. A three-sided conflict immediately erupted, involving royalist, neutralist, and Communist forces. In 1959 General Phoumi led a coup against the indigenous Pathet Lao (Communist) forces of Prince Souphanouvong. The Communists were driven into the bush, but aided and abetted by North Vietnam, China, and the Soviet Union, they retained military viability. Over the next decade and a half, the government alternated between various neutralist and royalist factions, which invariably brought on Pathet Lao offensives exploiting the chaos. By 1965, the Communists were poised to overrun the entire country before the United States intervened with direct air strikes against Pathet Lao positions and the Ho Chi Minh trail. Military advisers were also introduced, along with large-scale recruitment of Meo tribesmen as mercenaries.

For nearly a decade, the political and military situation in Laos revolved around control of the central highland region known as Plain of Jars. A seasonal succession of offensives and counteroffensives by both sides secured and lost this vital area with little diminution of fighting. At length, the Pathet Lao gained the upper hand, thanks to direct intervention by North Vietnamese forces. A cease-fire was agreed to in 1973, but two years later, with the retreat of U.S. forces from Indochina, the Pathet Lao took formal control of the country. Within two years, anti-Communist forces began a low-intensity war against the regime that lasted until 1990 and also involved incursions by neighboring Thai forces. Sporadic fighting lasted until 1991, when a final political accommodation was reached.

John C. Fredriksen

References and further reading:

Adams, Nina S., and Alfred W. McCoy, eds. *Laos: War and Revolution.* New York: Harper & Row, 1970.

Langer, Paul F. *Revolution in Laos: The North Vietnamese and the Pathet Lao.* Santa Monica, CA: RAND Corporation, 1969.

Larrey, Dominique Jean (1766–1842)

French military surgeon of the French Revolutionary and Napoleonic eras; renowned for pioneering rapid evacuation and treatment of wounded soldiers. Born at Beaudéan (Hautes-Pyrénées) on 8 July 1766, Larrey studied medicine at Toulouse. While serving with the Army of the Rhine in 1792, Larrey was appalled at the delay in treating the wounded. He helped organize mobile field hospitals, which closely followed the troops. He also recognized that rapid evacuation of wounded from the battlefield was crucial. Therefore he developed a light, sprung, horse-drawn, two-wheeled cart—the "flying ambulance"—to pick up wounded even under fire. A four-wheeled version to carry more wounded came later. In Egypt in 1798, he designed camel-mounted pannier baskets to transport the wounded.

Larrey served in every Napoleonic campaign after Egypt and was appointed chief surgeon of the Imperial Guard. Skilled in the accepted practice of rapid amputation of any severely injured limb, Larrey unwittingly pioneered the use of antiseptic dressings. He could be quite unorthodox. After the Battle of Aspern and Essling (20–22 May 1809), Larrey ordered the slaughter of horses, including officers' mounts, to provide broth for the wounded who were stranded without food.

Noted for his boundless energy in treating wounded of all ranks, Larrey distinguished himself by his courage, efficiency, ingenuity, and medical observations and writings. As surgeon general of the Grand Army in Russia in 1812, Larrey labored prodigiously to save the wounded while simultaneously making extensive observations of the effects of cold on them. He served at Waterloo, where the Duke of Wellington, noticing the brave surgeon at work under fire, ordered his gunners not to fire on him.

After Waterloo, Larrey devoted himself to a distinguished career in medicine and wrote many works dealing with military medicine. He died in Paris on 1 August 1842. In his "Testament" (15 April 1821), Napoleon described Larrey as "the most virtuous man" he had known.

James K. Kieswetter

See also: French Revolutionary Wars; Napoleonic Wars

References and further reading:

Haythornthwaite, Philip J. *Napoleon's Military Machine.* New York: Hippocrene Books, 1988.

Larrey, Dominique Jean. *Memoirs of Military Surgery and Campaigns of the French Armies on the Rhine, in Corsica, Catalonia, Egypt and Syria; at Boulogne, Ulm, Austerlitz; in Saxony, Prussia, Poland, Spain and Austria.* Trans. Richard Willmott Hall. 4 vols. Baltimore: Joseph Cushing, 1814.

Soubiran, André. *Le baron Larrey, chirurgien de Napoléon.* Paris: Fayard, 1967.

Vess, David M. *Medical Revolution in France 1789–1796.* Gainesville: University Presses of Florida, 1975.

Latin Empire–Byzantine Wars (1204–1267)

The Fourth Crusade shattered Byzantium and installed a Latin regime. In 1203, the knights of the Fourth Crusade captured Constantinople and drove out Emperor Alexius III (r. 1195–1203). The following year, after attempting to rule through several Byzantine puppets, the crusaders again took the city to suppress the anti-Latin regime of Alexius V Ducas Murtzuphlus (r. 1204). This time they thoroughly looted it and destroyed the Byzantine administration. Churches were converted from orthodox to Catholic (Latin) Christianity, and Count Henry of Flanders was crowned as the "Latin" emperor of Constantinople. Henry then parceled out provinces to his vassals, assuming that they could conquer them. Even as he did so, opposition was forming. In 1205, Alexius III's son-in-law, Theodore Lascaris (r. 1204–1222), created a Byzantine government in exile at Nicaea. The Latins also had to confront rivals in Epirus (present-day Albania and northwestern Greece) and in Trebizond, as well as predatory Turks and Bulgarians.

To challenge Lascaris, the Ducas family of Epirus began to expand into the Balkans. In 1216, Count Henry died, and his heir Peter fell in an Epiran ambush. With the Latins in disarray, Theodore Ducas moved in and captured Thessalonica in 1224, a great victory. Meanwhile, Nicaea, now under John Vatatzes (r. 1222–1254), was consolidating its hold on Anatolia after defeating both the Comneni of Trebizond and the Turks. With Ducas now claiming to be emperor of Byzantium, John Vatatzes, John Asen of Bulgaria, and even the Constantinople Latins united against him. In 1230, Ducas decided first to punish the Bulgarians, but John Asen crushed his army at the Battle of Klokotnitsa and annexed half of Ducas's former conquests.

With the Ducas family in eclipse, Vatatzes and the Bulgarians agreed in 1235 to divide the Balkans and besiege Constantinople together. The siege failed, and by 1237, the alliance had soured. Plagues and Mongol incursions delayed new operations, but circumstances still benefited Vatatzes. The Mongols crushed the Seljuqs, securing Nicaea's eastern flank. In 1246, Vatatzes invaded an enfeebled Bulgaria, securing a European base. In 1251, Michael II of Epirus invaded Nicaean holdings in Greece. Vatatzes intercepted the Epirans, pulverized their army, and forced Ducas into vassalage. Nicaea was now ascendant.

Vatatzes' sickly heir, Theodore II (r. 1254–1258), soon confronted a new Ducas plot, an alliance of Serbs, Bulgarians, Peloponnesian Latin knights, and the bellicose Manfred of Sicily. When Theodore II died, he left Nicaea to a child, John Lascaris (r. 1258–1261), and to his grand commander, Michael Paleologus. Paleologus immediately went on the attack. Although he inflicted severe defeats on the coalition, these campaigns were actually holding actions. Nicaea's real objective was not Epirus but Constantinople. Risking another invasion from Albania, Paleologus concentrated forces against the city in 1260 and took it, ironically, by stealth the next year. Now Emperor Michael VIII (r. 1259–1282), he played divide-and-conquer to force treaties on Bulgarians, Serbs, Venetians, the Latin knights in Greece, and the Ducas family. The death of Manfred of Sicily temporarily halted the menace from western Europe. By 1267, the "Latin Empire" of Constantinople was officially dead. It had taken the Byzantines over 60 years of convoluted war and diplomacy to overthrow it.

Weston F. Cook Jr.

See also: Seljuqs

References and further reading:

Bartutis, Mark. *The Late Byzantine Army.* Philadelphia: University of Pennsylvania Press, 1992.

Fine, John. *The Late Medieval Balkans.* Ann Arbor: University of Michigan Press, 1987

Laupen, Battle of (21 June 1339)

Swiss shock action that defeated mounted heavy cavalry. The Battle of Laupen pitted the Swiss city of Bern against a coalition of Burgundian cities in what boiled down to a land dispute. The city of Bern had aggressively acquired two Burgundian towns, Thurn and Laupen. In 1339, a Burgundian coalition formed to take back the disputed regions. In June 1339, the Burgundians (1,200 mounted knights and an unknown number of infantry auxiliaries) surrounded the town of Laupen, which was defended by 600 Bernese militia. The Swiss from the forest cantons came to the aid of the Bernese. On 21 June, the Bernese and their allies (about 6,000 men) moved to relieve the town.

The Burgundians, led by Count Gerard of Vallangin, intending to crush the Swiss by a strong attack against their left, deployed their horse on the right, with foot soldiers holding the center and left positions. The Swiss formed a staggered line, with the Bernese, armed with the pike, thrust forward onto the crest of a hill. Two other squares of Swiss halberdiers followed behind and were staggered to the left of the Bernese. There they awaited the Burgundian attack. After some minor skirmishing, the Swiss swept forward. Their right and center squares immediately drove into the enemy foot soldiers and dispersed them with great slaughter and panic. They then wheeled to the left to take the knights, who were engaged by the third Swiss square, in their flank. The knights had been launching successive charges against the Swiss with some effect, but they could not break the square, which bristled with halberds. With the field entirely in the hands of the Swiss, the knights were soon surrounded and forced to flee, leaving behind many of their fallen nobility.

Laupen marked the beginning of the end of the unquestioned dominance of the mounted warrior. Laupen was the first victory won by infantry attacking heavy cavalry. For nearly two hundred years afterward, the Swiss maintained the reputation for fearless and resolute offensive action.

Bryan R. Gibby

See also: Sempach, Battle of

References and further reading:

Delbruck, Hans. *Medieval Warfare.* Trans. Walter J. Renfroe, Jr. Lincoln: University of Nebraska Press, 1990.

Oman, Charles W. *The Art of War in the Middle Ages.* Ed. John H. Beeler. Ithaca, NY: Cornell University Press, 1953.

Lawrence, Thomas Edward (T. E.) (1888–1935)

Eccentric British scholar-adventurer, better known as "Lawrence of Arabia," who helped lead the Arab revolt against Turkey during World War I. Lawrence was born on 15 August 1888 in the Welsh town of Tremadoc. In 1910, he took a degree in modern history at Jesus College, Oxford University, while traveling regularly to the Middle East to study crusader castles. His reputation as an archaeologist and a linguist brought him to the attention of the War Office in 1914.

The writer and soldier T. E. Lawrence ("Lawrence of Arabia") c. 1918. (Hulton/Archive)

Lawrence was commissioned and went to work in the War Office's Geographical Department in London. In December 1914, he went to Cairo to help instigate a revolt on the Arabian peninsula.

In late 1916, Lawrence, now a captain, was part of a British delegation that met with Sharif Hussain of Mecca, whose son Feisal led a small insurgent army in southern Arabia. In November, Lawrence joined Feisal's army as an adviser and liaison. With British support, the Arab army launched attacks on the vital Hadjis Railroad. Feisal and Lawrence seized the Red Sea ports of Wejh (24 January 1917) and Aqaba (6 July 1917). Lawrence was promoted to major, and the army turned north in support of Edmund Allenby's offensive in Palestine. The Arabs played an important role in the fighting in 1918, taking Der'aa (27 September 1918) and Damascus (1 October 1918).

An outspoken supporter of Arab nationalism, Lawrence attended the Versailles Conference but was bitterly disappointed by continued Anglo-French influence in the region. Lawrence, now a colonel and uncomfortable with the publicity he received in Britain and the United States, resigned in 1922. He enlisted in the Royal Tank Corps and the Royal Air Force (RAF) under assumed names but was unmasked by the press. In 1926 he published his memoir, *The Seven Pillars of Wisdom.* On 19 May 1935, shortly after leaving the RAF, Lawrence died of injuries sustained in a motorcycle accident.

Adam R. Seipp

See also: Allenby, Edmund Henry Hyman, Viscount; World War I

References and further reading:

Graves, Robert. *Lawrence and the Arabs.* London: J. Cape, 1927.

Mack, John E. *A Prince of Our Disorder: The Life of T. E. Lawrence.* Boston: Little, Brown, 1976.

Wilson, Jeremy. *Lawrence of Arabia: The Authorised Biography of T. E. Lawrence.* London: Heinemann, 1989.

Laws of War

International laws, enforced sometimes by nations after war and sometimes by commanders in battle, governing both the decision to engage in war and the manner of its conduct, particularly the forms of violence used, the definition of combatants, the treatment of prisoners, and the treatment of neutrals and noncombatants. Throughout recorded military history, there have been limits on the conduct of war. These limits have been often breached, in the same manner that almost all laws are broken, but they have not only persisted but have grown more comprehensive, and whether a nation's armies and soldiers comply with them is a hallmark distinguishing that nation's military as professional.

Laws of war arose in ancient Greece from the custom of commanders as well as from the specific treaties concluded among cities. Thucydides recorded a high level of compliance with truces, armistices, alliances, and peace treaties between city-states. Further, commanders honored flags of truce and heralds, truces to bury the dead, conditions of surrender, and the sanctity of triumphant monuments erected to celebrate victory. The rights of neutrals were usually honored, as was the neutrality of religious temples and the right to travel to Olympic games. Soldiers and commanders obeyed these rules for three different reasons: they were defining habits of civilized Greeks, a status they highly valued; they were religious obligations; and they expected reciprocal treatment from their opponents.

Roman conquest was very little constrained by laws, although the army did maintain strict rules for discipline within its ranks, and there were detailed regulations for the treatment of conquered lands and people. Further, Rome concluded many treaties for truces and peace with both allies and opponents that were honored, at least for the time specified in the treaties. The most essential characteristics of the Roman *iustum bellum,* though, were that war be conducted *pium* (according to religious prescriptions) and only after unsatisfied demands had been made of the opponent or a declaration of war had been sent.

Medieval warfare was regulated only by religious doctrine. Christians were constrained in the treatment of opposing Christians, just as Muslims were constrained in their treatment of fellow Muslims. Neither, for instance, could enslave a captured enemy of the same religion. In both cultures, forms of chivalry emerged by the late Middle Ages that specified limits on the forms of battle and the treatment of prisoners, although these rules usually mandated such good treatment only of those with high rank.

Christian scholars from Ambrose and Augustine to Thomas Aquinas, Francisco de Vitoria, and Francisco Suárez argued that only some wars were just and that there was no justification in killing noncombatants. Despite their reflection in the Gratian decretals of canon law, these arguments for just wars were predicated on theology and found little adherence in national legal systems.

The modern law of war is the result of the development of the modern nation-state. Both were foreseen and described in the great text of Dutch scholar Hugo Grotius, *De Jure Belli ac Pacis* (1625), which argued (based in part on the system of Alberico Gentili) for national obligations of rational conduct through law, in peace and in war. Although initially few attempts were made at international agreement or enforcement, custom followed many of Grotius's observations and edits, such as the use of declarations of war and the honoring of pledges not to destroy surrendered cities.

With the balance of power created by the Treaty of Westphalia in 1648, states were subject to no obligations but those they voluntarily accepted, usually as treaties. There was no enforcement of a breached obligation other than by very powerful states or alliances. This process of "horizontal enforcement" has persisted for 350 years. As armies grew larger with massed men and as weapons became more capable of destruction, the identification of combatants, limitations of weaponry, and treatment of prisoners became more acute problems for all nations, and both internal military culture and international treaties began to set new standards.

The Declaration of Paris (1856) abolished privateering, leaving naval engagements solely to professional combatants and banning all others as pirates. In 1863, President Abraham Lincoln issued General Order No. 100, setting standards for the identity of combatants and treatment of prisoners of war. The first Geneva Convention (1864) set standards for the treatment of enemy wounded by the great states of Europe. Further international conventions, at The Hague in 1899 and 1907 and in Geneva in 1906, 1929, and 1949, refined the law of war as to battlefield conduct and weapons, civilians, prisoners of war, and wounded and sick military personnel. Other conventions banned particular weapons, beginning with the Geneva Protocol on Gas Warfare of 1925.

The Bryan Treaties of 1913 and 1914 and, perhaps most controversially, the Versailles Treaty of 1919 promoted limits on the grounds for commencing war, including requirements for investigation, arbitration, and peaceful settlement of disputes, and the Kellogg-Briand Pact (1928) condemned recourse to war in all cases but self-defense. None of these instruments prevented the horrors of World War II, and at the conclusion of the war, the victorious allies established tribunals at Nuremberg and Tokyo to try individuals accused of war crimes, particularly the new category of crimes against peace, which included planning, initiating, and waging wars of aggression in violation of international treaties and agreements; crimes against humanity, which included exterminations, deportations, and genocide; war crimes, or the violations of the laws of war on the battlefield; and conspiring to commit the criminal acts listed in the first three counts. In Germany, of 22 defendants, 3 were acquitted, 4 imprisoned from 10 to 20 years, 3 imprisoned for life, and 12 sentenced to hang. In Japan, of 25 defendants, 2 were sentenced to prison terms, 16 to life imprisonment, and 7 to hang. The most important change in law from these trials was the Nuremberg principle, holding the individual and not just the state accountable for violations of the laws of war.

With the adoption of the United Nations Charter in 1945, almost all nations of the world committed to the peaceful settlement of disputes and the renunciation of war except in self-defense. Among the signatory regimes, very effective conventions have been adopted outlawing genocide and crimes against humanity; further limiting the use of weapons of mass destruction, such as nuclear and biological weapons, and certain weapons of particular inhumanity, such as exploding bullets; and further refining standards for the treatment of prisoners and the wounded.

The UN Security Council created the International Criminal Tribunal for the Former Yugoslavia on 25 May 1993 and the International Criminal Tribunal for Rwanda on 8 November 1994. Both ad hoc tribunals are charged with the investigation of war crimes, and both have actively investigated and convicted individuals for violations of the Geneva Convention of 1949; genocide; violations of the laws and customs of war; and crimes against humanity. The specific articles for violations of the laws and customs of war include the use of poisonous weapons or other weapons calculated to cause unnecessary suffering; wanton destruction of civilian areas not justified by military necessity; attack or bombardment of undefended towns; seizing or harming buildings dedicated to religion, charity, education, and the arts and sciences, as well as historic monuments and works of art and science; and plundering public or private property.

The UN Rome conference (opened on 17 July 1998) drafted a treaty establishing an International Criminal Court with global jurisdiction to try individuals accused of crimes similar to those prosecuted by the tribunals for Yugoslavia and Rwanda and whose governments will not try them. The treaty will become effective when 60 states have ratified it; by December 2000, 120 states had signed it, and 25 had ratified it.

Steve Sheppard

See also: General Order No. 100; Geneva Conventions; Nuremberg Principle

References and further reading:

Best, Geoffrey. *War and Law since 1945.* Oxford: Clarendon Press, 1994.

Brownlie, Ian. *International Law and the Use of Force by States.* Oxford: Clarendon Press, 1963.

Holland, Thomas Erskine. *The Laws of War on Land (Written and Unwritten).* Oxford: Clarendon Press, 1908.

Lebanese Civil Wars (1958, 1975–2000)

Two civil wars that have devastated the Lebanese "nation" created by ill-conceived World War II peace settlements. The 1958 civil war was due to pro-Western president Camille Caiman's (1900–1987) wish to serve a second term, contrary to the constitution, and Lebanese Muslims' desire for a stronger pro-Arab relationship. To quell the riots of May 1958, Caiman asked the United States for help, and it responded by sending the Sixth Fleet with 14,000 U.S. troops. On 23 September 1958, Caiman was succeeded by General Fuad Chehab (1902–1973). The U.S. troops withdrew in October 1958.

The Lebanese civil war of 1975 to 2000 focused on the discontent that evolved from the unofficial, inequitable National Pact of 1943. The Maronite Christians governed Lebanon at the expense of the Shiite, Sunni, and Druze sects, which constituted 50 percent of the population by 1975. Disgruntled Palestinian Muslims supported the Palestine Liberation Organization's (PLO) guerrilla attacks on Israel.

Civil war was sparked on 13 April 1975, when some Christian Phalangists were attacked in a church; they retaliated by killing 27 Palestinian bus passengers. The PLO joined other Muslim groups in raids. Israeli became involved by supplying arms to the Christians. The League of Arab States, led by Syria, sent 30,000 troops to implement a peace plan in 1976. Beirut was divided into political and religious enclaves in 1977, with most groups fighting each other. Israeli troops invaded Lebanon on 14 March 1978 to eliminate PLO bases. Some 6,000 UN peacekeepers replaced the Israelis, who left later that year.

By 1981, Syria had intervened militarily and placed armed forces in Lebanon's Bekaa Valley, along with Soviet missiles. The Phalangists responded by occupying the area around the Beirut-Damascus highway, which sparked a Syrian offensive. The Israelis attacked the Syrians and bombed some Beirut sectors in retaliation for PLO rocket attacks into northern Israel. A cease-fire was called on 24 July 1981.

In June 1982, the Israelis reinvaded Lebanon, killing 18,000 Lebanese. Israel forced the PLO guerrillas to evacuate Beirut. On 14 September, President-elect Bashir Gemayel (1947–1982), a Phalangist, was assassinated, but he was succeeded by his brother Amin Gemayel (b. 1942). Then 328 Palestinian were killed by Phalangists in Beirut refugee camps from 16 to 18 September. Peace-keeping forces from the United States, the United Kingdom, France, and Italy arrived.

The U.S. Embassy was bombed on 18 April 1983, killing 50 people. Suicide bomb attacks on French and U.S. military headquarters in Beirut led to more than 300 deaths on 23 October 1983 and caused the international forces to withdraw. Israeli forces left the Shuf Mountains, which were then occupied by the Druze, who fought both the Lebanese army and the Christians. PLO Leader Yasir Arafat (1929–) was forced to leave Beirut on 20 December 1983 after some PLO dissidents supported by Syria attacked and besieged his stronghold.

By February 1984, Lebanon was occupied by both Israel

and Syria. Fierce fighting in Beirut between Druze and Shiite militias occurred. The extremist group Hezbollah (Party of God) emerged in 1985. Sheer anarchy reigned when Christian general Michel Aoun (b. 1935) became president in 1988, while Muslim prime minister Selim al Hoss (b. 1930) established a competing government. Their respective militias physically destroyed Beirut.

The League of Arab States drafted the National Reconciliation Charter for Lebanon in 1990, providing greater equality and diminished presidential power. It also called for the withdrawal of the militias and the destruction of the "'green line" that bisected Beirut; thus the civil war supposedly ended. However, more attacks and counterattacks continued to plague desolate Lebanon. Nearly 150,000 lives, civilian and military, have been lost in the civil war, and nearly 200,000 people have been wounded.

Annette Richardson

References and further reading:

Brogan, Patrick. *The Fighting Never Stopped.* New York: First Vintage Books, 1990.

Salibi, Kamal. *A House of Many Mansions: The History of Lebanon Reconsidered.* Berkeley: University of California Press, 1988.

Winslow, Charles. *Lebanon: War and Politics in a Fragmented Society.* London: Routledge, 1996.

Lechfeld (10 August 955)

Decisive defeat of Magyar raiders by Otto I. The Magyars, emerging from the steppes of Russia, migrated to the Danube River basin in the ninth century and settled in what is now Hungary. Fighting primarily as horse-archers, they sought to avoid close-quarter action, preferring to encircle their foes and engage them from afar.

As king of Germany, Henry the Fowler (r. 919–936) had transformed the Saxon nobility, hitherto used to fighting as light cavalry, into a disciplined force of armored horsemen. This "military revolution" gave the Ottonian dynasty the edge not only over its rivals in Germany but also over the Magyars. When Henry fought them at the Battle of Riade (933), he reminded his "men of iron" of the need to maintain their line, to use their shields to deflect the first discharge of arrows, and only then to spur their mounts to close contact, but it was left to his son, Otto I the Great, to banish the threat of the Magyars.

The Magyars resumed their attacks in 954 with a major invasion, followed by a second one in 955. Their numbers are unknown, but the chroniclers report that they had never been seen in such force before. Crossing Bavaria, they laid siege to Augsburg. Otto moved rapidly from Saxony, with an army amounting to some 8,000 horsemen, its various contingents coming from Saxony, Bavaria, Swabia, Franconia, and Bohemia. When Otto approached the Lech River, the Magyars broke camp. While their main body engaged the king, a smaller detachment, outflanking the German host, turned up in the rear of the Swabians and wreaked havoc among them. The Franconians under Conrad the Red, duke of Lotharingia, had to turn so as to face this surprise attack, but when Otto ordered a general charge against the main body of the enemy, everything favored his host. The Magyars, on their smaller mounts and lacking armor, discharged a volley of arrows before they were overtaken and slain, many as they attempted to negotiate the Lech River.

The Germans had suffered heavily—Conrad was killed the moment he lifted his helmet to get some air—but what turned defeat into irreparable disaster for the Magyars was the relentless pursuit of the vanquished by Otto. The remnants of the Magyar army were decimated and its captured leaders executed.

Nic Fields

See also: Otto I, the "Great"

References and further reading:

Leyser, K. J. *Medieval Germany and Its Neighbours, 900–1250.* London: Hambledon Press, 1982.

Lee, Henry ("Light Horse Harry") (1756–1818)

American cavalry commander and politician. Lee was born into a wealthy Virginia family in Prince William County on 29 January 1756. After graduating in 1773 from the College of New Jersey (later Princeton University) he volunteered for Captain Theodorick Bland's Virginia Cavalry in June 1776. This unit, with Bland as colonel and Lee as captain, was incorporated into the First Continental Dragoons on 31 March 1777 and saw action at Brandywine. Lee blamed Bland's poor reconnaissance of the northern fords for George Washington's being outflanked on the right and losing that battle.

Promoted to major on 7 April 1778 by virtue of distinctive service against Banastre Tarleton at Spread Eagle Tavern, Pennsylvania, on 20 January, he drilled his battalion into an effective force and led it to victory at Paulus Hook, New Jersey, on 19 August 1779. Promoted to lieutenant colonel on 6 November 1780, he named his regiment "Lee's Legion" and reinforced Nathanael Greene in South Carolina on 13 January 1781. Supporting the guerrilla warfare of Francis Marion, the "Swamp Fox," Lee excelled throughout the Carolinas in 1781 at Georgetown, Haw River, Guilford Court House, Fort Watson, Fort Motte, Fort Granby, Augusta, Ninety-Six, and Eutaw Springs. His raids on Charles Cornwallis's outposts were an important factor in the success of the Continental army's southern strategy.

After the war, Lee held several high political offices, including Virginia state legislator, Virginia governor, and U.S. congressman. In 1794 he commanded troops against the Whiskey Rebellion in western Pennsylvania. In 1799 he eulogized the just-deceased Washington as "First in war, first in peace, and first in the hearts of his countrymen." To recover from injuries he suffered while trying to impede an antiwar riot in Baltimore in July 1812, he retired to the Caribbean in 1813. He died on Cumberland Island, Georgia, on 25 March 1818, during the return voyage to Virginia. His third son was Robert E. Lee, the great Confederate general.

Eric v. d. Luft

See also: American Revolution; Brandywine; Greene, Nathanael; Guilford Court House; Lee, Robert Edward; War of 1812; Washington, George; Whiskey Rebellion

References and further reading:

Hartmann, John W. *The American Partisan: Henry Lee and the Struggle for Independence, 1776–1780.* Shippensburg, PA: Burd Street, 1999.

Lee, Henry. *The Campaign of 1781 in the Carolinas: Memoirs of the War in the Southern Department of the United States.* Reprint, Spartanburg, SC: 1975.

———. *The Revolutionary War Memoirs of General Henry Lee.* Edited with a biography of the author by Robert E. Lee. New introduction by Charles Royster. New York: Da Capo, 1998.

Royster, Charles. *Light-Horse Harry Lee and the Legacy of the American Revolution.* Baton Rouge: Louisiana State University Press, 1994.

Lee, Robert Edward (1807–1870)

Commander in chief of the Confederate armies in the American Civil War. Lee was born in Stratford, Virginia, on 19 January 1807, the third son of "Light Horse Harry" Lee. Ranking second in the U.S. Military Academy at West Point, class of 1829, and with no demerits, he was commissioned in the engineers and stationed in the southeastern states. Until 1846 he worked on bridges and fortifications in Georgia, Virginia, New York, and Missouri. In the Mexican-American War, he served first under John Ellis Wool and then under Winfield Scott, building bridges and securing important reconnaissance for the Battles of Saltillo, Veracruz, Cerro Gordo, Contreras, Churubusco, and Chapultepec. From 1852 to 1855, he was superintendent of the U.S. Military Academy.

Promoted to lieutenant colonel in the Second Cavalry, Lee served in Texas from 1855 to 1857. In October 1859 he led the expedition to capture John Brown at Harpers Ferry. He served again in Texas until February 1861, when Scott recalled him to Washington. When the Civil War broke out, both Scott and President Abraham Lincoln tried to persuade him to accept command of the Union armies, but choosing instead to support Virginia, he became major general of Virginia forces on 23 April. Confederate president Jefferson Davis promoted him to full general on 14 June.

Lee's debut as a Confederate field commander at Cheat Mountain, West Virginia, on 12–13 September was a failure caused by the insubordination of his junior officers. Davis reassigned him to the Carolinas and Georgia to oversee coastal defenses but recalled him to Richmond as a military adviser in March 1862. After Joseph E. Johnston was seriously wounded at Fair Oaks on 31 May, Davis ordered Lee to take over Johnston's command and renamed it the Army of Northern Virginia on 1 June. It was Lee's command for the remainder of the war.

Lee's brilliance as a field commander first became apparent in the Seven Days' Battles. Leaving only a small garrison in Richmond, Lee boldly attacked George B. McClellan north of the Chickahominy River. This bloody series of tactical defeats was in fact a strategic victory because it pushed the Union army away from Richmond. After a stunning victory over John Pope at Second Bull Run, Lee invaded Maryland, but McClellan eventually stopped him at Antietam. Lee tried a second invasion of the north after beating Ambrose Burn-

Photographic portrait of Robert E. Lee, 1869. (Library of Congress)

side at Fredericksburg and Joseph Hooker at Chancellorsville. He worsened his losses at Gettysburg on the third day by ordering "Pickett's Charge," a massive frontal infantry attack across a three-quarter-mile-wide plain under constant fire from the Union center.

In the wake of Gettysburg, the Army of Northern Virginia could not resume the offensive. Lee made full use of delaying tactics and entrenchments, forcing Ulysses S. Grant to waste huge numbers of Union troops assaulting his positions in the Wilderness, at Petersburg, and before Richmond. Davis named Lee commander in chief on 23 January 1865. In the end, Grant gave Lee generous terms of surrender at Appomattox on 9 April 1865.

Lee spent the rest of his life as a paroled prisoner of war. In October 1865, he became president of the nearly defunct Washington College, now Washington and Lee University in Lexington, Virginia. Unlike most Confederates, he was never able to regain his U.S. citizenship, even though he had opposed slavery before the war and epitomized reconciliation after the war. His greatest gift to his reunited nation, in fact, may have been his strong discouragement of any ideas of continuing the battle by guerrilla warfare, thus sparing the country the agony of prolonged insurgency and counterinsurgency conflict. He died in Lexington on 12 October 1870. A person of seemingly absolute integrity, Lee was revered throughout the South and honored in the North by the time of his death.

Eric v. d. Luft

See also: American Civil War; Antietam/Sharpsburg; Second Bull Run/Manassas Junction; Cerro Gordo, Battle of; Chancellorsville, Battle of; Fredericksburg; Gettysburg; Grant, Ulysses Simpson; Hill, Ambrose Powell; Jackson, Thomas "Stonewall"; Johnston, Joseph Eggleston; Lee, Henry; Lincoln, Abraham; Longstreet, James; McClellan, George Brinton; Meade, George Gordon; Mexican-American War; Petersburg, Siege of; Pope, John; Scott, Winfield; Seven Days' Battles; Veracruz, Siege of; Wilderness

References and further reading:

Chaney, William Franklin. *Duty Most Sublime: The Life of Robert E. Lee as Told through the Carter Letters.* Baltimore: Gateway, 1996.

Davis, Burke. *Gray Fox: Robert E. Lee and the Civil War.* Short Hills, NJ: Burford, 1998.

Fellman, Michael. *The Making of Robert E. Lee.* New York: Random House, 2000.

Gallagher, Gary W., ed. *Lee the Soldier.* Lincoln: University of Nebraska Press, 1996.

LeFebvre, Pierre-François-Joseph, Duke of Danzig (1755–1820)

French marshal. Pierre-François-Joseph LeFebvre was born at Rouffach on 25 October 1755. He enlisted in the Gardes Françaises in 1773 and rose to the rank of sergeant by 1789. During the French Revolution, he was promoted rapidly and served in the Army of the Moiselle. By December 1793, he was promoted to *general de brigade;* in 1794, he was appointed to command a division. From September to December 1797, he served as commander of the Army of the Sambre-et-Meuse after the death of Lazare Hoche. In March 1799, he was appointed to command the S17th Military Division, the district containing Paris. He remained quiet during Napoleon's coup of 18 Brumaire, thus ensuring its success. During the consulate, he served as president of the Senate.

Pierre-François-Joseph LeFebvre. (Library of Congress)

In May 1804, LeFebvre was made a marshal of the empire. Two year later, he commanded the V Corps and in October 1806 was appointed to command the infantry of the Imperial Guard, which he led at Jena. During the closing months of the campaign against Prussia, he was sent to besiege Danzig, in command of the X Corps. After the siege, lasting from January to May 1807, and the surrender of the city, he was created duke of Danzig.

In 1808, LeFebvre commanded the Fourth Corps in Spain, defeating Spanish armies led by Joaquin Blake and the marquis de la Romana. Recalled to Germany during the 1809 campaign, he commanded the VII Corps, composed mostly of Bavarians. Later, he was appointed to command the Army of the Tyrol, operating against pro-Austrian insurgents. He defeated the insurrection and restored order.

In 1812, LeFebvre again commanded the infantry of the Imperial Guard during the Russian campaign. He was thus present at most of the major battles of that invasion but figured little in the fighting. He did not participate in the 1813 campaign. In the 1814 campaign, he fought at Champaubert, Montmirail, and Monteneau, where, according to the diarist Coignet, he "fought so hard that he foamed at the mouth." At the end of the 1814 campaign, he was part of the group of marshals, including Michel Ney, MacDonald, and Nicholas-Charles Oudinot, who secured the first abdication from Napoleon, on 6 April 1814.

During the Hundred Days, he played no active role on behalf of the Bonapartists, pleading old age and thus avoiding exile or death. He lived in retirement until his death in 1820.

Joseph Isenberg

See also: Berezina River, Battle of; Borodino; French Revolutionary Wars; Jena and Auerstädt; Moscow, Retreat from; Napoleon I; Napoleonic Wars

References and further reading:

Chandler, David. *Napoleon's Marshals.* London: Weidenfeld and Nicholson, 1987.

Young, Peter. *Napoleon's Marshals.* Reading, Berkshire, UK: Osprey, 1973.

Leipzig, Battle of (16–19 October 1813)

Decisive victory for the allies over Napoleon, ending his last German campaign. When Austria declared war against France on 12 August 1813, Napoleon had about 443,000 field troops in Germany south of Berlin. Trying to surround him were three separate multinational armies, a total of about 512,000 men under Karl Philipp zu Schwarzenberg in the south, Gebhard Leberecht von Blücher in the east, and Jean Baptiste Jules Bernadotte, crown prince of Sweden, in the north. From a skirmish on 16 August to the great cavalry battle at Liebertwolkwitz on 14 October, they fought many engagements, and both sides suffered enormous losses.

Napoleon's main force on 16 October was deployed in and around the city of Leipzig. Schwarzenberg attacked the southern and eastern outskirts at 8:00 A.M. Meanwhile, Blücher tried to sever Napoleon's communication lines in the west. Inconclusive fighting raged all day. Little happened on 17 October; the crucial day was 18 October. At 9:00 A.M., Schwarzenberg advanced his left in the south and soon was able to send his center against Napoleon's diverted forces in the southeast. Napoleon's situation was precarious by early afternoon. Bernadotte attacked from the northeast and Blücher from the north, completing a three-quarters' circle around Napoleon's entire army, compressing it, and pushing it into the city. Schwarzenberg's final assault of the day came from the east, dramatically reducing Napoleon's perimeter and inflicting heavy casualties. Napoleon made a defensive stand inside the city on 19 October. The allies commenced urban warfare in the northwest, east, and southeast. Napoleon's main concern was to organize an orderly retreat to France without being cut off. His defeated army escaped through a swamp and over a causeway west of the city.

Leipzig is frequently called the Battle of the Nations because of the great numbers of troops actually engaged: about 300,000 Russians, Prussians, Austrians, Swedes, British, and Germans united against Napoleon's 190,000 French, Italians, Germans, and Poles. Napoleon's losses were about 40,000 and those of allied forces about 54,000. In terms of numbers of troops engaged, Leipzig was the greatest battle of the nineteenth century, eclipsing even the massive engagements of the American Civil War half a century later.

Eric v. d. Luft

See also: Bernadotte, Jean Baptiste Jules; Berthier, Louis-Alexandre, Prince of Neuchâtel and Valangin, Prince of Wagram; Murat, Joachim, Grand Duke of Cleves-Berg, King of Naples; Napoleon I; Napoleonic Wars; Ney, Michel, Duc d'Enchingen, Prince de La Moskova; Oudinot, Nicholas-Charles, Duc de Reggio; Schwarzenberg, Karl Philipp zu

References and further reading:

Hofschroer, Peter. *Leipzig 1813: The Battle of the Nations.* London: Osprey, 1993.

Jansson, Per-Eric. *Leipzig.* London: Almark, 1975.

Nafziger, George F. *Napoleon at Leipzig: The Battle of Nations, 1813.* Chicago: Emperor's Press, 1996.

Petre, Francis Loraine. *Napoleon's Last Campaign in Germany, 1813.* London: Greenhill, 1992.

Lend-Lease (1940–1945)

A program devised by President Franklin D. Roosevelt to provide material aid to England (and later the other Allied powers) during World War II. By late 1940, the United Kingdom had run out of gold and cash reserves and thus informed the United States that it would be unable to pay for any more war matériel. In response, President Roosevelt proposed the Lend-Lease Act, which Congress passed in March 1941. Under the act, the president was empowered to sell, transfer, or exchange matériel to any country deemed vital to the defense of the United States. The United States was still neutral, and Roosevelt had to deal with many Americans who took an isolationist view of the war in Europe. To get support for the act, Roosevelt appealed directly to the American people, using a water hose analogy: if your neighbor's house is burning down, you do not worry about selling him the hose, but you give him the hose to deal with the cri-

Russian militia during the Siege of Leningrad c. 1942. (Hulton/Archive)

sis at hand and worry about the cost later. In presenting the idea of Lend-Lease to Congress in January 1941, Roosevelt first conceived of the idea of the Four Freedoms (freedom of speech and expression, freedom of worship, freedom from want, and freedom from fear) that later became part of the Atlantic Charter.

One of the foundations for the Lend-Lease Act was the transfer, in September 1940, of 50 obsolete destroyers to the United Kingdom in exchange for 99-year leases on a number of bases in the Caribbean and Newfoundland. The initial act included $1 million for aid to the Allies. By the fall of 1941, China and the Soviet Union had been added to the list of recipients. In October 1941, the Office of Lend-Lease Administration was developed to handle the growth of the Lend-Lease program. By 1943, Lend-Lease had been taken over by the State Department. Although the United Kingdom was the first (and main) recipient of Lend-Lease, the program was later expanded to help more than 40 counties. By August 1945, when Lend-Lease was abruptly terminated, more than $49 billion in aid, ranging from fighter planes to canned meat, had been extended to Allied nations. The countries of the British Commonwealth received about 63 percent and the Soviet Union about 22 percent. The United States received about $8 billion in "Reverse Lend-Lease," in which host countries helped pay for U.S. troops overseas during the war.

Drew Philip Halévy

See also: World War II

References and further reading:

Dobson, Alan P. *U.S. Wartime Aid to Britain, 1940–1946.* New York: St. Martin's Press, 1986.

Leningrad, Siege of (1941–1944)

Monumental siege during World War II. Leningrad's 900-day ordeal began on 8 July 1941, when the German Fourth Panzer Army severed the city's land contact with the Soviet Union less than three weeks after invading Russia. Hemmed in by Finnish troops to the north and German forces to the south and west, the 2.5 million inhabitants of Leningrad depended on meager supplies brought across Lake Lagoda from the east. They were not prepared for a siege, the authorities having dismissed calls to stockpile supplies and prepare defenses as "defeatist."

The "siege" itself was really an extended blockade ordered by Adolf Hitler to annihilate the city. German forces remained within artillery range but were ordered not to accept any form of surrender. They dug in permanently after the diversion of troops for attacks against Moscow in 1941 made offensive schemes impossible, and their Finnish allies, reluctant to cross their pre-1940 border with the Soviet Union, refused to attack from the north.

For the next two and a half years, German artillery and aircraft pounded the city, and the Wehrmacht denied all Soviet attempts to break the blockade. Leningrad's inhabitants froze to death in the winter, died under the incessant shelling, or starved when no more animals or glue could be found for consumption. More than 850,000 were evacuated in 1942, but at least 1 million are estimated to have died by the time a Soviet offensive relieved the city in January 1944. No city in modern history has suffered such losses without surrendering.

Lance Janda

See also: Stalin; World War II

References and further reading:

Glantz, David M. *The Siege of Leningrad, 1941–44: 900 Days of Terror.* Staplehurst: Spellmount, 2001.

Salisbury, Harrison Evans. *The 900 Days: The Siege of Leningrad.* New York: Da Capo Press, 1985.

Wayne, Kyra Petroskaya, and Harrison E. Salisbury. *Shurik: A WWII Saga of the Siege of Leningrad.* New York: Lyons & Burford, 2000.

Leo III (c. 675–741)

Founder of the Isaurian dynasty, iconoclast, energetic military leader, and adept strategist. Leo III took power in 717, at a time when Byzantium seemed on the verge of disintegration and conquest. Seven emperors had reigned in two decades of coups, revolts, and murderous attacks by Arabs, Slavs, and Bulgarians (697–717). As Leo deposed the reluctant emperor, Theodosius III, and entered the capital, massive Arab armies converged behind him, determined to bring Constantinople under Islam.

Fortunately, Leo was a wily and experienced commander. His successes in the Caucasus had earned him command of the Anatolian-Syrian frontier. In that office, Leo had courted the Bulgars and Armenians and employed his fluent Arabic. He defended Constantinople against an overwhelming force in a masterful economy of force strategy, using fire ships, encouraging guerrilla raiding and ambushes by the Slavs and Anatolians, and provoking revolts in the enemy camp. The Umayyad caliph ended the siege in 718, and Leo quickly shifted forces to reclaim control of Sicily and southern Italy.

Although Arab raids into Anatolia continued throughout his reign, Leo had rescued the empire and restored the frontiers. He also reinforced the defense of many cities and updated the law codes of Emperor Justinian, but Leo's ban on the use of icons in Orthodox Christian worship ignited the iconoclastic struggle. It inflicted decades of internal strife upon Byzantium. His policies also fueled the growing alienation between eastern and western Christendom, when he attempted an invasion of northern Italy in 733.

Weston F. Cook, Jr.

See also: Constantinople, Siege of (717–718)

References and further reading:

Ostrogorsky, George. *History of the Byzantine State.* New Brunswick, NJ: Rutgers University Press, 1991.

Treadgold, Warren. *A History of the Byzantine State and Society.* Stanford, CA: Stanford University Press, 1997.

Lettow-Vorbeck, Paul Emil von (1870–1964)

Successful German guerrilla warfare leader in East Africa during World War I. Paul von Lettow-Vorbeck was trained as an officer at the Military Academy at Potsdam and served in the German expeditionary force that quelled the Boxer Rebellion in China (1899). As a captain in the Schutztruppe (German colonial troops), he saw action against local tribes in German South-West Africa (now Namibia) from 1904 to 1907.

In 1913, Lettow-Vorbeck was placed in command of the German forces in German East Africa (today Tanzania). When World War I broke out, he defeated the invading Allied forces on several occasions, for example, at Tanga harbor (November 1914); Jassini (January 1915); Kilbata (1916); and Narungombe, Mahiwa, and Lukuledi (1917). He led by example and was wounded on three occasions. At most, he commanded only 3,007 white soldiers and 12,100 Askaris (black soldiers). Lettow-Vorbeck succeeded in evading the vastly superior Allied forces (of approximately 150,000 men) commanded by the South African generals Jan Christiaan Smuts (1916) and J. L. van Deventer (1917–1918), both of whom had waged successful guerrilla campaigns against the British during the Boer War (1899–1902) but were incapable of implementing successful antiguerrilla warfare against the Germans. In fact, Lettow-Vorbeck was able to recruit a number of former Boer guerrilla fighters into his ranks, who assisted him in developing guerrilla tactics.

The German command attempted to resupply Lettow-Vorbeck by the only means possible in the face of British control of the seas—by dirigible. A German airship was dispatched from Bulgaria in 1916 and almost reached the guerrilla commander when it had to turn back because of adverse weather. It was the longest unrefueled flight in history until 1986.

In November 1917, Lettow-Vorbeck led his force across the border into Portuguese East Africa (Mozambique), defeated the Allies at Ngomano and Namakurra, and returned to German East Africa by September 1918. In November 1918, shortly before the armistice was signed, he occupied a strong position in Northern Rhodesia (now Zambia), but soon afterward he was ordered by his superiors in Germany to lay down his arms, which he and his remaining 155 white soldiers and 1,156 Askaris did reluctantly.

Lettow-Vorbeck's force contributed a brilliant chapter to the military history of irregular operations. His courageous resistance earned him worldwide fame, and he was honored and respected by both friend and foe. After the war, he became a symbol of inspiration for his humiliated fellow Germans. In 1919 he was promoted to brigadier general but was dismissed from the army in 1920 for taking part in the abortive right-wing Kapp Putsch. He was a member of the Reichstag (German parliament) from 1928 to 1933 and published three books on his war experiences in East Africa, two books on postwar visits to Africa, and his autobiography in 1957. Lettow-Vorbeck was a fervent patriot and strict disciplinarian but had good relations with his subordinates and was compassionate toward captured or wounded enemies. His Askaris called him *Bwana mkubwa ya akili mingi* (the big man who can do everything). His campaigns are still a cornerstone of unconventional warfare studies.

André Wessels

See also: Guerrilla/Partisan/Irregular Warfare; Smuts, Jan Christian

References and further reading:

von Lettow-Vorbeck, P. E. *Mein Leben.* Biberbach an der Riss: Koehlers, 1957.

———. *My Reminiscences of East Africa.* London: Hurst and Blackett, n.d.

Schnee, A. H. H. Deutsch. *Ostafrika im Weltkriege. Wie wir lebten und kämpften.* Leipzig: Verlag Quelle & Meyer, 1919.

Trümpelmann, G. P. J. "Von Lettow-Vorbeck, Paul Emil." In *Dictionary of South African Biography,* ed. C. J. Beyers. Vol. 4. Pretoria: Human Sciences Research Council, 1981.

Leuctra, Battle of (371 B.C.E.)

Epaminondas, with a force of approximately 6,000 soldiers, defeated the Spartan army, which numbered about 10,000 men, at Leuctra in 371 B.C.E. Epaminondas arrayed his force to meet the Spartan right in oblique order, with a reinforced left consisting of a deep column that was 48 ranks deep, compared to the customary eight. He may have protected this column's left flank with a terrain obstacle or with a detachment of the Theban Sacred Band. He held back the forces remaining to his right and assigned them the task of holding in place the numerically superior Spartan left. In standard phalanx warfare, the right flank tended to overlap the enemy's left because soldiers unconsciously inched to the right to find cover for their exposed side from their neighbor's shield. The resulting rightward drift of both sides often resulted in a quarter rotation of the two lines as each right wing bore against the enemy's less steady left. Epaminondas's oblique order allowed an overwhelming concentration to overthrow the enemy's strongest wing while immobilizing the remainder of the enemy force.

The battle opened, typically, with a cavalry skirmish, in which the Thebans had more success than the Spartans. The climax occurred soon after, when Epaminondas led his heavy column against the Spartan line. Following the impact there was considerable fighting, but the Spartan right could not resist the Theban mass. The Spartan center and left, held to their front by the remaining Theban line and the cavalry, took no part in the fight. When Epaminondas completed the destruction of the Spartan right, his column wheeled to the right and advanced on the flank of the remaining Spartan line. In short order, the Spartan line broke and fled, leaving Epaminondas master of the field. Although this new battle tactic had some shortcomings, it changed military tactics in ancient Greece and brought Sparta down from its preeminent military position.

Bryan R. Gibby

See also: Epaminondas; Mantinea, Battle of

References and further reading:

Delbruck, Hans. *Warfare in Antiquity.* Trans. Walter J. Renfroe, Jr. Lincoln: University of Nebraska Press, 1990.

Dodge, Theodore A. *Alexander.* New York: Da Capo Press, 1996.

Jones, Archer. *The Art of Warfare in the Western World.* Urbana: University of Illinois Press, 1987.

Leuthen, Battle of (5 December 1757)

Major battle of the Seven Years' War (1756–1763) between Prussia and Austria. The Austrian army occupied Silesia as Frederick the Great defeated the Austrian army at Rossbach on 5 November. Prince Charles of Lorraine's army overwhelmed the Prussian detachment guarding the province and captured both Schweidnitz and Breslau. On 2 December, Frederick returned to Silesia and marched toward Breslau with 39,000 troops and 170 guns. He planned to lure the

Austrians into a decisive battle that would end the war. Opposing him were 66,000 men and 210 guns.

The Austrians stood near the small village of Leuthen. Charles and Field Marshal Leopold Daun wanted to entice Frederick into making a frontal assault along their 4.5-mile line and lock his army in a battle of attrition. On the morning of 5 December, Frederick advanced his army directly toward Leuthen and discovered the Austrian left flank exposed and unguarded. He altered his army's angle of advance so that it would be oblique to the Austrian left flank. Feigning an advance against the Austrian main line, Frederick's army redeployed without the Austrians' knowledge. Around noon, Prussian forward units attacked and broke through the Austrian positions, followed by a large-scale cavalry charge that put the Austrian command in chaos. Charles's attempt to shift his front only contributed to a growing panic within the Austrian ranks. At 3:30 P.M., Frederick unleashed a final assault of 40 cavalry squadrons that resulted in a general Austrian retreat but failed to organize a general pursuit to annihilate the remnants of Charles's army.

Leuthen ranks as Frederick's greatest tactical masterpiece. Nearly 6,000 Prussians were killed or wounded. Austria losses included 3,000 dead, 7,000 wounded, 12,000 prisoners, and 130 guns. The battle did not decide the war, but it did reinvigorate Frederick's war effort and ensured the survival of Prussia.

Patrick J. Speelman

See also: Frederick the Great, King of Prussia; Rossbach; Seven Years' War

References and further reading:

Duffy, Christopher. *Frederick the Great: A Military Life.* London: Routledge & Kegan Paul, 1985.

Showalter, Dennis. *The Wars of Frederick the Great.* London: Longman, 1996.

Weigley, Russell F. *The Age of Battles: The Quest for Decisive Warfare from Breitenfeld to Waterloo.* Bloomington: Indiana University Press, 1991.

Lewis, Meriwether (1774–1809)

American explorer, leader of the Lewis and Clark expedition. Born near Charlottesville, Virginia, on 18 August 1774, the son of an American Revolutionary War officer, Lewis was an avid outdoorsman. He served during the 1794 Whiskey Rebellion in the Virginia Militia. Later, in the regular army, he served under Captain William Clark in the Chosen Rifle Company. Between 1796 and 1801, Lewis was assigned to the 1st U.S. Infantry Regiment on the Ohio and Tennessee frontier and was promoted to lieutenant in 1798 and captain in 1800. In 1801, Lewis became private secretary to President Thomas Jefferson, an old family friend.

In 1803, the United States acquired a enormous land tract, the Louisiana Purchase, from France, and Jefferson assigned Lewis and his old captain, William Clark, to explore the new territory with Lewis in command. Along with mapping and exploring, Jefferson wanted the team to look into the feasibility of a route to the Pacific Ocean and to bolster U.S. claims to western lands not included in the purchase.

The expedition began on 14 May 1804 from St. Louis, Missouri Territory, with a total of 50 men. The explorers went up the Missouri River to North Dakota, where they spent the winter before continuing across the Rocky Mountains toward Oregon, arriving at the Pacific Ocean in early November 1805. Along the way, they received valuable assistance from American Indians, most notably the Shoshone guide, Sacagawea. They wintered on the coast, waiting for a transport ship that never came.

In March 1806, they began the return journey and were back in St. Louis on 23 September 1806. Hailed as a hero, Lewis was nominated by Jefferson as governor of the Louisiana Territory in 1807. Lewis was a poor administrator and died during a trip from St. Louis to Washington, D.C., in a tavern 70 miles southwest of Nashville, Tennessee, on 11 October 1809. The cause of his death remains a mystery; most modern historians consider it a suicide.

Harold Wise

References and further reading:

Ambrose, Stephen. *Undaunted Courage: Meriwether Lewis, Thomas Jefferson and the Opening of the American West.* New York: Simon & Schuster, 1996.

Dillon, Richard. *H. Meriwether Lewis: A Biography.* New York: Coward-McCann, 1965.

Lexington and Concord (1775)

Traditionally, the first military engagement of the American Revolution. The clashes at Lexington and Concord on 19 April 1775 produced new pressures for independence within the British North American colonies and a new resolve to suppress colonial resistance on the part of the British government.

General Thomas Gage, commander of British forces in Massachusetts, received orders to act decisively against the leaders of colonial American resistance. Gage devised a plan to strike against the colonial militias and ordered 700 troops under Colonel Francis Smith and Major John Pitcairn to seize gunpowder and cannon reportedly hidden at Concord. News of this plan reached leaders of the resistance, including Paul Revere, who subsequently spread word of the planned British raid along the road from Boston to Concord.

Revere's ride brought him through the town of Lexington

Painting of the Battle of Lexington. (Library of Congress)

(and into immortality), where colonial militiamen dedicated to the resistance movement—the Minutemen—turned out in force under Captain John Parker to meet Smith and Pitcairn. On the village square, British and colonial American forces exchanged fire following a shot whose source remains a mystery, leaving 1 British and 18 American casualties.

Pressing his mission, Smith ordered his men to Concord, where they encountered a much larger and more organized force of Minutemen under Colonel James Barrett arranged on the heights above the settlement. Barrett moved his force toward the town center when he learned that British troops had began to burn houses and goods in their search for the gunpowder. Barrett's colonials met a British detachment at North Bridge on the outskirts of town, leaving a few casualties on both sides. Smith ended his futile search for the gunpowder and determined to withdraw, but the shots and alarm bells had drawn hundreds of new Minutemen from surrounding areas into his return path. Before their arrival back in Boston, the British withstood repeated guerrilla attacks, their retreat almost degenerating into a rout, and engaged a concentrated force at Menotomy, ultimately suffering 273 casualties in the entire operation. As a consequence, the British government reinforced Gage's army with thousands of new troops, while the American resistance movement recruited new adherents with their supposed evidence of British tyranny. Given the wider conflict that ensued, the exchange at Lexington and Concord eventually became known as "the shot heard round the world."

The brave and defiant performance of the citizen-soldiers at Lexington and Concord entered American mythology: the yeoman citizen-soldier, ready to leave his plow in its furrow and shoulder his musket to defend hearth and home. This ideal, given voice by Thomas Jefferson in particular and strengthened by the British heritage of distrust of a standing army and the Roman Republic's "Cinncinnatus at the Plow" for the classically literate British American elite, saw to it that the United States as late as 1939 had a standing army about the size of Romania's.

Jeffrey Webb

References and further reading:

Fischer, David Hackett. *Paul Revere's Ride.* New York: Oxford University Press, 1994.

Fleming, Thomas. *Liberty! The American Revolution.* New York: Viking, 1997.

Gross, Robert A. *The Minutemen and Their World.* New York: Hill and Wang, 1976.

Li Hongzhang (1823–1901)

Chinese imperial politician and military administrator, instrumental in modernizing the military infrastructure of China. Li was born into a Confucian scholarly family on 15 February 1823 in Hefei, Anhui Province, China. In 1844 he became a government official in Beijing under his mentor,

Zeng Guofan. Li's father, Zeng, and in 1847 Li himself both earned the terminal *jinshi* degree in the rigorous Confucian examination system.

Li raised militias to support the Qing Dynasty during the Taiping Rebellion. He was appointed a judge in 1856 and governor of Jiangsu Province in 1862. Militarily, he was both an independent field commander and a member of Zeng's staff. Li's negotiations brought Western personnel and weapons to the Qing side against the Taipings. After the death of Frederick Townsend Ward in 1862, Li held administrative command of the "Ever-Victorious Army," while Charles "Chinese" Gordon commanded this crack unit of foreign mercenaries in the field.

Convinced that China could never compete with the West, either militarily or economically, unless it adopted Western technology, Li dedicated the rest of his life to what he called after 1872 the "Self-Strengthening Movement." Under his leadership, China built railroads, shipyards, arsenals, factories, military academies, technological institutes, and communications systems. He grew increasingly wary of Japan, which was rapidly becoming a military threat to China. Because so few of his colleagues perceived this danger as accurately as he did, he was unable to persuade them to develop fleets or improve standing armies. The result was that Japan humiliated China in the 1894–1895 Sino-Japanese War, ending with the Treaty of Shimonoseki.

Li died on 7 November 1901 in Tianjin, brokenhearted by the Boxer Protocols signed on 12 September. Even though he had foreseen and tried to prevent both the Sino-Japanese War and the Boxer Rebellion, Li was ashamed that foreigners had twice so severely humbled China on his watch.

Eric v. d. Luft and Sarah Luft

See also: Boxer Rebellion; Chinese Imperial Wars; Gordon, Charles George; Hong Xiuquan; Religion and War; Sino-Japanese War; Taiping Rebellion; Wolseley, Garnet Joseph, Viscount; Yang Xiuqing; Yuan Shikai; Zuo Zongtang

References and further reading:

Cahill, Holger. *A Yankee Adventurer: The Story of Ward and the Taiping Rebellion.* New York: Macaulay, 1930.

Chu, Samuel C., and Kwang-Ching Liu, eds. *Li Hung-Chang and China's Early Modernization.* Armonk, NY: M. E. Sharpe, 1994.

Folsom, Kenneth E. *Friends, Guests, and Colleagues: The Mu-Fu System in the Late Ch'ing Period.* Berkeley: University of California Press, 1968.

Kuhn, Philip. *Rebellion and Its Enemies in Late Imperial China.* Cambridge, MA: Harvard University Press, 1971.

Li Shihmin (600–649)

Grand strategist, second emperor of the Tang Dynasty (618–907), and son of Tang Dynasty founder Li Yuan. Historians continue to debate how much Li Shihmin contributed to his father's rise and the precise nature of the coup that forced the latter's abdication in his favor in 626. Clearly he made contributions to the rise of Tang, but they may not have been as great as the historical tradition indicates, and equally clearly, Shihmin was no innocent party in 626.

In 630, Shihmin, later known as Emperor Tai Zong, defeated the eastern Turks and in several great campaigns brought the Tarim Basin and its Silk Road under Tang control. He eventually pushed Chinese power well beyond the Pamirs, its greatest extension in history. He also established a short-lived Chinese protectorate over Tibet and tried to annex Korea, a process completed in 668 by his successor, Emperor Gao Zong (643–683).

To maintain control over China's extended borders, Li Shihmin used permanent garrisons of soldiers who grew their own food and were otherwise self-supporting. He did so because the Tang tax base was still limited, and he wished to reduce the strain on government resources. The practice also drew upon a long northern tradition of similar forces (*fubing*) predating Tang.

Such garrisons tended to become more settled as they established families and grew more and more integrated into the local population over time. Thus they were less available as mobile forces. Mobilizing such local forces for distant campaigns had never been easy in any case. Later, to solve this problem, the Tang had to turn to expensive mercenaries, who often had their own agendas.

Among his many other contributions, Li Shimin restored local government after years of neglect. He continued the commitment of the Sui Dynasty (581–618) to a bureaucracy based on merit and primarily selected through a written examination system requiring mastery of Confucian philosophy and current topics. The energies of potential opponents were thus directed to passing the examinations and to moving ahead in the bureaucracy rather than to rebellion. Individual emperors (Empress Wu, for example) also used the examination system to recruit "new men," ones not associated with the traditional northern elite. It was largely thanks to Li Shimin's conquests and the institutions that he established that the Tang Dynasty lasted for nearly another three centuries, in spite of its near collapse in the aftermath of the An Lushan rebellion of 751 and the need for late Tang to reinvent itself.

Charles M. Dobbs

See also: Chinese Imperial Wars; Sino-Korean Wars and the Wars of Korean Unification; Talas River, Battle of

References and further reading:

Bingham, Woodbridge. *The Founding of the Tang Dynasty; the Fall of Sui and Rise of Tang: A Preliminary Survey.* New York: Octagon Books, 1975.

Fitzgerald, C. P. *Son of Heaven (A Biography of Li Shih-min, Founder of the Tang Dynasty)*. New York: AMS Press, 1971.
Pulleyblank, Edwin G. *The Background of the Rebellion of An Lu-shan.* New York: Oxford University Press, 1955.

Liberia (1989–1997)

Founded in 1822 by freed slaves from the United States, the Republic of Liberia quickly became an autocracy in which the freed slaves (Americo-Liberians) held power over the indigenous peoples. This, along with the growing unrest of the 1970s and a faltering economy, sowed the seeds of the Liberian civil war.

In 1980 a group of enlisted soldiers led by Samuel Doe entered the presidential palace and executed President William Tolbert and his ministers. Doe declared himself president; his 9-year rule was marked by corruption, brutality, and nepotism. Doe both showed favor to his own ethnic group, the Krahn, and violently suppressed rival ethnic groups to the north.

In December 1989, Charles Taylor, a former Doe minister, launched an invasion of Liberia with his rebel group, the National Patriotic Front of Liberia (NPFL), from bases in Ivory Coast. Taylor and his soldiers had received training and arms from Libya as well as Burkina Faso. Once the invasion began, the NPFL advanced rapidly, driving the impotent Armed Forces of Liberia (ALF) before it.

Even before the invasion, there were numerous factions vying for power and position within the NPFL. Once the invasion had begun, the warring factions quickly became more hostile. Prince Yourmie Johnson, who split with Taylor and formed the Independent National Patriotic Front (INPFL), was the first of many defectors.

Within seven months, the NPFL was on the outskirts of the capital, Monrovia, and in control of 95 percent of the country. With the international community obviously not willing to intervene, the surrounding West African states initiated a historic first: an all-African peace-keeping force for service in Africa. The Economic Community of West African States (ECOWAS) deployed ECOMOG (the Economic Community Monitoring Group) to Monrovia in early 1990.

The situation in Monrovia quickly became a stalemate and turned into a West African Beirut, with different factions controlling specific areas of the city. Doe was killed in an ambush on his way to peace talks with NPFL, ECOMOG, and INFLP in September 1990. After President Doe's death, the remnants of the AFL (which was mainly Krahn) regrouped under the banner of the United Liberation Movement for Democracy in Liberia (ULIMO).

The situation remained relatively static until elections were held in 1997. These elections, monitored by international observers, drew 90 percent of the 1 million registered Liberians to the ballots. Taylor won the presidency in a landslide and was installed as the president of the State of Liberia, and a measure of stability returned to the wounded nation.

James Corbin

References and further reading:

Beyan, Amos J., Carl P. Burrowes, and D. Elwood Dunn. *Historical Dictionary of Liberia.* 2d ed. Lanham, MD: Scarecrow Press, 2001.
Dunn, D. Elwood, and S. Byron Tarr. *Liberia: A National Polity in Transition.* Metuchen, NJ: Scarecrow Press, 1988.
Ellis, Stephen. *The Mask of Anarchy: The Destruction of Liberia and the Religious Dimension of an African Civil War.* New York: New York University Press, 1999.
Harold D. Nelson, ed. *Liberia: A Country Study.* Washington, DC: U.S. Government Printing Office, 1985.
Liebenow, J. Gus. *Liberia: The Quest for Democracy.* Indianapolis: Indiana University Press, 1987.

Liddell Hart, Sir Basil Henry (1895–1970)

British defense analyst. An infantry company commander when he was gassed in the Somme offensive, Liddell Hart became deeply involved in the development of infantry tactics in an attempt to restore mobility to the battlefield. His analyses caused senior officers to treat him with great courtesy, and he was unflinchingly proud of the ordinary British soldier, Britain's military leadership, and war aims.

In 1920, he made John Frederick Charles Fuller's acquaintance, and they sharpened each other's insights, writing for a wide audience about armored warfare. Both believed armor would profoundly change the nature of warfare, but Liddell Hart came close to advocating all-tank armies rather than Fuller's combined arms approach. In 1924, Liddell Hart was discharged for medical reasons from the service he loved, and his views of British military leadership deteriorated accordingly. As Adolf Hitler posed an increasing threat to Britain, Liddell Hart became convinced that British involvement in World War I had been a mistake. He therefore changed his policy positions to stress the primacy of the defense and became an appeaser as the Chamberlain government moved toward war.

His reputation shattered by the conquest of France, Liddell Hart lived quietly during World War II. After Germany's defeat, he began interviewing captured German officers, seeking to resurrect his reputation. Eventually, Generals Fritz Bayerlein and Heinz Guderian credited his writings with influencing German *offensive* armored doctrine at a time when he had stressed the *defensive* potential of armor. In turn, Liddell Hart vouched for the Wehrmacht leadership's blackened honor.

Israeli army commanders, thinking it wise to link the Israeli Defense Forces to the Wehrmacht's efficiency, proclaimed themselves his other best pupils, further enhancing his status. By the time of his death on 29 January 1970, the development of German and Israeli blitzkrieg doctrine was firmly associated with Liddell Hart's interwar writings, in defiance of the historical record.

Erin E. Solaro

See also: Academies, Military; Armored Fighting Vehicles; British Military, Twentieth Century Organization and Structure; France; Fuller, John Frederick Charles; Guderian, Heinz; Haig, Douglas; History, Military; Rommel, Erwin Johannes Eugen; The Somme; World War I; World War II

References and further reading:

Bond, Brian. *Liddell Hart: A Study of His Military Thought.* New Brunswick, NJ: Rutgers University Press, 1977.

Corum, James S. *The Roots of Blitzkrieg: Hans von Seeckt and German Military Reform.* Lawrence: University Press of Kansas, 1992.

Mearshheimer, John J. *Liddell Hart and the Weight of History.* New York: Cornell University Press, 1988.

Light Brigade, Charge of the (25 October 1854)

Near-suicidal British cavalry charge against Russian artillery in the Battle of Balaklava in the Crimean War. The British commander at Balaklava, General Fitzroy James Henry Somerset, Baron Raglan, saw from his headquarters on Sapoune Heights that the Russians on Causeway Heights were removing allied guns from the redoubts they had captured from the Turks that morning. Raglan's perhaps erroneous recollection that his hero, the Duke of Wellington, had never lost a gun roused him to action. He immediately tried to prevent the Russians from adding these guns to their own artillery.

Raglan routinely delegated tactical decisions to his staff and field officers, even when communication among them was poor. He chose to defer to General George Charles Bingham, Third Earl Lucan, nominal commander of the British cavalry, who was then with his troops east of Sapoune at the western end of the North Valley. From that vantage point, Lucan could not see the redoubts.

Raglan dictated the following order to his quartermaster general, Colonel Richard Airey: "Lord Raglan wishes the Cavalry to advance rapidly to the front, follow the Enemy & try to prevent the Enemy carrying away the guns. Troop Horse Attily may accompany. French Cavalry is on yr left. Immediate." The obscurity of this order has prompted much controversy among historians over the years, but most of them blame Raglan for the disaster.

Airey's aide-de-camp, Captain Lewis Edward Nolan, galloped the order downhill to Lucan. Nolan attempted to indicate which guns Raglan meant, but Lucan could see only the three main Russian batteries, aimed south from Fedioukine Heights, north from Causeway Heights, and west from the eastern end of the North Valley. Lucan ordered Brigadier General James Thomas Brudenell, Seventh Earl Cardigan, to charge the easternmost battery, about a mile and a quarter away. Cardigan simply obeyed. Disgusted with Lucan, Nolan voluntarily took part in the charge and was among the first to die. Of the 675 cavalrymen in the Light Brigade, only about 400 reached the guns, where they avenged their comrades by furiously sabering the Russian cannoneers.

"The Charge of the Light Brigade" soon entered legend as a symbol of bravery, perhaps blind bravery, against overwhelming odds. Poet Laureate Alfred Lord Tennyson's poem of the same title even included the line, "Someone had blundered," but the offending words were excised, supposedly at the behest of Queen Victoria.

Eric v. d. Luft

See also: Balaklava; Crimean War; Sevastopol, Siege of

References and further reading:

Adkin, Mark. *The Charge: Why the Light Brigade Was Lost.* London: Leo Cooper, 1996.

Bachrach, Deborah. *The Charge of the Light Brigade.* San Diego: Lucent, 1997.

Harris, John. *The Gallant Six Hundred: A Tragedy of Obsessions.* London: Hutchinson, 1973.

Lummis, William Murrell. *Honour the Light Brigade.* London: J. B. Hayward and Son, 1973.

Lin Biao (1907–1971)

Chinese Communist military leader. Lin Biao was, for many years, a close associate of Mao Zedong and a key figure behind the successful Communist effort to defeat the Nationalists and gain control of China and the more mixed effort to face American intervention in Korea. His downfall under mysterious circumstances only added to his image.

At age 18 years, he entered the famous Whampoa Military Academy in Guangzhou, and soon thereafter he served as a platoon leader and later battalion commander in the famous Northern Expedition in 1927–1928 to "unify" China under Chiang Kai-shek's Nationalist regime. When Chiang turned against the Communists, Lin defected to Mao's forces, and several years later, his corps was the vanguard in the Long March of 1934–1935, the long defeat—yet ultimately victory—as the Communists moved from southeastern to northwestern China.

When the anti-Japanese war (in which the Communist were little more effective than their Nationalist rivals) ended in 1945, Lin took command of Communist forces in Manchuria, and putting Mao's theories into practice, he abandoned the cities, gained the support of peasants, and took control of the countryside. By 1948, the Nationalists had suffered irreversible defeat in the northeast, despite massive American aid, and within a year had lost the battle for China.

In the late 1950s, Lin took over the army. He became a close ally of Mao during the Cultural Revolution of the mid-1960s that threatened to tear China apart. Lin compiled Mao's quotations into the famous book, *Quotations of Chairman Mao.* In 1966, Mao named Lin as his successor.

Then in 1971, it appeared—proof is sketchy—that Lin helped organize a plot against Mao (perhaps in opposition to the latter's opening to the Americans). When discovered, he tried to flee on an airplane to the Soviet Union; his plane supposedly crashed. But the reasons for and exact means of his demise remain shrouded in mystery.

Charles M. Dobbs

See also: Chinese Civil War; Korean War; Mao Zedong; Vietnam Conflict

References and further reading:

Chassin, Lionel Max. *The Communist Conquest of China: A History of the Civil War, 1945–1949.* Cambridge, MA: Harvard University Press, 1965.

Yao Ming-le. *The Conspiracy and Death of Lin Biao.* New York: Alfred A. Knopf, 1983.

Detail of a photograph by Alexander Gardner of Abraham Lincoln with General McClellan (facing Lincoln) at Antietam, 1862. (Library of Congress)

Lincoln, Abraham (1809–1865)

Sixteenth president of the United States and for many the model of how a commander in chief should conduct a war. The American Civil War dominated the Lincoln administration and consumed the president's daily thoughts and actions. Although it can be claimed that the South had better generals, at least at the beginning of the war, Lincoln's leadership was the decisive factor in the North's favor, and historians have often listed Abraham Lincoln as the Union's greatest "asset."

On a practical level, Lincoln made several strategic decisions that altered the course of the war. He visited the army in the field 11 times, spending 42 days with them, and had voluminous correspondence with commanders. He studied military strategy and spent long hours at the War Department telegraph office. In May 1862, he personally issued orders for the occupation of Norfolk and later tried to organize Union attempts to defeat Stonewall Jackson in the Shenandoah Valley. Fearing for Washington's safety, he transferred the Army of the Potomac from southeast of Richmond to northern Virginia. In September 1863, he later decided to transfer four divisions of that army to Chattanooga under General William Rosecrans after the loss of the Battle of Chickamauga. It was not uncommon for the president to study maps and make suggestions to his generals. Yet Lincoln left most military decisions to his commanders; he was not what a later generation would call a "micromanager." He insisted that commanders act promptly, not move slowly, and take advantage of numeric superiority. Such considerations led him to remove or demote generals such as George McClellan and remain fearlessly loyal in the face of criticism of commanders like Ulysses Grant.

Lincoln's greatest impact on the war was in the political arena, where he was able to promote and sustain northern participation. He strengthened and unified the Republican Party through the use of political and military appointments. He kept many of the border states in the Union and worked with Democrats who opposed emancipation and "subjugation" of the Confederate states. He was also able to dominate the Peace Democrats and their 1864 platform,

The Battle of the Little Bighorn. Painting by C. M. Russell, 1903. (Library of Congress)

which called for an armistice and a negotiated end to the fighting. Lincoln issued directives and urged the passage of laws that harnessed the industrial capacity of the Union for war production, promoted volunteerism, and stifled criticism. His declaration of martial law is perhaps the most controversial aspect of his war leadership. Through speeches, letters, and the Emancipation Proclamation, the president was able to bring a moral clarity and authority to the cause and conduct of the war. The conflict was transformed from one over states' rights and secession to a crusade for freedom and justice. For many, he had come to personify the northern cause, and his passing is often referred to as the last death of the Civil War. Abraham Lincoln was the only American president whose entire administration was conducted in time of war.

T. Jason Soderstrum

See also: Chickamauga, Battle of; Grant, Ulysses Simpson; McClellan, George Brinton; Rosecrans, William Starke

References and further reading:

Borritt, Gabor S., ed. *Lincoln's Generals.* New York: Oxford University Press, 1994.

Davis, William C. *Lincoln's Men: How President Lincoln Became Father to an Army and a Nation.* New York: Free Press, 1999.

Williams, T. Harry. *Lincoln and His Generals.* New York: Alfred A. Knopf, 1952.

Little Bighorn (25–26 June 1876)

Perhaps the most written about and hotly debated battle in U.S. military history. The deeper symbolism and mythology linked to what is popularly known as "Custer's Last Stand" have often outweighed in the minds of Americans what actually occurred on 25–26 June 1876. Even Americans severely ignorant of their own history know something of "Custer's Last Stand" and of that other "They Died with Their Boots On" epic—the Alamo.

In December 1875, under the direction of President Ulysses S. Grant, the commissioner of Indian affairs ordered all northern Plains Indians to report to their agencies by 31 January 1876 or be forced to do so by the army. General William Sherman and General Philip Sheridan had planned a winter campaign to break the hostiles, but General George Armstrong Custer had been delayed in reporting to his command because of a conflict with the president. On 17 May, General Alfred Terry, Custer, and the Dakota column left Fort Abraham Lincoln, in a coordinated effort with troops under the command of General George Crook, to round up renegade Sioux and Cheyenne warriors. On 22 June, Terry ordered Colonel John Gibbons and Custer to lead two columns into the valley of Little Bighorn, trapping any Indians found in the valley between them.

The nearly 600 soldiers of Custer's Seventh Cavalry and 35 Crow scouts marched south along Rosebud Creek. On the night of 24 June, from a tall peak in the Wolf Mountains, scouts saw the unmistakable signs of a large village in the Little Bighorn Valley. Believing they would scatter, Custer ordered a forced march to engage them before they could escape. A few miles from the camp, Custer ordered Major Marcus A. Reno to led three companies directly into the Little Bighorn and attack the southern end of the village. Custer would take the remaining five companies east of the river and attack the village's northern end. Captain Frederick Benteen would take three companies to the south, along the Wolf Mountains, to make sure no one escaped.

Although the exact size of the encampment is debated, it was the largest Indian village ever to congregate on the Plains. On the morning of the 25th, Reno's troops crossed the Little Bighorn River 2 miles south of the village and then advanced on the lodges. Just short of the encampment, Hunkpapa warriors met the oncoming soldiers. Able to hold his position for just 15 minutes, Reno ordered his men to retreat to a grove of cottonwood trees along the river. Feeling surrounded, Reno ordered his command to withdraw to the steep bluffs on the other side of the river. Of his 140 men, Reno had 40 killed, 13 wounded, and 17 stranded in the trees below. Benteen's troops arrived on the scene and dug in with Reno. Custer's companies attacked the village from a broad coulee know as Medicine Tail. As the troopers tried to cross the river, they received heavy fire from warriors. After they were driven back to the bluffs, it is debatable what exactly occurred. Whether they were overwhelmed by Indians led by the warrior Gall or encircled from the rear by Crazy Horse's Oglala, every soldier under Custer's command was killed. Although the exact number of Sioux and Cheyenne who died is unknown, 263 soldiers were killed and 60 wounded (of Reno's men). It is said that for the next four decades, every saloon in the United States had mounted over the bar either a full-length painting of a nude or a depiction of Custer's Last Stand.

T. Jason Soderstrum

See also: American Indian Wars; Crazy Horse; Custer, George Armstrong; Sitting Bull

References and further reading:

Gray, John S. *Custer's Last Campaign: Mitch Boyer and the Little Bighorn Reconstructed.* Lincoln: University of Nebraska Press, 1991.

Magnussen, Daniel O. *Peter Thompson's Narrative of the Little Bighorn Campaign 1876: A Critical Analysis of an Eyewitness Account of the Custer Debacle.* Glendale, CA: Arthur H. Clark Company, 1974.

Utley, Robert M. *Cavalier in Buckskin: George Armstrong Custer and the Western Military Frontier.* Norman: University of Oklahoma Press, 1988.

Livonian War (1558–1583)

A military conflict initiated by Ivan IV of the Muscovite state against Livonia in an attempt to gain an outlet to the Baltic Sea for trade with the West. Hostilities broke out in January 1558. Ivan invaded Livonia, which the grand master of the Livonian Order of Knights had occupied and ruled since the thirteenth century. His forces seized much of its territory, including the commercial port of Narva (Dorpat).

The Livonian knights, unable to face Ivan's offensive, placed themselves under the protection of the king of Poland. Subsequently, Livonia was partitioned among Poland, Denmark, and Sweden. This development precipitated the war between Lithuania and the Muscovite state. Ivan's army captured several towns, including the fortified city of Polotsk. Faced with complete collapse, Lithuania formed a political union with Poland in 1569, and Stepan Bathory was elected king of the Polish-Lithuanian kingdom. An able military commander, Bathory led his well-trained army against the Russians, defeated them repeatedly, and captured Polotsk and several border towns. His advance was finally halted at Pskov. The Swedes, meanwhile, took advantage of Ivan's unfavorable position, invaded the Baltic, seized Narva, and occupied the entire coast of the Gulf of Finland.

Finally, Ivan appealed to Pope Gregory XIII to mediate the conflict. Hoping to bring Muscovy into the Catholic fold, the pope dispatched the Jesuit Antonio Possevino, who arranged an armistice between Ivan and Bathory in 1582. The following year, Ivan ceded Livonia and Polotsk but kept his former possessions along the Lithuanian border. A year later, he signed a less favorable armistice with Sweden, surrendering most of the Baltic coastline. After 25 years of intermittent warfare, Ivan IV was no closer to gaining a window to the West, and Moscow had to wait another century to achieve this objective.

James J. Farsolas

See also: Ivan IV

References and further reading:

Attman, Artur. *The Struggle for Baltic Markets: Powers in Conflict, 1558–1618.* Goteborg: Vetenskaps, 1979.

Urban, William L. *The Livonian Crusade.* Washington, DC: University Press of America, 1981.

Lobengula (a.k.a. Lopenule, Nobengulu, or Ulopengule) (c. 1830–1894)

King of the Ndebele (Matabele), in what is today Zimbabwe. At the beginning of the 1840s, Lobengula's father, the Ndebele king Mzilikazi, ordered many of his subjects, including his sons, to be killed in an effort to stamp out possible opposition. However, Lobengula was hidden by his mother and lived in seclusion for several years.

Consequently, little is known about Lobengula until the death of Mzilikazi in 1868. Two years later, Lobengula was installed as king at the insistence of the witch doctors and *indunas.* However, not all the Ndebele tribes recognized Lobengula as their king, and he took action against his opponents, routing them in battle. In 1881 he moved to the new town he had built for himself at Gibexhegu, later renamed Bulawayo. Aggressive raiding against other tribes was an integral part of Ndebele life, which for several years ensured dominance in his sphere of influence. However, in due course many European hunters, traders, and concession seekers entered Matabeleland and Mashonaland. Against the background of Cecil John Rhodes's plans for British expansion northward from the Cape Colony, Lobengula first signed a treaty with the Boer Transvaal Republic (1887) and then with John Smith Moffat, a British representative (1888).

Also in 1888, Lobengula ceded his country's mineral rights to a group representing Rhodes. Rhodes then formed the British South Africa Company (BSAC), and soon British settlers started to occupy portions of what became known as Southern Rhodesia (now Zimbabwe). Soon clashes between white and black ensued, and the BSAC's forces were ordered to occupy Matabeleland. Lobengula set fire to his capital, Bulawayo, on 3 November 1893, the day before the company's forces arrived. Lobengula fled with several of his regiments, pursued by the company's men. A patrol under Major Allan Wilson caught up with Lobengula's forces on the Shangani River, but all 33 members of the "Shangani Patrol" were killed. Soon after, Lobengula reached Pashu's country, but there he died—of self-administered poison, smallpox, or arthritis. Lobengula was a man of high intelligence, but he lacked the military genius and ruthless cruelty of his father. He was not inclined to be a warrior, but his suspicious nature and the influence of witch doctors and *indunas* led him to commit acts of cruelty.

André Wessels

References and further reading:

Burke, E. E. "Lobengula." In *Dictionary of South African Biography.* Vol. 3. Eds. D. W. Krüger and C. J. Beyers. Pretoria: Human Sciences Research Council, 1977.

Hole, H. M. *Lobengula.* London: Philip Allen & Company, 1929.

Preller, G. S. *Lobengula: The Tragedy of a Matabele King.* Johannesburg: Afrikaanse Pers-Boekhandel, 1963.

Van Zyl, M. C. "Lobengula." In *Standard Encyclopaedia of Southern Africa,* ed. D. J. Potgieter. Cape Town: Nasou Limited, 1947.

Lodi (10 May 1796)

A battle fought in northern Italy between the French Army of Italy, commanded by Napoleon Bonaparte, and an Austrian army commanded by J. P. Beaulieu. Bonaparte opened the first Italian campaign in April 1796 with an attack on the Piedmontese army, commanded by General Colli, and a supporting Austrian force, commanded by Generals Provera and Argentau. The French assault led to several inconclusive actions and the withdrawal of the Piedmontese army.

By 24 April 1796, Bonaparte was threatening the Piedmontese capital, Turin. The king of Piedmont asked for an armistice, which Bonaparte granted. The effective neutralization of the Piedmontese allowed Bonaparte to attempt to trap the main Austrian army, which had been left in a dangerously exposed position southwest of Milan as a result of the Piedmontese negotiations.

The French army, 30,000 strong, thus began a 50-mile forced march in an attempt to seize crossings over the River Adda, including the town of Lodi, in order to trap the Austrian army. Beaulieu, aware of his danger, was in full retreat, and with a vigor unusual for Austrian generals of the period, managed to escape with most of his army across the Adda River, leaving only a 10,000-strong rear guard by the time the French reached Lodi on 10 May.

The Battle of Lodi itself consisted simply of determined French assaults upon a bridge over the River Adda. The first of these failed. The second, however, prevailed, and the French main column, assisted by a body of cavalry that had forded upriver, routed the Austrians. The Austrians lost about 150 men, and 1,700 were taken prisoner. The French lost 350 men.

Despite the relatively small scale of the action, the French victory at Lodi opened the way for the capture of Milan. As a result, the Kingdom of Savoy and the Duchies of Parma and Modena were forced to make peace with the French, and the Kingdom of Piedmont found it expedient to complete peace negotiations with the French. The French were now masters of the northwestern Italian peninsula, and Bonaparte was free to begin efforts to force the Austrians from Mantua, which would culminate in the Battle of Rivoli.

Joseph Isenberg

See also: French Revolutionary Wars; Napoleon I

References and further reading:

Chandler, David G. *Campaigns of Napoleon.* New York: Scribner, 1966.

Connelley, Owen. *Blundering to Glory.* Wilmington, DE: Scholarly Resources, 1999.

Logistics

Umbrella term for military activities other than strategy and tactics that emerged about two centuries ago. Today it is largely an American usage crystallized in World War II and encompassing military supply, transportation, medical service, and construction-maintenance.

Historically, there have been three solutions to the problem of supplying an army with the least sacrifice of power, mobility, and range: (1) self-containment, in which the force carries all its supplies, mortgaging power and range to mobility; (2) local supply, a forage system that narrows military activity to growing seasons and fertile areas; and (3) supply from bases, favoring power and range over mobility. Alexander the Great's army marched, self-contained, from Macedonia to India. Napoleon's armies foraged their way across Europe for a dozen years, but his Grand Army starved and froze while retreating from Moscow through country it had already denuded. The arrival of mass armies and greatly increased firepower after the Industrial Revolution, combined with highly developed systems of communication and economic support, brought widespread reliance on supply from bases. Generals continued to be more interested in strategy and tactics than in logistics, however, and thus took less advantage of manpower and munitions than they might have done. In 1870 the Germans used staged, continuous resupply by railroad to support their invasion of France by a mass army and found that even constant forward movement of supply depots was not enough to forestall the necessity of foraging. The long-planned envelopment of Paris by German armies was frustrated in 1914 in part because their plans called for more troops than the road system could bear and in part because rail lines used by the French to bring reinforcements from the Alsace-Lorraine front had not been targeted by German planners.

World War II was a breathtaking exercise in the logistics of total war. The Allies produced seven times as many planes as the Axis powers, five times as many trucks and artillery pieces, and more than four times as many machine guns and tanks. All these and millions of men and women had to be transported to fronts all over the world in the face of enemy resistance. But the inability of the Luftwaffe to resupply the German army trapped at Stalingrad, like the halting of General George Patton's offensive late in 1944, indicated the limits on logistical problem solving in total war. Nonetheless, the United States was able not only to lavishly supply (by the standards of the other belligerents) its own forces but also to provide millions of tons of equipment for the Nationalist Chinese, the Free French, the Soviets, and even the British forces.

At war's end, the advent of nuclear weaponry threatened to make conventional logistics irrelevant, and superpower rivalry raised new problems in the organization, deployment, and supply of mass armies. At the same time, Third World conflicts increasingly demanded rapid deployment of special forces. The United States solved these problems in the post-Vietnam era by elaborating AirLand, mechanized combined operations that could stop a Soviet offensive in Europe and be adapted to more limited scenarios, such as the deployment of 527,000 personnel and 3,500 aircraft in the Gulf War.

Joseph M. McCarthy

See also: Patton, George Smith, Jr.; World War II

References and further reading:

Lynn, John A., ed. *Feeding Mars: Logistics in Western Warfare from the Middle Ages to the Present.* Boulder, CO: Westview, 1993.

Shrader, Charles R. *United States Army Logistics, 1775–1992: An Anthology.* 3 vols. Washington, DC: Center of Military History, United States Army, 1997.

Van Creveld, Martin L. *Supplying War: Logistics from Wallenstein to Patton.* New York: Cambridge University Press, 1977.

Long Island, Battle of (22 August 1776)

A major defeat of the patriot American forces early in the Revolutionary War. In summer 1776, a huge British fleet with a large army arrived off New York City. The British occupied Staten Island, and the Americans, led by George Washington, defended Long Island along Brooklyn Heights as well as the Battery, Fort Washington, and other places in and around New York City. For seven weeks, the British strengthened their positions.

British general William Howe and 10,000 troops landed on Long Island on 22 August and proceeded to formulate a plan. The American defenders were at best untrained in warfare and inexperienced in battle; at worst, a mob without artillery. While some British and German troops demonstrated in front of the American position, Howe and about half his men marched around and behind the American left flank. They gained complete surprise, General John Sullivan's left wing was crushed, and the men fled. Washington ordered a retreat.

After considering a defense of Long Island at Gowanus Bay and realizing the British fleet could trap him, Washington had his men rowed across the East River to Manhattan, where after a battle at Harlem Heights and some fighting at Fort Lee and Fort Washington, he retreated to White Plains and later across the Hudson to New Jersey. General William Howe and his brother, Admiral Richard Howe, not wanting a repeat of the slaughter at Breed's Hill, pursued rather slowly. Howe also feared exasperating the Americans and hoped for some sort of negotiated reconciliation. Although the brothers Howe may have felt they had demonstrated the Americans' inability to withstand a proper British attack, they also had given Washington time to withdraw and save his army to fight another day.

Charles M. Dobbs

See also: American Revolution; Washington, George

Washington's retreat at Long Island, 1776. (Library of Congress)

References and further reading:
Bliven, Bruce. *Battle for Manhattan.* New York: Holt, 1956.
Gruber, Ira D. *The Howe Brothers and the American Revolution.* New York: Atheneum, 1972.

Longstreet, James (1821–1904)

Confederate field commander in the American Civil War, a skillful subordinate but unsuited for independent command. Longstreet was born in Edgefield District, South Carolina, on 8 January 1821. As a member of the West Point class of 1842, his roommate was William S. Rosecrans. An infantry lieutenant in the Mexican-American War, he won brevets to captain at Churubusco on 20 August 1847 and major at Molino del Rey on 8 September and was severely wounded at Chapultepec on 13 September. Promoted to captain in 1852 and major in 1858, he resigned on 1 June 1861 to join the Confederacy, which commissioned him brigadier general on 17 June.

Longstreet defeated Irvin McDowell's vanguard at Blackburn's Ford, Virginia, on 18 July and distinguished himself at First Bull Run. Promoted to major general on 7 October, he served under Joseph Johnston in the Peninsula campaign, fighting at Yorktown, Williamsburg, Seven Pines, and Fair Oaks. He excelled at Second Bull Run; fought at South Mountain, Maryland; commanded Robert E. Lee's right flank at Antietam; and held Marye's Heights at Fredericksburg. He made lieutenant general on 9 October 1862.

On the way to Gettysburg, Longstreet counseled Lee to maneuver between George Meade's army and Washington, D.C., thus forcing Meade to attack. Nevertheless, Lee attacked, with Longstreet commanding the right. By the third day, Longstreet was so disheartened that he had difficulty bringing himself to convey Lee's order to George Pickett to charge the Union center. Historians analyzing Gettysburg from both tactical and strategic viewpoints usually agree that Longstreet's plans were more reasonable than Lee's.

After Gettysburg, Lee detached Longstreet to Georgia to reinforce Braxton Bragg. Longstreet's arrival in time to command the left on the second day at Chickamauga ensured the Confederate victory. His siege of Knoxville, however, deprived the South of needed manpower at Chattanooga. Wounded at the Wilderness, he recovered for the final Petersburg and Richmond campaigns and was with Lee at Appomattox.

After the war, Longstreet became a Republican and held several federal offices in the Grant, Hayes, Garfield, Arthur, McKinley, and Theodore Roosevelt administrations. He died in Gainesville, Georgia, on 2 January 1904.

Eric v. d. Luft

See also: American Civil War; Antietam/Sharpsburg; Bragg, Braxton; Bull Run, First/Manassas; Bull Run, Second/Manassas Junction; Chickamauga, Battle of; Fredericksburg; Gettysburg; Grant, Ulysses Simpson; Hill, Ambrose Powell; Johnston, Joseph Eggleston; Lee, Robert Edward; Wilderness

References and further reading:

Connelly, Thomas Lawrence, and Barbara L. Bellows. *God and General Longstreet: The Lost Cause and the Southern Mind.* Baton Rouge: Louisiana State University Press, 1982.

Eckenrode, Hamilton James, and Bryan Conrad. *James Longstreet: Lee's War Horse.* Chapel Hill: University of North Carolina Press, 1986.

Piston, William Garrett. *Lee's Tarnished Lieutenant: James Longstreet and His Place in Southern History.* Athens: University of Georgia Press, 1987.

Wert, Jeffry D. *General James Longstreet: The Confederacy's Most Controversial Soldier.* New York: Simon & Schuster, 1993.

Louis XIV (1638–1715)

King of France and warlord for more than 70 years. In the eyes of a younger generation that had forgotten the former power of Spain, Louis XIV was a vain warmonger and enduring threat to the European balance of power, largely because of a policy directed at the destruction of Spain's power that continued long after Spain had apparently lost its influence on the international stage.

Louis led his armies in his youth but never fought a major battle. In later years, he sometimes assumed personal command at sieges because this form of war permitted him to establish permanent camps where he could carry out his administrative responsibilities. His letters reveal a lively understanding of siege craft, and he certainly had a gift for finding able commanders.

Louis inherited the Thirty Years' War (1618–1648), a long-drawn-out conflict with Spain, and the civil wars of the Fronde. In 1661 he launched the War of Devolution with Spain, only two years after the signing of the Peace of the Pyrenees. A Dutch War (1672–1678) soon followed, in which Franche-Comté fell into his hands. Between 1678 and 1688, Louis used armed force to intimidate his neighbors, annexing Strasbourg and other territory in Germany. This policy shaded into a general European conflict in 1688, the War of the Grand Alliance or War of the League of Augsburg (1688–1697). Primarily defensive in Europe, it ended with significant French gains in the Americas as Britain was driven to unfortunate terms by near-bankruptcy. In the long War of the Spanish Succession (1701–1714), Louis devastated France's economy while establishing a king of his house in Spain (although not in many of Spain's former European territories) and ending the Spanish menace, but in the process he sacrificed his earlier gains in the Americas. He died in 1715, admitting on his deathbed that he had "loved war too much."

Erik A. Lund

See also: Blenheim-Höchstädt, Battle of; Condé, Louis II de Bourbon, Fourth Prince de; Denain, Battle of; Franco-Spanish War; Fronde, Wars of the; Grand Alliance, War of the; Louvois, François-Michel Le Tellier, Marquis de; Luxembourg, François Henri de Montmorency-Bouteville, Duc de Piney; Luxembourg, Siege of; Malplaquet, Battle of; Oudenaarde, Battle of; Queen Anne's War; Spanish Succession, War of the; St. Gotthard Abbey; Turenne, Henri de la Tour d'Auvergne, Vicomte de; Vauban, Sébastien Le Prestre de

References and further reading:

Bluche, François. *Louis XIV.* Trans. Mark Greenglass. French edition, 1984. Oxford: Blackwell, 1990.

Chandler, David G. *The Art of Warfare in the Age of Marlborough.* London: Batsford, 1976.

Rowen, Herbert Harvey. *The King's State: Proprietary Dynasticism in Early Modern France.* New Brunswick, NJ: Rutgers University Press, 1980.

Vault, Françoise Eugène de, and [J. J.] Pelet. *Mémoires militaire relatifs à la Succession d'Espagne sous Louis XIV.* 11 vols. Atlas. Paris: Imprimérie Royale, 1835–1862.

Louisbourg, Expedition against (May–June 1758)

Successful British and colonial operation that forced the surrender of the linchpin of the defense of New France. Early in 1757, the new British prime minister, William Pitt, ordered the Earl of Loudoun to seize Louisbourg, a fort on Cape Breton Island guarding the entrance to the Gulf of St. Lawrence. This effort failed miserably. By the time 10 regiments arrived from Ireland to join forces already gathered in Halifax, Nova Scotia, a large French fleet had reached Louisbourg and brought 2,500 reinforcements. Stormy weather halted British operations for the rest of July and August. The British naval commander, Vice Admiral Francis Holbourne, believed offensive action was hopeless, and Loudoun agreed and abandoned the attack and retreated to New York City.

General William Pepperrell at the siege of Louisburg in 1745. (Library of Congress)

The next year, Pitt wisely promoted three junior officers who all would play major roles in the eventual British victory over the French in North America. One of these officers, Jeffrey Amherst, commanded the attack on Louisbourg. A British fleet sailed to Halifax in winter 1758, and reinforcements arrived several months later in early May. On 28 May, the expedition set out. Amherst followed the plan New Englanders had used in their successful attack in 1745. Led by James Wolfe, men landed at Gabarus Bay, west of Louisbourg, and soon established a siege that greatly damaged the town. On 26 July 1758, the governor raised the white flag of surrender.

The loss of Louisbourg imperiled the French colony in Quebec, which depended on seaborne transportation through the Gulf and past the fort to France. Defeat at Louisbourg foreshadowed France's defeat in North America several years later.

Charles M. Dobbs

References and further reading:

Anderson, Fred. *Crucible of War: The Seven Years' War and the Fate of Empire in British North America, 1754–1766.* New York: Alfred A. Knopf, 2000.

Schwartz, Seymour I. *The French and Indian War, 1754–1763: The Imperial Struggle for North America.* New York: Simon & Schuster, 1995.

Louvois, François-Michel Le Tellier, Marquis de (1639–1691)

The most outstanding military organizer of the seventeenth century. Louvois was the son of one of the most powerful official of Louis's XIV early reign. In 1655, the senior Le Tellier brought his dissolute teenaged son into the war department to teach him military administration. He emerged as a hard worker, supremely confident in his own ability to be a brilliant administrator. His administrative career is exceptional; as early as 1661 he was working with his father in the foreign affairs council and was appointed state minister in 1672, in charge of military affairs and administration, after his father's retirement. With Louis's backing, Louvois transformed the French army from a feudal semi-independent force to the first modern army. The reform of the financial and tax system gave Louvois the money he needed to increase the king's troops both in quantity and quality.

His first task was to build a centralized army control: he used civilian inspectors as war commissioners or army intendants whose job was to reduce corruption by regular inspections of troops. Officers, whatever their rank of birth or their commission, were responsible for obedience to orders and regulations, which were prescribed by Louvois. Corrupt or insubordinate officers were dismissed. Officers were also expected to be conversant with current military theories and practices. The purchasing of officers' commissions was fought by Louvois. He instituted ranks that were appointed by the king rather than bought: from 1661, lieutenant colonels were promoted solely on merit, the rank of brigadier general (given by the king) opened the way to high command to poorer nobility (Sébastien Le Prestre de Vauban's career is the best example). Louvois's work included the reform of various administrative branches: creating militia for second-line duties, which was the first attempt at a national conscription system; constructing barracks for the troops instead of quartering then in citizens' houses; providing regular pay and a uniform; implementing tighter discipline and a military justice code; and improving standardized weapons.

All these reforms were conducted to improve the soldier's lot and to ensure his loyalty to the king, as well as to heighten morale and corps pride. Louvois supported the first veterans' hospital, Les Invalides. The French army reached the incredible number of 450,000 soldiers by Louvois's death. He had constructed the military tool needed by Louis XIV for his aggressive foreign policy.

Gilles Boué

See also: Grand Alliance, War of the; Louis XIV; Vauban, Sébastien Le Prestre de

References and further reading:

Chartrand René. *Louis XIV's Army.* London: Osprey, 1988.

Corvisier, André. *Louvois.* Paris: Fayard, 1983.

Ludendorff, Erich Friedrich Wilhelm (1865–1937)

World War I general and postwar politician. Ludendorff was born on 9 April 1865, near Posen. He entered the army in 1883 and was appointed to the general staff in 1895. On 2 August 1914, he was appointed deputy chief of staff for the Second Army. He saw action on the western front and immediately won fame through his contribution to the capture of Liège. On 22 August 1914, he was appointed chief of staff of the Eighth Army, serving under Paul von Hindenburg. Their spectacular victories over the Russians at Tannenberg and the Masurian Lakes (August–September 1914) made them the most popular generals in Germany. In November 1914, Ludendorff was made chief of staff of the Supreme Command on the eastern front, again serving under Hindenburg. Convinced that the war could be won on the eastern front, Ludendorff came into increasing conflict over strategy with Erich von Falkenhayn, chief of the general staff. Falkenhayn's dismissal in August 1916 resulted in his replacement by Hindenburg, with Ludendorff serving as first quartermaster general. Ludendorff and Hindenburg were now in charge of German military strategy and increasingly of German domestic policy, a situation that by 1917 had led to the creation of a "silent dictatorship." Domestically, Ludendorff and Hindenburg sought to place the German economy on a total war footing. Militarily, they were responsible for the reintroduction of unrestricted submarine warfare in April 1917 and the annexationist peace treaties imposed on Russia and Romania in 1918. Following victory in the East, Ludendorff oversaw Germany's final attempt to break the stalemate on the western front in 1918. After the war, Ludendorff became active in right-wing politics. He participated in Hitler's failed Beer Hall Putsch in 1923 and served in the Reichstag from 1924 to 1928. Ludendorff died on 20 December 1937 in Bavaria.

J. David Cameron

See also: Falkenhayn, Erich von; Hindenburg; Paul von Beneckendorf und von; William II

References and further reading:

Ludendorff, Erich. *Meine Kriegserinnerungen, 1914–1918.* Berlin: E. S. Mittler und Sohn, 1921.

Kitchen, Martin. *The Silent Dictatorship: The Politics of the German High Command under Hindenburg and Ludendorff, 1916–1918.* New York: Holmes and Meier, 1967.

Lundy's Lane, Battle of (25–26 June 1814)

The most sanguinary battle of the War of 1812, a draw. The Americans sought to follow up their victory several weeks earlier at Chippewa on the Niagara frontier. General Winfield Scott and about 1,000 troops were in the vanguard, with General Jacob Brown in command of the main unit. Scott was aggressive and unexpectedly encountered a British force of 1,600 to 1,800 troops. Although outnumbered, he believed he had to attack because a retreat might result in panic among his main body of troops.

So, in the early evening of 25 July 1814, Scott ordered an attack uphill against British troops and a gun battery. The attack failed, for British artillery was extremely effective, and Scott had to retreat. As more and more Americans arrived, they once again assumed the offensive as dusk turned into night. The British too received reinforcements, and the fighting became intense with heavy casualties—more than 850—on each side.

After dark, the Americans began to run out of ammunition, and General Brown ordered them to retreat. The British and Canadians held the field but were too exhausted to give chase as the Americans retreated to Fort Erie. The earlier American victory at Chippewa was undone, and bloody Lundy's Lane ended this last U.S. effort to invade Canada.

Charles M. Dobbs

See also: War of 1812; Scott, Winfield

References and further reading:

Graves, Donald E. *The Battle of Lundy's Lane: On the Niagara in 1814.* Baltimore: Nautical and Aviation Publishing Company of America, 1993.

Hitsman, J. Mackay. *The Incredible War of 1812.* Toronto: University of Toronto Press, 1965.

Stanley, George F. G. *The War of 1812: Land Operations.* 1983.

Lützen, Battle of (16 November 1632)

The high tide of Swedish strategic dominance under Gustavus Adolphus during the Thirty Years' War. Following the Swedish victory at Breitenfeld in the fall of 1631, the Swedes under Gustavus marched into Bavaria to attack the senior member of the Catholic League. The Hapsburg general Albrecht von Wallenstein skillfully rallied the imperial troops and wore down the Swedish force. After the imperial victory at Nuremberg on 3 September 1632, a series of inconclusive engagements brought the combatants back into Saxony.

The two forces clashed again at Lützen on 16 November 1632. Eighteen thousand Swedes faced 25,000 imperial troops. Wallenstein occupied a strong position with cavalry on the wings, four *tercios* composed of pikemen and musketeers in the center, and artillery emplaced in the center and on the right flank. Additionally, a ditch defended by musketeers extended across his front. The Swedes took up their usual linear formation of two lines with infantry in the center and cavalry-infantry combinations on the wings. Gustavus, commanding his right wing of cavalry, planned to attack Wallenstein's left flank to push him back and away from Lützen. After an intense artillery barrage, Gustavus led his cavalry to penetrate the imperial musketeers and crash into Wallenstein's cavalry. Swedish infantry likewise advanced and captured the imperial artillery in the center. This success was temporary, however. Imperial cavalry charged into the flanks of the Swedish infantry, throwing them back. At this point, Gustavus moved across the field to rally his infantry and personally lead his final charge against the enemy. He died with musket balls in his arm, back, and head. The king's subordinates quickly marshaled all available forces and plunged ahead. The battle seesawed as infantry formations pushed with pikes and cavalry repeatedly charged and countercharged. The Swedes finally rallied and swept the imperial forces off the field, capturing by nightfall all their artillery and killing upward of 12,000 men. Swedish losses were about 6,000. Though a technical victory for the Swedes, the loss of their king brought the military balance into equilibrium. The Swedes lost much of the strategic initiative and direction Gustavus provided. The Battle of Nordlingen (1634) completed the shift of fortunes back to the Catholic cause.

Bryan R. Gibby

See also: Breitenfeld; Gustavus II Adolphus; Nordlingen; Thirty Years' War

References and further reading:

Dodge, Theodore A. *Gustavus Adolphus.* New York: Da Capo Press, 1998.

Parker, Geoffrey, ed. *The Thirty Years War.* London: Routledge, 1997.

Luxembourg, François Henri de Montmorency-Bouteville, Duc de Piney (1628–1695)

The most brilliant tactical commander of Louis XIV's early reign. The son of a duelist beheaded in 1627, he was educated at a prince's court and became a close friend of the Great Condé. At the age of 20, he was appointed brigadier general after the Battle of Lens (1648). Being loyal to Condé, he took part in the Wars of the Fronde on the rebels' side. His choice leading him straight to treason against the young king, he commanded Spanish troops during the Battles of Arras and the Dunes (1658). When the peace treaty of the Pyrenees was concluded, he was allowed to return to Paris in poverty. Once again, Condé helped him in finding a rich, noble young lady to marry. He claimed for his wife the restoration of the peerage of Luxembourg and eventually added this title to his own. He became the duke of Luxembourg and had to take legal action to be accepted as such by the king's courtiers.

Luxembourg's fortune had to wait 10 years before Louis XIV again allowed him to command French troops. The Dutch War of 1672–1678 gave him the opportunity to distinguish himself. Commanding the army in 1672 after the king's departure, he won the Battle of Senef with Condé in 1674 and was made marshal of France in July 1675. The victories accumulated in the following years: Valenciennes and Cassel in 1677 and Ypres and Saint Denis in 1678. His cleverness and his composure were the cornerstones of his tactical skill, but he took a hard line with those who didn't share his views and made numerous personal enemies, including François-Michel Le Tellier, Marquis de Louvois.

In 1679, Luxembourg was deeply involved in the famous poisoning of a king's mistress and spent 14 months in the Bastille jail. After being discharged the following year, he returned to court. The war of the Augsburg League gave him a further opportunity to add new victories to the king's glory: Fleurus in 1690, Leuze in 1691, Steinkeerk in 1692, and Neerwinden in 1693. This last battle crowned him as an outstanding tactical general. After besieging Huy, Luxembourg lured William of Orange from a very strong camp into a less sound position, brought him to battle, and successfully routed the allied army. His death in January 1695 left France without anyone of his quality to take his place. His nickname was "le tapissier de Notre Dame"—Notre Dame's decorator—in token of the dozens of captured standards displayed in that cathedral.

Gilles Boué

See also: Condé, Louis II de Bourbon, Fourth Prince de; Louis XIV; Louvois, François-Michel Le Tellier, Marquis de

References and further reading:

Bluche, François. *Dictionnaire du Grand Siècle.* Paris: Fayard, 1990.

Dussieux, Louis. *Les grands généraux de Louis XIV.* Paris: Lacoffre, 1888.

Luxembourg, Siege of (April–June 1684)

Probably the best example of siege warfare in the seventeenth century. During the seventeenth century, sieges were the rule and battle the exception. Fortified cities dominated communication lines and the most fertile parts of land. A field army could not allow harassing garrisons in its rear. Luxembourg was one of the most feared and well-defended fortified towns of this era. The five-stage siege of 1684 is archetypal.

The first stage was in January, when a French army under the Marechal de Créqui isolated Luxembourg from the Spanish main army. Then, a covering force of 20,000 took position between Brussels and Luxembourg to mislead the Spanish commanders. The main army approached Luxembourg with Marechal Sébastien Le Prestre de Vauban as commanding officer. A siege had to be conducted by specialist officers, who sometime overruled superiors, including the king. The besieging army was composed of more than 25,000 soldiers, including 40 royal engineers, and more than 70 guns. The besieged Spanish troops numbered no more than 3,000 under the governor, the prince de Chimay, and the comte de Tille. From 28 April to 8 May, defending lines were dug a few miles away from the town to protect the besieging troops. Vauban had to use 12,000 workers, forcing unwilling peasants into service. The inner lines were dug by troops under artillery fire.

The fortified town of Luxembourg was protected by high cliffs, a river, and modern fortifications made of a glacis-covered tunnel in front of ditches and bastions protecting the curtain walls. From early May, parallels were dug, and then zigzag trenches were constructed. Meanwhile, sappers had dug explosive mines. The explosion on 27 May was the sign of the assault on this first line by elite troopers. The French took the covered way and had to begin a new siege on the second defense line by a bastion. Hundreds of gabions were made to protect the head of the approaching trench. During the siege operations, the French artillery fired more than 55,000 rounds, night and day. The governor of Luxembourg, not expecting any relieving army and fearing the plunder and massacre that would follow a general assault, asked to surrender on 3 June. Four days later, he left the town with 2,000 survivors. The siege had cost more than 373,000 French livres, less than the million needed to rebuild new fortifications with Vauban as the main architect.

Gilles Boué

See also: Malplaquet, Battle of; Oudenaarde, Battle of; Ramillies, Battle of; Spanish Succession, War of the; Vauban, Sébastien Le Prestre de

References and further reading:

Dollar, Jacques. *Vauban à Luxembourg.* Luxembourg: RTL Editions, 1983.

Rorive, J. P. *La guerre de siège sous Louis XIV en Europe et à Huy.* Brussels: Racine, 1998.

Lyautey, Louis-Hubert-Gonzalve (1854–1934)

French colonial administrator and soldier. Born 17 November 1854 in Nancy, France, Lyautey studied at the Saint-Cyr Military Academy, spent time in a cavalry regiment, and served in Algeria from 1880 to 1882. He served in Indochina under the influential Joseph Simon Gallieni in 1894 and transferred to Madagascar in 1896. After successfully subduing the southern portion of the island, he returned to France to command the 14th Hussars at Alençon (1902–1903). Transferred to Algeria, he commanded the Ain Sefra region and gradually began expanding French territory into Morocco. In 1906, he became commandant of Oran and squelched Moroccan resistance to his expansion, particularly the rebellion of the Beni Snassen in late 1907. Lyautey returned to France and commanded the X Corps at Rennes from December 1910 to March 1912. He returned to Africa as resident general of the protectorate of Morocco in April

1912 and stepped into the middle of a revolt. He managed to reassert French rule and restore order fairly quickly and again was able to increase French holdings.

At the start of World War I, most of his troops left for France, but Lyautey kept a potentially explosive situation in hand by working within existing tribal institutions. From December 1916 to March 1917, he served as minister of war in Paris. Afterward, he assumed his former post in Morocco and successfully defended against a rebel force led by Abd-El Krim at Taza in spring 1925. Lyautey resigned on 5 September of that year, partly as a result of the appointment of Marshal Henri-Philippe Pétain as commander in chief in Morocco. He retired at Thorey, where he died on 21 July 1934.

Harold Wise

See also: French Colonial Wars; Galliéni, Joseph Simon

References and further reading:

Hoisington, William A. *Lyautey and the French Conquest of Morocco.* New York: St. Martin's Press, 1995.

Maurois, André. *Marshal Lyautey.* Trans. Hamish Miles. London: John Lane, 1931.

Lysander (d. 395 B.C.E.)

Spartan commander who combined land and sea strategies to defeat the Athenians in the final phase of the Second Peloponnesian War. In 406 B.C.E., Lysander, with a fleet of 140 ships, engaged the Athenian navy at Lesbos, destroying 30 of its 70 ships. The Athenians, in desperation, melted down the dedications to the gods, offered freedom to slaves and citizenship to the metics (resident foreigners), and built 150 additional ships. They engaged the Spartan navy at Arginusae, where they won their last naval victory of the war. The following year, Lysander ordered his ships to the Hellespont, where he observed the Athenian fleet. The Athenians attempted to draw the Spartan ships into battle, but Lysander ordered them to wait. Frustrated by the delays and needing fresh supplies, the Athenians anchored their ships and went ashore for provisions. Lysander seized this opportunity to dart across the straits separating the two fleets and captured 160 of the 180 Athenian ships. He then pushed all Athenians living outside Athens back to the city. After an eight-month siege, the people surrendered, and Lysander installed a new oligarchic government of the Thirty. In 403 B.C.E., Lysander put down an Athenian revolt intended to restore democracy.

After the death of the Spartan king Agis II, Lysander pushed the claim of Agis's brother Agesilaus as the rightful heir to the throne. Confident that he could exercise control over Agesilaus because of a personal relationship between the two men, Lysander received an appointment as the head of the board of 30 advisers for the new king. Agesilaus often rejected Lysander's advice, and at the beginning of the Corinthian War in 395 B.C.E., Lysander returned to Greece and was slain in the first battle of the war.

Cynthia Clark Northrup

See also: Peloponnesian Wars

References and further reading:

Mattingly, Harold B. *The Athenian Empire Restored: Epigraphic and Historical Studies.* Ann Arbor: University of Michigan Press, 1996.

M

MacArthur, Arthur, Jr. (1845–1912)

Prominent U.S. Army commander. Born in Springfield, Massachusetts, on 2 June 1845, Arthur MacArthur Jr. moved with his family to Milwaukee, Wisconsin, in 1849. Following the outbreak of the Civil War, MacArthur attempted to get an appointment to West Point, but when he was unable to do so, his politically influential father, Judge Arthur MacArthur Sr., managed to have him commissioned a second lieutenant and named the adjutant of the 24th Wisconsin Infantry Regiment on 4 August 1862. At the Battle of Missionary Ridge (25 November 1863), he seized the regimental colors at a critical moment and led his regiment to the crest of the ridge. The 24th Wisconsin's colors were the first to be planted on the enemy's breastworks, and for his daring action, MacArthur was awarded the Medal of Honor on 30 June 1890. By the end of the Civil War, MacArthur had been promoted to lieutenant colonel and brevetted to full colonel.

After being mustered out of the volunteers in June 1865, MacArthur was commissioned a first lieutenant in the regular army in February 1866. For the next 30 years, he served on the frontier, eventually being promoted to lieutenant colonel in May 1896. After the outbreak of the Spanish-American War, MacArthur was promoted to brigadier general of volunteers in May 1898 and commanded a brigade during the capture of Manila. Promoted to major general of volunteers in August 1898, he was given command of the U.S. forces in the Philippines, which were fighting against the insurrectionist army of Emilio Aguinaldo. MacArthur was promoted to brigadier general in the regular army in January 1901 and major general in February, which was followed by an appointment as the military governor of the Philippines in May 1901. In September 1906, MacArthur was promoted to lieutenant general and given command of all U.S. Army personnel in the Pacific. Despite being the most senior officer in the U.S. Army, he was passed over for the position of chief of staff and retired in June 1909. MacArthur died when a blood vessel in his brain burst while he was giving a speech at the 24th Wisconsin's fiftieth reunion in Milwaukee on 5 September 1912.

Alexander M. Bielakowski

See also: Aguinaldo, Emilio; Spanish-American War

References and further reading:

James, D. Clayton. *Years of MacArthur.* Vol. 1: *1880–1941.* Boston: Houghton Mifflin, 1970.

MacArthur, Douglas. *Reminiscences.* New York: Time, 1964.

Young, Kenneth R. *General's General: The Life and Times of Arthur MacArthur.* Boulder, CO: Westview Press, 1994.

MacArthur, Douglas (1884–1964)

The most successful and most controversial of any American general. His real and unchallenged accomplishments included the development of modern staff procedures, the foundation for American military expansion in the face of World War II, and the stunning employment of amphibious force in World War II and at Inchon in 1950. Still, his record has been marred by his own arrogance and by his refusal fully to disclose the reasons for many of the high command decisions.

MacArthur was born on 26 January 1880 into a military family. His father was a Civil War hero who was later to serve as the first U.S. governor of the Philippines and who would be rewarded by promotion to lieutenant general, then a rare rank in the American service. His older brother was a Naval Academy graduate who was himself a distinguished officer and whose death at a relatively early age was much lamented by his peers.

As is the case with most complex people, MacArthur was

Douglas MacArthur, after being fired by President Truman, making a speech, 1951. (Library of Congress)

a morass of contradictions. He was not an innate modernizer, but when the need for modernization was proven to him, he demanded it from his subordinates and from the military system. He detested staff work but, in World War I, developed and ran what might have been the finest divisional staff in that war. In World War II, he allowed his own staff to become rather slack at conducting routine chores while he developed elaborate plans on his own that emerged fully hatched and capable of implementation. His faith in the American fighting man—army, navy, Marine Corps, and air force was immense—yet he spent most of his career with the navy, air force, and Marine Corps distrusting him to the point at which he had to challenge them with barbs to achieve his ends. He sought closeness with political leaders but only achieved it either with those whose grip on power was slight, such as Newton Baker or Herbert Hoover, or those who failed fully to understand his capacities, such as Franklin D. Roosevelt. At the same time, he alienated the political leaders who could have worked with him for even greater accomplishments than were to be his due, such as Henry Stimson or Harry Truman. MacArthur's entire life is one of contradiction.

Although MacArthur did not develop the idea, he was the first major U.S. commander to accept the necessity of bypassing Japanese strong points in the Pacific. He was late in comprehending the significance of tactical air power, yet, once convinced, no U.S. commander has ever understood or employed air power to better advantage than did MacArthur. He had been an early advocate of strategic air power, but his advocacy was so shielded that it seemed nonexistent to many of the leaders of the army and air force in the buildup to World War II. In a similar vein, MacArthur alienated the navy, though his relationship with the chief of naval operations during MacArthur's tenure as army chief of staff marked the high-water level of army-navy relations for almost the first half of the twentieth century.

MacArthur committed few grave errors, but the arrogance of his personality caused him to be blamed with many. MacArthur was held to account by the public for perceived harshness in disbursing the Bonus Marchers in 1932, for laxness in allowing half of his heavy bomber force to be wiped out on the ground when World War II erupted over the Philippines in 1941, for the supposed cowardice of "Dugout Doug" in facing combat, for not recognizing the real threat of Chinese Communist intervention in the Korean War, and for treating the president of the United States in a dismissive and belittling matter. Yet, at the same time, there is far more to each of these tales than these bare outlines, and the complexity of MacArthur's character is matched closely by the intricacies of the crises in his life.

MacArthur was an outstanding field commander and staff officer in World War I. He was an innovative superintendent at the U.S. Military Academy at West Point. He was a successful corps commander and department commander in the Philippines and was noted for the leadership he projected in the military doldrums of the 1920s. He headed the successful U.S. Olympic Team in 1928, arguably the first occasion in which the nation mounted a major effort at these international games. His term as chief of staff was outstanding and lasted longer than that of any other officer in recent times save for George C. Marshall; during his term, MacArthur laid the foundations for the rapid mobilization that the United States was able to mount in the late 1930s and early 1940s and modernized military organizations and structures. He displayed great ability in establishing the Civilian Conservation Corps and established the beginnings of the army-navy cooperation that flourished in the decade after MacArthur ended his term as chief of staff in 1935.

MacArthur, following his withdrawal to Australia from the doomed Philippines, rapidly learned the application of modern warfare and proved a master of combined arms operations, integrating air, land, and sea power into a potent force that enabled those in the Pacific theater to handle immense distances, prepared enemy defenses, and meager resources and still advance from the Stanley Owens Mountains in New Guinea in late 1942 to the invasion of the Philippines barely two years later. His ability to seize the initiative and to combine overwhelming force with only short windows of opportunity marked him as perhaps the best-balanced of American senior commanders during World War II.

MacArthur, after having been designated to command DOWNFALL, the invasion of Japan, found himself instead designated to command the Allied occupation of the former enemy and was charged with converting a warlike state to a nation of peace. In this, he was successful beyond all expectation, balancing the demands of competing Allied requirements and often ambiguous guidance from Washington into a sure course of direction that rapidly turned Japan into both a democracy and the first of the economic "Asian Tigers."

MacArthur's final command ended in frustration and embarrassment, in some measure caused by his own failure to recognize the changed attitudes in both the United States and Europe toward warfare in Asia. From his initial chagrin at U.S. troops proving themselves to be ill-trained and ill-equipped to the magnificent stroke of CHROMITE (the Inchon Landings)—certainly one of the finest amphibious operations ever mounted—and then to the hectic advance north and the dismal retreat south, MacArthur made this war his, with his frequent appearances at the front and his even more frequent press releases. But the intervention of the Chinese Communists caused MacArthur to become a changed man, negative and complaining, and this attitude, in turn, seems to have led to his refusal to listen more carefully to how the winds were blowing in Washington. At the end, MacArthur was perceived by his superiors as being out of control, a conclusion with some basis in truth but also one tainted with personal envy from some of those involved. In any event, despite MacArthur's unrivaled seniority—he had been the senior eligible officer for the position of chief of staff in 1930, for instance, and both of his successors, and all of his rivals, had long ago retired—he was relieved of the far eastern command in a botched episode embarrassing to both Washington and Tokyo in April 1951.

MacArthur returned home to vast public accolades, and his address to Congress flooded the media. He was the keynote speaker at the Republican National Convention in 1952, but his political aspirations were blocked by the ready nomination of Dwight D. Eisenhower for the presidency.

MacArthur then moved to New York, where at the instigation of former president Herbert Hoover he lived at the Waldorf-Astoria. His birthday celebrations were events of great interest to the U.S. military community, as his former soldiers, many of them now risen to military power, paid homage to the man they credited with forming their careers. MacArthur did serve as a corporate officer with some success but otherwise avoided the limelight.

Although President Eisenhower declined contact with his former commander, President John F. Kennedy frequently consulted MacArthur as the United States became drawn into the Vietnam conflict, though MacArthur's analysis was that the United States should avoid military support to the South Vietnamese government, advice unwelcome to Kennedy. MacArthur enjoyed a tumultuous return visit to the Philippines in 1961 and completed his military duties as the graduation speaker at West Point in 1962. He died following a brief illness at Walter Reed Hospital in 1964 and is buried in his mother's home city of Norfolk, Virginia.

MacArthur was a soldier marred by an arrogant personality and one who failed properly to protect his record by explaining in detail the reasoning behind his actions but nevertheless a soldier first, last, and always.

Marc Small

See also: Philippines, U.S. Loss of; Philippines, U.S. Retaking of; World War I; World War II

References and further reading:

Appleman, Roy E. *South to the Naktong: North to the Yalu.* Washington, DC: Office of the Chief of Military History, 1961.

James, D. Clayton. *The Years of MacArthur.* Vol. 1, *1880–1941.* Boston: Houghton Mifflin, 1970.

———. *The Years of MacArthur.* Vol. 2, *1941–1945.* Boston: Houghton Mifflin, 1975.

———. *The Years of MacArthur.* Vol. 3, *Triumph and Disaster, 1945–1964.* Boston: Houghton Mifflin, 1985.

Linn, Brian McAllister. *Guardians of Empire: The U.S. Army and the Pacific, 1902–1949.* Chapel Hill: University of North Carolina Press, 1997.

MacArthur, Douglas. *Reminiscences.* New York: McGraw-Hill, 1964.

Morton, Louis. *The Fall of the Philippines.* Washington, DC: Center for Military History, 1953.

Perret, Geoffrey. *Old Soldiers Never Die: The Life of Douglas MacArthur.* New York: Random House, 1996.

Petillo, Carol Morris. *Douglas MacArthur: The Philippine Years.* Peru: Indiana University Press, 1981.

Maccabees, Revolt of the (168–143 B.C.E.)

The Jewish-dominated region of Judea rebelled against the religious oppression of the Seleucid king, Antiochus IV, and forged an independent nation-state in one of the world's first successful guerrilla campaigns. For about a century after Alexander the Great had conquered the Persian Empire, the coastal zone southwest of Syria became the pivot point of the rivalry between the Ptolemaic (Egypt-based) and Seleucid (Syria–Asia Minor) successor regimes. By 170 B.C.E., Antiochus III and his sons Seleucis IV and Antiochus IV Epiphanes, rulers of the Seleucid Empire, understood that they would have to confront the expanding influence of Rome. Antiochus IV felt that it was crucial to forge religious unity throughout his dominion, integrating all the various gods with Olympian Zeus at their head. Especially significant was Jewish-dominated Judea, the strategic fulcrum covering southern invasion routes. As a result, he violated the promise of his father Antiochus III to respect the religious autonomy of the Jews. To this end, Antiochus took sides in a power struggle between rival high priests in Jerusalem, as a pretext to intervene openly in Jewish religious matters. This confrontation culminated when Antiochus Epiphanes occupied Jerusalem. He destroyed the city walls, raided the Temple treasury to fund his dwindling war chest, and decreed the abolition of Jewish separatism. He next converted the temple into a pagan shrine, setting up a fortress opposite, and forbade the hallowed practices of circumcision and Sabbath observance.

In 168 B.C.E., Seleucid troops set up pagan altars in the countryside and, in the village of Modi'in, ordered a lower-ranking priest, Mattathias, to ritually eat pig's flesh. He refused and killed another villager who complied, leading the townsfolk in a massacre of the Greek garrison, thereby starting the revolt. Mattathias withdrew to a concealed and well-guarded training camp for irregular forces in the foothills near Gophna, northwest of modern Ramallah. The training went on for a year prior to conducting operations and included politico-religious indoctrination and the establishment of friendly ties with the populace in key localities, where they established logistical bases, intelligence networks, safe houses, and weapons hoards. The moribund Mattathias designated one of his sons, Judas (who became known as Maccabee, or "the Hammer") to take over for him.

In a series of brilliant guerrilla actions, Judas defeated a succession of Syrian generals. His most renowned victories occurred at Beth Horon Pass (166 B.C.E.), Emmaus (166 B.C.E.), and Beth Zur, in the vicinity of Hebron (165 B.C.E.). His success is attributed to the first recorded instances of successful irregular warfare: hit-and-run night raids, ambushes at defiles, and attacks on rear-echelon units and individuals. After Beth-Zur, Judas captured Jerusalem, liberating the temple, though a Seleucid garrison held out in the citadel.

In 165–164 B.C.E., Judas extended his control over most of Judea, maintaining a close siege of the Syrian troops in the citadel. Since Antiochus was preoccupied with a triumphant campaign in the East, it was left to the Syrian regent Lysias to lead an invasion of Judea to recapture Jerusalem. After defeating the Jews at Beth Zacharia, he had to cut the campaign short to suppress a revolt in Syria in 164 B.C.E..

In 164 B.C.E., Bacchides, in charge of Seleucid forces in Judea, defeated Judas, driving him from Jerusalem. Quickly rebounding from this reverse, Judas took the offensive and, in 160 B.C.E., routed and killed the Syrian general Nicanor at Adasa, close to his earlier victory at Beth Horon. Judas himself was killed in battle by Bacchides at Elasa later that year.

Leadership of the Maccabees passed to Judas's brother, Jonathan, who continued guerrilla campaigns against the Syrians. In 143 B.C.E., Syrian troops, in league with alienated Jews, captured and eventually executed Jonathan at Ptolemais (Acre). Subsequently, the Seleucids recognized another of Judas's brothers, Simon, as king of Judea, establishing the Hasmonean dynasty, which ended with the accession of Herod the Great, after his marriage to the last Hasmonean queen, Miriam.

James Bloom

See also: Syrian-Egyptian Wars

References and further reading:

Bar-Kochva, Bezalel. *The Seleucid Army: Organization and Tactics in the Great Campaigns.* Cambridge, UK: Cambridge University Press, 1976.

———. *Judas Maccabeus. The Jewish Struggle against the Seleucids.* Cambridge, UK: Cambridge University Press, 1989.

Farmer, William R. *Maccabees, Zealots and Josephus: An Inquiry into Jewish Nationalism in the Greco-Roman Period.* New York: Columbia University Press, 1956.

Gichon, Mordechai, and Chaim Herzog. *Battles of the Bible.* 2d ed. London, Greenhill Books, Lionel Leventhal, 1997.

Macedonian Wars (215–146 B.C.E.)

A series of wars during which the Romans gained control over Greece and destroyed the Macedonian kingdom.

The First Macedonian War (215–205 B.C.E.)

In 215 B.C.E. the Macedonian king Philip V signed a treaty with the Carthaginian general Hannibal, who had invaded Italy. Thereupon Philip invaded Rome's possessions in Illyria (Albania). Although the Romans succeeded in keeping the important city of Apollonia out of Philip's hands, the war effort in Italy prevented them from intervening until 211 B.C.E., when the Romans allied with the Greek confederacy of Aetolia.

The Romans left land warfare to the Greeks, confining themselves largely to naval support. In the following years, Rome's successes were mainly diplomatic. Several Greek states chose Rome's side. Philip was driven out of Greece by diplomatic means. Then, during a lightning campaign, Philip defeated the Greeks and their Balkan tribal allies, recovered his position in Greece, and attacked Aetolia. The Aeolians sued for peace (206 B.C.E.) after their Spartan allies were defeated by the Achaeans. After an unsuccessful campaign in Illyria, the Romans did so as well. The Peace of Phoenice (205 B.C.E.) left Philip in possession of his conquests in Illyria.

The Second Macedonian War (200–197 B.C.E.)

In 200 B.C.E., war broke out again. The Romans landed in Illyria with two legions and marched inland. They failed to push through into Macedonia but did succeed in coercing several states to join the many Greek states that had already joined them.

In 199 B.C.E., an army of Greek allies raided Thessaly and

southern Macedonia, but during a lightning campaign, Philip succeeded in fighting off both these invaders and Rome's tribal allies on the Balkan frontier. In the following year, Philip took the initiative and moved his army into a strategic position, where he threatened the lines of communication of the Roman army in Illyria. The Romans assaulted Philip's position, a costly but eventually successful campaign. Thereupon Philip retreated into Macedonia. In the meantime, the allies of Rome were successful at sea, and even more Greek states joined the Romans.

Philip advanced into Thessaly but was engaged by the Roman army before he had reached his objective. He was forced to do battle at Cynoscephalae and was defeated. He had to abandon all territories outside Macedonia and respect the independence of all Greek cities. The Romans assumed Macedonia's role of dominant power in Greece.

The Third Macedonian War (171–168 B.C.E.)

The Romans felt threatened in their hegemony when King Perseus, the son of Philip V, again started to acquire influence in Greece. Unscrupulously taking advantage of Perseus's diplomatic advances to avoid hostilities, they brought an army into Illyria and Greece. Perseus reacted with speed and outmaneuvered the Romans in Thessaly, cutting off their line of supplies.

In the meantime, the Romans alienated themselves from the Greeks by their brutality, heavy-handedness, and greed. Perseus, on the contrary, became increasingly popular. Moreover, he was successful, while the Romans suffered from bad discipline and command. Two invasions of Macedonia failed, and Perseus counterattacked, regaining territory and defeating Rome's Balkan tribal allies. During the following winter (169 B.C.E.), he campaigned successfully against the Romans on Macedonia's northwestern frontier and in Greece and Epirus.

In 168 B.C.E., the consul Lucius Aemilius Paullus assumed command of the Roman army. The Romans decided to attack on three fronts: a naval offensive in the Aegean Sea, an offensive from the west from Illyria, and an offensive from Thessaly. After initial Macedonian success, Perseus met the Romans at Pydna. The well-deployed Macedonian phalanx attacked the unprepared Romans, but the Macedonian line became disrupted. The Romans counterattacked and broke the Macedonians. Perseus was captured and brought to Italy. Macedonia was divided into four republics, tributary to Rome.

The Fourth Macedonian War (146 B.C.E.)

The so-called Fourth Macedonian War was in fact an insurrection. The Macedonians had always been very loyal to their royal house, and in 152 B.C.E., a pretender to the throne named Andriscus aroused the Macedonians into a rebellion to reinstate the royal dynasty. The insurgents initially succeeded in defeating an army consisting of a Roman legion and local militia, though another Roman army soon crushed the revolt.

Maarten van der Werf

See also: Cynoscephalae, Battle of; Hannibal Barca

References and further reading:

Errington, Robert Malcom. *A History of Macedonia.* Berkeley: University of California Press, 1990.

Hammond, Nicholas Geoffrey Lem Prière, and F. W. Walbank. *A History of Macedonia.* Vol. 3, *336–167 B.C.E.* Oxford: Clarendon Press, 1988.

Walbank, Frank William. *Philip V of Macedon.* Cambridge, UK: Cambridge University Press, 1940. Reprint, Hamden, CT: Archon Books, 1967.

Maceo y Grajales, Antonio (1845–1896)

Noted black general in the struggle for Cuban independence. Maceo y Grajales was born on 14 June 1845 in Majaguabo, San Luis, to a farming family of free blacks. At the outbreak of the Ten Years' War in 1868, he joined the revolutionary forces and rose to the rank of general. Although the war ended with the Pact of Zanjon, in which Spain promised various social and economic reforms, Maceo was one of a number of Cuban revolutionaries who refused to accept the pact's terms.

By 1880, Maceo was traveling outside Cuba attempting to acquire arms, munitions, and men to return to the battle. Though it would be 1895 before he returned to Cuba to fight, he worked tirelessly for independence. He met with Máximo Gómez and José Martí various times to plan the continued war for independence. During these meetings, Martí would have to mediate at various times because Maceo and Gómez were rivals.

With the renewal of the war, Maceo was wounded more than 200 times. He was emphatically against annexation of Cuba by the United States, a course of action considered by some revolutionaries. But Maceo, appalled by the increasingly restrictive "color line" being drawn in the post-Reconstruction United States, stated that if annexation were attempted, he would be forced to switch allegiance and fight on the Spanish side.

During a fierce battle at San Pedro in Havana province on 7 December 1896, Maceo and his aide, a son of Máximo Gómez, fell in battle.

Peter Carr

See also: Cuban War of Independence; Cuban Ten Years' War; Martí y Pérez, José Julián

References and further reading:
Carbonell y Rivero, Miguel Angel. *Antonio Maceo.* Havana: Imprenta "La Prueba," 1924.
Costa, Octavio R. *Antonio Maceo, el héroe.* Havana: Academia de la Historia de Cuba, 1947.

Machiavelli, Niccolò (1469–1527)

Secretary to the chancellor on diplomatic relations for the Republic of Florence, better known as the first great political philosopher of the Renaissance. Born in Florence, Italy, on 3 May 1469, Machiavelli was the son of a lawyer of modest means who provided his son with a strong background in the humanities. Over his remains stands a monument bearing, in Latin, the phrase, "No eulogy would do justice to so great a name."

In 1512, the Medici family overthrew the republic, and Machiavelli lost his position. He spent his forced retirement reflecting upon events, reading history, and writing political philosophy. It was during this time he wrote *The Prince* (1513), *Discourses on the First Ten Books of Titus Livius* (1513–1517), and *The Art of War* (1520).

Portrait of Niccolò Machiavelli. (Library of Congress)

In *The Prince,* his most famous work, Machiavelli discusses the political necessity of "vices" over traditional "virtues," the political benefits of deceitfulness and miserliness, and how a prince should prefer being feared to being loved while avoiding being hated by his subjects. The book is a technical manual on how a prince was to grasp and hold power.

Most of Machiavelli's later work focused on his love of republican values. In *Discourses,* he examines the elements of the ancient Roman Republic that led to its success and draws lessons for republican governments. In *The Art of War,* Machiavelli advocates replacing unreliable mercenaries with a patriotic militia imbued with civic virtue and possessing an intense desire to protect their republican rights.

Many of Machiavelli's works, especially *The Prince,* were favorite reading of history's great military minds, such as Frederick the Great, Napoleon, and Clausewitz.

Craig T. Cobane

See also: Mercenaries

References and further reading:
Pocock, J. G. A. *The Machiavellian Moment.* Princeton, NJ: Princeton University Press, 1975.
Skinner, Quintin. *Machiavelli.* New York: Farrar, 1981.

Machine Gun

A rapid-firing small arm, which today means a fully automatic weapon. Muzzle-loading firearms were slow to reload, inaccurate, and effective only at very short ranges. Since their first appearance, those who make and use them have striven to increase the guns' rate of fire and combine great rate of fire with accuracy. Muzzle-loading separate ball and powder prevented any development along these lines. Breech-loading weapons and the complete round (bullet and cartridge in one unit) made machine guns possible. The machine gun is the easiest method of putting heavy fire down quickly on unprotected troops and areas.

One of the earliest successful machine guns was the Gatling (1862), a hand-cranked gun, which had between 6 and 20 rotating barrels. By the end of the nineteenth century, machine guns were fully automatic, in that once the trigger was depressed the gun continued to fire until it either ran out of ammunition or the trigger was released. This effect was achieved by tapping some of the gases used to propel the bullet down the barrel or by using the recoil of the cartridge case to work the mechanism of the gun. Ammunition is fed to the gun from magazines or belts.

The machine gun has a purpose in attack (to suppress the enemy) and in defense (to mow down attackers who do not use practical anti–machine gun field craft and tactics). Its greatest effect was in World War I, when the machine gun took second place only to artillery in killing and wounding on both sides.

The machine gun is an infantry weapon and can be used for direct or indirect fire. In the direct fire role, the machine gun is a very effective defensive weapon and gives very good fire support for moving troops. In the indirect role, a machine gun or a battery of guns can deny the enemy unprotected movement well behind the forward battle lines.

Light machine guns are weapons carried by the infantry, and every infantry section has one or more light machine guns. Medium machine guns (used mainly in the indirect fire role) are concentrated normally at battalion level, as are heavy machine guns. All armored fighting vehicles carry a machine gun for local support. Machine guns have also been used in aircraft for air warfare and for ground strafing, but these roles have now mainly been taken on by missiles. But even in an age of high-tech electronic warfare, the machine gun, by general agreement, is still a most important weapon in any army's armory.

David Westwood

References and further reading:

Allen, W. G. B. *Pistols Rifles and Machine Guns.* London: English Universities Press, 1953.

Hobart, F. W. A., ed. *Jane's Infantry Weapons.* London: MacDonald and Jane's, 1975.

Mackensen, August von (1849–1945)

German field marshal who achieved a string of spectacular victories on the eastern front in 1914–1916. Born on 6 December 1849 in Leipnitz, near Wittenberg, Mackensen joined the Death's Head Hussars in 1869 as a cadet. Serving in the Franco-Prussian War as a junior officer, he was appointed to the general staff in 1882. Although not from the nobility, he rose rapidly through the ranks and was promoted to cavalry general in 1908.

As commander of XVII Corps on the eastern front in 1914, he suffered defeat at Gumbinnen (20 August) but contributed to victory at Tannenberg and in the first Battle of the Masurian Lakes. As commander of the Ninth Army, he conducted the successful offensive at Lodz (11–21 November). The following year, he succeeded in breaking through the Russian lines at Gorlice-Tarnów as commander of the Austro-German Eleventh Army, his advancing forces taking 120,000 prisoners, destroying the Russian Third Army, and capturing Lemberg and Brest-Litovsk. Promoted to field marshal in recognition of his achievements, he was ordered to renew the attack on Serbia and captured Belgrade on 9 October 1915 as commander of German, Austro-German, and Bulgarian armies. On 1 September 1916, he launched a successful attack on Romania with combined Bulgarian, Turkish, and German forces, entering Bucharest on 6 December. Mackensen was a modest man, and his battlefield successes have been attributed to his ability to work harmoniously with different chiefs of staff.

During the 1930s, he was used by Adolf Hitler at various public displays to symbolize the continuity of military tradition in the Third Reich. He died on 8 November 1945, at Burghorn, near Celle, having lived just long enough to witness Germany's utter defeat in World War II.

Alaric Searle

See also: Gorlice/Tarnow; Tannenberg, Battle of

References and further reading:

Mackensen, August von. *Briefe und Aufzeichnungen aus Krieg und Frieden.* Leipzig: Bibliographisches Institut, 1938.

Schwarzmüller, Theo. *Zwischen Kaiser und "Führer." Generalfeldmarschall August von Mackensen.* Paderborn: Schöningh, 1996.

Mactan, Battle of (1521)

An avoidable defeat of Spanish forces led by the Portuguese Fernao de Magalhaes (Ferdinand Magellan). The Battle of Mactan delayed Spain's colonization of the archipelago later named Las Islas Felipinas, or the Philippines.

With Pope Alexander VI's bull (decree) of 1493 and the Treaty of Tordesillas of 1494 (later approved by Pope Julius II), conflict between Catholic Spain and Portugal over prospective colonies in the Western Hemisphere was adjudicated. Spain then sought a direct water route to the Spice Islands in Southeast Asia.

Captain General Magellan commanded three ships sailing from Spain in 1519, intent on reaching the Spice Islands. He sailed from the Atlantic to the Pacific and thence through insular Southeast Asia. Magellan baptized the Muslim Rajah Humabon of Zebu (Cebu), whose gold and ginger attracted him, obtaining a pledge of loyalty to Spain. Although Rajah Lapulapu of Mauthan (Mactan) Island, 2 kilometers east, was refusing to submit, Magellan overconfidently declined military support from Humabon.

Magellan's three galleons anchored at low tide in the northern gulf of Mactan Island early on Sunday morning, 27 April 1521, leaving inland Mactan beyond the firing range of cannons on deck. In lieu of a surprise attack, Magellan sent an envoy on a fruitless mission seeking Lapulapu's obeisance. At daybreak, the Spanish contingent of less than 60 mostly inexperienced volunteers slogged shoreward over reefs. They confronted a crescent formation of 3,000 fighters. Invoking military analogies from Mexico, Magellan injudiciously ordered his forces inland. However, crossbows, muskets, and spears were ineffective against bolos, shields, longer iron-tipped bamboo lances, and poisoned arrows. Squeezed on two sides, the volunteer force retreated—first with discipline and then in disorder. In the hour-long rout, 7 Europeans and 15 Mactan Islanders were killed. Covering his unit's retreat in hand-to-hand fighting, Magellan perished.

Circumnavigating the globe, 18 survivors returned to Spain in 1522. Lapulapu's victory simply delayed Spanish colonization. In 1564, Spain returned to stay for 334 years.

Vincent Kelly Pollard

See also: Spanish Colonial Wars; Spanish-Portuguese Wars

References and further reading:

Joyner, Jim. *Magellan.* Camden, ME: International Marine, 1992.

Pigafetta, Antonio. *The Voyage of Magellan: The Journal of Antonio Pigafetta.* A translation by Paula Spurlin Paige from the edition in the William L. Clements Library, University of Michigan, Ann Arbor. First published, 1536. Englewood Cliffs, NJ: Prentice-Hall, 1969.

Spate, Oskar Hermann Khristian. *The Spanish Lake. The Pacific since Magellan.* Vol. 1. Canberra: Griffin Press for the Australian National University Press, 1979.

Transylvanus, Maximilianus. *De Moluccis Insulis* (Of the Moluccas Islands). Cologne, 1523. In *Documentary Sources of Philippine History,* comp. and ed. Gregorio F. Zaide. Manila: National Book Store, 1990, Vol. 1, Doc. 20.

Maczek, Stanislaw (1892–1994)

Polish World War II commander and the last surviving senior Allied general officer of World War II. Born in Szczerzec in Austro-Hungarian-occupied Poland on 31 March 1892, Maczek served in the Austro-Hungarian army during World War I. After active service during the Russo-Polish War of 1919–1921 and as an infantry officer during most of the interwar period, he commanded the 10th Motorized Mounted Rifle Regiment during the Polish campaign of 1939. Though his regiment, which was one of only two tank regiments in the Polish army, particularly distinguished itself against the Germans, it was overwhelmed by the vastly superior quantity and quality of German armor and was forced to seek refuge in Hungary. Promoted to major general, Maczek was reunited with many of his men in France, where he commanded the 10th Polish Mechanized Cavalry Brigade during the French campaign of 1940. Again forced into exile, he and his men eventually found their way to Scotland, where they formed the 1st Polish Armored Division. As part of the First Canadian Army, the 1st Armored fought its way across northern Europe after the Normandy invasion. During the Battle of the Falaise Gap in August 1944, it was Maczek and the 1st Armored that closed the "pocket" and prevented tens of thousands of German troops from escaping. Promoted to lieutenant general in May 1945, Maczek refused to return to Soviet-dominated Poland after the war and lived out his exile in Scotland. He was promoted to full general by Polish president Lech Walesa in March 1994 and died in Edinburgh on 11 December 1994, the only senior Polish World War II commander to witness the fall of the Soviet Union and of European communism.

Alexander M. Bielakowski

See also: Polish Campaign of 1939; Russo-Polish War; Sikorski, Wladyslaw Eugeniusz; World War II

References and further reading:

Keegan, John. *Six Armies in Normandy: From D-Day to the Liberation of Paris, June 6th–August 25th, 1944.* New York: Viking Press, 1982.

Stachura, Peter D., ed. *Themes of Modern Polish History—Proceedings of a Symposium on 28 March 1992 in Honor of the Centenary of General Stanislaw Maczek.* Glasgow: Polish Social and Educational Society, 1992.

Magdeburg, Siege of (1630–1631)

A symbol of the fury of the Thirty Years' War. Magdeburg was the first imperial town (Reichsstadt) to enter an alliance with the Swedish king on 1 August 1630. Thus the town became an enemy of the Habsburg emperor, but it did not become the center of the operations at that time because the main imperial army, commanded by Johann Tserclaes, Graf von Tilly, advanced to Pomerania to fight Gustavus Adolphus. As the Swedish king avoided a battle, Tilly turned his whole army against Magdeburg at the end of March 1631.

Now the siege became part of a war of diversion. Tilly intended to force Gustavus Adolphus to relieve his ally, who himself tried to distract the imperial army by advancing along the Oder River and posing a threat to the Habsburgian provinces of Silesia and even Bohemia. Ignoring this advance, Tilly reinforced his efforts in besieging the town instead, but the Magdeburgians relied on the Swedish promise to relieve the town and did not surrender. After several attempts, a general assault on 20 May 1631 was successful. In the course of fighting, a fire broke out and reduced almost the whole town to ashes, killing not only most of its inhabitants but also many of the invading imperial soldiers.

The question of who started the fire still remains unclear. Undoubtedly, the devastated town was of less worth for Tilly, who failed to gain a logistic stronghold for his campaign against Gustavus Adolphus. To the Swedish king, the fall of

Magdeburg served to damage his reputation as protector of the German Protestants, so massive Protestant propaganda (mostly by broadsheets) put the blame on the victorious Tilly.

Michael Kaiser

See also: Gustavus II Adolphus; Thirty Years' War; Tilly, Johann Tserclaes, Graf von

References and further reading:

Kaiser, Michael. *Politik und Kriegführung: Maximilian von Bayern, Tilly und die Katholische Liga im Dreißigjährigen Krieg.* Münster: Aschendorff, 1999.

Roberts, Michael. *Gustavus Adolphus: A History of Sweden 1611–1632.* 2 vols. London: Longmans, Green, 1953, 1958.

Magersfontein, Battle of (11 December 1899)

Second British defeat of "Black Week." In the opening months of the Boer War, Redvers Buller ordered Lord Paul Sanford Methuen to relieve the beleaguered garrison at Kimberley and remove all noncombatants. Methuen proceeded northward along the Western Railway to safeguard his supply line and to ensure the integrity of his only means of evacuating the civilian population. Anticipating the British strategy, the Boers positioned themselves along the railway. In late November, Methuen's force defeated the Boers in three successive battles at Belmont, Graspan, and Modder River.

On 10 December, British artillery opened fire upon Boer entrenchments at Magersfontein. Methuen ordered a night march, to be followed by a frontal attack. Despite heavy rain and poor reconnaissance, British troops managed to reach their destination, a few hundred yards from the Boer trenches. Orders to extend, however, came too late. Daybreak caught the advancing infantry in tight formation. Boer firepower left the brigade in a confused mass scrambling for cover. All attempts to reform and renew the advance failed. The British were forced to withdraw by late afternoon.

In 1899, no British soldier had ever come across such an elaborate design of trenches as those constructed at Magersfontein. British artillery failed to disturb them. British casualties approached 1,000; Boer casualties, 275. The failure at Magersfontein, one of three British defeats that week, demonstrated that the British army was not ready for modern warfare and led to major changes in leadership, mobilization, and organization.

Stephen M. Miller

See also: Boer Wars; Buller, Sir Redvers Henry; Kimberley, Siege of

References and further reading:

Duxbury, George. *The Battle of Magersfontein.* Johannesburg: National Museum of Military History, 1979.

Miller, Stephen M. *Lord Methuen and the British Army.* London: Cass, 1999.

Pemberton, W. Baring. *Battles of the Boer War.* Philadelphia: Dufour Editions, 1964.

Maginot Line

An extensive series of border fortifications that failed France in 1940. At the end of World War I, the dominant school of thought in the French army emphasized the value of a defensive stance in warfare. Based on experience from the early phase of the war, when frontal attacks against machine guns caused massive casualties, and the experience acquired at Verdun, the French general staff favored the option of "digging in" as a means to hold off the enemy while limiting losses. In addition, in the event of surprise attack, a massive fortification would gain the French army some valuable time as it assembled its forces. Throughout the 1920s, the French General Staff argued about what the best defensive attitude was and where to build fortifications. Eventually, the focus fell on the relatively flat area that extended from the Ardennes to Alsace. In this context, politician André Maginot came to oversee the design and construction of a defensive line that bore his name. As war minister from 1922 to 1924 (and again in 1929), he remained involved in the planning as the head of the Parliamentary Armament Committee. In 1927, the basic design was approved, and Paul Painlevé, then minister of war, authorized the call for bids. Private contractors built the Maginot line. The reason for naming it Maginot rather than Painlevé goes back to the level of involvement of the former and his successful lobbying of the French parliament to allocate funds at a time when Germany, prior to Adolf Hitler's takeover, was not considered an immediate threat to French security. By the time the Maginot line was built, it had cost twice the original estimate, exceeding 6 billion French francs at the time.

The design of the Maginot line posed several challenges to engineers, and no two forts (also known as *ouvrages*) were the same because of terrain and communication constraints. In addition, drainage was a constant worry, and several modifications were required in the 1930s to make the installations livable. Common to all forts were the garrison personnel, ranging from 200 to 1,200 men and divided into infantry, artillery, and engineering sections. The layout followed the same structure everywhere, with living quarters at the bottom of the installation, a railroad that brought supplies to a narrow-gauge network that linked forts, and a diesel-powered generating facility to supply electricity in times of war (in peacetime, the French national power grid fed the entire Maginot line). Armament was also standard to all installations and involved modern cannons, some specially modified to fit in the forts alone. Construction began in late 1929, and in 1936 the line was first used on the occasion of Hitler's military occupation of the Rhineland. Some installations were added later, but limited funding and wavering political will made them no more than perfunctory complements, especially near the English Channel.

Divided into sectors, the Maginot line was placed on war alert on 24 August 1939, nine days ahead of the general mobilization order. However, the state of war was not confirmed until 6 September, and garrison commanders were ordered to fire on the enemy only in case of incursion on French territory. The subsequent "Phony War" lasted until May 1940, when the German army invaded Belgium and circumvented the Maginot line. Germany's striking success encouraged the implementation of Operation ROT (red), whereby the Germans began testing the Maginot line's defenses. Although some sections held up extremely well against 88 mm cannon, turrets and other mobile steel gear were often damaged. The greatest weakness of the line was that even though the heavy cement foundations facing the border were further protected by earth, the rear was not, which made rear assaults easier. Several forts, however, held until the Armistice. Morale all along the line remained excellent by most accounts, and the Maginot cannons ceased firing only on 24 June 1940. Five days later, the men left their quarters and were made prisoners of war, even though they should have, in theory, been allowed to join French troops in the Free (Vichy) zone under the terms of the cease-fire.

German and American troops made sporadic use of the installations until 1944, after which the French army took over and maintained part of the installations for another 20 years. Since then, much of the Maginot line has been auctioned off to civilian businesses, from mushroom farms to dance clubs. The Maginot Line remains as a literal monument to unimaginative military thinking.

Guillaume de Syon

See also: France; French Army, Verdun, World War I, World War II

References and further reading:

Alexander, Martin. *The Republic in Danger: Gen. Maurice Gamelin and the Politics of French Defense.* 1992.

Chelminski, R. "The Maginot Line." *Smithsonian* (June 1997).

Hughes, Judith M. *To the Maginot Line: The Politics of French Military Preparation in the 1920s.* Cambridge: Harvard University Press, 1971.

Kemp, Anthony. *The Maginot Line: Myth and Reality.* New York: Stein and Day, 1982.

Mary, Jean-Yves, and Alain Hohnadel. *Hommes et ouvrages de la Ligne Maginot.* Vol. 1. Paris: Histoire & Collections, 2000.

Young, Robert M. *In Command of France: French Foreign Policy and Military Planning, 1933–1940.* Cambridge: Harvard University Press, 1978.

Magsaysay, Ramón (1907–1957)

Philippine guerrilla, counterinsurgency leader, and later president. Magsaysay was born into a poor rural family in 1907 in Zambales Province. After a brief career in business, he became a noted guerrilla leader when the Japanese invaded the Philippines in 1941. Later, appointed secretary of national defense, he was faced from the outset with the problem of putting down the Hukbalahap, a peasant guerrilla movement that by 1953 had been penetrated by left-wing cadres. He initiated a three-pronged program. Corrupt and inefficient officers and soldiers were removed; a ground-up development program in Hukbalahap areas was initiated to deny the guerrillas local support, and guerrillas who surrendered were given land grants (land hunger was supposedly the main reason for the Huk revolt) and an amnesty. By 1955, when Magsaysay had been elected president, the Huk rebellion had faded to a small hard-core group of communist cadres. Magsaysay himself died in office on 17 March 1957 in a plane crash.

Portrait of Ramón Magsaysay. (Library of Congress)

Magsaysay's success can be attributed to two main factors. In an environment rife with corruption, he was one of the few seen as uncorrupt. Second, as both secretary of national defense and later as president, he managed to inspire support from line soldiers and civilians by leading from the front, personally supervising operations, and demonstrating concern and an aptitude for leadership.

Magsaysay also oversaw a number of military innovations in his counterinsurgency campaign. Small units with overwhelming firepower were used to track down guerrilla groups. Heightened real-time intelligence identified and tracked guerrilla leaders and groups, as did the extensive use of bribed and "turned" informants from among guerrilla ranks themselves. Psychological warfare was deployed extensively to convince the Huks that they were on the losing side. Many of these tactics were absorbed by the U.S. Army in Vietnam. Magsaysay's death was a disaster for the Philippines, for much of his good work was undone, and persisting Marxist guerrilla war sprang up anew beginning in the 1960s.

Michael Ashkenazi

See also: Guerrilla/Partisan/Irregular Warfare; Vietnam Conflict

References and further reading:

Abueva, Jose Veloso. *Ramon Magsaysay. A Political Biography.* Manila: Solidaridad Publishing House, 1971.

Starner, Frances Lucille. *Magsaysay and the Philippine Peasantry. The Agrarian Impact on Philippine Politics, 1953–1956.* Berkeley: University of California Press, 1961.

Magyars

Seminomadic tribes, originally from western Siberia, that conquered the middle Danube and raided western Europe in the ninth and tenth centuries. The Magyars were the last invading people to establish a permanent presence in central Europe.

After destroying the Moravian state (902) and defeating the Bavarians at Breclavsburg (907), the Magyars established themselves in Pannonia. From this base, they raided neighboring lands, extorting tribute. Their armies, consisting mostly of light cavalry, were highly mobile. Attacking without warning, they quickly plundered the countryside and departed before any defensive force could be organized. If forced to fight, they would harass their enemies with arrows or suddenly retreat, tempting their opponents to break rank and pursue, after which the Magyars would turn to fight them singly. After 937, the Magyars began to range ever farther, across Germany and France and into Italy. The raids finally ended after emperor Otto I defeated the Magyars at the Lechfeld, near Augsburg (955). In the following centuries, the Magyars settled down in Hungary and adopted western European forms of feudal military organization, including the predominant use of heavy armored cavalry. The light cavalry tradition was partly revived through the settlement of nomadic Cuman tribes in southern Hungary in the thirteenth century, the employment of Serb mercenaries in the fifteenth century, and finally in the evolution of Hungarian *huszar* light cavalry in the sixteenth and seventeenth centuries, which served as the model for the later appearance of hussar units in western European armies.

Brian Hodson

See also: Lechfeld

References and further reading:

Macartney, C. A. *The Magyars of the IXth Century.* Cambridge, UK: Cambridge University Press, 1930.

Makkai, László. "The Hungarians' Prehistory, Their Conquest of Hungary, and Their Raids to the West to 955." In *A History of Hungary,* ed. Peter Sugar. Bloomington: University of Indiana Press, 1990.

Mahan, Dennis Hart (1802–1871)

American educator whose theories and insights had a great influence on American military strategists in both the Mexican War and the Civil War. Born in New York City on 2 April 1802, Mahan spent his childhood in Norfolk, Virginia. A gifted student and protégé of Sylvanus Thayer, he graduated from the top of his class at the U.S. Military Academy at West Point in 1824 and was named assistant professor of mathematics in his third year at the institution. A year after graduation, Second Lieutenant Mahan was transferred to the position of assistant professor of engineering. He then went abroad to study public engineering work and military institutions at the Military School of Application for Engineers and Artillerists in Metz, France, and was befriended by the Marquis de Lafayette. Returning to West Point in 1830, he was named professor of engineering and was promoted to chairman of the department two years later. In 1838, he was also named to the position of dean. He committed suicide on 16 September 1871 in Stony Point, New York, when he learned that he was going to be forced into retirement by an overseeing board. He was the father of Alfred Thayer Mahan.

Among Mahan's most important works are *Complete Treatise on Field Fortifications* (1836), *Summary on the Cause of Permanent Fortifications and the Attack and Defense of Permanent Works* (1850), and *An Elementary Course of Military Engineering* (2 vols., 1866–1867). He exposed cadets to the principles of Antoine Henri, Baron de Jomini.

According to student Henry Wager Halleck, Mahan stressed that war should be looked at as both an art and a science; a science as it analyzes general principles and military operations and an art when referring to the practical rules of conducting campaigns, sieges, battles, and so on.

T. Jason Soderstrum

See also: Jomini, Antoine Henri, Baron de; Thayer, Sylvanus

References and further reading:

Mahan, Dennis Hart. *Descriptive Geometry: As Applied to the Drawing of Fortification and Stereotomy: For the Use of the Cadets of the U.S. Military.* New York: J. Wiley & Sons, 1871.

———. *An Elementary Course of Civil Engineering.* Edinburgh: A. Fullarton, 1845.

Weigley, Russell F. *The American Way of War: A History of United States Military Strategy and Policy.* New York: Macmillan, 1973.

Mahmud of Ghazna (Yamin al-Daula Abu'l-Qasim Mahmud ibn Sebuktigin) (971–1030)

Founder of the medieval Ghaznavid dynasty, his conquests made the Turkish people and the Islamic faith a part of Indian civilization. Sebuktigin, Mahmud's father, held command of Ghazna, a military camp town in eastern Afghanistan. By the time Mahmud reached maturity, Ghazna had become virtually independent of Iran. Quickly proving himself an adept commander, he established himself as emir in 998 after a brief war with his brother Isma'il. At that time, the Samanid government of Iran was crumbling, and in the scramble for the pieces, Mahmud also annexed the northern territories of Khurasan. A rich and desirable province, Mahmud had to return repeatedly to Khurasan to defend his northern frontier from Turkish interlopers like the Kharakhanids.

Mahmud inherited from his father the practice of conducting annual raids into the Indus valley. A strict Sunni Muslim, he believed that these raids not only filled his treasury with loot but also served as jihad against infidel Hindus, Buddhists, and Shiite Muslim cities. Mahmud made his capital a rich center of Islamic culture but also invested large sums into organizing his state and army. He supplemented his Arab, Turkish, and Afghan units with Hindu infantry and elephants. The sultan's wars, wealth, and militancy also magnetized thousands of Turkish plainsmen to his standard.

Mahmud conducted over 17 campaigns in northeastern and central India and jihads against the Shiite Buyid state in central Iran. He imposed a unified Islamic regime over most of the northern Indus valley. In 1024, Mahmud marched across the Thar wastelands and plundered the great Hindu center at Somnath. Under Mahmud, Islam penetrated for the first time onto the Ganges plains. At his death, the sultan was contemplating the annexation of Iraq and a jihad against the Fatimid Shiites in Syria.

Weston F. Cook, Jr.

See also: Ghaznavid Empire

References and further reading:

Bosworth, C. E. *The Ghaznavids.* Edinburgh: Cambridge University Press, 1963.

Wink, Andre. *Al-Hind: The Making of the Indo-Islamic World.* Vol. 1. Leiden: E. J. Brill, 1991.

Majorian (Julius Valerius Majorianus) (d. 461)

Emperor of the western Roman Empire from 1 April 457 to 2 August 461. The date of his birth is unknown; he was executed on 7 August 461 at Dertona (Tortona, Italy). After a distinguished early military career, Majorian was appointed *comes domesticorum* (roughly, commander of the imperial bodyguard). In league with the Suevian commander Ricimer, he defeated the western emperor Avitus at Placentia (Piacenza, Italy) on 17 October 456. Subsequently promoted to *magister militum,* Majorian was acclaimed emperor by his troops; formal recognition from the eastern empire came on 1 December 457.

As emperor, Majorian ambitiously sought to strengthen the western empire by reintegrating with it former Roman territories in Gaul and North Africa. In Europe, he campaigned successfully against Huns, Vandals, Goths, and Alamanni and subdued Gallic rebels. In 460 and 461, he launched two expeditions intended to expel the Vandals from Africa but in both cases was defeated, the last before his transports left Nova Carthago (Cartagena, Spain). He initiated tax reforms and was admired greatly by Sidonius Apollinaris, bishop of Lyons, France. In 461, Ricimer, his erstwhile ally, deposed Majorian.

Ian Janssen

See also: Goths; Huns; Vandals

References and further reading:

Jones, A. H. M. *The Later Roman Empire, 284–602.* 2 vols. Baltimore: Johns Hopkins University Press, 1986.

Malayan Emergency (1948–1960)

An insurgency inspired by and modeled on Mao Zedong's success in China. The dates are misleading: emergency restrictions remained in several areas after 1960, and the communists remained in the field in southern Thailand until 1990. Nonetheless, by 1960 communist guerrillas had been reduced to a futile and ineffective existence.

British success in Malaya was largely the result of four factors. Perhaps the most important was the fact that at no stage did the government collapse in any part of Malaya: the British never faced the problem of creating government where none existed. Moreover, Malayan society was racially divided. With the communist movement overwhelmingly drawn from the Chinese population (physically, readily identifiable) the counterinsurgency effort could be focused on just one section of society. Furthermore, physical geography limited insurgency to no more than one-tenth of the country. The interior was all but uninhabited, and the Chinese were scattered along the jungle fringe where it met the main north-south roads. Britain never had a major numbers-to-space problem, and the fact that Malaya was a peninsula ensured the communists' isolation from outside support.

There were other factors. The uprising of 1947 miscarried and cost the communist movement some 6–12 months as it tried to recover from failure and initiate rural-based insurgency. Failure provided the British administration with breathing space, and over time, four strands of policy were bound together: the streamlining of all levels of government in order to ensure speed and implement decisions; the principle of civilian supremacy, specifically the primacy of the police, with the military assigned the supporting role; a comprehensive resettlement program as the means of isolating the insurgents from all sources of supply; and the policy of tackling the least affected areas first. Results were slow in manifesting themselves, and resettlement made the communist task of infiltration easier, but the long-term effectiveness of resettlement can be seen by the fact that only 2 of some 400 new villages were abandoned after 1960. The policy of providing the population with something to lose, which included independence, with the communists portrayed as the obstacle to its being granted, was underwritten by boom conditions in tin and rubber prices, but the basic point was that the main features of the Briggs Plan—integrated government structure, civilian primacy, and the new villages—worked in the very special conditions of Malaya at this time. It should also be noted that the British did not send National Servicemen (conscripts) to Malaya; all were professionals who either knew their jobs or were willing to learn them in good time.

Of course, British strategy and policy may seem obvious, even easy in hindsight, but at the time it was felt that the struggle could go either way, particularly after the assassination of the high commissioner, Sir Henry Gurney, in 1951.

H. P. Willmott

See also: Guerrilla/Partisan/Irregular Warfare

References and further reading:

Coates, John. *Suppressing Insurgency: An Analysis of the Malayan Emergency.* Boulder, CO: Westview, 1993.

Jackson, Robert, *The Malayan Emergency: The Commonwealth Wars 1948–1966,* London: Routledge, 1991.

MacKay, Donald. *The Malayan Emergency, 1948–1960. The Domino That Stood.* London: Brassey's, 1997.

Stubbs, Richard. *Hearts and Minds in Guerrilla Warfare.* Oxford, UK: Oxford University Press, 1990.

Maldon, Battle of (10–11 August 991)

Brave Saxon defense that failed to prevent Viking inroads. After nearly half a century of relative stability, Anglo-Saxon England was unprepared for a new wave of Viking invasions beginning in 991. Danish king Swein Forkbeard led several expeditions along the southern half of England; the English king Ethelred, consequently nicknamed "the Unready," was on the defensive. Maldon, located about 12 miles north of the mouth of the Thames River, near the east coast of England, was the site of one of the initial battles between the Anglo-Saxons and the invading Danes. We know about the Battle of Maldon because of the near-contemporary poem, of which most has been preserved.

The Danes had ravaged the town of Ipswich, and the Anglo-Saxon ealdorman Byrhtnoth prepared to engage them along the coast of Essex in August 991. Byrhtnoth and his local shire force, the *fyrd,* allowed the Danes to land near Maldon in order to incite them to pitched battle. The Anglo-Saxons formed "shield-walls," cohesive though mobile formations of troops, and used spears and shields to hold the Danes in check. Byrhtnoth, an ealdorman for 35 years, was portrayed as the brave leader in the poem, rallying his troops for battle. Only after his death did many of the Anglo-Saxons retreat. Three years after the battle, Ethelred was forced to make payments to the Danes as appeasement. In 1016, new Viking invasions culminated with the Danish king Cnut succeeding Ethelred's son, Edmund, as king of England.

Christopher P. Goedert

See also: British Dynastic Wars; Viking Raids; Vikings; William the Conqueror

References and further reading:

Cooper, Janet, ed. *The Battle of Maldon: Fiction and Fact.* London: Hambledon Press, 1993.

Laborde, Edward D. *Byrhtnoth and Maldon.* London: Heinemann, 1936.

Scragg, Donald, ed. *The Battle of Maldon, A.D. 991.* Oxford: Basil Blackwell in association with the Manchester Centre for Anglo-Saxon Studies, 1991.

Malplaquet, Battle of (11 September 1709)

The duke of Marlborough's last and most useless battle. After a long series of victories (Ramillies, Oudenaarde), the allied armies intended to destroy the French army and then invade France. The French main army was south of Mons, waiting behind field fortifications near the woods of Malplaquet. Marlborough and Prince Eugene, with their 7,500 men, intended to use the same tactical dispositions they had used formerly for Bleinheim and Ramillies, a straightforward advance on the enemy lines. The duc de Villars, commanding the French, had taken a defensive position, protected on his two wings by occupied forests forming a funnel-shaped line. The center was on higher grounds and the fortifications were defended by his elite regiments.

The first shots were fired at 7:30 A.M. on the French left wing by Eugene's troops; the wood of Sars was taken at 11:00, but the winning troops were too exhausted to follow the reforming French. The French right was attacked by Dutch troops, who were repulsed; the French commander was too cautious to give orders to pursue the hesitating Dutch. Villars had reinforced the wings from his well-defended center when no attack had been launched by noon. He wanted now to attack and gathered 50 battalions, but the British artillery covered the French front with a deadly fire. Two events turned the tide of the battle: Villars was wounded and taken away from the battlefield, and Marlborough and Eugene, seeing the weakened French center, launched a decisive attack. The fortifications were assaulted at a terrible human cost. Boufllers, now in command, ordered his cavalry to charge against the emerging infantry around 1:00 P.M., and six futile charges ensued. The French then decided to retire in good order, while the allies were too exhausted to pursue.

Malplaquet was the bloodiest battle of the eighteenth century, with no fewer than 11,000 killed and 22,000 wounded. The allied casualties were higher than those the French suffered; they were unable to follow their invasion plan. Malplaquet was seen as a glorious defeat in France and raised the fighting spirit of the army. Conversely, this dubious victory gave Marlborough's court enemies an argument to undermine Marlborough's position, and he was recalled in 1711.

Gilles Boué

See also: Denain, Battle of; Marlborough, John Churchill, First Duke of; Spanish Succession, War of the

References and further reading:

Corvisier, André. *La bataille de Malplaquet.* Paris: Economica, 1997.
Wijn, Jan W. "Les troupes hollandaises à la bataille de Malplaquet." *Revue Internationale d'Histoire Militaire* 19 (1957), 334–379.

Malta, Siege of (May–September 1565)

A defeat that blocked Turkish expansion to the west. The Ottoman emperor Süleyman, determined to seize Malta, the strategic gateway to the West, assembled nearly 30,000 men, including Janissaries and Spahis. The formidable Turkish artillery included specially made heavy artillery. One piece weighed nearly 40 tons and fired 200-pound balls. Two other pieces weighing nearly 20 tons each could fire 90-pound iron balls. The Turks also brought with them 100,000 cannonballs and 170,000 tons of powder.

These overwhelming odds could hardly be matched by Malta's 500 knights, around 5,000 Spanish soldiers, and approximately 4,000 other troops. The knights were led by Grand Master Giovanni Parisot de la Valette, who was able to strengthen Malta's fortifications before the Turkish onslaught. The knights also created a new weapon. After wrapping a circular iron band in tow, placing it in boiling pitch, and wrapping it with tow again, they lit the device and threw it at Turks scaling the fortifications. The knights also used entrenchments to stop the Turks.

The Turks began the bombardment of Saint Elmo on 10 June. Despite the death of their leader, Dragut, the governor of Tripoli, the Turks took the fortress. During the course of the siege, the fierce resistance by the knights caused the deaths of more than 24,000 Turks. Süleyman sent an additional 20,000 reinforcements, and by August Malta was nearing the end of its resistance. But the "Great Relief Force" of around 9,000 men led by Garcia de Toledo reached Mellieha Bay and refortified Malta's defenses on 7 September. Frustrated, the Turks began to evacuate Malta the following day.

Annette Richardson

See also: Süleyman I

References and further reading:

Blouet, Brian. *The Story of Malta.* Malta: Progress Press, 1993.
Ellul, Joseph. *The Great Siege of Malta.* Siggiewi, Malta: Ellul, 1992.
Sire, H. J. A. *The Knights of Malta.* New Haven: Yale University Press, 1994.

Malta, Siege of (June 1940–November 1942)

German siege of British-held island, the failure of which kept open the British supply line to the Middle and Far East. Malta's strategic position in the Mediterranean between Sicily and Libya led to the island's second great siege during World War II.

Italy's declaration of war against Britain brought numerous air raids against the island, for a period defended by only three Gloster Gladiator biplanes and a small assortment of antiaircraft guns. The arrival of German troops in North Africa (February 1941) was accompanied by frequent Luftwaffe attacks against the island and its vital supply convoys. Despite the Axis blockade, Malta's defenses steadily improved throughout the siege, with it becoming a crucial base for surface vessels, submarines, and aircraft to operate against Field Marshall Erwin Rommel's supply lines. An Italian naval attack against Malta by explosive motorboats and "pigs," two-man piloted torpedoes, was repulsed on 15 July 1941, while a renewed Axis air offensive commenced in January of the following year. The sinking of numerous Allied supply ships increased the threat of starvation during the summer of 1942; between March and August, only 7 of 35 merchant ships bound for Malta arrived, with the most urgently needed supplies delivered by submarine.

In recognition of its heroic struggle, Malta was awarded the George Cross in April 1942. A combined German-Italian invasion, Operation HERCULES, was proposed for late June 1942, once Tobruk had been captured, but was postponed after Rommel's decision to strike against Egypt instead. However, the subsequent Axis defeat at El Alamein and lengthy retreat to Tunisia removed the threat of invasion to Malta. Following a final effort to neutralize the embattled island by air in October, Axis bombing raids progressively decreased. An ironic postscript to the siege was the surrender of the Italian fleet in Malta's Grand Harbor on 8 September 1943 (the anniversary of the ending of the Great Siege of 1565) and the awarding of a presidential citation by U.S. president Franklin D. Roosevelt.

David Green

See also: World War II

References and further reading:

Bradford, E. *Siege: Malta 1940–1943.* New York: William Morrow, 1986.

Belfield, E. *Defy and Endure: Great Sieges of Modern History.* New York: Crowell-Collier, 1967.

Mamluks (1000–1600)

Soldiers who controlled the Abbasid Caliphate in Cairo between 1250 and 1517. The origins of the Mamluks lie in the famous regiment of the Abbasid caliph al-Mu'tasim (r. 833–841). They were the backbone of caliphate troops until the destruction of the caliphate at Baghdad in 1258 by the Mongols.

The Mamluks were essentially slaves recruited from the regions of Central Asia and Khorasan. They were a one-generation nobility, and their descendants were not allowed to join the same military aristocracy as their fathers, leading to rampant conflict and unrest. Therefore, in order to ensure the continuity of this aristocracy and to safeguard nomadic vitality, a constant supply of nomadic children was maintained. Furthermore, the persistent effort at investing this aristocracy with a superior status and segregating them from the remaining urban classes had important physical implications. In earlier times, a similar situation had caused the transfer of the Abbasid capital from Baghdad to Samarra and the development of an exclusive residential district. In the era of the Mamluk sultanate's residence in Cairo, it was responsible for the use of the Cairo citadel as segregated residential quarters.

In the complex political history of the Mamluk state, as many as 45 sultans ruled for varying periods of time. In the absence of a system of legitimacy, a sultan's son succeeded him only until another Mamluk gathered enough support to seize the throne. However, some rulers, such as Qalaun (r. 1279–1290), were still able to establish dynasties of continuing rulers. Several others were also able to provide a degree of internal stability and initiate foreign conquests in the course of their short reigns. The success of this system is attested by the important Mamluk victory over the Mongols at 'Ayn Jalut in 1260, which brought Baybars I (r. 1260–1277) into power. Under his leadership, the Mamluks campaigned successfully against the remaining crusader possessions in Palestine and Syria and concluded a truce with the Mongols in 1323 during the long reign of al-Malik an-Nasir (1293–1341).

Egypt continued to dominate eastern Arabdom after Nasir's death in 1341, though the first signs of political and economic decline had already set in. Beginning in 1348, the Black Death repeatedly struck Egypt with large losses. So did Timur's Syrian victory in 1400 and Egypt's loss of control over its Indian trade routes to the Portuguese. The final blow was dealt by the actions of unruly Mamluk corps, which the sultans failed to effectively control. The heyday of the Mamluk sultanate was hence long past when Qait Bay (r. 1468–1496) lost the Syrian Empire to devastating raids by the Turkoman states of Anatolia and Azerbaijan and the campaigns of the Ottoman Turks.

Manu P. Sobti

See also: 'Ayn Jalut, Battle of

References and further reading:

Ayalon, David. "The Muslim City and Mamluk Military Aristocracy." *Journal of Middle Eastern Studies* (1986), 311–329.

———. "Studies on the Structure of the Mamluk Army." *Bulletin of the School of Oriental and African Studies* 15 (1953), 208–228, 448–476; 16 (1954), 57–90.

Rogers, J. M. "Samarra: A Study in Medieval Town Planning," in *The Islamic City: A Colloquium,* ed. R. Stern and A. Hourani. Philadelphia: University of Pennsylvania Press, 1970.

Manchu Expansion, Wars of (1600–1681)

In the sixteenth century, the leader of one of the Jurchen tribes that lived outside the Great Wall in what is now Manchuria, Nurhaci, began to unite the Jurchen people, take on the trappings of a Chinese state, and gather talented Chinese political and military officials around him. In time, he became sufficiently powerful to threaten Ming control over the area outside the Great Wall in the northeast but not to take over China.

Nurhaci created mechanisms of government midway between nomadic rule and the bureaucratic Chinese system. One of his foremost creations was the banner system, in which companies of 300 warriors were grouped under four banners, colored either yellow, white, blue, or red; later, four more banners were added, the first three bordered in red and the last bordered in white. He appointed officers, and the system organized his people for peace and war. By 1644, when the Manchus occupied Beijing, there were 278 Manchu companies, 120 Mongol, and 165 Chinese—making an army of 169,000. Although this was a formidable striking force, it was not large enough to conquer China by itself.

Nurhaci's son, Abahai, sought to build greater power and to threaten the Ming in the north. He attacked Korea in 1627, and in 1636–1637, a renewed attack made Korea a vassal state of the Manchus. Abahai led his warriors through the Great Wall at least on three major occasions (1629, 1632, and 1634) and gained control of nearly all the areas to the north and northeast of the wall. To strengthen his appeal to those Chinese discouraged by the weaknesses and excesses of the Ming regime, he renamed his dynasty Qing, or "pure," and encouraged Chinese "defectors" where it would aid his effort.

The Qing victory owed a great deal to the efforts of a Ming general, Wu San-gui. Wu was called to the capital to help defend the dynasty against a Chinese rebel but arrived too late and turned to the Manchus for help in restoring control over these internal rebels. Wu allowed the Manchu banners to pass through the Great Wall unhindered and to gain control of Beijing; his armies worked with Manchu armies to defeat various rebel groups and local warlords. For more than 30 years, Wu worked with the Manchus to extend their control over the whole of China.

It appeared that Wu accumulated personal power in southern China as he helped the Manchus gain control over the whole country, and in time he revolted. He set himself up as a regional warlord of a sort, and with two fellow warlords, he rebelled in 1673. It would take the great-grandson of Nurhaci, the Kang-xi emperor, eight years to end this rebellion and to gain control over continental China proper.

However, the new Qing dynasty would continue to battle to extend its power over territory typically controlled by other expansive Chinese dynasties. Thus, the Manchus seized control of Chinese coastal areas opposite Taiwan, and the local warlord, Guo Xing-ye, fled to Taiwan, which he temporarily seized from the Dutch. The Dutch helped the Manchus gain control over Taiwan in 1683. Meanwhile, the Qing dynasty would take well into the eighteenth century to establish control over Tibet and over what is now western China and independent Mongolia, an area of traditional Chinese interest.

Charles M. Dobbs

See also: Nurhaci

References and further reading:

Chan, Albert. *The Glory and Fall of the Ming Dynasty.* Norman: University of Oklahoma Press, 1982.

Parson, James Bunyan. *The Peasant Rebellions of the Late Ming Dynasty.* Tucson: University of Arizona Press, 1970.

Rossabi, Morris. *The Jurchens in the Yuan and Ming.* Ithaca, NY: Cornell University Press, 1982.

Spence, Jonathan D., and John E. Wills Jr., eds. *From Ming to Ch'ing: Conquest, Region and Continuity in Seventeenth Century China.* New Haven: Yale University Press, 1979.

Mannerheim, Carl Gustaf Emil (1867–1951)

Finnish military leader and statesman. Mannerheim was born on 4 June 1867 in Louhisaari, Finland, to a noble family. He first studied unsuccessfully at the Hamina Cadet School (1882–1886) and then graduated from a private school in 1887. He completed his military training at the Nicholas Cavalry School in St. Petersburg (1887–1889). Mannerheim served in the Russian imperial army, making his way through the officer ranks and participating in the Russo-Japanese War (1904–1905).

During the initial years of World War I, Mannerheim was initially commander of a cavalry brigade and of a cavalry division in Poland and Galicia and then commander of a cavalry corps in 1917. He resigned his commission on 1 January 1918. In mid-January 1918, as a firm anticommunist, he took over the leadership of the Finnish White Guard. He was awarded the rank of general during his victorious command in the Finnish Civil War but was compelled to resign in May 1918. After Germany's defeat in November 1918, he was elected regent of Finland (1918–1919). He returned to Finnish military decisionmaking in the 1930s as the chairman of the Defense Council (1931–1939) and was promoted to the rank of field marshal in 1933.

In the Winter War with the USSR (1939–1940) and the Continuation War with Germany (1941–1944), Mannerheim was the commander in chief of the Finnish armed forces. He was awarded the title of marshal of Finland in 1942. It may well be that the stout Finnish resistance to Soviet demands induced Stalin, who respected only force and power, to refrain from making Finland another Soviet satellite. Finland would enjoy national independence, although it was always wary of offending its giant neighbor. Much of the credit for Finnish national survival therefore must go to Mannerheim.

After the wars, with Finland having to agree to harsh peace terms with the Soviet Union, Mannerheim was elected president (1944–1946) to steer the country toward peace. During the war crimes trials (1945–1946), which were meant to satisfy the Allies' demands to assign responsibility for the Continuation War, the possibility of his prosecution undermined his position. He resigned in March 1946, exhausted by illness. Mannerheim died on 28 January1951 in Lausanne, Switzerland.

Jari Eloranta

See also: Finnish Civil War; Mukden, Battle of; Russo-Finnish Wars; Russo-Japanese War; World War I

References and further reading:

"C. G. E. Mannerheim," http://www.mannerheim.fi.
Jägerskiöld, Stig. *Mannerheim: Marshal of Finland.* London: Hurst, 1986.
Mannerheim, Carl Gustaf Emil. *Muistelmat,* Part 1. Helsinki: Otava, 1951.
———. *Muistelmat,* Part 2. Helsinki: Otava, 1952.

Field Marshal von Manstein on an inspection tour in Russia, c. 1941. (Library of Congress)

Manstein, Fritz Erich von (1887–1973)

The most brilliant German strategist of World War II was born 24 November 1887 at Berlin as "von Lewinski" and was adopted by his aunt. Following family tradition, he joined a military college, becoming a lieutenant in 1907. After service in staff positions from 1914 to 1918, he entered the post-Armistice Reichswehr and made his way up (deputy chief of the general staff 1937–1938) but was removed to take over a division. When during the winter of 1939–1940 Germany prepared to attack France, Manstein managed to impress Adolf Hitler with his own plan of operations (attack through the Ardennes mountains). Hitler took Manstein's suggestions, and France surrendered within six weeks.

Considered a military genius, Manstein received higher commands in the Russian campaign (Eleventh Army from September 1941 onward). Being fully aware of the mass murders carried out by SS units, Manstein issued an order excusing harsh measures against Jews. After the conquest of the Crimean peninsula, he was promoted to field marshal on 1 July 1942. Beginning in the autumn of 1942, he commanded Army Group Don, trying in vain to relieve the Sixth Army at Stalingrad. He refused to order a withdrawal without Hitler's consent. After the disaster, Manstein managed to stabilize the southern part of the eastern front, but Hitler ignored his suggestions for a reorganization of defenses to allow flexible tactics under Manstein as supreme commander in the east. After several quarrels and Manstein's disregard of Hitler's "stand fast" orders, Manstein was dismissed 30 March 1944 but continued to hope for a comeback until the final surrender.

Manstein repeatedly refused to join military resistance circles but kept silent about contacts with conspirators. A witness during the Nuremberg trials, he stood accused in 1949 of the killing of civilians and commissars. His trial received worldwide attention: Winston Churchill, Bernard Montgomery, and others intervened for Manstein, who nonetheless was sentenced to 18 years' imprisonment but was released four years later. He acted as an adviser for the reestablished German army and in his memoirs blamed Hitler for "lost victories." He died 10 June 1973 at Irschenhausen, near Munich.

Although his strategic abilities are undisputed, Manstein's critics focused on his tolerance for, if not support of, war crimes in Russia and his unwillingness to act against Hitler. He despised the dictator but stayed loyal to him, refusing to draw political conclusions from military developments.

Martin Moll

See also: France; Hitler, Adolf; Stalingrad

References and further reading:

Manstein, Erich von. *Verlorene Siege.* Bonn: Athenäum, 1958.

Smelser, Ronald, Enrico Syring, eds. *Die Militärelite des Dritten Reiches: 27 biographische Skizzen.* Frankfurt am Main: Ullstein, 1995.

Mansûrah, Battle of (November 1249)

Pivotal battle of King Louis IX's (Saint Louis) crusade in Egypt. After wintering in Cyprus, King Louis marshaled his army of approximately 20,000 men and sailed for Egypt in May 1249. Despite attempts by the army of Sultan al-Salih to prevent a landing, the crusaders successfully captured Damietta. On 20 November 1249, King Louis began an advance southward along the Nile toward Mansûrah.

Arriving before Mansûrah in December, the crusaders found their army wedged between the Nile and a tributary. Louis intended to cross the tributary and strike Mansûrah from the rear, but it was not until 8 February 1250 that the army's vanguard successfully forced a crossing. Led by Robert d'Artois, Louis's brother, the crusaders crossed the river, attacked the Egyptian camp, and killed the Muslim commander, Fakhr al-Dîn ibn al-Shaykh. Emboldened by his success, Robert d'Artois then advanced into the city of Mansûrah rather than waiting for reinforcements.

The narrow streets of Mansûrah became a gauntlet for Robert's knights as arrows, stones, and tiles hailed down upon them from the rooftops. An Egyptian counterattack led by the Mamluks, the sultan's military slaves, annihilated the survivors. When King Louis and the main army later attempted to cross the river, they met stiff resistance from the reinvigorated Egyptians.

With the crusaders' forward advance thwarted, Muslim forces increased pressure on King Louis's army by harrying its supply lines. Disease also struck the Christian camp, leaving King Louis himself with dysentery. In March, the crusaders had no choice but to fall back on Damietta but were subject to constant attack along the way. Finally, on 6 April 1250, King Louis surrendered and offered himself as a hostage. The crusaders were too enfeebled to resist or renew the offensive. The invasion of Egypt ended with the exchange of King Louis for the city of Damietta and the ransoming of his army.

Timothy May

See also: Arsuf, Battle of; 'Ayn Jalut, Battle of; Crusades; Hattin, Battle of; Mamluk; Saladin

References and further reading:

Joinville, John de, and Geoffroy de Villehardouin. *Chronicles of the Crusades.* Translated by M. R. B. Shaw. London: Penguin Books, 1963.

Mayer, H. E. Desmond. *The Crusades.* Trans. John Gillingham. London: Oxford University Press, 1972.

Riley-Smith, Jonathan. *The Crusades: A Short History.* New Haven: Yale University Press, 1987.

Runciman, Steven. *A History of the Crusades.* Vol. 3. Cambridge, UK: Cambridge University Press, 1954.

Mantinea, Battle of (362 B.C.E.)

Thebes repeatedly clashed with Sparta over the Spartans' tyrannical rule following the conclusion of the Peloponnesian Wars. Epaminondas led the Theban army on four separate invasions. His final invasion occurred in 362 B.C.E. and culminated in the Battle of Mantinea, in which he managed to repeat his tactical victory at Leuctra against the allied army of Spartans, Mantineans, Arcadians, and others.

Epaminondas deceived the Spartan allies by the manner of his march. His best troops, the Theban Sacred Band, led the march column northward toward the allies but deftly maneuvered to the left, forcing the allies to rotate at right angles. Epaminondas pretended to set up camp without giving battle. Consequently, his enemies began to remove armor and break ranks. Epaminondas maintained the integrity of his formation and posted his cavalry to protect his flanks; he made special provisions for his left flank to prevent it from envelopment.

At the signal, the Theban line and its auxiliary cavalry began a rapid advance against the surprised allies. They managed to reform, but their haste ensured a disorganized and loosely formed line. In keeping with his tactical device at Leuctra, Epaminondas withheld the right portion of his line and vigorously pushed forward his left, which he reinforced in depth at the expense of breadth. The strong impetus of the Thebans smashed into the Spartan phalanx and broke its moral and physical cohesion. After a bloody struggle on the left, the Theban center and right advanced in good order against the weaker portion of the allied line, which quickly gave way. Epaminondas won but at the highest personal cost. Wounded in the chest by a spear, he died shortly thereafter. Although not as decisive as it would have been had he lived, Epaminondas's tactical genius won peace but not hegemony for Thebes.

Bryan R. Gibby

See also: Epaminondas; Leuctra, Battle of

References and further reading:

Delbruck, Hans. *Warfare in Antiquity.* Trans. Walter J. Renfroe Jr. Lincoln: University of Nebraska Press, 1990.

Dodge, Theodore A. *Alexander.* New York: Da Capo Press, 1996.

Mao Zedong (1893–1976)

Leader of an agrarian-based, Communist movement in China during the long period of anti-Japanese resistance and civil war against Chiang Kai-shek's Nationalist regime in the 1930s and 1940s who ultimately came close to destroying Chinese society in the Great Proletarian Cultural Revolution in the 1960s. Mao was born in Hunan Province in central China and moved to Beijing where, in the aftermath of World War I, he became active in student and revolutionary causes, joined the Communist Party, and, during the period of alliance with Chiang's Kuomintang, studied agrarian conditions in China's poverty-stricken countryside. He concluded that peasants had a great anger that could be harnessed to a revolutionary movement, and thereby he broke with the more orthodox Communists who sought the revolution among the limited number of urban proletariat in China's Western-dominated cities along the coast and the Yangtze River.

After Chiang crushed the urban Communists in 1927–1928, Mao gained more power; his "soviet" (revolutionary area) in the rural southeast became a haven for Communists. But in October 1934, after a great many Nationalist "extermination campaigns," Mao and his followers were forced to abandon the soviet and undertake a 12-month "Long March" from southeastern to western China and eventually to the northwest by the Great Wall, near the imperialist Japanese.

Portrait of Mao Zedong. (Library of Congress)

Mao espoused a philosophy that both revolutionized the peasantry and helped guide them in the desperate conflict against Japanese and Nationalist power. He helped them identify entrenched interests—landlords, government officials, businesspeople, the privileged—as being in league with one another and with foreign imperialists and thereby helped peasants identify them as enemies. He also helped them understand how to fight—to harass when weak, to combat when stronger, and always to propagandize the peasantry.

Although the Communists did not play a major role in the defeat of Japan (however they later claimed to have defeated the Japanese almost single-handedly), Mao helped direct the successful campaign in Manchuria that first tied Nationalist troops to big cities, then isolated them, and finally forced them to surrender. Thereafter, as many Nationalist troops deserted or changed sides as were beaten in battle.

Before the final battle of the long civil war could take place—the invasion of Taiwan and the destruction of Chiang's remaining forces and resources—Mao felt forced to intervene in the Korean conflict as Republic of Korea troops and United Nations forces neared the sensitive Yalu River border with Manchuria. For nearly three years, Chinese troops fought better-armed and better-supplied UN forces to a draw, reestablishing the North Korean regime and the thirty-eighth parallel, but at a fearsome human cost.

During the late 1950s, Mao turned his attention inward to remake China. Frustrated with what he viewed as entrenched interests in the government and party bureaucracies, he unleashed the power of youth, backed by a highly politicized army, in the destructive Great Proletarian Cultural Revolution of the 1960s. His later Great Leap Forward was an economic disaster (in which peasants were "encouraged," for example, to build backyard blast furnaces, producing useless metal), and millions died of starvation. Eventually, Mao had to concede the breakdown in power, and he most likely died frustrated with his failure to secure his "Continuing Revolution."

Charles M. Dobbs

See also: Chinese Civil War; Lin Biao

References and further reading:

Schram, Stuart R. *Mao Zedong: A Preliminary Reassessment.* New York: St. Martin's Press, 1983.

Spence, Jonathan D. *Mao Zedong.* New York: Viking Press, 1999.

Terrill, Ross. *Mao: A Biography.* Stanford: Stanford University Press, 1999.

Wilson, Dick, ed. *Mao Tse-tung in the Scales of History: A Preliminary Assessment.* New York: Cambridge University Press, 1977.

Maps and Cartography

The utilization of cartography and topographical mapping for military strategy and operations. Throughout history, considerations of terrain have influenced land warfare. Basic knowledge or ignorance of the lands in which armies traveled and fought sometimes determined their victory or defeat. However, until the invention of the scientific tools and methodologies necessary for composing precise maps, cartography held limited value for soldiers. Scouts, spies, and travelers fulfilled their ever-pressing needs for information about enemy landscapes. Because of the small scale of most campaigns in the premodern world, reliance on such nongraphically expressed intelligence was neither surprising nor particularly injurious to the conduct of war. Even the exceptionally long-distance land campaign of Alexander the Great against the vast Achaemenid Persian Empire or the Mongol incursions into Russia and eastern Europe were not expedited greatly by any formal cartographic organization of knowledge about their enemies' territories and deployments, but rather were facilitated through intelligence obtained from mounted scouts and local informants in a gradual, unfolding fashion. Likewise, the successful administration and defense of small premodern polities did not require exceptionally strong cartographic skills.

These conditions do not mean that the strategic and tactical values of landscape went undetected and unexploited by ancient and medieval commanders. As small chiefdoms and city-states expanded into kingdoms and empires with diplomatic and commercial connections of continental scope, the need for graphic representations of geographic space acquired a heightened significance. The earliest known examples of methodical collations of geographic information occurred soon after the advent of writing among the peoples of ancient Mesopotamia, where cuneiform lists of towns, rivers, and mountains appear as early as the third millennium B.C.E. Simple maps, building plans, and property surveys emerged in the next millennium, both in Mesopotamia and Egypt. Whether the traditions of the ancient Near East and Egypt considerably influenced the evolution of Mediterranean cartography presents a contentious issue, but mapping certainly reached its pinnacle in the premodern West with the Greeks and Romans, especially with the massive influx of geographic data produced by Alexander's conquests and the proliferation of long-distance trading routes connecting Europe with Central Asia, Arabia, India, and the coasts of sub-Saharan Africa in the last four centuries B.C.E. Global mapping, at least in terms of the world known to them, and mathematically grounded cartography emerged in this period, as seen in the works of Eratosthenes, followed by Marinus of Tyre and Ptolemy. The latter's *Geographike Hyphegesis* (*Manual of Geography*) served as the standard for centuries and strongly influenced both European and Arab cartographers, the latter translating his work into Arabic as early as the ninth century.

However, these achievements existed predominantly within the civilian realm; intelligence and maps typically followed conquest in classical Europe. When produced, maps rarely incorporated significant amounts of expressly military data, as seen in the Peutinger Table, a medieval copy of a third-century map of the Roman Empire that lacks any references to military installations. Geographic and ethnographic literature was written after campaigns and oriented toward civilian audiences, such as the fantastic descriptions of India composed by Alexander's admiral Nearchus. Land surveying, an art practiced by every literate culture with increasing precision since the Sumerians, was a vital aspect of Greek and Roman cartography but was employed primarily for civilian or civil administrative purposes, such as the planning of cities and land apportionments. *Agrimensores* (land measurers) accompanied Roman legions, but their tasks principally consisted of laying out fortified camps and buildings, constructing roads, and demarcating lands for veterans, not producing maps; intelligence about territory and terrain was acquired by *exploratores* (scouts). Roman road itineraries constituted the main cartographic tool exploited for military purposes in premodern Europe. Itineraries were written descriptions of roads accompanied by enumerations of the settlements, way stations, and other important features situated along them, along with their intervening mileages, thus allowing for some marching-rate calculation. They are clearly referred to in the military textbook of the late Roman author Vegetius and sometimes were paired with rough graphic illustrations.

With Rome's demise, most of these cartographic developments were lost and replaced by unrealistic, fanciful depictions of the world, shaped more by Christian theological considerations than actual geographic data. This trend is seen most plainly in the *mappaemundi* (literally, "table-cloth worlds" for the size of their media) manufactured in monasteries as didactic tools. Itineraries retained some importance, but systematic, mathematically based cartography, military or otherwise, largely was unpracticed and ignored. Production of maps increased slightly during the Crusades, but again the chief motivation was religious, as demonstrated by the maps of holy sites and pilgrimage destinations in Palestine created by the English monk Matthew Paris.

Mapping reached a sophisticated level very early in China and was applied with considerably greater frequency to military affairs than in contemporary Europe. Dating to 168 B.C.E., silk maps clearly depicting topography, fortifications, depots, and other military sites have been unearthed by archaeologists from a tomb of an officer at Mawangdui (near Changsha, China). There are several unambiguous references to military maps contained within the historical literature of the Han dynasty, such as passages in the *Guanzi* (*Book of Master Guan*), a military text of the third century B.C.E., that urge their use for planning marches and exploiting terrain for strategic advantage. Three-dimensional military maps dating to the early first century and constructed of wood and molded rice are known, and precise, mathematically based topographical maps were drawn up as early as the third century by the imperial cartographer Pei Xiu, whose methods possibly are reflected in extremely accurate gridded maps of the entire Chinese coastline that survive in stone copies dating to the twelfth century. Throughout Chinese history, maps provided by tributary states and peoples signified their submission and allowed Chinese military leaders to amass a substantial amount of strategic geographic intelligence. Their precocious cartographic methods spread to Korea and Japan, where military administrators also adopted them. Beginning in the mid-1400s, Korean cartographers produced particularly high-quality maps for arranging the defense of their Manchurian frontier against potential Manchu invasion.

The history of medieval Islamic cartography is lengthy and rich, but its military relevance remained unrealized until the rise of the Ottoman Empire. One of the few early examples of military Islamic cartography is a literary reference to maps drafted for al-Hallaj ibn Yusuf, an eighth-century administrator who relied on them to coordinate military activities near the Caspian Sea from his palace in Iraq. Arab geographers, cosmographers, and mathematicians, although certainly gifted, drew maps from illustrative rather than strategic intent. However, the Ottoman army definitely exploited small-scale military mapping in its European operations. The *kulaguz* (reconnoiterer) figured prominently in Ottoman military practice prior to the adoption of European cartographic methodology in the nineteenth century, drafting maps and plans of enemy fortifications for use in future conflicts. The earliest example is a late fifteenth-century map of Kiev and its suburbs prepared for Sultan Bayezid II; it proposed a never-executed naval assault on the city, thus revealing its intended role in the planning of campaigns. Süleyman I probably relied upon a still-extant plan of Belgrade, drafted by an army reconnoiterer, during his successful siege of the city in 1521; similar plans for operations in Malta and Szigetvár (Hungary) also exist, as well as a map drawn much later for the ill-fated second siege of Vienna in 1683. For the most part, these "maps" were impressionistic artistic views of the targeted cities and fortresses but stand as concrete illustrations of cartographic-based advance military planning.

Mapping traditions also flourished in the Americas prior to European contact, although most of these materials were lost and what survives is known mainly from European copies of varying quality and frequently dubious veracity. The best examples of pre-Columbian military cartography are maps allegedly utilized and drawn by Aztec *pochteca* (long-distance traders), sent as spies into adjacent towns and regions in order to collect geographic intelligence under cover of their commercial endeavors. According to an illustration contained in the *Codex Florentine,* a Spanish-Nahuatl "encyclopedia" of preconquest Mexico written about 1570, it seems that the Spanish integrated Nahuatl information into new maps, which then guided the troops to their objectives; unfortunately, no actual *pochteca* maps exist today. Also, the conquistador Hernando de Cortez mentioned Aztec ambassadors who brought to him cloth maps detailing the Gulf of Mexico coast, whereupon he ordered his staff to make copies in European form and used them to plot further expeditions.

Comprehensive and accurate cartography useful for military applications in the modern sense emerged only toward the close of the medieval period in Europe. New technologies and social forces coincided to produce the enormous upsurge in map production during the Renaissance. Directional compasses appeared in China around 1150 and passed to Europe about a century later, eventually revolutionizing Western navigation and cartography. The revived study of classical urban planning and military architecture intensified interest in surveying and mapping generally, especially in Italy, where district maps and diagrams of fortifications prepared by military engineers, including the famous artist Leonardo da Vinci, appeared throughout the fifteenth century. This is a trend reflected most clearly in the military district maps commissioned in 1460 by the Council of Ten of Venice and the large regional maps of Lombardy produced as early as the 1440s. Triangulation surveying techniques, introduced by Gemma Frisius in 1533, allowed for considerably more precise measurements of distances than previously available, enabling the development of scale mapping. True-to-scale local and property maps began to be drawn in Italy, the Netherlands, and England, and English engineers produced accurately scaled maps of their coastal fortifications by the mid-1500s after French raids along the Channel coast. From the fifteenth to the seventeenth centuries, the escalation of border and frontier disputes between the emergent absolutist nation-states, extensive nautical exploration and the construction of transoceanic empires, massive religious warfare, and insurrections like the Fronde in France emphasized the need for reliable maps for the rulers and military leaders of Europe, who then enthusiastically employed surveyors to map their territories to meet such dire military and diplomatic concerns. The first known official military cartographic project in France began in 1495 with Charles VIII's order to Jacques Signot to map the mountain passes by which the French army could traverse the Alps and invade Italy. In Habsburg Spain, where military cartography evolved slowly and to an arguably lesser extent than in other European realms, Philip II nonetheless often utilized maps to coordinate information about his far-flung empire and charted the route of his doomed armada with maps and nautical charts, and his subordinate, Fernando Alvarez de Toledo, the Duke of Alba, relied extensively on rough maps of the Netherlands to plan marches and attacks during his attempts to subdue the Dutch insurgents.

Despite these advances, before 1700 most military maps were simplistic and schematic, drafted more frequently by and for civilians and bureaucrats than soldiers, and not exploited regularly by commanders in the field. Pamphlets published in the 1750s urged British officers in India to use their maps and avoid overreliance on native guides. Frederick II constantly complained about the dearth of good military maps and was compelled to rely on captured Austrian maps for his campaigns in Silesia.

The eighteenth century brought the formalization of military cartography requisite for the production of maps serviceable for strategic planning and combat operations. Surveyors and engineers increasingly were incorporated into formal army structures, beginning with the organization of the French army corps of surveyors in 1696. Improvements in road construction, the desire for better control over larger numbers of troops, which required detailed advance logistical and operational planning, and the realization that successful defense from foreign invasion rested significantly upon geographic intelligence led to the first truly scientific efforts to map entire countries. Important examples include the topographical surveys of France undertaken by the Cassini family between 1733 and 1788, General William Roy's mapping of Scotland for the British army in the wake of the Jacobite Rebellion, F. W. Schetten's survey of Prussia in the 1780s, the mapping of Austrian crown lands ordered by Joseph II in the same decade, and the initiation of the Board of Ordnance surveys in Britain in 1791. Topographic mapping, a necessary component of modern military cartography, began to be standardized during the 1700s. First proposed in 1777 by Jean-Baptiste Meusnier, a French lieutenant of engineers, contour lines dramatically increased the military efficacy of topographical maps, especially at the tactical level; however, they did not replace entirely older topographical maps drawn with hachure lines until the next century. Thoroughly map-based advanced military planning emerged toward the end of the eighteenth century, noticeable as early as 1775 with General Pierre-Joseph de Bourcet's work, *Les principes de la guerre de montagne.* Based on his detailed topographical surveys in the Savoy and Piedmont border regions of France, the work presented a carefully organized system by which all rates of march and supply issues for a campaign could be anticipated through reliance on detailed topographical maps. Coupled with the creation of divisional units, modern topographical maps contributed to the expansion of commanders' abilities to control significantly larger armies than existed in previous ages, thus transforming European warfare.

This process of formalization and large-scale strategic mapping continued throughout the nineteenth century. Napoleon I organized his Imperial Corps of Surveyors in 1809, whose efforts facilitated the speed with which his armies penetrated Russia a few years later. The implementation of general army staffs, which brought the art of preparing for future wars during peacetime to an unprecedented level, sustained interest in military cartography throughout the century. The predecessor of these bodies was the Great General Staff of the Prussian army, created during the Napoleonic Wars to coordinate technical and logistical information for field commanders; these goals required the systematic compilation of immense amounts of topographical data collected well before hostilities began. By the 1840s, general staff maps were available both in France and Prussia, where they exercised a strong influence on military strategy and planning, seen most clearly with the formulation of the Schlieffen Plan in Germany prior to World War I. Military cartography disseminated outside Europe, replacing older traditions in China, Japan, and the Ottoman state.

Army surveyors proved invaluable in exploring and mapping unsettled regions in the western United States throughout the nineteenth century, beginning with the famous expeditions led by Captains Meriwether Lewis and William Clark, Lieutenant Zebulon Pike, and Lieutenant John Frémont, the latter an officer with the Army Corps of Topographical Engineers, formed in 1838. The corps' work, as well as numerous surveys undertaken by the War Department, allowed for the rapid settlement and railroad construction that occurred in the American West after the Civil War. Although the western and "Indian" territories were mapped systematically, that conflict also highlighted the lack of scientific surveys of the country's eastern and southern sectors, further stimulating the development of American military cartography, so that by the Civil War's end, the Coast Survey and Army Corps of Engineers supplied Union forces with approximately 43,000 printed maps per year. Similar increases in the scale of map production took place elsewhere, especially in connection with trench warfare during World War I, which necessitated highly accurate large-scale maps for accurate, long-range artillery fire. For example, the British Expeditionary Force (BEF) originally landed in France with two cartographers, an officer, and a clerk responsible for the provision of all maps; by 1918, the BEF contained 5,000 cartographic personnel who produced over 35 million maps throughout the course of the war.

It was in the twentieth century that the most substantial advances in scientific military cartography were made, as mapping moved into the skies. Although surveyors and artillery observers working from balloons participated effectively in nineteenth-century wars, notably the American Civil War, the invention of the airplane utterly transformed their work. Significantly more mobile than balloons and dirigibles, aircraft were acknowledged to have an advantage quite early, with the first examples of aircraft reconnaissance occurring in 1911 during the Italian campaign in Libya. The armies of all participating countries employed them during World War I, eventually equipping them with machine guns and primitive bombs and transforming them into the first fighter and bomber aircraft; the American army flew reconnaissance missions as early as 1916 during the Mexican Punitive Expedition directed against Pancho Villa.

By the outbreak of World War II, aerial operations were regarded everywhere as vital components of land warfare, leading to a demand for detailed maps for strategic bombing and aerial support of land combat and, when coupled with photography, allowing for the composition of extremely accurate maps. Two examples from the experience of the German Luftwaffe clearly illustrate this double facet of modern warfare: Nazi bomber crews relied on British Ordnance Survey maps to locate targets in England and then in preparation for the invasion of the Soviet Union flew modified high-altitude bombers over Soviet territory to collect intelligence about geography and troop deployment. Similar photo-reconnaissance missions enabled the amphibious landing of their Allied adversaries at Normandy a few years later.

During the Cold War, aerial reconnaissance and mapping saw extensive application as nuclear threats emerged. The United States conducted high-altitude reconnaissance flights over Soviet territory beginning in 1946, successfully charting their bomber bases and revealing their nuclear capabilities, although the constant emphasis that Strategic Air Command placed on using aircraft instead of missiles or rockets throughout the 1950s hampered the development of American space and satellite programs. Between the Apollo moon landing program of the 1960s and the space shuttle program of the 1980s, this disadvantage was rectified, and American satellites now provide the most accurate military cartographic services ever known. Without global positioning system (GPS) and geographic information system (GIS) satellites and computer software that produces precise three-dimensional maps of enemy terrain, the pinpoint accuracy of armor fire achieved by U.S. forces during the Gulf War or in later cruise missile strikes against antiterrorist objectives in Sudan and Afghanistan would have been unachievable. Recent space cartography projects, such as the hyperaccurate digital terrain maps generated by the new Shuttle Radar Topography Mission, certainly hold potentially enormous consequences for the nature of land warfare in the twenty-first century.

Ian Janssen

References and further reading:

Black, Jeremy. *Maps and Politics.* Chicago: University of Chicago Press, 1997.

Buisseret, David, ed. *Monarchs, Ministers, and Maps: The Emergence of Cartography as a Tool of Government in Early Modern Europe.* Chicago: University of Chicago Press, 1992.

Delano-Smith, Catherine, and Roger Kain. *English Maps: A History.* Toronto: University of Toronto Press, 1999.

Harley, J. Brian, et al., eds. *The History of Cartography.* Vols. 1–2. Chicago: University of Chicago Press, 1987–1998.

Harvey, P. *The History of Topographical Maps.* London: Thames and Hudson, 1980.

Konvitz, Josef. *Cartography in France, 1660–1848.* Chicago: University of Chicago Press, 1987.

Luebke, Frederick, et al., eds. *Mapping the North American Plains.* Norman: University of Oklahoma Press, 1987.

Maratha Wars (1775–1818)

Three wars that doomed the Maratha Confederacy. By the late eighteenth century, the Maratha Confederacy was one of the greatest powers in the central Indian subcontinent. During the reign of Shivaji (d. 1680), the Marathas erupted from their mountain domain of the Western Ghats on the Arabian Sea and were transformed from Hindu mercenaries into warlords in their own right. Significant as was their military proficiency in the rise of the Marathas, equally important were the dissensions that afflicted Mogul rule of India. The reign of Shivaji paralleled that of the Mogul emperor Aurangzeb, whose vigorous persecution of non-Muslims in the last half of the seventeenth century served to encourage revolt among not merely the Marathas but the Rajputs and Sikhs as well. The resulting overextension of Mogul forces meant that, by the time of Aurangzeb's death in 1707, the Marathas had established themselves as the dominant power in the Deccan. In the succession crises that followed the death of the emperor, the Marathas were able to extend their power still further, until by 1740, their ruler, the Peshwa of Pune, governed from the Arabian Sea to the Bay of Bengal.

Given the nature of the Maratha rise to power, it was fitting, if not ironic, that the ultimate British victory in the three Maratha Wars had as much to do with dissension among the Marathas as to particular proficiency on the part of their European enemy. As the Marathas extended their power across India, governance of lands seized from the Mogul emperor was left in the hands of Maratha commanders. Consequently, rather than governing a centralized state, the Peshwa of Pune oversaw what the nineteenth-century historian James Duff described as a "communion of interests." The same tendency to internal dissension that so afflicted the Mogul empire and that largely accounted for the rise of the Marathas soon became a feature of Maratha political life.

Matters took a serious turn in the early 1770s, when the British East India Company's Bombay presidency saw in the succession crises of that time an opportunity to expand its interests in the region. In 1775, Bombay recognized Raghunath Rao as the legitimate claimant to the Peshwaship in exchange for territorial gains and in so doing set the scene for the First Maratha War (1775–1782). It was a conflict that ran in fits and starts. At Aras (18 May 1775), Raghunath and his British allies were defeated by the Maratha commander, Hari Pant. Facing war with France and its primary Indian ally, the Sultan of Mysore, Governor of India Warren Hastings took the opportunity of this defeat to condemn Bombay's actions and ordered the company troops back to their quarters. Subsequent negotiations with the Maratha Regency Council failed—despite British offers to abandon Raghunath Rao for territorial concessions—and in 1778 troops from Bombay again marched against the Marathas. Though their defeat at Talegaon (11–17 January 1779) represented a serious setback to British interests in the region, 1779 also marked an important turning point in British strategic interests in India. Concerned that Bombay's actions could increase French interest in the region, Hastings ordered six battalions to march from Bengal. When the commander of this force, Colonel Thomas Goddard, heard of the defeat at Talegaon, he did not turn back but pushed on, covering 300 miles in 19 days. When negotiations with the Regency Council failed, Goddard was joined by the Gaikar, Maratha princes from Baroda, and successfully stormed Ahmadabad. Meanwhile, in 1780, a second Bengal force under Captain Thomas Popham captured the Marathas' mountaintop fortress at Gwalior (November 1780). Just as British victory over the Marathas seemed to be assured, however, Haidar Ali, Sultan of Mysore, invaded the Carnatic, opening the Second Mysore War. As a result of the very real threat to Madras and the British position on the Carnatic, the East India Company opened negotiations with the Marathas in 1781 that would end with the Treaty of Salbai (1783). Although the latter forced the British to relinquish their support of Raghunath Rao, the expeditions of Goddard and Popham nonetheless demonstrated the British ability to strike at will anywhere on the subcontinent.

Peace between the British and the Marathas would last for the next two decades, until a succession crisis shook the confederacy in 1803. Defeated by his rival, Holkar of Indore, Baji Rao II entered into the Bassein Treaty (1803), by which the British agreed to restore Baji as Peshwa in return for the Marathas accepting and paying for British troops in their capital, together with other obligations. To restore Baji Rao and bring those princes who rejected the Bassein Treaty to heel, Governor General Sir Richard Wellesley planned a twofold campaign against the Marathas. First, Wellesley's brother, Arthur, would lead a force of 9,000 Europeans and 5,000 Indian troops into the Maratha homeland. A second force under Gerard Lake invaded Hindustan. In March 1803, Wellesley's force captured Pune and restored Baji as Peshwa. On 23 September 1803, Wellesley's army met and defeated the Marathas under Doulut Rao Sindhia at Assaye. Though victorious, Wellesley would later recall this campaign as the hardest-fought action of his long career. Meanwhile, Lake captured Delhi on 16 September 1803 and in the Battle of Laswari (1 November) finally destroyed the forces of the Maratha prince, Sindhia. In the meantime, the British government had grown concerned with the extent of these operations. In particular, the siege of Bhurtpore (January–April 1805) had claimed 3,100 men before the British were victorious. Accordingly, Lord Wellesley was recalled, and with the capitulation of Holkar at Amritsar (December 1805), the Second Maratha War came to an uneasy close.

The Third Maratha War (1817–1818) was in large part the consequence of the turmoil that gripped India as Maratha power finally crumbled. In the aftermath of the Second Maratha War, a vast horde of former Maratha soldiers known as the Pendaris spread out across central and southern India in an organized campaign of violence and depredation. When the governor of India, Francis Hastings, Lord Moira, decided to move against the Pendaris with two large armies, he expected Maratha support. Instead, the Peshwa Baji Rao II, justifiably resentful of the conditions imposed on him by the British in return for their support in the 1803 war, turned on the British and attacked and destroyed their residency at Pune with a force of 27,000 men (5 November 1817). Holkar likewise took to the field but suffered defeat at the hands of Sir Thomas Hyslop at Mahidput (21 December 1817) before being forced to surrender. Nor did the Peshwa fare any better, for on the same day his forces destroyed the British residency at Pune, they were defeated at Kirkee by a mere 2,800 British soldiers. Defeated again at Koregaon (1 January 1818) and Ashti (20 February), the Peshwa finally surrendered to Hastings's army on 2 June 1818. With Baji Rao's surrender, the hereditary office of Peshwa was abolished by the victorious British, and with it the political and military power of the Maratha Confederacy ceased to exist.

Adam Lynde

See also: Mysore Wars

References and further reading:

Duff, James G. *History of the Mahrattas.* Ed. J. P. Guha. New Delhi: Associated Publishing House, 1971.

Gordon, Stewart. *The Marathas, 1600–1818.* Cambridge, UK: Cambridge University Press, 1993.

Keay, John. *India. A History.* London: Harper Collins, 2000.

Mehra, Parshotam. *A Dictionary of Modern Indian History, 1707–1947.* Delhi: Oxford University Press, 1987.

Marathon, Battle of (490 B.C.E.)

In August 490, a Persian force of some 30,000 men under the command of Darius landed at Marathon in Attica. Nine thousand Athenians and 1,000 Plataean allies, all under Miltiades, defeated the enemy, despite having been refused immediate help from Sparta.

Who took the initiative for battle is still under debate, though it seems that the Greeks decided to attack first after they heard a rumor saying that the Persian cavalry was withdrawing. Miltiades, wanting to make his army look equal in length to the Persian army, made its center only a few ranks deep but kept the wings deeper and stronger. The Athenians occupied the center and the right side of the line, and the Plataeans were on the left. Little is known of the Persian dispositions, except that the Persians and Sacae (a warlike people from Central Asia) formed the very strong center of the line.

After the usual sacrifice, the Greeks charged at the double (according to Herodotus, the first Greeks to have done so) across no-man's-land, taking the Persians by surprise and thus reducing the effectiveness of their archers. The fighting, according again to Herodotus, was severe and lasted a long time. The Persians broke the weak Athenian center and pursued the survivors inland. Meanwhile, the stronger Greek wings, which had already managed to route their opponents, reformed (most probably joining forces) and attacked the Persian troops who had broken through their center. The Persians started to flee toward their ships, with the Greeks in close pursuit. Large numbers of Persians perished in a nearby marsh, and even more were killed by the pursuing

Greeks attacking Persian ships during the Battle of Marathon. (Bettmann/Corbis)

Greeks. Most of the Persian navy was already at open sea, but seven Phoenician ships that were still lying close inshore, waiting for the last fugitives, were captured by the Greeks. Herodotus gives the losses as 6,400 Persians and 192 Athenians dead. The former figure may seem exaggerated, but the latter can surely be accepted as precise.

Despite the Greek victory, the Persian fleet laid course for Sounion in order to attack Athens. Miltiades immediately ordered his troops to march post-haste to Athens and managed to reach the city before the enemy fleet. When the Persians arrived soon afterward and saw an army waiting for them, they set off toward Asia.

This amazing victory of the Athenians and their Plataean allies had a huge impact on Athens's later history, and many scholars have praised the strategy and tactical brilliance of Miltiades. It should be noted, however, that although all these tactics appear to be quite sophisticated and planned well ahead (even down to what becomes, according to some views, the "falling back of the Athenian center"), it is more likely that what happened was almost accidental. If we are to believe Herodotus, the thinning of the Greek center was a purely defensive move rather than a specific plan for the wings to first crush the enemy wings and then move on to smash their center by a "double envelopment." In addition, there is no reason to believe that the victory was due to the superiority of Greek discipline because most of the Greek *hoplitai* were just common citizens and not professional soldiers. All these caveats do not decrease the importance of the victory but on the contrary enhance it and make it more astonishing.

Ioannis Georganas

References and further reading:

Hackett, John, ed. *Warfare in the Ancient World.* London: Sidgwick & Jackson, 1989.
Hammond, Nicholas. "The Campaign and Battle of Marathon." *Journal of Hellenic Studies* 88 (1968), 13–57.
Lazenby, John. *The Defence of Greece 490–479 BC.* Warminster: Aris & Phillips, 1993.

Marcellus, Marcus Claudius (c. 275–208 B.C.E.)

Probably the most popular commander in Rome during the Second Punic War. Middle-aged when the Second War began, Marcellus had already won his spurs. While serving in the First Punic War, he saved the life of his adopted brother. As consul, he campaigned against the Gallic tribe of the Insubres in 222 B.C.E. He relieved the city of Clastidium and killed the Gallic chief Viridomarus in single combat, by which he won the so-called Spolia Opima (the spoils of honor), that is, the right to offer his vanquished opponent's personal spoils to Jupiter. This honor was given only twice before in Roman history.

When in 216 B.C.E., Rome was disastrously defeated by Hannibal at Cannae, Marcellus was sent to take command of the remnants of the defeated army. He reformed it into two legions and followed Hannibal into Campania. Using the delaying tactics advised by the general Fabius Maximus, Marcellus dug in on a strategically important position, afterward known after him as "Castra Claudiana." From there he could cover a large part of Campania, threaten the defecting town of Capua, and secure important lines of communication without risking battle with Hannibal. During the following years, Marcellus frustrated Hannibal's attempts to extend his foothold in Campania.

In 213 B.C.E., Marcellus was dispatched to Sicily and assaulted Syracuse. Because of the defensive machinery created by the scientist Archimedes, the Romans were repelled, and Marcellus laid siege to the city. Although the Syracusans held out for three years, in 211 the city was taken and sacked. In later years, Marcellus remained faithful to the Fabian method. He doggedly followed Hannibal's footsteps on the Italian mainland without engaging his army. However, in 208 B.C.E., Marcellus was attacked and killed reconnoitering the battlefield. Hannibal gave him a hero's funeral, a fitting end for the commander who was called "the Sword of Rome."

M. R. van der Werf

See also: Cannae, Battle of; Fabius Maximus Verrucosus "Cunctator"; Hannibal Barca; Punic Wars

References and further reading:

Bagnall, Nigel. *The Punic Wars. Rome, Carthage and the Struggle for the Mediterranean.* London: Pimlico, 1999.
Caven, Brian. *The Punic Wars.* London: Weidenfeld and Nicholson, 1981.
Lazenby, J. F. *Hannibal's War. A Military History of the Second Punic War.* London: Aris & Phillips, 1978.

March, Peyton (1864–1955)

American general of World War I, sometimes called the "Father of the Modern U.S. Army." Born 27 December 1864 in Easton, Pennsylvania, March graduated from the U.S. Military Academy at West Point in 1888 and served in the Philippine Insurrection of 1899–1902, having field command in the Battle of the Clouds at Tilad Pass on 2 December 1899. He served on the general staff from 1903 to 1907, acted as an observer during the Russo-Japanese War of 1904–1905, and served as commander of the 1st Battalion, 6th Field Artillery

Regiment in Fort Riley, Kansas, from 1911 to 1916. As a colonel, March commanded the 8th Field Artillery on the Mexican border in August 1916. In June 1917, after the United States entered World War I, March was promoted to brigadier general and led the 1st Field Artillery Brigade in the American Expeditionary Force in France. He became acting chief of staff of the army in March 1918 and chief of staff on 19 May of that year and held the position until 30 June 1921. During these crucial years, he presided over the buildup of U.S. forces in the closing months of the war, as well as the demobilization of those forces. Although today a little-remembered figure, Peyton March is credited with creating the Air Service, Tank Corps, and Chemical Warfare Service during the war. He died 13 April 1955 in Washington, D.C.

Harold Wise

See also: Philippine Insurrection; World War I

References and further reading:

March, Peyton C. *The Nation at War.* Garden City, NY: Doubleday, Doran and Company, Inc., 1932.

Statue of Emperor Marcus Aurelius. (Library of Congress)

Marcus Aurelius (Antoninus) (121–180)

Roman emperor, philosopher, and soldier. Born Marcus Annius Verus, Marcus Aurelius succeeded Antoninus Pius as Roman emperor (Augustus) in 161. Marcus appointed Lucius Verus coemperor to help rule and consolidate the large empire, reserving the title of chief priest (*pontifex maximus*) for himself. In 162, Marcus sent Lucius to the eastern part of the empire to campaign against the Parthian ruler Vologases III, who had placed his brother on the throne of Armenia and had attacked Roman garrisons along the Armenian border. Lucius defeated Vologases and reinforced the border along the Euphrates River before returning to Rome in 166. Marcus and Lucius suppressed rebellions in Britain and Africa and impeded an invasion of Italy by a Germanic group, the Marcomanni, who under their leader, Ballomar, besieged the strategic frontier town of Aquileia. Marcus and Lucius retook Aquileia and pushed the Marcomanni back across the Danube River among the other Germanic tribes. Lucius died on the journey north in 169, and Marcus was left to carry on the Danubian campaigns for another 11 years.

Marcus temporarily left these campaigns when Avidius Cassius, a once loyal governor of Syria, claimed for himself the title of Augustus in 175. Although Avidius was killed by his own soldiers before Marcus could reach Syria, Marcus used the opportunity to secure his power in the east and returned to the Germanic wars in 176. He campaigned separately against the Marcomanni, Quadi, and Sarmati tribes in order to break up any Germanic unity. Marcus planned to extend the empire past the Danube River and to place these tribes into the new provinces, thus creating a larger buffer zone between the tribes and Italy. Only the last step in his project remained when Marcus died in his camp at Vindobona on 17 March 180.

Christopher P. Goedert

References and further reading:

Garzetti, Albino. *From Tiberius to the Antonines: A History of the Roman Empire,* C.E. *14–192.* Trans. J. R. Foster. London: Methuen, 1974.

Grant, Michael. *The Antonines: The Roman Empire in Transition.* London: Routledge, 1994.

Watson, Paul Barron. *Marcus Aurelius Antoninus.* 1884. Reprint, Freeport, NY: Books for Libraries Press, 1971.

Marengo, Battle of (14 June 1800)

French victory over Austria in northern Italy. In early 1800, Napoleon sought to defeat Austria, his one active enemy. Crossing the Alps into Lombardy, he believed the Austrians would flee. Therefore he detached units of his army to block their escape. However, Austrian commander Michael Melas decided to fight and deployed around Alessandria. On 13 June Napoleon, increasingly convinced Melas would retreat, sent one division north to the Po River and ordered another, under Louis Charles Desaix, south to block the road to Genoa. Thus the Austrians had concentrated 31,000–34,000 troops around Alessandria, whereas Napoleon's were reduced to less than 28,000.

Early on 14 June, three strong Austrian columns surprised Napoleon by marching from Alessandria to attack. Battle was joined just west of the village of Marengo, 3.5 miles east of Alessandria. Not until late morning did Napoleon realize he confronted the bulk of Melas's army. He then ordered the recall of units he had previously detached. But the situation deteriorated rapidly for the French. Retreating eastward, by noon they had no reserves, were short of ammunition, and faced being outflanked on their right.

The Austrians, confident of victory, paused to regroup. They resumed the attack about 1:00 P.M., pushing the French back to San Giuliano, nearly 5 miles from Marengo. About 3:00 P.M. a confident Melas turned over command to his chief of staff, Anton Zach. Then Desaix arrived, having marched directly to the sound of the guns. Zach did not press the attack until approximately 4:30. Desaix led a counterattack in which he was killed, but Auguste Marmont and François Kellermann (the younger) rallied the French, who then routed the Austrians. The battle ended about 10:00 P.M. The French suffered some 4,700 killed and wounded, the Austrians 6,500.

Marengo was a very close call because Napoleon had badly miscalculated. Nevertheless, Marengo enhanced his image, strengthened his position as first consul, and quelled possible political opposition at home.

James K. Kieswetter

See also: French Revolutionary Wars; Masséna, André, Duc de Rivoli, Prince d'Essling; Napoleon I; Napoleonic Wars

References and further reading:

Chandler, David G. *The Campaigns of Napoleon.* New York: Macmillan, 1966.

Connelly, Owen. *Blundering to Glory: Napoleon's Military Campaigns.* Wilmington, DE: Scholarly Resources, 1987.

Rodger, Alexander Bankier. *The War of the Second Coalition: A Strategic Commentary.* Oxford: Clarendon Press, 1964.

Sargent, Herbert Howland. *The Campaign of Marengo.* 6th ed. Chicago: A. C. McClurg, 1914.

Marignano, Battle of (13–14 September 1515)

Marignano ended the myth of Swiss invincibility. At 20 years of age, François I became king on New Year's Eve, 1515. He was determined to bring the Duchy of Milan back to his crown. Gathering his army at Lyons the following spring, he faced an alliance of Massimiliano Sforza, Duke of Milan, the Habsburg emperor, and the cardinal of Sion. Their army, mainly Swiss mercenaries, occupied the easiest pass to cross the Alps. Francis I chose a smaller and more difficult draw to bypass the waiting Swiss. The two sides now looked for a financial agreement to avoid battle. The Swiss, followed by the French troops, marched to Milan. The king joined a Venetian army, and on 8 September, the agreement was to be signed. But the cardinal of Sion persuaded the Swiss to attack the king in his camp at Marignano on 13 September. With the Venetian army encamped at Lodi, the French were left on their own. The battlefield was difficult: a large plain cut by hedges and small irrigation ditches that would disrupt any French cavalry charge.

The surprised French placed their artillery in front of the large blocks of Swiss pikemen. The French king charged at the head of the royal gendarmerie more than 30 times, only to be repulsed by the wall of pikes of the Swiss phalanx. The falling night stopped the fight, with the armies resting less than 50 yards from each other. During the night, Francis I sent a messenger to Alviano's Venetian troops to join as soon as possible.

The dawn of the 14th saw a new battle, as the 20,000 Swiss attacked, again facing deadly artillery fire. The German mercenaries on the French side were overwhelmed by the Swiss, some of the latter reaching the French artillery only to be cut to pieces by the gendarmerie's heavy knights. The first Venetians reached the battlefield by 8:00 A.M., and the main Swiss pike block was assaulted on its front by the king's cavalry and on its left flank by Venetian infantrymen. By 1:00 P.M., the surviving Swiss retired to Milan, leaving 14,000 dead on the battlefield. Milan surrendered the following day, giving the duchy to the king. This battle was won by the superior French artillery and the king's stubborn defense. The most important result was the Perpetual Peace, signed in 1516, which gave France the exclusive use of Swiss soldiers. The treaty lasted until 1792.

Gilles Boué

See also: Cerisolles, Battle of; Pavia, Battle of

References and further reading:

Contamine, Philippe. *Histoire militaire de la France.* Vol. 1. Paris: PUF, 1992.

Oman, Charles. *A History of the Art of War in the Sixteenth Century.* London: Greenhill, 1997.

Marion, Francis (1732–1795)

American partisan leader in the Revolutionary War. Born in Winyah, South Carolina, and by occupation a planter, Francis Marion first saw military action as a lieutenant of South Carolina militia in campaigns against the Cherokees in 1759 and 1761. In 1775, he took a captaincy in the 2d South Carolina Regiment of the Continental army.

After being promoted to major the following year, he helped defend Fort Sullivan during the British attack on Charleston, firing the last shot at their departing fleet. As lieutenant colonel, he commanded the regiment until he was injured in the spring of 1780.

After the disastrous American defeat at Camden in August had cleared the Southern Department of practically all regular U.S. troops, Marion began a partisan campaign. Commanding about 50 militiamen, he defeated a Loyalist militia force five times larger in September and then squelched a Tory uprising. British lieutenant colonel Banastre Tarleton fruitlessly chased his guerrillas fighters through the swamps in November and commented disgustedly, "but as for this old fox, the devil himself could not catch him," thus giving Marion his famous nickname, the "Swamp Fox." Through 1781, now a brigadier general of militia, he harassed the British from bases in the swamps and woods, often in tandem with "Light Horse Harry" Lee, capturing Forts Watson and Motte. His brilliant and ceaseless guerrilla campaign distracted the British, while General Nathanael Greene's Continentals reestablished control of the area. In September, Marion joined Greene and commanded the militias of North and South Carolina in the Battle of Eutaw Springs. An abstemious and nonviolent man in an age of hard-drinking fighters, Marion is supposed to have clambered out of a second-story window to avoid a round of alcoholic toasts and, when forced to draw his sword (presumably in battle), found it rusted into its scabbard! After this bitter war, Marion was a leader in the reconciliation between patriot and Tory.

Elected to the South Carolina Senate in December, he was subsequently reelected twice. From 1784 to 1794, he was militia general and commandant of Fort Johnson in Charleston Harbor.

Joseph McCarthy

See also: American Revolution; Camden, Battle of; Cowpens; Greene, Nathanael

References and further reading:

Bass, Robert D. *Swamp Fox: The Life and Campaigns of General Francis Marion.* New York: Henry Holt, 1959.

Rankin, Hugh F. *Francis Marion, the Swamp Fox.* New York: Thomas Y. Crowell, 1973.

Weigley, Russell F. *The Partisan War: The South Carolina Campaign of 1780–1782.* Columbia: University of South Carolina Press, 1970.

Marius, Gaius (157–86 B.C.E.)

Roman general, statesman, and military reformer who led the Populares Party during the civil war. Born in 157 B.C.E. at Arpinum, Marius—a "new man" since he achieved his position through ability and talent instead of by birth—represented the interests of the plebeian class. In 116 B.C.E., he administered Further Spain, suppressing bandits and establishing his personal wealth through mining investments. During his consulship, Marius initiated numerous military reforms, including the recruitment of troops through a headcount system in the cities, which replaced the old volunteer plebeian army of farmers. He developed a strict training program and required his men to carry their own equipment and supplies. He is credited with redesigning the *pilum* (Roman spear) so that the shaft bent after hitting a target, making it impossible to throw back on his own men. In 107 B.C.E., as consul, he led the Roman forces against Jugurtha, King of Numidia (present-day Algeria), but his rival Sulla received credit for the victory after arranging for the capture of the king. A rivalry developed between Marius and Sulla that resulted in years of bloodshed within Rome.

At the conclusion of hostilities in North Africa, Marius and Sulla fought together against the Germanic tribes. Their rivalry continued to intensify until civil war broke out in 88 B.C.E., when Marius arranged to have Sulla's command, to lead the Roman army against the Asian king Mithradates VI, transferred to himself. Sulla returned to Rome with his army, and Marius lost his status as consul and was forced to flee. Many of his supporters lost their property and lives. After Sulla departed for Asia, Marius returned to Rome, murdering Sulla's supporters and ruling the city. In 86 B.C.E., Marius declared himself consul but died a few days later.

Cynthia Clark Northrup

See also: Sulla, Lucius Cornelius

References and further reading:

Kildahl, Phillip A. *Caius Marius.* New York: Twayne Publishers, 1968.

MARKET GARDEN (10–24 September 1944)

The largest airdrop in history and the last defeat for British forces in World War II. In September, Allied forces had liberated most of France and Belgium. Supreme Allied Commander General Dwight Eisenhower wanted to continue along a broad front, but Field Marshal Bernard Montgomery and other commanders wanted a quick thrust along a narrow front through Holland, outflanking the Siegfried Line, breaking the paper-thin German defenses, and then turning eastward into Germany's Ruhr Valley. Such a move would cut the heart out of Germany's industrial capacity.

The success of such an operation depended on securing bridges on the Rhine River at Grave, the Waal River at Nijmegen, and the Mass River at Arnhem. Montgomery decided that airborne troops would seize and hold each bridge, while the Second British Army moved northward along what was called Hell's Highway. In the largest airborne operation in history, the British 1st Airborne Division was to capture the bridge at Arnhem, while the 82nd American Airborne Division was to capture the crossings at Nijmegen and Grave and the 101st Airborne Division was to secure crossings between Grave and Eindhoven.

On 10 September, the first part of the operation, called Operation MARKET and involving the seizure of bridges at Eindhoven and Nijmegen, was successful. Operation MARKET GARDEN, the British seizure of the Mass River bridge at Arnhem, turned into a logical and strategic nightmare. British forces found themselves confronted by 9th and 10th SS Panzer Divisions, which were refitting in the area. The British 1st Airborne Division was able to seize and hold one of the two bridges until 20 September, when they surrendered after waiting for the British 2nd Army, which was not able to keep to the schedule. The 1st Airborne Division was effectively wiped out, with 1,000 killed and 6,000 taken prisoner. With German reinforcements gathering around Arnhem, Montgomery ordered British forces to withdraw on 24 September. For students of military strategy, Operation MARKET GARDEN provides numerous examples of faulty decision-making on the part of commanding officers but also of simple bad luck.

Jason Soderstrum

See also: Airborne Operations; Montgomery, Bernard Law; World War II

References and further reading:

Harclerode, Peter. *Arnhem: A Tragedy of Errors.* London: Arms and Armour, 1994.

Hibbert, Christopher. *The Battle of Arnhem.* London: B. T. Batsford, 1962.

Middlebrook, Martin. *Arnhem 1944: The Airbone Battle, 17–26 September.* Boulder, CO: Westview Press, 1994.

Marlborough, John Churchill, First Duke of (1650–1722)

Led the British armies in the War of the Spanish Succession with great success and made the fortune of the house of Churchill in British affairs. John Churchill, born to a wealthy but far from prominent family, rose to prominence thanks to the patronage that the Duke of York, the heir to the British throne and subsequent king, and later Queen Anne conferred upon his family. On the duke's accession as James II (1633–1701, r. 1685–1688), Churchill, a prominent member of James's clique of young officers, received a senior command in the king's large new army and took part in the campaign leading up to Sedgemoor. Nevertheless, he betrayed James II in the revolution of 1688 and then turned coat again and conspired with the deposed pretender during the reign of his successor, William III. These political efforts kept Churchill from much active service in 1689–1702, but Queen Anne made him her captain general upon Britain's entry into the War of the Spanish Succession.

Painting of John Churchill, First Duke of Marlborough. (Library of Congress)

As commander on the continent, Marlborough conquered the Lower Palatinate at the head of an Anglo-Dutch army in 1702 and won the Battle of Blenheim-Höchstädt (1704) in combination with Prince Eugene. For this, Queen Anne conferred upon him the title duke of Marlborough. The years 1703, 1705, and 1707 were fallow periods of failed campaigns, but in 1706 Marlborough led the Anglo-Dutch army into Brabant in a brilliant campaign of maneuver that made possible the victories of Ramillies and Turin. In 1708, the Anglo-Dutch forces and the imperial Habsburg army, at last combined in a single theater under the joint command of Marlborough and Eugene, won the Battle of Oudenaarde, and, showing great strategic and logistical daring, took Lille. The year 1709 saw the more ambiguous victory of Malplaquet and the fall of Mons. In subsequent years, Eugene and Marlborough took many fortresses and devastated northern France, conducting an economic warfare that strained the French economy yet could not force peace upon the enemy. By 1712, Queen Anne faced state bankruptcy. She maneuvered her way out of the war, and Marlborough and his aggressive allies fell from office in the process.

Some historians have exaggerated Marlborough's abilities, portraying him as a prophet rising above the limits of his age and making his Dutch allies scapegoats for his failure to execute a presumed "Napoleonic" vision. Although one of history's great captains, Marlborough's genius was in keeping with the spirit of eighteenth-century warfare, and it was nowhere better exhibited than in his operational masterwork, the passage of the determinedly defended ne plus ultra French lines (1711).

Erik A. Lund

See also: Blenheim-Höchstädt, Battle of; Coehoorn, Baron Menno van; English Wars in Ireland; Eugene of Savoy; Jacobite Rebellions; Malplaquet, Battle of; Northern War, Great; Oudenaarde, Battle of; Ramillies, Battle of; Sedgemoor; Spanish Succession, War of the; Turenne, Henri de la Tour d'Auvergne, Vicomte de

References and further reading:

Chandler, David. *Marlborough as Military Commander.* London: Batsford, 1977.
Churchill, Winston. *Marlborough, His Life and Times.* 4 vols. London: Harrap, 1933–1938.
Marlborough, John Churchill, Duke of. *Letters and Dispatches from 1702–1712.* Ed. George Murray. 5 vols. London: J. Murray, 1845.
———. *The Marlborough-Godolphin Correspondence.* Ed. Henry L. Snyder. 3 vols. Oxford: Clarendon, 1975.

Marne, Battle of the (5–10 September 1914)

Crucial battle in the opening days of World War I. Heinrich von Kluck, commander of the German First Army and right wing of the Schlieffen Plan, advanced through Belgium and northern France in August 1914. Approaching Paris, von Kluck lost contact with the German Second Army on his left and opened a gap between the two advancing armies. He also exposed his right flank when he turned southeast to roll up what he believed to be the French left flank in front of Paris. Taxicabs transported French troops from Paris and caught von Kluck unaware. He quickly transferred two corps from his left flank to the west, further opening the gap north of the Marne River between his army and the German Second Army.

The British Expeditionary Force, under Sir John French, and the French Fifth Army crossed the Marne River and surged into the breach between the two German armies. The German Second Army tenaciously attacked the French Ninth Army under Ferdinand Foch near the marshes of St. Gond. These attacks failed, and the German chief of the general staff, Helmuth von Moltke the younger, ordered a withdrawal of the First and Second Armies to the Aisne River on 10 September 1914. The Germans held this line in the face of stiff attacks, and the "race to the sea" ensued when each side attempted to outflank the opponent. Both sides established a network of linked trenches that would characterize the next four years of warfare on the western front.

The German defeat at the Marne proved a decisive Anglo-French strategic victory and has been termed "the miracle of the Marne." Despite a string of costly defeats on the frontiers, the Anglo-French forces seized the strategic initiative with the victory. As a result, Germany had to fight on two fronts, which ultimately cost it the war.

Mark A. Mengerink

See also: Foch, Ferdinand; French, John Denton Pinkstone, First Earl of Ypres; Joffre, Joseph Jacques Césaire; Moltke, Graf Helmuth Johannes Ludwig von; Schlieffen, Graf Alfred von; World War I

References and further reading:

Asprey, Robert B. *The First Battle of the Marne.* Westport, CT: Greenwood Press, 1962.
Keegan, John. *The First World War.* New York: Alfred A. Knopf/Random House, 1999.
Tuchman, Barbara. *The Guns of August.* New York: Macmillan, 1962.

Marne Counteroffensive (15 July–16 September 1918)

Allied response to the final German offensive push of the war, also known as the Second Battle of the Marne. This battle marked the final turning of the tide for the Allies in World War I. In early July 1918, a German offensive menaced Paris. Many residents of the French capital prepared for evacuation in a situation that bordered on panic. Worse, German long-range artillery sporadically bombarded vital war industries in and around the capital. In the middle of July, the offensive ran out of energy 50 miles east of Paris, along the Marne River.

On 15 July, the U.S. Army's 3d Infantry Division held staunchly against strong local attacks, even though the American troops were nearly surrounded. British, French, Italian, and American reinforcements were rushed to the area and thrown into a large-scale attack. Now began a multinational battle, the outcome of which could very well decide the war.

The Germans, faced with the choice of imminent retreat versus reinforcing their troops along the Marne River at the expense of their impending Flanders offensive, chose the latter. For the first month of the battle, Allied soldiers advanced eastward against the entrenched, reinforced German defenders. Some of the fiercest fighting took place near Soissons, where the Americans encountered fanatical enemy resistance. For much of August, the Germans dug in along the Aisne and Vesle Rivers and held fast against American and French attacks. A break for the Allies came on 2 September, when the American 32d Infantry Division captured the key town of Juvigny, effectively cutting off a major German supply route. Meanwhile, French troops in the south and British troops in the north steadily pushed the Germans eastward.

Day by day, Allied soldiers fought and died to reduce the German salient and eliminate the threat to Paris. Eventually, they succeeded in reducing that salient to such an extent that Paris was no longer in range of German artillery. By mid-September the question was no longer if the Germans would take Paris, but rather if they could stave off the Allies from pushing any further eastward.

The ultimate significance of this battle is that the initiative passed from the Germans to the Allies for the rest of the war. In the spring and early summer of 1918, the Germans had hoped to launch one last great offensive to win the war before fresh American manpower could have any impact on the battle fronts. At the Marne, in the summer of 1918, the Germans ran out of time. From this point forward, the Allies would launch a series of offensives designed to drive the Germans from France, a goal never completely fulfilled, even though World War I would conclude in November 1918 on Allied terms.

John C. McManus

See also: Marne, Battle of the; World War I

References and further reading:

Coffman, Edward. *The War to End All Wars.* Lexington: University Press of Kentucky, 1998.

Toland, John. *No Man's Land.* Garden City: Doubleday, 1980.

Marshall, George Catlett (1880–1959)

U.S. Army chief of staff and one of the foremost soldier-statesmen of the twentieth century. Born in Uniontown, Pennsylvania, on 31 December 1880, George Marshall graduated from the Virginia Military Institute in 1901 and was commissioned in the infantry in 1902. He held a variety of assignments, including in the Philippines and Oklahoma. He attended the Infantry and Cavalry School in Fort Leavenworth (1906–1907) and in 1908 graduated from the Army Staff College there. After working as an instructor at the Staff College (1908–1910), he was an instructor-inspector for the Illinois National Guard and an infantry company commander. He again served in the Philippines until 1916.

General George Marshall, c. 1944. (Library of Congress)

Marshall established his reputation as a brilliant staff officer following U.S. entry into World War I. Sent to France in June 1917, he served on the staff of American Expeditionary Force commander General John J. Pershing and planned the September 1918 American offensive at St. Mihiel. Made operations officer for the First Army, Colonel Marshall planned the transfer of some 400,000 U.S. troops, carried out in just six days, for the September–November Meuse-Argonne offensive.

After the war, Marshall was aide to then army commander General Pershing (1919–1924). He served in China (1924–1927) and afterward was deputy commander of the Infantry School at Fort Benning (1927–1932). He held several command positions before he was promoted to brigadier general (1936). Marshall became deputy chief of staff of the army in 1938, won a promotion to major general that July, and became chief of staff on 1 September 1939.

President Franklin D. Roosevelt advanced Marshall over many more senior officers to appoint him chief of staff of the army with the rank of temporary general in September

1938. Promoted to general of the army in November 1944, he continued in that capacity, earning the unofficial title of "Organizer of Victory" for his masterful leadership, until his retirement in November 1945.

President Harry S. Truman recalled Marshall to serve as special envoy to China (1945–1947) and secretary of state (1947–1949). He was serving as president of the American Red Cross when Truman again recalled him in September 1950 as secretary of defense to preside over the 1950–1953 Korean War military buildup. He held that post until he retired altogether in September 1951. He was awarded the Nobel Prize for peace in 1953, the first soldier so honored. Marshall died in Washington, D.C., on 16 October 1959.

Spencer C. Tucker

See also: Meuse-Argonne; Pershing, John J.; Roosevelt, Franklin D.; St. Mihiel; Truman, Harry S.

References and further reading:

Pogue, Forrest C. *George C. Marshall.* 4 vols. New York: Viking Press, 1963–1987.

Marston Moor (2 July 1644)

Largest battle of the English Civil War. By the middle of 1644, the Scots had joined Parliament against King Charles I, threatening decisively to tip the scales against the royalists. Scottish forces joined parliamentary soldiers to besiege York, the center of royalist power in the north. Charles believed that his survival depended upon York and stripped his own army to send a relieving force under Prince Rupert. The allies lifted the siege to intercept Rupert and force him into decisive battle.

The two armies met 6 miles west of York, on Marston Moor. Each side had about 7,000 cavalry. Parliamentary cavalry included Oliver Cromwell's superbly trained Ironsides. Rupert was heavily outnumbered in infantry, however, with only 13,000 men to his opponents' 20,000. Both armies drew up into traditional battle formations on 2 July, with the infantry in the center and cavalry on either wing. The afternoon was spent in scattered exchanges of artillery, but at 5:00 P.M., Rupert concluded that there would be no fighting and retired to his quarters. At 7:00, Alexander Leslie, parliamentary commander, ordered his army to attack, catching the royalists by surprise. Cromwell's Ironsides dispersed the royalist horse on the left and began to attack the unprotected infantry. When George Goring's royalist cavalry threatened the parliamentary right, Cromwell moved his disciplined force to the other wing and defeated Goring. Although the unsupported royalist infantry put up a brave fight, they were enveloped and crushed. York and northern England were lost to Charles. Although the Civil War continued for another year, Rupert's defeat at Marston Moor made a military victory for Charles impossible.

Tim J. Watts

See also: Cromwell, Oliver; English Civil War; Rupert, Prince

References and further reading:

Newman, P. R. *The Battle of Marston Moor, 1644.* Chichester, UK: Bird, 1981.

Woolrych, Austin. *Battles of the English Civil War: Marston Moor, Naseby, Preston.* New York: Macmillan, 1961.

Young, Peter. *Marston Moor, 1644: The Campaign and the Battle.* Kineton: Roundwood Press, 1970.

Martí y Pérez, José Julián (1853–1895)

Cuban patriot, guerrilla fighter, poet, and philosopher. Born in Havana, Cuba, on 28 January 1853 of Spanish parentage, Martí's father was an artillery sergeant. Martí began his writing career early, publishing various autonomist articles by 1869. Because of a letter he wrote to a friend, Martí and his companion Fermín Valdés Dominguez were sentenced in April 1870 to hard labor at the Quarries of San Lázaro, where he was put in leg irons. In January 1871, he was deported to Spain, where he wrote his famous work, *El presidio politico en Cuba.* Martí and Valdés Dominguez moved to Zaragoza, Spain, to continue their studies in 1872, and in 1875, he was reunited with his parents and siblings in Veracruz, Mexico. He was again deported to Spain in 1879 but escaped to France and then to New York. His article written about the arrival of the Statue of Liberty in New York for the newspaper *La Nacion* of Venezuela stands as one of the finest pieces written on the subject in any language.

In 1887, he became consul for Uruguay in New York and then for Argentina and Paraguay. In 1889, he began the journal *La Edad de Oro* (Age of Gold, i.e., childhood), dedicated to children and their needs. And in 1892, he founded in New York the Cuban Revolutionary Party in New York, with the goal of winning Cuban independence. In April 1894, Martí and Máximo Gómez met in New York. Gómez returned to Santo Domingo to begin preparations and planning for the eventual invasion of Cuba. In January 1895, Martí traveled to Montecristi, Santo Domingo, to meet with Gómez again. In March of the same year, Martí wrote the *Manifesto of Montecristi,* in which he put forth his political views. By this time, war in Cuba was already a fact, having started on 24 February 1895. Martí landed in Cuba and joined the fighting. On 19 May, during a clash at Dos Rios, he fell, mortally wounded. One of the most erudite philosophers of nineteenth-century Cuba and perhaps the whole of Latin America, José Martí is remembered as the "father of the Cuban Republic."

Peter Carr

See also: Cuban Ten Years' War; Cuban Revolution; Weyler y Nicolau, Valeriano, Marquis of Tenerife

References and further reading:

Mañach, Jorge. *Martí: Apostle of Freedom.* Trans. Coley Taylor. Preface by Gabriela Mistral. New York: Devin-Adair, 1950.

Masada, Siege of (72–73)

Mountaintop fortress in the Judean desert of Israel used as a stronghold by Jewish Zealots, the Sicarii, one of the numerous groups who revolted against Rome in 66. Originally fortified by the Maccabees, Masada was improved by Herod the Great, who constructed two palaces, added heavy walls and defensive towers, and developed a cachement system to supply water for his royal citadel. After Herod's death, the Romans controlled Masada until Jewish Zealots captured the fortress by surprise in 66. After the fall of Jerusalem in 70, this group of about 1,000 men, women, and children refused to surrender. The Roman X Legion under the command of Flavius Silva besieged Masada, but the elaborate defensive system proved superior to Roman siege machines. Assembling an army of 15,000 soldiers, the Romans built a wall around the mountain to prevent any escapes and then constructed a sloping ramp up the west side of the mountain until they were in reach of the walls. After two years, Roman forces finally penetrated the fortress, only to find that the Jews, led by Eleazar ben Yair, had committed suicide rather than be enslaved. Only two women and five children survived; the rest had drawn lots to determine who would die first, with each father responsible for killing his family before taking his own life. The provisions, except for the food, were set on fire. Roman historian Josephus Flavius provides an account of the events provided to him by the survivors. Except for a brief period of Jewish control in the second century during the Bar Kochba revolt, the fortress remained abandoned until the twentieth century, when Masada became a symbol of Jewish independence.

Cynthia Clark Northrup

See also: Jewish Revolts; Josephus, Flavius

References and further reading:

Tamarin, Alfred H. *Revolt in Judea: The Road to Masada, the Eyewitness Accounts by Flavius Josephus of the Roman Campaign against Judea, the Destruction of the Second Temple, and the Heroism of Masada.* New York: Four Winds Press, 1968.

Yadin, Yigael. *Masada: Herod's Fortress and the Zealots' Last Stand.* New York: Random House, 1966.

Masséna, André, Duc de Rivoli, Prince d'Essling (1758–1817)

An extremely aggressive field commander of the French Revolutionary and Napoleonic Wars. Massena was born in Nice (6 May 1758) and enlisted in 1775. He left the army in August 1789 and became lieutenant colonel of a volunteer regiment in 1792.

In the siege of Toulon, he gained Napoleon's attention and a promotion to division general (20 December 1793). In Italy in 1794–1795, he achieved successes but also revealed the rapacity that marred his career. Masséna played crucial roles at Lodi (10 May 1796), where he led the charge that took the bridge, and at Rivoli in January 1797.

Masséna commanded the combined Armies of Helvetia and the Danube in his most significant campaign, defeating an Austro-Russian army at Zurich (25–28 September 1799) and then crushing a Russian relief army. Thus he decisively turned the tide of war and ended the allied invasion threat in that theater.

In November 1799, Napoleon sent Masséna to Genoa, which the Austrians were besieging. After a heroic defense, he surrendered (4 June 1800) with full military honors. Relieved of command, partly because of looting, Masséna spent the next five years in civilian life. Nevertheless, Napoleon appointed him a marshal in 1804.

Masséna contributed to Napoleon's Austerlitz campaign by keeping the Archduke Charles occupied in Italy. In July 1807, Masséna again returned to civilian life, and Napoleon named him duc de Rivoli in March 1808. In the 1809 campaign, Masséna fought bravely at Aspern-Essling (20–22 May), where, covering the evacuation to Lobau Island, he was the last man across the bridge before its destruction. At Wagram (6 July), he audaciously sent his troops laterally across the enemy front to fill a gap in the French lines. Napoleon awarded him the title prince d'Essling in January 1810.

Reluctantly, Masséna accepted command of the Army of Portugal in May 1810. He captured Ciudad Rodrigo (10 July) and Almeida (28 August) but failed to defeat Arthur Wellesley, the Duke of Wellington, at Torres Vedras. Failure in Iberia ended Masséna's field command. Thus closed the active career of one of Napoleon's most capable generals. He died in Paris on 4 April 1817.

James K. Kieswetter

See also: Austerlitz, Battle of; French Revolutionary Wars; Napoleonic Wars; Rivoli; Toulon, Siege of; Wagram; Wellington, Arthur Wellesley, Duke of

References and further reading:

Chandler, David G. *The Campaigns of Napoleon.* New York: Macmillan, 1966.

Horward, Donald D. *Napoleon and Iberia: The Twin Sieges of Ciudad*

Rodrigo and Almeida. Tallahassee: University Presses of Florida, 1980.

Macdonnell, Archibald Gordon. *Napoleon and His Marshals.* New York: Macmillan, 1934.

Marshall-Cornwall, James H. *Marshal Masséna.* New York: Oxford University Press, 1965.

Klaniczay, Tibor, and József Jankovics, eds. *Matthias Corvinus and the Humanism in Central Europe.* Budapest: Balassi, 1994.

Kovács, Péter E. *Matthias Corvinus.* Budapest: Officina Nova, 1990.

Létmányi, Nándor. *Párhuzam Hunyadi János es fia Mátyás között* (A comparison of John Hunyadi and his son Matthias). Budapest: Atheneum, 1885.

Vég, Gábor. *Magyarország királyai és királynöi* (Hungary's kings and queens). Budapest: Maecenas, 1991.

Matthias I (Mátyás Hunyadi) (1443–1490)

The first Hungarian king not of the House of Árpád and one of Hungary's greatest kings, known as "the Truthful." Matthias's father was János Hunyadi, a popular warlord who led several campaigns against the Turks. The Hungarian estates chose Matthias as king on 24 January 1458. His rule was at first tenuous, and he had to put down several attempts to overthrow him; he also had to prevent Holy Roman Emperor Frederick III from taking the Hungarian throne.

Once his throne was secure, Matthias devoted his attention to strengthening his authority over the nobility and centralizing the government. He expanded his power base within the lesser nobility but failed to win the permanent allegiance of the great nobles. Matthias reformed the army, known as the "Black Troops," which he used to keep order and collect taxes. Taxes now became permanent and provided him with a regular source of income. Not stopping his reforms with the army, he recodified Hungarian common law, reorganized the legal system, established a civil service, improved the means of communication, and promoted the development of towns. He also founded the University of Pressburg (now Bratislava), revived the University of Pecs, and introduced the Renaissance to Hungary.

Matthias saw the Ottoman Turks as Hungary's chief enemy and sought to build a united European coalition against them under his leadership. He defeated the Turks in 1479 and only after his death did they again become a serious threat, in part because of the enmity of Vienna. Matthias devoted the last 20 years of his life to establishing a Danubian empire. He became king of Bohemia in 1479 and laid siege to Vienna and took it in 1485, annexing Austria, Styria, and Carinthia. Although he failed to win his desired election as Holy Roman Emperor, he transferred his court to Vienna and died there in 1490. His strong rule provoked a reaction under his successors. His reforms were largely abandoned, and the country fell into anarchy.

Ákos Tajti

References and further reading:

Bánlaki, József of Doberdo. *A magyar nemzet hadtörténelme* (The military history of the Hungarian nation). Budapest: Grill, 1934.

Maurice of Nassau (1567–1625)

Dutch general who significantly contributed to the development of early modern warfare. Maurice was born to William the Silent, Prince of Orange, in 1567, and his family sought to free the Netherlands from Spanish control. He attended university at both Heidelberg and Leiden, but his father's assassination in 1584 thrust Maurice into leadership, and he became president of the United Provinces. He soon assumed the duties of admiral general and captain general, making him commander in chief of all Dutch military forces.

Maurice recognized the need to efficiently organize his limited manpower resources to fight the Spanish empire. His knowledge of Roman warfare and mathematics led him to develop small, maneuverable battalion formations that joined both musket and pike in a linear formation. Maurice also instituted rigorous drills for individuals and formations to increase the rate of fire and maneuverability. He experimented with artillery capability embedded within infantry formations, an early attempt at combined arms synchronization. To ensure adequate manpower, Maurice provided consistent pay and encouraged education by establishing the first military academy for officers.

With a responsive and dependable army, Maurice often inflicted disproportionate casualties during battle and soon wrested control of key provinces from the Spanish. To secure terrain, he developed an integrated defensive system of fortified towns and rivers. His success resulted in a 12-year truce with Spain in 1609.

Maurice eventually died from liver disease at The Hague in April 1625. Other commanders, such as Gustavus Adolphus, soon adopted his military innovations. Maurice's legacy of state-supported professional armies and linear gunpowder tactics mark him as one of the founders of modern warfare.

Steven J. Rauch

References and further reading:

McNeill, William H. "Keeping Together in Time." *Military History Quarterly* (Winter 1994).

Parker, Geoffrey. *The Military Revolution.* Cambridge, UK: Cambridge University Press, 1988.

Mauricius Flavius Tiberius (539–602)

One of the eastern Roman Empire's greatest rulers. Maurice became emperor in 582, at a time of great crisis: the Justinian system was crumbling as epidemics, population loss, falling state revenues, and Slav incursions into Thrace threatened to destroy the imperial position throughout Byzantium; the latest in a long line of wars with Sassanid Persia also fared badly.

Maurice's place in history is assured on three separate counts. First, he was the author of a military manual, the *Strategikon,* which remained in imperial service for several hundred years and even today remains in print. Second, he was the architect of comprehensive victory over the Sassanid Empire. His victories at Nisbis and the Araxes (589) led to the overthrow of the Sassanid emperor Hormizd. A disputed succession allowed imperial intervention on behalf of Chosroes, the deposed emperor's son. With Chosroes installed as emperor, Maurice then imposed peace based on the status quo ante bellum and without gain: his calculation was that Sassanid indebtedness would ensure peace and stability in the east.

In the Haemus the empire faced not single, successive invasions by different tribes but simultaneous and continuous invasion by many different groupings: by the time of Maurice's accession, the imperial position had been compromised. Nonetheless, in a series of deliberate campaigns, Maurice curbed the Slavic influx and then defeated the Avars (598–601). His main problem, however, remained inadequate state revenues: his rule was noted for a series of mutinies that attended cost-cutting measures. It was Maurice's decision that the army remain on the Danube River through the coming winter that provoked the mutiny that saw him deposed and decapitated, his four youngest sons having been executed before him.

H. P. Willmott

References and further reading:

Haldon, John. *Warfare, State and Society in the Byzantine World.* London: UCL, 1999.

———. *The Byzantine Wars.* Tempus, Stroud, 2001.

Treadgold, Warren. *Byzantium and Its Army, 284–1081.* Stanford, CA: Stanford University Press, 1995.

Mauryan Empire, Conquests of (321–232 B.C.E.)

Resulted in a rare, internal unification of Hindu India that had taken place only twice before outside invasions became common after 1100 C.E. The Gangetic kingdom of Magadha, with its capital at Patna, was the center of both unifications. By 500 B.C.E., 16 petty Hindu kingdoms established during the Aryan invasions of India competed for control of the Ganges River trade routes in northern India. The unfinished invasion of India by Alexander the Great in 326 B.C.E. appears to have forced India toward unification politically and militarily. Conflicting accounts of Alexander's expedition suggest that huge military forces under King Porhus in western India numbered 60,000 men, 20,000 cavalry, 2,000 chariots, and 3,000 war elephants. Further east, Gangetic forces encountered by Alexander's forward probes are listed by Pliny and Plutarch as numbering 500,000 foot soldiers, 30,000 cavalry, 8,000 chariots, and 9,000 war elephants. It is no wonder Alexander's men rebelled!

In 321, Chandragupta Maurya (325–280 B.C.E.) seized the Magadha throne in northeastern India as Alexander turned south down the Indus River in western India and returned to Persia and eventually Babylon. Chandragupta took advantage of the power gap left by Alexander's victory over King Porhus at the Battle of Hydaspes in western India. He conquered all the land between the Indus River and the Narbada River to the south. The Magadha king then closed the mountain passes in northwestern India used by Alexander and others to invade northern India. He did so by supposedly defeating the Macedonian general Seleucus Nicator in 305 B.C.E. In reality, Seleucus realized he could not defeat the huge Indian forces and negotiated a treaty with Chandragupta while both armies faced each other on the field.

In 280 B.C.E. Bindusara (298–273 B.C.E.), son of Chandragupta, inherited the throne. He extended the empire south into the Deccan plateau near Mysore. Chandragupta's grandson, Ashoka (269–232 B.C.E.), completed the empire with bloody conquests of the Kalinga kingdom on the northeast coast. The Mauryan Empire now controlled all but the southern tip of India, and Ashoka turned toward developing empire, resulting in the "golden age" of the Mauryan Empire. However, his emphasis on Buddhism over the army left India open to invasions from the northwestern mountain passes by Bactrian, Scythian, and Parthian forces. In 150 B.C.E., Indo-Hellenic forces reached Patna (Patiliputra) and found the empire in ruin.

Christopher Howell

See also: Alexander's Wars of Conquest; Aryan Conquest of India; Chandragupta Maurya; Hydaspes, Battle of the

References and further reading:
Kulke, H. and D. Rothermund. *A History of India.* New York: Barnes & Noble Books, 1986.
Majumdar, R. C. *Classical Accounts of India.* Calcutta: Mukhopadhyay Publishers, 1960.
Singh, Sarva Daman. *Ancient Indian Warfare.* Reprint, Dehli: Motilal Banarsidass Publishers, 1997.

Maximilian I (1459–1519)

Holy Roman Emperor who made the Habsburg family into a European power. Maximilian von Habsburg was born in Wiener Neustadt, Austria, on 22 March 1459, the son of Holy Roman Emperor Frederick III, whom he succeeded on 19 August 1493. His marriage in Ghent on 19 August 1477 to Mary, daughter of Charles the Bold, Duke of Burgundy, gained him the Netherlands, much Burgundian territory, and the enmity of France. French king Louis XI immediately attacked. Maximilian defended his lands well and decisively defeated the French at Guinegate on 7 August 1479, but the Franco-Austrian War continued sporadically until 1493, with Maximilian keeping almost all the disputed area.

Maximilian pursued his lifelong ambition to unite all of Europe under the Habsburgs. His three main tactics were diplomacy, arranging marriages, and waging war. His main rival was France. From 1482 to 1485, he fought the Netherlands States General, finally wresting from them the regency of his son, Philip. When Hungarian king Matthias I Corvinus died in 1490, Maximilian resumed control of Austrian lands that had been seized by Hungary and declared himself a candidate for the vacant throne. When Ladislas II of Bohemia was elected instead, Maximilian forced the Treaty of Pressburg upon him in 1491 so that the throne of Bohemia and Hungary would pass to a Habsburg if ever vacant again. In 1495 he joined the Holy League of Spain, Venice, Milan, and the papal states to drive the French out of Italy and took an active role in the league's military efforts. Having lost his war against Switzerland in 1499, he was compelled to recognize Swiss independence. Allied with English king Henry VIII, he beat the French on 16 or 17 August 1513 in a second battle at Guinegate, called the "Battle of the Spurs" because of the speed with which the French retreated. He continued fighting the French, mostly in Italy, until 1516, and died in Wels, Austria, on 12 January 1519.

Eric v. d. Luft

See also: Austro-Swiss Wars; Charles the Bold, Duke of Burgundy; Holy Roman Empire; Hungarian War with the Holy Roman Empire; Marignano, Battle of; Matthias I; Ravenna; Valois-Habsburg Wars

References and further reading:
Andrews, Marian. *Maximilian the Dreamer: Holy Roman Emperor, 1459–1519.* London: Paul, 1913.
Benecke, Gerhard. *Maximilian I, 1459–1519: An Analytical Biography.* London: Routledge & Kegan Paul, 1982.
Burgkmair, Hans. *The Triumph of Maximilian I.* New York: Dover, 1964.
Seton-Watson, Robert W. *Maximilian I, Holy Roman Emperor.* Westminster, UK: Constable, 1902.
Waas, Glenn Elwood. *The Legendary Character of Kaiser Maximilian.* New York: Columbia University Press, 1941.

Mayaguez Operation (12 May 1975)

On 12 May 1975, Khmer Rouge naval forces operating in Cambodian territorial waters seized the U.S. merchant ship *Mayaguez* and removed its crew of 41. U.S. president Gerald Ford ordered a military response to punish the Khmer Rouge and retake the ship and crew, thought to be on the island of Koh Tang. On 15 May, 11 U.S. Air Force helicopters launched from Utapao, Thailand, and transferred 70 men to the *Holt,* which subsequently came alongside the *Mayaguez* in the first hostile ship-to-ship boarding since the War of 1812; they found it empty.

Eight helicopters carrying approximately 200 men assaulted the eastern and western beaches of Koh Tang's northern neck: four were shot down in the opening minutes of the battle, and only one escaped undamaged. Thirteen survivors were rescued from the water after swimming four hours to the *Wilson* offshore, and three isolated contingents were left on the island, the largest numbering only 60 men. Unknown to the United States, the Khmer were well entrenched in anticipation of a Vietnamese attack over an ongoing territorial dispute.

As the remaining helicopters organized as the second wave, the *Mayaguez* crew was freed from an island 40 miles away. The desperately needed second wave was nearly recalled by the U.S. Joint Chiefs of Staff before the marine assault commander on Koh Tang persevered in arguing that the second wave be landed before the western beach was overrun.

The last available helicopter rescued the last group of marines as darkness closed 14 hours after the initial landings. In all phases of the operation, 50 servicemen were wounded and 41 killed, including three men believed to have been left behind alive and subsequently executed, and 23 air force personnel killed earlier while en route to the staging area at Utapao. It is believed that approximately 60 Khmer Rouge soldiers were killed out of a land and sea force of about 300. Although there was initial rejoicing in the United States over the successful rescue of the *Mayaguez* crew, as news surfaced of the heavy loss of life in the operation, Americans became appalled. The operation, following closely on the fall of South Vietnam, seemed yet another indication that the U.S. military still could not handle operations in less than all-out war.

John N. Warren

See also: Cambodian Wars; Vietnam Conflict

References and further reading:

Guilmartin, John F. *A Very Short War.* College Station: Texas A & M University Press, 1995.

Rowan, Roy. *The Four Days of Mayaguez.* New York: W. W. Norton, 1975.

McClellan, George Brinton (1826–1885)

American Civil War army commander. Born on 3 December 1826 in Philadelphia, McClellan was educated at the University of Pennsylvania before entering the U.S. Military Academy at West Point, New York. After graduating second from his class in 1846, he was commissioned a second lieutenant in the Corps of Engineers. During the Mexican-American War, McClellan won three brevets for gallantry, but he later decided to resign from the army and eventually became the vice president of the Illinois Central Railroad. Soon after the outbreak of the Civil War, he was commissioned a major general in the regular army. In November 1861, after Lieutenant General Winfield Scott's retirement, McClellan was appointed general in chief of the U.S. Army. McClellan proved to be highly effective at organizing and training the Union army, but his skill as an organizer was not matched by his art as a combat commander. After his failures during the Peninsular campaign and at the Battle of Antietam, McClellan was relieved of his command and ordered home to await further orders, which never came.

In 1864, McClellan was nominated by the Democratic Party as its candidate for president on a peace platform (despite the fact that he personally believed that the war should continue until the Union was victorious), but he was easily defeated by Lincoln. After serving as the governor of New Jersey (1878–1881), McClellan died in Orange, New Jersey, on 29 October 1885. He was typical of so many failed high commanders: a superb staff officer who lacked the ability to "think on his feet" rapidly on the battlefield and who invariably took counsel of his fears—the service academies and staff colleges turn them out by the hundreds.

Engraved portrait of General George B. McClellan, with a border of Antietam battle scenes. (Library of Congress)

Alexander M. Bielakowski

See also: American Civil War; Lee, Robert Edward; Lincoln, Abraham

References and further reading:

McClellan, George B. *McClellan's Own Story: The War for the Union.* New York: C. L. Webster & Company, 1887.

Sears, Stephen W. *George B. McClellan: The Young Napoleon.* New York: Da Capo Press, 1999.

McDowell, Irvin (1818–1885)

Union general defeated in the American Civil War's first major battle, First Bull Run. Irvin McDowell was born on 15 October 1818 in Columbus, Ohio. He attended the U.S. Military Academy, graduating in 1838 in the middle of his class, and began his career as an artillerist. During the Mexican-American War, he fought at Buena Vista, earning a brevet promotion. Joining the adjutant general's corps in 1848, he served in staff positions until 1861.

McDowell was promoted to brigadier general at the outbreak of the Civil War and, because of political connections, was given command of the Washington, D.C., military district. He built an army in record time but could do little about its lack of combat experience. Under political pressure, McDowell methodically launched an offensive toward Richmond, hoping to end the war in a single battle.

Facing Confederate generals Pierre Gustave Toutant Beauregard and Joseph E. Johnston, McDowell did a capable job of deploying his divisions for the initial Battle of Bull Run on 21 July 1861 but was unable to steady his fatigued recruits when the rebels poured fresh troops into the battle after a daylong stalemate. McDowell soon faced a rout, as thousands of terrified Union troops ran back to Washington.

McDowell was soon relieved by General George McClellan and later reassigned as a corps commander. He again commanded the Washington garrison during the Peninsular campaign in 1862. At Second Bull Run, under General John Pope, McDowell's performance was suspect, resulting in his relief for cause. A court of inquiry exonerated him, but his fighting career was over. McDowell subsequently commanded several military departments, retiring in 1882. He died in San Francisco on 4 May 1885. McDowell was that very ubiquitous commander in military history: one who could achieve high command for his ability to train and supply troops but lacked the blood instinct to win on the battlefield.

Michael S. Casey

See also: American Civil War; Beauregard, Pierre Gustave Toutant; Johnston, Joseph Eggleston; McClellan, George Brinton

References and further reading:

Davis, William C. *Battle at Bull Run: A History of the First Major Campaign of the Civil War.* New York: Stackpole Books, 1995.

Hassler, Warren W. Jr. *Commanders of the Army of the Potomac.* Westport, CT: Greenwood Press, 1962.

McNair, Lesley J. (1883–1944)

Commander of U.S. Army Ground Forces in World War II. McNair, a combat veteran of World War I, is usually credited as the general most responsible for training American ground combat forces in World War II. He saw active duty in North Africa and was wounded at a forward observation post in Tunisia in 1943.

After his recovery, he was given "command" of a fictional organization designed to deceive the Germans about the upcoming Normandy invasion. McNair's First Army Group was ostensibly slated to cross the channel at its most narrow point and invade in the Pas de Calais area. This deception plan, generally known as Operation FORTITUDE, had the goal of convincing the Germans the invasion would come anywhere but Normandy, the site of the real invasion. It succeeded mightily. Even after a lodgement had been secured at Normandy, Hitler continued to insist that the Allies were making a feint to draw German attention from the Calais area.

In late July 1944, roughly two months after the invasion, McNair—as was his penchant—went to a forward area to watch the carpet bombing preceding the American attack at St. Lo. The heavy bomber crews that day were told to fly horizontally along enemy lines, instead of vertically across Allied lines, in an effort to avoid friendly casualties. But, thanks to heavy German antiaircraft fire and a steady wind that blew marking smoke toward American lines, many of the bomber crews accidentally dropped their loads on American troops, including McNair's observation trench. He and at least 100 other Americans were killed. A story quickly circulated among American combat troops that the only trace of McNair ever found was his bloody ring finger, West Point class ring still attached. McNair was the highest-ranking military American to die in World War II.

John C. McManus

References and further reading:

Kahn, E. J., Jr. *McNair: Educator of an Army.* Washington, DC: Office of the Chief of Military History, 1945.

Palmer, Robert R. *The Procurement and Training of Ground Combat Troops.* Washington, DC: Office of the Chief of Military History, 1948.

McNamara, Robert Strange (1916–)

Secretary of defense during much of the Vietnam conflict. Born in California, McNamara obtained a position at the Harvard Business School that led to his employment as an

Defense Secretary Robert McNamara at a news conference, 1967. (Library of Congress)

analyst with the U.S. Army Air Forces's strategic bombing campaign. This duty brought about his hiring by the deteriorating Ford Motor Company, where he ultimately became the firm's president before being selected as secretary of defense by President John F. Kennedy.

McNamara arrived at the Pentagon determined to apply contemporary statistical management techniques to achieve "cost-effectiveness" in terms of procurement and strategy and was indifferent to service self-conceptions of mission and image. Considered as one of those urging the escalation of American involvement in the Vietnam conflict, McNamara tried to "manage" the war in the same statistical fashion as he directed the administration of Ford and the defense establishment, apparently ignoring the historical and emotional elements of war.

Paradoxically, the supposedly "bloodless" McNamara proved unable to stand the stress of the war, failing to win concessions from Hanoi or from the turmoil his strategy provoked in American society. Resigning in 1968 before the conclusion of the Johnson administration, McNamara continued in public life as president of the World Bank and (bafflingly, considering his record) as a commentator on the United States role in the world.

George R. Shaner

See also: Castro Ruz, Fidel; Cuban Missile Crisis; Dominican Civil War; Ho Chi Minh; Vietnam Conflict; Vo Nguyen Giap; Westmoreland, William

References and further reading:

McMaster, H. R. *Dereliction of Duty: Lyndon Johnson, Robert McNamara, the Joint Chiefs of Staff, and the Lies That Led to Vietnam.* New York: HarperCollins, 1997.

Shapley, Deborah. *Promise and Power: The Life and Times of Robert McNamara.* Boston: Little, Brown, 1993.

Vandiver, Frank E. *Shadows of Vietnam: Lyndon Johnson's Wars.* College Station: Texas A & M University Press, 1997.

Meade, George Gordon (1815–1872)

Union field commander in the American Civil War, victor at Gettysburg. Meade was born in Cadiz, Spain, to American parents on 31 December 1815. Commissioned in the artillery after his graduation from West Point in 1835, he resigned in 1836 after brief service against the Seminoles, became a civil engineer, but rejoined the army in 1842. In the Mexican-American War under Zachary Taylor, he saw action at Palo Alto on 8 May 1846, Resaca de la Palma, and Monterrey, where he was brevetted first lieutenant. He participated in the siege of Veracruz under Winfield Scott in 1847. As a military surveyor and engineer after the war, he made first lieutenant in 1851 and captain in 1856.

On 31 August 1861, Meade was commissioned brigadier general of Pennsylvania volunteers. After duty in the Washington, D.C., garrison, he fought in the Seven Days' Battles at Mechanicsville, Beaver Dam Creek, Gaines' Mill, White Oak Swamp, and Glendale, where he suffered a terrible lung wound that troubled him for the rest of his life. Nevertheless, he was able to lead a brigade at Second Bull Run; a division at South Mountain, Antietam, and Fredericksburg; and a corps at Chancellorsville. As major general of volunteers since 29 November 1862, he replaced Joseph Hooker in command of the Army of the Potomac on 28 June 1863. Meade then won his great defensive victory at Gettysburg.

For winning at Gettysburg, Meade received the thanks of Congress and a brigadier general's commission in the regular army but was criticized for his failure to pursue Robert E. Lee. The press conspired to mention him only unfavorably because his bristly temper had riled some reporters. His Bristoe Station, Rapidan Ring, and Mine Run campaigns against Lee misfired. Except for the period from 30 December 1864 to 11 January 1865, Meade commanded the Army of the Potomac until 27 June 1865, but in March 1864, Lieutenant General Ulysses S. Grant established headquarters in Meade's camp, which essentially reduced Meade to Grant's executive officer. He served Grant ably at the Wilderness, Spotsylvania, Cold Harbor, Petersburg, Five Forks, and Appomattox, achieving a promotion to major general on 18 August 1864. Debilitated by his wound, he died of pneumonia in Philadelphia on 6 November 1872.

Eric v. d. Luft

See also: American Civil War; Antietam/Sharpsburg; Bull Run, Second/Manassas Junction; Chancellorsville, Battle of; Cold Harbor, Battle of; Fredericksburg; Gettysburg; Grant, Ulysses Simpson; Hancock, Winfield Scott; Hooker, Joseph; Lee, Robert Edward; Mexican-American War; Monterrey; Petersburg, Siege of; Resaca de la Palma; Scott, Winfield; Seven Days' Battles; Spotsylvania Court House; Taylor, Zachary; Wilderness

References and further reading:

Cleaves, Freeman. *Meade of Gettysburg.* Norman: University of Oklahoma Press, 1960.

Lyman, Theodore. *With Grant and Meade from the Wilderness to Appomattox.* Lincoln: University of Nebraska Press, 1994.

Pennypacker, Isaac Rusling. *General Meade.* New York: Appleton, 1901.

Sauers, Richard Allen. *A Caspian Sea of Ink: The Meade-Sickles Controversy.* Baltimore: Butternut and Blue, 1989.

Medals and Decorations

Throughout history, rulers and states have found ways to recognize heroic achievement and military service. Ancient Greek literature refers to the award of arms and armor to commanders victorious in war. These gifts were often adorned with metal ornaments bearing martial symbols. This practice was later adopted by the Romans, who awarded circular medallions, or phalerae, worn on the breastplate of the recipient. Both Greeks and Romans also issued large coins, or medallions, to commemorate military victories. This practice was lost to Europe with the collapse of the Roman Empire, not to be revived (incredibly) until the fifteenth century.

The bestowing of awards in recognition of military and spiritual achievement resumed with the establishment of religious orders of knighthood during the Crusades. The pope officially recognized the oldest of these, the Order of the Knights of St. John of Jerusalem, in 1113.

As Europe emerged from the early Middle Ages, rulers established their own secular orders of chivalry, using the religious orders as models. These orders strategically bound knights, exclusively feudal nobility, to the sovereign through precepts of chivalric honor and religious duty. One of the earliest of these orders, the English Order of the Garter, was believed to have been founded by Edward III in 1348.

Awards recognizing military service were initially limited to a select number of officers. In 1588, Queen Elizabeth I of England presented medals of gold and silver to her senior commanders to mark the defeat of the Spanish Armada in 1588. Her Stuart successors continued the practice. In 1643, England's King Charles I instituted one of the first awards for gallantry when he authorized a medal awarded to any man who succeeded in a "forlorn hope." Medals, gold to officers and silver to enlisted men (the first recorded instance), celebrated Oliver Cromwell's victory over the Scots at the Battle of Dunbar in 1650.

Although the practice of awarding medals subsequently fell into disuse in England, other nations adopted the tradition. The Russian monarchs Peter the Great and Catherine the Great authorized both gallantry and service medals. During the American Revolution, General George Washington issued a heart-shaped cloth decoration known as the Badge of Military Merit as a reward for conspicuous gallantry.

The Napoleonic Wars brought a renewed interest in medals and decorations. In 1804, Napoleon established the Legion d'Honneur, an award for both bravery in action and distinguished civil or military service, regardless of the rank of the recipient. Five years later, Czar Alexander I of Russia established the Cross of St. George to honor the bravery of noncommissioned officers and enlisted men. In 1813, Frederick William III of Prussia first instituted the Iron Cross (das Eiserne Kreuz) as a gallantry award.

Great Britain hesitatingly resumed rewarding senior officers with medals, but it was not until the issuance of a silver service medal for the Battle of Waterloo in 1815 that all ranks shared the same award. The Waterloo Medal set the pattern for subsequent British campaign medals. With the exception of those awarded for World War II, most British medals bear the name, rank, and regiment of the recipient. As Britain's imperial wars increased, so did the issuance of campaign medals. Rather than award a specific medal for every battle, medals were issued for entire wars, with separate bars affixed to denote participation in particular engagements.

The first official decoration solely for gallantry in the British army was the Distinguished Conduct Medal, first instituted in 1845, but it was awarded only to sergeants. At the suggestion of the prince consort, Queen Victoria authorized the Victoria Cross for acts of conspicuous valor, a simple bronze cross cast from Russian cannon captured during the Crimean War. From the award's creation in 1856 to the Falkland Islands War (1982), only 1,354 Victoria Crosses were awarded to officers and men. It remains Britain's preeminent gallantry decoration.

At the outbreak of the American Civil War, there were no American medals for distinguished service or gallantry. The Medal of Honor was authorized by Congress in December 1861 to recognize Union officers and soldiers who displayed conspicuous gallantry in battle. Originally intended for only the duration of the Civil War, the medal's authorization was extended to cover subsequent conflicts.

The first American service or campaign medals were issued for action in the Spanish-American War (1898). President Theodore Roosevelt, an enthusiastic advocate of military medals and awards, pressed Congress and the War Department to honor veterans of previous wars. During his presidency, service medals were issued to veterans of the Civil War, the Indian wars, the China Relief Expedition, and many other campaigns.

In the profusion of medals and decorations established during World War I, the United States created a hierarchy of decorations. The Distinguished Service Cross (1917), the Distinguished Service Medal (1918), and the Silver Star (1918) all recognized levels of heroism that did not meet the high standard set for the Medal of Honor. The British government also established auxiliary honors, such as the Military Cross (1914) and the Military Medal (1916) to meet the huge demand for awards. The Central Powers, just like the Allies, liberally created and awarded medals during the war. The Prussian Iron Cross, never a permanent decoration, was reauthorized on 5 August 1914 and issued in great numbers.

In the aftermath of war, the Romanov, Habsburg, and Hohenzollern Empires disappeared, along with their complex systems of honors and awards. In Russia, the Bolshevik leadership, slow to recognize the propaganda and loyalty value of awards, later enthusiastically embraced them. The militaristic Nazi Party in Germany established its own extensive system of badges and honors well before it assumed power in 1933.

World War II precipitated a rash of awards. All of the belligerent nations and most of the neutral nations issued medals to mark the event. In recent years, the United Nations has increasingly played a role in settling international disputes, and it issues service medals to its peacekeeping forces dispatched to monitor the peace in ethnic and regional conflicts.

There are instructive differences between the democracies and other powers in the awarding of the higher medals: the former often honors soldiers who have saved lives; the latter awards only those who have killed or captured the enemy. The democracies also have rigid rules for the awarding of the highest awards; and rarely is it even charged that politics, favoritism, or nepotism were involved in the process. The same cannot be said for other nations.

Eric Smylie

References and further reading:

Dorling, H. Taprell. *Ribbons and Medals.* London: Osprey Publishing, 1983.

Kerrigan, Evans E. *American War Medals and Decorations.* New York: Mallard Press, 1990.

Litherland, A. R., and B. T. Simkin. *Spink's Standard Catalogue of British Orders, Decorations, and Medals.* London: Spink and Son, 1990.

Meriecka, Vaclav. *The Book of Orders and Decorations.* London: Hamlyn, 1975.

Purves, Alec A. *The Medals, Decorations, and Orders of the Great War, 1914–1918.* London: J. B. Hayward & Son, 1975.

———. *The Medals, Decorations, and Orders of the World War II, 1939–1945.* London: J. B. Hayward & Son, 1986.

Medici, Giovanni de (a.k.a. Pope Leo X) (1475–1521)

Vivacious warrior-pope who made major contributions to the reestablishment of Rome as a center of European cultural activity and political power. Giovanni was the second son of Lorenzo the Magnificent, ruler of the Florentine Republic at the height of the Italian Renaissance. His education was the finest Europe had to offer at the time; he studied under the tutelage of figures like philosopher Pico della Mirandola and from early on was destined for clerical service. Perhaps his most notable action was the excommunication of Martin Luther in 1521, but Giovanni made other significant historical contributions, such as expediting the construction of St. Peter's Basilica and substantially increasing the holdings of the Vatican library.

In general, Giovanni was committed to the arts in a manner befitting a Renaissance ruler, spending much of his personal wealth and the money of the church on cultural enterprises. As head of the Catholic Church, temporal ruler of the papal states, and head of the ruling Medici family, Giovanni engaged in political struggle and what some might consider an overabundance of nepotism. He granted, for example, the archbishopric of Florence to his cousin (who would later become Pope Clement VII) and called on his nephew Lorenzo and brother Giuliano to be Roman patricians.

These political maneuvers were initiated in an attempt to dominate Italy, the central European power at the time, and they often brought with them considerable danger from rival factions and outside powers. France, in particular, felt it had claims to key Italian cities like Milan and Naples, resulting in Louis XII's march on Italy in 1513. Giovanni grudgingly formed an alliance with the militarily powerful Spanish, and the French were defeated at Novara, forcing Louis to withdraw. When France's Francis I rose to power in 1515, however, the war was renewed, and Giovanni revived his alliance with Spain and England. Giovanni's defeat at Marignano on 14 September 1515 forced him to make peace and draw up the Concordat of Bologna, which regulated church and state relations until the 1790s.

David J. Tietge

See also: Marignano, Battle of

References and further reading:

Gobineau, Arthur, Comte de. *The Golden Flower.* Trans. Ben Ray Redman. Freeport, NY: Books for Libraries Press, 1968.

Mee, Charles L. *White Robe, Black Robe.* New York: Putnam Books, 1972.

Vaughan, Herbert Millingchamp. *The Medici Popes.* Port Washington, NY: Kennikat Press, 1971.

Medicine, Military

The medical and surgical specialty concerned with the ailments of soldiers and sailors. Warfare provides opportunities to expand medical and surgical knowledge but, at the same time, frustrates battlefield doctors who are unable to prevent death, relieve suffering, cure disease, or mend wounds. But military doctors and surgeons are unique in their ambivalent position: they are employed in their healing tasks by the same organization that inflicts wounds and pain, more sometimes on their own patients.

Detailed descriptions of wounds in the *Iliad* show that the Greeks knew basic human anatomy very well. Ancient Chinese and Indian texts reveal similar levels of understanding. Such knowledge is prerequisite for effective trauma surgery. That does not mean that ancient trauma surgery was effective; usually, it was not. There was little a surgeon could do except pull out the arrow or spear, bandage the wound, splint or amputate the shattered limb, numb the patient with alcohol, and hope for the best. Yet there is compelling evidence in Greek and Roman literature that army surgeons were revered. The bravest soldiers and highest-ranking officers were attended by the most skillful surgeons. Thanks to his doctors, Alexander the Great survived dozens of grim wounds before dying of fever at 33. Ancient military surgeons frequently failed, but obviously they were serious about their practical science.

Like medieval medicine in general, medieval military surgery regressed from the progress made in ancient cultures. Except for Paul of Aegina (625–690), the Chinese, the Arabs, the School of Salerno, Lanfranc (fl. 1290), and Guy de Chauliac (c. 1298–1368), few doctors made advances in surgery between the fall of Rome and about 1500. Medieval medical students learned anatomy from the inaccurate works of Galen (130–200), not by direct experience. Until laboratory dissection of cadavers began to be allowed in the sixteenth century, studying battlefield casualties was the main way for surgeons to gain firsthand knowledge of human anatomy.

Ambroise Paré (1510–1590) was the father of modern military surgery. He gained fame through his treatment of a relatively new phenomenon in warfare, gunshot wounds. Earlier surgeons studied gunshot wounds, but Paré was the first to learn how to attend to them effectively. For two centuries after Paré, the French dominated surgery in general and military surgery in particular.

The Thirty Years' War, the early colonial conflicts between England and France, and other seventeenth- and eighteenth-century European wars led to noteworthy increases in medical and surgical knowledge. John Woodall (1570–1643) wrote the first textbook of naval surgery. Johann Schultes (Johannes Scultetus) (1595–1645) wrote the standard text on surgical instruments and procedures. Richard Wiseman (1622–1676) added to the knowledge of gunshot wounds. Lorenz Heister (1683–1758) developed tourniquets. François-Michel Disdier (1708–1781) contributed to what eventually resulted in the superior first-aid bandaging techniques of Johann Friedrich August von Esmarch (1823–1908). John Hunter (1728–1793) gained new insight into gunshot wounds while serving in the Seven Years' War.

Perhaps the greatest military surgeon of all time was Dominique Jean Larrey (1766–1842), who participated in all major engagements of the Napoleonic Wars. In 1792 he invented the "flying ambulance," by which wounded soldiers could be quickly and safely evacuated. He emphasized first aid and improved the mobile battlefield hospital. The men adored him, and Napoléon himself called him "the most virtuous man I have ever known."

The American Civil War established the United States as the world leader in military medicine. *A Manual of Military Surgery* (1861) by Samuel D. Gross (1805–1884) was the standard text. The surgical potential of anesthesia, introduced in the 1840s, was just beginning to be exploited. Because infection and disease proved more deadly than battles, doctors finally began to notice that sanitation and hygiene were important to military health. New knowledge appeared in several classic works, including *Outlines of the Chief Camp Diseases of the United States Armies as Observed during the Present War* (1863) by Joseph Janvier Woodward (1833–1884) and *A Treatise on Military Surgery and Hygiene* (1865) by Frank Hastings Hamilton (1813–1886).

Antisepsis, anesthesia, and hemorrhage control, the three prerequisites for intricate surgical procedures, were all firm medical facts by the start of the twentieth century. The primary medical concerns in World War I were gas warfare, artillery wounds, disease, and shell shock. During that war, the motorized ambulance first appeared, and the field hospital became more complex.

The American Medical Association's book *War Medicine,* published in eight volumes from 1941 to 1945, was the basic medical and surgical manual for World War II. American medical schools in cooperation with the War Department founded permanent or semipermanent general military hospitals throughout the world. American leadership in surgical innovation was so renowned that Nazi intelligence routinely monitored Allied medical correspondence in order for German military surgeons to acquire techniques from the Americans.

Helicopter evacuations of wounded from battlefields to mobile army surgical hospital (MASH) units began during the Korean War. Thus the speedier use of more sophisticated care than medics could provide on the battlefield became possible.

Military medicine is not only surgery. Disease and filth are sometimes greater threats than the human enemy. In the eighteenth century, beginning with the work of John Pringle (1707–1782), the British began to succeed against some of the diseases that had plagued soldiers and sailors since ancient times. James Lind (1716–1794) and Gilbert Blane (1749–1834) conquered scurvy in the British navy. An American, Walter Reed (1851–1902), discovered the control for yellow fever in 1900 while stationed with the occupation force in Cuba. Another American, Edward B. Vedder (1878–1952), stationed in the Philippines in 1911, developed a cure for amoebic dysentery.

Florence Nightingale founded the modern profession of military nursing during the Crimean War. Before her time, military nurses were typically camp followers, prostitutes, or blowsy girlfriends. Clara Barton attended the Union wounded as an independent nurse during the Civil War, served with the International Red Cross in the Franco-Prussian War, and founded the American Red Cross in 1881.

In times when it was common to spend a lifetime within a few miles of one's birthplace, simple homesickness or "nostalgia" could sap a young soldier's or sailor's will to live, causing his debility or even death. In the twentieth century, this problem was ameliorated by initiatives such as the United Service Organization (USO) and by the fact that young adults had become more accustomed to travel far from home.

Challenges to military medicine at the beginning of the third millennium include chronic health problems such as posttraumatic stress disorder (PTSD), formerly called "shell shock" or "battle fatigue," characterized by psychologically damaging flashbacks to combat situations; the physical aftereffects of exposure to the defoliant Agent Orange in Vietnam; and Gulf War syndrome (GWS), the mysterious biological ailment of veterans of that 1991 conflict. But if there has been one field of undoubted progress in modern times, it has been medicine—and military medicine.

Eric v. d. Luft

See also: American Civil War; Ancient Warfare; Barton, Clarissa; Chemical and Biological Warfare; Ethics of Warfare; Gulf War; Korean War; Laws of War; Napoleonic Wars; Nightingale, Florence; Prisoners of War; Seven Years' War; Thirty Years' War; Vietnam Conflict; War Crimes; World War I; World War II

References and further reading:

Binneveld, J. M. W. *From Shell Shock to Combat Stress: A Comparative History of Military Psychiatry.* Amsterdam: Amsterdam University Press, 1997.

Curtin, Philip D. *Disease and Empire: The Health of European Troops in the Conquest of Africa.* Cambridge, UK: Cambridge University Press, 1998.

Denney, Robert E. *Civil War Medicine: Care and Comfort of the Wounded.* New York: Sterling, 1995.

Ginn, Richard V. N. *The History of the U.S. Army Medical Service Corps.* Washington, DC: Office of the Surgeon General and Center of Military History, 1997.

Megiddo (September–October 1918)

An engagement that ended Turkey's participation in World War I. General Edmund Allenby's effective strategy in Palestine used battle-hardened soldiers, including Australians, New Zealanders, Indians, and Arabs, as well as British troops, and Arab guerrilla fighters led by Thomas Edward Lawrence ("Lawrence of Arabia").

Allenby deployed 57,000 infantry, 12,000 cavalry, and more than 500 guns against the Turks' 32,000 infantry, 200 cavalry, and 400 guns. With superiority in cavalry and mastery of the air, Allenby was well placed to overwhelm the numerically inferior and exhausted Turkish troops. His strategy, however, was based on mobility, surprise, and depriving the enemy of all communications by attacking the Turkish road and rail systems, particularly the Hejaz Railway south of Damascus, the feeder line for supplies for the Fourth, Seventh and Eighth Armies.

Dummy camps and horses were set up, mules raised dust, and a small number of soldiers marched back and forth to create the impression of a much larger force to make the Turks think an attack would come in the Jordan Valley. Allenby deployed his force to the west, with the bulk of his cavalry riding north along the coast before swinging in behind the Turks' Seventh and Eighth Armies and taking their communications centers. Lawrence and his Arab force destroyed railway lines north, south, and west of Deraa on 16 and 17 September, while British and Australian pilots bombed the track and station buildings.

On 19 September, Allenby's bombardment opened along a 24-kilometer (15-mile) front along the coast, punching a hole in the Turkish line. With communications destroyed, German general Liman von Sanders, in Nazareth, had no idea that the Allied forces were sweeping through the breach in the Turkish lines and barely escaped the advancing Desert Mounted Corps.

The retreating Turks were bombed repeatedly by Allenby's aircraft as they fell back from Nablus toward the Jordan River. The Turkish Fourth Army east of the Jordan began retreating on 22 September, surrendering near Amman and at Damascus. By 1 October, the key cities of Beirut, Homs, Aleppo, and Damascus had fallen to Allenby's army, and for Turkey the war was over.

Roslyn Russell

See also: Allenby, Edmund Henry Hynman, Viscount; Lawrence, Thomas Edward; World War I

References and further reading:

Gullett, Henry. *The Australian Imperial Force in Sinai and Palestine, 1914–1918.* Sydney: Angus and Robertson, 1940.

James, Lawrence. *Imperial Warrior: The Life and Times of Field-Marshal Viscount Allenby, 1861–1936.* London: Weidenfeld and Nicolson, 1993.

Livesey, Anthony. *Great Battles of World War I.* New York: Macmillan, 1989.

Wavell, Archibald Percival. *Allenby: Soldier and Statesman.* London: George G. Harrap, 1946.

Megiddo, Battle of (1469 B.C.E.)

In an attempt to regain land, especially cities controlling the Via Maris, the major trade route from Egypt to Syria, Pharaoh Thutmose III of Egypt invaded Canaanite territory with a large army, which may have had as many as 20,000 men. Opposed by the Canaanites under the leadership of the king of Kadesh, the Egyptians chose to attack through the central pass (probably modern Wadi 'Ara), passing into the Jezreel valley with only a small skirmish against a Canaanite guard force. Surprised, the Canaanite army, which had expected an attack through the broader northern or southern approaches, rearranged its lines. The Egyptians deployed their chariots in a line across the pass mouth, with Thutmose III in the center and the Egyptian left wing overlapping the Canaanites to the right. The Canaanites broke under the charge and retreated into the walled city of Megiddo. Because the Egyptians paused to loot the camps of the Canaanites, especially that belonging to the king of Kadesh, the besieged were able to immediately seal the city gate, which necessitated hoisting recovered men over the wall with ropes. Thutmose III then besieged the city for seven months, after which it surrendered, yielding rich plunder, including 350 slaves and the chariots and horses used by the Canaanites.

Although Megiddo is the first recorded battle in history, the Egyptian records show that warfare was already highly developed, with the Egyptian army able to quickly move large numbers of men on forced march, supply them through a long siege, and support the manufacture of weapons and chariots for a large force. The strategy chosen by Thutmose III was closely mirrored by that of Sir Edmund Allenby in his own attack on Megiddo in 1918.

Cynthia Clark Northrup

References and further reading:

Cline, Eric. *Battles of Armageddon.* Ann Arbor: University of Michigan Press, 2000.

Davies, Graham I. *Megiddo.* Cambridge, UK: Lutterworth, 1986.

Herzog, Chaim, and Mordechai Gichon. *Battles of the Bible.* New York: Random House, 1978.

Meigs, Montgomery Cunningham (1816–1892)

The leading American engineering officer of his era and quartermaster general of the U.S. Army during the American Civil War. Born 3 May 1816 in Augusta, Georgia, he grew up in Philadelphia, graduating fifth in his class from the U.S. Military Academy at West Point, New York, in 1836. He entered the Army Corps of Engineers after graduation and supervised the construction of the Washington Aqueduct, the construction of the wings and dome of the U.S. Capitol, and the expansion of the General Post Office Building before the war. As quartermaster general during the Civil War, he provided huge quantities of materials to the Union armies. He commanded Ulysses S. Grant's base of supplies during the Overland campaign (1864) and commanded War Department employees in the Washington fortifications during Jubal Early's raid (July 1864). He personally supervised the resupply of General William Tecumseh Sherman's army at Savannah and a few months later in North Carolina, reopening Sherman's lines of supply. He was brevetted major general on 5 July 1864. Meigs's duties as quartermaster general included the oversight of government land use for military purposes. In this capacity, he first suggested that Arlington would be an appropriate site for a national cemetery.

After the war, Meigs supervised plans for the new War Department building, the National Museum, and the extension of the Washington Aqueduct. He died on 2 January 1892 in Washington, D.C., and is buried in Arlington National Cemetery.

Robert D. Bohanan

See also: American Civil War

References and further reading:

Dickinson, William C., Dean A. Herrin, and Donald R. Kennon, eds. *Montgomery C. Meigs and the Building of the Nation's Capital.* Athens: Ohio University Press, 2001.

Miller, David W. *Second Only to Grant: Quartermaster General Montgomery C. Meigs: A Biography.* Shippensburg, PA: White Mane Books, 2000.

Weigley, Russell Frank. *Quartermaster General of the Union Army: A Biography of M. C. Meigs.* New York: Columbia University Press, 1959.

Mercenaries

Hired professional soldiers who fight for any state without regard to political interests or issues. The use of paid foreign military troops is as old as warfare itself. Mercenary soldiers have been utilized in every period of recorded history. Although possessing a long and rich history, the profession of mercenary has an unsavory reputation. Historically, mercenary use is almost universal in advanced societies, and they have played many key roles in history.

Nearly every ancient empire, including the Israelite, Persian, Chinese, Greek, and Roman Empires, used mercenaries at one time or another. It should be remembered that even Xenophon was a mercenary leader. Without mercenaries, Carthage could never have challenged Rome, and Hellenistic civilization would never have spread to Italy and Afghanistan. Later, mercenaries would be an essential and underrated element in medieval warfare. Flemish mercenaries allowed King Stephen of England (r. 1135–1154) to fight off the Plantagenets (a rival royal house) for nearly 20 years. By the end of the medieval period, mercenaries were abundant in Europe. During this time, the mercenary profession earned its fame and history's scorn.

Following the Hundred Years War (1337–1457), Europe was replete with thousands of men whose only training was in the arts of war. During the fifteenth century, these unemployed men formed "free companies" and sold their services to various princes. Most famous among these mercenary groups were the *Condottieri,* named after the *condotta* or contracts they signed, who fought prominently in the wars of the ministates of Renaissance Italy (the Italian Wars of 1494–1559). The other famous mercenary formation of the time was the Swiss pikemen, who were so impressive in battle that many kings were eager to hire them, including Julius II, who recruited them as a papal police corps, a function they serve to this day.

By the late eighteenth century, conscription and standing armies had largely replaced ad hoc military formations. As a result, the use of mercenaries declined markedly, although the British used a great number of German mercenaries during the American Revolution. The change in the stigma associated with using mercenaries can be seen in the American Declaration of Independence, which lists the king of England's use of "foreign mercenaries" as a specific offense. The French Revolution, with its ideals of patriotism, universal conscription, and fighting for the nation, ideas that spread throughout Europe, made the concept of fighting simply for personal gain unacceptable. Work for mercenaries continued, only now it lacked the status it had enjoyed in an earlier time.

In the second half of the twentieth century, the reputation of the mercenary profession continued to come under assault. Modern concepts of national sovereignty required the suppression of nonstate military activities. Foreign nationals would henceforth be uniformed, trained, and given rank as units of the national army, such as the French Foreign Legion and the British Gurkhas. The 1977 protocol to the Geneva Convention of 1949 sought to codify disgust for mercenaries. For signatories to this protocol, mercenaries are considered outlaws, placing them in the category of criminals or worse.

The end of the Cold War, in much the same fashion as the end of the Hundred Years' War, has created new opportunities for mercenaries. As global military competition disappeared, thousands of highly trained soldiers were in need of employment. At the same time, the disintegration of the bipolar international structure meant that the great powers were less concerned about events happening in Third World countries. True to free market principles, the existence of a demand for military expertise and the existence of a supply invariably created a market.

The post–Cold War environment has led to the creation of private military organizations run, in a professional manner, by retired senior military officers. Among these new mercenaries are Sandline International and Military Professional Resources Incorporated (MPRI). These organizations tend to deal exclusively with national governments and for a fee will provide advice on defense strategy, train units in the nation's armed forces, help the government procure arms, or fight the government's battles.

The new era of the mercenaries has produced mixed reviews, ranging from condemnation for profiteering and, supposedly, for exacerbating civil wars in Africa to praise for providing assistance to Croatian forces in their battle with the Serbian military. The latter intervention, in fact, is credited with bringing both sides to the negotiating table.

It can be argued that precisely because the mercenary fights for money and is thus not nearly so driven by national, ethnic, or racial animosities, he is something of a moderating force in battle. Further, the professionalism of many mercenaries sometimes makes national armies look inept in comparison, and thus not all of the criticism leveled against mercenaries has been entirely disinterested.

Craig T. Cobane

See also: American Revolution; French Foreign Legion; Hundred Years War; Xenophon

References and further reading:

Shearer, David. *Private Armies and Military Intervention.* Oxford, UK: Oxford University Press, 1998.

Thompson, Janice E. *Mercenaries, Pirates, and Sovereigns: State Building and Extraterritorial Violence in Early Modern Europe.* Princeton, NJ: Princeton University Press, 1994.

Yalichev, Serge. *Mercenaries of the Ancient World.* London: Constable and Company, 1997.

Meroe (antiquity–300 C.E.)

Ancient Ethiopian city-state eclipsed by Christian Ethiopians of Aksum. The earliest written account of Meroe dates from 738 C.E., when Arab chronicler Wahb Ibn Munabbeth described Meroe as a city and state by the same name. The tenth-century Arab chronicler al-Masudi of Baghdad argued that the capital, a flourishing market town, was made of gold, meadows, and gems and was the home of the "sons of Kush" and the "sons of Canaan." Meroe was known for its fine architecture and an elaborate system of temples. It was also particularly renowned for its iron smelting.

For hundreds of years, East African coastal trade was carried northwest to the town. From there caravan routes, by which the ancient Kushites traded incense and metal over long distances, led to the highlands of Abyssinia and to the Indian Ocean along the Atbara River. The Meroites probably had ancestral ties to dynastic Egypt. The ancient Kushites of the Nile Valley have left a record of the transfer of their capital to Meroe and include among their former capitals Napata, well-known from dynastic Egyptian records.

During the first century B.C.E., invaders from Arabia conquered northern Ethiopia, forming Aksum. By the fourth century C.E., following their conversion to Christianity, the Axumites had cut Kush's major caravan routes. Ultimately, the Arabian invaders blocked Meroe's access to the Indian Ocean ports, initiating a time of sustained warfare between the city-states. Ultimately, Kush was defeated, and Meroe declined as Aksum gained in power.

Tekla Johnson

References and further reading:

Jackson, John G. *Introduction to African Civilization.* New York: Citadel Press, 1970.

Trigger, B. G., and B. J. Kemp et al. *Ancient Egypt: A Social History.* New York: Cambridge University Press, 1983.

Merovingians

A dynasty of Frankish kings descended, according to tradition, from Merovech, a chieftain of the Salian Franks. Merovech's grandson was Clovis (r. 481–511), founder of the Frankish monarchy. The Merovingians were known as the "long-haired kings," and the cutting of a king's hair represented his loss of royal power.

Originally little more than a tribal chieftain, Clovis became the sole leader of the Salian Franks by force of perseverance and a free use of assassination. Expanding his kingdom with a ruthless single-mindedness, Clovis consolidated the position of the Franks in northern Gaul. In 486 he defeated Syagrius, the last Roman governor in Gaul and, in a series of subsequent campaigns with strong Gallo-Roman support, occupied an area situated between the Frankish kingdom of Tournai, the Visigothic and Burgundian kingdoms, and the lands occupied by the Ripuarian Franks and the Alamanni.

Clovis came to believe that his victory over the Alamanni at Tolbiacum in 496 was due to the help of the Christian God, whom his wife Clotilda, a Burgundian princess, had been encouraging him to accept. With the support of Remigius, bishop of Reims, Clovis converted with some 3,000 of his army. Thereafter, Clovis was the champion of orthodox Christianity against the Arian heretics, the Burgundians and Visigoths. He attacked the Burgundians at Dijon (500), and the Visigoths at Vouillé (507), where he killed their leader Alaric II in single combat.

Clovis instituted a law code (*Lex Salica*), and for the next 200 years, only his descendants were entitled to rule. When he died, having united all Franks under his rule and gained the support of the Gallo-Roman clergy, he was master of most of Gaul. He thus laid the foundation, which even four hundred years of chaos and misrule could not destroy, of the French monarchy. Clovis personifies the metamorphosis of barbarian warrior into the ruler of a state.

The Merovingians followed the Frankish custom regarding patrimony, and on the death of Clovis the kingdom was divided among his four sons. This partition was not made according to ethnic, geographical, or administrative divisions. The only factor taken into account was that the portions be of equal value (defined in terms of the royal fisc and tax revenues). Although boundaries were poorly defined, the new political units became the kingdoms of Austrasia, Neustria, and Burgundy.

These kingdoms, whose borders were constantly shifting, were for a short period united in a single realm under Chlotar I (r. 558–561), again under Chlotar II (r. 613–623), and once again under Dagobert I (r. 629–639). The rule of the Merovingians before Dagobert, who was able to preserve this unity, was troubled by chronic warfare among aristocrats (both Gallo-Romano and Frankish) and rivals for power. Dagobert was the last active ruler, and his descendants were called the "idle kings." With the decline of the royal authority in Austrasia, the office of mayor of the palace developed into the real seat of power. This appointment was hereditary in the family of the Carolingians, who became the nominal as well as the actual rulers when Pepin the Short deposed the last Merovingian king, Childeric III, in 751.

Nic Fields

See also: Carolingian Empire; Charles Martel; Franks

References and further reading:

Wallace-Hadrill, John Michael. *Long-Haired Kings and Other Studies in Frankish History.* London: Methuen, 1962.

Wood, Ian N. *Merovingian Kingdoms, 450–751.* London: Longman, 1994.

Merrill's Marauders

Defeated the Japanese in the Burmese jungle during World War II using guerrilla tactics, duplicity, and Nisei interpreters. Nicknamed for their commanding officer, Brigadier General Frank D. Merrill, the Marauders, also known as Merrill's Raiders, were conceived during the Quebec Conference in August 1943 as a counterpart to Charles Wingate's Chindits. Allied leaders envisioned a guerrilla-style unit that would wreak havoc behind Japanese lines, disrupt communication and supply lines, and aid in attempts to reopen the Burma road. President Franklin D. Roosevelt called for volunteers for "a dangerous and hazardous mission," and 3,000 army personal offered their services.

Code-named GALAHAD and given the obscure designation of 5307 Composite Unit (Provisional), in October they were sent to India for preliminary training. Frontline troops were divided into six combat teams of 400 each. In February 1944, the regiment was transferred to a location near Ledo in the northeastern corner of India. Their only contact with the outside world by radio and plane, three Marauders battalions marched 500 miles down the Ledo road beginning on 7 February and over the next three months engaged the enemy in five major battles and 17 skirmishes. In March, supported by a Chinese division, they engaged the Japanese 18th Division at Walawbum, and even though the second division went without food or water for 36 hours, the Marauders killed 1,500 and pushed the Japanese south. In late March, they were able to establish an airstrip north of Hsamshingyang, even though Merrill, who was suffering from heart trouble, had to be evacuated soon after. Under the new command of Colonel Charles Hunter, the Marauders were able to withstand a Japanese attack, even though the battles at Inkangahtawg and Nhphm Ga cost the 5307th casualities of 59 dead and 314 wounded. The Marauders' greatest accomplishment was the seizure of the vital airstrip at Myitkyina in May. By 4 June, the regiment's casualties in northern Burma totaled 2,394, and only 200 of the original 3,000 men were considered fit for duty. Weakened by dysentery, skin diseases, fatigue, and malaria, the remaining members of the 5307th could not withstand a Japanese assault on 3 August from Myitkyina. After the war, the Marauders were immortalized in poems, on film, and even in comic books.

T. Jason Soderstrum

See also: Burma, Retreat from; Chindits; Wingate, Orde

References and further reading:

Hunter, Charles Newton. *Galahad.* San Antonio: Naylor Company, 1963.

Ogburn, Charlton. *The Marauders.* New York: Harper, 1959.

United States War Department General Staff. *Merrill's Marauders (February–May 1944).* Washington, DC: Historical Division, War Department, 1945.

Mesoamerican Warfare (1200 B.C.E.–1521 C.E.)

Highest development of Stone Age warfare, with some variations. Pre-Columbian Mesoamerica provides an excellent study area for the development of warfare on a different path than in the old world. The lack of draft and pack animals, wheels, metallurgy, and ships in quantity and quality all led to developments different from those in Europe.

The Olmecs (1200–400 B.C.E.) first used warfare to expand trade and access to resources. Fighters from the Olmec city of San Lorenzo utilized obsidian-edged weapons, hand-to-hand elite combat, and small, elite forces numbering in the tens to hundreds to control local trade routes from the Veracruz region. La Venta assumed power from 900 to 400 B.C.E. and introduced the sling, clay projectiles, and yucca-cotton armor to gain superiority. Tortillas were also used to feed the hundreds of troops deployed in enemy territory. By 400, trophy heads, stone knives, obsidian-tip spears, spear throwers, wood shields, upper-torso armor, and hide helmets were common for elites and, to a lesser extent, for supporting commoner forces.

Fortifications also became common, especially in the lowland Mayan area where captive taking and elite warfare dominated. In the Zapotec region, Monte Alban developed as a heavily fortified city that controlled a regional kingdom through its defensive location and warfare based on thrusting spears and hand-to-hand combat. Skull racks indicate probable religious-based warfare centered on captives and sacrifice. By 100 C.E., Monte Alban was challenged by the huge city-state of Teotihuacán in the Mexico City area. From 100 to 700 Teotihuacán, which numbered perhaps 100,000 people, spread its influence over trading partners partly by emphasizing spear throwers, shields, and stone axes and knives. The Teotihuacanos utilized military orders of eagles, jaguars, and so on, special housing, regular production of weapons, and nodal control of trade centers over 1,500 miles distant. Astronomy and religion seem to have played a large role in how and why war was carried out at the end of Teotihuacán hegemony.

In 378, the Teotihuacanos brought projectile warfare into the Mayan region and tipped the balance of power in favor of large Mayan cities like Tikal, with rulers like Smoking-Frog. These lowland Maya developed religious- and astronomy-based warfare among elites that became known as "star wars." The kin-city competitions for resources, natural and supernatural, dominated classic Mayan warfare from 378 to 900, when warfare may have helped to collapse classical Maya civilization.

In most cases, these early and classic period civilizations in Mesoamerica focused on elite warfare and weaponry, with religion and trade as key motivating factors. Most "armies" numbered less than a thousand soldiers, were supported logistically by commoners, and sought out captives as a way of removing rival dynasties and usurping power. It was as important to take religious items of power as it was to take a city. By the early post-Classic period, between 700 and 900, warfare began to change significantly.

At places like Xochicalca, Cacaxtla, or Bonampak, people like the Olmeca-Xicallanca increased warrior numbers, used backpacks in long-distance attacks on cities like Teotihuacán, and involved commoners in guerrilla activities. After the collapse of classic Mesoamerican civilizations, the Toltecs rose to power in central Mexico between 900 and 1200, and their ascendance marked the rise of territorial warfare, combined arms, and highly militaristic society. They would have a great influence on the later Aztecs (Mexica).

Tollan and its Toltec capital of Tula in central Mexico used large armies in the tens of thousands, concentrated projectile fire of spear throwers, obsidian blades on wood clubs and swords, siege warfare with firing platforms, and watercraft, when necessary. One leader, Topiltzin Quetzalcoatl, may have invaded Yucatan territory after 1100 and spread full-scale warfare into the region from the site of Chichén Itzá. Itzá fought with Coba for control of Yucatan for several centuries. The Itzá eventually prevailed in a conflict that saw the fortifications, attrition, and logistics of the Coba defeated by Itzá Mexican military might. However, both sides had exhausted their resources, and soon a series of smaller kingdoms returned control of the peninsula to Maya polities by 1350.

In the post-Classic period, waves of Chichemecan invaders from the north, such as the Toltecs and Aztecs, combined their nomadic, commoner-based, bow-and-arrow warfare with the elite, trained, central Mexico warfare traditions. The Maya region struggled to keep up but was about to be overrun by the time of Spanish invasions in 1519.

The Aztecs established their capital Tenochtitlán on an island in Lake Texcoco and used this combined approach to establish a huge tributary empire by war between 1300 and 1521. They eventually controlled much of Mesoamerica, notable exceptions being the west Mexican Tarascan kingdom, the Tlaxcallan kingdom, and the Maya lowlands.

Tlacaelel was most responsible for the building of the Aztec Empire. He ruled as a warrior-priest, supporting relative after relative as emperor, for most of the fifteenth century. When he died at 96, he left a legacy of military training schools for elites and commoners, arms production, the ability to field huge armies of 100,000 or more for long campaigns, a religious-military system that promoted and supported war and captive taking, and the largest, most powerful empire in the pre-Columbian Americas.

The Aztecs, like the Inca, often defeated enemies by logistics and numbers, not by military superiority. Time and again, the Aztecs were actually defeated on the battlefield by Tarascan metal weaponry and fortifications, Tlaxcallan volley bow and arrow fire, or even in hand-to-hand combat. Still, the Aztecs usually prevailed in the end.

Christopher Howell

References and further reading:

Hassig, Ross. *War and Society in Ancient Mesoamerica.* Berkeley: University of California Press, 1992.

Sahagun, Bernardino de. *General History of the Things of New Spain.* Trans. Arthur J. Anderson and Charles E. Dibble. 13 vols. Salt Lake City: University of Utah Press, 1950–1982.

Tsouras, Peter. *Warlords of the Ancient Americas: Central America.* London: Arms and Armour Press, 1996.

Metz, Siege of (1870–1871)

A siege that made the Prussian defeat of France almost inevitable. After briefly skirmishing with the Prussians immediately after the start of the Franco-Prussian War, an entire French army, consisting of five corps (155,000 men), fell back to Metz in order to regroup. Led by the incompetent Marshal Achille-François Bazaine, this army was then trapped by the Prussians, who bypassed Metz and began to invest it on 19 August 1870. Bazaine never intended to remain in Metz, yet he made only one halfhearted attempt to break out, on 31 August, to link with the army advancing from the direction of Sedan under Marshal Marie-Edme-Patrice-Maurice de MacMahon, duc de Magenta. When this army was destroyed on 1 September, Bazaine made no further attempts to break out, and the Prussians intensified the ring around the city.

The problem for Bazaine after the defeat at Sedan was that his was an imperial army, and the empire no longer existed. He considered himself a representative of the imperial government and made no efforts to coordinate his defense of Metz with the Republican government in Paris. During early October, Bazaine sent an emissary to Otto von Bismarck to negotiate surrender terms entirely on his own initiative and without even bothering to let the government in Paris know what he was doing. On 27 October, the army unconditionally surrendered and was simply taken prisoner while Bazaine sneaked out to avoid his troops. Bazaine's imperial army thus fought no major battles during the Franco-Prussian War, and it surrendered without having engaged the enemy in any full-scale battle.

After the war, Bazaine was put on trial for treason. He was found guilty and sentenced to death, but President MacMahon commuted it to 20 years' imprisonment, which Bazaine avoided by escaping after nine months. The Siege of Metz is important because the surrender of the city freed troops, allowed the Prussians to more effectively encircle Paris, and ensured that the Prussians would not be amenable to an armistice.

Lee Baker

See also: Franco-Prussian War; Sedan

References and further reading:

Howard, Michael. *The Franco-Prussian War.* New York: Collier Books, 1961.

Williams, Roger. *The French Revolutions of 1870–1871.* London: Weidenfeld and Nicolson, 1969.

Meuse-Argonne (26 September–11 November 1918)

The largest and most important offensive of the American Expeditionary Force (AEF) during World War I and perhaps the largest American battle to date. After successful operations at Amiens and Albert in 1918, Marshal Ferdinand Foch decided to reward the AEF for their success at St. Mihiel with an attack on German forces in the Argonne Forest. This was part of a larger strategy to attack at interlocking points along the line, exhausting German reserves and allowing Allied forces to break German lines of communication and logistics. The southern thrust of this pincer movement was to be led by American general John J. Pershing. His 400,000-man force was to attack an area deemed impregnable by some military commanders. The hilly, rough terrain of the Argonne Forest had been reinforced with defensive fortifications by the German army since 1915. The Americans were backed by 300 tanks under the control of General Hunter Liggett and 500 aircraft of the U.S. Air Service under General William Mitchell. They were opposed by 40 German divisions under the leadership of General Max Carl von Gallwitz.

Launched on 26 September, the plan was for Pershing's First Army to attack the Meuse and Aire valleys. To its left, the French Fourth Army would also move north. They were to break through the 10 miles of rough terrain, turn right, and continue to Sedan and Mezieres. Although progress slowed as German resistance increased, in the first three days of fighting, American forces were able to penetrate 3 to 7 miles at some points in the line, capture 10,000 prisoners, and gain the villages of Montfaucon, Exermont, Gercourt, Cuisy, Septsarges, Malancourt, Epinonville, Charpentry, and Very. Yet the lack of roads created traffic jams, and inexperienced American divisions were able to gain little ground. On 4 October, the First Army began a major attack along the entire front. The harsh fighting gave rise to some of the heroic moments in American history, including the famed "Lost Battalion" and Sergeant Alvin York's capture of 132 Germans. By 10 October, Allied forces had nearly cleared the Argonne Forest of the enemy.

The heavy fighting continued until November, when the Americans and French were able to break through the German fortifications and advance some 20 miles, while the French Fourth Army captured the railroad hub at Sedan. This advance broke the transportation network that supported the German army in France. On 11 November, the Meuse-Argonne offensive ended; during the six weeks of combat, the AEF suffered 26,277 dead and 95,786 wounded.

T. Jason Soderstrum

See also: Pershing, John J.; World War I

References and further reading:

Braim, Paul F. *The Test of Battle: The American Expeditionary Forces in the Meuse-Argonne Campaign.* Newark: University of Delaware Press, 1987.

Keegan, John. *The First World War.* London: Hutchinson, 1998.

Stokesbury, James L. *A Short History of World War I.* New York: William Morrow, 1981.

Mexican Revolution (1810–1821)

Revolution that achieved independence from Spain. The revolt was ignited by Father Miguel Hidalgo y Costilla in the village of Dolores in the state of Guanajuato on 16 September 1810. Hidalgo called his parishioners and supporters to revolt with "El Grito de Dolores" (the cry of Dolores), shouting "Long live the Lady of Guadalupe" and "Death to the Spaniards." Hidalgo was a Creole (someone born in the colonies of European descent). His army consisted of more than 50,000 troops, whom he often could not control.

The first objective was the city of Guanajuato, and after its surrender, both Creoles and Spaniards were slaughtered. Such atrocities caused both of these groups to join forces against Hidalgo. After attempting to take Mexico City itself and failing, Hidalgo and his troops were forced north. Though his army was able to take a few other cities, Hidalgo was captured and shot on 31 July 1811. His head was exposed on a stake for 10 years.

Hidalgo's death did not halt the revolution. What was left of his army was taken over by Father Jose Maria Morelos y Pavón. He was able to seize much of Mexico, put a form of government together, and call for a constitutional convention at Chilpancingo in 1813. During this convention, a formal declaration of independence was drafted, along with the Constitution of Apatzingan. However, on 22 December 1815, Morelos was also captured and shot by Spanish troops. By now, the only remaining rebel force still in the field was that

Mexican insurrectos *with a homemade cannon in Juarez, c. 1911. (Library of Congress)*

commanded by Vicente Guerrero, an Indian. But for the next five years, until 1820, peace reigned throughout much of Mexico.

Events in Europe forced the Spanish king Ferdinand VII to promulgate the liberal constitution that had been put in place in 1812 and that he later had rescinded. On 24 February 1821, Augustín de Iturbide, a Mexican landowner, issued his three-point Plan de Iguala, which called for a Catholic nation, independence under a monarchy, and equality between Europeans and Creoles. Iturbide's army joined forces with those of Guerrero and entered Mexico City on 27 September 1821. Mexico had finally won its independence from Spain. Though Hidalgo's efforts did not result in an immediate victory, Mexico still celebrates its independence on 16 September.

Peter Carr

See also: Santa Anna, Antonio López de

References and further reading:

Atwater, James D., and Ramón Eduardo Ruiz. *Out from Under: Benito Juárez and the Struggle for Mexican Independence.* Garden City: Doubleday, 1969.

Van Young, Eric. *The Other Rebellion: Popular Violence, Ideology, and the Mexican Struggle for Independence, 1810–1821.* Stanford, CA: Stanford University Press, 2001.

Mexican Unrest and Civil War (1911–1929)

Series of coups and countercoups, revolts, and civil wars that did not address the basic Mexican problem of mass poverty and that twice drew in American intervention. As Mexico prepared in 1910 to celebrate the centennial of the republic's independence in 1810, the superficial signs of prosperity could not mask the widespread poverty and discontent that would soon erupt into revolution and plunge the nation into years of civil war. In 1910, Mexico was one of the world' s most lucrative and alluring economies. The credit fell to the nation's longest-serving president, Porfirio Díaz. However, the prosperity was an illusion created by the selling of trading concessions and appropriated communal lands. Fewer than 1,000 landowners controlled 97 percent of all of Mexico's land. In the 1910 election, a wealthy liberal landowner, Francisco Madero, challenged Diaz, demanding expanded suffrage, limits on presidential succession, and agrarian reform. The resulting surge of public support for Madero and growing antiregime violence shocked Díaz, who resigned the presidency and left Mexico for exile.

Madero was inaugurated as president in November 1911 amid great expectations. However, timidity and compromise characterized his administration. He failed to institute promised agrarian reforms, thus alienating his rural supporters. His willingness to work with the elites cost him the support of the liberals. In a conservative-backed counterrevolution, General Victoriano Huerta forced the resignation of President Madero and his vice president. Three days later, on 23 February 1913, both men were shot while under the general's protection. Huerta assumed the presidency, incurring the wrath of Madero's one-time supporters. Huerta's resistance to agrarian or social reforms mobilized his domestic opposition. Emiliano Zapata and Pancho Villa raised revolutionary armies in rural Mexico. In the north, the revolutionary army under the command of Venustiano Carranza was a formidable threat to Huerta. The regime was further destabilized by the U.S. Navy's occupation of Mexico's largest port city, Veracruz, following a minor affront to an American naval officer. Huerta resigned the presidency in July 1914, leaving Mexico for exile, while Mexico's revolutionary commanders battled for supremacy.

Carranza won broad popular support when, in January 1915, he issued a decree that outlined a program of land redistribution. The U.S. government and Mexico's Latin American neighbors recognized Carranza as the de facto head of state. His rivals, particularly Villa, sought to destroy international support for Carranza. Villa's forces attacked the town of Columbus, New Mexico, in March 1916, killing a number of Americans. President Woodrow Wilson's response was to dispatch a punitive expedition into Mexico to track down Villa. The incursion rallied Mexicans behind Carranza. A liberal constitution was ratified on 5 February 1917, the same day the United States withdrew its forces from Mexico. Carranza became the first president under the new constitution. Mexicans expecting dramatic reforms were soon disappointed. Carranza bowed to international pressure, suspending decrees that threatened foreign business interests. When he hesitated to enact the agrarian reforms called for in the constitution, his popular support eroded.

Constitutionally prohibited from succeeding himself in the election of 1920, Carranza backed a puppet candidate. This action prompted Alvaro Obregón, the former minister of war, to challenge the president's handpicked candidate. The governor of the state of Sonora called upon his fellow governors to rise up militarily against Carranza. Thirteen states followed his lead. Carranza fled the capital, only to be assassinated en route to Veracruz. Obregon was elected president and moved quickly to implement agrarian reforms. He also imposed restrictions on foreign ownership of Mexican land and resources. The election of Obregon is considered by many historians as marking the end of the Mexican Revolution of 1910. The relative peace that Obregon's presidency brought to Mexico was shattered in 1923, however. In the elections that year, Obregon threw his support to Plutarcho Calles. Rival candidate Adolpho de la Huerta urged his supporters to take up arms against the government. Obregon personally led federal troops in suppressing the rebellion.

As president, Calles was cautious in limiting foreign investment in Mexico. He did not show the same restraint in dealing with the Catholic Church, aggressively restricting the rights and activities of the clergy. Calles's anticlerical measures sparked violent resistance, known as the Cristero Rebellion, that continued throughout his presidency. Peace was elusive until the 1940s. Provisions of the Constitution of 1917 continued to be implemented by successive governments. Yet the twentieth century ended as it began for Mexico, with the ownership of land and disparities in wealth dominating political debate.

Eric Smylie

See also: Mexico, U.S. Punitive Expedition in; Pershing, John J.; Villa, Francisco "Pancho"; Zapata, Emiliano; Zapatista Rebellion

References and further reading:

Brenner, Anita, and George R. Leighton. *The Wind That Swept Mexico: The History of the Mexican Revolution, 1910–1942.* Austin: University of Texas Press, 1996.

Gilderhus, Mark T. *Diplomacy and Revolution: United States–Mexico Relations under Wilson and Carranza.* Tucson: University of Arizona Press, 1977.

Hall, Linda B., and Don M. Coerver. *Revolution on the Border: The United States and Mexico, 1910–1920.* Albuquerque: University of New Mexico Press, 1988.

Knight, Allen. *The Mexican Revolution.* Cambridge, UK: Cambridge University Press, 1986.

Mason, Herbert Molloy, Jr. *The Great Pursuit.* New York: Random House, 1970.

Sweetman, Jack. *The Landing at Veracruz: 1914.* Annapolis, MD: United States Naval Institute Press, 1968.

Mexican-American War (1846–1848)

Disastrous Mexican defeat at the hands of the United States, resulting in enormous losses of territory. President James Polk wanted land from Mexico and Canada in his drive to expand the United States from the Atlantic to the Pacific Ocean. It was an era of Manifest Destiny, when many Americans assumed they had a right to overflow the continent from coast to coast (and perhaps the Americas from pole to pole as well). When the breakaway Republic of Texas joined the United States in March 1845, Mexico was angered, and tensions increased along the disputed Texas-Mexico border, one side claiming the Rio Grande and the other the Nueces River as a border.

Polk then settled the Oregon Territory boundary dispute with Great Britain in 1846; that left Mexico and the vast and underpopulated lands in its north as a barrier to westward expansion. In March 1846, Polk ordered General Zachary Taylor and his "Army of Observation" to the north bank of the Rio Grande to strengthen the Texan and American boundary claim. That decision soon led to fighting and formal, mutual declarations of war.

The Mexican-American War fell into three broad phases. The first phase centered on General Taylor in the north. American and Mexican armies soon clashed, first at Palo Alto and then at Resaca de la Palma near current Brownsville, Texas. The Americans won both battles, and the Mexicans retreated. Taylor slowly pursued and, in September, neared Monterrey. The Mexicans had formidable defenses. Still, Taylor sent a flanking movement that soon gained control over the dominating two hills, emplaced artillery, and caused the Mexican forces to abandon the town. Taylor proceeded somewhat south, and in February 1847, after most of his regular army troops were detached to form the main force for General Winfield Scott's amphibious invasion, Taylor was near the Hacienda de la Buena Vista when General Antonio López de Santa Anna attacked him. The Americans had good defenses, but the Mexicans sought to outflank them on the American left. Militia units rushed to the battle, fought very well, and were able to throw back the Mexican assault. This battle largely ended fighting in north-central Mexico, as Santa Anna moved to contest Scott's invasion.

There was, to be sure, fighting on the periphery, which could not affect the ultimate outcome nor compel a Mexican surrender. General Stephen Watts Kearny marched from Fort Leavenworth, Kansas, to take Santa Fe, New Mexico, an important trading point. Kearny proceeded to California, where other Americans, including John C. Frémont and Richard Stockton, helped take control of that Mexican province.

These American gains in the north did not translate into a Mexican surrender or cession of territory. Thus, in early 1847, President Polk somewhat reluctantly agreed to a plan by General Winfield Scott to attempt a seaborne invasion of the port city of Veracruz, then to proceed along the relatively traditional route to attack and seize the capital, Mexico City, and thereby compel surrender.

Scott's resulting campaign was remarkable. Polk feared that if Taylor or Scott enjoyed too much success, the victorious general might make a formidable presidential campaign opponent; Scott also had to deal with shortages of equipment and limited manpower throughout the campaign. He had to attempt the first major contested American amphibious assault, and he had to cooperate well with the U.S. Navy, on whose logistical support he depended. He had to follow a mostly predictable route into the heartland of his enemy and win a series of battles mostly on grounds of his opponent's choosing, without being able to afford losing many men. That is, he operated under a remarkable series of constraints and surmounted all of them.

Scott gathered his invasion force at New Orleans and then, after a stop at Tampico, accepted the advice of Commodore David Conner, who was commanding the naval flotilla, and landed his command on a beach south of the heavily fortified city of Veracruz. By nightfall of the first day, 9 March 1847, some 100 ships had landed 10,000 men, their animals, and supplies—a remarkable accomplishment. Scott then established a siege line across Veracruz, and within several weeks, the city surrendered.

Scott needed to proceed up the national highway to move his men above the dreaded "yellow fever" line before the season of illness began. General Santa Anna established seemingly strong defenses at Cerro Gordo in early April, where he expected Scott to proceed up the national highway and be denied further progress. Scott's engineering officers, led by Captain Robert E. Lee, found a goat path—a trail—that could be widened to allow the Americans to proceed around, behind, and above the Mexican defenses from the right and thereby force the Mexicans to attack or cede their positions, which they did on 17–18 April 1847. Scott then rested midway at Puebla, while he massed supplies and dealt with the enlistment terms of his militia (for many, their terms were up, and Scott wanted them out of his way before proceeding to the Mexican capital).

Again, the deluded Santa Anna felt that he had established a formidable set of defenses before the capital, Mexico City. He assumed Scott would approach from due east, and he was ready. There were deep lakes to the north, a supposedly impenetrable lava bed to the south, and several lakes in the center that he expected would channel the American invaders into the strength of his defenses. Once again, Scott's engineers found a way around these obstacles and avoided the expected line of advance. They found a path across the lava bed to the south, and Scott managed to outflank Santa Anna, first by moving south, fighting at Contreras and Churubusco, and thereby moving south of the capital. The American commander then attacked Mexico City from the lightly defended south and west. The Americans won at El Chapultepec and then descended from the heights to take the city. After some months of negotiation, both sides agreed to the Treaty of Guadalupe Hidalgo in February 1848, in which Mexico ceded California, Nevada, Utah, Arizona, and New Mexico, along with much of Colorado and the disputed territory in southern Texas.

Taylor's campaigns in the north did not greatly advance the military arts and sciences. Mexican troops were poorly trained and mostly poorly led. Their copper cannonballs dented rather than exploded; Americans soldiers literally jumped over the cannonballs rolling along the ground. The fighting in New Mexico and California involved few troops. However, Scott fought an exemplary campaign of maneuver reflecting pre-Napoleonic values; that is, he could not afford the massive firepower and extensive loss of life of battles and campaigns from the Napoleonic Wars. Instead, relying on military strategy and tactics from the previous era, he mostly avoided expected lines of advance, gained psychological advantage by an indirect advance, and won a great series of battles. Scott's benign treatment of the civil populace also ensured a smooth passage along his lines of communication.

Charles M. Dobbs

See also: Santa Anna, Antonio López de; Scott, Winfield; Taylor, Zachary

References and further reading:

Bauer, K. Jack. *The Mexican War, 1846–1848.* Lincoln: University of Nebraska Press, 1993.
Eisenhower, John S. D. *So Far from God: The U.S. War with Mexico, 1846–1848.* New York: Random House, 1989.
Singletary, Otis. *The Mexican War.* Chicago: University of Chicago Press, 1960.

Mexico, U.S. Punitive Expedition in (1916–1917)

U.S. Army expedition sent into Mexico to seize the bandit and revolutionary Pancho Villa. Continued political instability in Mexico after the Revolution of 1910 led to a growing concern over the safety and security of the U.S.-Mexican border. On 9 March 1916, perhaps upset at the loss of American support or just desperate to once again be a player in Mexican politics, Pancho Villa, a major figure in the Mexican Revolution, attacked the town of Columbus, New Mexico. When Villa and his mounted raiders withdrew, 16 U.S. citizens had been killed, and the town center had been burned to the ground. The unprovoked attack created a firestorm of outrage in the United States, and President Woodrow Wilson dispatched General John "Blackjack" Pershing in pursuit of Villa. It took a few days to assemble a force, and Pershing did not cross into Mexico until 15 March 1916.

An 11-month-long incursion by U.S. troops hundreds of miles into the Mexican state of Chihuahua failed to find the elusive Villa. Although a military failure, it did provide the U.S. Army with much-needed field experience and a chance to develop the staff skills needed to run and support a large army in Europe. In particular, Pershing pioneered the use of aircraft (which failed in most cases even to get off the ground) and motor transport, which was more successful.

American and Constitutionalist forces went out of their way to avoid each other, and the Americans were forbidden to enter any towns. What occurred was not peace and was not war. Provisional president Venustiano Carranza at first simply wanted to contain the penetration of American forces and then get them out Mexico as fast as possible. Pershing wanted only to capture Villa, not confront Constitutionalist forces.

The Mexicans demanded that first the Americans leave and then that they jointly resolve the problem of cross-border raids. The United States countered by offering to work out a plan after it had captured Villa. Both sides tried to avoid open confrontation, but the political strain started to show as each side was unwilling to concede to the other.

To resolve this impasse, both sides formed a joint commission to find a solution. The commission met many times in New London, Connecticut, from September 1916 to January 1917, but it never reached an accord. The expedition would end only when Woodrow Wilson chose.

Militarily, Constitutionalist and American forces did clash twice, in the towns of Parrazal and Carrizal. Although there were some losses (at Carrizal, both sides suffered 25 percent casualties), commanders on both sides moved to keep the conflict from escalating into full-scale war, something that neither Wilson nor Carranza wanted or could easily afford.

In January 1917, Wilson saw that the threat from Germany was greater than the threat posed by Mexico, and he ordered Pershing to return with his command to the United States. The "hot pursuit" never came close to catching Villa, and it served only to degrade an already strained relationship between the United States and Mexico. Wilson's attempts to "teach the Mexicans democracy" (he also sent troops to occupy Veracruz for more than a year) proved an abject failure. But that did not stop the president from mounting two further military essays into other lands for ill-defined purposes. Expeditions into Murmansk and Vladivostok, Russia, toward the end of and after World War I, like the Mexican expedition, had little purpose and no lasting effect except to create hatred of the regime.

Drew Philip Halévy

See also: Pershing, John J.

References and further reading:

Camin, Hector, and Lorenzo Meyer. *In the Shadow of the Mexican Revolution.* Austin: University of Texas Press, 1993.
Gilderhus, Mark T. *Diplomacy and Revolution: U.S.-Mexican Relations under Wilson and Carranza.* Tucson: University of Arizona Press, 1977.
Haley, P. Edward. *Revolution and Intervention: The Diplomacy of Taft and Wilson with Mexico, 1910–1917.* Cambridge, MA: MIT Press, 1970.

Mexico City, Battles for (20 August–14 September 1847)

The concluding battles for the Mexican capital, which ended

the Mexican-American War. After the battle of Cerro Gordo, General Antonio López de Santa Anna established formidable defenses around Mexico City; a series of lakes would channel the invading Americans into his prepared positions, or so he hoped. He believed that Lake Texcoco limited an attack from the north and that Lake Chalco, Lake Xochimilco, and a vast lava bed limited an advance to the south; his strongest defenses anticipated an attack headlong from the east.

American general Winfield Scott faced further challenges, including his limited number of troops and supplies, capturing a capital city some 225 miles inland, and avoiding the set defenses, since he could not afford many casualties. He solved his problems brilliantly by engaging in a strategy of marching south and past the defenses, eventually to attack Mexico City from the underdefended southwest and western approaches.

There were several battles in this campaign. After resting at Puebla for several months, Scott's advance units arrived in the valley of the capital in early August. The Americans fought at Contreras, Churubusco, and El Molina del Rey and outflanked Santa Anna's defenses.

Finally, on 13 September, the Americans attacked the city itself, beginning with defenses around the Mexican military academy, El Chapultepec. After hard-fought battles, the invaders gained control of the hill on which the academy sat and thus gained entrance into the capital, which formally surrendered to Scott soon after, paving the way for the Treaty of Guadalupe Hidalgo some months after that.

Charles M. Dobbs

See also: Mexican-American War; Scott, Winfield; Santa Anna, Antonio López de

References and further reading:

Bauer, K. Jack. *The Mexican War, 1846–1848.* Lincoln: University of Nebraska Press, 1993.

Eisenhower, John S. D. *Agent of Destiny: The Life and Times of General Winfield Scott.* Norman: University of Oklahoma Press, 1999.

Johnson, Timothy D. *Winfield Scott: The Quest for Military Glory.* Lawrence: University Press of Kansas, 1998.

Miles, Nelson Appleton (1839–1925)

Distinguished American commander, a military leader for four generations, one of few to achieve the highest rank without having attended the U.S. Military Academy at West Point. Miles was born in Westminster, Massachusetts, on 8 August 1839. A store clerk in the 1850s, he studied military science in his spare time.

As soon as the Civil War began, Miles enlisted in the 22d Massachusetts Volunteers, where he was quickly commissioned first lieutenant. By September 1861, he was captain and then aide-de-camp to Major General Oliver Otis Howard. Miles was wounded at Fair Oaks, Fredericksburg, Chancellorsville, and Petersburg. He fought at Antietam, the Wilderness, Spotsylvania, and Cold Harbor, was brevetted three times, and commanded a division at Appomattox. In 1892, he received the (Congressional) Medal of Honor for his service at Chancellorsville.

In October 1865, Miles became major general of volunteers and in 1867 brevet brigadier general. As commandant of Fort Monroe, Virginia, until July 1866, he was criticized for rough treatment of his prisoner, Jefferson Davis. After 1868, as husband of the niece of William T. Sherman, he sought special favors, but Sherman resisted.

From 1869, as colonel of the U.S. Army 5th Infantry, until 1894, as major general of the Department of the Missouri, Miles fought the Indians of the American West. He defeated the Cheyenne in 1874 and 1875, drove Sitting Bull into Canada in 1876, and captured both Crazy Horse and Chief Joseph in 1877 and Geronimo in 1887. Soldiers under his command massacred the Sioux at Wounded Knee in 1890.

As general in chief of the army from 1895 until his retirement in 1903 (the title was changed to chief of staff in 1903), he planned campaigns for the Spanish-American War, the Philippine Insurrection, and the Boxer Rebellion, observed the Turco-Greek War, and personally led the assault on Puerto Rico in 1898. He achieved the permanent rank of lieutenant general in 1901.

Before the emergence of John J. Pershing, Miles was the best-known soldier in the United States. At the time of his death in Washington, D.C., on 15 May 1925, he was the last surviving regular Union major general.

Eric v. d. Luft

See also: American Civil War; Antietam/Sharpsburg; Apache Wars; Boxer Rebellion; Chancellorsville, Battle of; Cochise; Cold Harbor, Battle of; Crazy Horse; Custer, George Armstrong; Fredericksburg; Geronimo; Joseph the Younger, Chief; Little Bighorn; Nez Percé; Pershing, John J.; Petersburg, Siege of; Philippine Insurrection; San Juan Hill/El Caney; Sherman, William Tecumseh; Sioux Wars; Sitting Bull; Spanish-American War; Spotsylvania Court House; Wilderness; Wounded Knee, Battle of

References and further reading:

Amchan, Arthur J. *The Most Famous Soldier in America: A Biography of Lt. Gen. Nelson A. Miles, 1839–1925.* Alexandria, VA: Amchan, 1989.

DeMontravel, Peter R. *A Hero to His Fighting Men: Nelson A. Miles, 1839–1925.* Kent, OH: Kent State University Press, 1998.

Johnson, Virginia Weisel. *The Unregimented General: A Biography of Nelson A. Miles.* Boston: Houghton Mifflin, 1962.

Wooster, Robert. *Nelson A. Miles and the Twilight of the Frontier Army.* Lincoln: University of Nebraska Press, 1993.

Military and Society

The relationship between the soldier and society has been discussed and studied since human societies were formed and individuals or groups within them were armed. The nature and implications of this relationship center on those who manage political relationships within any given society. Plato juxtaposes Spartan society and Athenian society in *The Republic.* In the former, society revolves around the military, and the two are intertwined at every level from cradle to grave. In the latter, the military serves society as a distinct entity that is both apart from the rest of society but stems from it, serves it, and remains a part of society as embodied and represented by the Athenian city-state.

More recently, the field of civil-military relations has attempted to identify and describe the key elements involved in the relationship between modern military organizations and their political masters within the modern nation-state. Since the early 1950s, particularly with Samuel Huntington (*The Soldier and the State,* 1957) and Morris Janowitz (*The Professional Soldier,* 1960), the fundamental questions have revolved around how to provide for the defense of the state and concurrently keep those who dominate the use of force from applying that force to exert control over the political decisionmaking processes or to control the society within the state or both.

Two principal currents of thought have consumed most of the work on civil military relations since the 1950s in the democracies. Huntington set forth the terminology of objective and subjective control as two distinct ways to manage political-military relations. He has been viewed as the proponent of the former method of control through what he calls professionalism. Janowitz has been viewed as a proponent of subjective control. In both cases, the objectives are similar: to prevent a so-called praetorian military from dominating society and the political system.

Although either method of political control can be applied in both democratic and nondemocratic systems of government, the debate is most heated where democratic systems are at potential risk of being overthrown by military action through the use or threatened use of force. To prevent this outcome, objective control seeks to create a distribution of power between military and civilian groups that can lead to the emergence of professional attitudes and behavior among military officers. The goal is an autonomous professional military that is apolitical and focused on its missions. Subjective control also advocates a professional military, understood as expertise in the use of force, but not autonomous and uninvolved with the political dynamics of the state. Control is essentially exerted through an integration of the military into the political structures. The essential idea is, make military officers a part of the political aspects of the state, and they are unlikely to overthrow themselves. Objective control has been crudely interpreted as "give them toys and keep them busy."

Regardless of the method used, these theorists and their predecessors and successors have all worked with a complex but limited number of variables and issues to explain why militaries might or might not threaten societies and the governments that govern them and how one might prevent or reverse that threat when and where it exists. The key issues to understand are the nature of the state, military missions, and the relationship between these two.

The state is three things: it is a nation-state, a political system that governs relationships within the boundaries of the nation-state, and the government organs that physically exist. The nation-state is a psychological construct that includes concepts such as nationalism and notions with particular cultural attributes. It is also a physical entity. Armed forces' missions stem from this conception of the state. Military forces defend against aggression from other states in a world that is assumed to work in what international relations theorists call the "realist paradigm." It assumes that states in the international system work as unitary actors first and foremost to ensure their survival as states. But states are bound to clash and conflict to ensue. Thus, militaries exist to defend against other militaries when such a clash occurs.

Militaries also exist to defend the existence of the state from internal enemies. Generally, civil wars, guerrilla or separatist challenges, or other armed groups that threaten the existing system of governance are threats to the second conception of the state. The government, regardless of whether it is a democracy or not, is that part of the state that directs and regulates relations within society, between society and the state, and between state organs. The government of a state ostensibly defines what those institutions are supposed to do and also manages resources and allocates those it possesses to state institutions such as the military.

Finally, the state is physically manifested in its third dimension by state institutions such as governing bodies (legislatures, executive offices, courts) and by organizations such as the social security administration, highway department, and the armed forces.

The armed forces are directly related to the nation-state because they exist to defend its existence, and they are a real part of the state as physical entities. The government and society surround the military as an organization with interests that stem from their conception of the nation-state and what they need to do to ensure the survival of the state in all its manifestations.

Here lies the crux of political-military relations. The government allocates the resources that permit the military to succeed or fail in its missions of defense. Whether fighting an external enemy or an internal enemy, the mission is conceived as a zero-sum game. That is, either one wins or one loses. Where the use of force is involved, losing often means dying (but, then, so also can winning). Thus the government is under pressure by the controllers of the use of force to ensure that adequate resources are provided to accomplish the mission.

What that mission is and how it is conceived differently by the armed forces and by the government will greatly determine the day-to-day relationship between the military and society. Internal missions will tend to involve the military in domains within society that are not within the military's traditional competence. External missions will tend to focus the military on the expertise needed to apply force most effectively to defeat a like organization (i.e., another country's armed forces). Such a mission will tend to separate the military from society, but not in an unhealthy way.

The actual relationship between the military and society is dependent on how the military is organized, supplied with personnel, and trained and educated. The field of military sociology focuses in part on these issues. For example, Charles Moskos has written much on the nature of the U.S. military. He has looked at the results on the linkages between society and the armed forces of a conscript-based versus a volunteer-based military. He has tracked the composition of various components of the armed forces in terms of percentages of minorities, women, or people from a certain geographical region to ascertain whether manipulations of these variables affect the degree of understanding of the military by society at large or of currents within society by the armed forces. The great fear is that military and society will develop excessively distinct cultures and perspectives to the point at which they may clash. A military alienated from the society within the state it defends may become a danger to that society.

In the end, militaries reflect the societies whence they come. But they do so in the context within which they must exist. Is their mission primarily to defend from potential external threats, or is it to defend against internal threats? One nation, at least, is in the happy position of having no convincing threat. Canada, invincible, protected from external threats by the United States, and domestically relatively tranquil, is hesitant to define any mission for its armed forces beyond the benign role of peace keepers. New Zealand, enjoying even more domestic tranquility, has gone even farther than Canada in transmogrifying its armed forces into UN peace keepers, but New Zealand does face some conceivable external threats in the Pacific Rim.

The answer to the mission question will greatly determine the relationship between the military and those elements of the state that represent and manage society. How is the military to be organized, deployed, and manned? The answers to these questions will affect how the military relates with various elements of society. How is the military trained and educated? What is its cultural perspective? An understanding of these issues will in part determine the quality of the relationship of the armed forces with society.

An understanding of why the military exists, what it does, and how it accomplishes the missions laid on it by civilian policymakers is an important element in ensuring healthy civil-military relations in both the political and societal realms, most particularly in democracies.

Frédéric Ruiz-Ramón

See also: Military-Industrial Complex

References and further reading:

Finer, S. E. *The Man on Horseback: The Role of the Military in Politics.* 2d ed. Boulder, CO: Westview Press, 1988.

Harries-Jenkins, Gwyn, and Charles C. Moskos. *Armed Forces and Society.* London: Sage Publications, 1981.

Huntington, Samuel P. *The Soldier and the State: The Theory and Politics of Civil-Military Relations.* New York: Vintage Books, 1957.

Janowitz, Morris. *The Professional Soldier: A Social and Political Portrait.* New York: Free Press, 1960.

Military Justice

The law governing the army. It is also the system of justice exercised by the military over society during emergency situations of military government or martial law.

Prior to the development of societal organization, which we term *civilization,* there was armed conflict. Civilization is associated with the establishment of a system of law or conduct of behavior. Governance and the regulation of the civilian population were considered necessities for the semblance of order. However the concept of law as a defined set of principles was not applied or was considered inapplicable to the battlefield, since war was an anarchic activity and contest of strength.

Nevertheless it became apparent to rulers that in the interest of state preservation, order, and prosperity, limits should be placed upon the destructive potential, to population and property, of warfare. Prior to concerted efforts by governments/states to regulate warfare, philosophers and military theorists were social advocates providing the first notions of military law.

With the aggrandizement of Rome, the military became the foundation of the state, necessary to garrison, fortify, and defend the territory and perimeter of the empire. Julius Caesar's subversion of the Republic and its senatorial basis of government brought imperial rule where civil and military law became intertwined and almost indistinguishable. The concept of *citizenship,* that of civil rights under state protection, was extended to the barbarians of the conquered lands as a reward based upon military service within the legions of Rome. Desertion, mutiny, cowardice, violence to a superior, and the sale of arms were some of the military offenses recognized and punished by the Romans.

The collapse of the Roman Empire led to a period of anarchy in western Europe due to the absence of a strong established political order with a corresponding military enforcement. This period of medieval history, known as the Dark Ages, marked the decline of professional infantry. Petty bands of cavalry rose to prominence as powers unto themselves, able to terrorize or maintain overlordship of a given territory. Rulers/princes/lords, in order to maintain and expand their political control, instituted a system for the hire of these cavalrymen, rewarding them with land for military service. This lord-vassal relationship of military obligation for service fiefs became known as *feudalism.*

A system of military law and conduct for cavalry was established as the property and birthright of the nobility, which in this period became an exclusive military caste. This code of ethics and regulation of warfare became known as *chivalry.*

The first written military laws of Europe were within the Salic Code (circa 400) and revised by successive Frankish kings. There was no separation of civil and military jurisdiction. Civil judges were also military commanders. The first French military law (Ordonnance) was written in 1379, while the German version (Kriegsartikel) appeared in 1487. Habsburg emperor Charles V's penal code of 1532 is considered to be the model for the existing military codes of modern Europe. This system of military law, known as Carolina, was expanded and given national versions as the Articles of Gustavus Adolphus of 1621, the Regulations of Louis XIV of 1651 and 1665, the Articles and Regulations of Czar Peter the Great of 1715, and the penal code of Empress Maria Theresa of 1768.

The British military code, from which the American and Canadian counterparts originate, comprises the statute of the Army Mutiny Act and Articles of War. The Mutiny Act of 3 April 1689 was created after the desertion of Scottish troops loyal to the Stuarts who refused to obey the order of William III. Thereafter, any soldier causing mutiny or sedition in the army could be punished by death or alternate penalty judged by a court-martial. The Mutiny Act was replaced on 24 July 1879 by the Army Discipline and Regulation Act, which itself was revised as the Army Act of 27 August 1881.

The American military code differs from that of Great Britain in several ways. It does not have a Mutiny or Army Act that must be annually renewed, and although the American Articles of War are derived from the British, they are nonetheless wholly statutory, being enacted by Congress as the legislative power. American military law consists of a written and an unwritten component, the former including the statutory Code of Articles of War, other statutory enactments relating to the discipline of the army, the Army Regulations, and General and Special Orders.

After resolving to raise an army to fight the British, the Continental Congress adopted a set of Articles of War on 7 November. New articles followed on 20 September 1776, dealing with treason and providing intelligence to the enemy. After the adoption of the Constitution, the Articles were readopted by an act of 29 September 1789. A further revision occurred as the Articles of 1806. The present American Articles of War consists of 128 articles from the revised Code of 1874, which prohibited punishments such as flogging and branding.

Military justice is administered through the tribunal of court-martial. Among the Romans this consisted of justice delivered from the legionary tribunes and the Magistri Militum. The early Germanic tribes during times of peace assembled courts of free men, while in times of war a duke or military chief and priests sat in judgment. This system developed into a court of regiments, which was presided by a colonel who carried a mace (*regiment*) as his emblem of judicial authority.

Specific military courts were established in France as Conseils de Guerre in 1655. In ascending hierarchy of jurisdiction, they were the courts of the Mayor of the Palace, the Constable, and the Provost Marshal. German military courts (spear courts) were established as the Militärgerichts of Emperor Frederick III in 1487.

The British tradition of court-martial derives from the King's Court of Chivalry, alternatively known as the Court of the High Constable and Marshal of England, the Court of Arms, and the Court of Honour. Presiding were the Lord High Constable and Earl Marshal. However not until the subdivision of the tribunal system into separate courts by Edward I did the Court of Chivalry actually derive its distinct existence. Moreover, since the Court of Chivalry extended jurisdiction over civil and criminal matters, successive acts of Parliament restrained and curtailed its power until it practically ceased to exist as a military tribunal by the time of the English Revolution.

The American Continental Congress adopted the British military tribunal system of courts-martial: general, regimental, and garrison courts. The Fifth Amendment of the Constitution, through the act of 29 September 1789, made the distinction between civil offenses and those cognizable by a military forum. Courts-martial do not fall under the jurisdiction of the American judiciary as inferior courts. Rather, they are instruments of executive power provided by Congress for the president as commander in chief to enforce discipline in the army through his authorized military representatives. Therefore, court-martial is not a court by definition, but a creation by an order that is subject to a superior military body or person.

Courts-martial are not courts of record, and their judgment is simply a recommendation that is not made operative until approved by a revisory commander. The proceedings of a court-martial cannot be reviewed by an federal court. The only appeal process is via the judge advocate general to the president or the secretary of war/defense.

The British North American Act of 1867 gave the Dominion of Canada responsibility for its own defense and the maintenance of military forces during peacetime. The Dominion Parliament passed the Militia Act in 1868. Guidelines were provided in 1884 by the British Manual Military Law, whose fourteen chapters covered a history of military law, military crimes and punishments, English criminal law applicable to soldiers, courts-martial, and customs of war.

With the introduction of the National Defense Act in 1950, the Canadian armed forces obtained a national Code of Service Discipline. It was accompanied by the Queen's Regulations and Orders. The repatriation of the Constitution and the creation of the Canadian Bill of Rights and the Charter of Rights and Freedoms in 1982 provided the last amendments regarding standardization and fairness in Canadian judicial military procedure.

At present most member states of the United Nations recognize a large body of international law applied to soldiers during conflict known as the Law of War/International Humanitarian Law/Law of Armed Conflict. This governs the rights and obligations of combatants and aims to temper the destruction of war by setting limits to warfare. The Law of War also seeks to protect noncombatants.

The Red Cross conference of 1864 provided the original Geneva Convention for the protection of war victims. The present Law of Armed Conflict has three sources: the Hague Convention of 1907, which placed limits on the methods of conduct during military operations; the four Geneva Conventions of 1949, which provide the protection of wounded, sick, and POWs; and the Additional Protocols to the Geneva Convention of 1977, which further limits the use of unnecessary force causing suffering.

Additionally, there is the Martens Clause, which first appeared as a preamble to the Hague Convention II of 29 July 1899 and has been added to most international humanitarian treaties. The Martens Clause expresses the notion that there are universal minimum standards of behavior during warfare and customary law that all states recognize. But there will always be a tension between military law/justice, which provides for penalties for offenses that would be meaningless in civil society (e.g., absence without leave, conduct unbecoming an officer, adultery, and so on), and the civil law, which recognizes no such offenses. The tension becomes all the more acute when the military is flooded with mass conscript troops, fresh from civilian society.

Neville G. Panthaki

See also: Military and Society

References and further reading:

Great Britain War Office. *Manual of Military Law.* London: H.M. Stationery Office, 1968.

Madsen, Chris. *Another Kind of Justice: Canadian Military Law from Confederation to Somalia.* Vancouver: University of British Columbia Press, 1999.

Rowe, Peter. *Defense: The Legal Implications: Military Law and the Laws of War.* Washington, DC: Brassey's Defense Publisher, 1987.

Simpson, James. *Law Applicable to Canadian Forces in Somalia 1992/93: A Study Prepared for the Commission of Inquiry into the Deployment of Canadian Forces to Somalia.* Ottawa, ON: Minister of Public Works and Government Services Canada, 1997.

Winthrop, William. *Military Law and Precedents.* New York: Arno Press, 1979.

Military-Industrial Complex

In his farewell address in 1961, President Dwight D. Eisenhower warned that America must "guard against the acquisition of unwarranted influence by the military-industrial complex" (Eisenhower 1965, 616). Thus entered into the American public realm the term that captures the reality that the institutions and people for planning, procuring, and fighting a war shape the economy, the political realm, and the wider society. Although other developed nations also support extensive military structures, with the fall of the Soviet Union, the United States remains as the world's only military superpower; therefore the question of the importance and the influence of the military-industrial complex (MIC) is basically an American issue.

Advanced technological weapons and communication devises are the cutting edge for the military today. Based upon the hard lessons of World War II, the U.S. government and military assumes as a guiding tenet that it must possess the hardware for the next war before that war begins. The United States can no longer put its national defense at risk, trusting that, in the words of William Jennings Bryan, "a million men will spring to arms." The defense of the nation requires permanent armaments and a defense establishment built in the United States by American manufacturers.

This is the military-industrial complex. A constellation of

people and institutions play a guiding role in the modern United States. The constellation includes the military professionals and the Pentagon, the scientific-technological elite, the universities, and the entrepreneurs—the investing class and the corporation. Of course, money is what keeps the system operating.

A very early example of MIC occurred when Alexander Hamilton recognized that the country needed arms and armories to provide for a common defense. Seeing the expected procurement of 40,000 muskets, Eli Whitney obtained a contract to build 10,000 and succeeded in establishing the first factories making muskets with interchangeable parts. The economic boon was obvious.

The Civil War generated a massive need for arms. Consequently, arms spending increased more than a hundredfold. The procurement of cannon alone required a massive increase in coal and iron production that established Pittsburgh as the iron-making capital of the country.

By World War II, the United States had become known as the "Arsenal of Democracy," producing 300,000 airplanes, 124,000 ships of all types, 100,000 tanks and armored vehicles, and 2,400,000 trucks. The expense for this hardware reinvigorated American corporations, in the doldrums from the Depression during the 1930s.

Similarly, the success of the Manhattan Project, the most expensive wartime undertaking in American history, revolutionized the economic landscape by creating entirely new industries, including "think tanks," the infrastructure for fighting a nuclear war. Also, since World War II, "black projects" have likewise funneled billions of U.S. dollars into corporate coffers.

Thus, certain military contractors become essential to the defense of the country. For example, the United States financed the financial bailout of Lockheed Corporation in 1969 because of its importance to the national defense. There is also the reality of people moving from one institution to another in the military-industrial complex. When procurement officers in the Pentagon retire, they have an opportunity to become employed by the contractors with whom they had been dealing.

The problem that President Eisenhower noted was that the vested interests of both the military and the corporations may generate harmful outcomes as well. At present, the extremely large nuclear arsenals of the major powers are generally superfluous and thus pose more danger than deterrent effect, as even the recent U.S. commander of the intercontinental ballistic missile force publicly stated.

Similarly, there remains strong congressional support for the Strategic Defense Initiative (SDI) and for the next-generation fighter. Thus the atmosphere created by the Cold War ideology continues, after the demise of the Soviet Union, to influence decisions on weapon systems development, whether the military leadership wants them or not. The argument for such spending assumes the underlying economic reality. Without such massive spending, the needed corporate infrastructure will deteriorate quickly, perhaps leaving the United States unable to build and deploy the necessary weapon systems to defend itself against its future enemies.

Some of these debates appear in Pentagon planning for U.S. military needs. Must the armed forces be able to deploy and fight two wars simultaneously? This standard foresees simultaneous wars in the Middle East and in Asia. Military readiness is defined as being combat-ready for such wars. However, during the year 2000, the United States deployed military forces in peace-keeping roles in numerous and various localities. The weapons and training required for this task are far different.

The military-industrial complex, an amorphous collection at best, had its heyday in the 1950s and 1960s, at the height of the Cold War. It even affected population patterns, as Americans moved in large numbers from the old industrial upper Great Plains and Northeast to the Sun Belt states, where the newer, more militarily oriented industries, like aircraft and electronics, were concentrated. But in the twenty-first century, its influences are waning, as the percentage of U.S. gross national product devoted to the military steadily declines from its Korean War, post–World War II peak high. Only a changed context with a new significant military threat to the United States will reverse this trend.

John R. Popiden

References and further reading:

Eisenhower, Dwight D. *The White House Years.* Vol. 2, *Waging Peace, 1956–1961.* Garden City, NY: Doubleday, 1965.

Kapstein, Ethan Barnaby. *The Political Economy of National Security: A Global Perspective.* Columbia: University of South Carolina Press, 1992.

Koistinen, Paul A. C. *The Military-Industrial Complex: A Historical Perspective.* New York: Praeger, 1980.

Markusen, Ann R., and Sean S. Costigan, eds. *Arming the Future: A Defense Industry for the 21st Century.* New York: Council on Foreign Relations Press, 1999.

Van Creveld, Martin. *Technology and War: From 2000 B.C. to the Present.* New York: Free Press; London: Collier Macmillan, 1989.

Milne Bay (1942)

The first defeat of a Japanese invasion force. The Japanese completed the conquest of their planned "Southern Economic Zone" in the South Pacific with the capture of Rabaul in early 1942. However, they were surprised by the rapid consolidation of Allied forces in Australia and the aggressive air campaign that followed. Plans were rapidly made to

A depiction by Peter Paul Rubens of the Battle of the Milvian Bridge. (Philadelphia Museum of Art/Corbis)

capture all of New Guinea, bases in the Solomons, New Caledonia, and Fiji to isolate Australia from the United States. To this end, the Japanese sent a force overland along the Kokoda Trail toward Port Moresby in August.

An airstrip was to be built at Milne Bay, on the far eastern tip of New Guinea, to support the Port Moresby attack and provide a base for bombing northeastern Australia. Japanese intelligence suggested that only a small garrison was present. However, the Allies had already constructed airstrips at the western head of the bay, and the defenders numbered 7,500: two Australian Infantry Brigades—the veteran 18th and the 7th Militia—accompanied by 1,300 U.S. Army engineers.

The 1,200-strong Japanese Special Naval Landing Force landed on the northern side of the bay on the night of 25 August 1942 and was reinforced two nights later by 1,200 more troops. However, they landed further east than planned. P-40 fighter-bombers, operating within their own landing pattern, destroyed the Japanese shore depot on 26 August, adding to their difficulties. Australian resistance was unrelenting as they advanced westward, and in spite of nightly fire support from destroyers, the Japanese had reached only the first airfield by the night of 28 August. Fierce fighting continued at the airstrips until 31 August. Lack of success then caused Imperial Headquarters to order withdrawal, and the 1,300 survivors were evacuated by the Japanese navy on the night of 6 September.

Michael Hyde

See also: Guadalcanal; Kokoda Trail

References and further reading:

Brune, P. *The Spell Broken: Exploding the Myth of Japanese Invincibility.* Sydney: Allen and Unwin, 1997.

Japanese Monograph No. 37, "South-East Asian Operations Record: 18th Army Operations on New Guinea and Rabaul (January 1942–June 1943)"; "The Southern Area (Part II)." In *War in Asia and the Pacific,* vol. 7., ed. D. Detwiler. New York: Garland Publishing, 1980.

McCarthy, D. *Australia in the War of 1939–1945.* Series One, Army, Vol. V. *South West Pacific Area—First Year, Kokoda to Wau.* Canberra: Australian War Memorial, 1959.

Odgers, George. *Army Australia—An Illustrated History.* New South Wales: Child and Associates, 1988.

Milvian Bridge, Battle of (28 October 312)

Victory that brought Constantine to power. With troops from the garrisons of Britain, Gaul, and the Rhine, Constantine invaded Italy. His aim was to wrest power from the coemperor of the West, Maxentius, son of Diocletian's old colleague Maximian.

Victorious over Maxentius's northern forces near Turin and Verona, Constantine marched on Rome. Maxentius opted to defend the walls of Rome and thus cut the pons Mulvius, the bridge that carries the Via Flaminia across the Tiber River, on the northern approach to the city. Constantine then crossed the Tiber River on a pontoon bridge moored just downstream of the stone bridge and gave battle at Saxa Rubra. Constantine's army, although outnumbered, was battle-hardened and confident. Maxentius's army was thrown back in confusion, and as it retreated across the Tiber River, the pontoon bridge collapsed. Maxentius and his armored cavalry were drowned in the swollen river, a scene depicted on the Arch of Constantine, erected at Rome to commemorate Constantine's victory "by divine inspiration." The Senate welcomed Constantine as liberator and proclaimed him sole emperor in the West.

It was prior to the battle, so records his biographer Eusebius, bishop of Caesarea, that Constantine saw a sign in the sky, a cross of light superimposed on the sun. He took this as a sign of victory—he stated, under oath, that he saw the words "Be victorious in this" written in stars around the cross—a message from the God whose symbol was the cross. Since Constantine was heavily outnumbered, this vision may explain his bold decision to attack. He certainly put his faith to the test when he ordered his men to paint the Greek monogram for Christ (*chi-rho*) on their shields. Victorious at Milvian Bridge, Constantine continued to wear the symbol for Christ against every enemy he faced.

Nic Fields

See also: Constantine the Great
References and further reading:

Burckhardt, J. *The Age of Constantine the Great.* Trans. Moses Hadas. German original, 1898. New York: Pantheon Books, 1949.

Minamoto, Yoshitsune (1159–1189)

Principal Minamoto commander during the Gempei War (1180–1185). Minamoto was instrumental in the formation of the first shogunate at Kamakura under his half-brother, Yoritomo (1147–1199). Over the centuries, Minamoto has been transformed through poetry, stories, and *No* and *Kabuki* plays into one of Japan's quintessential tragic heroes, making history difficult to separate from legend.

Minamoto was placed in a monastery after his father, Yoshitomo (1123–1160), was killed warring against the virtual dictator of Japan, Kiyomori Taira (1118–1181), head of the rival Taira (or Heike) clan. Escaping in 1180, Minamoto joined Yoritomo's rebellion against the Taira, fighting a campaign across the island of Honshu and defeating the enemy in a series of brilliant, swift maneuvers that secured the Minamoto victory over the Taira.

In 1184, Minamoto won a decisive victory in the Battle of Ichinotani, attacking the enemy castle from the Hiyodori Impasse by leading a body of 70 horsemen down a treacherously steep mountain path reportedly used only by wild boar, deer, rabbits, and foxes. He then led a small force across the Inland Sea during a fierce storm, capturing the fortress of Yashima in March 1185. On 25 April, he crushed the Taira in the naval Battle of Dannoura at the western end of the Inland Sea. Following the battle, Taira's widow leapt into the sea with the boy-emperor, Antoku. The Sacred Sword was lost, but the other imperial regalia, the Sacred Seal and the Sacred Mirror, were recovered and returned to Kyoto.

After the war, Yoritomo grew jealous of his half-brother's success and suspicious of his close relationship with Cloistered (Retired) Emperor Go-Shirakawa. Minamoto soon rebelled, fleeing to northern Honshu, where he committed suicide in 1189.

Michael C. Paul

See also: Gempei War; Samurai
References and further reading:

Morris, Ivan. *The Nobility of Failure.* New York: Holt, Rinehart and Winston, 1975.
Shinoda Minoru. *The Founding of the Kamakura Shogunate 1180–1185.* New York: Columbia University Press, 1960.

Minden (1 August 1759)

Major battle of the Seven Years' War in Germany between the Anglo-Hanoverian-Prussian army under Ferdinand, Duke of Brunswick, and the French army under Louis Georges Érasme, Marquis de Contades.

In July 1759, Contades occupied the village of Minden on the Weser River, 30 miles west of Hanover. He wanted to concentrate his scattered forces in order to advance on Ferdinand's recently defeated allied army. Minden was a strong position, with the Weser River and marshes covering the flanks of his army of 60,000 men. Ferdinand's allied army of 45,000 men lay to the west, but that skilled general began to advance toward Contades on 31 July to force battle.

Contades broke camp that same day and arrayed his superior force to take advantage of the terrain. He placed his cavalry in the middle of his line to give still-absent detachments room to deploy on the flanks. The battle began when Charles-François, Comte de Broglie, attacked and failed to break Ferdinand's surprised left flank. Contades considered withdrawing and had no further plan for the battle beyond Broglie's attack. Ferdinand's Anglo-Hanoverian troops had advanced far ahead of the main army, which prompted the French cavalry to charge. Armed only with swords, the infantry drove the cavalry back. The French infantry advanced against the exposed allies as their cavalry reformed and enveloped the entire formation, which nonetheless held fast against the onslaught. The French center collapsed as the cavalry once again retreated. At this moment of decision, the allied cavalry failed to advance and deliver the charge. Lord George Sackville had repeatedly refused to advance, thus allowing the French army to withdraw across the Weser River. Allied casualties totaled 2,600, but the French suffered the loss of 7,000 casualties, 10,000 prisoners, and 45 guns.

Minden had the potential to be a decisive battle like Leuthen. Sackville was court-martialed for his insubordination, and the French army continued to be a threat to Hanover. Ferdinand followed close on its heels but abandoned his pursuit after Frederick the Great's disastrous defeat at Kunersdorf. As with most battles in the war, Minden proved indecisive, yet Ferdinand gained both time and space. The war continued.

Patrick J. Speelman

See also: Seven Years' War

References and further reading:
Elliott, Charles Winslow. "The Men That Fought at Minden." *The Journal of the American Military History Institute* 3, no.2 (Summer 1939), 80–103.
Mackesy, Piers. *The Coward of Minden: The Affair of Lord George Sackville.* New York: St. Martin's Press, 1979.
Savory, Reginald A. *His Britannic Majesty's Army in Germany during the Seven Years' War.* Oxford: Clarendon Press, 1966.

Minié Ball

An improved bullet that increased the effective kill range of rifles and had a dramatic impact on the casualty rate in the American Civil War. Claude-Etienne Minié, a French army officer and part-time machinist, perfected the bullet in 1849. Along with a rifled barrel that he designed, Minié invented a conoidal-shaped bullet with a hollow base that deformed and expanded when a rifle was fired. This created the much desired tight seal around the projectile that increased the accuracy and velocity of the weapon but allowed it to be easily dropped into a barrel. Rifles equipped with the new projectile had the same reloading capability as a smoothbore musket but an effective kill range four to five times that of the older weapon.

Nearly all senior ranking U.S. and Confederate officers gained their combat experience in the Mexican-American War. This war was fought with smoothbore muskets and a reliance on closed-rank linear infantry formations. The imbalance between technologically improved infantry weapons with greater velocity and accuracy, combined with tactics better suited to weapons of a previous generation, sent casualty rates soaring. (It is not for nothing that critics accuse most of the world's armies of "fighting the last war.") During the Civil War, Minié balls caused the majority of battlefield casualties. In fact, in light of those casualties, it can be argued that the Minié ball was the single greatest killer of American young men, even more so than automobiles or liquor or their combination.

Lincoln Bramwell

See also: American Civil War

References and further reading:
Brodie, Bernard, and Fawn M. Brodie. *From Crossbow to H-Bomb.* Bloomington: Indiana University Press, 1973.
Fuller, J. F. C. *Armament and History: A Study of the Influence of Armament on History from the Dawn of Classical Warfare to the Second World War.* New York: Scribner's Sons, 1945.
Jamieson, Perry D., and Grady McWhiney. *Attack and Die: The Civil War, Military Tactics and the Southern Heritage.* Montgomery: University of Alabama Press, 1982.
O'Connell, Robert L. *Of Arms and Men: A History of War, Weapons, and Aggression.* New York: Oxford University Press, 1989.

Mithradatic Wars (88–63 B.C.E.)

Series of three wars between Republican Rome and King Mithradates VI Eupator of Pontus for control of Asia Minor. Mithradates VI ascended the Pontic throne at age 11, about 121, escaped his mother's plot to kill him, and solidified his power about 114 by murdering his mother and her supporters. Always wary of conspiracy throughout his long reign, he regularly drank tiny amounts of a wide variety of poisons to immunize himself; kept a supply of antidotes handy; and is supposed to have killed his brother, three sons, and three daughters. Gradually and secretly, by murder and intrigue, he replaced neighboring kings friendly to Rome with usurpers friendly to him. His ambitions included Cappadocia to the south, Armenia to the east, the Crimea to the north, and Bithynia and Galacia to the west.

About 89, when Roman legate Marcus Aquillius refused Mithradates' request for Roman aid against the encroachment of King Nicomedes III of Bithynia into western Pontus, Mithradates decided to wage open war on Rome and its allies. Lucius Cornelius Sulla received command of the expeditionary force against Mithradates in 88, but challenges to his consulship by Gaius Marius and others delayed his operations. Meanwhile, Mithradates took the war into Greece.

Sulla recaptured Athens in 86 and defeated a larger army under Pontic general Archelaus at Chaeronea in 86 and again at Orchomenus in 86. After Lucius Valerius Flaccus won at Philippi and Gaius Flavius Fimbria captured Pergamum, the First Mithradatic War concluded in 85 with the Treaty of Dardanus.

Mithradates rebuilt his army and navy after Dardanus. A maverick Roman commander in Asia Minor, Lucius Licinius Murena, led a preemptive strike against Mithradates in 83, starting the Second Mithradatic War, which lasted only one year. Mithradates decisively defeated Murena, who was then punished by Sulla for disobeying orders and violating the treaty.

Bithynia quietly became a Roman province in the mid-70s at the bequest of Nicomedes. Now that Rome controlled the Bosporus, Mithradates again feared for the safety of his kingdom and launched an offensive. As the Third Mithradatic War began in 74, Lucius Licinius Lucullus led five legions against Mithradates, winning at Cyzicus in 73 and Cabira in 72. When Mithradates retreated and allied with Armenian king Tigranes, Lucullus invaded Armenia in 70 and defeated a vastly superior force, perhaps 100,000 Pontic-Armenians to 10,000 Romans, at Tigranocerta in October 69.

Pompey replaced Lucullus as eastern commander in late 67 or early 66 because of Lucullus's harsh leadership that led to mutinies after his victory at Artaxata. Quickly successful, Pompey compelled Tigranes to surrender in 65. The remainder of the war was a mop-up campaign against Mithradates, who fled to the Crimea, where he committed suicide. Pompey established direct Roman rule over the provinces of Asia Minor and returned to Rome in triumph in 62.

Eric v. d. Luft

See also: Alexander the Great; Caesar, Julius; Chaeronea, Battle of; Marius, Gaius; Pompey the Great; Roman Republic, Wars of the; Sulla, Lucius Cornelius

References and further reading:

Bellinger, Alfred Raymond. *The End of the Seleucids.* New Haven: Connecticut Academy of Arts and Sciences, 1949.

Duggan, Alfred Leo. *He Died Old: Mithradates Eupator, King of Pontus.* London: Faber & Faber, 1958.

Macartney, Carlile Aylmer. *Studies on Early Hungarian and Pontic History.* Aldershot, England: Ashgate, 1998.

McGing, B. C. *The Foreign Policy of Mithridates VI Eupator, King of Pontus.* Leiden: E. J. Brill, 1986.

Mogul-Persian Wars (1622–1653)

A series of limited clashes, never growing to full-scale war, over Kandahar.

Mogul-Persian War of 1622–1623

Kandahar, in what is now modern-day Afghanistan, had represented a source of tension and rivalry between the Safavid Persian and Mogul Empires since Akbar (1542–1605) had acquired it for the Moguls when two Safavid princes defected in 1595. Patiently building his forces and taking advantage of division within the Mogul court, Shah Abbas "the Great" (1571–1629) personally led his forces against Kandahar in the winter of 1622. After a 45-day siege, the ill-prepared 300-man Mogul garrison surrendered to the Safavids. Shah Abbas then seized control of the fortress, town, and province of Kandahar before the Mogul emperor, Jahangir (1569–1627), could marshal an army to relieve the garrison. Jahangir planned to recapture Kandahar. He sent his son Khurram (1592–1666), who would later become Shah Jahan, to recapture Kandahar. However, before the Moguls could do so, Jahangir fell seriously ill, leaving his wife, Nur Jahan, and his son Khurram locked in a dynastic struggle for control of the Mogul Empire. The Moguls finally sent a force against the Safavids in 1623, but by that time the Mogul force that reached Kandahar was too weak to recapture the province.

Mogul-Persian War of 1638

Although initially distracted by the dynastic struggle within the Mogul Empire, Shah Jahan saw an opportunity to recover Kandahar in 1638. Ali Mardan Khan, a Persian noble and commander of the fortress, feared his life was in danger from the capricious Safavid emperor, Shah Safi (1629–1642), and so surrendered the fortress to Shah Jahan without bloodshed. As a reward for his defection, Ali Mardan Khan received a substantial monetary reward and a political appointment within the Mogul Empire. Upon reacquiring the fortress, Shah Jahan began to bolster the fortifications of Kandahar.

Mogul-Persian War of 1648–1653

In the decade after Ali Mardan Khan's defection, the Safavid emperor, Shah Abbas II (r. 1642–1666), regarded Mogul military setbacks in the Balkh region against the Uzbeks as a sign of weakness. In the winter of 1648, sensing his opportunity, Shah Abbas II sent an army into the region to retake the fortress at Kandahar. After a two-month siege, the Mogul garrison surrendered. Although aware of the Safavid attack, Shah Jahan's advisers convinced him that a winter campaign to relieve the city was unwise. This decision gave precious time to the Safavids to reinforce their recent reconquest.

Shah Jahan mounted three unsuccessful campaigns to retake Kandahar between 1649 and 1653. The Moguls mounted their first campaign in the summer of 1649, under the leadership of his son, Aurangzeb. Commanding a force of

50,000 men, Aurangzeb laid siege to the fortress but withdrew because he could not defeat the Safavid garrison before the onset of winter. The Moguls did not again try to take Kandahar until the fall of 1652, when they again laid siege to the fortress. Although the Moguls repulsed a relief force sent by the Safavids, they could not complete their siege of the fortress. The Moguls made their final attempt to recapture Kandahar in the spring of 1653. Led by Shah Jahan's favorite son, Dara Shukoh, the latest Mogul force came close but could not fully penetrate the defenses. Dara Shukoh employed siege guns, which breached some of the fortress walls but were not enough to force the capitulation of Kandahar by the winter. Foul weather and thinning supply lines forced the Moguls to withdraw from the battlefield.

The Moguls' Kandahar campaigns were a failure. The estimated deaths of 30,000–40,000 soldiers were unable to achieve for the Moguls what diplomacy and bribery had earlier achieved. Throughout the battles for Kandahar, the Moguls favored bows and arrows over artillery and firearms. Indeed, the Moguls considered archers to be the most prestigious of warriors during this period. At the same time, the Safavids consistently outgunned the Moguls. Safavid artillery was accurate, reliable, and inflicted very heavy casualties upon the Moguls during their sieges. Strangely, the Moguls felt little incentive to invest in systematic efforts to develop an army backed by gunpowder. In any case, Kandahar remained a part of the Safavid Empire until the beginning of the eighteenth century.

Eric D. Pullin

See also: Akbar the Great; Abbas the Great; Aurangzeb

References and further reading:

Habib, Irfan. *The Agrarian System of Mughal India, 1556–1707.* New York: Oxford University Press, 1999.

Richards, John F. *The Mughal Empire.* Cambridge: Cambridge University Press, 1993.

Zaman, M. K. *Mughal Artillery.* Delhi: Idarah-I Adabiyat-I Dellii, 1983.

Mohács, Battles of (29 August 1526, 12 August 1687)

Turkish-Hungarian battles. The first battle of Mohács took place on 29 August 1526. Over 30,000 Hungarians under King Louis II and Bishop Tomore made a heroic stance to defend Hungary against the Turks under Süleyman the Magnificent. The Turks numbered more than 100,000 troops and had 300 guns that proved decisive in routing the Hungarians, who lost 22,000 casualties, their king, many clergy and nobility, and eventually control of their capital at Budapest. The sultan went on to besiege Vienna, although unsuccessfully, at the height of Turkish power in eastern Europe.

The second battle took place 160 years later and marked a reversal of fortune for the Turks. A combined Austro-Hungarian force crushed the Turks under the Sultan Mohammed IV on 12 August 1687. The sultan was deposed by the soldiery and succeeded by Süleyman III. The Turks were badly overstretched, fighting wars against Venice, Russia, and the Holy League with Austria and Hungary at the same time. Turkish power, which had seen a brief military renaissance with this war against Austria, would never recover.

Christopher Howell

See also: Austro-Turk Wars; Süleyman I; Vienna, Sieges of

References and further reading:

Goodwin, Jason. *Lords of the Horizons: A History of the Ottoman Empire.* New York: Owl Books, 2000.

Turfan, Naim. *Rise of the Young Turks: Politics, the Military and Ottoman Collapse.* Istanbul, London: I. B. Tauris & Company, 2000.

Molnar, Miklos, and Anna Magyar, trans. *A Concise History of Hungary.* London: Cambridge University Press, 2001.

Mohi or Sajo River, Battle of (April 1241)

Battles in which the Mongols destroyed the Hungarian army and ransacked the kingdom. After conquering Russia, Mongol armies led by Sübedei and Batu invaded eastern Europe in February 1241, advancing as five separate but closely coordinated forces to deceive their enemies, who remained unclear regarding the Mongols' real targets until the last minute. Two advanced into Poland, one into Bohemia, and two into Hungary. At this time, Hungary, which appears to have been the primary Mongol target with its good pastures, possessed perhaps the finest army in Europe. Initially invaded by only a part of the Mongol army, it was soon invaded by the rest, after the Mongol victory against the Saxons at Liegnitz, in Silesia.

Although King Bela IV of Hungary had fortified the passes of the Carpathian Mountains, the Mongols had broken through by 14 March 1241. On 9 April 1241, King Bela advanced with an army that may have numbered 70,000 men, although there is some question whether or not he had his entire army with him because of a well-managed Mongol campaign of misinformation, including false mobilization orders. In response, the Mongols withdrew before the Hungarians for several days, until they had led the Hungarians to the plain of Mohi, between the Sajo and Tisza Rivers. The Hungarians camped in the plain, unaware that the Mongols had specifically chosen this site as a battlefield.

When the Mongols advanced to the Sajo River, prepared to do battle, Bela formed his wagons into a circle, thus fortifying them against a sudden cavalry charge. He stationed 1,000 men at the only bridge to prevent a crossing.

Around dawn, Batu attacked the bridge with archers and a rolling barrage of catapults firing naphtha. The Hungarians retreated from the bridge before the Mongols. In the ensuing melee, both sides suffered heavy casualties.

Sübedei, who had meanwhile crossed the river farther upstream on pontoons, then appeared behind the Hungarians, forcing them to fall back on their camp, which the Mongols surrounded, leaving a gap on the western flank, and bombarded with catapults and arrows. Eventually, the Hungarians detected the opening and soon poured from their camp in that direction, often dropping their weapons as they ran. As the unarmed Hungarians fled, the Mongols now wheeled upon them and slaughtered the fleeing men.

The Mongols continued the pursuit for three days, ravaging Hungary. Bela IV barely escaped, and only after a long flight into the southern Balkans with Mongol forces close behind. After taking up residence in Hungary, even issuing coins and dispatching raids as far as the suburbs of Vienna, the Mongols then abruptly withdrew in late 1241 and early 1242 because of the death of Great Khan Ögödei. Hungary remained a shadow of its former might for decades.

Timothy May

See also: Genghis Khan; Mongol Empire; Ögödei

References and further reading:

Chambers, James. *The Devil's Horsemen.* New York: Atheneum, 1985.

Grousset, Rene. *The Empire of the Steppes.* Translated by Naomi Walford. New Brunswick, NJ: Rutgers University Press, 1970.

Hildinger, Erik. *Warriors of the Steppe.* New York: Sarpedon, 1997.

Marshall, Robert. *Storm from the East.* Berkeley: University of California Press, 1993.

Moltke, Graf Helmuth Johannes Ludwig von (1848–1916)

Born at Gersdorf, Mecklenburg, on 23 May 1848, Helmuth Moltke joined the army in 1869. He was a nephew of Helmuth von Moltke ("the Elder"), who commanded Prussian armies to victory over Austria and France. Although similar greatness was expected for the younger Moltke, he unfortunately possessed little of his uncle's innovative military genius.

Moltke joined the Prussian army in 1869. He served as adjutant to his uncle and the kaiser and held a variety of field commands. Promoted to colonel (1895) and brigadier general (1899), in 1900 he became a major general commanding the 1st Guards Division. He was then quartermaster general (1903). Kaiser Wilhelm II named him chief of the general staff in 1906, succeeding General Alfred von Schlieffen. Moltke accepted the post with reservations, knowing that he was incapable of quick decisions.

Engraved portrait of General Helmuth J. L. von Moltke. (Library of Congress)

As German army chief of staff, Moltke believed war with the Entente powers was inevitable and pushed for it to be sooner rather than later. His major contribution to World War I was his ill-conceived revision of the Schlieffen Plan. Because he feared a French thrust into Alsace and Lorraine, he strengthened the German left wing at the expense of the right, which made it much more difficult for the right wing's encircling movement to succeed. Then with the offensive already under way, on 25 August he exacerbated matters by taking two corps and a division from the right wing and sending them east against the Russians. Moltke exercised little leadership during the fighting and, on 14 September following the critical Battle of the Marne, he was relieved of his post and demoted to deputy chief of staff. Moltke died suddenly of a heart attack in Berlin on 18 June 1916.

Spencer C. Tucker

See also: Moltke, Graf Helmuth Karl Bernhard von; Schlieffen, Graf Alfred von

References and further reading:

Craig, Gordon A. *The Politics of the Prussian Army, 1640–1945.* London: Oxford University Press, 1964.

Görlitz, Walter. *History of the German General Staff, 1657–1945.* New York: Frederick A. Praeger, 1953.

Moltke, Graf Helmuth Karl Bernhard von (1800–1891)

Prussian field marshal and architect of Prussia's victories in the nineteenth-century wars of German unification. Born on 26 October 1800 in Parchim, Mecklenburg, Helmuth von Moltke joined a Danish regiment on graduation from the Royal Cadet Corps in Copenhagen. After visiting Berlin in 1821, he decided to enter the Prussian army. Not wealthy, Moltke supplemented his income through writing.

Moltke attended the Prussian War Academy during 1823–1826 and joined the Prussian General Staff in 1833. Sent to Turkey in 1835 to study the language and advise the sultan on military matters, he entered the Turkish service contrary to instructions and campaigned in Egypt and Syria, distinguishing himself in the Battle of Nezib (Nizip) in July 1839.

Returning to Prussia in 1839, Moltke was aide-de-camp to Prince Henry of Prussia and then rejoined the general staff. Promoted to colonel in 1851, he was then aide-de-camp to Prince Frederick William (later Kaiser Frederick III). He traveled to Britain and Russia and in October 1858 became chief of staff of the Prussian Army.

Moltke and Minister of War Albrecht von Roon helped secure the appointment of Otto von Bismarck as minister-president of Prussia in 1862. These three men worked closely in the cause of German unification, reforming and increasing the size of the regular army. Moltke, who had written about railroads, well understood the implications of the railroad and telegraph for modern war. He soon reorganized the general staff into three geographical divisions and a railways department.

In 1864, Moltke oversaw Prussian military operations during a war with Denmark. His success in that campaign earned him the complete support of Kaiser William I. Moltke then drew up plans for the 1866 war against Austria, which involved a quick campaign of rapid concentration in which three armies would advance on different routes by rail, their movements coordinated by telegraph. Although communication broke down, Moltke nonetheless won a decisive victory over the Austrians in the Battle of Königgrätz (Sadowa). This Seven Weeks' War ended 120 years of rivalry between Prussia and Austria for domination in the Germanies.

Moltke noted flaws and corrected them in the final war of German unification, against France in 1870–1871. Although he allowed his subordinates considerable latitude, Moltke directed the military campaigns of the war, including the September 1870 Battle of Sedan, the October 1870–January 1871 Siege of Paris, and the final battles against the French Army of the Loire.

Advanced to both graf (count) and field marshal in June 1871 in recognition of his accomplishments, Moltke continued as chief of the general staff. In the early 1880s, he began to turn over responsibility to others, retiring altogether in 1888. He died in Berlin on 24 April 1891. Moltke wrote a number of books, most of them on military subjects.

Spencer C. Tucker

See also: Franco-Prussian War; German Wars of Unification; Königgrätz, Battle of; Sedan

References and further reading:

Craig, Gordon A. *The Politics of the Prussian Army, 1640–1945.* New York: Oxford University Press, 1956.

Howard, Michael. *The Franco-Prussian War: The German Invasion of France, 1870–1871.* New York: Macmillan, 1962.

Moltke, Helmuth K. B. von. *Strategy: Its Theory and Application: The Wars for German Unification, 1866–1871.* Westport, CT: Greenwood Press, 1971.

Wawro, Geoffrey. *The Austro-Prussian War. Austria's War with Prussia and Italy in 1866.* New York: Cambridge University Press, 1996.

Mongol Empire (1206–1259)

The world's greatest steppe empire was traditionally founded in 1206, when Genghis Khan (c. 1162–1227) was first elected khan; expansion had begun even before that date with raids on the northern Chinese state of Xixia. They continued with other raids on Xixia, and against the Chinese Jin dynasty, culminating in the capture of the Jin capital by the Mongols in 1215. In 1217, a new stage was reached as preparations were made for a general assault on the Khwaraz Empire of western Turkistan and Iran in response to mistreatment of some envoys under Mongol protection. After initial moves to shore up positions in eastern Turkistan and in the north, the main Mongol advance began in mid-1219. The Khwarazmians, outflanked on several fronts, quickly collapsed, and their last ruler died on an island in the Caspian Sea in late 1220, seeking to avoid the relentless Mongols.

Freed by the death of their adversary, the Mongols now pressed on into Iran. From there, Jebe and Sabutai (1172–1245) mounted their famous reconnaissance in force around the Caspian Sea (1221–1223). They reunited with other Mongolian forces under Prince Joci, eldest son of Genghis Khan, in late 1223 or 1224.

The death of Genghis Khan in 1227, while subduing Xixia, interrupted the Mongol advance, but it was quickly resumed under his successor. Ögödei (r. 1229–1241) focused Mongol efforts in two directions. One was China, where the Jin had reestablished themselves along the Yellow River. The other was toward the distant west, where Jebe and Sabutai had fought a battle against the Russians in 1223.

The Jin campaign began in 1231, after Ögödei had put his financial house in order. In a pattern typical of Mongolian warfare, separate Mongolian armies closed in on the Jin capital and forced the last Jin emperor to flee. He committed suicide in 1234, ending the dynasty. Although new hostilities developed with Jin's southern neighbor, Song China, that were to continue until that state was finally subdued in 1279, the major Mongol advance south was, for the time being at least, ended.

Ögödei's second major campaign began in 1235, with the convening of a council to discuss what was to be done about the west. A campaign was decided on, and armies began to move toward the Kipchak Steppe and Russia in 1236. They were under the titular command of Batu Khan, son of Joci, but Sabutai took overall strategic control. Initially, the Mongols attacked the Volga Bulghars and then the various Qipchaq tribes. Next was Russia: Ryazan was stormed on 21 December 1237, followed by Vladimir on 7 February 1238. After a pause for consolidation, the Mongols moved west again. Kiev fell on 6 December 1240, and from Kiev the Mongols advanced into eastern Europe.

Although the main Mongol target appears to have been Hungary, which had received some refugees fleeing the Mongols, the assault was a general one, with no less than five major lines of advance intended to prevent any single adversary from uniting against them. The following winter, the Mongols took the double cities of Buda and Pest, while raiding parties penetrated as far as the suburbs of Vienna. Only the death of Ögödei saved Europe from further invasion.

After Ögödei's death, there was an interregnum of nearly five years with few major endeavors. Although Ögödei's son Güyük was finally elected khan in 1246, he died two years later, and the interregnum continued. It was ended in 1251 by a veritable coup that brought a new Mongol house to the throne, that of Genghis Khan's youngest son, Tolui (c. 1190–1231/1232), in the form of Khan Möngke (r. 1251–1259), the last of the four khans to preside over a unified empire.

Under Möngke, the Mongolian advance resumed in two primary directions, against China through the southwest in an effort to outflank the Song and into Iran. The leader of the Iranian advance was Möngke's younger brother Hüle'ü (d. 1265), later founder of the Ilqan dynasty.

After Möngke, there were pretenders to the vacant throne of the khan, principally his brothers Kublai (1215–1294) and Arigh Böke (d. 1266), but none was able to impose himself on the other Mongols. Serious antagonisms between the various Mongol houses also prevented any reconciliation and a reuniting of empire.

Paul D. Buell

See also: 'Ayn Jalut, Battle of; Genghis Khan; Kublai Khan; Ögödei

References and further reading:

Allsen, Thomas T. *Mongol Imperialism.* Berkeley: University of California Press, 1987.

Buell, Paul D. "Sübötei-ba'atur." In *In the Service of the Khan: Eminent Personalities of the Early Mongol-Yuan Period (1200–1300),* ed. Igor de Rachewiltz, Chan Hok-lam, Hsiao Ch'i-ch'ing, and Peter W. Geier, 13–26. Wiesbaden: Otto Harrassowitz, 1993.

———. "Early Mongol Expansion in Western Siberia and Turkestan (1207–1219): A Reconstruction." *Central Asiatic Journal* 36 (1992): 1–2, 1–32.

Ratchnevsky, Paul. *Genghis Khan, His Life and Legacy.* Trans. Thomas Nivison Haining. Oxford, UK: Blackwell, 1991.

Rossabi, Morris. *Khubilai Khan: His Life and Times.* Berkeley: University of California Press, 1988.

Mongol-Song Wars (1267–1279)

The Mongols' crushing of the Song Dynasty. Kublai Khan waited for some years to consolidate his power before beginning his final assault on the surviving Chinese state, Southern Song (1126–1279). The campaign began in 1267, went on for 12 years, and was one of the most sophisticated, protracted, and hard-fought in history, not only because of the size of the armies involved, but also because of the rich pyrotechnical resources available to both sides and the sophistication of torsional artillery by that date.

The Mongols, to the greatest degree possible, sought to provoke a war of maneuver that the Song, always short of horses, were ill-equipped to counter. The Song, by contrast, relied upon enormous armies sited in fixed fortresses, knowing that the Mongols had either to assault these fortresses, advance through unsuitable terrain in central and south China, or attempt a naval envelopment, unlikely in the face of a technologically superior Song force that included some of the world's largest warships, also armed with pyrotechnical weapons.

The Mongols, well aware of Song plans, sought to counter them by using Chinese tactics against the Song fortresses, relying upon what was now a substantial siege train and large forces of Chinese foot soldiers. They were also aware of the need not just to advance but to defeat the Song morally, and thus set about destroying Song field armies piece by piece in a strategy reminiscent of Ulysses S. Grant's before Richmond in 1864–1865.

The lynchpins of the Song position in defending their capital at Hangzhou were the dual fortresses of Fancheng and Xiangyang, facing each other across the Han River, directly athwart the best line of Mongol advance. It took Kublai Khan's armies, led capably by Marshal Bayan (1237–1295), six years to reduce them, and it was late 1274 before Mongol armies finally penetrated to the Yangtze River, but Song resistance continued, and it was another year and a half before the Song capital was reached. Only after a massive land and sea battle in March 1275 and a protracted last-ditch resistance did the inevitable become clear to the Song court, which surrendered to the Mongols, who entered Hangzhou peacefully on 10 February 1276.

Before the Mongols could complete their occupation, loyalists fled with two young princes and took to the seas, supported by a still-powerful Song fleet. What followed was a remarkable resistance movement paralleling that of 1126–1230, in which Southern Song had once saved itself in the face of an equally determined invasion by the Jurchen of the Jin Dynasty (1122–1234). Thanks to unexpected problems encountered by Kublai Khan due to an invasion of his Mongolian homeland by Central Asian competitors, the resistance movement, based first in the province of Fujian and then in Guangdong and Guangxi, was able to rally much of the southeast and interior central China to the Song.

In the end, the Mongols had to launch a coordinated land and sea campaign to overcome Song resistance. Advancing simultaneously into the various regions supporting resistance along several land routes, they also used increasingly capable naval forces, added to as the campaign went on, in part through Song commanders going over to the Mongols, to seize coastal points behind loyalist lines. By late 1278, loyalist efforts had become confined to the province of Guangdong and to surviving units of the Song fleet carrying the surviving Song prince (one had died).

Increasingly outmaneuvered and isolated, the Song navy prepared for a final battle in early 1279, at Yaishan, an island located not far from modern Macao. Comprised of perhaps 1,000 oceangoing junks plus smaller supporting ships, the Song fleet, giving up all mobility, was drawn up in a long rectangle, tied to each other, with sterns outward. Wooden palisades were built on top so that not only the sailors, but Song land forces then on board, could participate in the battle. To a large extent, this arrangement was more a reflection of Song desperation and low morale than it was of a sound tactical judgment. It also reflected a realistic appraisal of increasingly numerous and very well handled Mongol naval forces.

Because of limited supplies of food and wood, which was important for making arrows, the Song fleet was anchored close to land. Its position gave Li Heng, one of the Mongol commanders, the opportunity to seize positions there and mount catapults to bombard the Song with stones and incendiaries and possibly exploding bombs.

On 19 March 1279, the Mongols were ready. Their fleet was at most half the size of the Song fleet, and apparently some ships arrived too late to participate in the battle. Mongol ships were also smaller, but their size proved an advantage in the waters in which the battle was fought, midway between two islands. Actually, despite the large number of ships involved, the ensuing battle was fought more as a land conflict than a naval battle.

The battle went on most of the day, with the Mongol fleet using its mobility to the utmost and the Song unable to respond since their ships were tied to one another. Later, the Mongols were able to penetrate the Song line and begin operating within the Chinese rectangle. As the afternoon tide came in, the Mongols used its force to charge in again and boarded several Song ships, braving the Greek fire.

By late afternoon, the Song rectangle was in disarray, and ships began to surrender. Some 800 ships are said to have been taken. Some 100,000 corpses were left floating in the water, among them that of the last Song prince. Not only had the Mongols won a notable victory, but they had bested the Song in their own element, on the water.

Paul D. Buell

See also: Chinese Imperial Wars; Kublai Khan; Mongol Empire; Song-Jin Wars

References and further reading:

Buell, Paul D. "The Sung Resistance Movement, 1276–1279: The End of an Era." *Annals of the Chinese Historical Society of the Pacific Northwest* 3 (1985–1986), 138–186.

Deng, Gang. *Maritime Sector, Institutions, and Sea Power of Premodern China.* Westport, CT: Greenwood Press, 1999.

Mote, F. W. *Imperial China, 900–1800.* Cambridge, MA: Harvard University Press, 1999.

Monmouth (27–28 June 1778)

A drawn battle in the American Revolution that marked the last major clash in the northern states. Faced by imperial obligations in the expanding conflict, the British decided to withdraw from Philadelphia to New York City. British general Henry Clinton began to march the 70 miles to Sandy Hook, New Jersey, and the protection of the Royal Navy. At the same time, American commander George Washington wanted to demonstrate the new American army forged over the winter at Valley Forge. The battle would take place during the British retreat and American pursuit at Monmouth Court House.

For a month, it was clear the British were making preparations to quit Philadelphia. Washington intended to pursue and catch them. The retreat was difficult in very hot and humid weather. The Americans met the British on 27 June, but General Charles Lee hesitated to attack. The next day, the British began moving to Sandy Hook and, to cover the retreat, readied to attack the American vanguard; meanwhile, it seemed that Lee had ordered a retreat, which was countermanded heatedly by Washington when he arrived on the battlefield.

The British attacked three times. The newly trained American army held its ground, and as more troops arrived, it pushed the British back. By evening, both sides were exhausted from the fighting and from the weather. Washington rested his troops, and Clinton continued his withdrawal to Sandy Hook and the safety of the Royal Navy. Although the Americans may have missed an opportunity to destroy the British, the battle made clear that what had been a ragtag group of militia had become a trained army and that the war of attrition increasingly favored the American republic.

Charles M. Dobbs

See also: American Revolution; Washington, George

References and further reading:

Smith, Samuel Steele. *The Battle of Monmouth.* Monmouth Beach, NJ: Philip Freneau Press, 1964.

Stryker, William. *The Battle of Monmouth.* Princeton, NJ: Princeton University Press, 1970.

Mons Graupius, Battle of (September 83)

Agricola's great victory over the Caledonians. The culmination of Tacitus's eulogy for his father-in-law describes the Battle of Mons Graupius. There have been many attempts to locate the site, but Agricola's marching camps near Huntly, Speyside, are the only pointers.

Assembled under the leadership of Calgacus (Swordsman), "the full force" of the Caledonians, 30,000 warriors, occupied Mons Graupius. The size of Agricola's army is not given, but Tacitus does say the enemy had "great superiority in numbers." Agricola certainly had 8,000 auxiliaries and probably 5,000 cavalry, together with vexillations from the four legions of Britain. The total force numbered some 20,000. Agricola placed the auxiliary infantry in the center, with their ranks spread out, and 3,000 cavalry on the wings. The vexillations were to the rear, drawn up in front of the Roman camp. The Caledonians were deployed in tiers on the gentle slope, with the vanguard on the level ground.

The battle began with Caledonian chariots racing across the ground between the two armies, only to be routed by the Roman cavalry. Next came a brisk exchange of missiles, followed by the Roman advance up the slope. The auxiliaries were initially successful and were soon joined by the cavalry.

The sheer number of Caledonians, combined with the roughness of the ground, soon halted the advance. Gradually, the auxiliaries began to be outflanked. As a counter, Agricola sent in his reserve cavalry. They stemmed the flanking movement and fell on the rear of the war bands, which broke. The legionaries were never engaged.

Nic Fields

See also: Agricola, Gnaeus Julius; Celts

References and further reading:

Maxwell, G. S. *A Battle Lost: Romans and Caledonians at Mons Graupius.* Edinburgh: Edinburgh University Press, 1989.

Montcalm-Gozon, Louis-Joseph de, Marquis de Montcalm de Saint-Véran (1712–1759)

French general who, according to his admirers, almost prevented a British takeover of Canada during the Seven Years' War and, according to his detractors, was the primary cause of it. Before he was given command of French regular forces in North America during the Seven Years' War (1756–1763), Montcalm had served in the War of the Polish Succession (1733–1738) and the War of the Austrian Succession (1740–1748). He arrived in New France in May 1756 and soon found himself at odds with the colony's Canadian-born governor, Pierre de Rigaud, the Marquis de Vaudreuil. Despite their differences, they managed to take Fort Oswego on Lake Ontario from the English. The following year, Montcalm captured Fort William Henry on Lake George. Even after the British government had determined to win the war in North America and sent over thousands of regular troops for the purpose, Montcalm's successes continued. In July 1758, he prevented a large British force from taking Fort Carillon (Ticonderoga) on Lake Champlain.

Elsewhere, the tide of war began to turn. Facing what he considered overwhelming odds, Montcalm wanted to use his regulars to defend the St. Lawrence Valley against the inevitable British onslaught, whereas Vaudreuil persisted in his plans for a continued guerrilla war, using the Canadian militia. Although the government in Paris sided with Montcalm and gave him command of all forces in New France, ample opportunity remained for Vaudreuil to frustrate Montcalm's efforts.

Throughout the summer of 1759, Montcalm managed to thwart General James Wolfe's British regulars from getting below the walls of Quebec. When at dawn on 13 September, however, the British surprised him by scaling the escarpment just west of the fort, Montcalm precipitously gave battle. He lost and died of his battle wounds the day after. Quebec surrendered soon thereafter. The war in North America was not yet lost, but given France's reluctance to come to the aid of its colony, the fate of New France was sealed.

N. F. Dreisziger

Montcalm trying to stop Native Americans from attacking the British as they leave Fort William McHenry. (Library of Congress)

See also: Austrian Succession, War of the; French and Indian War; Seven Years' War; Wolfe, James

References and further reading:

Eccles, W. J. "Montcalm." *Dictionary of Canadian Biography.* Vol. 3. Toronto: Oxford University Press, 1974.

Frégault, Guy. *Canada: The War of the Conquest.* Toronto: Macmillan, 1969.

Stacey, C. P. *Quebec 1759. The Siege and the Battle.* Toronto: McClellan, 1959.

Stanley, G. F. G. *New France: The Last Phase, 1744–1760.* Toronto: McClelland and Stewart, 1968.

Montecuccoli, Raimondo, Prince (1609–1680)

Italian commander in the service of the Habsburg emperors Ferdinand III (r. 1637–1657) and Leopold I (r. 1658–1705). One of the foremost generals and military theorists of the seventeenth century, Montecuccoli fought in the Thirty Years' War (1618–1648), the Second Northern War (1655–1660), the Austro-Turk War (1660–1664), and the Dutch War (1672–1678) against the numerous enemies of the house of Austria.

Montecuccoli entered military service as a child and progressed rapidly through the ranks. In 1664, he became supreme commander of the imperial armies and in 1668 president of the Supreme War Council. Four years earlier, he had thwarted Grand Vizier Fazil Ahmet Köprülü's plan to march against Vienna, for which he was acclaimed as "the savior of Christendom." The middle period of the Dutch War saw him pitted against worthy opponents: Louis XIV's great generals Henri de la Tour d'Auvergne, Vicomte de Turenne (1611–1675), and Louis II de Bourbon, fourth prince de Condé (1621–1686). Montecuccoli relinquished his command in 1675 and retired.

Whether in captivity or on peacetime duty and after his retirement, he studied the sciences, classical authors, and the art of war. His most influential works on that subject are *Dell'arte militare* and *Memoire della guerra.* Though above all a soldier, Montecuccoli on occasion also served as the Habsburg Court's diplomatic emissary. A military reformer, an advocate of "methodical warfare," and a skilled practitioner of the war of maneuver, Montecuccoli was a master of seventeenth-century warfare. He is the author of the famous dictum: to wage war, three things are needed—money, money, and money.

N. F. Dreisziger

See also: Condé, Louis II de Bourbon, Fourth Prince de; Louis XIV; Thirty Years' War; Turenne, Henri de la Tour d'Auvergne, Vicomte de; Turkish Wars of European Expansion

References and further reading:

Barker, Thomas Mack. *The Military Intellectual and Battle: Raimondo Montecuccoli and the Thirty Years' War.* Albany: State University of New York Press, 1975.

Campori, Cesare. *Raimondo Montecuccoli: La sua famiglia e i suoi tempi.* Florence: G. Barbera, 1876.

Montecuccoli, Raimondo. *Opere di Raimondo Montecuccoli.* Turin: G. Favale, 1821.

Perjés, Géza. *Army Provisioning, Logistics, and Strategy in the Second Half of the 17th Century.* Budapest: 1970.

Tomassini, Luciano. *Raimondo Montecuccoli: Capitano e scrittore.* Rome: Stato Maggiore Dell'esercito, Ufficio Storico, 1978.

Monterrey (20–24 September 1846)

Major U.S. Army victory in the Mexican-American War. At the opening of the Mexican-American War (1846–1848), American general Zachary Taylor advanced with an army of 3,080 regulars and 3,150 volunteers from the town of Matamoros on the south bank of the Rio Grande to Monterrey, defended by 7,000 regulars and 3,000 militia under the command of General Pedro de Ampudia. Taylor arrived on the northern outskirts of Monterrey on 19 September and found the approach guarded by a massive citadel known as the Black Fort. Despite the Mexican's numerical advantage, he decided to divide his army into two wings and dispatch one wing to the west of the city and the other to the east. On 20 September, the west wing, commanded by William J. Worth, swung to the west, avoiding the guns of the Black Fort. The following day, Worth led his men across the Saltillo road, forded the Santa Catarina River, turned east, and stormed Federacon Hill, capturing Fort Solidado on the eastern end of the promenade. On 21 September, the eastern wing of Taylor's army, commanded by Colonel John Garland, attacked the stoutly defended fortification, El Teneria, and took it but was unable to dislodge the Mexicans from another strategic position, the earthwork fort, El Diablo. Two days later, Worth's men recrossed the Santa Catarina River, stormed Independence Hill, and took the Bishop's Palace. Worth's men next advanced into the western end of the city. On the eastern side of Monterrey, the Mexicans abandoned El Diablo and retreated to the central plaza and the cathedral. General Ampudia requested a truce on 24 September, but Taylor did not agree until the next day. Without consulting President James K. Polk, Taylor agreed to allow Ampudia and his men to evacuate the city. American loses were 120 killed and 368 wounded, and Mexican casualties totaled 367.

George M. Lauderbaugh

See also: Mexican-American War; Santa Anna, Antonio López de; Taylor, Zachary

References and further reading:

Eisenhower, John S. D. *So Far from God: The U.S. War with Mexico, 1846–1848.* New York: Random House, 1989.

Singletary, Otis. *The Mexican War.* Chicago: University of Chicago Press, 1960.

Smith, George W., and Charles Judah, eds. *Chronicles of the Gringos: The U.S. Army in the Mexican War, 1846–1848.* Albuquerque: University of New Mexico Press, 1968.

Smith, Justin. *The War with Mexico.* New York: Macmillan, 1919.

Montgomery, Bernard Law (1887–1976)

British field marshal best known for his victory at El Alamein, 1942. Born on 17 November 1887 in London, Montgomery entered Sandhurst in 1907. His military talent was recognized in World War I, and he became a general staff officer in January 1917. After attending the staff college at Camberley in 1920, he went on to hold staff and command posts in Ireland, England, Palestine, and India and served as an instructor at the staff colleges at Camberley and Quetta.

During the Battle of France (May–June 1940), Montgomery commanded the 3rd Division energetically, and during the final days of the Dunkirk evacuation, he briefly commanded II Corps. Back in England, he was promoted to lieutenant general, becoming commander of V Corps. After the dismissal of General Claude Auchinleck, Montgomery was selected to command the Eighth Army in North Africa, halting Erwin Rommel's forces at the Battle of Alam Halfa (31 August–2 September 1942) and then grinding down the Germans' tank strength at El Alamein, the battle that turned the tide in the desert. Finally, here was a British general who could win victories, albeit with massive superiority over the enemy, and "Monty" became a popular figure with the British masses.

After commanding the Eighth Army in Italy, Montgomery took over command of the Twenty-first Army Group, which played a central role in the western European campaign of 1944–1945. Montgomery favored a single thrust to defeat Germany but, like George Patton and Omar Nelson Bradley, was forced to bow to Dwight D. Eisenhower's broad front strategy.

Montgomery was an efficient general, albeit extremely cautious, possibly remembering horrific British casualties in World War I. But he could be tactless and arrogant, often expressing the need to teach the "naive" Americans battle truths. The latter, bearing in mind Singapore, Greece, Crete, and so on, were not about to be so "instructed." Montgomery was chief of the Imperial General Staff from June 1946 to November 1948 and deputy supreme Allied commander in Europe from 1951 to 1958. He died at Islington Mill on 24 March 1976.

Alaric Searle

See also: El Alamein; MARKET GARDEN; Normandy Landings

References and further reading:

Hamilton, Nigel: *Monty: The Making of a General, 1887–1942.* New York: McGraw-Hill, 1981.

———. *Monty: The Final Years of the Field-Marshal, 1944–1976.* New York: McGraw Hill, 1987.

Montgomery, Field Marshal Bernard Law. *Memoirs.* London: Collins, 1958.

Montmorency, Anne, Duc de (1493–1567)

The constable Anne de Montmorency was a distinguished warrior during his long life, serving five French kings. During the first half of the sixteenth century, as the French monarchy struggled to gain control of France and its nobles, the Valois kings faced considerable opposition to their attempts to centralize royal authority. The death of Henry II in a jousting accident in 1559 began a long period of royal weakness that would not end until the Bourbon Henry of Navarre took the throne in 1589. The Duke of Montmorency, constable of France, had immense landholdings and a personal following of several hundred vassals. When the Huguenot Montmorency converted other major nobles of France to the new religion, they became a dangerous political threat to the Catholic Valois. Montmorency is a good example of how the French kings managed to control their nobles by offering them titles in exchange for loyalty.

Montmorency was made a marshal in 1522 by Francis I and was captured with Francis at Pavia in 1525. He helped negotiate Francis's release in 1526 and soon after the king's return received the governorship of Languedoc, which remained in his family until 1632. He was made constable in 1537. Montmorency's enemies at court and his policy of peace with Holy Roman Emperor Charles V finally led to his disgrace in 1541, which lasted until Francis's death in 1547.

Henry II restored him to a degree of favor, and in return he took Metz from the Spanish in 1552. Dismissed by his successor, Francis II, Montmorency was restored to office by Catherine de Medici. He joined the Guises in the Wars of Religion, was captured at Dreux in 1562, and was killed in the siege of St. Denis, near Paris, in 1567.

David C. Arnold

See also: French Wars of Religion; Guise, François de Lorraine, Second Duke of; Pavia, Battle of; Valois-Habsburg Wars

References and further reading:

Briggs, Robin. *Early Modern France, 1560–1715.* London: Oxford University Press, 1998.

Hartmann, Cyril Hughes. *The Magnificent Montmorency: The Life and Death of Henri Duc de Montmorency, 1595–1632.* New York: E. P. Dutton, 1928.

Palm, Franklin Charles. *Politics and Religion in Sixteenth-Century France: A Study of the Career of Montmorency-Damville, Uncrowned King of the South.* Gloucester, MA: Peter Smith, 1969.

Montrose, James Graham, Marquis of (1612–1650)

Leading royalist general of Scottish "Covenanter wars." James Graham was born in 1612 of a prominent Lowlands noble family. His brief career played out against the complex religious, social, and political turmoil of the seventeenth-century British Isles.

The Scottish Reformation conveyed the Roman Catholic Church's considerable estate into the power of a nobility, many of whom saw profit in Protestantism. Siding first with the Covenanters against Charles I's attempts to impose episcopacy, the young Montrose soon rejected the rebellion's religious absolutism and political chicanery. In his struggle to win adherents to the Royalist cause, he advocated a monarchy strong enough to uphold fundamental liberties against factionalism and fanaticism.

Obtaining Charles's commission, Montrose raised loyalist Irish and highland Scots and during his "year of miracles" (1644–1645) virtually destroyed the Covenant's larger armies with superior tactics and leadership, until his dwindling force was surprised at Philiphaugh. Montrose escaped, while his men were slaughtered after surrendering. On the king's orders, he disbanded his remaining followers and went to Europe to raise support. After Charles I's execution, he landed in the Orkney Islands, but his small force of foreign regulars and local levies was routed at Carbisdale on 27 April 1650. Montrose was captured, hanged, and quartered without a trial in Edinburgh on 21 May.

Despite repeated victories against great odds, his mostly irregular clansmen, who fought fiercely under his personal leadership, could not hold territory or establish a lasting power base. Without effective and timely support by the Royalist leadership, his victories were as ephemeral as they were remarkable, and his legacy was more one of personal example than military effectiveness.

Anne L. Angstadt

See also: Cromwell, Oliver; English Civil War (1642–1649)

References and further reading:

Buchan, John. *The Marquis of Montrose.* Reprint, London: Prion, 1996.

Wedgwood, C. V. *Montrose.* New York: St. Martin's Press, 1995.

Mormon War (1838–1839)

Major nineteenth-century American internal conflict. The first "Mormon War" began in northwestern Missouri in 1838, when members of the Church of Jesus Christ of Latter-Day Saints (LDS, or Mormons) battled units of the Missouri state militia. This conflict escalated into a massacre of Mormons at Haun's Hill, Missouri, and prompted governor Lillburn Boggs to issue an October 1838 extermination order against Mormons, calling for their execution if they did not leave Missouri immediately.

The Mormons understandably fled to Hancock County, Illinois, where they founded Nauvoo, which became the biggest city in Illinois. Local residents lynched LDS founder Joseph Smith and his brother Hyrum in 1844, prompting a Mormon exodus to Mexico's Alta California Province, beginning in 1847. The province was transferred to the United States following the Mexican-American War and was renamed Utah. Conflict quickly developed between LDS leaders and federal officials and grew into the second Mormon War, or the Utah War of 1857–1858.

Lance Janda

See also: Utah War

References and further reading:

Furniss, Norman F. *The Mormon Conflict, 1850–59.* New Haven, CT: Yale University Press, 1960.

Hafen, LeRoy R., and Ann W. Hafen. *The Utah Expedition: A Documentary Account.* Glendale: Arthur H. Clark Company, 1958.

LeSuer, Stephen C. *The 1838 Mormon War in Missouri.* Columbia: University of Missouri Press, 1987.

Mortars

A muzzle-loaded weapon firing its bomb at a high angle to attack protected positions and trenches. The mortar has been known for many centuries and was most effective as a naval weapon for shore bombardment and as a land weapon for attacking the defenders behind walled defenses. It is the artillery of the infantry, supporting them at all levels from section up to regiment, and infantry have always held a healthy respect for their opponent's mortars.

Mortars were prevalent in the trench warfare of World War I, firing high-explosive (HE), smoke, and gas shells. Some were rifled and had separate firing mechanisms for safety. In World War II, infantry mortars ranged in caliber from 5 centimeters (cm) (used for smoke and illumination mainly) to 12 cm (firing mostly HE bombs).

Mortars nowadays have ranges up to 10 kilometers and more, and a good mortar team can have many bombs in the air at once, adding to the effect on target. Bombs are HE, smoke, illuminating, and antitank. Mortars are used mainly for indirect fire against targets unseen by the mortar teams.

The mortar is usually intended to be man-portable, although some heavier versions are vehicle-mounted. Every infantry battalion has mortar support, giving fire for attack and defense. Mortars are normally grouped in pairs and sets of pairs in battle and can operate in the front line from trenches because of their high angle of fire. Each mortar has a baseplate, a bipod (or similar support) with sights attached, and a barrel, and each segment is normally man-portable. Ammunition supply is paramount, for mortars can achieve a very high rate of fire; in battle, many infantrymen will carry one mortar bomb plus their own equipment and spare machine gun ammunition.

David Westwood

References and further reading:

Hobart, Frank William Arthur, ed. *Jane's Infantry Weapons.* London: MacDonald and Jane's, 1975.

Freytag, Viktor. *Infanteriegechuetz und s GrW 34.* Berlin: Mittler and Sohn, 1939.

Mosby, John Singleton (1833–1916)

Confederate cavalry commander and raider and leader of Mosby's Rangers. Mosby was born in Edgemont, Virginia, on 6 December 1833 and practiced law in Bristol, Virginia, after 1855. Enlisting in the Confederate cavalry early in the war, he saw action at First Bull Run and then, under James Ewell Brown "Jeb" Stuart, in the Peninsular campaign and at Second Bull Run and Antietam. Stuart ordered Mosby to create a free-moving cavalry unit in December 1862 to harass the enemy. This unit, Mosby's Rangers, was so successful that the area it controlled between the Potomac and Rappahannock Rivers became known as "Mosby's Confederacy."

Raiding usually at night in small groups armed with Colt 44 pistols, Mosby's men diverted thousands of federal combat troops to guard duty. Their most daring exploit was the

Soviet troops manuever a piece of anti-tank artillery through the snow in the German attack on Moscow, 1941. (Hulton/Archive)

capture of Brigadier General Edwin Stoughton at Fairfax Court House, Virginia, on 8 March 1863. Their presence prevented flank attacks as Robert E. Lee marched from Chancellorsville to Gettysburg. By late 1863, several federal cavalry units had standing orders to pursue Mosby full-time. Mosby eluded them all, and on 18 November 1864 killed or wounded all but two of the handpicked 100 men that Philip Sheridan had sent after him.

Mosby surrendered only after word came of Joseph E. Johnston's surrender. He practiced law in Warrenton, Virginia, until his death on 30 May 1916.

Eric v. d. Luft

See also: American Civil War; Antietam/Sharpsburg; Bull Run, First/Manassas; Bull Run, Second/Manassas Junction; Chancellorsville, Battle of; Gettysburg; Johnston, Joseph Eggleston; Lee, Robert Edward; Sheridan, Philip Henry; Stuart, James Ewell Brown

References and further reading:

Evans, Thomas J., and James M. Moyer. *Mosby's Confederacy: A Guide to the Roads and Sites of Colonel John Singleton Mosby.* Shippensburg, PA: White Mane, 1991.

Jones, Virgil Carrington. *Ranger Mosby.* McLean, VA: EPM, 1987.

Ramage, James A. *Gray Ghost: The Life of Col. John Singleton Mosby.* Lexington: University Press of Kentucky, 1999.

Siepel, Kevin H. *Rebel: The Life and Times of John Singleton Mosby.* New York: Da Capo Press, 1997.

Moscow (30 September 1941–April 1942)

First land defeat of the Wehrmacht during World War II, marking the failure of the German Barbarossa campaign to defeat the USSR in a single operation. Adolf Hitler's Directive 21, Operation BARBAROSSA, listed Moscow as a secondary objective after the capture of Leningrad and Kiev. On 19 July 1941, because of the nonuniform advance of the three German army groups (North, Center, and South), Directive 33 instructed Panzer Group 2 to be redeployed from Center to South to assist in the capture of Kiev (21 August–27 September). At Leningrad, the German assault became a siege.

The first phase of Operation TYPHOON, the attack on Moscow, was mounted from 30 September to 30 October.

World War II: Barbarossa, 1941
Miles 0 100 200
Kms 0 100 200
Viipuri
Lake Ladoga
Northwest Front (Voroshilov)
Helsinki
Leningrad
Hango
Gulf of Finland
Narva
SOVIET UNION
Baltic Sea
Tallinn
Lake Peipus
Luga
Vokay River
Novgorod
Lake Ilmen
Volga River
DAGO
ESTONIA
Demyansk
West Front (Timoshenko, Zhukov)
OESEL
Tartu
Staraya Russa
Kalinin
Kholm
Pskov
Gulf of Riga
Rzhev
Klin
Moscow
Velikiye Luki
Riga
Army Group North (Leeb)
Beloj
LATVIA
Nevel
Mozhaisk
Oka River
Vyazma
Dvinsk
Kaluga
Tula
Dvina River
LITHUANIA
Vitebsk
Smolensk
Memel
Don River
Kaunas
Orsha
Roslavl
Minsk
Bryansk
Beresina River
Mogilev
Vilna
Niemen River
Orel
Konigsberg
Livny
Voronezh
Suvalki
EAST
Grodno
Southwest Front (Budenny, Timoshenko)
Kursk
Gomel
Desna River
Glukhov
Bialystok
Army Group Center (Bock)
Bug River
Pripet River
Warsaw
Vistula River
Sumy
Brest
Knontop
Korosten
Kharkov
POLAND
Kowel
Lubny
Kiev
Lublin
UKRAINE
Poltava
Rowne
Dnieper River
GERMANY
Zhitomir
Kremenchug
Cherkassy
Stalino
Lwow
Tarnopol
Uman
Dnepropetrovsk
Przemysl
Kirov
Mariupol
Dniester River
Nikopol
Bug River
Melitopol
Cernauti
Nikolayev
Stalin Line
Front Line, 21 June 1941
Front Line, 9 July 1941
Front Line, 1 Sept. 1941
Front Line, 30 Sept. 1941
German Routes of Attack
Army Group South (Rundstedt)
Prut River
Perekop
Sea of Azov
Odessa
Kerch
Feodosiya
CRIMEA
ROMANIA
Danube River
Yevpatoriya
Sevastopol
Black Sea
Yalta

The German force amounted to 74 German divisions, including 14 panzer divisions of Panzer Groups 2, 3, and 4. They were opposed by the Western, Briansk, and Reserve Fronts, a Soviet force totaling 1.25 million men.

The Germans launched pincer movements to encircle 81 Soviet divisions in two separate pockets, Viazma and Briansk. Eliminating these pockets stalled the German advance until the second phase of Typhoon (15 November–8 December), the attempt to capture Moscow via pincer attacks from Klin and Tula. The German logistical situation was weakened, many battle formations were severely under strength and unprepared for winter, and equipment was wearing out.

On 5 December, the Soviets launched a counterattack planned by Marshal Georgy Zhukov, employing a strategic reserve of 10 armies, mostly fresh Siberian troops. The Soviet industrial plants evacuated in July–November began supplying the improved weapons from their reconstructed locations in the Urals. The German were sent reeling back.

By 6 January 1942, the Germans had retreated beyond the Volkhov River along the Orel-Rzhev axis. The Soviets expanded their action into a counteroffensive, attempting to destroy Army Group Center and break through to Leningrad. They did not succeed, although Viazma and Rostov-on-Don were liberated by the time the Soviets halted their operations in March 1942.

Neville G. Panthaki

See also: Guderian, Heinz; Hitler, Adolf; Kiev; Konev, Ivan Stepanovich; Leningrad, Siege of; Rokossovsky, Konstantin Konstantinovich; Smolensk; Stalin; Timoshenko, Semen Konstantinovich; World War II; Zhukov, Georgy Konstantinovich

References and further reading:

Erickson, John. *The Road to Stalingrad.* New York: Harper & Row, 1975.

Fugate, Bryan, and Lev Dvoretsky. *Thunder on the Dnepr.* Novato, CA: Presidio Press, 1997.

Overy, Richard. *Russia's War.* London: Penguin Books, 1998.

Werth, Alexander. *Russia at War, 1941–1945.* London: Pan Books, 1964.

Moscow, Retreat from (19–23 October 1812)

The abandonment of a city whose capture Napoleon had thought would provide supplies, shelter, and an armistice. On 13 September 1812, the Russian commander, Prince Mikhail Kutuzov, decided to abandon Moscow, retreating from Fili southeast along the Kolomna road. The population evacuated, with only 25,000 of Moscow's 250,000 inhabitants remaining. The city's mayor, Count Fyodor Rostopchin, arranged for arsonists to set the city ablaze. From 15 to 18 September, four-fifths of Moscow was destroyed.

Napoleon expected the Russian nobility to greet him and negotiate an armistice. His appeals (20 September, 4 October, 14 October) to Kutuzov and Czar Alexander I were rebuffed. Left with a ruined city, without stores, supplies, or winter quarters, Napoleon decided to abandon Moscow on 19 October. The French rearguard remained until 23 October.

Napoleon had brought with him 87,500 infantry, 14,750 cavalry, 533 guns, and an enormous baggage train consisting of 40,000 wagons, most of which was loot. The French faced Kutuzov and 100,000 infantry, 20,000 Cossacks, and 600 guns. Theoretically, Napoleon had provisions for 20 days and fodder for a week. The partisans menaced French logistics so that convoys from Smolensk had to be guarded by 1,500 men.

The French marched at 10 miles per day on the Kaluga road. Russian forces pursued and forced battle on 25 October at Maloyaroslavets. The ensuing battle cost the Russians 7,000 men and the French 4,000. Napoleon now decided to retreat to Smolensk via Borovsk-Mozhiask-Gzhatsk-Viazma.

Kutuzov followed Napoleon on a parallel route, Medyn-Smolensk, permitting only limited engagements and allowing the fatigue and famine of withdrawal to destroy the French. At Viazma on 3 November, 20,000 cavalry and infantry attacked Louis Nicolas Davout's rearguard and separated it from the main French army, while Michel Ney was also under attack.

By 7 November, it was snowing heavily. Maintaining a march pace of 12 miles per day, 41,000 French reached Smolensk on 9–12 November. Napoleon learned that the Russian armies of the Baltic and Danube were converging to cut off his retreat at Borisov on the Berezina River. Napoleon's retreat from Moscow would soon become a rout.

Neville G. Panthaki

See also: Berezina River, Battle of; Borodino; Kutuzov, Prince Mikhail Illarionovich Golenishchev; Napoleon I

References and further reading:

Austin, Paul. *1812: The Great Retreat.* London: Greenhill Books, 1996.

de Ségur, Philippe-Paul. *Napoleon's Russian Campaign.* Boston: Houghton-Mifflin, 1980.

Nafziger, George. *Napoleon's Invasion of Russia.* Novato, CA: Presidio, 1988.

Nicolson, Nigel. *Napoleon 1812.* New York: Harper & Row, 1985.

Riehn, Richard. *1812: Napoleon's Russian Campaign.* New York: John Wiley and Sons, 1991.

Mount Badon, Battle of (c. 490–516)

Unknown location of a famous victory by the Britons over invading Anglo-Saxons. After 410, the last Roman legions were withdrawn, and Britain was left to fend for itself. During the rest of the century, large numbers of Germanic peoples (Angles, Saxons, Jutes, and others) poured into Britain and established foundations for their kingdoms. For several years after midcentury, the invaders gradually attempted to expand but met strong resistance from the Britons. During a lengthy period of warfare, both sides alternately experienced defeats and victories.

Gildas, a native Briton living just after that period of conflict, wrote a brief account of the Battle of Mount Badon (Mons Badonicus). The site of the three-day siege is unknown, and the date is uncertain. Gildas implied that the British leader was Ambrosius Aurealianus, the last Roman leader in Britain. According to Gildas, the victory provided 40 years of comparative peace. The ninth-century chronicler Nennius tells us that the Battle of Mount Badon was the twelfth and last battle fought by a British captain named Arthur. Nennius describes how Arthur fought the Saxons in the company of the British kings and how 960 Saxons were killed by Arthur at Mount Badon. Living a generation after Ambrosius and more chronologically correct, Arthur has been generally credited with the victory at Badon. Tradition and scholarship have also suggested that he utilized cavalry against Saxon foot soldiers.

Mount Badon was probably a hill-fort in southern England. Scholars have favored Badbury, Bath, and Solsbury as the location. The dating of the battle falls broadly between the years 490 and 516.

Brigitte F. Cole

See also: Ancient Warfare

References and further reading:

Alcock, Leslie. *Arthur's Britain.* London: Penguin, 1971.
Gildas. *Works.* Trans. Hugh Williams. London: Cymmrodorian, 1899–1901.
Nennius. *History of the Britains.* Trans. E.W. Wade-Evans. London: Church History Society, 1938.

Mountbatten of Burma, Louis Francis Albert Victor Nicholas (1900–1979)

Very influential royally related British naval and land commander and final viceroy of India. Mountbatten joined the Royal Navy in 1913 and saw action aboard capital ships *Lion* and *Queen Elizabeth* during World War I. Continuing in the Royal Navy until World War II, Mountbatten was promoted to the rank of captain and given command of the Fifth Destroyer Flotilla in 1939. In May 1940, a German E-boat torpedoed Mountbatten's own destroyer, the *Kelly,* in the North Sea. Luftwaffe Ju–87 Stuka dive-bombers sank the *Kelly,* still under Mountbatten's command, at Crete on 23 May 1941.

Lord Louis Mountbatten (right) discusses the war with General George Patton at Camp Anfa, near Casablanca, 1943. (Library of Congress)

Noel Coward's play and film, *In Which We Serve,* was based on this action.

In the summer of 1941, Prime Minister Winston Churchill promoted Mountbatten to chief of combined operations; as such, he was responsible for preparing the Allied invasion of Europe. As part of the preparations, Mountbatten developed the organizational framework for Operation OVERLORD. He also planned the commando raids, among them the disastrous Dieppe raid of 19 August 1942, which were a series of probing missions designed to assess the requirements of the future invasion force, gauge the strength of German coastal defenses, and raise morale among citizens of German-occupied countries. Churchill appointed Mountbatten as supreme commander of the Allied forces in Southeast Asia in August 1943.

Mountbatten's experience in Asia during World War II and his somewhat left-wing politics (as much as would be feasible for one of such blue blood that he looked down on the royal Windsors) made him the ideal choice of Britain's ruling Labour Party to succeed General Archibald Wavell as India's final viceroy on 22 March 1947. After India's independence in August 1947, he served as India's first governor general until 1948. Mountbatten became fourth sea lord in 1950, commander in chief of the Mediterranean Fleet in 1952, and first sea lord in 1955. He served as chief of the United Kingdom Defense Staff and chairman of the Chiefs of Staff Committee from 1959 to 1965. The Irish Republican Army murdered Mountbatten and several members of his family by a remotely detonated bomb on his boat in Donegal Bay, Ireland, on 27 August 1979.

Eric D. Pullin

See also: Churchill, Sir Winston; Crete; Dieppe; Normandy Landings; Wavell, Archibald Percival, First Earl; World War I; World War II

References and further reading:

Campbell-Johnson, Alan. *Mission with Mountbatten.* New York: Atheneum, 1985.
Hough, Richard. *Mountbatten.* New York: Random House, 1980.
Mountbatten, Vice Admiral the Earl of Mountbatten of Burma. *Report.*
Thorne, Christopher. *Allies of a Kind.* New York: Oxford University Press, 1978.
Ziegler, Philip. *Mountbatten.* New York: Alfred A. Knopf, 1985.

Mountjoy, Charles Blount, Lord (1562–1606)

Most successful Elizabethan military commander in Ireland. Charles Blount, Lord Mountjoy, repulsed a Spanish intervention at Kinsale, successfully ending nine years of war that followed the rebellion of Hugh O'Neill, the Earl of Tyrone.

Mountjoy's military career began in 1586, when he joined the earl of Leicester's forces fighting the Spanish in the Netherlands. He distinguished himself at the Battle of Zuthpen in 1587 and was subsequently knighted. In the next few years, he learned the art of war by serving with Sir John Norreys in Brittany but was forbidden further field service by Elizabeth I, when he succeeded his brother as the Eighth Baron Mountjoy in 1594. Despite the queen's admonition to learn about war from books, Mountjoy took part in the Cadiz expedition under the earl of Essex. His first substantial command came in 1600, when he was appointed lord deputy of Ireland in place of Essex, who had been disgraced by embarrassing defeats at the hands of O'Neill. Though physically weak and considered a hypochondriac, Mountjoy displayed an intuitive grasp of the central problem of Irish warfare, supply. He launched a policy of campaigning in the winter, which prevented the Irish from moving their cattle, and ordered the destruction of agricultural areas that supported the rebel forces.

His first offensive against O'Neill foundered against Irish fortifications in the indecisive Battle of Moyry Pass in October 1600, but he won a decisive victory at Kinsale in late 1601. In the later campaign, Mountjoy's brilliance as a logistician was confirmed when he managed to deploy and supply a large army with siege equipment in an isolated part of Ireland. He subsequently negotiated O'Neill's submission in early 1603. His health broken by extended campaigning in the Irish climate, Mountjoy died of illness in 1606.

John S. Nolan

See also: Kinsale, Siege of; Nine Years' War

References and further reading:

Falls, Cyril. *Mountjoy: Elizabethan General.* London: Odhams Press, 1955
Fissel, Mark Charles. *English Warfare, 1511–1642.* London: Routledge, 2001.
Wernham, R. B. *The Return of the Armadas.* Oxford, UK: Oxford University Press, 1994.

Mozambican War of Independence (1963–1974)

The Portuguese occupation of Mozambique was a particularly grim affair, relying heavily on slave and forced labor. Resistance to colonial rule ranged from work stoppages to outright armed resistance. All of these factors coalesced in 1962 with the formation of the Front for the Liberation of Mozambique, or Frelimo, which comprised exiled political groups, radical intellectuals, and underground organizations that had begun to operate within the country.

To understand the situation in Mozambique, one has to understand that with numerous challenges facing it, the Portuguese government of Antonio Salazar tied its prestige to the fate of its African colonies. Much the same way that France viewed Algeria as an integral part of the republic, Portugal had declared its African holdings to be "overseas provinces."

Portugal had been quite effective in keeping a tight grip on potential resistance movements in Mozambique. During the Angolan Luanda insurrection of 1961, there were, surprisingly, no similar rural uprisings in Mozambique. Much of this lack of opposition was due to the activities of the state security police, which had been systematically detaining people known to be hostile to the regime. As a result, the most effective resistance movement flourished outside the country. In 1962, Frelimo was founded in Tanzania, led by the charismatic Eduardo Mondlane, an academic and official at the United Nations in New York. On 25 September 1964, Frelimo launched an attack on the Portuguese in northern Mozambique, at the same time issuing a call to arms.

The Portuguese set the tone of the conflict by rounding up and detaining some 1,500 Frelimo activists in the cities, putting to an end any hope for an Algerian-style protracted urban conflict. Frelimo southern and central fronts having virtually collapsed under the weight of the Portuguese attacks, the focus turned to the north, where the Portuguese forces were minimal. However, the successes of late 1965 were soon reversed; in 1966 the Portuguese counterattacked along Lake Malawi. With the policy of grouping the population into camps, some 250,000 people were resettled in 150 villages by the end of the year, removing much of Frelimo's support base.

By 1968, the war had focused on the ambitious Portuguese civil works project, the Cabora Bassa dam on the Zambezi River. Even though Frelimo's attacks on the fortified construction sites were unsuccessful, the protection of the dam absorbed a great deal of effort and rendered the Portuguese forces static, allowing Frelimo for the first time to outflank the defenses and begin operations south of the Zambezi River.

After the death of Salazar and Marcello Caetano's succession in 1968, Portugal launched a counteroffensive. The military planned a massive sweep in the north of Mozambique in which reconnaissance and airborne assault would search out and destroy Frelimo. The group was taken by surprise by the scale of the Portuguese operation, but rather than try to hold on to the north, Frelimo withdrew troops and transferred them, through Malawi, to Tete in the center. Portugal's grand offensive succeeded, but Caetano was not pleased with the cost of the campaign; Lisbon halted further offenses.

The reopening of the Tete front proved to be a breakthrough for Frelimo. It moved units south of the Zambezi River in 1971, and in July 1972, for the first time, guerrilla activity threatened an important section of the settler population. These campaigns were psychologically successful and in the period 1972–1974 contributed to a rapid crumbling of the colonial structure.

In Portugal, there was a growing sense that an African empire was passé in the twentieth century. With the Portuguese military coup of 1974, the new government sought immediately to end the hostilities and remove all Portuguese military units from the country. On 7 September, the Lusaka Accord was signed, allowing for the rapid and unequivocal transfer of power to Frelimo, and on 28 September 1974, the granting of Mozambique independence was signed, making it an independent country with Frelimo in command.

James Corbin

See also: Angolan Civil War; Angolan War of Independence

References and further reading:

Ciment, James. *Angola and Mozambique: Postcolonial Wars in Southern Africa.* New York: Facts on File, 1997.

Finnegan, William. *A Complicated War: The Harrowing of Mozambique.* Berkeley: University of California Press, 1993.

Newitt, Malyn. *A History of Mozambique.* Bloomington: Indiana University Press, 1995.

Muhammad Ahmad (al-Mahdi, Muhammad Ahmad Ibn As-Sayyid' Abd Allah) (1844–1885)

Muslim holy man from Dongola in the Sudan who declared himself the "Mahdi," or "Guided One," and raised the banner of revolt against the excesses of the Anglo-Egyptian administration in the Sudan.

Born 12 August 1814, Muhammad Ahmad was deeply religious from childhood. At age 20, he was already a sheikh with a reputation for sanctity. His call for a jihad in 1881 to restore Islam to its pristine purity received enthusiastic response and attracted both Muslims and non-Muslims alike. The violence that accompanied the conquest of the Sudan engendered deep-seated hatred for the Turco-Egyptians. Charles Gordon's efforts to suppress the slave trade in the 1870s were bitterly resented by Muslim traders. The cattle-owning nomads of Kordofan smarted under heavy taxation, and pious Muslims were scandalized by the corruption and lack of Islamic observance by Turkish and Egyptian officials. The increasing use of European officials in the administration accentuated the loss of independence and emphasized the alien quality of the Egyptian presence.

Muhammad Ahmad knit together these disparate groups in the Sudan through his piety and stirring oratory. To the people of the Nile banks, his message was oppression of the tax collector; around the plains of Gedir, it was defilement of an ancient faith by cowardly Turks and renegade foreigners ousting the rightful owners of the land.

Ahmad and his closest advisers acted as a high command, disseminating propaganda and articulating the discontent in the Sudan. From 1881 through 1885, the bravery and fervor of the Mahdist forces won impressive victories over the better-armed Egyptian armies sent against them. In 1885, they took Khartoum, killing Gordon and the remnants of the Egyptian soldiers and officials in the city. (Gordon's death was taken as a personal blow by Queen Victoria.) Five months later, Muhammad Ahmad died, leaving the organization of the Mahdist state to his closest disciple, Abdallahi.

Edmund Abaka

See also: Gordon, Charles George; Wolseley, Garnet Joseph, Viscount

References and further reading:
Holt, Peter Malcolm. *The Mahdist State in the Sudan 1881–1898.* Oxford, UK: Clarendon, 1970.
———. *A History of the Sudan from the Coming of Islam to the Present Day.* London: Weidenfeld & Nicolson, 1979.
Wingate, Francis Reginald. *Mahdism and the Egyptian Sudan.* London: Macmillan, 1968.

Muhammad Ali (c. 1770–1849)

Ottoman *wali* (governor) regarded as the founder of modern Egypt. Born in Kavala, Greece, around 1770, Muhammad Ali came from a family of Albanian soldiers long in Ottoman service. In 1801, he sailed to Alexandria with troops sent to repel Napoleon's invasion of Egypt. Exploiting ethnic and political rivalries, he obtained military command, deposed the *wali* Kurshid Pasha, and grudgingly was confirmed as *wali* of Egypt by the Ottomans in 1805. He consolidated his rule by massacring the Mamluks, exiling dissident religious leaders, and revoking tax-farming privileges for the Egyptian elite.

Through conquest and modernizing reforms, Muhammad Ali tried to establish Egypt as the foremost power in the eastern Mediterranean. At the Ottoman government's request, his armies invaded the Hijaz in 1811, quelling the Wahhabi revolt there by 1818. From 1820 to 1822, Muhammad Ali conquered the northern Sudanese territories of Nubia, Sennar, and Kordofan, using the captives to construct a new army trained by a French officer, marking a developing relationship between Egypt and France. Native Egyptians replaced the Sudanese slaves, who rapidly died from exhaustion and disease. Led by his son Ibrahim Pasha, they fought Greek rebels in Crete, Cyprus, and the Morea throughout the 1820s, capturing Athens in 1827. But the destruction of the Ottoman-Egyptian fleet obliged their withdrawal the following year.

Unhappy at not receiving compensation for his services in Greece, Muhammad Ali attacked the Ottoman Empire itself three years later, capturing Palestine and Syria by 1833. The considerably weakened Ottoman state caused Britain, which feared disruption of communications with India and encroaching Russian and French interests in the Near East, to demand his withdrawal. Ottoman forces unsuccessfully counterattacked in 1839. Subsequently, British forces occupied Beirut and shelled Acre, compelling the Egyptians to withdraw and negotiate. With the London Convention of 1841, Muhammad Ali exchanged his Levantine acquisitions for Ottoman recognition of Egypt as an autonomous province ruled by a hereditary *wali,* namely himself. Increasingly mentally incompetent, Muhammad Ali abdicated in 1847 and died in Alexandria on 2 August 1849. At least nominally, his dynasty governed Egypt until it was toppled by Gamal Abd al-Nasir in 1952.

Ian Janssen

See also: Alexandria; French Revolutionary Wars; Greek War of Independence; Mamluks; Ottoman Empire

References and further reading:
Lawson, Fred. *The Social Origins of Egyptian Expansionism during the Muhammad 'Ali Period.* New York: Columbia University Press, 1992.
Marsot, Afaf. *Egypt in the Reign of Muhammad Ali.* Cambridge, UK: Cambridge University Press, 1984.
Sabini, John. *Armies in the Sand: The Struggle for Mecca and Medina.* London: Thames and Hudson, 1981.

Muhammad of Ghur, Conquests of (1175–1206)

The Ghurid conqueror of northern India, who was among the founders of Muslim rule in India. Muhammad of Ghur, also called Muhammad Ghuri or Shihab-ud-din Muhammad Ghuri, followed his brother, Ghiyas-ud-Din, who had acquired power east of Herat in the region of Ghur (present-day Afghanistan) in 1162. Among his early military expeditions, Muhammad Ghuri assisted his brother against the Oguz Turkmen nomads to regain control of the city of Ghazna (Ghazni) in 1173 and against the ruler of Khwaraz in gaining the former Seljuq holdings in the region of Khorasan. In 1204, two years after Ghiyas-ud-Din's death, Muhammad Ghuri made yet another successful attack on the Khwaraz capital of Gurganj (in present-day Uzbekistan). His victories in Hindustan were also significant, including the capture of Uch and Multan in 1175 and the annexation of the Ghaznavid principality of Lahore in 1186. In addition, he answered his rare defeat by the coalition of Rajput kings under Prithviraj III at Taraori in 1191 with a resounding victory in the following year at the same site and another at Chandawar in 1194. These two battles are considered most decisive in the course of Muslim history, and as a result, the Ghurid forces occupied Delhi in 1192–1193. Over the next two decades, the entire region of northern India also fell under their control. Muhammad Ghuri left much of the control of his territories in north India with his lieutenant Qutb-ud-Din Aybak and his armies. Aybak is credited with building some of the most important Muslim monuments in northern India, which emulate aspects of Ghaznavid and Ghurid architecture in several ways. In addition, the Ghurid soldiers retained their political connections with Ghur until Delhi was established as the permanent capital under Iltutmish (r. 1211–1236).

Manu P. Sobti

See also: Akbar the Great

References and further reading:
Bosworth, Clifford E. "The Early Islamic History of Ghur." *Central Asiatic Journal* 6 (1961).
Fischer, Klaus. "From the Rise of Islam to the Mongol Invasion." In *The Archaeology of Afghanistan from the Earliest Times to the Timurid Period,* ed. F. Raymond Allchin and Norman Hammond. London: Academic Press, 1978.
Moline, Jack. "The Minaret of Gam (Afghanistan)." *Kunst des Orients* 9 (1975).
Scarcia, Gianroberto, and Maurizio Taddei. "The Masjid-i Sangi at Larvand." *East and West* 23 (1973).

Muhlberg, Battle of (24 April 1547)

The only battle of the Schmalkaldic War. In the spring of 1547, Emperor Charles V turned against the Elector John Frederick of Saxony, one of the main leaders of the Schmalkaldic League. By the fall of 1546, Charles had expelled the league's troops from upper Germany, almost without a fight.

Coming from Bohemia on 11 April, Charles invaded the electorate Saxony with 17,000 men on foot and 6,300 horsemen. He marched toward the encampment of the Elector John Frederick near Meissen. Charles easily defeated the elector's troops, forcing them into disorganized retreat. John Frederick was captured by the cavalry when he tried to escape to the citadel of Wurzburg. This clash marked the end of the Battle of Muhlberg and the Schmalkaldic War itself.

The myth of the Battle of Muhlberg glorifies Charles V as the invincible military leader in the medieval sense of the ideal of the knight. This atavistic attitude stands in stark contrast to the actual modern techniques of war used by the emperor.

Michael Herrmann

See also: Schmalkaldic War

References and further reading:
Held, Wieland. 1547. *Die Schlacht bei Muhlberg.* Beucha: Sax-Verlag, 1997.

Mukden, Battle of (21 February–10 March 1905)

Final land battle of the Russo-Japanese War. In the winter of 1905, the land war between Russia and Japan moved from the siege at Port Arthur and fighting around Liaoyang to the contest for Mukden in central Manchuria.

The Battle of Mukden took place between 21 February and 10 March 1905. Until the massive battles of World War I, this clash involved the greatest number of land troops of any battle in history. Japanese field marshal Oyama Iwao commanded a force of more than 200,000 soldiers and nearly 1,000 artillery pieces, and Russian general Aleksey Kuropatkin commanded nearly 300,000 men and more than 1,200 artillery pieces.

Oyama realized the need to attack before Russian reinforcements arrived from Europe. Although outnumbered and outgunned, he attacked first along a 40-mile front, beginning in late February. He wanted to turn the flanks of the Russian defense and thereby create a classic envelopment. Massed infantry attacks soon bent the Russian right so that it was facing as much west as south. Kuropatkin shifted reserves to restore his right wing, and Oyama threw more troops in the effort to continue to bend the Russian right flank.

By early March, the Japanese had pushed the Russian right so far that it seemed they might be able to threaten the Russian line of communication north to Harbin and then eventually across the Trans-Siberian Railroad. Kuropatkin withdrew in good order and very carefully, until he established a new defensive position at Harbin, where he was replaced in command.

Although more than 100,000 Russian troops had been killed or seriously wounded and much equipment had been abandoned in the retreat from Mukden, the Japanese had also suffered proportionate losses, and the Russians could more easily replace men and equipment. There would be no more major land campaigns.

Charles M. Dobbs

See also: Russo-Japanese War

References and further reading:
Okamoto, Shumpei. *The Japanese Oligarchy and the Russo-Japanese War.* New York: Columbia University Press, 1970.
Warner, Denis, and Peggy Warner. *The Tide at Sunrise: A History of the Russo-Japanese War, 1904–1905.* New York: Charterhouse, 1974.
Westwood, J. N. *Russia against Japan, 1904–1905: A New Look at the Russo-Japanese War.* Houndmills, Basingstoke, Hampshire: McMillan, 1986.

Murat, Joachim, Grand Duke of Cleves-Berg, King of Naples (1767–1815)

French cavalry commander during the French Revolutionary Wars and the Napoleonic Wars. Joachim Murat was born 25 March 1767 in La Bastide-Fortunide in Gascony. He enlisted in the French cavalry in 1787 as an ordinary trooper and rose quickly after the onset of war, reaching the rank of *chef d'escadron* in May 1793.

In October 1793, Murat provided critical support to Napoleon Bonaparte during the suppression of the Parisian mob on 13 Vendémiaire—Murat secured the cannon from which the famous "whiff of grapeshot" was fired. Bonaparte, placed in command of the Army of Italy, secured the promotion of Murat to *general de brigade* in 1793. Murat commanded the French cavalry in the first Italian campaign and accompanied Bonaparte to Egypt, where he again served as cavalry commander.

Accompanying Bonaparte on his return to France from Egypt, Murat again proved invaluable to Bonaparte. During the coup of 18 Brumaire, Murat led troops into the legislative chamber to remove protesting legislators. The creation of the Consular Guard led to his appointment to that unit, the forerunner of the Imperial Guard. Murat married one of Bonaparte's sisters, Caroline, in December 1800.

Murat commanded the cavalry of the Army of Italy during the second Italian campaign. After a brief hiatus, he was sent to command operations in southern Italy in 1801. Upon the creation of the empire, he was made both marshal and grand admiral of France.

From 1805 to 1812, Murat usually served as commander of the French cavalry, often, as in the aftermath of Jena, with spectacular results. He proved much less adept at the command of mixed formations or in independent roles. Thus, his mishandling of the occupation of Spain led to a revolt by the residents of Madrid that was suppressed only with great difficulty. Similarly, his attempt in 1809 to invade Sicily ended in failure and the capture of most of the troops landed there.

Murat was created grand duke of Cleves-Berg in March 1806. In 1808, he was made king of Naples by the Emperor Napoleon, in place of Joseph Bonaparte, who became king of Spain. In Naples, Murat continued the reform work begun by Bonaparte and attempted to fan public sentiments for the unification of Italy.

After the failure of the Russian campaign, Murat returned to Naples and began reorganizing the Neapolitan army. Although he rejoined Napoleon for the 1813 campaign in Germany and commanded the imperial cavalry at Dresden and Leipzig, he simultaneously negotiated treaties with Austria and Britain allowing him to withdraw from the war and retain his throne. His volte-face completed, he spent the 1814 campaign moving very slowly against French positions in northern Italy.

During the Hundred Days, he attempted to switch sides again, but the Neapolitan army was decisively defeated by the Austrians at Tolentino on 2 May 1815. The Neapolitan Bourbons then seized the opportunity to return to their mainland territory. Murat attempted to incite a revolution against them. This failed, and he was captured and executed at Pizzo on 13 October 1815.

As a general, he introduced few if any innovations. He is instead better remembered for flamboyance, treachery, and his failed early attempt to unify the Italian peninsula.

Joesph Isenberg

See also: Aboukir; Austerlitz, Battle of; Berezina River, Battle of; Borodino; Dresden, Battle of; French Revolutionary Wars; Jena and Auerstädt; Leipzig, Battle of; Lodi; Marengo, Battle of; Napoleon I; Napoleonic Wars; Pyramids; Retreat from Moscow; Rivoli; Wagram

References and further reading:

Chandler, David G. *Napoleon's Marshals.* London: Weidenfeld and Nicholson, 1987.

Young, Peter. *Napoleon's Marshals.* Reading, Berkshire, UK: Osprey, 1973.

Murfreesboro (31 December 1862–2 January 1863)

Important Union victory in the American Civil War, ending Confederate hopes of invading the North through Tennessee. At dawn on 31 December 1862, near Widow Smith's house across Stones River from Murfreesboro, Tennessee, Braxton Bragg threw a massive surprise attack from his left into the right flank of William S. Rosecrans. Confederate infantry under William Hardee immediately gained about 3 miles' worth of territory and threatened to push the Yankees into the river. Confederate cavalry under Joseph Wheeler and Nathan Bedford Forrest harassed the Union left. If not for Philip Sheridan's valiant defense, Rosecrans might have been routed. George H. Thomas managed to regroup around William B. Hazen's artillery, turn the line, create a salient around Rosecrans's headquarters, and hold the center so that by the end of the day the battle lines were perpendicular to the river on its western shore.

Little action occurred on 1 January, but on 2 January, Bragg made a gigantic tactical error by ordering John C. Breckinridge to charge across an open field on the eastern shore into a superior Union position. Union artillery on the western shore had a clear shot into the Rebel left. Union reinforcements swarming across the river forced Breckinridge to retreat, and the battle was over. Total casualties were 12,000 Confederate and 13,000 Union. That Bragg squandered the decisive advantage he had on the first day of this engagement went far toward undermining confidence in his leadership throughout the South.

Eric v. d. Luft

See also: American Civil War; Bragg, Braxton; Chickamauga, Battle of; Forrest, Nathan Bedford; Rosecrans, William Starke; Sheridan, Philip Henry; Thomas, George Henry

References and further reading:

Cozzens, Peter. *The Battle of Stones River.* Conshohocken, PA: Eastern National Park and Monument Association, 1995.

Hess, Earl J. *Banners to the Breeze: The Kentucky Campaign, Corinth, and Stones River.* Lincoln: University of Nebraska Press, 2000.

Reid, Richard J. *Stones River Ran Red.* Owensboro, KY: Commercial, 1986.

Vance, Wilson J. *Stones River: The Turning-Point of the Civil War.* New York: Neale, 1914.

Shaban, M. A. *Islamic History: A New Interpretation.* London: Cambridge University Press, 1971.

Musa ibn Nusayr (c. 640–714)

Conqueror of North Africa and Spain during the period of Islamic expansion. Born in 640, Musa spent part of his early career fleeing from the authorities for suspected embezzlement in Basra. Musa, however, evaded the troops of Caliph 'Abd al-Malik and took refuge with the caliph's brother, 'Abd al-Aziz, the governor of Egypt. 'Abd al-Aziz helped extricate Musa from his legal difficulties by paying half of his 10,000-dinar fine. In addition, he allowed Musa to return to Egypt with him. In 698 or 699, 'Abd al-Aziz granted Musa the governorship of Ifikiya, or North Africa. It was at this point that Musa's military career began.

Because Muslim control of North Africa was incomplete, Musa led expeditions against Zaghwan and Sadjuma as well as defeating numerous tribes. After the new caliph, al-Walid, confirmed him in his position of governor, Musa continued his conquests by pursuing the Berber tribes, who had fled west into modern Morocco. His armies pushed as far west as Tangiers. He left his freedman Tariq ibn Ziyad there as his deputy and returned victorious to Egypt.

Tariq took advantage of his position, led an army across the straits, and invaded Spain in 710–711. Musa soon learned of Tariq's success in Spain and followed in 712 with another army, partially out of jealousy. Rather than following the army of Tariq, Musa and his son 'Abd al-'Aziz bin Musa took a different route, capturing several cities, including Seville, before joining Tariq en route to Toledo. Musa reprimanded Tariq for his unauthorized invasion and then resumed his campaign and conquered northern Spain.

In 713 or 714, Musa ibn Nusayr departed from Spain with a large amount of booty. He left his son 'Abd al-Aziz in Spain to rule as governor. Musa died in 714 after a long, successful career.

Timothy May

See also: 'Amr ibn al-'As; Byzantine-Muslim Wars; Charles Martel; Khalid ibn al-Walid; Leo III; Muslim Civil War (656–661); Muslim Conquests; Tariq ibn Ziyad; Yarmuk, Battle of

References and further reading:

Abun-Nasr, Jamil. *A History of the Maghrib in the Islamic Period.* New York: Cambridge University Press, 1987.

Donner, Fred M. *The Early Islamic Conquests.* Princeton, NJ: Princeton University Press, 1981.

Julien, Charles Andre. *History of North Africa: Tunisia, Algeria, Morocco, from the Arab Conquest to 1830.* Trans. John Petrie. London: Routledge and Kegan Paul, 1970.

Music, Military

Music played in accompaniment to military activities, usually for regulating the pace of drills and marches, signaling, intimidating enemies, and enhancing morale. Even though the recognizable genre of military marches traditionally played on a combination of wind and percussion instruments is only about five centuries old, martial music possesses a far greater history that reaches deep into antiquity. Ancient Egyptian depictions of musicians playing horns and drums during regal processions and parades of soldiers attest to this fact, as do several references to music in classical military texts by Aelian and Vegetius. However, the history of this music prior to the European Renaissance largely is lost and its reconstruction conjectural at best. The standard duty accorded to musicians in most premodern cultures was the relaying of signals, usually to initiate or disengage from combat or to warn of enemy movements. Ancient and medieval horns created a piercing sound audible above the din of battle, providing somewhat effective battlefield communications for centuries. Roman commanders relied on legionary trumpeters to coordinate movements among multiple units. Medieval European chronicles and ballads frequently refer to the use of simple wind instruments as signals during combat. As for other applications of ancient and medieval military musicians, little is known for certain. Greek hoplites trained and marched to flute music. Medieval kings and rulers frequently employed musicians for processions and ceremonies.

In contrast to the simple horn-based music of premodern Europe, Islamic armies integrated Central Asian percussion traditions with a variety of horns that were the basis for many modern wind instruments, notably fifes and oboes. Crusaders encountered ensembles of Arab horn and drum players accompanying the standard-bearers of their armies; according to medieval texts, as long as the musicians played, the soldiers fought, confident that their standards were safe. As the Ottoman Empire rose to preeminence in the Islamic world, it continued and elaborated on these musical traditions, using military bands for signals, intimidation, and ceremonies. As it expanded into the Balkans and eastern Europe, it also transmitted these ideas and instruments to its Christian adversaries.

The evolution of modern Western military music coincided with other significant transformations in the manner in which European armies trained and fought. The initial trajectory of this development was the application of field music to drill and march. In the early 1500s, soldiers playing drums, fifes, and oboes began to appear in western Europe, first among the ranks of Swiss mercenaries and then within the forces of their French employers. In 1543, a French royal ordinance delegated two drummers and two fifers for each company of 1,000 infantry. The traditional arrangement of assigning drummers, fifers, and oboists to infantry and trumpeters and buglers to cavalry and artillery emerged by midcentury. As regular military drill grew in importance, especially after the reforms of Maurice of Nassau, fife and drum music acquired a heightened significance. Drums were particularly necessary for keeping soldiers marching in step, and fifes, oboes, and bagpipes provided some aesthetic diversion and boosted the soldiers' morale. By the mid-1700s, every European military establishment considered these musicians as essential components of their armies, employing them for signal, drill, and camp calls. The subsequent process of standardization is visible in the creation of fife, trumpet, and drum major ranks in the British army and the regulation of their training, pay, and uniforms by the 1740s; in this same period, young boys also began to be used as field musicians. Fifers and drummers retained their importance until the twentieth century, by which time military bands replaced fife and drum corps and field music lost importance in the face of changing tactics and technologies.

The other standard component of military music, the formal military band, also traces its origins to early modern Europe. Descendants of medieval town bands, early military bands of oboes (known as *hautbois* or *hoboys*) appeared among a few units during the seventeenth century, although they held a tenuous, quasi-legal existence sustained only by the largesse of a regiment's officers or royal patronage; notable examples include the oboe bands of the French dragoons acquired during the reign of Louis XIV and the wind band created for the British Horse Grenadier Guard in 1678. In the early 1720s, the Ottoman government sent full military bands to Poland and Russia as diplomatic gifts, sparking a craze for "Janissary" music throughout Europe. The fad quickly spread, first to Austria and Prussia and then on to France and Britain, fulfilled by imported Ottoman bands or imitation "Janissary" musicians, usually Africans attired in exotic "Turkish" or "Moorish" uniforms. The instruments of these bands—kettledrums, side and bass drums, oboes, bassoons, trombones, cymbals—prefigured the brass, woodwind, and percussion composition of future military bands. Official acknowledgment and regulation of bands began in the mid–eighteenth century, as seen in the British government's recognition of preexisting bands for the Royal Artillery, Life and Horse Guards, Foot Guards, and other elite units and allowance for the creation of regular regimental bands in the 1760s. The ideological services that military bands provided, especially in terms of summoning patriotic and nationalist enthusiasm during times of crisis and for recruiting drives, was recognized during the French Revolution, which witnessed the massing of gigantic bands for republican fêtes and the formation in 1792 of the earliest school for military music, the École Gratuite de la Garde Nationale Parisienne.

Formalization proceeded in the nineteenth century, as military bands achieved their greatest prominence. The British army began to curtail the long-standing practice of using Africans, civilians, and foreigners as bandsmen during the Napoleonic Wars. In 1857, the Royal Military School of Music was formed after a particularly bad performance given at a grand review during the Crimean War. The United States followed the European model, forming its Marine Band in 1798 and authorizing regular army bands in 1834, although American military bands remained a disorganized, local affair until after the Civil War; the Army Music School was not created until 1911. In the 1820s, military bands in Prussia and Austria standardized their instruments, training, and personnel, but the most significant changes occurred in France with the reforms of Adolphe Sax, who standardized the instrumentation of the Imperial Guard in 1854, establishing the pattern for most continental European bands. Military band music reached its pinnacle in the highly militarized and competitive atmosphere of the decades leading up to World War I, as international band competitions became both a very popular means for expressing nationalist sentiment and a means for voicing diplomatic dissent. Throughout the late nineteenth and twentieth centuries, military bands of the European and American style spread through the rest of the world, either as an inheritance of colonial rule in India and most of Africa or as part of modernizing military reforms and growing nationalism, as occurred in Japan. Military band music also affected "civilian" classical music, influencing the work of such notable composers as Ludwig van Beethoven and Hector Berlioz. Some works, such as the "Colonel Bogey March," and certain bandleaders, such as John Philip Sousa, have enjoyed enormous popularity in their native lands to this day. And eminent army bands, such as the Band of the Coldstream Guards in Great Britain and the Marine Corps Band in the United States, give performances internationally of concert hall quality. Even though military bands seem to have little place on the modern battlefield, these units nonetheless have now established themselves as a permanent and valued part of most of the world's militaries.

Ian Janssen

References and further reading:
Camus, Raoul. *Military Music of the American Revolution.* Chapel Hill: University of North Carolina Press, 1976.
Farmer, Henry. *The Rise and Development of Military Music.* London: W. M. Reeves, 1912.
Winstock, Lewis. *Songs and Music of the Redcoats: A History of the War Music of the British Army, 1642–1902.* Harrisburg, PA: Stackpole, 1970.

Muslim Civil War (656–661)

Civil war that nearly destroyed new Arab empire. When Uthman ibn Affan became caliph in 644, factions were starting to emerge within the Arab conquest state. Uthman's tribe, the Umayyads, numerous, talented, and adept at both trade and arms, had once been the Prophet Muhammad's fiercest enemies. Other Meccans and Medinans of the Quraysh confederation, earlier converts to Islam, resented the Umayyad upstarts intensely. Third came the Shiites, devotees of Ali ibn Abu Talib, son-in-law of the Prophet. Convinced that Muhammad had appointed Ali his successor, the Shiites felt that Uthman and the two previous caliphs had thwarted God's prophet by cheating Ali of his birthright. Finally, throughout the army camps of Syria, Iraq, and Egypt, Arabs quarreled over privileges accorded some tribes and discrimination shown toward others.

In 656, disgruntled soldiers from Egypt surrounded Uthman's palace and, when he resisted, murdered him. The dissidents then persuaded the Shiites and many Quraysh to raise Ali to the caliphate, but az-Zubayr, a prestigious and pious Muslim, rejected Ali as tainted by the regicide. Seeking allies, az-Zubayr's party set off for Iraq, but the new caliph chased them down and defeated them at the Battle of the Camel. The battle killed az-Zubayr and many of the Prophet's closest friends, further tarnishing Ali's image.

A more serious threat arose from Muawiyah, governor of Syria and Umayyad champion. In 657, Ali left Iraq and marched against Syria. His army encountered Muawiyah at Siffin. Halfway through the Battle of Siffin, Umayyad forces called for a truce and a negotiated settlement based on the Quran. To end the shedding of Muslim blood by Muslims, Ali agreed. Muawiyah demanded the execution of Uthman's killers and the retention of all Umayyad officeholders and secretly courted Ali's wavering allies in Iraq. Ali insisted that his power derived from his religious reputation and lineage, not from the mutineers, and he refused to punish them.

Infuriated that Ali might compromise with Umayyad "apostates," several thousand soldiers denounced and deserted the caliph. Labeled "Kharijites," these men declared jihad against Ali and Muawiyah alike with their slogan, "No judgment but God's." After several incidents, Ali wiped out a Kharijite force at the Battle of Nahrawan in July 658. As the balance of power shifted his way, Muawiyah aggressively cajoled, bribed, and strong-armed others into Umayyad ranks. In January 661, Kharijite assassins killed Ali at the Kufa mosque in Iraq.

With Ali dead, Muawiyah moved quickly. He browbeat Hassan, Ali's son and heir, into paying homage to the Umayyad house. He suppressed resistance in Iraq and made himself caliph. The Muslim civil war was now over. The Umayyad century had begun, and so had the alienation of Shiite Muslims from the rest of the Islamic community.

Weston F. Cook, Jr.

See also: Muslim Conquests

References and further reading:
Madelung, Wilferd. *The Succession to Muhammad.* Cambridge, UK: Cambridge University Press, 1997.
Shaban, M. A. *Islamic History, 600–750.* Cambridge, UK: Cambridge University Press, 1971.

Muslim Civil War (861–870)

A conflict that marked the end of a unified Muslim empire under the Abbasid caliph. The Muslim world would never again be united under a single ruler or ethnicity.

Conflict developed in two major areas. The first involved a dispute over control of the highest office in Islam, that of the caliph, which fell under the control of Turkish military leaders. The dispute drained the treasury and left the empire open to rebellions from Kharijites (secessionists opposed to both the main Sunni and Shiites), slaves, and royal pretenders, to mention a few. A second area of conflict found expression in the infamous Zanj Rebellion of black slaves in Mesopotamia.

Turkish nomads from the steppes of Asia had been streaming into the eastern Islamic world of southwest Asia since the ninth century. To control them, the Turks converted them to Islam and integrated into the Muslim military structure as superb archery horsemen, generals, and royal guards. The Turks used these exalted soldiers to control the office of caliph. From 861to 870, the Turks dethroned or killed no less than four caliphs who did not adhere to Turkish demands.

The loss of Abbasid Arabic control over the caliphate encouraged factional and ethnic rebellions in the empire. Rebellions broke out in Persia, Transoxiana, Mesopotamia, Egypt, and in Arabia itself. The worst was the 15-year Zanj Rebellion by black slaves in Mesopotamia who mined salt. Ali ibn-Muhammad, a Kharijite Persian, led the slave rebellion, which built two base cities in Mesopotamia. The rebellion forces consistently defeated caliphate forces sent against them because the caliphate no longer controlled the Turks and their generals, who made up the bulk of the caliphate army. As a result, the caliphate had to send African soldiers, who often deserted the caliphate armies for the rebellion. Now unstoppable, the forces of Ali ibn-Muhammad sacked and destroyed the wealthy city of Basra and killed over 300,000 people in the region.

Finally, after draining the caliphate treasury, the Turks lost interest in control of the caliph. Their disinterest allowed Muslim forces to besiege the two African slave cities in Mesopotamia, capturing the last in 883, but the unified caliphate had been destroyed for ever.

Christopher Howell

See also: Abbasid Revolution; Muslim Civil War (656–661)

References and further reading:

Brockleman, Carl. *History of the Islamic Peoples.* Rev. ed. New York: Capricorn Books, 1973.

Popovic, A. *The Revolt of African Slaves in Iraq.* New York: Markus Weiner, 1999.

Muslim Conquests (624–982)

Wars that transformed a religion into an empire. Islam's enemies, particularly the Byzantine Empire and Persia, which had been engaged in a protracted war, were weak and exhausted and thus ripe for conquest. Islam also brought a new vitality into the loosely organized regions in North Africa, the Middle East, and Spain, although one that built upon late Roman achievements in most cases.

After a few preliminary probes of Byzantine defenses, including victories at al-Aqaba (633) and Ajnadayn (634), the first battle in which Arabic invaders fought as an army rather than a band of raiders, Arabic armies under Khalid ibn al-Walid, and others, invaded Syria, taking Damascus in 636. Although temporarily forced back by a Byzantine counterattack, the Byzantine disaster at Yarmuk that same year signaled the permanent loss of Syria and adjacent areas. Jerusalem, left behind and isolated, like many Byzantine fortified cities, surrendered in 638, not to be recovered by Christians until the First Crusade (1096–1099).

Moving in several directions simultaneously, the Arabs, who had already taken much of Iraq in their initial raids, began a serious invasion of Persia proper in 636. In 637, they decisively defeated the Sassanids in the Battle of Qadisiya, seized the capital of Ctesiphon, and forced the last Sassanian emperor to flee to Central Asia. Most of Iran was under their control by 649, although the conquest of Khorasan was completed only in 654. From Khorasan and eastern Iran, Muslim armies slowly advanced into what is now western Turkistan and then India, laying the foundation of modern-day Pakistan and Bangladesh.

Other Arabic forces moved into Byzantine Egypt, largely captured by 643, although Alexandria, isolated from its hinterland, was able to hold out a few years longer. Even before the final subjugation of Egypt, Arab armies began moving down the African coast, where Tripoli was captured in 643. Armenia was invaded in 642. In 650, Cyprus was invaded for the first time, and again, along with Crete and Rhodes, in 654.

The victorious Arabic advance was temporarily interrupted by the civil war of 656–661, during which Umayyad forces defeated Ali, whose supporters became known as Shiites. The Umayyads then moved the Muslim capital to Damascus.

Resuming the advance, Umayyad naval forces appeared in the Sea of Mamora in 670, although the Byzantines, using Greek fire, heavily defeated the Arabs in a naval battle in 677. Elsewhere, other Arabic armies completed the conquest of Byzantine Africa, taking Carthage in 698. From Africa, they crossed the Straits of Gibraltar in 711, whose name ("rock of Tariq") recalls their general, Tariq ibn-Ziyad, whose overwhelmingly outnumbered army crushed the Visigoth king Roderick at the week-long Battle of Rio Barbate. Although a number of Christian princes fled to refuge in the Pyrenees and held out against Islam, most of Spain now came under Arabic control.

From Spain, Muslim forces invaded the Merovingian kingdom of the Franks but were halted by Charles Martel at Tours and Poitiers in 732, although the importance of these Christian victories has been overstated, since Muslim armies were operating well beyond their safe range during their invasions of France. In addition, Charles's victories did not end the direct threat to Europe since Arabs were able to invade and seize Sicily from the Byzantines in the early ninth century and retain their position there for some time.

The same year that the Arabs entered Spain, 711, they also began serious raids and advances into Anatolia, which the Byzantines had hitherto defended successfully. This move inaugurated a struggle that went on well into the tenth century, although the Arabs suffered a decisive repulse by land and by sea in the failure of their siege of the Byzantine capital of Constantinople in 717–718. Although the Byzantines were attacked on two sides, by Arabic armies below the Long Walls and by Arabic ships operating in the Sea of Mamora, the experienced Byzantine Emperor Leo III was able both to defeat and to rout the depleted Arab armies.

The Umayyads, some of whom took refuge in Spain, were overthrown by the Abbasids in the mid-eighth century. The Abbasids moved the capital to Baghdad, which became a great trading city, and continued the war against Byzantium:

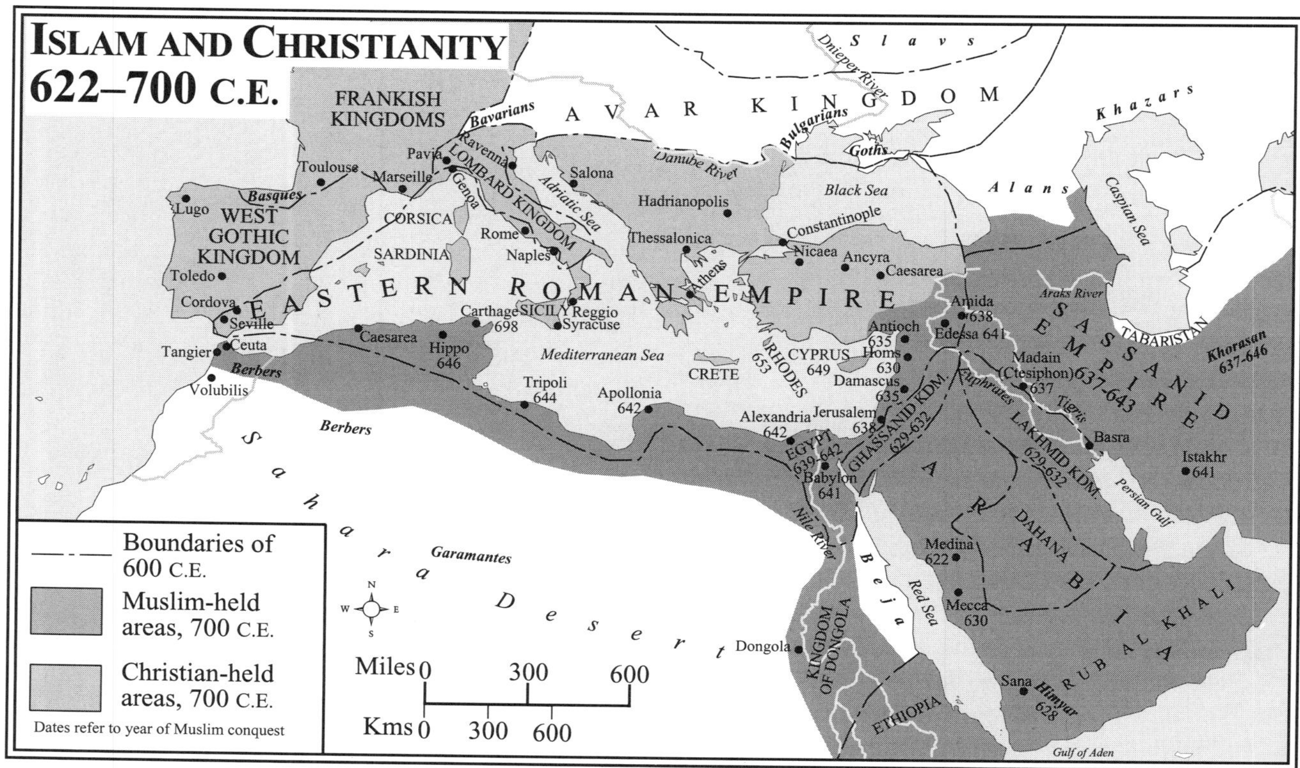

it was under their rule that the advance against Sicily took place, and they won the Battle of the Talas River in 751 against a weakening Chinese Tang dynasty (618–907). Nevertheless, the reign of Harun al-Raschid (r. 786–809) was, in every way, the high watermark of Muslim military power. Centralized authority declined sharply after his time, particularly during the civil wars of 861–870, which permanently lamed the caliphate as a central, Arabic authority.

The period also saw an increasingly powerful Byzantine *reconquesta,* as Byzantine armies recovered Crete, major parts of northern Mesopotamia, and Syria and even threatened Jerusalem. Among the emperors taking the lead were Constantine V (r. 741–775) and his son, Leo the Khazar (r. 775–780), who gradually extended Byzantine power in Anatolia.

Later, under Leo VI (r. 886–912), the Byzantines were able to invade the emirate of Tarsus successfully and then Armenia, which also came under Byzantine control, and continued the process of the recovery of frontier territory. Subsequently, Emperor Romanus Lecapenus (r. 920–944) attacked and sacked Melitene, an Arab base, and in 928 formally restored it to the empire. Although local Arab forces counterattacked, the area was brought definitely under Byzantine control by 936.

The culmination of these efforts came during the reigns of Constantine VII (r. 913–959), his son Romanus II (r. 959–963), Nicephorus II Phocas (r. 963–969), and John I Tzimisces (969–976). The Byzantines expanded their control in northern Mesopotamia, Armenia, and Cyprus. In 961, Nicephorus II Phocas, then the general of Romanus II, recaptured Crete. Meanwhile, Tzimisces, then still a general, took Aleppo and, as emperor, advanced into northern Palestine. The following century, the Byzantines even sought to reconquer Sicily, although it was the Normans who were the ultimate beneficiaries. Only in Spain did an era of Arabic conquest persist, despite what was by and large a stalemate existing between Muslims and Christians, thanks to the infusions of raw Berber energy from North Africa that reinvigorated the Arabic advance. Elsewhere, it was the Turks who took over the role of expanding the frontiers of Islam.

Annette Richardson

See also: Abbasid Revolution; 'Abu al-'Abbas; Basil II Bulgaroctonus; Byzantine-Muslim Wars; Byzantine-Persian Wars; Constantine V; Constantinople, Siege of (717–718); Heraclius; John I Tzimisces; Khalid ibn al-Walid; Leo III; Muslim Civil War (656–671); Muslim Civil War (861–870); Nicephorus II Phocas; Tariq ibn Ziyad; Talas River, Battle of; Tours; Yarmuk, Battle of

References and further reading:

Belyaev, E. A. *Arabs, Islam, and the Arab Caliphate in the Early Middle Ages.* London: Pall Mall Press, 1969.

Donner, Fred. *The Early Islamic Conquests.* Princeton, NJ: Princeton University Press, 1981.

Hawting, G. *The First Dynasty of Islam: The Umayyad Caliphate.* Carbondale: Southern Illinois University Press, 1987.
Kaegi, Walter. *Byzantium and the Early Islamic Conquests.* Cambridge, UK: Cambridge University Press, 1992.
Treadgold, Warren. *A History of the Byzantine State and Society.* Stanford, CA: Stanford University Press, 1997.
Whittrow, Mark. *The Making of Byzantium, 600–1025.* Berkeley: University of California Press, 1996.

Mutaguchi, Renya (1888–1966)

Imperial Japanese army general who conceived and commanded the Imphal campaign of March–July 1944. Born in Saga Prefecture in Kyushu, southwestern Japan, a region renowned for breeding tough soldiers, Mutaguchi graduated from the Army's Military Academy in 1910 and the Military Staff College in 1917. After serving in the War Ministry and General Staff Headquarters, he assumed command of the 1st Infantry Regiment, stationed in northern China in 1936. In July of the following year, he played a role in developing the "Marco Polo Bridge incident" into a pretext for expanded war against China.

At the opening of World War II in the Pacific, as commander of the 18th Division, Mutaguchi participated in the conquest of Malaya, Singapore, and Burma in 1941–1942 and was promoted to commander of the Fifteenth Army, headquartered at Rangoon, in 1943.

Mutaguchi was initially lukewarm toward plans for an offensive into northeastern India. However, the success of Orde Wingate's first "Chindit" guerrilla operation behind Japanese lines in February–June 1943 convinced him that if British soldiers could breach the thickly jungled hills between Burma and India, his own men, aided by the Indian National Army of Subhas Chandra Bose, could break through British defenses, occupy the Imphal Plain, and inspire Indian patriots to rise up against their British masters.

Mutaguchi had grandiose visions of toppling the British Raj, but his offensive lacked proper logistical support and adequate lines of communication, especially during the monsoon rains. Some 50,000 of the 100,000-man strong Fifteenth Army died in combat or during the terrible retreat back into Burma. Mutaguchi's name became synonymous with the Japanese militarists' cavalier disregard for the lives of their men.

Donald M. Seekins

See also: Imphal and Kohima; Indian National Army; Wingate, Orde

References and further reading:

Allen, Louis. *Burma: The Longest War, 1941–1945.* London: Phoenix Press, 2000.

Mysore Wars (1767–1799)

A series of four conflicts, beginning in 1767, that by 1799 established British supremacy in the Deccan and southernmost regions of India. The First Mysore War (1767–1769), however, hardly anticipated any such British triumph. Despite its concern with the growing power of the sultan of Mysore, Haidar Ali Khan, whose territories bordered the Carnatic coast and thus threatened the trading stations at Madras and Cuddalore, the British East India Company not only failed to form an alliance to challenge Haidar but soon found itself facing invasion. Haidar defeated the British at Malbagal (4 October 1768) before being driven from the Carnatic. Invading again the next year, Haidar dictated the Treaty of Madras to the British before the gates of their city (3 April 1769).

The First Mysore War resolved none of the issues that had provoked it and, not surprisingly, sowed the seeds for the renewal of conflict. Haidar's ferocious Anglophobia was reinforced when the British, despite unequivocal mutual assistance provisions in the Madras Treaty, failed to come to his aid when his capital of Seringapatam was besieged by the Marathas in 1771. Moreover, Haidar's hatred of the English was matched only by the esteem in which he held the French. During the British siege of Pondicherry in the First Carnatic War, Haidar had led his horsemen to the assistance of the French, from whom he would later gain technical experience, gunners, and guns. When Britain and France found themselves at war in 1778 and the British captured the French posts of Pondicherry, on the Carnatic, and Mahe, within Mysore territory, Haidar needed no further compunction to go to war again. The Second Mysore War (1780–1784) opened with Haider's invasion of the Carnatic with 80,000 men and 100 guns. Taking Arcot, Haidar destroyed a British force at Pollilur (10 September 1780), forcing his enemies to flee for the safety of Madras's fortifications.

Despite this initial success, Haidar was unable to capture Madras before Eyre Coote arrived with a relieving force from Calcutta. At Porto Novo (1 July 1781), Coote, with 8,000 Europeans and Sepoys, defeated Haidar's force of some 60,000. Madras thus relieved, Haidar was again defeated at the scene of his earlier victory, Pollilur (27 August 1781), and yet again at Sholingur (28 September 1781). British victory remained limited, however, because of the greater mobility of Haidar's forces, while Haidar's son, Tipu, defeated the British at Annagudi (17–18 February 1782). The British in India likewise suffered from the greater demands in manpower and munitions made by the ongoing war in North America and the West Indies. The consequences of this wider conflict were made clear when a French squadron under Admiral Pierre du Suffren captured Trincomalee (30 August 1782). Though enabling Haidar to successfully defend Cuddalore from British attack (13 May 1783), the arrival of French reinforcements in fact proved too late to measurably influence the outcome of the war. The Treaty of Versailles (20 January 1783) ended the war between Britain and France (and the United States), and Haidar Ali himself had died earlier (2 December 1782). It was therefore hardly surprising that his successor, Tipu, was amenable to peace, especially as the Treaty of Mangalore (11 March 1784) restored the status quo ante bellum.

If Tipu's respect for the French, inherited from his father, had been tempered by what he believed to be their failure to give adequate support in the recent war, it did not prevent his sending ambassadors to the French court in 1787. Arriving at Toulon in June 1788, the envoys were received by Louis XVI two months later. Yet if Tipu thus demonstrated his willingness to achieve his ends through European diplomatic as much as military means, the effort ultimately proved to be too little, too late. The flames of revolution soon would sweep across France, eventually consuming the ancien regime. At the same time, the global conflict that the French Revolution was to become would provide the setting for the two final Mysore Wars.

Soon after the revolution had swept the French monarchy from power, it became clear that "Citoyen Tipu" could not be counted on to support the British against revolutionary France. Sir Charles Cornwallis, governor of India, accordingly sought to strengthen British ties with the traditional foes of Mysore, such as the Marathas, while military aid was given to the Raja Rama Verma of Travancore, then at war with Tipu. It was evident to Cornwallis, however, that Tipu could only be suitably chastised by direct action, and the Third Mysore War (1790–1792), opened with General Sir William Medows invading Malabar with some 30,000 men. After Tipu proved more than capable of avoiding Medows's forces, Cornwallis himself assumed command in January 1791, while Maratha forces attacked on Tipu's northern frontier. Losing his capital of Mangalore to the British (21 March 1791), Tipu fell back on Seringapatam. With the end of the rainy season in early 1792, Cornwallis moved against Tipu, opening the siege of Seringapatam on 6 February 1792. When the citadel was captured on 21 February, Tipu had no choice but to open the negotiations that would end the war with the Treaty of Seringapatam (16 March 1792).

If the inconclusive nature of the first two Mysore Wars had ensured the outbreak of their successor, the apparent conclusiveness of the Third War, represented in the harsh terms imposed on Tipu by the British, equally ensured the outbreak of the fourth and final conflict. Despite being forced to cede half of his territory to the British, Tipu's abilities as an administrator ensured a quick recovery of Mysore. The continued threat from Mysore seemed all the greater to the British, moreover, when Napoleon invaded Egypt in 1798. Fearing a French invasion of India in support of Tipu, Richard Wellesley, Lord Mornington, governor of India, ordered a force of 42,000 to invade Mysore (14 February 1799). Though the Fourth Mysore War (1799) would help establish the reputation of Wellesley's younger brother, Arthur, the future duke of Wellington, Tipu's defeat owed as much to the defection of his three senior generals as it did to British generalship. Defeated at Siddeswara (5 March) and again at Malavalhi (25 March), Tipu fell back on Seringapatam. There, having refused the exorbitant demands of General George Harris, Tipu died defending his citadel from the final British assault (4 May). With Tipu died the threat posed by Mysore to British dominion in southern India.

Adam Norman Lynde

See also: Carnatic Wars; Cornwallis, Sir Charles; Harun al-Raschid

References and further reading:

Keay, John. *India: A History.* London: Harper Collins, 2000.

Mehra, Parshotam. *A Dictionary of Modern Indian History.* Oxford, UK: Oxford University Press, 1987.

N

Nadir Shah (a.k.a. Tahmasp Qoli Khan) (1688–1747)

Ruler who reunited Iran after the collapse of the Safavid Dynasty, campaigning from Arabia and Iraq to Azerbaijan and the Ganges Valley. Nadir Shah rose to power in Iran at the beginning of Persia's eighteenth-century civil wars. His tribe, the Afshars, belonged to the Qizilbash, a tribal alliance that helped found the ruling Safavid Dynasty. However, in 1722, Afghan invaders seized Esfahan and deposed the Safavid shah, throwing Iran into chaos. Urban revolts, dissident tribes, and seceding provinces fragmented the state. Both Russia and the Ottoman Empire seized Persian territory.

Nadir Shah rallied the Afshar to his leadership and aligned them with Tahmasp II, a northern Safavid prince. In 1729–1730, he defeated the Afghans as well as his rivals in the Qizilbash, the Qajar. Having pacified Persia, the "Slave of Tahmasp" drove out the Ottomans while simultaneously pressuring Russia into evacuating Baku and the southern Caspian. After deposing Tahmasp's son in 1736, Nadir claimed the throne himself, becoming Shah Nadir Khan Afshar. Additionally, he secured the Persian Gulf by occupying Oman.

Nadir invaded Afghanistan in 1737. Running over the Afghans, he plunged through the Khyber Pass and east to Lahore. At the Battle of Karnal (1739), he defeated the Mogul emperor of India, marched across the Ganges plain, and sacked Delhi. Looting the Mogul treasury and the bejeweled Peacock Throne, the shah then turned north to wage war against the Uzbeks of central Asia. By 1742, Merv, Bukhara, and Khiva were Iranian vassals. In his last campaigns, Nadir crushed an Ottoman force in Iraq in 1745.

Nadir Shah was an abusive ruler, more feared than respected, and insensitive to Persia's Shiite Islamic faith. His assassination by his troops in 1747 renewed Iran's civil wars.

Weston F. Cook, Jr.

See also: Persian Civil Wars

References and further reading:

Abraham of Erevan. *History of the Wars, 1721–1738.* Costa Mesa, CA: Mazda Publishers, 1999.

Lockhart, Laurence. *Nadir Shah.* London: Clarendon Press, 1938.

Nagashino, Battle of (1575)

Battle fought by Nobunaga Oda (1534–1582) and his ally Ieyasu Tokugawa (1543–1616) with Takeda Natsunori, around the strategic fortress of Nagashino. In this encounter, the forces of Tokugawa and Nobunaga Oda were the first to rely primarily on massed firepower in the form of Western armaments, helping to transform samurai warfare while pushing both houses closer to hegemony over Japan.

Ieyasu Tokugawa had actually forged a familial alliance with the Takedas, whose territories bordered his own in central Honshu. He married both a son and daughter into the Takeda household in the 1560s, but in the world of shifting alliances and steady warfare that characterized Japan at the time, the alliance quickly foundered. The Takedas were soon at war with the Tokugawa again.

The death of the elder Takeda (Shingen) in 1573, at the hands of a sniper in battle, placed his son Natsunori at the head of the Takeda house. The rising fortunes of the Tokugawa had made them fierce rivals of the Takedas, and when in 1575 a traitor to Tokugawa offered to hand over the vitally strategic castle of Ozaki to the Takedas, Natsunori Takeda jumped at the opportunity. Ozaki was the capital of Mikawa Province, the heart of Tokugawa territory, and its castle was guarded by Tokugawa's own son.

Takeda led a force of 15,000 warriors in what was expected to be a near-bloodless seizure of Ozaki Castle. Instead, they discovered en route that the treachery had been discovered by Tokugawa. Rather than face a humiliating retreat, Takeda opted to send his troops instead against the nearby fortress of Nagashino, another strategic castle sitting at the convergence of three rivers and guarding the entrance to Mikawa and Totomi Provinces.

Takeda began his siege of the castle in May 1575 but was still unsuccessful when word came that relief forces led by Tokugawa and Oda were on their way. Takeda opted to stand his ground near Nagashino and engage the approaching allied armies, though his forces were outnumbered more than two to one. At the Battle of Nagashino in June 1575, the alliance's greater numbers and, more important, overwhelming firepower, including musket volley fire by alternating ranks (the first time that this technique is known to have been employed in warfare), carried the day. Takeda lost almost two-thirds of his men and generals, and the mortally wounded Takeda clan would linger only until 1582, when it was overrun for good.

Daniel Kane

See also: Japanese Wars of Unification; Oda, Nobunaga; Tokugawa, Ieyasu

References and further reading:

Parker, Geoffrey. *The Military Revolution: Military Innovation and the Rise of the West, 1500–1800.* Cambridge, UK: Cambridge University Press, 1988.

Sadler, A. L. *The Maker of Modern Japan: The Life of Tokugawa Ieyasu.* Tokyo: Charles E. Tuttle,1937.

Napalm

A jell weapon made up of naphthenic acids, palmitic or fatty acids, and the salts of aluminum. One of the enduring images of the Vietnam conflict is the photograph of a naked nine-year-old Vietnamese girl running toward the camera screaming in pain, her flesh burned by napalm and gasoline. In popular terms, any hydrocarbon incendiary weapon is referred to as "napalm." It is most commonly dispensed from airplanes or helicopters.

The origins of napalm can be traced back to attempts to improve the flamethrowers used in World War I. It was first developed by Dr. Louis Fieser of Harvard University during World War II. Because of the short supply of magnesium in 1942, napalm became the most widely used ingredient in incendiary bombs, such as the M-69. It was used in both the Atlantic and Pacific Theaters, especially on target cities in Japan. More than 50 percent of the bombs that destroyed Dresden were incendiaries. Napalm was also used by U.S. forces in the Korean War and by the French in Indochina and Algeria. Yet, it was the use of napalm during the Vietnam conflict on suspected Vietcong villages, livestock, crops, and strongholds that led to a reaction among many Americans and Europeans. It is estimated that the United States used a total of 338,237 tons of napalm in the Vietnam conflict between 1963 and 1971.

T. Jason Soderstrum

References and further reading:

Björnerstedt, Rolf, et al. *Napalm and Other Incendiary Weapons and All Aspects of Their Possible Use: Report of the Secretary-General.* New York: United Nations, 1973.

Chong, Denise. *The Girl in the Picture: The Story of Kim Phuc, the Photographer and the Vietnam War.* New York: Viking Press, 2000.

Mountcastle, John W. *Flame On! U.S. Incendiary Weapons, 1918–1945.* Shippensburg, PA: White Mane Publishing Company, 1999.

Napier, Sir Charles James (1782–1853)

British general and colonial governor of Sindh. Born 10 August 1782 in London, Napier served in the Peninsular War against Napoleon and was wounded in the Battle of Corunna on 16 January 1809. He was wounded again at Busacco on 27 September 1810 and served at Fuentes de Onoro on 5 May 1811. During the War of 1812, he saw duty on the eastern coastline of the United States. Beginning in September 1814, he attended military college at Farnham, volunteered to serve under the Duke of Wellington in Belgium, and saw action following the Battle of Waterloo in 1815. After graduating from Farnham in 1817, he was appointed inspecting field officer for the Ionian Islands in May 1818 and then became resident for Cephalonia in March 1822, governing the island until 1833. Napier was then promoted to major general in 1837, assigned to India in 1841 and to the Sindh command in August 1842. In February 1843, Edward Law, Earl of Ellenborough and governor-general of India, compelled Sindh to sign a treaty that the inhabitants considered unfair and humiliating, provoking unrest in the region. The treaty stipulated that Napier could seize territory if he decided the Sindhi rulers were disloyal.

Soon afterward, war began, and Napier occupied Sindh, winning battles at Miani (17 February 1843) and Dabo (24 March 1843) with an outnumbered army. He then was appointed governor of Sindh, serving in that capacity until 1847. He was to have been the commander of British forces during the Second Sikh War (1848–1849) but arrived from England too late. In his retirement, Napier published books about his experiences. He died on 29 August 1853 in Portsmouth, Hampshire, England.

Harold Wise

See also: Napoleonic Wars; War of 1812

References and further reading:

Napier, Lieutenant General Sir William. *The Life and Opinions of Sir Charles James Napier, G.C.B.* 4 vols. London, 1857.

Napoleon I (1769–1821)

French field commander, revolutionary hero, and emperor, among the greatest military strategists and tacticians of all time. Born as Napoleone di Buonaparte in Ajaccio, Corsica, on 15 August 1769, he enrolled in 1779 at the military academy of Brienne le Château as Napoleon Bonaparte. He was commissioned a second lieutenant of artillery in 1785 and promoted to first lieutenant in 1791. Increasingly revolutionary, he joined both the Corsican nationalist movement and the Jacobin Club of Grenoble. In 1792, he became lieutenant colonel of Corsican volunteers and captain of French artillery. He fled Corsica in June 1793, opposed to Pasquale Paoli's anti-French and pro-British policies. He was promoted to brigadier general in December for distinguished service with the Army of Carteaux during the siege of Toulon.

Napoleon at Fontainebleau, 1814. (Library of Congress)

Briefly imprisoned in August 1794 after the fall of Maximilien Robespierre but back on active duty in 1795 with the rank of general, Napoleon "with a puff of grapeshot" saved the revolutionary convention from a popular royalist uprising on 5 October (13 Vendémiaire in the French revolutionary calendar). From that point, his rise was phenomenal. Two weeks later, the convention named him commander in chief of the Army of the Interior and on 2 March 1796 commander in chief of the Army of Italy.

Immediately taking the offensive against Austria and its allies, Napoleon won at Montenotte on 12 April, Mondovi on 21 April, Lodi on 10 May, Milan on 15 May, Castiglione on 5 August, Bassano on 8 September, Arcole on 17 November, Rivoli on 14 January 1797, and Mantua on 2 February. The coup d'état of 18 Fructidor (4 September) augmented his status. Back in Paris for only a few months, he sailed on 19 May 1798 to invade Egypt. He easily conquered Lower Egypt by routing the Mamluks at the pyramids on 21 July but was marooned by British admiral Horatio Nelson's victory over the French fleet in the sea battle of Aboukir on 1 August. After defeating the English-Turkish alliance in the land battle of Aboukir on 25 July 1799, he escaped back to France, arriving on 9 October. His coup d'état of 18 Brumaire (9 November) gave him significant political power. Quickly solidifying that power, he defeated the Austrians at Marengo on 14 June 1800, concluded peace with England by the Treaty of Amiens on 25 March 1802, became first consul for life by a national vote in May, raised money for war by selling Louisiana to the United States on 3 May 1803, and crowned himself emperor of the French on 2 December 1804 and king of Italy on 17 March 1805.

England, Austria, and many German states, fearful of Napoleon's growing power, influence, and ambition, launched the Napoleonic Wars in 1803. The British naval blockade of France was successful, especially after Nelson won at Trafalgar on 21 October 1805, but on land the French prevailed. Napoleon defeated the Austrians at Ulm on 17 October 1805; the Russians at Oberhollabrunn on 16 November; the Austrian-Russian alliance decisively at Austerlitz on 2 December; the Prussians at Jena on 14 October 1806; and the Russians at Eylau on 7–8 February 1807, Heilsberg on 10 June, and Friedland on 14 June.

Napoleon appeared only briefly in Iberia for the peninsular campaign but defeated the Spanish at Somosierra on 30 November 1808. He beat the Austrians (who were persistent, if nothing else) at Abensberg on 20 April 1809, Landeshut on 21 April, and Ratisbon on 23 April. After losing at Aspern-Essling on 21–22 May, he crushed the Austrians at Wagram on 5–6 July.

Napoleon's downfall began when, overconfident, he invaded Russia in 1812. He won at Vitebsk on 28 July,

Smolensk on 17 August, Valutino on 19 August, Borodino (barely) on 7 September, Krasnyi on 16–17 November, and Berezina on 26–28 November but was defeated by the Russian winter and endured a miserable retreat. Encouraged by Napoleon's failure in Russia, German states rose against him in 1813. He beat them and their many allies at Lützen on 2 May, Bautzen on 20–21 May, and Dresden on 26–27 August, but was hard-pressed, overextended, and finally suffered a major defeat in the gigantic Battle of Leipzig on 16–19 October. Pushed back toward Paris, he still managed to win tactical victories at Hanau on 30–31 October, Brienne on 29 January 1814, La Rothière on 30 January, Champaubert on 10 February, Montmirail on 11 February, Chateau-Thierry on 12 February, Vauchamps on 14 February, Montereau on 18 February, Craonne on 7 March, and Rheims on 13 March but lost the strategic war. The allies beat him at Laon on 9–10 March and Arcis-sur-Aube on 20–21 March. Paris fell on 30 March. He abdicated on 4 April and was exiled to the Mediterranean island of Elba on 4 May 1814.

Napoleon escaped from Elba on 26 February 1815, landed in France on 1 March, and arrived in Paris, triumphant, on 20 March. The allies immediately mobilized against him. He engaged them in Belgium, won at Ligny on 16 June, but met disaster at Waterloo on 18 June. Thus ended his "Hundred Days." But to the end, Napoleon retained much of his military genius. Wellington himself is supposed to have remarked of the Battle of Waterloo, "It was a damned close-run thing."

Prevented from escaping to the United States, Napoleon surrendered on 15 July to Captain Frederick Maitland of the *Bellerophon.* The allies sentenced him to permanent exile on the British island of St. Helena in the South Atlantic, where he died on 5 May 1821, probably poisoned by arsenic.

Napoleon was more than a military conqueror. Like Alexander the Great, he aspired to "improve" his conquests. In the spirit of the Enlightenment, he led the reform of the continental legal system, introduced rational weights and measures and money, emancipated the serfs, freed the Jews from legal disabilities, and strove to create a "European Community" or "Common Market." Had Europe possessed railroads and telegraphs at the time, he might have pulled it off. In the end, it was the sea power and money of the British, combined with British-subsidized but often-defeated Continental armies, that brought Napoleon down. Napoleon provided a focus of fear and opposition that rallied the reactionary, class-ridden British, Austrians, and Russians, as well as Spanish and Russian peasants/serfs, to combine for his final defeat, but Europe as a whole may have been the loser.

Eric v. d. Luft

See also: Abercromby, Sir Ralph; Aboukir; Alexandria; Artillery; Austerlitz, Battle of; Berezina River, Battle of; Berthier, Louis-Alexandre, Prince of Neuchâtel and Valangin, Prince of Wagram; Blücher, Gebhard Leberecht von; Borodino; Brunswick, Frederick William, Duke of; Carnot, Lazare-Nicholas; Davout, Louis-Nicolas, Duke of Auerstädt, Prince of Eckmühl; Dresden, Battle of; Ferdinand, Duke of Brunswick; French Revolution; French Revolutionary Wars; Friedland; Gneisenau, August Neidhardt von; Jena and Auerstädt; Jomini, Antoine Henri, Baron de; Kléber, Jean-Baptiste; Kutuzov, Prince Mikhail Illarionovich Golenishchev; Lannes, Jean, Duke of Montebello; LeFebvre, Pierre-François-Joseph, Duke of Danzig; Leipzig, Battle of; Lodi; Marengo, Battle of; Masséna, André, Duc de Rivoli, Prince d'Essling; Moscow, Retreat from; Murat, Joachim, Grand Duke of Cleves-Berg, King of Naples; Napier, Sir Charles James; Napoleonic Wars; Ney, Michel, Duc d'Elchingen, Prince de La Moskova; Oudinot, Nicholas-Charles, Duc de Reggio; Pyramids; Quatre Bras and Ligny; Rivoli; Scharnhorst, Gerhard Johann von; Schwarzenberg, Karl Philipp zu; Soult, Nicolas-Jean de Dieu; Toulon, Siege of; Wagram; Waterloo; Wellington, Arthur Wellesley, Duke of

References and further reading:

Asprey, Robert B. *The Rise of Napoleon Bonaparte.* New York: Basic Books, 2000.

Lachouque, Henry. *The Anatomy of Glory: Napoleon and His Guard: A Study in Leadership.* London: Greenhill, 1997.

Lyons, Martyn. *Napoleon Bonaparte and the Legacy of the French Revolution.* New York: St. Martin's Press, 1994.

Marrin, Albert. *Napoleon and the Napoleonic Wars.* New York: Viking, 1991.

Schom, Alan. *Napoleon Bonaparte.* New York: HarperCollins, 1997.

Napoleonic Wars (1803–1815)

The military campaigns from 1803 to 1815, during which Napoleon fought against Austria, Prussia, Russia, Britain, and their allies; conquered and dominated much of western and central Europe; and established the French Empire with its dependencies and allies. It is the story of Napoleon the soldier, the statesman, the emperor, whose uncompromising will and military genius propelled him to rule France and dominate Europe for more than a decade.

The Napoleonic Wars were actually a continuation of the French Revolutionary Wars that began in 1792 and ended with the conclusion of the Anglo-French Treaty of Amiens in 1802. But the peace of Amiens turned out to be a temporary rather than a long-lasting armistice. Territorial disputes between France and Britain brought them into a new confrontation. Napoleon encamped an army around the port of Boulogne on the English Channel, in anticipation of an invasion of Britain. The British retaliated and declared war on France on 16 May 1803. By the end of 1805, Europe once again entered a new round of wars of larger proportions.

Britain organized a new anti-French alliance, the Third Coalition, which included Austria, Russia, and Sweden. Napoleon (crowned emperor of the French in 1804) hastily removed his troops from the English Channel and sent them to the Rhine and northern Italy. He assumed command of the armies in Germany, routed the Austrian general Karl Mack at the Battle of Ulm (October 1805), and took 30,000 Austrians prisoner. Almost simultaneously, the British Royal Navy under Admiral Horatio Nelson destroyed the French fleet at Trafalgar (21 October), thus breaking France's naval power and confirming Great Britain as the mistress of the seas. Trafalgar made up for Ulm and served to restore the balance of power.

While Britain dominated the seas, Napoleon continued the conquest of central Europe. He marched down the course of the Danube River and captured Vienna. The Russian army under General Mikhail Kutuzov and a second army under Czar Alexander arrived at Olmütz (Olomouc), a city in Moravia, to join the Austrians in an attempt to stop the French advance.

On 29 November 1805, Napoleon and his army took position at Austerlitz (Slavkov) in expectation of a collision with the allied forces. His strength of 73,000 men faced a combined Austro-Russian army numbering 86,000. On 2 December, he defeated the Austro-Russian armies at the Battle of Austerlitz, called "the most perfect battle in history" and Napoleon's masterpiece. He then dispersed the Russians after frightful losses, while Czar Alexander was galloping as fast as his horse could carry him. Emperor Francis II of Austria escaped the carnage but later accepted the humiliating Treaty of Pressburg (Bratislava), ceding territories to France's southern German allies and adding Venetia to Napoleon's Italian kingdom. Napoleon's brother Joseph became king of Naples, while another, Louis, was proclaimed king of Holland. After Austerlitz, France gained immeasurable prestige throughout Europe.

In August 1806, Napoleon dissolved the anachronistic Holy Roman Empire, which he pejoratively referred to as being "neither Holy, nor Roman, nor Empire." In its place he organized the Confederation of the Rhine under French auspices and with himself as its protector. He then entered Vienna, and at his bidding, Francis II abandoned his imperial crown of Holy Roman Emperor for the more restricted title of Francis I, Emperor of Austria.

Napoleon still faced Britain and Russia, however, and Prussia now felt threatened by the creation of the Confederation of the Rhine and the stationing of French troops throughout much of Germany. The Prussians prepared for war and boastfully promised a lightning victory over Napoleon, the "revolutionary anti-Christ"! On 1 October 1806, Prussia delivered an ultimatum to Paris, while Prussian troops seized Saxony.

But no sooner were hostilities under way than events took a very different course. Without waiting for a formal declaration of war, Napoleon launched his own lightning campaign against the Prussians and routed them in two simultaneous battles at Jena and Auerstädt in October 1806. He then advanced and occupied Berlin. Within a month, Prussia ceased to exist as a military power.

Napoleon then turned against Britain and tried to destroy the "nation of shopkeepers" (his term) by imposing an economic blockade known as the "continental system." He issued the Berlin Decree (November 1806) that banned trade and importation of British goods into continental Europe. It was the first large-scale application of economic means to win a war. But to make the blockade more effective, he had to control the entire European coastline, either directly or through allies.

On the Continent, Russia continued to pose a threat to Napoleon's grandiose designs even after the disaster at Austerlitz. He pursued the retreating Russian army and fought an obstinate battle on ice and snow at Preussisch-Eylau in February 1807. Despite tremendous losses on both sides, the outcome of the battle was indecisive. At the Battle of Friedland, however, he routed the Russians, rendering further resistance useless. On June 23, Alexander concluded an armistice.

On 7–9 July 1807, the two emperors and King Frederick William of Prussia met on a raft on the Nieman River and concluded the Treaties of Tilsit. Alexander and Napoleon agreed to divide Europe between them: Russia recognized Napoleon's dominance in western and central Europe, and France supported Russia's claims in eastern Europe and Turkey. Alexander also agreed to join Napoleon's economic blockade against Britain.

The treaty with Prussia, however, was extremely harsh. That country lost half its territory to France, and all its acquisitions from the partition of Poland went to the newly established Grand Duchy of Warsaw. French troops occupied Berlin, and Napoleon's brother Jerome became king of Westphalia.

Napoleon had reached the zenith of his power and glory by 1808. He was now the master and arbiter of Europe. He created new republics, deposed royal dynasties, established the French Empire, set up a series of dependencies ruled through relatives or close friends, and ruled 70,000,000 people. Russia maintained friendly relations with him. Only Britain, Sweden, and Turkey remained outside French influence. For all practical purposes, Napoleon had achieved complete hegemony over continental Europe.

But soon Napoleon's power began to show signs of decline. The rise of romantic nationalism among the defeated European nations and Britain's persistent opposition to his expansionist policy turned the tide against him. Nationalism was most evident in the Iberian peninsula. When Portugal opened trade with Britain, Napoleon invaded Spain, precipitating the costly Spanish or Peninsular War (1808–1814).

Napoleon defeated the Spaniards, deposed King Ferdinand VII, and installed his brother Joseph as king of Spain. A Spanish guerrilla war, which the British supported and financed, tied down 200,000 French troops. When British troops invaded Spain with the support of Spanish guerrillas, Joseph relinquished the throne and fled Madrid. The Peninsular War marked Napoleon's first major defeat.

In 1809, Austria announced, rather prematurely, a "war of liberation" of the German people and launched an army of 170,000 into Germany. Napoleon left Spain and once again took command of the French army against the Austrians. He defeated them at the Battle of Wagram (5–6 July) and compelled them to sign the Treaty of Schönbrunn, depriving them of considerable territory and population.

Relations between France and Russia also began to deteriorate. Alexander lifted the economic blockade and opened the Russian ports to British trade. Napoleon, furious, embarked on his perilous invasion of Russia. On 24 June 1812, he crossed the Nieman River with his "Grand Army" of 500,000 men—Poles, Swiss, Dutch, Italians, Germans, Prussians, and Austrians. The French advanced rapidly, capturing one town after another. Near Smolensk, Napoleon tried to engage the Russian army, hoping to destroy it quickly. But the Russians evaded a pitched battle and allowed the French to press on through burning villages, towns, and cities.

After Smolensk, Napoleon faced the army of Kutuzov at Borodino, a village near Moscow. On 7 September 1812, he fought the Battle of Borodino, one of the bloodiest engagements in Russia. Despite repeated French attacks, the Russian defense did not break. Finally, the two armies retired toward the evening to their earlier positions, after more than 90,000 French and Russian soldiers had died on the battlefield.

Kutuzov did not renew the attack next day. He decided to withdraw his troops beyond Moscow and allowed the French to enter the city. His generals insisted on defending the city, but the veteran general told them: "When it becomes a matter of Russia's salvation, Moscow is only a city, like any other. But the loss of the Russian army means the loss of Russia. Let us, therefore, retreat!"

On 14 September, the last Russian detachment left Moscow, and next the entire population followed. Napoleon's vanguard entered the deserted city. Mysterious fires broke out throughout Moscow, burning it to the ground and devouring supplies and everything upon which the enemy had depended for shelter and subsistence.

Napoleon offered Alexander a truce but, after waiting five weeks without an answer, decided to retreat from Moscow. But the French retreat became a complete catastrophe, as swarms of angry Cossacks and infuriated peasants constantly harassed and attacked the French army, committing horrific atrocities upon the starving, freezing, and dying soldiers. The Russian army made surprise attacks on the French at the Battles of Tarutino, Maloyaroslavets, and Vyazma. At the crossing of the Berezina River, the Russians caused thousands of French soldiers to drown or freeze to death.

Napoleon, seeing the destruction of his Grand Army, abandoned it on 5 December 1812 and returned to Paris to raise another army. Early in 1813, he returned to meet the Russians, who had already made their way into Germany.

This time, however, Napoleon confronted not only the Russians but a new European coalition as well, the Sixth, which began with the Russo-Prussian alliance to wage the "war of liberation" in Germany. In a series of battles during the spring of 1813, Napoleon defeated the Prussians and Russians at Lützen and Bautzen.

Austria soon joined the coalition. Napoleon again overwhelmed the allied armies at the Battle of Dresden, his last major victory. But at the Battle of Leipzig, called the "Battle of the Nations," the allies destroyed Napoleon's forces (16–19 October 1813). On 31 March 1814, Czar Alexander entered Paris at the head of the allied armies and dictated the terms of surrender. Napoleon abdicated, and Louis XVIII became king of France.

Honorable, if not outright generous, Napoleon's captors, following the unwritten freemasonry of monarchy, exiled him to the island of Elba, assigning it to him as a sovereign principality and allowing him to retain the title of emperor. The French treasury provided him with an annual income of 2,000,000 francs.

The Elba exile, however, lasted only 10 months. In February 1815, Napoleon escaped from Elba aboard a small ship and landed in southern France. King Louis dispatched troops to intercept the escaped exile, but the soldiers went over to Napoleon! On 20 March, he entered Paris and began his ephemeral "Hundred Days" rule.

The alarmed allies, meeting at the Congress of Vienna, raised an army under Arthur Wellesley, the Duke of Wellington. Napoleon, too, somehow gathered a new army, marched to the north, and repelled the Prussian attack under General Gebhard Blücher at Ligny. On 18 June, the Battle of Waterloo ensued. Napoleon first assaulted Wellington's British army. At one point in the battle, when it seemed that the French would carry the day, Blücher returned and joined Wellington with reinforcements. Soon Napoleon's army was decimated. Waterloo signaled the end of the Napoleonic Wars and Napoleon's incredible military career. Almost to the very end, he could win battles against heavy odds, and, as the Duke of Wellington remarked of Waterloo itself, "It was a damned close-run thing."

The British exiled Napoleon to the distant volcanic island of St. Helena, off the west coast of Africa, where he arrived on 15 October 1815. He lived on this remote island until his death on 5 May 1821 at the age of 52.

To the French and continentalists, Napoleon represented the forces of the Enlightenment, reforming, rationalizing, sweeping away the frowzy remnants of the feudal past, an armed Voltaire seeing Europe whole. To the British and their allies, he was a monster of ambition, threatening to extinguish crowns and kingdoms if not stopped. The major differences between the nations of the Continent and Great Britain can still in large measure be attributed to whether they were conquered by Napoleon.

James J. Farsolas

See also: Berezina River, Battle of; Blücher, Gebhard Leberecht von; Kutuzov, Prince Mikhail Illarionovich Golenishchev; Moscow, Retreat from; Napoleon I

References and further reading:

Nosworthy, Brent. *With Musket, Cannon and Sword: Battle Tactics of Napoleon and His Enemies.* New York: Sarpedon, 1996.

Riehn, Richard K. *Napoleon's Russian Campaign.* New York: McGraw-Hill, 1990.
Connelly, Owen. *Blundering to Glory: Napoleon's Military Campaigns.* Wilmington, DE: Scholarly Resources, 1987.

Narses (c. 478–c. 574)

An Armenian eunuch and Byzantine general, born around 478 of obscure parentage. A bureaucrat by experience and training, he was sent in June 538 to reinforce Belisarius, then fighting the Goths.

In 551, Narses was sent by Justinian to resume Byzantine efforts to reconquer Italy from the Goths. In June or July 552, Narses won the Battle of Taginae, halfway between Ravenna and Perugia, and killed the Gothic king, Totila. He then defeated Totila's successor, Teias, in the Battle of Mons Lactarius, near Naples, in October 552. After Narses fought an inconclusive battle at Rimini in late 553 against Frankish and German invaders, the invading army divided. The smaller force, attempting to return north, was severely mauled at the Battle of Fano by a subordinate of Narses. The larger force was defeated by Narses at Capua in 554. As a result of these victories, Narses was granted the last triumph ever held in Rome. In 561 and 562, Narses defeated a Gothic revolt and in 565 a revolt by Heruli mercenaries. In 565 the death of the Emperor Justinian removed Narses's great patron. The new emperor, Justin II, recalled Narses in 566 or 567, shortly before the Lombard invasion. Narses died sometime thereafter.

Joseph M. Isenberg

See also: Belisarius; Byzantine-Persian Wars; Franks; Gothic War; Goths

References and further reading:

Fauber, Lawrence. *Narses: Hammer of the Goths.* New York: St. Martin's Press, 1990.
Norwich, John Julius. *Byzantium, The Early Centuries.* New York: Alfred A. Knopf, 1989.

Naseby (14 June 1645)

The last major battle of what has been called the First English Civil War. Naseby marked the entry of Parliament's New Model Army into the conflict and with it a new professionalism of arms. It also signaled the destruction of Charles I's hopes in the first part of this conflict and marked a major turning point in a struggle that would ultimately end in the execution of Charles I and the exile of Charles II.

By the spring of 1645, the Royalist cause in Britain was reeling. The defeat at Marston Moor the previous summer had meant the loss of northern England; various successes in Scotland had helped to offset that reverse. But Parliament had finally decided to reorganize its arms and had appointed Sir Thomas Fairfax to lead the new army. In early June, Fairfax's New Model Army of nearly 13,000 (approximately 7,500 of them horse or dragoons) was on the march, looking for Charles I, who himself was in the field with a force of around 7,400 (3,300 cavalry and 4,100 foot, although the numbers given on both sides represent compromises between differing claims).

The Battle of Naseby, 14 June 1645. (Hulton/Archive)

On the morning of 14 June 1645, the two sides drew up their lines north of the village of Naseby. The Royalists had assembled half a mile from Fairfax's men. Their right wing, under the command of the veteran Prince Rupert of the Rhine, consisted of 1,600 horse and 200 musketeers. The numbers of the center and left wings are less certain, although it appears probable that 3,500 foot comprised most of the center, with an unknown number of cavalry on the left. In reserve was King Charles with perhaps 700 foot and a contingent of horse. Opposing them, the parliamentary lines consisted of 3,200 horse on the left and another 3,500 horse to the right (the latter under Oliver Cromwell), with the foot in the center and one regiment of dismounted dragoons deployed along the left flank.

In midmorning the Royalist line advanced, with the cavalry soon engaged. On their extreme left, the parliamentary cavalry were dispersed, and Prince Rupert's horse rode behind their lines to attack the baggage train. In the center, the outnumbered Royalist foot soldiers held their ground but were soon attacked on both flanks; their left wing was broken by Cromwell's horse, and their right flank, exposed by the absence of Rupert's cavalry, was attacked by the remounted dragoons. By the time Rupert regathered his cavalry and returned to the field, the center of the Royalist lines was doomed. The reserves Charles held under his command fled, and with them went the last chance for Charles to make a stand.

The rout of the Royalist forces at Naseby was fairly complete: between 400 and 1,000 men were killed, and a further 4,500 were taken prisoner. Worse than this for the Royalist cause, all of Charles's papers were captured, and the terms of the sensitive negotiations they revealed crippled the Royalist plans. With the parliamentary cause in the ascendancy, Charles was incapable of fielding an army, and for all intents and purposes the first measure of the English Civil War was ended.

Daniel German

See also: Cromwell, Oliver; English Civil War (1642–1649); Marston Moor; Rupert, Prince

References and further reading:

Kenyon, John. *The Civil Wars of England.* London: Weidenfeld and Nicolson, 1989.

Young, P. *Naseby, 1645, the Campaign and the Battle.* London: Century Publishing, 1985.

Woolrych, Austin. *Battles of the English Civil War.* London: B. T. Batsford, 1961.

Nashville, Battle of (2–15 December 1864)

A Union victory in the American Civil War that basically destroyed the Confederate Army of Tennessee. It was a ragged, battered army that approached Nashville, Tennessee, in December 1864. Turning north after the fall of Atlanta, Confederate general John B. Hood hoped to draw General William T. Sherman out of Georgia, threaten his lines of supply, and

The Battle of Nashville, fought in December 1864, during the American Civil War. (Library of Congress)

retake Tennessee. Instead, Sherman launched his march to the sea, leaving General George H. Thomas to deal with Hood. Thomas quickly organized regular and garrison troops from scattered commands.

In a vicious battle at Franklin on 30 November, Hood shattered his army in frontal charges on federal earthworks. Attacking across open ground, the Confederates suffered atrocious losses. Thomas pulled back to Nashville and began to fortify the city. Hood arrived before the city on 2 December and began to dig in. The winter weather took a heavy toll on the Confederates, and their supply system broke down.

Within Nashville, Thomas received supplies and fresh men daily. Rather than besieging the city, the Confederates could only fortify the high ground below the city. By 15 December, Thomas was ready to strike, and he launched a feint against the Confederate right, while his main attack struck their left. Driven back, the Confederates hastily established a new line behind the first. The next day the federal attack continued, and Hood's army disintegrated. The left, at Shy's Hill, and the center both broke. Several African-American units distinguished themselves in the assaults.

Thomas lost 3,061 men and Hood 6,500. The Confederate Army of Tennessee was finished as an effective combat force. Hood was removed as commander, and the remnants transferred to North Carolina, where they surrendered to Sherman at Durham in 1865. The 1864 Tennessee campaign was the last Confederate offensive of the war.

Robert Dunkerley

See also: American Civil War; Hood, John Bell; Thomas, George Henry

References and further reading:

Groom, Winston. *Shrouds of Glory.* New York: Atlantic Monthly Press, 1996.

Sword, Wiley. *Embrace an Angry Wind.* New York: HarperCollins, 1994.

National Security Agency/ Central Security Service

Largest, most expensive, and perhaps least known of all the U.S. intelligence agencies. The National Security Agency (NSA) was established by President Harry S. Truman on 24 October 1952 as a separately organized agency within the Department of Defense to be in charge of signals intelligence (SIGINT) and communication security (COMSEC) for the federal government. The Central Security Service (CSS) was created as the central agency for cryptology. The head of the NSA is also in charge of the CSS.

The three principle functions of the NSA are information systems security, operations security training, and foreign intelligence information. It collects, deciphers, interprets, and disseminates information gathered from a vast array of global listening posts. The NSA was first brought to world attention when the North Korean navy seized the *Pueblo* in 1968. Later, congressional investigation revealed the ship was on an intelligence gathering mission for the NSA.

As the world becomes increasingly digital, so do the means states use to wage war. The NSA, with its technical assets and expertise, will become increasingly vital to national security in the information age.

Craig T. Cobane

See also: Central Intelligence Agency; Electronic Warfare; Intelligence, Military

References and further reading:

Bamford, James. *Puzzle Palace.* Boston: Houghton Mifflin, 1982.

Breckinridge, Scott D. *The CIA and the U.S. Intelligence System.* Boulder, CO: Westview Press, 1986.

Brownell, George A. *The Origin and Development of the National Security Agency.* Laguna Hills, CA: Aegean Park Press, 1981.

Richelson, Jeffrey T. *The U.S. Intelligence Community.* Boulder, CO: Westview Press, 1995.

Navarro, Pedro, Count of Olivetto (c. 1460–1528)

Military engineer and infantry commander. Pedro Navarro contributed greatly to the art of military mining and fortification, but his role is not widely known. He arrived in Italy in the 1490s and served as a *condotiere* for several different armies, including that of Florence. He fought for Ferdinand V of Spain in the Italian campaigns of 1502–1503, engineering the defense of Canossa and the capture of several Neapolitan fortresses using mining operations. He was given the title Count of Olivetto and made captain general in 1508. He commanded the Spanish campaigns in North Africa, capturing the island and town of Velez de la Gomera in 1508, the city of Oran in 1509, and the major ports of Bougie and Tripoli in 1510.

In 1513, Navarro led the infantry of the Holy League against the French at the Battle of Ravenna. He incorporated his own invention, a mobile cart featuring harquebuses and a protruding spear, into his infantry. He implemented a defensive strategy for the battle with trenches, but it failed because the artillery was weak. He was captured during the battle but never ransomed by Ferdinand. Navarro changed sides and, in 1515, led a French army through the Swiss Alps to campaign again in Italy. In 1522, he led troops on the French side at the Battle of Bicocca, where his field fortifications were successfully set up by the opposing side. That same year, Navarro was captured by the Spanish at Genoa and imprisoned at Naples until 1526. He lost his title as Count of Olivetto but engaged in one last campaign at Naples in 1527.

Christopher P. Goedert

See also: Marignano, Battle of; Ravenna

References and further reading:

Merriman, Roger Bigelow. *The Rise of the Spanish Empire in the Old World and in the New.* New York: Cooper Square Publishers, 1962.

Taylor, F. L. *The Art of War in Italy, 1494–1529.* Westport, CT: Greenwood Press, 1973.

Ndlela kaSompisi Ntuli (?–1840)

Commander in chief of the Zulu army and chief councillor to King Dingane kaSenzangakhona during the Voortrekker invasion of Zululand (1837–1840). King Shaka appointed Ndlela, who was connected through marriage to the Zulu royal house, chief of the Ntuli people in southern Zululand and, in recognition of his prowess as a warrior, raised him to high military command. When Dingane assassinated his brother Shaka in 1828, he also eliminated many of his favorites. Ndlela was an exception, for the usurper appointed him commander in chief and also made him his chief councillor.

In mid-1837, Ndlela led an inconclusive campaign against the Ndebele people, who were already weakened by defeats at the hands of the Voortrekkers, or Boers, who were advancing into the South African interior in search of lands to settle. When in late 1837 the Voortrekkers invaded Zululand, Ndlela persuaded Dingane to resist rather than negotiate. During the ensuing war of 1838, Ndlela undoubtedly planned the campaign, which turned on destroying the Voortrekkers in their fortified encampments of wagons (laagers) and in repulsing any Boer offensives. The turning point in the war was reached on 13–15 August 1838, when the Zulu army, led by Ndlela, failed repeatedly to penetrate the all-round fire from the Boer laager at Veglaer. The Boers then mounted a counterthrust, and Ndlela was in joint command of the great army that on 16 December disastrously failed at Blood River (Ncome) to stem their advance. Following this crushing defeat, Dingane withdrew to northern Zululand and ceded the lands south of the Thukela River to the Boers.

Dynastic conflict ensued in the weakened Zulu kingdom, and in September 1839, Mpande, Dingane's brother, fled to Boer territory with a large following. Mpande entered a compact with the Boers, and in January 1840 he marched against Dingane with Boer forces in support. Ndlela commanded Dingane's army, which Mpande's forces defeated at the Maqongqo hills on 29 January 1840. Ndlela was wounded but escaped. However, Dingane, now also a fugitive, executed him for his military failure.

John Laband

See also: Blood River (Ncome); Shaka kaSenzangakhona

References and further reading:

Knight, Ian. *Great Zulu Commanders 1838–1906.* London: Arms and Armour Press and Sterling Publishing, 1999.

Laband, John. *The Rise and Fall of the Zulu Nation.* London: Arms and Armour Press and Sterling Publishing, 1997.

Německý Brod (Deutschbrod) (1422)

Major Hussite victory over the Holy Roman emperor. After the failure of the First Crusade against the Hussites at the Battle of Prague (1420), Emperor Sigismund neglected to join with other German princes in the Second Crusade, which failed in its siege of Žatec. In October 1421, he finally entered Moravia and advanced into eastern Bohemia, meeting the Hussite army under Ján Žižka outside Kutná Hora (December 21). While Sigismund's Hungarian knights charged Žižka's wagon-fort, other troops entered the city, which was opened to them by German townsmen. Trapped between the town walls and Sigismund's army, Žižka attacked the king's lines, using his war wagons offensively for the first time as field artillery, and escaped with his army.

While Sigismund put his forces in winter quarters, Žižka gathered reinforcements from Prague and Tabor. With the support of local partisans, he attacked and overran the Hungarian garrison at Nebovidy (6 January 1422). Unable to gather his scattered forces quickly, Sigismund evacuated Kutná Hora and retreated toward Moravia. Žižka caught up with Sigismund north of Německý Brod on January 8. The Hussites attacked immediately and smashed the rear guard, causing the rest of the army to flee. Sigismund escaped with his life, but more than 500 knights drowned in the icy Sázava River. A small number of survivors, who sought refuge in Německý Brod, were massacred when the town fell to the Hussites two days later, after a short siege. The defeat of his second campaign against the Hussites marked the end of Sigismund's active involvement in the Hussite Wars, though he continued to press his claim for the Bohemian crown, finally achieved in the Compacts of Jihlava (1436), which brought the wars to a close.

Brian Hodson

See also: Hussite Wars; Žižka, Ján

References and further reading:

Heymann, George. *John Žižka and the Hussite Revolution.* Princeton, NJ: Princeton University Press, 1955.

Neville's Cross, Battle of (17 October 1346)

Scottish defeat during wars with England. In 1346, Scotland chose to honor her French alliance and take advantage of English commitments in France by invading northern England with an army of 12,000. It included a sprinkling of French knights, weaponry, and armor. Crossing the border above Carlisle, the Scots arrived before Durham on 16 October.

Forewarned of Scottish intentions, the English had two formations in the field as the Scots crossed the border. One, some 4,000 levies drawn from Cumberland, Northumberland, and Lancashire and commanded by the archbishop of York, immediately moved via Barnard Castle to Durham, where it scattered Scottish foraging parties on the morning of the 17th. The Scots immediately formed themselves into three formations below an Anglo-Saxon stone cross (Neville's Cross) on high ground heavily broken with ditches and walls. With memories of defeats at Dupplin Moor and Halidon Hill, the Scots had no intention of undertaking offensive action. The English were likewise inclined. The standoff was broken when the English advanced and their longbowmen wrought havoc in Scottish ranks. The men of the first echelon, rather than being killed where they stood, advanced, but the few who reached English positions were quickly dispatched. The second Scottish echelon, seeing the destruction of its sister formation, broke, whereupon the English advanced on the third Scottish force. Although this formation resisted fiercely, the day belonged to the English. King David of Scotland, along with many nobles, was captured and his army scattered.

H. P. Willmott

See also: Anglo-Scots Wars (1290–1388); Anglo-Scots Wars (1513–1560); Bannockburn, Battle of; Flodden, Battle of

References and further reading:

Prestwich, Michael. *The Three Edwards. War and State in England, 1272–1377.* London: Weidenfeld and Nicolson, 1980.

———. *Armies and Warfare in the Middle Ages: The English Experience.* New Haven, CT: Yale University Press, 1996.

Sumption, Jonathan. *The Hundred Years War: Trial by Battle.* London: Faber & Faber, 1990.

New Orleans, Battle of (8 January 1815)

Decisive American victory in the War of 1812, fought two weeks after the war ended. To defend the strategically, politically, and psychologically important port of New Orleans from imminent British attack, Andrew Jackson established a strong defensive position 6 miles downriver at Chalmette, Louisiana. His 5,800 mostly irregular troops, including Choctaw Indians, local bayou-dwellers, Tennesseans under John Coffee and William Carroll, the Louisiana Free Men of Color Battalion, and Jean Laffite's Baratarian pirates, built a line about a mile and a quarter long, perpendicular to the Mississippi River, extending along the northwestern bank of the Rodriguez Canal from the Mississippi levee across three-quarters of a mile of dry ground and another half mile into a cypress swamp. They widened and deepened the canal, using the mud to create breastworks. They had two dozen guns, the largest a 32-pounder. Coffee commanded the left, Carroll the center, and Jackson himself the right.

General Edward Pakenham sent 5,400 of his 8,000 regulars to attack frontally on the dry ground, providing clear targets for American marksmen. Samuel Gibbs led the main attack against the American center at the edge of the swamp, while Robert Rennie's column on the far left advanced parallel to the river. The 4,000 of Jackson's troops who found themselves engaged easily thwarted Gibbs with small arms and antipersonnel cannon fire but nearly allowed Rennie to gain the ramparts. Under John Keane, the 93rd Highlanders ran obliquely across the field from the left to reinforce the failing right, but to no avail. British artillery was bogged down in the mud too far behind the lines to be effective. Pakenham himself was killed while rallying the right. John Lambert assumed command and ordered retreat. Casualties numbered 2,000 British and 13 American. The British, especially their general, Colin Campbell, learned hard lessons at New Orleans that served them well at the similar Battle of the Alma 39 years later. But rarely has history recorded so one-sided a victory.

Eric v. d. Luft

See also: Alma; Campbell, Colin; Creek War, Jackson, Andrew; War of 1812

References and further reading:

Albright, Harry. *New Orleans: Battle of the Bayous.* New York: Hippocrene, 1990.

Brown, Wilburt S. *The Amphibious Campaign for West Florida and Louisiana, 1814–1815: A Critical Review of Strategy and Tactics at New Orleans.* Tuscaloosa: University of Alabama Press, 1969.

Owsley, Frank Lawrence. *Struggle for the Gulf Borderlands: The Creek War and the Battle of New Orleans, 1812–1815.* Tuscaloosa: University of Alabama Press, 2000.

Remini, Robert Vincent. *The Battle of New Orleans.* New York: Viking, 1999.

Ney, Michel, Duc d'Elchingen, Prince de La Moskova (1769–1815)

French field commander. Born the son of a cooper in Alsace on 10 January 1769, Ney enlisted in 1787 in the 5th Hussars and was commissioned a lieutenant after Valmy in 1792. He

Death of General Edward Pakenham at the Battle of New Orleans. (Library of Congress)

fought at Jemappes in 1792 and Mainz in 1794. Promoted to brigadier general on 15 August 1796, he won at Kirchberg on 19 April 1797 but was captured at Giessen on 20 April. After he was exchanged, he fought under André Masséna at Winterthur in 1799 and under Jean Victor Marie Moreau at Hohenlinden in 1800. Already a corps commander, Ney was promoted to marshal on 19 May 1804. He shone at Elchingen on 14 October 1805; captured Innsbruck in November; and fought well at Jena, Erfurt, and Magdeburg in 1806 and Eylau, Güttstadt, and Friedland in 1807. He led the VI Corps under Masséna from 1808 to 1810 in Iberia, capturing Ciudad Rodrigo in 1810. After setbacks at Bussaco in 1810 and Torres Vedras in 1811, Masséna accused him of insubordination and relieved him of command. During the 1812 invasion of Russia, Ney fought at Krasnoye, Smolensk, and Borodino and held the rear guard on the retreat from Moscow. In Napoleon's last German campaign, Ney fought at Weissenfels on 1 May 1813, was wounded at Lützen on 2 May, commanded the left at Bautzen on 20–21 May, lost at Dennewitz on 6 September, and proved tenacious at Leipzig.

Changing sides just before Napoleon's first abdication in 1814, Ney served King Louis XVIII, while Napoleon was exiled on Elba. Ordered to capture the escaped Napoleon, Ney instead joined him for the Hundred Days, commanding Napoleon's left on the march to Belgium, engaging Arthur Wellesley, the Duke of Wellington, at Quatre Bras, and fighting ferociously at Waterloo.

Ney was an outstanding cavalryman with extraordinary courage but was frequently criticized, especially after the Russian campaign, for his questionable battlefield decisions. Some historians have blamed him for the French shortcomings at Bautzen, Dennewitz, Quatre Bras, and even Waterloo. The humbly born Ney's rise to high command also illustrated the revolutionary and Napoleonic principle of "careers open to all talents." The restored Bourbons executed him by firing squad for treason on 7 December 1815.

Eric v. d. Luft

See also: Berezina River, Battle of; Bernadotte, Jean Baptiste Jules; Borodino; French Revolutionary Wars; Friedland; Jena and Auerstädt; Leipzig, Battle of; Masséna, André, Duc de Rivoli, Prince d'Essling; Moscow, Retreat from; Murat, Joachim, Grand Duke of Cleves-Berg, King of Naples; Napoleon I; Napoleonic

General Nelson Miles charging the Indian camp, Nez Percé war, Montana, 1877. (Library of Congress)

Wars; Quatre Bras and Ligny; Valmy; Waterloo; Wellington, Arthur Wellesley, Duke of

References and further reading:

Foster, John T. *Napoleon's Marshal: The Life of Michel Ney.* New York: Morrow, 1968.

Horricks, Raymond. *Marshal Ney: The Romance and the Real.* London: Archway, 1988.

———. *Military Politics from Bonaparte to the Bourbons: The Life and Death of Michel Ney, 1769–1815.* New Brunswick, NJ: Transaction, 1995.

Morton, John Bingham. *Marshal Ney.* London: Barker, 1958.

Nez Percé (June–October 1877)

In 1877, the flight of the Nez Percé captured the American public's imagination and made the U.S. Army look inept. Under the leadership of Chief Joseph and his namesake father, the Nez Percé had tried to live peaceably with impinging white society. In 1855, they agreed to a reservation in Idaho and, following the discovery of gold within their boundaries, had renegotiated the reservation to land surrounding the Clearwater River. Yet leaders like Chief Joseph the Elder and White Bird refused to live within the boundaries of this new agency. In 1871, the younger Chief Joseph was made chief and repeatedly insisted that the Nez Percé had never sold the Wallowa Valley in Oregon. Authorities insisted that Joseph had to report to the reservation and threw the Wallowa open to settlement.

While disagreeing with the decision, Joseph and his followers moved slowly to the reservation in June 1877. Three young warriors from White Bird's band disagreed with the decision and killed four white settlers. Fleeing to the gorges of the Salmon River, the Nez Percé pleas for peace went unheralded by local militia and cavalry. The Nez Percé were able to fend off their attackers and flee eastward to the inhospitable land on the south fork of the Clearwater River. General Oliver Howard soon caught up with them on a plateau above the Clearwater and engaged them for two days before the Nez Percé escaped.

On 15 July at Weippe Prairie, the Nez Percé chiefs decided the best course of action was to flee to Canada. While resting at Big River Hole in Montana on 9 August, the 900 Indians were attacked by 200 soldiers, who killed 89 Indians. But the warriors were able to pin down the soldiers for two days, allowing their families to escape. Joseph and his followers continued to dodge their pursuers and escape at places like Canyon Creek. On 30 September, at Snake Creek, less than 40 miles from the Canadian border, Colonel Nelson Miles engaged the hostiles. Three hundred Nez Percé led by White Bird were able to make it to Canada, but on 5 October, Joseph surrendered to Miles, and the Nez Percé war was at an end.

T. Jason Soderstrum

See also: American Indian Wars; Joseph the Younger, Chief; Miles, Nelson Appleton

References and further reading:

Brown, Mark Herbert. *The Flight of the Nez Percé.* New York: Putnam, 1967.

Hampton, Bruce. *Children of Grace: The Nez Percé War of 1877.* New York: H. Holt, 1994.

Lavender, David Sievert. *Let Me Be Free: The Nez Percé Tragedy.* New York: HarperCollins, 1992.

Nicaragua, Walker's Invasion of (1855–1857)

Failed filibustering expedition to Nicaragua led by the American William Walker. Known to many as the "Grey-Eyed Man of Destiny," William Walker was both a pro-slavery southerner and a firm believer in America's Manifest Destiny to rule the Americas. Possessing a strong desire to not only spread the institution of slavery but also to lead an independent state himself, Walker organized and led a filibuster (soldier-of-fortune) expedition to "liberate" Baja California and Sonora from Mexico in 1853. From the start, the expedition was a fiasco, and Walker and his ragged band returned to the United States in 1854. Although Walker's foray into Mexico was a failure, it did attract the attention of citizens throughout the United States and beyond, thereby allowing him to gain experience and luring him to continue such activities in the future.

In May 1855, Walker again set out to filibuster, this time in Central America. This time Walker had chosen to meddle in Nicaragua. It should not be overlooked that Nicaragua was the primary transit point for people and goods headed for the recently discovered gold fields of California. Furthermore, Nicaragua was in the midst of a civil war between two factions—the Granadans (conservatives) and the Leonese (liberals)—so named from their respective capital cities. Losing the conflict, the Leonese forces requested Walker's aid. Walker landed near Realejo on 16 June 1855 with 58 followers grandiosely calling themselves Walker's "Immortals" and soon brought military success to the liberal faction. Walker was given the rank of colonel by the Leonese authorities and placed in command of La Falange Americana, or the American Phalanx. (The term was eerily evocative of twentieth-century European fascism, with which Walker shared some attributes.)

After some military success and the seizure of a vessel run by Cornelius Vanderbilt's Accessory Transit Company, friction between Walker and the liberal leadership soon developed. As a result, in 1856 Walker staged a coup d'état and named himself commander of the armed forces and president of Nicaragua. In addition, Walker legalized slavery in Nicaragua and made English the official language of the state. However, Walker's tenure as president of Nicaragua was to be brief, as both the conservatives and liberals would soon unite, along with military forces from neighboring states, to oust the troublesome Walker and his fellow Yanquis. Facing a coalition of Central American states and hoping to avoid capture, Walker surrendered to U.S. naval forces on 1 May 1857 and left Nicaragua.

But Walker had not learned his lesson and, after leading another ill-fated expedition, was executed by a Honduran firing squad in 1860. William Walker was perhaps the most notorious of the nineteenth-century filibusterers.

Andrew G. Wilson

References and further reading:

Greene, Lawrence. *The Filibuster: The Career of William Walker.* Indianapolis: Bobbs Merrill, 1937.

May, Robert E. *The Southern Dream of a Caribbean Empire: 1854–1861.* Baton Rouge: Louisiana State University Press, 1973.

Nicaraguan Civil War (1925–1933)

Internal conflict that paved the way for the Somoza family dictatorship. In 1925, Conservative Party candidate Carlos Solórzano was elected president, and U.S. Marines withdrew from Nicaragua after a 13-year occupation. However, opposition to Solórzano was strong, a revolution quickly ensued, and the Marines returned in 1926. Emiliano Chamorro deposed Solórzano, but his efforts did not bring peace to Nicaragua as liberal vice president Juan Bautista Sacasa led another revolt. The U.S. Department of State then brokered a deal resulting in former conservative president Adolfo Díaz's return to power. Despite this diplomatic effort, the civil war was renewed and intensified. U.S. secretary of state Henry Stimson was appointed a special envoy by U.S. president Calvin Coolidge and sent to Nicaragua in 1927. Stimson negotiated an agreement between many of the warring factions that allowed Díaz to remain as president until 1928, at which time there would be U.S.-supervised elections. In addition, the United States agreed to help pacify the country and to establish and train a National Guard to maintain law and order.

Augusto César Sandino, one of the guerrilla leaders, rejected the accord and continued to fight both the government and the Marines. Sandino's hit-and-run guerrilla tactics frustrated all attempts to capture him and boosted his reputation. The failure of the Marines to capture Sandino caused embarrassment for the administration of incoming U.S. president Herbert Hoover, who sought a means to disengage. In 1932, the Liberal Party gained power with the election of Sacasa, and Anastasio Somoza García assumed command of the newly created National Guard. A truce was negotiated with Sandino, and the Marines left on 1 February 1933. Soon after the Marines withdrew, the National Guard attacked a rebel town, causing Sandino to declare a resumption of the war. President Sacasa offered to negotiate with Sandino, and they met with Somoza in Managua on 21 February 1934. After the meeting, Sandino was kidnapped and murdered by members of the National Guard, allegedly under Somoza's orders. Sandino's murder made him a martyr and a symbol of opposition to U.S. intervention in Central America. Anastasio Somoza used his power base as National Guard commander to overthrow Sacasa in 1936 and to establish a family dictatorship that made Nicaragua his personal family fiefdom until 1979.

George M. Lauderbaugh

See also: Sandino, Augusto César

References and further reading:

Macaulay, Neil. *The Sandino Affair.* Chicago: Quadrangle Books, 1967.
Walker, Thomas W. *Nicaragua, the Land of Sandino.* Boulder, CO: Westview Press, 1981.

Nicaraguan Civil War (1979)

The Nicaraguan Civil War began in 1961 with the creation of the Sandinista National Liberation Front (FSLN), a guerrilla group dedicated to the overthrow of the Somoza dynasty that had ruled the Central American republic as its private fiefdom since 1936. The movement gained adherents but was brutally suppressed by Luis Somoza Debayle, the president of Nicaragua, and his brother Anastasio, who commanded the National Guard. In 1963 Anastasio assumed the presidency and continued to fight the FSLN and all other opposition. In 1972, Nicaragua suffered a massive earthquake that devastated the capital, Managua, and the surrounding countryside. The Somoza regime demonstrated ineptitude and greed during the earthquake relief effort, thus intensifying opposition. Nevertheless, Anastasio Somoza was again elected president in 1974.

On 27 December 1974 FSLN guerrillas seized the minister of agriculture and several of Somoza's relatives and held them for ransom. The government accepted the rebels' demands, paid $1 million for the hostages' release, and provided safe passage to Cuba for the perpetrators. This event greatly enhanced the prestige of the FSLN but led the regime to increase attempts to crush the rebels militarily. By 1976, FSLN losses were high and one of the movement's founders, Carlos Fonseca, had been killed. However, the brutal tactics and atrocities committed against the civilian population supporting the FSLN drew international attention and condemnation. This pressure led in turn to a weakening of support for the Somoza government from the United States.

The FSLN struck the National Guard barracks at San Carlos in October 1977 and followed up by taking and temporarily holding several towns. Although not conclusive, these military successes resulted in moderate and conservative elements in Nicaragua throwing support to the FSLN. On 9 January 1978, Joaquin Chamorro, editor of the opposition paper *La Prensa* and a moderate opponent of Somoza rule, was murdered. Chamorro's assassination resulted in a general strike, street demonstrations, and a call for Somoza to resign. On 22 August 1978, Sandinistas commanded by Eden Pastora, whose nom de guerre was Comandante Cero, seized the National Palace and held hostage all the members of Nicaragua's Congress and some 200 government employees. Somoza was forced to pay $500,000 in ransom, release 60 Sandinista prisoners, and grant safe passage to Venezuela or Panama for Pastora and his men. This humiliation resulted in fissures within the National Guard, but Somoza arrested rebellious officers and remained in control of much of the country.

Somoza renewed his efforts to win a military victory by calling up reserves and creating a special combat unit commanded by his son, Major Anastasio Somoza Portacarerro, and ordering the capture of the Sandinista stronghold at the town of Matagulpa. However, in early September 1978, the FSLN gained control of several other towns and most of León, Nicaragua's second-largest city. The National Guard was on the verge of collapse but concentrated its tanks, artillery, and air power on the Sandinista-held towns and drove them out by 19 September.

The counteroffensive was conducted without regard for the civilian populations, and the Somoza regime was subjected to mounting international pressure for a negotiated settlement. In addition, U.S. support for the Somoza dictatorship continued to wane. However, all attempts at a negotiated settlement by international organizations and the United States failed.

On 4 June 1979, the FSLN launched its final offensive by calling for a general strike, which soon shut down most of the businesses in the country. The guerrillas had received new shipments of arms from Venezuela, Cuba, and Panama and by 6 June had taken control of major portions of León. A few days later, fighting broke out in Managua's poorer neighborhoods, and the National Guard responded with air attacks on residential sections of the city. Throughout June and early July, international pressure by the nations of the Andean Pact and the Organization of American States was exerted on Somoza to leave the country, but he stubbornly clung to power despite the fact that he had lost the support of the United States and controlled only some sections of Managua.

With his forces running out of ammunition, Somoza finally fled Nicaragua on 17 July. On 19 July, Sandinista troops entered Managua in triumph and were enthusiastically greeted by masses of Nicaraguans from all walks of life. On 20 July, a junta took control of the country.

The Nicaraguan Civil War was costly, with an estimated 30,000 to 50,000 Nicaraguans killed, 100,000 injured, and 300,000 left homeless or displaced to other countries. The economy was in a shambles, with most of the infrastructure of the country in ruin and a war debt of $1.5 billion. And Nicaragua would soon be facing another conflict, this time between the Sandinistas and the Contras.

George M. Lauderbaugh

References and further reading:

Black, George. *Triumph of the People: The Sandinista Revolution in Nicaragua.* London: Zed Press, 1981.
Christian, Shirley. *Nicaragua, Revolution in the Family.* New York: Random House, 1985.
Kinzer, Stephen. *Blood of Brothers: Life and War in Nicaragua.* New York: Putnam, 1991.
Lake, Anthony. *Somoza Falling.* Amherst: University of Massachusetts Press, 1989.
Millet, Richard, *Guardians of the Dynasty.* Maryknoll, NY: Orbis Books, 1977.

Nicephorus II Phocas (r. 963–969)

Byzantine general and emperor. Son of another Byzantine general, Bardas Phocas, Nicephorus Phocas began his military career in 955 as the successor to his father as domestic of the *scholai* (field forces). His father had been noted for his mastery of mobile tactics in defending against the Arabs, but the family itself, in spite of its military successes, had been under a cloud for some years because of the attempt of Bardas's brother, Leo, to seize power in 919.

Nicephorus came to a position of influence just as the Byzantine *reconquesta* was gaining ground, and he was soon actively involved. His greatest accomplishment came in 961, under Emperor Romanos II (r. 959–963), when he successfully recovered Crete for the empire, an act for which he won considerable public recognition. Still more recognition came the next year as a result of a highly successful raid against Arab Syria. It was primarily because of this recognition that Nicephorus was proclaimed emperor by his troops at Kaisareia in Cappadocia on 2 July 963, soon after the death of the emperor and a few months after a well-deserved triumph in Constantinople in recognition of his achievements.

This time, the Phocas usurpation was successful, and Nicephorus became emperor. As such, he continued his military successes in 965 by capturing Cyprus, Tarsos, and Mopsuestia. He was also successful in dealing with the Bulgarians, always a threat to the Byzantines of the time; his generals took Antioch in 969.

In support of the army, he increased land allocations to his soldiers and attempted to limit the growth of church lands by restricting bequests, although he supported the church in other respects. Despite the fact that Nicephorus was very much the military man of action, he fulfilled his ritual role as well, as we know from the account of papal envoy Liudprand of Cremona, although not as well as the well-liked Constantine VII, for whom the people continued to long.

Despite his success as ritual figure, there is also evidence that Nicephorus's reign was unpopular, in part on account of the heavy costs of the *reconquesta* itself, which seemed to lay a heavy burden upon the population of Constantinople. As a result, Nicephorus had constantly to be on the defensive as emperor. He was murdered by his nephew, the general John I Tzimisces, in cooperation with his empress, Theophano, the widow of Romanus II, whom Nicephorus had married to cement his claim to power. John (r. 969–976) became his successor.

Paul D. Buell

See also: Byzantine-Muslim Wars; John I Tzimisces; Muslim Conquests

References and further reading:

Norwich, John Julius. *Byzantium: The Apogee.* New York: Alfred A. Knopf, 1991.
Rosser, John H. *Historical Dictionary of Byzantium.* Latham, MD: Scarecrow Press, 2001.
Wittrow, Mark. *The Making of Byzantium, 600–1025.* Berkeley: University of California Press, 1996.

Nicholas, Grand Duke (1856–1929)

Russian general, commander in chief during the opening stages of World War I, and one of Russia's best commanders in that conflict. Nephew to Czar Alexander II, Nicholas was born on 18 November 1856 in St. Petersburg. After attending general staff college, he served with his father, Grand Duke

Nikolay Nikolayevich, commander in chief in the Russo-Turkish War of 1877–1878. He commanded the Guard Hussar Regiment in 1884 and served as inspector general of the cavalry from 1895 to 1905, where he instituted a much-needed modernization plan. His reform efforts continued in his next post as commander of the St. Petersburg Military District. From 1905 to 1908, he served as president of the Imperial Committee of National Defense, which was then dissolved.

Nicholas was not involved in war planning during the turbulent period from 1909 to mid-1914, but when World War I started, Czar Nicholas II named him commander in chief. Nicholas did a superb job of rallying the underprepared Russian forces against the Germans and the Austro-Hungarians, but the czar relieved Nicholas in September 1915 following defeats the previous summer. The czar, disastrously, assumed personal command of the military and assigned Nicholas command of Russian forces in the Caucasus. There he enjoyed success in campaigns in Armenia, where he captured the fortress of Erzurum in February 1916 and the port of Trabzon in April 1916. He successfully defended his gains against the Turkish offensive later that summer.

On the eve of the March 1917 revolution, the czar named Nicholas full commander in chief once again, but he held the post only a very short time. After being relieved by Prince Georgy Y. Lvov, Nicholas retired to the Crimea until 1919, when he moved to France. He died on 5 January 1929 in Antibes.

Harold Wise

See also: Bolshevik Revolution; Russo-Turkish Wars; World War I

References and further reading:

Danilov, Yuri N. *Le premier généralissime des armies russes, le grand duc Nicolas.* Paris: 1937.

Keegan, John. *The First World War.* New York: Alfred A. Knopf/Random House, 1999.

Nieuport (1600)

The first test of the Dutch army following Maurice of Nassau's reforms. Against his better judgment, Maurice was ordered by the Dutch government to "liberate" the Flemish coast from Spanish control. This move was strategically unwise, as the only Dutch base in the region was the isolated port of Ostende, but Maurice executed a brilliant logistical maneuver, moving his army of 14,000 to Ostende and marching down the coast to Nieuport. The capture of this city would deny the Spanish Netherlands access to the sea, so the Spanish governor-general, Archduke Albert of Austria, needed to break the siege. Many of his veteran units were in mutiny, but Albert convinced them to rejoin the army, gathering 10,000 men.

Archduke Albert's army made for the coast, falling on Maurice's rear guard at Leffinghem. This force was scattered, blocking any Dutch retreat toward Ostende. The Spanish then moved rapidly down the coast, hoping to fall on the rear of Maurice's siege positions. Meanwhile, Maurice abandoned the siege and moved his army across the Yser River to face the Spanish.

The battle, fought on 2 July 1600, demonstrated the advantages of the smaller, more maneuverable companies with a higher proportion of musketeers instituted by Maurice. Both armies were forced to redeploy inland as a result of the rising tide, a maneuver that the Dutch executed with ease. The Spanish *tercios* (infantry regiments) were held at bay by the firepower of Maurice's English contingent, under the command of Sir Francis Vere. While this fight raged in the center of the battle, Maurice successfully concentrated his cavalry on the inland flank and routed the Spanish horse, exposing the flank of the Spanish infantry.

A final charge by Maurice's army then drove the Spaniards from the field. It was a brilliant tactical victory, but Albert had forced the Dutch to give up the siege of Nieuport.

John S. Nolan

See also: Anglo-Spanish War; Ostende, Siege of

References and further reading:

Arnold, Thomas. *The Renaissance at War.* London: Cassell, 2001.

Oman, Charles. *The Art of War in the XVIth Century.* London: Methuen, 1937.

Parker, Geoffrey. *The Dutch Revolt.* London: Penguin, 1979.

Nigerian Civil War (1967–1970)

A brutal civil strife that exacerbated distrust and antagonism and has plagued Nigeria from independence to the present. Nigeria was bedeviled by regional differences at independence. Indirect rule under the British had created a north-south dichotomy. Then the 1957 Macpherson Constitution transformed regional councils into parliaments, making Nigeria a federation of three self-governing states at independence in October 1960, under Prime Minister Abubakar Tafewa Balewa. The north, the largest region, was predominantly Muslim and Hausa, the east largely Christian and Ibo, and the west religiously mixed but predominantly Christian Yoruba.

Although the federal system was touted as a model of diversity and achievement, regional differences sowed seeds of discontent. In 1965, the northern region again gained a majority in the federal legislature, and thereafter a climate of lawlessness gradually enveloped parts of the country in

1965–1966. Easterners and westerners chafed under "northern domination." A coup by young Ibo army officers achieved very little, but in rapid succession, prominent politicians (Prime Minister Tafewa Balewa; the western prime minister, Chief Akintola; and the northern prime minister, the Sardauna of Sokoto) were assassinated in January 1966. Anarchy was temporarily averted by the coup d'état of Major General Jounson Aguiyi-Ironsi. However, the calm lasted only until mid-1966, when General Aguiyi Ironsi was kidnapped and murdered in a countercoup on 29 July by mostly northern Hausa soldiers who detested his attempts at a unified government and the failure to punish the Ibo officers responsible for the earlier coup.

In a climate of accusation and counteraccusation, thousands of Ibos working in different parts of Nigeria as clerks and civil servants were killed by Hausas in retaliation. Lieutenant Colonel Yakubu Gowon emerged as head of state and called a conference in September 1966 to determine the form of national government. The effort met with very little success because of deep-seated divisions between the three regions. Concomitant with the conference's collapse in early October was a new and vicious rebellion by part of the army in the northern region. Mobs of Hausas again mercilessly slaughtered Ibos, especially those leaving the region. Consequently, Ibos boycotted the reconvened constitutional conference in November and threatened secession.

After months of unproductive negotiations in early 1967, Colonel Odumegwu Ojukwu assumed control of the eastern region and proclaimed the sovereign state of Biafra. It attained initial military success, but by 1969, Ibos were slowly driven into a smaller part of the eastern region with the capture of Enugu. The international community and African nations were dragged into the war. Ivory Coast, Zambia, Haiti, Gabon, and Tanzania recognized Biafra. The Nigerian federal government used Soviet aircraft and Egyptian pilots for bombing runs in Biafra. Britain also provided arms, but France, Spain, and Portugal supported Biafra, albeit on humanitarian grounds. The United States officially supported the federal government but provided medical supplies, foodstuffs, and other materials to Biafra.

After Biafra's initial military victories, the federal government gradually imposed a stranglehold on Biafra, cutting off all arms, food, and medical supplies to the region, leading to starvation and malnutrition. Children were collected into orphanages, but with little food to go around, many ended up in mass graves.

By early 1970, Biafra was no longer able to prosecute the war and surrendered, and Ojukwu fled the country. International efforts were mounted for relief supplies, but the operation was weakened by the Cold War rivalry of the United States and the Soviet Union.

Edmund Abaka

References and further reading:

Obasanjo, Olusegun. *My Command: An Account of the Nigerian Civil War 1967–70.* London: Heinemann, 1980.

Uwechue, Raph. *Reflections on the Nigerian Civil War.* New York: Africana Publishing, 1971.

Nightingale, Florence (1820–1910)

Near-legendary founder of modern nursing. The daughter of wealthy English parents, Nightingale was born in Florence, Italy, in 1820. She became interested in nursing after she claimed that God had spoken to her in 1837 and directed her to serve others. Florence studied with nurses in England, Alexandria, Egypt, and Germany. Nursing was held in low esteem at the time, and Nightingale chose not to marry in order to pursue her vocation with a passion.

When the Crimean War began in 1853, British secretary of war Sidney Herbert asked Nightingale to assist British forces. She trained 38 nurses for work in army hospitals and found horrifying conditions in the war zone. Thousands of casualties suffered in primitive hospitals with poor medical care and insufficient supplies, and the experience left Night-

Photograph of Florence Nightingale, c. 1845. (Hulton/Archive)

ingale with acute posttraumatic stress disorder (PTSD) for the rest of her life. She returned to England when the war ended in 1856 and, tormented by her memories, never again made a public appearance or statement.

Yet her widely publicized service in the Crimea had made her a legend, and Nightingale used her fame to encourage the professionalization of nursing. Arguing that a nurse's care was noble and never-ceasing, she established the foundation of modern nursing by writing numerous books and pamphlets and in 1860 founded the Nightingale School and Home for nurses in St. Thomas's Hospital, London. She received the British Order of Merit in 1907 and upon her death in 1910 was buried at her family's plot in East Wellow, England. Her casket was carried by six sergeants of the British Army. Britain honored her with the Crimean Monument in London in 1915, and the international community did so by creating the Florence Nightingale International Foundation in 1934. It is due primarily to Florence Nightingale's nearly obsessive efforts that nursing, military and civilian, is the respected profession that it is today.

Lance Janda

See also: Crimean War; Medicine, Military

References and further reading:

Dossey, Barbara Montgomery. *Florence Nightingale: Mystic, Visionary, Healer.* Springhouse Publishing, 2000.

Small, Hugh. *Florence Nightingale: Avenging Angel.* New York: St. Martin's Press.

Nine Years' War (1595–1604)

Also known as the O'Neill Rebellion, the result of increasing English involvement in Ireland in the 1580s. Ironically, Hugh O'Neill, the Earl of Tyrone, was the product of efforts to bring the island under control, having been taken to England at a young age and educated there. He was returned to Ireland in the late 1570s to rise to leadership of the long recalcitrant O'Neill clan of Ulster, bringing them to some degree of submission and in 1593 was elevated to the English title earl of Tyrone.

Though O'Neill had been considered a loyal subject, English officials in Ulster now reported that he was preparing rebellion. Though he was probably motivated by personal grudges, these reports were taken seriously by London, which sanctioned garrisons around O'Neill's territory. Caught between two cultures, O'Neill elected for the Gaelic in late 1594; he began negotiations with Spain and started forming an army equipped with modern firearms. In defiance of Elizabeth I's orders, he assumed the Gaelic title of "The O'Neill" in 1595. From that point on, he was considered to be in rebellion.

Fighting began in 1595, when O'Neill's brother Art attacked English garrisons on the Blackwater River. In May, O'Neill demonstrated his military talents by ambushing the English at Clontibert. He expanded his army to more than 10,000 men during a shaky truce he negotiated with Sir John Norreys in 1596. In 1597, as rebellion broke out in other parts of the island, the English decided to rebuild the forts on the Blackwater. O'Neill promptly laid siege to them, and in August 1598, an attempt by 4,000 English troops to relieve the forts led to their greatest defeat in the war at Yellow Ford, with more than half of the relief force lost. Subsequently, the province of Munster rose in bloody revolt against its English plantation.

In 1599, the Queen's favorite, the earl of Essex, brought over 16,000 troops in an attempt to salvage the situation. O'Neill whittled this force down to a mere 4,000 in just 21 weeks through the use of guerrilla tactics, combining traditional Irish tactics with modern firearms.

Essex was replaced by Charles Blount, Lord Mountjoy, who instituted new tactics, campaigning in winter and devastating the countryside to deprive O'Neill's forces of food. Though his first battle, against positions O'Neill had fortified at Moyry Pass (2 October 1600), was a draw, it was clear Mountjoy was gaining control of the situation, when on 21 September 1601, long-awaited Spanish forces arrived in Ireland. Unfortunately for O'Neill, they landed at Kinsale in the extreme south and were promptly besieged by Mountjoy. O'Neill had to face Mountjoy's army in an open field to lift the siege and was decisively defeated in the attempt on 24 December 1601. The Spanish surrendered soon after. O'Neill's rebellion was effectively crushed with the defeat at Kinsale, and he made his submission on 30 March 1603, having been defeated by the superior resources of a powerful state.

John S. Nolan

See also: Yellow Ford; Mountjoy, Charles Blount, Lord

References and further reading:

Falls, Cyril. *Elizabeth's Irish Wars.* London: Methuen, 1950.

Silke, John J. *Kinsale: The Spanish Intervention in Ireland.* Liverpool, UK: Liverpool University Press, 1970.

Wernham, R. B. *The Return of the Armadas.* Oxford, UK: Oxford University Press, 1994.

Nivelle, Robert (1856–1924)

One of the more disastrous of the French generals. Born at Tulle on 15 October 1856, Nivelle graduated from the École Polytechnique in 1878 and entered the artillery. Promoted to colonel (1911) and then brigadier general (October 1914), he commanded III Corps at Verdun and developed tactics that won him prominence. These consisted of training selected units to assault objectives in small groups. Attacks were preceded by deception barrages that would be halted to encourage the Germans to reveal their artillery positions. With the enemy guns silenced, attacks would then resume.

In April 1916, General Joseph Joffre gave Nivelle command of the Verdun Front (Second Army). Nivelle proclaimed "We have the formula!" and launched a series of local attacks beginning on 1 May that led, after initial setbacks, to the recapture of Fort Vaux (7 June) and Fort Douaumont (24 October). Because of his Verdun success and skill at self-advertisement, Nivelle was named commander in chief of the French armies of the north and northeast in December 1916, replacing Joffre. Nivelle's fluent English helped him secure approval from Prime Minister David Lloyd George for a plan to secure victory. The focus of the attack was in Champagne, and the key to success would be the "Verdun" formula, despite the difficulty of applying these tactics at the army level. The "Nivelle Offensive" (16 April–9 May 1917) was widely anticipated by the Germans. Aware of the French plan, they shortened their front and prepared defenses in depth. The offensive produced only minimal gains and 130,000 French casualties. It also led to widespread mutinies in the army and to Nivelle's replacement in May by General Henri-Philippe Pétain.

Nivelle declined command of an army group and submitted to review by a military inquiry in October that whitewashed him. He commanded French troops in Algeria in 1918 and served on the Supreme War Council after the war. He died in Paris on 23 March 1924.

Spencer C. Tucker

See also: Foch, Ferdinand; French Army; Joffre, Joseph Jacques Césaire; Pétain, Henri-Philippe; World War I

References and further reading:

King, Jere Clemens. *Generals and Politicians.* Berkeley: University of California Press, 1951.

Terrail, Gabriel. *Nivelle et Painlevé: La deuxième crise du commandant (décembre 1916–mai 1917).* Paris: P. Ollendorff, 1919.

Watt, Richard M. *Dare Call It Treason.* New York: Simon and Schuster, 1963.

Nogi, Maresuke (1843–1912)

Japanese general famous for siege of Port Arthur during Russo-Japanese War. Born in Tokyo in 1843 to a Choshu clan samurai father, Nogi served in the Restoration War of 1868, attained the rank of major in 1871, and fought in the Satsuma Rebellion in 1877. He was part of the Japanese officer contingent that studied military science in Germany in 1885–1886. He saw action during the 1894–1895 Sino-Japanese War in the siege of Port Arthur (24 October–19 November 1894) and in the Battle of Yingkow (9 March 1895) as a brigade commander. Nogi commanded the Third Army during the 1904–1905 Russo-Japanese War and oversaw the costly siege of Russian defenses at Port Arthur (22 June 1904–2 January 1905). Japan suffered 100,000 casualties before the Russians finally surrendered. Following the long siege, Nogi rushed his army to participate in the Battle of Mukden, another Japanese victory. Later, as headmaster of a private school, he tutored the future emperor Hirohito. Hailed as a hero, Nogi demonstrated his loyalty to the emperor by committing ritual suicide on 30 June 1912 following his ruler's death. Understandably, his home is today a shrine.

Harold Wise

See also: Mukden, Battle of; Port Arthur, Siege of; Russo-Japanese War; Sino-Japanese War (1894–1895)

References and further reading:

Warner, Denis, and Peggy Warner. *The War of the Rising Sun and Tumbling Bear: A Military History of the Russo-Japanese War.* London: Routledge, 1988.

———. *The Tide at Sunrise: A History of the Russo-Japanese War, 1904–1905.* London: Frank Cass, 2001.

Nongovernmental (Extranational) Organizations: Their Role in War and in the Wake of War

Civilian organizations that mobilize resources and individuals to alleviate human suffering in peace war and war. Since the mid-nineteenth century, people in the developed nations have founded organizations, such as the Red Cross, Cooperative for Assistance and Relief Everywhere (CARE), Catholic Relief Services, and Oxfam, aiming to provide humanitarian aid beyond local boundaries. Naturally, these efforts are applied to war-torn areas as well. The staff members of nongovernmental organizations (NGOs), neither established nor controlled by any government, bring the essentials of survival, food, clothing, shelter, and health care to people who have lost everything.

After 1945, the United Nations High Commissioner for Refugees (UNHCR) became a focal point for NGO efforts internationally. In most instances, UNHCR coordinates all major humanitarian relief efforts by NGOs in a particular country with that country's government.

Generally, the most influential and effective NGOs are religious-based organizations founded in the prosperous countries of the Northern Hemisphere. Most of their efforts are aimed at relieving major human disasters that are found usually in the poorer countries of the Southern Hemisphere. Because most NGOs have a long history, they are well-established bureaucracies having various levels of management and even perhaps competing suborganizations. Moreover, the NGOs frequently know each other's strengths and do not duplicate efforts. For example, among Rwandan refugees in Zaire, Oxfam alone established a water supply system for 800,000 people in 18 days.

In most cases, there are ongoing military conflicts either causing or caused by the human disaster. Thus, a range of important matters must be resolved in the relations between military forces and the NGOs. First, there may be a civil war in progress. The central government may oppose and refuse to permit NGO relief efforts from reaching those in rebellion. NGOs generally seek to remain neutral and even-handed in all conflicts. But their purpose of providing humanitarian aid to any and all people in need may lead to their staging their relief efforts in a neighboring country and crossing the international border directly into rebel territory. The government could see their efforts as rendering aid to its enemies, as happened in East Timor.

In Bosnia-Herzegovina, UNHCR and various NGOs providing relief took a different tack. Their convoys had to travel roads through areas controlled by Bosnian Serb forces in order to reach Bosnia Muslims who had been victims of ethnic cleansing. To obtain a peaceful accommodation, standard practice was to give a part of the relief aid to the Bosnian Serb forces that had ethnically cleansed the area in exchange for being allowed to proceed to deliver aid to the victims.

Second, occasions such as Somalia may arise in which the central government has ceased to exist. UNHCR and NGOs may seek military intervention to protect and assist them in their efforts to move relief supplies into the country and to the people suffering in the interior. As happened in Somalia, the results can lead to new levels of violence or new causes for military action. The U.S. military termed this effect "mission creep," and it cost American lives in the streets of Mogadishu.

In addition, some NGOs have the purpose of moving beyond emergency relief for saving people's lives to the nation-building or development phase. Here the task is to create new social and indigenous governmental institutions to sustain the people. Their concerns include the protection of human rights and the need for a war crimes tribunal. In these circumstances, repatriation or implementation of a peace settlement may require facing the issues that caused the military conflict originally. The various military forces in question may need to shift from a combat mode to a peacekeeping or peace-establishing mode.

Finally, NGOs have had to work out agreements with relief military units sent in to suppress violence. The NGOs looked upon the military as akin to those armed forces that started the problem, while the relief units, particularly those from the developed world, viewed the NGO personnel as "disaster groupies." Since approximately the time of the Kurdish protection operation in 1991, both sides have come to realize that they work much better through mutual cooperation; the NGOs need the military for its unsurpassed logistics and transportation facilities and skills, and the military has become mindful that its members are not trained for the complex tasks of running a civil economy over time and also realize that the NGOs, which generally will stay much longer than expensive military units, are their "tickets out of here."

John R. Popiden

See also: Red Cross; Refugees and Victims of Ethnic Cleansing

References and further reading:

Fernando, Jude L., and Alan W. Heston, eds. "The Role of NGOs: Charity and Empowerment." *Annals of the American Academy of Political and Social Science* (November 1997).

Maynard, Kimberly A. *Healing Communities in Conflict: International Assistance in Complex Emergencies.* New York: Columbia University Press, 1999.

Moore, Jonathan, ed. *Hard Choices: Moral Dilemmas in Humanitarian Intervention.* New York: Rowman & Littlefield, 1998.

Weiss, Thomas G., and Larry Minear, eds. *Humanitarianism across Borders: Sustaining Civilians in Times of War.* Boulder, CO: Lynne Rienner, 1993.

Nordlingen (1634)

A watershed battle in the Thirty Years' War. After two disastrous years, the battle ensured the survival of the Catholic and Habsburg cause and produced a balance of Protestant and Catholic forces within Germany.

From 1632 to 1634, the Swedish and Protestant position slowly unraveled. Imperial (Catholic) forces registered a series of small but cumulatively significant successes, until September 1634, when they won a battle in Bavaria that radically changed the situation within Germany.

At Nordlingen, a numerically superior Catholic army crushed a Swedish army that was committed first to a frontal attack on an entrenched hilltop and then, after having taken but lost this position, to a withdrawal across the front of the main part of the Catholic army. The attack by this uncommitted part of the Catholic army turned a retreat into a rout: the Swedish army lost 21,000 dead and prisoners from an initial strength of just 25,000 troops. Sweden's defeat marked the point at which it could no longer lead the Protestant cause, and Catholic France, unless it were to tolerate a Habsburg victory, was obliged to lead the war against Austria and Spain.

H. P. Willmott

See also: Gustavus II Adolphus; Thirty Years' War

References and further reading:

Parker, Geoffrey. *The Thirty Years' War.* London: Routledge & Kegan Paul, 1984.

Wedgwood, C. V. *The Thirty Years War.* London: Cape, 1953.

Polisensky, V. *The Thirty Years War.* Trans. Robert Evans. London: Batsford, 1970.

Norman Conquest (1066–1072)

William conquers and restructures England after victory at Hastings. The Norman Conquest of England was more than the military victory of one of three contenders for the English throne. It marked a complete restructuring of England's society, with some changes imposed and others constituting an effective application of native systems already in place. The Norman Conquest changed the ruling house, ruling class, and the legal languages of England. Changed too was ownership of the land. Before the conquest, individuals might own areas of land. Afterward, even church land was held by the king on feudal terms. This change allowed greater control over a feudal system in which many portions were held in fief from different liege lords. In England all loyalty, in the end, was to the monarch, and subinfeudation was mostly eliminated as a divisive element. The Anglo-Saxon ruling class was largely replaced by Norman supporters of William the Conquerer. As part of his administrative reorganization, a string of castles was built. The language of the court and the courts changed to French and Latin, respectively.

From 1068 to 1071, a series of regional revolts against William occurred. They were largely localized. William ended them with brutal efficiency. He laid waste to Yorkshire, killing all males and pursuing a scorched-earth policy that was apparent even 20 years later in the *Domesday Book.*

The Norman Conquest should be regarded as the seminal event in English history until the Reformation. It substantially altered the institutional structures of the church, the monarchy, and feudalism. It also changed the political, intellectual, and social framework of England, enhancing the existing rules and reinterpreting them. The character of medieval England was created in the crucible of the Norman Conquest.

Tamsin Hekala

See also: William the Conqueror; Hastings, Battle of

References and further reading:

Douglas, David C. *William the Conqueror: The Norman Impact upon England.* Berkeley: University of California Press, 1964.

Loyn, H. R. *Anglo-Saxon England and the Norman Conquest.* New York: St. Martin's Press, 1963.

Previté-Orton, C. W., ed. *The Shorter Cambridge Medieval History,* Cambridge; Cambridge University Press, 1962.

Norman-Byzantine Wars (1081–1108)

Wars through which Normans tried twice to conquer Byzantium through the Balkans but were repulsed by Emperor Alexius I Comnenus (r. 1081–1118). Around 1017, the first Norman warriors landed in southern Italy, looking for lands and loot. Byzantium held southern Italy and Sicily, but revolts by the Lombard population had enfeebled its grip. Supported by constant infusions of their kinsmen, the Normans carved up southern Italy, and by 1042, very few cities remained to Byzantium. In 1053, the Norman Robert Guiscard compelled the pope to recognize him as duke of Apulia and Calabria. In turn, Guiscard became a papal vassal, just as relations between the papacy and Byzantium devolved into mutual hostility and excommunication. In 1071, after a siege and blockade of nearly three years, the Normans captured the port of Bari, ending forever the Byzantine presence in Italy.

That same year, Byzantium faced a mortal crisis more dire than the loss of Italy. The 1071 Battle of Manzikert had destroyed the Byzantine army in Asia, and Turks now flooded into Anatolia. Additionally, Manzikert plunged Byzantium into civil war. As Alexius I Comnenus won the throne in 1081, Guiscard resolved to conquer Constantinople. The empire was in tatters, Norman hirelings in the Byzantine army threatened to defect, and a deposed emperor, Michael VII (r. 1071–1078), had betrothed a son to Robert's daughter. Thus, Robert Guiscard and his son, Bohemond, took sail that year and landed on the Epirus (Albanian) coast.

Alexius persuaded the Venetians to sink the Norman fleet but could not save Dyrrhachium from Robert's siege. A Byzantine relief force, heavy with Bosnian and Turkish mercenaries, suffered complete defeat, and by 1082, Robert held northwestern Greece. Byzantine money inspired rebels in Italy, forcing Robert to return home, but Bohemond continued to occupy Greek and Bulgarian lands. Alexius lost three more battles, until the Byzantines finally stopped the Normans in the spring of 1083. The alliance with Venice now paid off by blocking support to Bohemond, and the Normans evacuated the region. Robert Guiscard was preparing for a rematch when he died in 1085, but his aggression had cost Alexius almost all of Anatolia.

The First Crusade delayed the next Norman-Byzantine war, and Bohemond's Normans provided a major contingent to the Crusaders. After taking Antioch, Bohemond fell into Turkish captivity for several years. Once released, he struggled with Alexius's Armenian allies no less than with the Turks. By 1106, apoplectic at perceived Byzantine treachery, Bohemond returned to Italy to plan a second Balkan invasion. In 1107, Normans again landed in Epirus and threw up another siege around Dyrrhachium. Alexius then encircled the besieging army, as Venice sealed the coast. After months of relentless attrition, Norman forces finally collapsed in 1108. Pledging homage to Alexius, Bohemond returned to Italy. Norman threats to Byzantium remained dormant until the 1147 Sicilian crisis.

Weston F. Cook Jr.

See also: Alexius I Comnenus; Crusades; Guiscard, Robert

References and further reading:

Comnena, Anna. *The Alexiad of Anna Comnena.* Translated by E. R. A. Sewter. New York: Penguin Books, 1969.

Fine, John. *The Early Medieval Balkans.* Ann Arbor: University of Michigan Press, 1983.

Normandy Landings (1944)

The greatest amphibious landing operation in the history of warfare. Allied plans for an invasion of western Europe in World War II began soon after Germany declared war against the United States on 11 December 1941, with the appointment of General Dwight D. Eisenhower to design a plan for Allied victory in Europe. Eisenhower quickly developed two plans, one for 1942, called Operation SLEDGEHAMMER in case the Soviets were routed in the east, and a 1943 invasion plan called Operation ROUNDUP. British officials persuaded Americans leaders to focus their principal operations on North Africa and later on operations in Sicily and Italy. Soviet leader Stalin continued to press for a "second front" to lessen the German pressure on Russia.

Finally, at the Tehran Conference (November–December 1943), President Franklin D. Roosevelt and Stalin insisted to British prime minister Winston Churchill that May 1944 be the date for the invasion and that the Soviets would mount an attack on German forces to coincide with the European invasion.

Even though the British had been reluctant, Lieutenant General Frederick Morgan had worked on an invasion plan called Operation OVERLORD since the Casablanca Conference in January 1943. The landings were to be at Normandy, between Caen and the Cotentin Peninsula. Three Allied divisions were to be part of the landing, and two other divisions were to be air-dropped, with 11 other divisions to land within 14 days. Two artificial harbors were to be towed from England, and once a foothold in Europe had been established, several hundred divisions would be shipped from the United States and from across the channel.

The German high command had been aware of Allied cross-channel invasion planning for a long time, but with their forces dispersed in the Mediterranean and campaigns in the east, they were unable to fortify western Europe until November 1943, when Adolf Hitler issued Fuhrer Directive 51. Hitler appointed Field Marshal Erwin Rommel to oversee coastal defenses and command Army Group B. Although Rommel was able to lay 4 million mines, he was not able to position German tank divisions where he wanted because of the divided German command.

In January 1944, British general Bernard L. Montgomery was named commander of the ground invasion forces under Eisenhower. Montgomery demanded that five divisions (two British, two American, and one Canadian) make the initial landing and that the landing zone include the Orne River estuary. American landing forces would be led by General Omar Bradley and Canadian and British forces by General Miles Dempsey. Each of the five beaches where forces were to land was assigned a code name from east to west: Sword, Juno, Gold, Omaha, and Utah. One British airborne division was to land behind coastal defenses in the east and two American divisions in the west, while amphibious forces would swim ashore to prepare for the landing. To soften up German defenses, between 1 April and 5 June, 11,000 Allied aircraft flew 200,000 sorties, dropping 195,000 tons of bombs on strategic locations in France. Many of these raids were designed to persuade German forces that the landing would be northeast of the Seine. The Allies also created an entire phantom army in England under the command of George S. Patton, as well as false images of an invasion fleet sailing toward the Pas-de-Calais area on the night of the invasion.

Because of difficulties with assembling landing craft, the invasion was moved to June 1944. The invasion, threatened by foul weather, was nonetheless given the go-ahead on the morning of 5 June by Eisenhower. The cross-channel armada contained 3,000 landing craft, 500 naval vessels, and 2,500 other ships. Although the Luftwaffe had fewer than 400 airplanes in the area on D-Day, 13,000 fighters, bombers, and other Allied aircraft aided ground forces. The American 82d and 101st Airborne Divisions dropped into the Cotentin Peninsula and, although suffering heavy casu-

American soldiers wade from a Coast Guard landing craft toward the beach at Normandy on D-Day, 6 June 1944. (Library of Congress)

alties, secured their objectives, and the 6th British Airborne Division captured key bridges over the Caen Canal and Orne River.

At 6:30 A.M. on 6 June, British and Canadian forces landed on Gold, Juno, and Sword beaches with little opposition. The American forces at Utah faced a similar situation. But the 1st American Division at Omaha Beach was confronted by the 352d, the best German coastal division. The 6-mile section of beach between Port-en-Bession and the Vire River had 12 German strong points called Widerstandsnester and numerous other fighting positions on the cliffs surrounding the beach. By 8:30, landings had ceased at Omaha, leaving surviving American forces slowly to secure the beach and scale the cliffs. Navy destroyers steamed close in to shell German fortifications. By noon, German fire had noticeably decreased as U.S. troops took German defensive positions from the rear. An exit from the beach was finally opened, but not before the Americans had suffered 2,400 casualties and the Germans of the 352d 1,200 casualties.

German forces were caught in disarray, with Rommel on leave at home. At first, Hitler was unwilling to release an armored division for the counterattack, but he relented by midday, allowing the 21st Panzer Division to move to an area between Juno and Sword beaches, which almost reached the sea. But the Germans had long since lost any opportunity of throwing the Allies back into the sea; considering the vast superiority of the Allies across the spectrum of land, sea, and air power, it was a forlorn hope from the beginning.

T. Jason Soderstrum

See also: Eisenhower, Dwight David; Hitler, Adolf; Rommel, Erwin Johannes Eugen; World War II

References and further reading:

Ambrose, Stephen E. *D-Day, June 6, 1944: The Climactic Battle of World War II.* New York: Simon & Schuster, 1994.

Hunt, Robert. *The Normandy Campaign.* London: Cooper, 1976.

Kershaw, Robert J. *D-Day: Piercing the Atlantic Wall.* Annapolis, MD: Naval Institute Press, 1994.

Tute, Warren, John Costello, and Terry Hughes. *D-Day.* New York: Collier Books, 1974.

North Atlantic Treaty Organization (founded 4 April 1949)

Mutual defense alliance presently comprising 19 members from Western and Central Europe and North America and formed after World War II to offset the large conventional military advantage supposedly possessed by the USSR. Immediately following World War II, Belgium, France, Luxembourg, the Netherlands, and the United Kingdom signed a collective defense alliance termed the Brussels Treaty. It was soon recognized that the Brussels Treaty was no match for the Soviet military. Almost immediately, negotiations began with the United States and Canada to enlarge the collective defense arrangement. Negotiations culminated in the signing of the North Atlantic Treaty.

The original members of the North Atlantic Treaty Organization (NATO) included Belgium, Canada, Denmark, France, Iceland, Italy, Luxembourg, the Netherlands, Norway, Portugal, the United Kingdom, and the United States. During the next 50 years, NATO expanded to include Greece and Turkey (both joined in 1952); West Germany (1955); Spain (1982); and the Czech Republic, Hungary, and Poland (1999).

Harry S. Truman holding the NATO treaty he signed on 25 July 1949. (Library of Congress)

The heart of the NATO alliance is Article 5 of the treaty. In Article 5, signatories declared that an armed attack upon one member shall be considered an attack against all. In such cases, NATO members have the right, recognized by Article 51 of the Charter of the United Nations, to take whatever actions necessary to safeguard their security and territorial integrity. Post-1945 proponents of such a treaty used the argument that had Adolf Hitler been faced with a similar mutual defense network in the 1930s, he would not have gone to war.

One of the early issues confronting NATO in the first half of the 1950s was negotiating the participation of West Germany in the alliance. It was less than a decade since the end of World War II, and with Nazi occupation still fresh in the minds of many, the European powers were understandably wary of rearming West Germany. But it was recognized that a revived West Germany was key to NATO's success. The large German population, its growing economy, and its geostrategic location astride probable Soviet invasion routes made its membership in the alliance critical. The Soviet Union reacted to West Germany accession to NATO by creating the Warsaw Pact alliance in Eastern Europe.

In 1966, President Charles de Gaulle of France informed U.S. president Lyndon Johnson that France, although adhering to the basic tenets of the Atlantic Alliance, would take steps to exercise her full sovereignty. Subsequently, NATO troops were permitted use of French airspace or territory. Additionally, France withdrew from the integrated command structure and denied NATO the use of her troops. De Gaulle managed to have it both ways: France was free of the obligations of NATO but knew full well that the organization would not sit by and watch the country be again the victim of an aggressor.

Although NATO was assumed to have better-equipped and trained militaries, the huge numerical advantage supposedly possessed by the USSR and the Warsaw Pact meant that Western European security rested partly on the deterrent effect of U.S. nuclear retaliation. In 1979, NATO's Nuclear Planning Group agreed to station medium-range U.S. nuclear missiles (Pershing IIs) in Western Europe. Some member-states worried that deploying such weapons would accelerate the arms race. Additionally, several members had to contend with widespread civilian protests concerning deployment of the missiles. Many believed that the deployment of the missiles led to the 1987 Intermediate-Range Nuclear Forces (INF) Treaty banning medium-range missiles.

By the early 1990s, NATO was suffering from a crisis of identity. For half a century, the raison d'être for NATO had been to protect Western Europe from Soviet aggression. With the collapse of the Soviet Union in 1991, NATO's purpose became more difficult to define. (The members of the defunct Warsaw Pact engaged in no such navel gazing; they all wished to join NATO.) As leaders struggled with justifying not only the existence of NATO but a rationale for expanding NATO, events in the Balkans provided possible new missions and opportunities.

A new chapter in NATO's history began in the 1990s, when for the first time it engaged in military action. In April 1993, NATO warplanes began patrolling the skies over Bosnia and later began air strikes against Serbian military targets. Later, as part of the Dayton (Ohio) Peace Accords, NATO provided ground troops as part of a multinational peacekeeping mission in Bosnia.

In 1998, the Serbian province of Kosovo was the scene of widespread Serb persecution of its secession-threatening Albanian population. NATO responded with a 78-day bombing campaign, forcing Serbian leaders to capitulate. NATO ground forces were again inserted as peacekeepers. Critics wondered publicly about just how far NATO could go as the policeman of Europe and about the extent of American forces in this policing. Further, labeling the "aggressor" to be punished was much more complex than in 1949. For example, Albanians were "victims" when persecuted by Serbs but then "aggressors" when they turned upon the Serbs in Albanian-dominated areas.

Craig T. Cobane

See also: Yugoslavian Civil Wars

References and further reading:

Carpenter, Ted. *Beyond NATO.* Washington, DC: Cato Institute, 1994.

Gordon, Philip H., ed. *NATO's Transformation.* Lanham, MD: Rowman & Littlefield, 1999.

Northern Ireland, Civil War in (1969–present)

Conflict, known as "the Troubles," related to British control over six northeastern counties of the island of Ireland. The conflict has a long history, going back to the Norman conquest of England (1066). For almost a millennium, the fighting has ebbed and flowed with the tide of English control of the region. Casualties related to the Troubles (1969–2000) are in excess of 3,300 dead and 42,000 injured.

Early in the twentieth century, Britain negotiated the divestment of 26 Irish counties to the newly formed Republic of Ireland. The remaining six counties (Northern Ireland), possessing a 2–1 Protestant majority, were given their own parliament, known as the Stormont. From 1921 to 1968, Northern Ireland was ruled as a Protestant state whose purpose was to serve the interests of the Protestant majority, who felt that they had already given up more than enough to the "papists."

In the late 1960s, a civil rights movement, modeled on Dr. Martin Luther King Jr.'s movement in the United States, developed to address inequities and seek political changes. Some of the more radical and violence-prone groups demanded union with the Republic of Ireland. On 5 October 1968, nightstick-wielding members of the Royal Ulster Constabulary (RUC, the Protestant-dominated police force of Northern Ireland) attacked 400 peaceful marchers who were singing "We Shall Overcome." The entire episode was caught on film and led to riots erupting in Catholic sections of Northern Ireland's capital, Belfast.

As rioting erupted throughout the province, the exhausted RUC soon realized that they needed assistance, and the 2,000-strong garrison of British soldiers was pressed into service. At first, Catholics saw the British troops as saviors from the brutal RUC. Within a year, the British army's welcome had worn thin among Catholics. Over time, Catholics began to see British troops as an army of occupation that favored the Protestants. Tensions came to a climax on 30 January 1972, when British paratroopers fired upon a group of marchers, killing 14, an incident ever afterward known as "Bloody Sunday." The official version of the incident claims that paratroopers were returning fire from the marchers. No evidence to support this contention has ever been found.

Violence quickly escalated, and soon more troops were sent, ultimately reaching a total of approximately 21,000 in 1972. Soon, a near full-fledged civil war was being waged between Catholic and Protestant paramilitaries, with the RUC and British army caught in the middle.

During most of the 1970s, the "security phase" of the conflict dominated. Local police were put under control of army commanders. A large number of the elite British Special Air Service (SAS) troopers were introduced into the conflict as undercover operatives, with controversial results. The security measures were seen as counterproductive, and by 1977, a new policy of "police primacy" was implemented.

What British politicians originally saw as a relatively brief military deployment extended to more than a third of a century. The British army learned a lesson that has been taught many times in history: military force, no matter how well trained, equipped, and dedicated, cannot resolve a political conflict.

Craig T. Cobane

See also: Guerrilla/Partisan/Irregular Warfare; Special Operations Forces

References and further reading:

Coogan, Tim. *The Troubles: Ireland's Ordeal 1966–1996 and the Search for Peace.* Boulder, CO: Roberts Rinehart, 1996.

O'Brien, Brendan. *The Long War: The IRA and Sinn Fein, 1985 to Today.* Syracuse, NY: Syracuse University Press, 1995.

Northern War, Great (January 1700–August 1721)

Conflict involving Sweden against the Baltic powers, resulting in the replacement of Sweden by Russia as a European great power. Swedish expansion during the sixteenth and seventeenth centuries had antagonized the other Baltic powers. Russia's access to the Baltic was blocked; Denmark-Norway resented its loss of Scania; Brandenburg coveted Swedish Pomerania; and Poland desired Swedish Livonia. When Charles XII ascended the throne in 1697, Denmark-Norway began to organize an anti-Swedish coalition including Saxony-Poland, Denmark-Norway, and Russia.

The elector of Saxony, Augustus II, who was also king of Poland, attacked Livonia in January 1700. King Frederick IV of Denmark-Norway marched into Schleswig and Holstein in March 1700. In October 1700, Czar Peter I of Russia laid siege to Narva.

Charles made a daring landing a few miles from Copenhagen, compelling Frederick to sign the Treaty of Travendal in August 1700. Next, Charles raised the siege at Narva on 30 November 1700. Then he occupied Courland and forced Augustus to retreat into Poland. After Charles invaded Saxony, Augustus agreed to relinquish the Polish crown to Stanislaw Leszczynski and signed the Treaty of Altranstädt in September 1706.

Peter used this respite after Narva to undertake a series of reforms, the prime purpose of which was to reorganize and strengthen the Russian army. Charles resumed his attack on Russia in January 1708 with a force of 50,000. The Russians defeated an auxiliary Swedish force of 15,000 men at Lesnaia in October 1708. The main Swedish force was then trounced at Poltava in July 1709.

Charles fled to Turkey, where he convinced the sultan to declare war on Russia in 1710. However, after the Turkish victory at Jassy on the Pruth River in July 1711, the sultan decided to end the war with a negotiated settlement that returned control of the Azov region to the Ottomans.

Russia's victory at Poltava revived an anti-Swedish coalition with Saxony, Poland, Denmark, Prussia, and Hannover. Peter captured Viborg/Viipuri and Reval in 1710. During 1713–1714, the Russians occupied most of Finland. In 1714 the Russians defeated the Swedish fleet at Hanko and, having captured the Åland Islands, threatened Stockholm. Charles returned to the Swedish territory of Stralsund in November 1714 and made his way the following year to southern Sweden. He opened peace negotiations in 1717–1718 while simultaneously organizing an army of 60,000 men in anticipation of a new offensive.

In September 1718, Charles invaded southeastern Norway, but he was killed at the siege of Frederikshald in December 1718. The Swedish throne passed to his sister Ulrika Eleonora and later to her husband, Frederick I of Hesse-Kassel. Frederick negotiated a series of peace settlements from 1719 to 1721.

By the Treaties of Stockholm (1720–1721), Sweden settled with Saxony, Poland, Denmark, Prussia, and Hannover. Denmark ceded its conquests to Sweden in return for a substantial sum of money. Sweden ceded Bremen to Hannover and gave up Stettin and part of Swedish Pomerania to Prussia. By the Treaty of Nystadt (30 August 1721), Sweden ceded Ingria, Estonia, Livonia, and a strip of Finnish Karelia to Russia. Thanks to his battle victories and his diplomacy, Peter the Great had made Russia the dominant power in the Baltic.

Neville G. Panthaki

See also: Charles XII; Peter I, Romanov, Czar of Russia; Poltava; Russo-Turkish Wars (1676–1878)

References and further reading:

Anderson, Matthew Smith. *Peter the Great.* New York: Longman, 1995.

Kliuchevskii, Vasilii Osipovich. *Peter the Great.* London: Macmillan, 1958.

Lisk, Jill. *The Struggle for Supremacy in the Baltic, 1600–1725.* New York: Funk & Wagnalls, 1968.

Sumner, Benedict Humphrey. *Peter the Great and the Emergence of Russia.* London: English Universities Press, 1964.

Northern War, Second (1655–1660)

War among Sweden, Poland, Austria, the Dutch Republic, Denmark, and Brandenburg. (The First Northern War was fought almost a century earlier, in 1563–1570.) In 1655, Charles X Gustav, King of Sweden, decided to abandon his peace talks with King John Casimir of Poland and to attack his neighbor instead with an overwhelming force of 50,000 troops in Poland and Lithuania. This marked the beginning of the Second Northern War. The Swedes entered Warsaw without opposition on 29 August 1655. Polish noblemen, displeased with their king, surrendered to the Swedes, as did most of the Polish forces. Only Cracow offered a two-week resistance but had to surrender to Charles X on 9 October after running out of supplies. King John Casimir fled to Glogau (Silesia). But the monastery of Jasna Gora, near Czestochowa, resisted all Swedish attacks in a manner that was deemed miraculous.

The Protestant regime established by the Swedes in Poland provoked an outburst of national and religious feeling. In 1656, a general insurrection expelled the Swedes from southern and western Poland. King John Casimir gathered his troops and marched on Warsaw at the head of 25,500 regulars and 18,000–20,000 soldiers from the noble levy, undisturbed by the fact that he had neither infantry nor cannon at hand to besiege the city. The dismounted nobles and their hordes of servants attacked the walls of Warsaw repeatedly until it capitulated on 1 July 1656. A combined Swedish-Brandenburg relief army only a few miles away defeated the Polish forces because of the superiority of its cavalry in a three-day battle (28–30 July) at Warsaw. The Polish losses were relatively insignificant, and John Casimir was able to regroup his army. Even more important, he was able to convince Frederick William of Brandenburg to take his side.

With Charles X under heavy Polish pressure, the Danish National Assembly took the opportunity to launch the kingdom on a war of revenge against Sweden in 1657. Using Bremen and Verden as the base for their operations, Swedish troops marched north and struck deep into Jutland. The Danes withdrew most of their forces to the islands but left 6,000 soldiers in the newly rebuilt fortress of Fredericia to guard the passage from Jutland across the Little Belt to the island of Fyn. The Swedes pierced the bulwark on the night of 23–24 October, killing many of its defenders.

Even more unfortunate for the Danes, during the winter of 1657–1658, the water around the Danish islands froze harder than usual. In February 1658, Charles led an army of 5,000–10,000 across the waters of the frozen Little Belt. On 25 February, the Swedes surprisingly appeared in the suburbs of Copenhagen, forcing King Frederick of Denmark to sign the humiliating Treaty of Roskilde (8 March) that stripped Denmark of all of its possessions in southern Sweden.

In July 1658, a Polish-Austrian force laid siege to Swedish-occupied Thorn. Charles attacked Denmark again. This time, however, he had no success. Furthermore, a Dutch fleet broke the Swedish sea blockade of Copenhagen, while 10,600 Austrians under Prince Raimondo Montecuccoli, 14,500 Brandenburgers under Frederick William, and 4,500 Poles under Stefan Czarniecki marched from Hamburg through Schleswig into Jutland. The Swedes were trapped in the Danish islands between the Dutch and Danish fleets and a superior allied army. After the fall of Thorn in December and successful operations of Austrian, Brandenburg, and Polish troops in Pomerania in 1659, the Swedes were in retreat on all fronts. In 1660, the unexpected death of Charles X on 23 February led to the Peace Treaty of Oliva (3 May) among Poland, Austria, Brandenburg, and Sweden and the Treaty of Copenhagen between Denmark and Sweden, bringing the conflict to a close.

Juergen Luh

See also: Northern War, Great

References and further reading:

Frost, Robert I. *After the Deluge: Poland, Lithuania and the Second Northern War, 1655–1660.* Cambridge, UK: Cambridge University Press, 1993.

———. *The Northern Wars: War, State and Society in Northeastern Europe, 1558–1721.* London: Longman, 2000.

Opitz, Eckhardt. *Osterreich und Brandenburg im Schwedisch-Polnischen Krieg 1655–1660: Vorbereitung und Durchfuehrung der Feldzuege nach Daenemark und Pommern.* Boppard am Rhein: Harald Boldt Verlag, 1969.

Norway and Denmark, Invasion of (9 April–10 June 1940)

One of the British army's worst-fought campaigns. "Weserübung" was the code name for the German occupation of Norway and Denmark, aimed at securing Swedish iron ore deliveries coming from the port of Narvik (northern Norway) as well as the German domination of the Baltic Sea.

The German military sensed when Allied intervention in the Soviet-Finnish Winter War became likely. British and French plans included aid for Finland and the interruption of German iron ore supplies that were vital to Adolf Hitler's war economy. An armistice ended the Winter War on 12 March 1940, but German as well as Allied planning for some abrogation of Norwegian sovereignty continued. It is still not clear what one side knew about the other, but German claims that its invasion was launched only to prevent an Allied breach of Denmark's and Norway's neutrality are doubtful.

According to Hitler's order of 1 March 1940, a small staff prepared a combined operation of army, navy, and air force. This planning aimed at a peaceful occupation. Allied intelligence expected a German attack against France and was struck by surprise when naval forces (detected too late by the Royal Navy) landed troops at several Norwegian ports on the morning of 9 April 1940. Denmark, invaded by land and by sea, surrendered almost immediately. The sinking of the German heavy cruiser *Blücher* by a Norwegian coastal battery south of Oslo delayed the occupation of the capital. The Norwegian government and King Haakon VII gained time to escape Oslo and to mobilize the country. Elsewhere, the German navy had more success, taking by surprise main ports against little resistance. By April, the main Norwegian ports (Oslo, Stavanger, Kristiansand, Bergen, Trondheim, Narvik) were in German hands.

Resistance by the small Norwegian army continued in the interior. A coup attempt by Vidkun Quisling, the leader of the Norwegian Nazi Party who had talked to Hitler in December 1939 (presumably on the invasion of Norway), failed. The Germans, who were interested in negotiating with the legal government to achieve an agreement, dismissed Quisling. But fighting increased when Allied forces landed at western Norwegian ports between 14 and 18 April 1940. They retook Narvik and forced German mountain troops to withdraw toward the Swedish border. Meanwhile, German divisions, supported by massive air attacks, fought their way north. When the German invasion of France proved successful, the Allies had to withdraw their troops from Norway. The situation turning hopeless, King Haakon and his government left for London 7 June 1940; three days later the Norwegians surrendered but continued the war from exile.

Wehrmacht casualties reached 3,700 dead; the Allies lost 3,900 and the Norwegians 1,350 troops. The German navy, with almost all surface units engaged, suffered heavy casualties (3 cruisers, 10 destroyers sunk) and was unable for months to profit from its new Atlantic bases. Denmark and Norway remained under German occupation until May 1945.

Martin Moll

See also: British Military, Twentieth Century Organization and Structure

References and further reading:

Ottmer, Hans-Martin. *"Weserübung": Der deutsche Angriff auf Dänemark und Norwegen im April 1940.* Munich: Oldenbourg, 1994.

Novgorod, Muscovite Conquest of (1471–1479)

Grand Prince Ivan III of Moscovy annexes Novgorod. Novgorod was administered by an assembly called the *veche.* It usually elected the grand prince of Moscow, although he was forbidden to station troops or reside in the city. Lacking a military capacity and dependent on imported food, Novgorod's reputation was based on its merchants.

In 1456, boyars of the *veche* advocated alliance with Lithuania-Poland, contrary to the existing treaty with Muscovy. In retaliation for their efforts, Grand Prince Vasili II of Muscovy refused any longer to recognize the right of the *veche* to pass laws without his approval. Despite this, Novgorod boyars continued to push their agenda, led by Marfa Boretskaya. They gained the support of Prince Ivan Andreevich of Mozhaisk and Vasili II's cousin, Prince Ivan Dmitrievich. In 1470, the boyars invited Prince Mikhail Olelkvich of Kiev to defend Novgorod with troops.

In February 1471, the boyars forced the *veche* to recognize Casimir of Lithuania-Poland as Novgorod's sovereign. After a failed attempt at reconciliation by Metropolitan Filip of Moscow, Grand Prince Ivan III of Muscovy declared war in June 1471.

Muscovite and Tartar forces reached Torzhok by July. The main battle took place along the Shelon River. A Muscovite advance guard of 5,000 cavalry routed a Novgorod force of 40,000, killing 12,000 and capturing 2,000. Ivan III's peace terms were lenient. He imposed a 15,500 ruble fine, reinstated the Treaty of 1456, ordered Novgorod to accept the authority of the metropolitan of Moscow, and forbade future alliance with Lithuania-Poland. Ivan returned to Moscow in January 1476.

In March 1477, Novgorod sent a petition for Ivan's review, addressing him as *gosudar* (sovereign), rather than the usual *gospodin* (lord). Ivan took this as an indication that Novgorod was willing to strengthen ties. He immediately sent envoys to Novgorod. They were detained in Novgorod for six weeks and returned to Moscow with a negative reply. Personally insulted, Ivan declared war on 30 September 1477. By the end of November, a Muscovite army and the Kasimov Tartar cavalry from Tver laid siege to Novgorod. Novgorod capitulated in December and swore an oath to their new *gosudar,* Ivan. He dissolved the *veche,* abolished the office of *posadnik* (mayor), annexed parts of Novgorod's territory, and subjected the rest to tribute.

In 1479, the boyars sought an alliance with Khan Ahmad of the Golden Horde. Simultaneously, Novgorod received support from Ivan's brothers, Prince Andrei of Uglich and Prince Boris of Volok, who were negotiating with Casimir. Ivan learned of these actions in October 1479 and, without declaring war, laid siege to Novgorod. He entered the city on 15 January 1480. One hundred boyars were executed, and many of the gentry were exiled to Suzdal. Archbishop Feofil, who had been elected archbishop by the *veche* at the death of his predecessor in 1470, was deposed. Ivan and his brothers were reconciled in October 1480.

Neville G. Panthaki

See also: Ivan III

References and further reading:

Alef, Gustave. *The Origins of Muscovite Autocracy: The Age of Ivan III.* Berlin: In Kommission bei Harrassowitz, 1986.

Fennell, John Lister Illingworth. *Ivan the Great of Moscow.* London: Macmillan, 1961.

Grey, Ian. *Ivan III and the Unification of Russia.* London: Pelican Books, 1973.

Vernadsky, George, and Michael Karpovich. *A History of Russia.* Vol. 4, *Russia at the Dawn of the Modern Age.* New Haven, CT: Yale University Press, 1968.

Atomic bomb mushroom cloud over Hiroshima, 1946. (Library of Congress)

Nuclear and Atomic Weapons

Weapons that use nuclear explosives. With the discovery of fission in early 1939 came the possibility of building a bomb having unprecedented destructive power. The great Danish physicist Niels Bohr announced the discovery of fission to the scientific community during a theoretical physics conference organized by Edward Teller and George Gamov at George Washington University. Alarmed by the prospect that Germany might be able to develop an atomic bomb, Albert Einstein, persuaded by Leo Szilard, Teller, and Eugene Wigner, sent a letter to President Franklin D. Roosevelt advising the president of such a possibility. Einstein's letter led, ultimately, to the creation of the Manhattan Project to construct nuclear bombs.

As World War II grew more deadly, two physicists—J. Robert Oppenheimer and Enrico Fermi—made significant contributions to the American atomic effort. In the summer of 1942, Oppenheimer convened a study conference in his offices at the Berkeley campus of the University of California to explore the theoretical basis for developing a fission weapon. Attended by many notable physicists, including Hans Bethe and Teller, the conferees concluded that a fission bomb was possible and that gun assembly of uranium or plutonium, the only two metals known to be fissionable, offered the best hope of success. Fermi, working at the University of Chicago, achieved the first self-sustaining nuclear chain reaction in December 1942. Because an atomic bomb is an uncontrolled self-sustaining chain reaction, Fermi's achievement, along with the theoretical knowledge developed during Oppenheimer's summer study, allowed the United States to pursue a full-scale nuclear weapon development program.

World War II research and development of the atomic bomb had two principal components. The first component was to produce enough plutonium and uranium to make one or more atomic bombs. Production of these materials was difficult, and by August 1945, barely enough of each was available to build a mere two nuclear bombs, termed Fat Man and Little Boy. The second component of the wartime atomic program was to design and build an atomic bomb. This job was assigned to the newly created Los Alamos weapons laboratory and its director, Oppenheimer.

Established formally in April 1943, Los Alamos had the single mission of designing and building a fission bomb for use in World War II. Based on the conclusions of the Berkeley summer conference, primarily that gun technology was both well understood and relatively simple, Oppenheimer organized most of the Los Alamos effort on developing gun assembly. Such a gun, essentially a naval cannon, would shoot one piece of uranium or plutonium at a second piece. When the two pieces of material came together, a supercritical mass would be formed, causing a nuclear detonation.

Experiments conducted in the spring of 1944 showed, however, that light element impurities in plutonium would cause a premature, low-order detonation in a gun assembly. Such a detonation would be, in nuclear terms, a fizzle. This discovery was disturbing, particularly since Oak Ridge was having problems producing significant quantities of uranium. Without a method of using plutonium, development of a combat atomic bomb could be delayed and might not be available for use in World War II. Recognizing that high explosives could be used to implode, or crush, a ball of plutonium, causing fission and a high-order nuclear explosion, Oppenheimer reorganized Los Alamos in August 1944, centering most of the laboratory's work on developing implosion. Doubts about implosion, an untried and radical departure from established knowledge, remained until the successful Trinity test in July 1945.

Little Boy, the gun gadget using uranium, exploded over Hiroshima with a force of approximately 16 kilotons on 6 August 1945. Fat Man, the implosion device using plutonium, exploded over Nagasaki with a force of 20 kilotons on August 9, 1945. The use of atomic bombs against Japan ended World War II and inaugurated the nuclear era.

As soon as World War II ended, the entire nation, including the Los Alamos laboratory, demobilized. Senior scientists at Los Alamos returned to their prewar university positions, and younger staff left to enter graduate school. As a result, nuclear weapons work languished, and the United Stated possessed only a handful of such weapons. However, some research did continue on improving fission bombs, particularly the implosion device. The two wartime weapons were laboratory devices that could not be easily reproduced if needed.

In the summer of 1946, two slightly improved Fat Man bombs were used in Operation CROSSROADS at Bikini Atoll in the Marshall Islands. These tests, one an airburst and the other an underwater detonation, were designed to see how well atomic bombs worked against naval vessels. The tests were not very dramatic in that only a dozen ships in all were sunk, although the newsreel footage was spectacular enough and has been used in countless "message" films since 1946. Because of wide international press coverage, the not-so-dramatic effects of CROSSROADS may have led the Soviet Union to believe that atomic bombs were not to be feared and probably encouraged Stalin to increase Soviet international belligerence.

By early 1947, the United States had made the decision to use atomic bombs as a key part of the U.S. defense posture. The weapons laboratories at Los Alamos, New Mexico, Oak Ridge, Tennessee, and Hanford, Washington, started to rebuild from their postwar demobilization. In addition, the military began planning new weapons systems, including an expanded role for atomic bombs. Los Alamos tested new designs of fission weapons that met the new military requirements in Operation SANDSTONE, conducted in 1948. These designs made possible significant increases in stockpile numbers and delivery capabilities. Los Alamos continued to make fission bomb improvements into the 1950s, primarily working to make such bombs smaller and more efficient.

Simultaneous with fission bomb development in the late 1940s, work continued and accelerated on hydrogen bomb development. First studied in 1942, the idea for a hydrogen bomb came from the thermonuclear study of stars conducted in the 1930s by Hans Bethe. Unlike fission weapons that derive their energy from splitting atoms of the heavy elements uranium and plutonium, hydrogen bombs derive their power from fusing atoms of the light element hydrogen, particularly the isotopes deuterium and tritium. Because fusion can only be achieved with stellar temperatures, hydrogen bombs were not possible until such a heat source became available. The improved fission bombs of the late 1940s offered the promise of near-stellar temperatures.

After years of study conducted primarily on computers and the discovery of radiation implosion, the first hydrogen bomb was detonated in October 1951. The success of the first thermonuclear test ushered in a new era in nuclear weaponry—significantly increased destructive power. Fission bombs explode with energy levels measured in thousands of tons of trinitrotoluene (TNT) equivalents. Fat Man, for instance, exploded with a force of 20,000 tons of TNT and destroyed most of the city of Nagasaki. The first hydrogen bomb, code-named Mike, exploded with a force of over 10 million tons of TNT and vaporized the entire island on which the device stood. Although civilization could survive a war fought with atomic weapons, such was not the case with thermonuclear weapons.

Just as fission weapons started with crude designs and were continually improved, so too were thermonuclear weapons. The first hydrogen bomb relied primarily on the use of liquid deuterium, a cryogenic material. Its size, three stories high and weighing more than a million pounds, made it a "bomb" only in the explosive sense; obviously it was not a deliverable weapon. From 1951 through 1956, hydrogen bomb research focused on using dry fuel. This change made it possible to reduce the size of thermonuclear bombs and made them deliverable by a wider range of aircraft, including smaller naval planes flying off aircraft carriers.

Beginning in the late 1950s, delivery systems such as ballistic missiles governed design changes in nuclear weapons. Both land- and submarine-based missiles began to take on primary importance in potential nuclear weapons delivery. Nuclear weapons had to be reduced in size dramatically in order to fit into the much smaller spaces of nose cones. Although nuclear weapons had always been constrained in size by the lift capacity of bombers, the constraints imposed by missiles were several orders of magnitude more difficult to meet. Miniaturization of weapons became a dominant theme in nuclear weapons development throughout the 1960s.

By the early 1970s, the number of new weapons designed and built began to decline. Increasing emphasis began to be placed on improving and upgrading weapons already in the stockpile, as well as enhancing safety. It became increasingly important to know that nuclear weapons would only detonate on command and not by accident. Weapon accidents at Palomares, Spain, and Thule, Greenland, underscored this need. Many of the underground nuclear tests in the 1980s and early 1990s conducted by the United States were safety tests of stockpiled weapons. With the current ban on nuclear weapons testing, other methods, primarily computer simulation, are being used in ensure the safety of the U.S. stockpile. This activity, called Science-Based Stockpile Stewardship, is of critical importance as the age of individual weapons increases. As the cessation of nuclear weapons testing continues, the safety and reliability of the stockpile will be the key weapons concern well into the twenty-first century.

Roger A. Meade

See also: Hiroshima and Nagasaki, Atomic Bombings of

References and further reading:

Hewlett, Richard G. *A History of the United States Atomic Energy Commission.* Berkeley: University of California Press, 1989–1990.

Hewlett, Richard G., and Oscar E. Anderson Jr. *Atomic Shield, 1947–1952.* Berkeley: University of California Press, 1990.

Nuremberg Principle

A doctrine of the international law of war holding individuals accountable for their own actions. On 8 August 1945, representatives from the United States, Great Britain, the Soviet Union, and the provisional government of France entered into the London Agreement, establishing the International Military Tribunal, which would try individuals in the Nazi German government and military who had been accused of war crimes. Twenty-four major leaders were indicted variously for crimes against peace, crimes against humanity, war crimes, and conspiracy to commit such crimes. Trials commenced on 18 October 1945.

The principle of individual responsibility for actions in war was established at these trials. There was no defense available to an individual who pled that his or her actions were made only under orders from a superior, although such a pleading might lead to a mitigation of sentence.

This principle was also applied at the International Military Tribunal for the Far East and in the ad hoc Tribunals for Yugoslavia and Rwanda and is a doctrine of the International Criminal Court contemplated by the Rome Treaty of 1998. It is also a principle of military training in NATO member-states and most other states.

Steve Sheppard

See also: General Order No. 100; Laws of War

References and further reading:

Taylor, Telford. *The Anatomy of the Nuremberg Trials: A Personal Memoir.* New York: Alfred A. Knopf, 1992.

Trial of the Major War Criminals before the International Military Tribunal: Nuremberg, 14 November 1945–1 October 1946. Nuremberg, Germany, Allied Military Government, 1947–1949.

Nurhaci (1559–1626)

Founder of the Manchu state. Much of the early life of Nurhaci is shrouded in legend, but his military career began in his early twenties. From his youth, Nurhaci had close contact with the Chinese Ming Dynasty (1368–1644), which bordered his homeland of Manchuria. Indeed, his father and grandfather, Taksi and Giocangga, respectively, were allies of the local Ming garrison. Both died under mysterious circumstances.

After an internecine struggle, Nurhaci successfully united the surrounding villages and tribes. Using marriage alliances and carefully planned military campaigns, Nurhaci increased his strength before embarking on a war against the Ming Dynasty. During this time, he continued to demonstrate the utmost respect for the Chinese dynasty. By 1607, many eastern Mongol tribes recognized him as khan. By 1613, all but one of the Jurched (Manchurian) tribes submitted to Nurhaci. The final tribe, the Yehe, was aided by the Ming in their resistance.

Nurhaci's armies consisted mainly of horse archers, as well as cannon made by Jesuit priests. His primary achievement in military science was the banner system. In this, he organized companies of men under four banners of yellow, white, red, and blue. Soon the number of banners increased to eight, but the new ones added a fringe to their standard. The new banners consisted of 7,500 men divided into five regiments consisting of five companies. The banners replaced the tribal structure and created an efficient fighting machine.

In 1616, Nurhaci declared the creation of the Qing state. In 1618, he invaded the Ming Empire. His armies annihilated all the armies that opposed him, including the recalcitrant Yehe tribe. From 1621 to his death in 1626, Nurhaci campaigned extensively in the modern Liaoning Province of China. His death did not end the conquests because the new dynasty of Manchurian ethnicity he founded went on to conquer an empire larger than modern China.

Timothy May

See also: Chinese Imperial Wars; Manchu Expansion, Wars of

References and further reading:

Barfield, Thomas J. *The Perilous Frontier: Nomadic Empires and China, 221 BC to AD 1757.* Cambridge, UK: Blackwell Publishers, 1992.

Crossley, Pamela Kyle. *The Manchus.* Cambridge, UK: Blackwell Publishers, 1997.

Spence, Jonathan D., and J. Wills, eds. *From Ming to Ch'ing: Conquest, Region and Continuity in Seventeenth-Century China.* New Haven, CT: Yale University Press, 1979.

O

October War (1973)

The fourth Arab-Israeli War, a doctrinal watershed providing world military powers with lessons on the latest techniques in armored and air warfare and the first Arab-Israeli clash since 1948 in which the issue was not in doubt after the first few hours. Six years after Israel had humiliated its Arab neighbors in the Six-Day War, Egypt and Syria launched simultaneous attacks from the west and the northeast on Israel.

Israeli intelligence failed to read accurately the incipient two-front attack of 6 October 1973 principally because they were convinced that the Arabs would not attempt to move forward without absolute air supremacy and could not mount a cooperative, two-front effort. Further, the Israelis believed that their air force had developed effective tactics to foil surface-to-air missile defenses (SAMs) following the War of Attrition in 1970. Nor did the Israeli Defense Forces (IDF) contemplate Arab willingness to settle for a *limited* objective under the protection of a static, tightly integrated, multilayered air defense shield. Finally, the Israelis did not anticipate the precision of the Egyptian attack plan, a well-rehearsed, scrupulously orchestrated, shallow mass assault on a broad front. Inconceivable as well, based on the lessons of 1967, was the very idea of Arab initiative and multifront coordination between allies. In short, the Israelis were complacent on the eve of a major assault.

The fact that the attack came on the holiest Jewish day of the year, when reservists were at prayer, perhaps added to the surprise but actually facilitated mobilization by leaving roads bereft of civilian traffic. Exceptional Egyptian ingenuity and the adaptation of Soviet doctrine and technology, combined with a successful deception plan, contributed to the proficient cross-canal assault. It began with a massive artillery preparation, which covered the opening stages of the assault. Once across, teams of sappers skillfully cut pathways through the Israeli sand ramparts and blew holes for bridging units as 70,000 infantry fanned out laterally from the crossing points to set up recoilless rifle and antitank missile ambushes. The Israeli Air Force's scramble to wipe out the widening bridgeheads was foiled by the deadly high-level SAMs umbrella covering radar-guided antiaircraft gun batteries and handheld infrared SAMs, the last directed at treetop-level attacks. Israeli reserve armor was sent forward as soon as each sub-unit mobilized—that is, piecemeal. The advance company–sized packets were badly mauled two days after landing as they blindly charged into infantry-manned antitank killing grounds.

Meanwhile, two corps-sized Egyptian armies crossed the canal and consolidated shallow bridgeheads along an 80-kilometer (50-mile) front. On the second day, the bulk of the IDF Air Force was redirected to the northern front to try to stem the Syrian advance, also begun on 6 October. Syria had committed about 75 percent of its total armor (800 tanks) to the attack, which sent four columns westward north of the Sea of Galilee. Preceded by heavy artillery fire, three mechanized infantry divisions (in no less than 2,800 armored personnel carriers) were followed by two armored divisions, ultimately 1,400 tanks, against less than 200 Israeli tanks that redeployed to specially prepared chokepoint ambushes with interlocking fields of fire. By this method, the Israeli armor was able to make the Syrians pay dearly for their initial breakthrough. An assault by Syrian heliborne infantry seized the fortified Israeli observation on the commanding heights of Mount Hermon.

Because the Syrian encroachment posed the most immediate threat to Israeli territorial integrity by crossing the narrow neck of northeastern Galilee to threaten Haifa, the IDF had quickly devoted attention to this front, even though the Egyptian deployment was more menacing. By the second day, Israeli reserves were arriving in Galilee in sufficient numbers (an entire division) to put their highly accurate long-range tank gunnery to good use. Israeli ground attack planes at first flew into the missile umbrellas, regardless of cost. However, they soon developed evasive tactics and were able to hit a fresh column of armor advancing along the southernmost axis by coming in at treetop level over Jordanian territory, stopping the column after it had progressed almost 29 kilometers (18 miles)—the Syrians' deepest penetration. The Syrians soon outran their lines of communication and then changed their formation to line abreast, whereupon Israeli air decimated them. In this way, the Israelis bought 36 vital hours. Without a follow-on echelon to extend its incursion and lacking the improvisational capacity to regroup and explore alternative lines of advance, the Syrians were driven back with hammer blows, mounting a stubborn fighting withdrawal toward Damascus and Sasa, clear off the Golan Heights, and back to their start line by 10 October. The next day, advancing Israeli tanks were able to turn to deal decisively with the Iraqi and Jordanian armored attacks on the southwestern flank of the northern front.

On 14 October, the Egyptians responded to desperate Syrian appeals by breaking out of their secure defensive laagers and mounting a major assault. Backed by uncontested air cover, the Israelis were able to neutralize the infantry antitank teams with artillery fire, while precise long-range tank fire picked off advancing Egyptian T-62 tanks before the latter could bring their turret guns to bear, disabling more than 250 of the Soviet-built vehicles.

The next day, exploiting a seam between the two Egyptian bridgeheads discovered during the early containment probes, the IDF activated a contingency plan to span the canal into Egypt proper. Using improvised bridging equipment, the Israelis advanced to the canal through the gap between the two Egyptian army sectors. The Egyptian Second Army, on the northern flank of the crossing, slowly recognized the threat and mounted a delayed concerted effort to pinch off the corridor (Battle of the Chinese Farm). This effort was repulsed by General Abraham (Bren) Adan's division, which then crossed the canal into the bridgehead held by General Ariel Sharon's division. As Adan passed through and turned toward the southwest, Sharon attempted to surge northward and seize Ismailia but was stopped cold. Consequently, Adan's southerly push toward Suez City established the Israeli main effort. The Egyptian Third Army—astride the canal—was encircled from its rear and faced strangulation. By this time international pressure, including a direct Soviet threat and a United States counterthreat, brought about a cease-fire, just as Adan was turned back from Suez City by tenacious Egyptian urban tactics. Israel broke several successive cease-fires, as its forces tried to enhance its negotiating position. Israel had managed to turn a near disaster into a muted victory, losing 3,000 soldiers in the effort. The losses were commensurate with those of the other belligerents but unacceptable by Israeli standards. On the grand strategic level, the winner appears to have been Egypt, which broke the diplomatic stalemate that had been underpinned by Israeli military superiority and secured eventual return of the Sinai and a "cold peace" with Israel five years later.

Jim Bloom

See also: Israeli-Arab Wars; Six-Day War; Sinai-Suez Offensive

References and Further Reading:

Adan, Avraham. *On the Banks of the Suez: An Israeli General's Personal Account of the Yom Kippur War.* San Rafael, CA: Presidio Press, 1980.

Bartov, Hannoch. *Dado: 48 Years and 20 Days.* Trans. Ina Friedman. Tel Aviv: Ma'ariv Book Guild, 1981.

Cordesman, Anthony H., and Abraham R. Wagner. *The Lessons of Modern War.* Vol. 1, *The Arab-Israeli Conflicts, 1973–1989.* Boulder, CO: Westview Press, 1990.

Dupuy, Trevor N. *Elusive Victory: The Arab-Israeli Wars, 1947–1974.* New York: Harper & Row, 1978.

El-Badri, Hassan, Taha El-Magdoub, and Mohammed Dia El-Din Zohdy. *The Ramadan War, 1973.* Dunn Loring, VA: T. N. Dupuy Associates, 1978.

El-Shazly, Saad. *The Crossing of the Suez.* San Francisco: American Mideast Research, 1980.

Gawrych, George W. *The Albatross of Decisive Victory: War and Policy between Egypt and Israel in the 1967 and 1973 Arab-Israeli Wars.* Westport, CT: Greenwood Press, 2000.

Oda, Nobunaga (1534–1582)

In the mid–sixteenth century, Nobunaga Oda was a minor daimyo who rose from obscurity to become one of the unifiers of Japan. Oda first came to prominence when Imagawa Yoshimoto attempted to seize Kyoto by passing through Oda's territory of Owari. Oda, with an army of 2,000, routed Yoshimoto's force of 20,000 men. Then in 1568, Oda proceeded to Kyoto, captured the city, and installed Ashikaga Yoshiaki as shogun.

Oda then attempted to conquer all of Japan. At the time, implacable enemies surrounded him. The first venture in his attempt to unify Japan led Oda to attack the Buddhist monastery of Hieizan in 1571 to counter its temporal influence. This action resulted in the deaths of hundreds of monks and the burning of the monastery.

After initial successes in 1573, Oda attacked the fortress of Ishiyama. At times, an army of 60,000 men surrounded it, but the fortress did not fall until 1580. In 1573, he also deposed his puppet shogun, Yoshiaki, thus effectively ending the Ashikaga shogunate.

Oda then turned to strengthening his own territories. Between 1576 and 1579, he built the castle of Azachi on the shores of Lake Biwa. It was the first Japanese fortress specifically built to withstand the effects of cannon fire. Then in 1577, his general, Toyotomi Hideyoshi, led the attack against the Mori. Oda's dreams of conquest ended abruptly, however, when one of his own generals, Akechi Mitsuhide, assassinated him while the two marched with Hideyoshi's reinforcements in 1582.

Oda's legacy laid the basis for the unification of Japan, as he had conquered a third of it. He also changed Japanese warfare by using massive armies rather than retainers. To support his conquests, he restructured the system of taxation and disarmed peasants to prevent uprisings.

Timothy May

See also: Hideyoshi, Toyotomi; Japanese Invasion of Korea; Japanese Wars of Unification; Samurai; Sekigahara; Tokugawa, Ieyasu

References and further reading:

Okuno, Takahiro. *Nobunaga to Hideyoshi.* Tokyo: Shibundo, 1966.

Weston, Mark. *Giants of Japan: The Lives of Japan's Greatest Men and Women.* New York: Kodansha International, 1999.

Offa's Wars (771–796)

Anglo-Saxon king and builder of Offa's Dyke. Offa, son of Thingfrith, was the ruler of Mercia (757–796). He is best remembered for the immense barrier that carries his name, built in 787, although its history has remained obscure. Its main purpose seems to have been the defense of Mercia from the Welsh.

During the 770s, Offa gradually extended his influence over the whole of England south of the Humber River. Mercia had no natural boundaries. It was open on all sides to hostile kingdoms. It was thus a continuous struggle for Mercian kings to keep it intact. The only way for them to create natural boundaries was to subdue all others to their authority.

In 771, the Mercians crossed the Thames River into Sussex and overcame the men of West Sussex. The move may have been planned to consolidate Offa's influence in Kent, the most settled and civilized kingdom in England. In 776, according to the *Anglo-Saxon Chronicle,* the Mercians and Kentishmen fought at Otford. The outcome is not recorded, but it is significant that Offa possessed little authority in Kent over the next ten years.

Whatever happened at Otford did not stop Offa. He launched another expedition in 778, this time deep into Wales. He devastated the land and seized plunder. The next year, Offa moved south to attack Cynewulf of Wessex. The two kings fought at Benson, a West Saxon royal village on the north bank of the Thames River. Offa carried the day. A large tract of what is now Berkshire was annexed. Offa, now the most powerful king in Britain, could with justification call himself a *Bretwalda* (Britain-ruler).

In the mid-880s, Offa aspired to be accepted as an equal by continental monarchs. If any single event contributed to his European perspective, it was Offa's taking direct control of Kent in 785, either due to internal dissension or by direct invasion. The following year, Offa made a pact with Pope Adrian I, who formally addressed him as the *Rex Anglorum* (king of England). In exchange, the pope increased his control over the English church while acceding to Offa's request for the creation of an archbishopric of Lichfield. Thereby he freed, albeit temporarily, the Mercian clergy from the authority of the archbishop of Canterbury. Archbishop Jaenberht of Canterbury, a Kentishman through and through, had always been Offa's staunch adversary.

Offa brought Anglo-Saxon southern England to its highest level of political unification. He ruled East Anglia, Kent, and Sussex and maintained superiority over Wessex and Northumbria. After his death, Mercian power gradually gave way before Wessex.

Nic Fields

See also: Æthelbald's Wars

References and further reading:

Fox, Cyril Fred. *Offa's Dyke.* London: British Academy, 1957.

Stenton, Frank Merry. *Anglo-Saxon England.* Oxford, UK: Clarendon Press, 1987.

Office of Strategic Services

The U.S. intelligence, intelligence-gathering, and psychological warfare coordinating agency during the last three years of World War II and the ancestor of today's Central Intelligence Agency (CIA). The need for such an organization began to be felt in Washington after Nazi victories in northern and western Europe in the spring and summer of 1940. On the advice of Secretary of the Navy Frank Knox, President Franklin D. Roosevelt dispatched World War I hero and prominent New York lawyer William J. "Wild Bill" Donovan to England to study Britain's intelligence establishment, especially the Special Operations Executive (SOE). Later Donovan also toured the Mediterranean. In the winter of 1940–1941, preparations began for the establishment of an agency to handle intelligence, counterintelligence, and psychological warfare. As a result, in July 1941 the Office of Coordinator of Information (COI) was established under Donovan's leadership. Because the COI did not fulfill its creators' expectations, a year later it was replaced by a more powerful organization, the Office of Strategic Services

(OSS), also under Donovan's directorship. He reported directly to FDR and received his funding from him.

The new agency quickly expanded its budget, staff, and scope of activities. It gathered strategic information, disseminated propaganda and disinformation, and engaged in espionage and sabotage in enemy-occupied territories. At the height of its activities, the OSS employed 12,000 individuals as staff and agents and relied on the services of a great many part-timers and volunteers. One of the OSS's most successful missions was in northern Burma, where its Detachment 101 led hill tribesmen against the Japanese occupiers and, by coordinating with the British Chindits and Merrill's Marauders in its guerrilla warfare, cleared the area of the enemy.

The OSS was disbanded in the fall of 1945. Roosevelt's successor, the militantly plebeian president Harry Truman, had no use for the society blue bloods that dominated the "Oh, So Social," and for nearly two years the United States had no coordinated intelligence-gathering or unconventional warfare capability. Some OSS functions and staff were absorbed by the State and War Departments. In 1947, the CIA was established to replace the OSS but without the earlier agency's psychological warfare mission.

N. F. Dreisziger

See also: Guerrilla/Partisan/Irregular Warfare; Special Operations Executive; World War II

References and further reading:

Roosevelt, Kermit, ed. *War Report of the OSS.* New York: Walker & Company, 1976.

———. *War Report of the OSS: The Overseas Targets.* New York: Walker & Company, 1977.

Smith, Bradley F. *The Shadow Warriors: O.S.S. and the Origins of the C.I.A.* New York: Basic Books, 1983.

Troy, Thomas F. *Donovan and the CIA: A History of the Establishment of the Central Intelligence Agency.* Frederick, MD: University Publications of America, 1981.

Ögödei (c. 1186–1241)

Second of four Mongolian khans ruling the empire established by Genghis Khan. Ögödei was probably not his father's first choice as successor but was elected khan with a reasonable majority in 1229. He was immediately faced with two major problems: an empty treasury and the need for continuing expansion to reward his followers. The first problem he dealt with through a more rational approach to the conquered territories, emphasizing revenues over expropriation. The second, Ögödei solved by initiating new campaigns in almost all directions, with efforts to complete the conquest of north China coming under his personal control and culminating in the fall of the last Jin capital in 1234. Even before this event, another, even greater campaign was being prepared.

Joci, the oldest son of Genghis Khan, had been assigned the most distant pastures controlled by his father, in the extreme west. After Joci's death in 1225, his son Batu had taken over these pastures and had further expanded them. With the accession of Ögödei, Batu received further increments of manpower and the promise of a major western campaign. Although Batu, seconded by various other Mongol princes representing all the major lines, was theoretically to be in command, the actual organizer of the advance was the veteran general Sabutai (1172–1245). The result was a masterpiece of the tactician's art: an advance first into the Turkic areas bordering Russian on the south; then into Russia itself (1237), which was brought under Mongolian control for centuries; and finally into eastern Europe, as far as Liegnitz in Silesia and the outskirts of Vienna (1241), using almost the same lines of advance as those employed by the Soviets in 1944–1945. Only the death of Ögödei, news of which reach the Mongols around Christmas 1241, halted this attack, probably saving Austria and Germany from disaster.

Paul D. Buell

See also: Genghis Khan; Kublai Khan; Mongol Empire

References and further reading:

Allsen, Thomas T. *Mongol Imperialism.* Berkeley: University of California Press, 1987.

Buell, Paul D. "Sübötei-ba'atur." In *In the Service of the Khan, Eminent Personalities of the Early Mongol-Yuan Period (1200–1300),* ed. Igor de Rachewiltz, Chan Hok-lam, Hsiao Ch'i-ch'ing, and Peter W. Geier. Wiesbaden: Otto Harrassowitz, 1993, 13–26.

———. "Chinqai (1169–1252): Architect of Mongolian Empire." In *Opuscula Altaica, Essays Presented in Honor of Henry Schwarz,* ed. Edward H. Kaplan and Donald W. Whisenhunt. Bellingham, WA: Center for East Asian Studies, 1994, 168–186.

Okinawa (1 April–21 June 1945)

World War II's last great battle. The large island of Okinawa was a part of metropolitan Japan and could provide a staging base for the projected invasion of the Japanese home islands. After ferocious naval and air bombardments, the first wave of U.S. Marines and army troops landed on 1 April to very light resistance. The Japanese, after losing on the beaches in their previous attempts to halt American island invasions, had devised the strategy of drawing their 500,000-man enemy to the rough terrain of the southern half of the island, where their 120,000-strong garrison would hold while kamikaze aircraft would pound the invasion warships. Meanwhile, the gigantic new battleship *Yamato* would beach itself and destroy what remained of the

A Marine of the 1st Marine Division draws a bead on a Japanese sniper during the Battle of Okinawa in 1945. (National Archives)

U.S. fleet. The Japanese commander, General Ushijima Mitsuru, understandably had his doubts about such a plan, but he faithfully followed his orders from Tokyo.

Okinawa's northern half was secured fairly early against scattered resistance, but then the invaders began to encounter stiff resistance from Japanese troops dug into a series of mutually supporting caves, ancient tombs, and ridge lines with interlocking forward and reverse slope defenses. The American offensive slowed drastically.

The Japanese then unleashed their counteroffensive. *Yamato* headed for Okinawa. On 7 April, it was sunk by U.S. naval warplanes, a loss that also spelled the end of Japan as a major naval power. But the kamikazes proved a far more effective weapon. In 1,900 one-way attacks, these manned projectiles killed more Americans than had been lost in all the United States' naval wars to date.

On the ground, the fighting had degenerated into a slogging match, transforming Okinawa's fields into a landscape reminiscent of World War I's western front, with gains measured in feet. Home critics began to criticize the way the fighting was going on the island. Fleet Admiral Chester Nimitz, Pacific fleet commander, took the unprecedented step of holding a press conference on Guam to defend his land commander, General Simon Bolivar Buckner. On 18 June, General Buckner was killed by Japanese artillery fire, the highest-ranking American to die by enemy action during World War II. Buckner was succeeded by General Roy S. Geiger (who thus became the only U.S. Marine officer to command an American field army).

By then, the Japanese were being steadily pushed back; they were finally also running out of aircraft and pilots for suicide missions. American troops and supplies flowed ashore in increasing numbers, tonnage, and safety. Three days after General Buckner's death, General Geiger was able to declare the island basically secured. General Ushijima and his staff had already committed ritual suicide, contemptuously rejecting a soldier-to-soldier demand for surrender from General Buckner.

The butcher's toll on Okinawa was grim: No less than 107,000 Japanese troops had been killed in battle and some 27,000 sealed in caves to die more slowly; only 7,400 prisoners were taken. U.S. Army forces suffered 7,613 dead and the Marines 3,561. The worst losses, however, were suffered by the civilians of Okinawa. Of a prewar population of 450,000, between 60,000 and 160,000 were lost; many were persuaded by Japanese soldiers to commit suicide. Okinawa was the

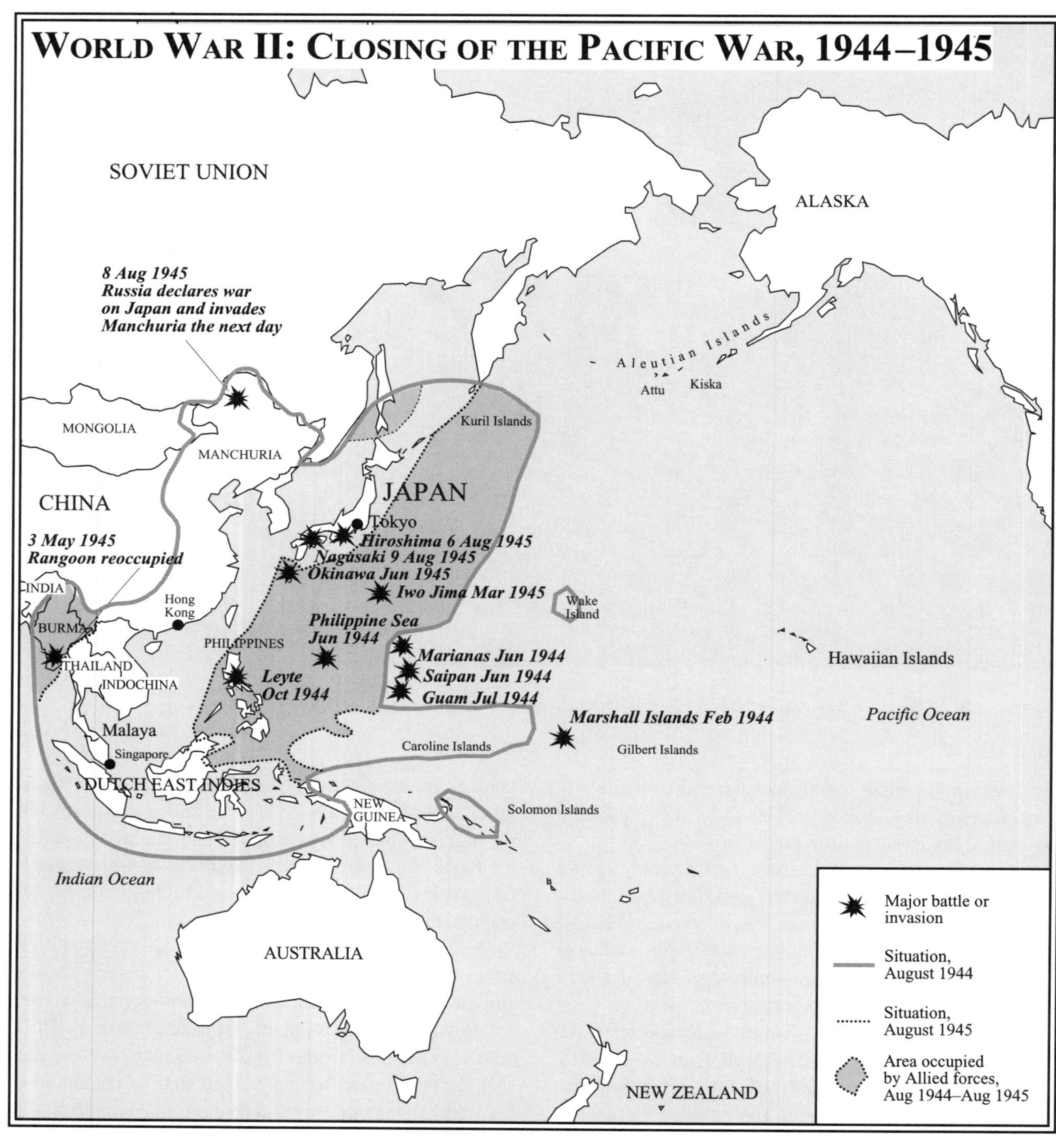

only battleground in the Pacific War in which large numbers of enemy civilians were encountered by the Americans. Yet Okinawa seemed to present a mere prelude to the greatest Pacific battle of all: the invasion of the Japanese home islands, a bloody scenario averted by the dropping of the world's first atomic bombs in warfare at Hiroshima and Nagasaki.

Stanley Sandler

See also: World War II

References and further reading:

Appleman, Roy E. *Okinawa: The Last Battle.* Washington, DC: U.S. Army Office of the Chief of Military History, 1948.

Feifer, George. *Tennozan: The Battle of Okinawa and the Atomic Bomb.* New York: Ticknor & Fields, 1992.

Gow, Ian (W. P. Willmott, consultant). *Okinawa, 1945: Gateway to Japan.* Garden City, NJ: Doubleday, 1985.

Omani Conquest of East Africa (1622–1730)

Conquest leading to the decline of Portuguese power on the Swahili coast. Asian traders (before 900) and Muslim traders (after 900) sailed across the Indian Ocean, linking the East African coast from the Horn of Africa to southern Mozambique and the adjacent islands in a network of seagoing commerce between Asia and East Africa. Ships and merchants from Arabia, Persia, and India participated in the trade in search of gold, ivory, tortoise shell, and other products. These exchanges led to the development of many coastal and island towns (Manda, Pemba, and Zanzibar; Pate, Lamu, Mombasa, and Vumbu in Kenya; and Kilwa in Tanzania) suffused with commercial activities and Islam, which became the nucleus of Swahili civilization (African and Muslim). Many traders and settlers from Oman and the Persian Gulf also intermarried with local women and settled down.

Vasco da Gama's trip around the Cape of Good Hope in 1497 and into the Indian Ocean brought the Portuguese to the East African coast. They attacked and occupied Kilwa in 1502, Zanzibar in 1503, Sofala and Kilwa in 1505, and Mozambique in 1507. By 1508, they had established control over the Swahili coast.

To break the Portuguese stranglehold, the people of Mombasa turned to the Omanis, who had already expelled the Portuguese from Muscat, their capital, in 1508. Utilizing the Mombasa appeal for help as the excuse, Omani sultan Ibn Saif sent a fleet that attacked the Portuguese settlements at Pate and Zanzibar. In 1696, Ibn Saif sailed to Mombasa with more than 3,000 men and, in 1698, took Fort Jesus.

The Omanis had imperialist designs, however; after freeing Mombasa from the Portuguese, they imposed their rule over the Swahili states, garrisoned Pemba, Kilwa, and other cities, and set governors (*walis*) over them. Limited rebellion and Swahili refusal to pay taxes between 1710 and 1740 led to political upheaval on the East African coast. In 1724, Kilwa broke away from Omani rule with the support of Europeans in Mozambique. By 1745, Pate, Malindi, Pemba, Zanzibar, and Mafia had all revolted against Omani overlordship.

Recognizing that only by closer attention to the coast would Omani control be effective, the Omanis made Zanzibar the focal point of their East African empire. Beginning with Sayyid Said, who came to power in Muscat in 1806, the Omanis strengthened their garrisons in East Africa and gradually asserted military and commercial control along the East African seaboard. Thus, the Omanis came to dominate Zanzibar and parts of the East African coast. They then replaced the Portuguese as the imperial power and monopolized Indian Ocean–Swahili trade. Omani overlordship reached its climax in 1840, when Sayyid Said transferred his political headquarters from Muscat to Zanzibar.

Edmund Abaka

References and further reading:

July, Robert. *A History of the African People.* Prospect Heights, IL: Waveland Press, 1998.

Woodfork, Jacqueline. "The Omani Empire." In *Africa.* Vol. 1, *African History before 1885,* ed. Toyin Falola. Durham, NC: Carolina Academic Press, 2000.

Omdurman (1898)

Anglo-Egyptian victory that effectively destroyed the Mahdist state, one of the most one-sided victories in modern military history, and the last large-scale cavalry charge by a major military power. The Mahdist army, which had taken Khartoum and killed General Charles "Chinese" Gordon in 1885 under Muhammad Ahmad (a.k.a. al-Mahdi), had warded off British attempts to reassert control over the region. In 1896, the British government, propelled by public opinion and concerns over French and Italian ambitions in the Sudan, prevailed upon the Egyptian government to launch an offensive toward Khartoum. Led by Horatio Herbert Kitchener, sirdar of the Egyptian Army, a mixed British and Egyptian force moved south. Using Nile gunboats and building a railroad to keep the army supplied, the 26,000-man force took all of two years to reach Khartoum.

The Mahdist army, now under the command of al-Mahdi's successor, Khalifa Abdullah al-Taashi, launched a number of strikes against Kitchener but was driven back each time. By late summer, the Anglo-Egyptian army was within a few miles of Khartoum. There, at Omdurman, the Khalifa launched a substantial assault on the morning of 2 September. The initial attacks focused on Kitchener's fortified camp along the Nile and the cavalry units protecting its right flank. Against well-protected Anglo-Egyptian troops armed with Maxim guns, the assaults made little headway. By noon, an Anglo-Egyptian counterattack had driven the Mahdist army from the field in more of a slaughter than a battle.

The Mahdists suffered more than 10,000 killed in a few hours of fighting. The Anglo-Egyptians lost 48. Omdurman effectively destroyed Mahdist power in the Sudan. The Khalifa, who was captured a year later, lost his capital city and many of his best commanders.

Kitchener, now a national hero, turned his attention to the French expedition encamped at Fashoda. After a brief standoff, the French withdrew in late September, securing British influence in the region.

Adam Seipp

See also: Churchill, Sir Winston; Gordon, Charles George; Kitchener, Horatio Herbert; Muhammad Ahmad

References and further reading:
Cassar, George. *Kitchener: Architect of Victory.* London: William Kimber, 1977.
Neillands, Robin. *The Dervish Wars: Gordon and Kitchener in the Sudan, 1880–1898.* London: John Murray, 1996.
Pollock, John. *Kitchener: The Road to Omdurman.* London: Constable, 1998.

Onin War (1467–1477)

Intensified period of civil war during the Onin era (1467–1469) that began in a succession dispute. The struggle soon engulfed the Ashikaga capital of Kyoto and led to its almost complete destruction before the war ended 10 years later. The period is also aptly known as "the epoch of a warring country."

When the eighth Ashikaga shogun, Yoshimasa (1435–1490), more interested in pleasure and the arts than in politics, announced his plans to retire at the tender age of 30, an effort ensued to find a successor to the heirless shogun. Hosukawa Katsumoto (1430–1473), a member of one of the most influential families supporting the shogun and the *kanrei* (the highest civil official in the shogunate, comparable to a prime minister), recommended Yoshimasa's brother Yoshimi, then living as a monk. Not long after Yoshimi's reluctant arrival in Kyoto to prepare for his duties, Yoshimasa's wife unexpectedly gave birth to a son and heir, Yoshihisa. The chief rivals of the Hosukawa, the Yamana clan, saw their opportunity and sided with Yoshimasa's wife, who wished to see her newborn son succeed. Only the weakness of the Ashikaga allowed this minor crisis to erupt into open war, which it soon did.

In 1467, the forces of the Yamana and Hosukawa houses came to blows in Kyoto. The decade of street warfare in Kyoto that followed was intermittent but still destructive. The once proud city and cultural center of Japan was reduced in size and population by more than half, and its culturally rich cityscape was utterly decimated.

In the end, the dispute settled nothing, and when the two original disputants, the respective heads of the Yamana and Hosukawa families, both died, the war came to an end. The decade did decisively weaken the Ashikaga shogunate, which became a powerless bystander to extended warfare that spread out into the countryside from Kyoto.

Daniel Kane

See also: Japanese Civil Wars; Samurai

References and further reading:
Berry, Mary Elizabeth. *The Culture of Civil War in Kyoto.* Berkeley: University of California Press, 1994.
Varley, H. Paul. *The Onin War.* New York: Columbia University Press, 1967.

Orleans, Siege of (12 October 1428–8 May 1429)

Most famous siege of the Hundred Years' War. During the later years of the Hundred Years' War, France responded to English tactical superiority on the battlefield (Cravant in 1423, Verneuil in 1424) by making use of positional warfare, forcing its enemy to engage in costly sieges.

In the summer of 1428, English regent John, Duke of Bedford, decided to invade southern France and its kingdom of "Bourges." The key bridgehead was Orleans, located 90 miles south of Paris on the Loire River. The campaign was intended as training for taking many small towns downstream and upstream of Orleans. Because of the need to deploy garrisons in many captured towns, English and Burgundian forces under the earl of Salisbury are estimated to have numbered no more than 4,000.

The people of Orleans, before being surrounded behind their walls, burned the suburbs to deny the English food or any comfort. The town militiamen were assigned to defend the 34 towers of the city wall, and the professional soldiers (first 500 and then 6,000), under Jean le Batard d'Orleans, better known as Dunois, were to make sallies. Before being killed by a cannonball (26 October 1428), Salisbury gave orders to isolate the city by a line of redoubts, or bastilles, on the western side. These strongholds were to be linked by ditches and earthworks manned by artillery. The northern side facing a forest was not covered by the English, which gave the besieged troops the opportunity to keep in touch with the Dauphin Charles's relief army.

The southern side of the Loire River was occupied by the English, and the fortification called "les Tourelles," protecting the bridge on the Loire River, was taken. The town was to be reduced by famine rather than by assault. But by April 1429, the Burgundians allies had quit the siege, leaving the English, who were too few to surround the city effectively.

The dauphin's army marched from Blois to relieve Orleans. Within its ranks was "the Maid," Joan of Arc, who had recently convinced Charles that he would soon be crowned King of France. Joan decided to move on ahead of the main French force and entered Orleans on 27 April to raise the spirits of the defenders.

Exploiting the weakness of the English forces, French troops (with Joan) sallied out on 4 May to seize the bastille on the eastern side. Two days later, they crossed the river to secure the southern bank. On 7 May, Joan attacked les Tourelles. The surrender of its English defenders persuaded Lord Salisbury to abandon the siege on 8 May. Joan of Arc cleared the way for Charles's coronation.

Gilles Boué

See also: Hundred Years' War; Joan of Arc

References and further reading:

Blanchard, Anne, ed. *Histoire militaire de la France.* 4 vols. Paris: PUF, 1992–1994.

Bradbury, Jim. *The Medieval Siege.* Woodbridge, Suffolk, UK: Boydell Press, 1997.

Corfis, Ivy A., and Michael Wolfe, eds. *Medieval City under Siege.* Woodbridge, Suffolk, UK: Boydell Press, 1995.

Osaka Castle, Siege of (1614–1615)

The final act of resistance by samurai on the losing side at the Battle of Sekigahara (1600). Ieyasu's Tokugawa assumption of hegemonic power in 1598, on the death of Toyotomi Hideyoshi, was opposed by forces led by Ishida Mitsunari (1560–1600). They backed Hideyoshi's chosen successor, his infant son Hideyori.

Tokugawa's victory at Sekigahara confirmed his mastery of Japan and his status as successor to the great project of Japanese unification begun by Nobunaga Oda and continued by Hideyoshi. After Sekigahara, the estates of the losers were largely curtailed, but the house of Hideyoshi was allowed to retain three provinces centered on Osaka Castle. Tokugawa, a ruthless strategist, would no doubt have preferred the complete elimination of Hideyoshi's family, including Hideyori, a potential opposition rallying point, but a narrow victory at Sekigahara and a still unconsolidated position initially precluded such a move.

Tokugawa bided his time while winning over many former Hideyoshi supporters. In 1614, he finally made his move. No daimyo came to Hideyori's defense, although almost 100,000 *ronin,* or masterless samurai, did. These *ronin* were the real losers at Sekigahara. They had been left destitute and desperate by the defeat of their lords.

Tokugawa's first assault against Osaka Castle, in the winter of 1614, was a costly failure, with over 35,000 casualties. Reverting to wile, Tokugawa offered an armistice to the Hideyori forces barricaded and besieged within their castle, provided that they allowed Tokugawa's men to fill in the castle's outer moat. When this was agreed to, Tokugawa instead filled in both the inner and the outer moat of the fortress. By the time that Hideyori's army realized what was happening, it was already too late. Tokugawa's forces overran the fortress on 3 June 1615. The destruction of the castle and the annihilation of Hideyori and his supporters, followed by the confiscation of the Hideyoshi estates, removed the final barrier to complete Tokugawa dominance in Japan.

Daniel Kane

See also: Hideyoshi, Toyotomi; Japanese Wars of Unification; Nagashino, Battle of; Samurai: Sekigahara; Tokugawa, Ieyasu

References and further reading:

Sadler, A. L. *The Maker of Modern Japan: The Life of Tokugawa Ieyasu.* Tokyo: Charles E. Tuttle, 1937.

Osan, Battle of (5 July 1950)

The opening ground clash between the invading North Korean forces and U.S. troops. In the days immediately following the North Korean attack in late June 1950, General Douglas MacArthur sought to delay the onslaught and buy time until U.S. units could arrive in strength to stiffen the South Korean defense and repel the invaders. MacArthur ordered elements of the U.S. 24th Division—two rifle companies, an artillery battery, and a few other supporting units—all lightly and inadequately armed—to Osan, south of the capital, Seoul, on the west side of the peninsula, by 5 July. MacArthur referred to this 540-man force—called Task Force Smith after its commander, Lieutenant Colonel C. B. Smith—as "an arrogant display of force."

The [North] Korean People's Army (KPA), 4th Korean Division, with its 33 Soviet T-34 tanks, struck Task Force Smith around 8 A.M. on 5 July. It suffered slight losses; the Americans did not have the numbers of men and equipment or the appropriate position to resist well, and the North Korean infantry flowed around them and turned their flanks. Two (and possibly three) KPA tanks were destroyed, however. The men of Task Force Smith had two choices—be captured or retreat—and thus retreated to the south.

Over the next several weeks, the 24th Division continued to seek to slow the North Korean advance, while the North Koreans—with greater numbers, tanks, and artillery—would seek to find them, fix them, and turn their flanks to crush them. The result was a steady American retreat down the west side of the Korean peninsula and a serious morale deflator for U.S. armed forces. However, the brief battle at Osan and others like it did create the breathing space to establish the perimeter at Pusan.

Charles M. Dobbs

See also: Korean War; MacArthur, Douglas

References and further reading:
Appleman, Roy E. *South to the Naktong, North to the Yalu, United States Army in the Korean War.* Washington, DC: Office of the Chief of Military History, 1961.
Sandler, Stanley. *The Korean War: No Victors, No Vanquished.* London: Routledge; Lexington: University of Kentucky, 1999.
Schnabel, James F. *U.S. Army in the Korean War: Policy and Direction: The First Year.* Washington, DC: U.S. Military Office of Chief of Military History, 1972.

Ostende, Siege of (1601–1604)

An epic siege that captured the attention of Europe. Habsburg forces commanded by Ambrogio Spinola labored to take the city, which was surrounded by water and reputed to be one of the strongest fortifications in Europe, from the Dutch Republic. An Italian skilled in siege warfare, Spinola employed the leading military engineers in Europe gradually to reduce the city one bulwark at a time. During the siege, Spinola showcased how far the fine art of military engineering had developed in the Habsburg forces, employing a wide range of innovative devices.

The Dutch and their English allies used their control of the sea to constantly replace the losses of the garrison. Maurice of Nassau, the general of the Dutch field army, had been repulsed in his attempt on the Flemish coast at Nieuport in 1600 and declined to attempt a relief operation, considering the isolated outpost to be hardly worth the cost of defending it. He instead used the distraction to make extensive gains further inland along the Maas and Rhine Rivers while the Spanish were fixated on Ostende.

The siege became an ongoing battle of attrition and a trial of wills, with the Dutch eventually recording losses of more than 30,000 people in the siege and nearly twice that many Habsburg troops dying in the assaults or from exposure and the diseases that ran unchecked through the trenches. Altogether, the city held out for three years and 77 days, surrendering in September 1604 only after every one of the outer bulwarks had been lost and the harbor closed by Spanish batteries. By taking the city, Spinola had solidified Habsburg control of the Flemish coast, but it was at best a Pyrrhic victory.

John S. Nolan

See also: Anglo-Spanish War; Nieuport, Battle of

References and further reading:
Arnold, Thomas. *The Renaissance at War.* London: Cassell, 2001.
Oman, Charles. *The Art of War in the XVIth Century.* London: Methuen, 1937.
Parker, Geoffrey. *The Dutch Revolt.* London: Penguin, 1979.

Ostrogoths

The Ostrogoths (Eastern Goths) were a Germanic tribe first organized into an empire of sorts in the third century in the region extending north from the Black to the Baltic Seas. They first grew to prominence under Ermaneric (fl. 350–376) just before being invaded by the Huns. The Ostrogoths, as vassals of the Huns, were moved westward into Dacia during the early fifth century. After Attila the Hun died in 453, the Ostrogoths asserted their independence and followed other Germanic groups by invading the disintegrating Roman Empire, first under Theodemir and then under Theoderic. The Ostrogoths received territory in Dacia and Lower Moesia from the eastern emperor, Zeno, in 483, but they continued to raid Thrace and threaten Constantinople. In 488, Theoderic, convinced by Zeno, invaded Italy, which was ruled by the Germanic barbarian Odovacar. After three years of campaigning, Theoderic and his Ostrogoths defeated Odovacar and conquered the Italian peninsula.

Theoderic strengthened alliances by marrying off two of his daughters and his two sisters to other Germanic kings. He supported the Alemanni against the Frankish king, Clovis, and took on the remnants of the Visigoths in France and Spain. At the height of his reign, Theoderic controlled Italy, Sicily, Provence, Rhaetia, and lands south and west of the Upper and Middle Danube River, and as regent for his grandson, Amalaric of the Visigoths, he had influence in Spain. In 535, nine years after Theoderic's death, the Ostrogothic king Totila successfully fended off Belisarius, the commander under the eastern emperor Justinian, who wanted to reunite the old Roman Empire. In 552, Totila was ultimately defeated by another of Justinian's commanders, Narses, and the power of the Ostrogoths that had built up over the previous two centuries came to an end.

Christopher P. Goedert

See also: Goths; Huns; Justinian I; Visigoths

References and further reading:
Burns, Thomas. *A History of the Ostro-Goths.* Bloomington: Indiana University Press, 1984.
Heather, Peter. *Goths and Romans, 332–489.* Oxford: Clarendon Press, 1991.
Goffart, Walter. *Barbarians and Romans, A.D. 418–584: The Techniques of Accommodation.* Princeton: Princeton University Press, 1980.

Otto I, the "Great" (912–973)

Real founder of the medieval German kingdom. Otto I is the only medieval German ruler to be called "the Great."

In Otto's time, Germany was made up of five largely independent duchies: Saxony, Franconia, Swabia, Bavaria, and

Lorraine. Otto took over Franconia and ruled Saxony by inheritance, putting down other ducal rebellions and consolidating control in Germany. He also made his brother Bruno archbishop of Cologne, a bastard son archbishop of Mainz, and another close relative archbishop of Trier, thus giving Otto control over the Catholic Church in Germany.

Rebellions by Otto's brother Henry and by Duke Eberhard of Franconia were ended by the Battle of Andernach in 939. This victory ensured German control over Lorraine. The following year, Otto campaigned deep into France. In 950, he campaigned against the Slavic Wends and gained suzerainty over Bohemia.

In 955, Otto won his most famous and important victory, defeating the Magyars (Hungarians) at Lechfeld, near Augsburg. After the battle, the Magyars ceased raiding into Germany and established an organized polity in what is now Hungary.

Otto was crowned emperor by the pope in 962. Hereafter, the papacy was fatefully linked with the German kingdom, and the German kings increasingly came to meddle in Italian affairs. It is thought that Otto's threatening posture toward pagan Poland probably led to Prince Mieszko's decision to convert Poland to Christianity in 966.

Michael C. Paul

See also: Holy Roman Empire; Lechfeld

References and further reading:

Barraclough, Geoffrey. *The Origins of Modern Germany.* New York: W. W. Norton, 1984.

Ottoman Empire (1300s–1922)

The Turkish ruler Osman founded the Ottoman state in 1299, utilizing the military capabilities of his people to consolidate control over Arab lands. Known for their endurance, discipline, mobility, warrior spirit, and equestrian skill, the Turks relied on equestrian archers to win their battles. In 1326, Sultan Orkhan organized the military into three principal contingents. The feudal armed forces received fiefs in exchange for military service and the provision of soldiers, but the land reverted back to the sultan if the recipient failed to fulfill his military duties or committed a crime. Janissaries, recruited Christian youths trained in the ways of Islam, served as the standing infantry. Organized by Murad II in the fourteenth century, these troops served as escorts, security guards, and defenders of the city gates during times of peace. Auxiliary troops consisting of scouts, armed nomads, and defenders of outlying fortresses rounded out the military structure.

After establishing administrative control over Anatolia, the Ottomans invaded Europe many times during the next 500 years. In 1354, the Gallipoli peninsula fell under their control. Under Murad I (1359–1389) their light cavalry moved further into the continent. With internal strife dividing the Christians, European leaders failed to prevent further expansion. By 1400, the Ottomans had defeated the Serbs and their allies at Kosovo and, at Nicopolis, the Macedonians, the Bulgarians, and the Hungarian king Sigismund, leader of the anti-Ottoman crusade organized by Pope Boniface IV. The Ottoman troops were poised for a strike at Hungary when Tamerlane's Mongol forces captured the sultan and defeated his men at Ankara in 1402. The Venetians and the Byzantines briefly recaptured Gallipoli and Salonika, respectively, but after Mehmed I emerged as the successor in 1413, Ottoman troops once again controlled these areas. His successor, Murad II, continued the expansionist military policies, defeating the Albanians, Greeks, and Romanians as well as another crusading army organized by Pope Eugene IV in 1444. Although the Ottomans had achieved many victories and expanded their territory considerably during the fourteenth and early fifteenth centuries, the beginning of the empire period dates from the reign of Mehmed II in 1451. After expanding and improving the army and establishing a navy, Mehmed conquered the Balkans and pushed into central Europe, the Ukraine, the Caucasus region, Arabia, and North Africa. After capturing Athens, Bosnia, and Herzegovina, the new sultan won a decisive victory against the Venetians at Lepanto. Then the Ottomans turned their attention back to the east to deal with the Persian challenge. The Persians, under the Safavids, and the Ottomans waged a series of wars until the eighteenth century, when they agreed on their borders.

With the Persians checking their advance in the east, the Ottomans shifted their expansionist efforts back to the west. Selim the Grim, a great warrior, conquered Syria and Egypt, leaving his son and successor, Süleyman the Magnificent, with a full treasury and an experienced army. In 1521, Süleyman captured Belgrade and then waged a campaign against the Hungarians and the Austrians. The Hungarian defeat at Mohács led to the division of the country, with half falling under Ottoman control and the rest controlled by Austria. After forming an alliance with the French king, Francis I, against Emperor Charles V, Süleyman resumed the war against the Austrians while intermittently halting the campaigns to fight the Persians. By 1562, peace treaties had been signed with both Persia and Austria. After experiencing two major naval defeats in the Mediterranean, Süleyman once again led his army against Austria. Before he could wage war against the forces of Maximilian II, who had refused to pay tribute, Süleyman died. The sultanate passed to his son Selim II, known as "the Sot," and the military strength of the Ottoman began a rapid decline.

In 1683, the Ottoman forces experienced a crushing defeat at the hand of the Viennese. Recognizing the superiority of European arms after the introduction of gunpowder, the Ottomans attempted to reform their military. Relying on Prussian advisers to train their troops, the Ottomans fell under their influence. When World War I broke out, Turkey, after initial hesitation, allied with the Central Powers and paid the price after the defeat of Germany, when the Allies dictated armistice terms to the Ottomans. Several political factions battled over the future of the country, and finally in 1922, Mustafa Kemal abolished the sultanate, drove Greek forces out of Turkey, and officially ended the Ottoman Empire.

Cynthia Clark Northrup

See also: Austro-Turk Wars; Hungarian Civil Wars; Mohács, Battles of; Rhodes, Sieges of; Vienna, Sieges of

References and further reading:

Peers, Douglas M., ed. *Warfare and Empires: Contact and Conflict between European and Non-European Military and Maritime Forces and Cultures.* Brookfield, VT: Variorum, 1997.

Trumpener, Ulrich. *Germany and the Ottoman Empire, 1914–1918.* Princeton, NJ: Princeton University Press, 1968.

Wittek, Paul. *The Rise of the Ottoman Empire.* New York: B. Franklin, 1971.

Oudenaarde, Battle of (11 July 1708)

The perfect illustration of the difficulties of double command. In 1708, John Churchill, Duke of Marlborough, wanted to raise the morale of his Dutch allies by winning a battle in Flanders. His main objective was to retake all the territories lost the two previous years. On the French side, the king had sent his grandson, the Duc de Bourgogne, to command the field army with the Marechal de Vendôme on a secondary front. Eugene of Savoy's army was far away, and Marlborough's troops were deployed all over northern Flanders, with Brussels as headquarters. On 16 May, the French army advanced toward Brussels, its superior number pushing away Marlborough's troops. Then Bourgogne stopped waiting for orders from Versailles, 200 miles away. A very religious man, Bourgogne was also very cautious and was always at variance with Vendôme's orders. On the other side, Marlborough asked Prince Eugene to join his army as soon as possible to coordinate an aggressive defense.

At the beginning of July, a sycophantic noble follower of Bourgogne suggested an attack toward Bruges and Ghent. The two towns were easily taken, and the royal army decided to encircle Oudenaarde on the River Scheldt. But Marlborough had discerned this move and sent his army to cross the river before the French arrived.

On 11 July, the French general Biron discovered the waiting allied troops and asked for orders. Vendôme refused to believe Biron and left his army without deployment orders until it was too late. Marlborough, urging his troops on, arrived at noon and deployed on a line of low hills north of Oudenaarde. His lines were protected by meadows and hedges. By 3 P.M., Bourgogne gave the order to the marching French to assault the waiting English lines. The attack began on the French right, soon supported by the center. All this uncoordinated movement gave predictable results, as all the columns were repulsed. The French left, under Vendôme, remained useless.

Eventually, with Eugene's army facing Vendôme, Marlborough took the initiative. Following the retiring French right, he managed to encircle them, forcing thousands to surrender. The French rout sent them back to Bruges. Marlborough's victory restored allied morale. The French had lost more than 15,000 soldiers and were no longer able to protect their northern border. France lay open to an invasion.

Gilles Boué

See also: Marlborough, John Churchill, First Duke of; Spanish Succession, War of the

References and further reading:

Belloc, H. *The Tactics and Strategy of the Great Duke of Marlborough.* London: Arrowsmith, 1933.

Bluche, François. *Dictionnaire du Grand Siècle.* Paris: Fayard, 1990.

Oudinot, Nicholas-Charles, Duc de Reggio (1767–1847)

Military commander during the Revolutionary and Napoleonic Wars of France. Nicholas-Charles Oudinot was born on 25 April 1767 at Bar-le-Duc, France. He enlisted in the Royal Army in 1784 and served until just before the outbreak of the French Revolution. The revolution provided opportunities for men of humble origins, like Oudinot, with military experience and even command, and he was one of the many beneficiaries.

In 1789, Oudinot was appointed captain and rose to the rank of lieutenant colonel by 1791. Between 1792 and 1796, he campaigned with the Army of the Rhine, rising to the rank of *general de brigade* by June 1795. Frequently wounded and once captured, he was promoted to *general de division* in 1799 and made chief of staff of the Army of Switzerland in that year.

During the second Italian campaign, Oudinot served under André Masséna and so took part in the defense of

Genoa. In August 1800, he was appointed chief of staff of the Army of Italy and participated in G. M. A. Brune's campaign of 1800–1801 that led to the capture of Verona.

In February 1805, Oudinot was appointed to command the Reserve Grenadier Division, which ultimately became the 1st Division of Jean Lannes's corps during the campaign against Austria. Though the grenadiers distinguished themselves at Austerlitz, Oudinot was wounded early in the campaign and did not receive another command until 1807, when he served under the command of François-Joseph LeFebvre, Duke of Danzig, at the siege of Danzig, and again under Jean Lannes, Duke of Montebello, at Friedland.

In July 1808, Oudinot was created a count of the empire and in April 1809, duke of Reggio. He was elevated to the rank of marshal of the empire in July 1809. After receiving command of the Second Corps in 1812, he distinguished himself at Polotsk and at the Berezina crossing during the disastrous retreat from Moscow.

In the 1813 campaign, Oudinot was given command of the XII Corps and fought at Bautzen. After the conclusion of the armistice, the XII, together with the IV and VII Corps, were detached from the Grand Armeé, and the whole force, under the command of Oudinot, was directed to march on Berlin. Oudinot was promptly defeated by a mixed force of Prussians, Russians, and Swedes under the command of the crown prince of Sweden, Jean Bernadotte. Oudinot was replaced in command of the Army of Berlin by Michel Ney, who was in turn defeated by Bernadotte at the Battle of Dennewitz. Oudinot commanded the remnants of his corps at Leipzig and in 1814 fought at Brienne, La Rothiere, and Arcis-sur-Aube.

After the Bourbon Restoration, Oudinot was appointed commander of the Metz area and made a peer of France. During the Hundred Days, he was not employed by Napoleon and so was able to continue his career after the Second Restoration. He commanded a corps during the Spanish campaign in 1823 and became governor of Madrid. In 1842, he became governor of the Invalides. He died on 13 September 1847. Overall, Oudinot was a failure as an independent army commander but was a capable corps commander and administrator.

J. Isenberg

See also: Austerlitz, Battle of; Berezina River, Battle of; Borodino; Dresden, Battle of; French Revolutionary Wars; Friedland; Lannes, Jean, Duke of Montebello; Leipzig, Battle of; Masséna, André, Duc de Rivoli, Prince d'Essling; Moscow, Retreat from; Napoleon I; Napoleonic Wars

References and further reading:

Chandler, David G. *Napoleon's Marshals.* London: Weidenfeld and Nicholson, 1987.

Young, Peter. *Napoleon's Marshals.* Reading, Berkshire, UK: Osprey, 1973.

P

Pachacutec Yupanqui (r. 1438–1471)

Sapa Inca (first ruler) responsible for the growth and development of the Inca Empire. Although Spanish and native sources differ on specifics, Pachacutec Yupanqui clearly took the early reforms and successes of his father, Viracocha, and transformed the Inca from one of several ethnic chiefdoms in highland Peru to a huge empire controlling much of the coast and highlands of western South America.

In 1438, at around 16 years of age, Yupanqui took control of the defense of the Inca capital Cuzco from his ailing father. He defeated the 30,000-man Chanca army by using allied troops in surprise flanking movements at key moments in the battle. After this victory, he was crowned Pachacutec Yupanqui, Sapa Inca, and ruled for 33 years. He would conquer the highland kingdoms of Lupaca and Cajamarca, form alliances with the Quechua and Charca, conquer the coastal states of the Ica and Nazca, and eventually oversee the conquest of the powerful coastal Chimu state by 1471. His development of cycling in fresh troops to threatening realms was crucial to his success.

Pachacutec developed a permanent military system and grand strategy for the empire in carrying out this expansion. The military system consisted of ethnic Inca nobility trained in the arts of war and leadership at schools in Cuzco. Other ethnic Inca were trained at military-style schools and formed the core of Inca armies. He used alliances to provide the bulk of troops from loyal provinces, utilizing their alternative weapon and fighting systems to complement the Inca core. Fortifications like Sacsahuaman in Cuzco were used to protect road systems and supply depots, and the llama was the pack animal for the expeditions.

Pachacutec's grand strategy consisted of overwhelming logistics, defense-in-depth fortifications, and a variety of alliance offers, made both peacefully and forcefully to acquire new territory. He successfully incorporated many peoples by moving around loyal subjects to rebellious areas and vice versa. His use of the *mitmae* (labor tax) allowed for one of the most rapid developments of an empire infrastructure in world history.

Christopher Howell

See also: Chan Chan, Battle of; Cuzco, Battles of; Inca Empire Imperial Wars

References and further reading:

Adorno, Rolena. *Guaman Poma Del Ayala.* New York: Americas Society, 1992.

D'Altroy, Terrence, ed. *Provincial Power in the Inka Empire.* Washington, DC: Smithsonian Institution Press, 1992.

Pacific, War of the (1879–1884)

Major war resulting from a dispute between Chile and Bolivia. The dispute centered on control of the Atacama Desert, important because of rich deposits of nitrates used for fertilizer, on the western coast of South America. Peru soon entered the war on the side of Bolivia. Chile and Bolivia had argued over border delineation since their independence. In 1874, the dispute seemed to be resolved when Chile agreed not to pursue its claim for control over the southern portion of the Atacama in exchange for a generous tax concession for Chilean companies exploiting nitrates in the Bolivian-controlled area.

When the Bolivian dictator General Hilarón Daza increased taxes in an apparent violation of the 1874 accord, Chile protested vociferously, and Daza declared war. Chile soon learned that Peru and Bolivia had a secret alliance and that Peru intended to honor its commitments to Bolivia. These revelations resulted in an immediate declaration of war by Chile on Peru.

Naval power proved to be of great importance in the early phase of the war. Chile's navy, under the command of Admiral Juan Williams Rebolledo, established a blockade with several wooden ships off the Peruvian port of Iquique for the purpose of cutting Peru's nitrate trade. Williams then sailed north with his two ironclad monitors to attack the Peruvian navy, which he believed was defending Peru's main port of Callao. However, Peruvian admiral Miguel Grau had sailed south with his two ironclads, the *Huascar* and the *Indepedencia,* and on 21 May 1879 attacked the Chilean blockade, sinking the *Esmeralda* and damaging the *Covadonga.* Unfortunately for Grau, the Battle of Iquique proved a hollow victory because the *Independencia* was run aground and lost. With only one ironclad, the *Huascar,* remaining, Peru was at a decided disadvantage for the remainder of the war. Nevertheless, Grau used the *Huascar* to harass Chilean shipping lanes, resulting in Williams's resignation. On 8 October 1879, a refurbished Chilean fleet, including the ironclads the *Blanco Encalada* and the *Cochrane,* finally forced an engagement with the *Huascar.* Superior Chilean firepower soon reduced the *Huascar* to a burning hulk, resulting in the death of most of the crew, including Admiral Grau. (*Huascar* is still in existence as a Chilean memorial.)

With control of the sea assured, Chile launched an invasion of the southern Peruvian province of Tarapac in October 1879, led by General Erasmo Escala. General Hilarón Daza led a Bolivian army from the sierra to counter Escala's move and to join a Peruvian army led by General Juan Daza. But Daza's troops were ill-equipped and unprepared for the arid conditions of the Atacama, and Daza abandoned his plan. On 19 November 1879, Escala repulsed an allied attack and forced a retreat. It was followed by an assault on the city of Tarapac, which proved costly but was ultimately successful and led to the capture of Iquique.

On 8 April 1880, Chile renewed land operations to gain total control of Peru's nitrate-rich province of Tacna. The campaign resulted in extraordinarily high casualties for the invaders, but by June Chile had control of most of Tacna. When peace negotiations failed, Chile decided to attack Lima, which fell on 17 January 1881. Peruvian resistance continued despite the loss of the capital. Finally, in 1883, the Chilean army defeated the forces of Andre's Céceras at Huamchaca, and Peru signed a peace treaty ceding Tarapac to Chile and permitting occupation of Tacna and Arica for 10 years. The Chileans took complete possession of the disputed areas in 1884. Bolivia lost its Pacific coast when it turned over the Atacama to Chile. Thus, Chile became the leading power on the west coast of South America, but Bolivia never forgot its lost access to the sea.

George M. Lauderbaugh

References and further reading:

Sater, William F. *Chile and the War of the Pacific.* Lincoln: University of Nebraska Press, 1986.

Pacifism/War Resistance

The opposition to war, killing, or violence. The word comes from the Latin pax or *pacis,* which means "peace," and *facere* which means "to make." Pacifists believe that nations should settle their conflicts as peacefully as possible and are often opposed to participating in military activity. Even though peace and justice are the objectives of all pacifists, the degree and circumstances of nonviolence vary from person to person and circumstance to circumstance. Although absolute pacifism declares that violence is wrong always and in every situation, most pacifists are on a moral and ethical continuum as it relates to force. For example, some pacifists refuse to enter the military service in any capacity, whereas others find their witness for peace as unarmed army medics. Thus much of the writing of those advocating peace debates under what circumstances nonviolence should be national, group, or individual policy and the degree of coercive or disciplinary violence that should be used to achieve social or personal goals.

The roots of pacifism are as old as war itself and can be traced to Asia, especially Buddhism, several of the indigenous peoples of the Americas, and the writings of Greek philosophers like Plato. Pacifism as a dominant form of philosophy emerged in western thought with first-century Christianity. After hearing passages like Jesus' Sermon on the Mount, most early Christians believed that their Christ called for nonviolent resistance to pagan political power and the ways of the world. Christianity did not change its stance toward violence until the third century, when it increasingly gained followers in power in the Roman Empire, particularly the Emperor Constantine. By the fifth century, Christian thinkers, particularly St. Augustine, developed a "just war" theory. Although no longer the dominant strain of thought, pacifism still held power in many ecclesiastical circles and later reappeared in the sects founded during the Protestant Reformation. Often called the "peace churches," the groups that elevated nonresistance to doctrinal position included Mennonites, Anabaptists, Friends (or Quakers), Moravians, Brethren, and Dukhobors. Leaders from these groups have been the heart of most peace societies founded after 1815 and have been the most vocal in the cause of peace. More philosophical advocates of pacifism can be found in the writings of Immanuel Kant, Erasmus, Adin Ballou, and William James.

Modern pacifism began with the founding of peace societies in Massachusetts (1815) and New York (1815) and in England (1816); France, Switzerland, and other countries soon followed suit. William Ladd brought many of these groups together in the United States, establishing the American Peace Society in 1828. These groups advocated various proposals to smooth relations between nations. Yet many of these societies or individuals, like William Lloyd Garrison, the most prominent American abolitionist, allowed for some degree of violence, particularly in support of the antislavery cause. In 1843, the first peace congress met in London, and momentum seemed to be building for pacifistic reform in international relations until the American Civil War shattered the peace movement in the United States. While American peace societies were rebuilding during the latter half of the nineteenth century and European efforts were set back by the Crimean War and the wars of Italian and German unification, Sir William Randal Cremer of Great Britain and Frederic Passy of France spearheaded efforts to establish the Inter-Parliamentary Union in 1889, which brought members of national electoral bodies together in periodic conferences. The same year, the International Peace Bureau was founded in Berne, Switzerland. Alfred Nobel (1833–1896), the Swedish inventor of dynamite, established the Nobel Peace Prize to recognize and reward work for peace and humanitarian causes.

During the mid-1860s, socialist thinkers such as Cesar de Paepe developed the First International of Working Man, an organization of socialists, pacifists, and union supporters who believed the cause of peace was almost impossible until private property and class inequality could be abolished. A Second International was found in 1889, and its members advocated general strikes in case of war, arbitration treaties, arms reduction proposals, and much of colonialism. Militants such as Gustave Herve urged sabotage in the cause of pacifism. Vladimir Lenin urged the dissolution of international boundaries as the only means of true peace. Still, most peace societies were ethnocentric and nationalistic in their viewpoint, and the association with socialism (and vegetarianism, antivivisectionism, and other "fads") in the public's mind would hurt their efforts in the twentieth century.

Yet with conferences at The Hague in 1899 and 1907 and mainstream political leaders like William Jennings Bryan advocating international treaties and courts to settle disputes, many pacifists believed an end to war was within sight. World War I shattered these illusions, but pacifist sentiment quickly reappeared with the conclusion of the war. Many peace advocates pushed for the League of Nations as the forum to settle international disputes. In the United States, pacifists were often actively involved in the growing women's rights movement and sought to distance themselves from events in Europe. Pacifism was again dealt a blow by the events leading to World War II when pacifists were blamed for the isolationism and appeasement that led to that war. Still, the number of conscientious objectors in the United States and England was larger than in World War I, and most were treated with far more respect for their beliefs than in the previous conflict.

The "McCarthyite" 1950s were the low point for peace movements in the United States, and the cause was harmed by the Communists and Soviets hijacking the term *peace* for their own use. There was very little vocal opposition to the Korean War, and those who advocated measures and resolutions toward maintaining world peace were labeled "fellow travelers" or seen as disloyal to their country. Still, pacifist sentiments were nurtured by the writings of Jane Addams, Leo Tolstoy, Albert Schweitzer, Dorothy Day, Mohandas Gandhi, and Martin Luther King. They inspired efforts to work toward world peace, and by the 1960s and 1970s, pacifists and other antiwar groups were vocal in their opposition to the Vietnam conflict. They organized marches, rallies, and protests against the war, and the movement pressure was responsible in part for U.S. withdrawal from that conflict.

After the war, President Gerald Ford allowed conscientious objectors who had fled the draft to return home. The threat of nuclear weapons particularly enlivened the peace movement and helped pacifists to be taken seriously in their urging of unilateral disarmament and an end to nuclear testing.

Pacifists flourish unmolested in the developed democracies, but it can be argued that this is the case primarily because they are so few in number that they pose no threat to those countries' military-industrial complex. A major question that will arise in any future U.S. conflict, however, is whether "secular" pacifists, that is, those who hold sincere nonviolent beliefs but do not belong to any of the state-recognized "historic peace churches," will be given draft-exempt status.

T. Jason Soderstrum

References and further reading:

Brock, Peter. *Freedom from War: Nonsectarian Pacifism.* Toronto: University of Toronto Press, 1991.

Brock, Peter, and Nigel Young. *Pacifism in the 20th Century.* Syracuse, NY: Syracuse University Press, 1999.

Chatfield, Charles. *For Peace and Justice: Pacifism in America, 1914–1941.* Boston: Beacon Press, 1973.

Martin, David A. *Pacifism: An Historical and Sociological Study.* New York: Schocken Books, 1966.

Paekche (attributed 18 B.C.E.–660 C.E.)

One of three kingdoms dominating the Korean peninsula. Situated in the southwest, Paekche's origins and early history remain obscure. Most sources agree that its founders were warrior-refugees from the Manchurian state of Fuyu (Korean Puyo), which met its demise in 285 C.E. The oldest extant Korean history places Paekche's foundation at 18 B.C.E., but Paekche does not appear in written records until the third century C.E.

Despite purported warrior origins, Paekche was better known for its cultural achievements than for any military prowess. Its emergence coincided with the appearance of two primary rivals, Silla and Koguryo, located in the southeast and north, respectively, the other two kingdoms giving the period its name. From the mid–fifth century, the three waged an increasingly bitter struggle for hegemony.

In this climate, Paekche forged an alliance with Yamato Japan, a partnership whose nature continues to be debated. As a result, Paekche served as a conduit for technology and culture to the Japanese islands, while Yamato troops were engaged on the peninsula.

From the fifth century, Paekche was subjected to increasing pressure from Koguryo advancing south and Silla intent on going north, in a general atmosphere of winner-take-all. A Paekche-Silla alliance crumbled in 552, and in 660 Paekche was finally destroyed by Silla, which took advantage of a military alliance with the new Tang Dynasty in China to defeat both Paekche and Koguryo and unify the peninsula.

Daniel Kane

See also: Koguryo; Silla; Sino-Korean Wars and the Wars of Korean Unification

References and further reading:

Gardiner, K. H. J. *The Early History of Korea: The Historical Development of the Peninsula Up to the Introduction of Buddhism in the Fourth Century A.D.* Honolulu: University of Hawaii Press, 1969.

Iryon. *Samguk yusa: Legends and History of the Three Kingdoms of Ancient Korea.* Trans. Tae-Hung Ha and Grafton K. Mintz. Seoul: Yonsei University Press, 1972.

Lee, Ki-baik. *A New History of Korea.* Trans. Edward W. Wagner, with Edward J. Shultz. Cambridge, MA: Harvard University Press, 1984.

Pagan Kingdom (1044–c. 1300)

The founder of the Pagan Kingdom, King Anawrahta (r. 1044–1077), established the first state unifying Upper and Lower Burma, including most of the territory of the modern nation, except for Shan State and the remoter border areas. He and his successors recognized Theravada Buddhism as the state religion, building magnificent pagodas at their royal capital of Pagan and making generous donations to the *sangha* (community of Buddhist monks). The Pagan dynasty's 12 kings dealt with the challenges of a multiethnic society (principally Mon, Burmese/Myanmar, and Pyu) both by absorbing non-Burmese cultural influences (especially Mon culture) and by preserving the privileges of an ethnic Burmese ruling class.

In 849, the Burmese built a fortified city at Pagan (near Nyaung-U, in Mandalay Division) that was strategically located on the banks of the Irrawaddy River and near the irrigated districts of Kyaukse and Minbu, which provided the small state with surpluses of rice. The availability of rice was the economic foundation of Pagan's military power. Linguistically related to the Tibetans, the Burmese originally lived in eastern Tibet or Yunnan but had migrated into the Irrawaddy Valley (Upper Burma) because of the power vacuum created by attacks by the Nanchao Kingdom of Yunnan (now China's Yunnan Province) on states in Burma ruled by an earlier people, the Pyu. The Upper Burma Dry Zone is a harsh, semidesert environment, and the Burmese quickly gained a reputation as aggressive warriors. They gave their capital of Pagan the Pali name of Arimaddanapura, "the city that is a crusher of enemies."

Anawrahta conquered Lower Burma (the Irrawaddy Delta and Tenasserim), capturing the Mon city of Thaton in 1057 and bringing its king, the devout Buddhist Manuha, as a hostage to Pagan. In the first recorded instance of political protest in Burmese history, the Mon king built a small and unspectacular temple claustrophobically housing large Buddha images in cavelike chambers, expressing his distress at being Anawrahta's prisoner. Although Anawrahta, Kyanzittha (r. 1084–1111), and other Pagan monarchs patronized Mon culture, more refined than their own, and venerated Mon monks as teachers of Theravada doctrine, this Lower Burma people staged numerous revolts against the Burmese that were harshly suppressed until c. 1281, when Pagan, hard-pressed by the Mongols, could not prevent the emergence of an independent Mon state at Pegu.

The Mongol emperor Kublai Khan's conquest of Yunnan in the 1250s set the stage for Pagan's fall. King Narathihapate (r. 1256–1287) rejected Kublai's repeated demands for submission, and in 1277 the Mongols invaded. In his *Description of the World,* Marco Polo chronicles the defeat of Burmese soldiers mounted on elephants by Mongol archers, a terrible rout. In 1286–1287, Narathihapate's continued intransigence led to a second invasion in which Pagan was occupied. By 1300, the Pagan Kingdom was no more. Tai (Shan) peoples came into Burma in the wake of the Mongol incursions and established a power base at Ava in Upper Burma.

Donald M. Seekins

American forces in formation at the Battle of Palo Alto, 1846. (Library of Congress)

See also: Anawrahta; Kublai Khan

References and further reading:

Aung-Thwin, Michael. *Pagan: The Origins of Modern Burma.* Honolulu: University of Hawaii Press, 1985.
Hall, D. G. E. *A History of South-East Asia.* 2nd ed. London: Macmillan, 1964.

Palo Alto (8 May 1846)

Early battle in the Mexican-American War. In preceding months, General Zachary Taylor and his "Army of Observation" had moved from the Nueces River to the Rio Grande, which was disputed territory between Mexico and what had formerly been the Republic of Texas and now was the United States. He was opposed by General Mariano Arista and the Mexican Army of the North.

On 8 May 1846, the two armies clashed at Palo Alto. American artillery was more mobile and far superior; the Mexican army had antiquated muskets and inferior gunpowder and shot. The fighting began around 2:00 P.M. with an artillery exchange and the U.S. troops literally dodging the solid copper Mexican shot, while the U.S. artillery caused great damage. In early evening, Arista tried to turn Taylor's flank and failed; meanwhile, the Mexican left began to break, and the high grass caught fire. As the infantry fighting halted for the fire, the artillery duel continued, with the Americans having the better of it. The battle was probably a draw but was costly for the Mexicans.

Charles Dobbs

See also: Mexican-American War; Resaca de la Palma; Taylor, Zachary

References and further reading:

Hamilton, Holman. *Zachary Taylor: Soldier of the Republic.* 1941.
Nichols, Edward J. *Zach Taylor's Little Army.* 1963.
Singletary, Otis. *The Mexican War.* Chicago: University of Chicago, 1960.

Panama Incursion (1989–1990)

Quick U.S. military operation against corrupt Panamanian ruler. Panama had been ruled by the military from the 1960s, and by the 1980s, General Manuel Antonio Noriega Moreno had become the power behind the throne in Panama. Noriega had links with the Central Intelligence Agency (CIA) dating back to the 1960s.

Panama, cut in two by the American-built and administered Panama Canal, had always had a close, albeit one-way, relationship with the United States, but by the mid-1960s, this relationship was beginning to show signs of strain. Although Noriega assisted the United States in its war against the Sandinistas in Nicaragua, he also helped Cuba break the U.S. blockade by reselling goods to the Caribbean island. In 1986, the journalist Seymour Hersh published an article in the *New York Times* contending that Noriega was involved in gun running, drug trafficking, and money laundering.

Noriega was becoming an embarrassment for the United States, and in mid-1987, the Reagan administration initiated economic sanctions against Panama. These sanctions were tightened in December of that year, when all assistance from the United States was stopped. The situation worsened when, in February 1988, two Florida grand juries found Noriega guilty of drug trafficking and money laundering.

In the May 1989 presidential elections, qualified observers argued that Guillermo Endara Galimary had won three times as many votes as Noriega's candidate. Noriega simply annulled the elections and appointed his own candidate, Francisco Rodriguez, as president. In October, Noriega survived an attempted coup, and on 15 December he became head of the government with the title "Maximum Leader."

Relations with the United States approached the crisis stage on 16 December, when a U.S. serviceman, Lieutenant Robert Paz, was shot and a U.S. Navy officer and his wife were arrested and harassed by the Panama Defense Force (PDF). These affronts were the last straw for U.S. president George Bush, who set in motion Operation JUST CAUSE on 20 December.

This operation, which involved more than 20,000 U.S. troops, had two functions: the invasion of Panama and the seizing of Noriega at H-hour before transporting him to the United States to face charges. The PDF quickly disintegrated, with U.S. forces facing more resistance from the paramilitary Dignity Battalions. Both U.S. Special Operations and conventional forces were completely successful and suffered very few casualties. But the invading force could not locate Noriega. He eventually surfaced at the Papal Nunciature on Christmas Eve, leading to a standoff with U.S. forces. Finally, on 4 January, the deposed dictator was persuaded that he had no choice but to give himself up and face the charges against him in the United States.

Panama moved quickly during 1990 toward democratization and demilitarization, and the May 1989 election results were upheld. Operation JUST CAUSE had ended Noriega's rule, but it also gave rise to questions of the legitimacy of Endora's presidency. The operation also was a flexing of the muscles of the post-Vietnam U.S. military, rejuvenated by former U.S. president Ronald Reagan.

M. J. Bain

See also: Bay of Pigs Invasion; Nicaraguan Civil War (1979); Peruvian Guerrilla War; Salvadorian Civil War

References and further reading:

Black, J. N. *Latin America: Its Problems and Its Promise.* Boulder, CO: Westview Press, 1998.

Loser, E. *Conflict Resolution and Democratization in Panama: Implications for U.S. Policy.* Washington, DC: Center for Strategic and International Studies, 1992.

Scranton, M. E. *The Noriega Years: U.S.-Panamanian Relations, 1981–1990.* Boulder, CO: Lynne Rienner Publishers, 1991.

Skidmore, T. E., and P. E. Smith: *Modern Latin America.* New York: Oxford University Press, 1997.

Panipat, Battles of (21 April 1526, 5 November 1556, 14 January 1761)

Series of Persian-Afghan-Indian battles. The first Battle of Panipat took place on 21 April 1526. Ibrahim led at least 10,000 Delhi Muslims with 100 war elephants against Babur and his 2,000 handpicked Moguls. It is likely that more conscripts were involved, but only the number of professional soldiers is known. Babur scored a complete victory, with gunpowder weapons playing a significant role in frightening the elephants. Ibrahim was killed, and the Mogul Empire began in India from the ashes of the Afghan Dynasty that had ruled from Delhi. This third invasion of India by the Moguls was easily the most successful.

The second Battle of Panipat took place on 5 November 1556. Akbar Khan and 20,000 troops of the Mogul Empire faced Hemu, who commanded about 100,000 Hindu Rajah troops, 1,500 war elephants, and a chaotic baggage train full of loot from rebel-held Delhi, the former Mogul capital.

The Moguls repulsed an initial charge by the war elephants and then directed the panicked Hindu elephants toward the Hindu rear baggage train area, all but stopping any movement of Hindu reinforcements. The Moguls scored a complete victory, capturing and executing Hemu, retaking Delhi, and building a tower of Hindu heads.

The assassination of Nadir Shah, last of the Safavid-linked Persian leaders, in 1747 caused the collapse of his Persian empire to Russian, Ottoman, and Afghan interests and resulted in the third Battle of Panipat. Shah Ahmed Durani created the Afghan empire from its ashes by conquering parts of Persia and sections of Maratha India, namely the Punjab and Delhi. In response, Sedashao Bhao, cousin of the Maratha Peshwa (ruler), went forth with the largest Maratha army ever assembled, perhaps 300,000 strong, pushing back the Durani Afghans. Shah Ahmed then led 90,000 Afghan and Indian troops to face the Marathas at the third Battle of Panipat in 1761. Bhao attacked first and dispersed Ahmed's Indian allies on 14 January, but Ahmed, preaching a jihad (holy war) against the predominantly Hindu Marathas, rallied his Islamic Afghan forces and crushed the Maratha army, killing 75,000 and capturing and ransoming another 30,000. The Mogul throne, used as a pawn by Afghans, Marathas, and the British, now effectively ceased to exist, and the remnants of the once-mighty Mogul empire were divided up among the three.

Christopher Howell

See also: Persian-Afghan Wars; Maratha Wars

References and further reading:

Adamec, Ludwig. *Dictionary of Afghan Wars, Revolutions, and Insurgencies.* Kennikat: Scarecrow Press, 1996.

Gordon, Stewart. *Marathas, Marauders, and State Formation in Eighteenth-Century India.* Oxford, UK: Oxford University Press, 1994.

Kadam, V. S. *Maratha Confederacy: A Study in Its Origin and Development.* Delhi: South Asia Books, 1993.

Paramilitary Organizations

A wide range of groups organized along military lines yet lacking the traditional role or legitimization of conventional or "genuine" military organizations. Typical characteristics include a hierarchical organization with clear lines of authority and strict discipline, military-style ranks or uniforms, and usually an explicit ideological mission. Light weaponry may also be included. Party militias like the Nazi Stormtroopers (SA) or Italian Squadristi (Black Shirts); militarized police forces such as the armed units of the Soviet secret police or the French gendarmerie; veteran's organizations such as the German Stahlhelm; U.S. state police and Canadian provincial police; and even many youth groups such as the Boy Scouts all may be termed paramilitary for different reasons.

Paramilitary organizations exist to perform tasks for which conventional military forces are either ill-suited or considered unworthy, for example, domestic police duties or state terrorism. They also represent an attempt to apply military forms of organization to nonmilitary or political ends because of the military's assumed greater efficiency or to appropriate and imitate the prestige and aura of conventional military forces. These latter reasons were especially true in the first half of the twentieth century because of the great prestige that conventional military establishments had gained as symbols of national unity and was only intensified (though not without challenge) by the series of great wars that swept Europe in the late nineteenth and early twentieth centuries. By the end of World War I, military ways of organization came to be seen as possible alternatives to liberal democracy, and millions of veterans searching for meaning after the carnage of war could find in them a familiar way of life.

The most characteristic form of paramilitary organization in the early and mid–twentieth century was the party militia typified by the Squadristi of the Italian Fascist Party. Before the Fascists came to power, the Squadristi served as a way for the Fascists to organize violence against their opponents and at the same time appear to be more dynamic and effective than their conservative and liberal competitors. After the Fascists came to power, the Squadristi were institutionalized as a mechanism for mobilizing, organizing, and indoctrinating the population, yet they kept their original role as an extralegal means of exercising violence. Nearly all fascist or radical conservative movements of the period between the two world wars established similar paramilitary auxiliaries. The success of the Bolshevik Revolution and the adoption of the Soviet model of development by newly independent states in the former European colonies or by the puppet states of Eastern Europe also led to the widespread establishment of paramilitary state youth organizations, particularly after 1945, most of which have now largely disappeared with the collapse of the Communist states that organized them.

Today, paramilitary organizations are often formed in cases in which established social groups and interests seek to exercise power yet are either unwilling or unable to use conventional military forces, which they may not fully control or which may be unwilling to dirty their own hands. Examples include private death squads established with government connivance, such as in Guatemala or El Salvador, or the ethnic Serbian paramilitaries established in Bosnia in the 1990s.

In the democracies, paramilitary organizations were not unknown, but their goals were usually entirely benign, such as the search-and-rescue mission of the U.S. Civil Air Patrol or the woodcraft of the Boy Scouts.

Bruce Campbell

See also: Death Squads; SA; SS

References and further reading:

Diehl, James M. *Paramilitary Politics in Weimar Germany.* Bloomington: Indiana University Press, 1977.

Morgan, Philip. *Italian Fascism, 1919–1945.* New York: St. Martin's Press, 1995.

Reichardt, Sven. "Faschistische Kampfbünde in Italien und Deutschland. Ein Vergleich der Formen, Funktionen und Ursachen politischer Gewalt in der Aufstiegsphase faschistischer Bewegungen." Ph.D. diss., Freie Universität Berlin, 2000.

Tobler, Hans Werner, and Peter Waldmann, eds. *Staatliche und Parastaatliche Gewalt in Lateinamerika.* Frankfurt am Main: Vervuert Verlag, 1991.

Williams, Warren E. "Paramilitarism in Inter-State Relations: The Role of Political Armies in Twentieth Century European Politics." Ph.D. diss., London University, 1965.

Paris, Siege of (1870–1871)

The climax of the Franco-Prussian War, which destroyed the French Second Empire and led to the creation of the Third Republic. After the collapse of the French armies, the Prussians surrounded Paris in September 1870. A spontaneous popular movement in the city deposed Emperor Napoleon III and created a republic. General Louis Trochu, appointed to lead the city's defense, was competent, but not very zealous in actively ending the siege. The French National Guard, the main force available within Paris for its defense, made two poorly planned attempts to break through the Prussian lines but failed to coordinate their efforts with French forces outside the city. Both ended in total fiasco. The Prussians made no attempt to storm Paris, preferring to starve it into surrender. French forces outside Paris, led by Léon Gambetta, were never able to mount a serious effort to relieve the capital. The siege saw the first extensive wartime use of hot air balloons for communication with the outside world; unfortunately, given the state of technology at the time, it was difficult to navigate the balloons and flights into Paris were impossible. The siege laid bare the fissure lines between conservatives and radicals in Paris. The "Reds" were increasingly critical of the way Trochu and the government handled Paris's defense and the way the government handled the economic problems resulting from the siege. The government surrendered Paris in January 1871 largely because it feared an incipient revolt by Parisians. Shortly after the surrender, there was, in fact, a rebellion that chased a newly elected government to Versailles and led to the creation of the Paris Commune.

Lee Baker Jr.

See also: Bismarck, Otto von; Franco-Prussian War; German Wars of Unification

References and further reading:

Horne, Alistair. *The Fall of Paris: The Siege and the Commune, 1870–71.* New York: Penguin Books, 1985.

Howard, Michael. *The Franco-Prussian War.* New York: Collier Books, 1961.

Tombs, Robert. *The War against Paris, 1871.* New York: Cambridge University Press, 1981.

Williams, Roger. *The French Revolutions of 1870–1871.* London: Weidenfeld and Nicolson, 1969.

Parma and Piacenza, Alessandro Farnese, Duke of (1545–1592)

Spanish general and statesman. Parma was the greatest soldier of his time in western Europe. He came close to defeating the Dutch revolt against Spanish rule, but interference and lack of support from Philip II prevented his victory.

Parma was the son of Margaret of Austria, Emperor Charles V's natural daughter, and Ottavio Farnese, Duke of Parma. He spent part of his boyhood in Philip II's court, where he became friends with Don Juan of Austria, his cousin. Parma accompanied his mother to the Netherlands in 1565, where she was regent. Parma became very familiar with the country and the leaders of society. He volunteered for duty with the Holy League fleet under Don Juan against the Turks and distinguished himself in the victory at Lepanto on 7 October 1571. Parma continued to serve in the Mediterranean until 1574.

In 1577, Don Juan requested Parma join him in the Netherlands. At the Battle of Gembloux, 31 January 1578, Parma led the cavalry charge that smashed the opposing infantry and nearly destroyed the Dutch army. After Don Juan's death on 1 October 1578, Parma became Spanish commander in the Netherlands. His knowledge of the country and people was a great advantage. In May 1579, he signed a peace treaty with Catholic leaders of the southern provinces, bringing them back into allegiance with Philip. With his base secure, Parma concentrated on taking the centers of Protestant power in the north. A master of maneuver and sieges, he did not undertake any operations beyond his army's power, which numbered only 27,000 men, but isolated cities before reducing them. Parma was merciless to his avowed enemies but persuasive in winning over others. His greatest triumph was the capture of Antwerp in August 1585, after blockading it from the sea with a barrage of boats. The opportunity to crush the revolt for good was lost when Philip ordered Parma to intervene in the French wars of religion and the invasion of England with the Spanish Armada. While he was in France, much of Parma's gains were lost to Maurice of Nassau and his reorganized army. Frustrated by Philip, Parma became disheartened. He was wounded in the arm in a skirmish at Caudebec, fell ill, and died soon afterward. No soldier who followed him could duplicate his successes.

Tim J. Watts

See also: Don Juan de Austria; Dutch War of Independence

References and further reading:

Hoeven, Marco van der. *Exercise of Arms: Warfare in the Netherlands, 1568–1648.* New York: Brill, 1997.

Mattingly, Garrett. *The Armada.* Boston: Houghton Mifflin, 1959.

Parker, Geoffrey. *The Army of Flanders and the Spanish Road, 1567–1659: The Logistics of Spanish Victory and Defeat in the Low Countries' Wars.* New York: Cambridge University Press, 1995.

Parthian Empire (247 B.C.E.–226 C.E.)

The Parthians liberated Persia from Hellenistic domination and made Persia a power to rival the Roman Empire. They originated as nomadic Persian speakers living southeast of the Caspian Sea and south of the Oxus River.

Under Shah Mithradates I, the Parthians expanded through Iran and, by 141 B.C.E., reached modern-day Iraq. In 139 B.C.E., Mithradates captured the Seleucid prince, Demetrius II, and occupied the Tigris-Euphrates Valley. Under Mithradates II the Great (124–87 B.C.E.), the Parthians managed to decisively secure their eastern borders as well. Ctesiphon in Babylon became the capital.

The Parthian army was primarily a cavalry force, provided mostly from feudal levies, especially from the powerful landed nobility. Heavy cavalry wore body armor and fought at close quarters with sword and lance. Light cavalry used the compound bow, firing continuous volleys of arrows and javelins from a distance. The Parthian "lights" developed a technique of firing to their rear at a pursuing enemy, a tactic Romans called "the Parthian shot." Infantry and mercenaries, recruited mostly from feudal landlords, played largely supporting but vital roles. This military system made the Parthians formidable and frustrating opponents. Conversely, poor logistics and dependence on an unreliable nobility severely limited Parthian capacities for sustained offensive operations.

Parthian-Roman relations began on friendly enough terms in 96 B.C.E. However, when General Pompey subjugated Armenia, traditionally a Persian vassal, frictions began. Marcus Licinius Crassus attempted a conquest of Parthia in 53 B.C.E. and died at Carrhae. Mark Anthony lost thousands of men invading Persia 15 years later. Caesar Augustus fortified Syria as a base against Persia and, in 20 B.C.E., imposed a puppet king on Armenia. Using this strategy, Rome controlled Armenia for decades. However, Shah Vologases wrecked this hegemony, waging a decade of war (53–63), until Nero accepted Vologases's brother as king of Armenia.

In 113, Emperor Trajan invaded Armenia and, in 115, captured Mesopotamia and Ctesiphon itself. Occupation unleashed popular revolts throughout Mesopotamia, leading Emperor Hadrian to evacuate in 117. In the First Parthian War (161–166) Shah Vologases III, responding to noble and popular anti-Roman pressures, launched invasions into Syria and Armenia. Lucius Verus drove him out, reconquered northern Mesopotamia, but avoided Ctesiphon. Vologases IV started the Second Parthian War (197–199), trying to drive the Romans out of northern Mesopotamia. Rome again repulsed the shah and once more sacked Ctesiphon. In 215, the shah defeated the armies sent against him by Caracalla, granting a truce to Caracalla's beleaguered successors in exchange for heavy tribute.

Ardashir Sassan revolted against Parthian ineptitude and venality caused by centuries of warfare and defeated Artabanus at Hormizdagh in 225, bringing an end to the Parthians and founding the Sassanian Empire.

Weston F. Cook, Jr.

See also: Cyrus II the Great; Persian Empire

References and further reading:

Wiesehofer, Josef. *Ancient Persia.* Trans. Azizeh Azodi. London: I. B. Tauris Publishers, 1996.

Yarshater, Ehsan, ed. *The Cambridge History of Iran.* Vol. 3. London: Cambridge University Press, 1985.

Patton, George Smith, Jr. (1885–1945)

U.S. Army general and pioneer in modern armored warfare. Born in San Gabriel, California, on 11 November 1885, he inherited a warrior's legacy from his father.

Patton's family possessed a military tradition dating back to the American Revolution, and from an early age, he knew that a military career was his destiny. When he graduated from high school, there were no appointments to the U.S. Military Academy at West Point. Therefore, he enrolled at the Virginia Military Institute (VMI), the school from which his father, grandfather, and three great-uncles had graduated.

After one year at VMI, Patton secured his appointment to West Point. During his time at West Point, he became an expert fencer and demonstrated the drive, aggressiveness, and flair that would define his career. The skills developed at West Point and his competitive nature earned Patton the right to represent the United States in the 1912 Olympics. As the first American to compete in the modern pentathlon, he finished a respectable fifth.

With the start of World War I, Patton requested permission to serve with the French cavalry but was turned down. In 1916, he was an aide to General John J. Pershing on the punitive expeditions into Mexico against Pancho Villa. During one mission, Patton killed General Julio Cardenas, the

Portrait of George Patton. (Library of Congress)

head of Villa's bodyguard, using the same Colt pistol that would become his trademark.

With the U.S. entry into World War I, Patton was selected on 15 May 1917 to join Pershing's American Expeditionary Force. In August 1918, Patton commanded a tank brigade during the Meuse-Argonne Offensive. He was wounded and was awarded both the Purple Heart and Distinguished Service Cross.

During the interwar years, the size of the U.S. Army, especially armored units, was severely reduced. Patton used this time to attend the Army War College, learn to fly, and publish articles on armored unit tactics.

U.S. entry into World War II necessitated the preparation of the army's newly formed armored units. Patton was given the task. On 8 November 1942, Patton landed on the west coast of Africa. In the wake of the defeat at Kasserine Pass, General Dwight D. Eisenhower put Patton in command. His success led to his command of the Seventh Army during the invasion of Sicily. Chafing at his role of providing flank protection for his rival, British general Bernard L. Montgomery, Patton looked for an opportunity to play a more active role. Taking advantage of stiffer than expected resistance to the British advance, he received permission to drive toward Palermo, capturing it on 22 July and then capturing Messina ahead of Montgomery.

Patton missed the Italian campaign and was denied the opportunity to be the American ground commander for Normandy because of an incident in which he slapped a soldier whom he believed to be a malingerer (an action that he would repeat). On 6 July 1944, Patton was sent to France to take command of the Third Army. It was the zenith of his career, as his Third Army made a dramatic sweep across northern France in a campaign marked by great initiative, ruthless drive, and disregard of classic military rules.

When a German counteroffensive threatened to cut through thin American lines, Patton saw possibilities in this dire situation. He disengaged his troops, hurled them northward during a terrible winter storm, and attacked the German's flank, relieving the encircled troops at Bastogne. Patton's actions, considered impossible when he suggested them, are credited in relieving Bastogne and defeating the Germans in the Battle of the Bulge.

As the war ended, controversy continued to surround Patton. After Germany surrendered, Patton, a staunch anti-Communist, argued for a combined Allied-German campaign against the Soviet Union. When he later argued to keep former Nazis in administrative positions, he was removed from command.

Patton died in Heidelberg, Germany, on 21 December 1945, the result of an automobile accident. He is buried among the soldiers who died in the Battle of the Bulge in Hamm, Luxembourg. Probably the most admired and controversial of all American generals in World War II, Patton was known for carrying ivory-handled pistols, using racy language, and having an intemperate manner but was also regarded as one of the most successful American field commanders of any war.

Craig T. Cobane

See also: Ardennes, Battle of; Armored Fighting Vehicles; TORCH, Operation; World War II

References and further reading:

D'Este, Carlos. *Patton: A Genius for War.* New York: HarperCollins, 1995.

Essame, Hubert. *Patton: A Study in Command.* New York: Charles Scribner's Sons, 1974.

Pavia, Battle of (24 February 1525)

The turning point of the "Italian wars" and the end of the era of chivalry. By 1525, French kings had been claiming territories in Italy for 30 years. To reach their political goals, they had to face the thrones of Spain and Austria, which were combined in 1519, forming a threatening neighbor. The nature of the Italian wars changed as the new king, Charles V, ruled countries surrounding France on three sides. In 1524, the imperialist forces invaded Provence, but facing failure at the siege of Marseille, they had to retire in front of the main French army. Francis I, the king of France, decided to follow the retiring army in Italy.

The imperialists resisted the French invasion but had to fall back on their fortified garrisons of Pavia and Lodi. Francis decided (against the advice of his wiser commanders) to avoid a direct fight against the main imperialist army, led by the Marquis of Pescara. He chose instead to besiege Pavia.

The siege began on 28 October 1524. Facing superior French artillery, the Spanish commander Antonio de Levya made a stubborn defense. Unable to storm the town rapidly, Francis decided to make his winter quarters in a walled park, north of the siege work. The desertion rate among the mercenaries began to rise (8,000 Swiss on 20 February 1525 alone). Pescara's army of 40,000, mainly *Landsknecht* (mercenary soldiers from the Holy Roman Empire), pikemen, harquebusiers, and light artillery, left Lodi and reached Pavia to find a waiting French army. The besieger was besieged in Mirabello Park.

The battle took place on 24 February 1525. During the night of the 23d–24th, the imperialists (23,000 soldiers) took the initiative. Their approach march turned around the high wall, and a breach was made in an unsuspected spot. Dawn took the French army of 22,000 unprepared and sepa-

The USS Shaw explodes during the Japanese attack on Pearl Harbor on December 7, 1941. (National Archives)

rated in three groups. Following the king, the French cavalry impetuously charged the *Landsknecht* as soon as they emerged from the wall while still masking their own artillery. Facing deadly fire, the French cavalry was cut to pieces, and the reinforcements, unable to stop the imperialists, were destroyed piecemeal. Francis I, wounded in the thick of the fray, was taken prisoner, and 10,000 French were killed, including hundreds of lords, as no mercy was given by either side.

This crushing defeat marked the beginning of a period of imperial control of Italy. "Tout est perdu, fors l'Honneur" ("All is lost but honor) was the comment made by Francis I, writing to his mother to announce his defeat.

Gilles Boué

See also: Cerisolles, Battle of; Marignano, Battle of

References and further reading:

Cornette, Joël. *Chronique de la France moderne, le XVIème siècle.* Paris: SEDES, 1995.

Hardy, Etienne. *Origines de la tactique française.* Paris: Dumaine, 1881.

Konstam, Angus. *Pavia 1525.* London: Osprey Publishers, 1996.

Pearl Harbor Attack (1941)

The devastating Japanese aerial attack on Pearl Harbor in the Hawaiian Islands on 7 December 1941 caused the United States to enter World War II with almost unanimous public support. Japan sought to neutralize the U.S. Pacific Fleet in order to invade and fortify its planned empire, which included the Philippines, Malaya, Netherlands East Indies, China, Thailand, and Burma, without U.S. naval interference. The operation was approved only 13 weeks beforehand, after the personal intervention of Admiral Isoruku Yamamoto. A fleet of six aircraft carriers, *Akagi, Kaga, Shokaku, Ziukaku, Hiryu,* and *Soryu* (by far the largest combat combination of carriers), accompanied by two battleships, two cruisers, nine destroyers, and eight supply ships, was to sail by a northwesterly route to an aircraft launch point 275 miles north of Pearl Harbor. The Japanese task force sailed on 26 November, receiving the final attack order and confirmation of the date seven days later.

Pearl Harbor was unprepared for an air attack, although war in the Pacific was thought imminent. The Imperial Japanese Navy was considered incapable of mounting any operations additional to the invasion convoys that were being reported in the world's press and known to be moving southward from Japan and Formosa. It was also believed that Japan would not commit the strategic error of unnecessarily forcing the United States into war. As a result, the eight air groups that commenced flying off from the Japanese carriers at 6:00 A.M. on Sunday, 7 December, achieved complete surprise when they dropped their first bombs at 7:55.

The 353 strike aircraft launched in two waves, 45 minutes apart. Their targets were battleships and cruisers and U.S. Army and Navy airfields. Attacks were made on the ships by torpedo bombers, level bombers, and dive-bombers, and many aircraft also strafed after dropping their bombs. The escort fighters strafed airfields, while level bombers and dive-bombers destroyed the planes and facilities. Antiaircraft gunfire was initially sporadic, and only about 18 U.S. Army fighters managed to get airborne during the two-hour attack. Twenty-nine Japanese aircraft were lost during the raid, and approximately 20 more were destroyed by landing accidents in rough weather.

U.S. losses were severe: 2,403 dead and 1,178 wounded; the battleships *Arizona, California,* and *West Virginia* destroyed; the *Oklahoma* capsized; and the *Nevada, Tennessee, Pennsylvania,* and *Maryland* damaged. The target battleship *Utah,* two destroyers, and a minelayer were also sunk. Additionally, four cruisers, a destroyer, and three tenders were damaged. Of the approximately 400 aircraft based in Hawaii, 239 were destroyed or severely damaged. It was the most one-sided naval air assault in history.

The Japanese themselves blundered in not scheduling the attack to destroy the American aircraft carriers based at Pearl Harbor, in not hitting the oil tank farms, in not destroying the machine shop complex that would help to restore many of the sunken and damaged warships, and in sinking the warships in waters shallow enough to permit the raising of all but one of the sunken U.S. battleships. But Japan's worst blunder was that of underestimating American resolve, industrial capacity, and fighting power. Japan would pay for those blunders with total defeat in a war that it could not hope to win.

So successful was the attack on focusing a once-divided nation's belligerent rage against Japan that the conspiratorial-minded have ever since suspected that President Franklin D. Roosevelt at least had some foreknowledge of the attack. They ignore the obvious fact that Roosevelt was preparing the United States for conflict with Germany and would hardly have welcomed a two-front war. Further, he would have had no idea that Adolf Hitler, in an act of gratuitous folly, would declare war on the United States.

Michael Hyde

References and further reading:

Japanese Monograph No. 97. "Pearl Harbor Operations: General Outline of Orders and Plans (5 November–2 December 1941)"; "The Naval Armament Program and Naval Operations (Part I)." In *War in Asia and the Pacific,* ed. D. Detwiler. Vol. 4. New York: Garland, 1980.

Morison, S. E. *The Rising Sun in the Pacific 1931–April 1942.* Vol. 3, *History of United States Naval Operations in World War II.* Boston: Little, Brown, 1948.

Prange, G. W., in collaboration with Donald M. Goldstein and Katherine V. Dillon. *At Dawn We Slept: The Untold Story of Pearl Harbor.* New York: Viking, 1991.

Worth, Roland H., Jr. *Pearl Harbor: Selected Testimonies, Fully Indexed, from the Congressional Hearings (1945–1946) and Prior Investigations of the Events Leading Up to the Attack.* Jefferson, NC: McFarland, 1993.

Peleliu (15 September–27 November 1944)

One of the most costly, least known, and perhaps most unnecessary of the Pacific island invasions during World War II. In September 1944, General Douglas MacArthur was planning the invasion of the Philippines and wanted his flank protected by an attack on Peleliu in the Palau Islands, located between New Guinea and the Philippines. The attack, Operation STALEMATE, would be just that.

U.S. planners had little useful information on Peleliu, including the strength and nature of Japanese defenses. The pre-invasion bombardment did not inflict much damage on the Japanese, who were well-protected in deep caves and other defenses away from the landing beaches. The invasion began well on 15 September, and then concealed machine guns and mortars opened fire, followed by tanks and troops in the afternoon. That evening, the Japanese launched suicide attacks against the Marines, who were still mostly on the invasion beach.

In the first week, the Marines Corps suffered 4,000 casualties, and some units were reduced to throwing chunks of coral at and using bayonets on the Japanese. Marine Corps fighter planes taking off from the landing strip on the island did not raise landing gear—they commenced their bombing runs too soon.

By the time that flamethrowers, bombs, naval bombardment, and the courage of the marine and army troops finally won the island, the United States had suffered grievously. The 1st Marine Division suffered some 54 percent casualties; the 5th Marine Division suffered 43 percent killed, wounded, and missing in action; and the 7th Marine Division lost 46 percent of its strength. Of 19 medals of honor given to members of the 1st Marine Division, eight were earned in the fighting on Peleliu. Worse, taking the island did not speed up MacArthur's timetable for the attack on Leyte or help defend the flank of his advance. The attack was both unnecessary and unmindful of the lessons learned in earlier amphibious invasions in the Pacific theater.

Charles M. Dobbs

See also: Saipan, Battle of; Tarawa; Tinian

References and Further reading:

Gailey, Harry A. *Peleliu, 1944.* Annapolis, MD: Nautical and Aviation Publishing Company of America, 1983.

Gayle, Gordon D. *Bloody Beaches: The Marines at Peleliu.* Washington, DC: History and Museums Division, HQ, U.S. Marine Corps, 1996.

Ross, Bill D. *Peleliu: Tragic Triumph: The Untold Story of the Pacific War's Forgotten Battle.* New York: Random House, 1991.

Wheeler, Richard. *A Special Valor: The U.S. Marines and the Pacific War.* New York: Harper & Row, 1983.

Peloponnesian Wars (460–456, 431–404 B.C.E.)

Wars between Athens and Sparta that spelled the end of the former's role as a major Mediterranean power. The First Peloponnesian War was sparked when Athens renounced its alliance with Sparta against the Persians and allied itself with Sparta's enemy, Argos. Soon after, Megara, following a border dispute with Corinth, withdrew from the Peloponnesian League, to which they had both belonged, and made an alliance with Athens. The defection of Megara meant Sparta was now unable to strike overland at Attica.

For the alliance with Argos to be of any benefit, Athens needed to acquire a foothold in the Peloponnese. The Athenian seaborne landing at Haliae was the result, but the Corinthians successfully repulsed it (458 B.C.E.). Athens now turned its attention to Aegina, the strategy being to clear the nearby seas of hostile navies and thus secure maritime communications to Argos. Matters went well for Athens, which won two naval engagements off Aegina before laying siege to the island's chief town. Even when a Spartan army crossed the Corinthian Gulf and defeated the Athenians at Tanagra (457 B.C.E.), Athens's immediate response was to invade Boeotia, defeat the Boeotians at Oenophyta, and bring all central Greece under its control. Shortly afterward, Aegina surrendered, and the confidence of Athens was well illustrated when an Athenian fleet sailed around the Peloponnese, raiding as it went (456 B.C.E.).

Athens's success was cut short by defeat in Egypt at the hands of the Persians (454 B.C.E.). Furthermore, Athens was forced to surrender control of central Greece after the Boeotians defeated the Athenians at Koroneia (447 B.C.E.). Worse still, with Megara rejoining the Spartan alliance, a Peloponnesian army invaded Attica (456 B.C.E.). Athens had had enough, and a 30-year truce was concluded with Sparta. Athens gave up its claims to central Greece and ceased to interfere in the Peloponnese. However, it retained a grip on Aegina and secured the recognition of its maritime empire. With these diplomatic gains, the First Peloponnesian War ended.

What made the next war between Athens and Sparta inevitable, according to the contemporary historian Thucydides, was Sparta's fear of Athens. Yet this "truest cause" was least discussed because Sparta could hardly stand before its allies and announce its fears. In Thucydides' eyes, the Spartans were not warmongers, being traditionally slow to go to war unless forced. However, when Athens started to meddle with Sparta's allies, namely Corinth, and antagonism arose between the Athenians and the Corinthians over the control of Corcyra (433 B.C.E.) and Potidaia (432 B.C.E.), Sparta was left with little choice. This was especially so when another important ally, Megara, added its voice to the clamor for war.

Now able to invade Attica through the Megarid, Sparta did so during the initial phase of the war. On Pericles' advice, the Athenians took refuge inside the walls surrounding Athens and the Peiraeus and responded to the Spartan ravaging merely by minor cavalry operations, seaborne raids on the Peloponnese, and invasions of the Megarid. But after Pericles' death (429 B.C.E.), Athens, now dominated by Kleon, adopted a more daring strategy. In addition to establishing bases on the Peloponnesian coast—notably at Pylos—it also attempted to knock Boeotia out of the war, but the second invasion ended in defeat at Delion (424 B.C.E.).

The same year saw the Spartan Brasidas surprising Athens with a campaign in northern Greece and winning over a number of Athens's dependencies, including Amphipolis. His own death and that of Kleon in battle outside Athens (422 B.C.E.) led to the conclusion of peace. The "hollow peace," as Thucydides so aptly calls it, was soon in tatters when Alcibiades cobbled together an anti-Spartan coalition in the Peloponnese. Yet it came to naught when the Spartans destroyed the coalition forces, led by Athens and Argos, at Mantinea (418 B.C.E.).

At Alcibiades' urging, Athens launched an expedition against Syracuse (415 B.C.E.), with him, along with his rival Nikias, as the commanders. Before the attack on Syracuse had begun, however, Alcibiades was recalled to answer charges of sacrilege. He fled to Sparta, and on his advice, the Spartans established a permanent base at Dekeleia in Attica (413 B.C.E.). Bogged down in the siege of Syracuse, the expedition ended in total disaster.

Athens was dependent on maritime imports, particularly grain and flax from the Black Sea region, and thus needed a navy for the protection of commerce. But sea power was of little use for the defeat of Sparta, a stalwart land power. Sparta was fully aware of this shortcoming and of Athens's dependence upon seaborne supplies. Still, Sparta had been unable to match the might of the Athenian navy and thus could only dispatch its fleets to stir up revolts within the Athenian empire. Sparta had never been a naval power, but Athens's Sicilian debacle presented Sparta with the opportunity to become one.

Sparta sent a fleet to attempt a blockade of the Hellespont and thus cut Athens off from the Black Sea. Despite this stratagem, King Agis, who was holding Dekeleia, reckoned it was a waste of time attempting to sever Athens's supply lines when he could still see the grain ships putting into the Peiraeus. The alternative was to engage Athens on the high seas, but in doing so Sparta was to suffer absolute disaster at sea on a number of occasions.

Kynossema (411 B.C.E.) was a moral victory for the Athenians, who, lacking their former confidence, had been afraid of the Peloponnesian fleet with its Syracusan allies. Kyzikos (410 B.C.E.) was a scrambling fight along the Hellespontine coast. Off Arginousai (406 B.C.E.), the Peloponnesian fleet, with its more skillful crews, attempted to outmaneuver the Athenians. Sparta ultimately gained the upper hand, and its admiral Lysander resoundingly defeated the Athenians at the naval engagement off Aegospotami (405 B.C.E.). The following year, Lysander was able to strangle Athenians into submission, his naval victory effectively cutting the city off from Black Sea grain supplies.

The ultimate result of the Pelopponesian wars was to weaken all the protagonists. In the end, notwithstanding the resurgence of some, such as Thebes, the Greek polis fell prey to outside barbarians, as the Macedonians swept all before them.

Nic Fields

See also: Alcibiades; Cimon; Syracuse, Siege of

References and further reading:

Kagan, D. *The Fall of the Athenian Empire.* Ithaca, NY: Cornell University Press, 1987.

Peng Dehuai (1898–1974)

China's field commander in the Korean War. Of peasant stock from Hunan province, Peng sought a military career by joining the local Nationalist Kuomintang (KMT) forces in his home province in 1916. By 1921, he had become an officer and remained with the GMD through the Great Northern Expedition. With the collapse of the alliance between the Nationalists and the Communists, Peng joined the latter, having always been concerned with social reform.

One of the People's Liberation Army's first professional soldiers, he emphasized the military verities of discipline, organization, and chain of command, as opposed to guerrilla war tactics. Despite this focus, Peng retained Mao Zedong's confidence and came to respect Mao's military thought.

The pinnacle of Peng's career was leading the People's Volunteer Army in Korea and sending the United Nations forces reeling back across the 38th parallel. The inability of the volunteers to follow up this victory and conclude the war on Communist terms rekindled Peng's concern with conventional approaches to war (he had seen how the United Nations' air and sea power had kept his forces from complete victory in Korea) and possible friction with Mao.

After being raised to the rank of marshal in 1955, Peng was dismissed from command in 1959 for openly challenging Mao over the failures of the Great Leap Forward. Despite partial rehabilitation in 1962, Red Guards arrested Peng in 1966, and he spent the remainder of his life imprisoned and tortured, refusing to apologize for past criticisms. The party posthumously rehabilitated Peng in 1978.

George R. Shaner

See also: Chinese Civil War; Korean War; Mao Zedong

References and further reading:

Domes, Jurgen. *Peng Te-Huai: The Man and the Image.* Stanford, CA: Stanford University Press, 1985.

Hsiung, James C., and Steve I. Levine, eds. *China's Bitter Victory: The War with Japan, 1937–1945.* Armonk, NY: M. E. Sharpe, 1992.

Zhang, Shu Guang. *Mao's Military Romanticism: China and the Korean War, 1950–1953.* Lawrence: University Press of Kansas, 1995.

Pequot War (1636–1637)

An early colonial war that was in practice genocide against an American Indian tribe. The Pequot War began as a contest between the Pequot and Narragansett tribes over trading rights in southern New England. Both groups coveted the European textiles, tools, handicrafts, and contraband (guns and alcohol) that the Dutch and English exchanged for pelts. When the Dutch erected a trading post on the Connecticut River in 1633, Pequots murdered rival Narragansett traders. The Dutch responded by assassinating the Pequot sachem, Tatobem. In retaliation, the Pequots then murdered the captain and crew of an English trading vessel, thinking they were Dutch.

Threatened by the Dutch and the Narragansetts, the Pequots sought assistance from Massachusetts Bay Colony. In 1634, the Puritan leaders in Boston offered to negotiate peace in return for heavy tribute payments and the surrender of those responsible for the deaths of the English traders. The Pequots rejected the offer. For strategic, political, and economic reasons, Massachusetts then constructed Saybrook fort at the mouth of the Connecticut River and planted three settlements upriver.

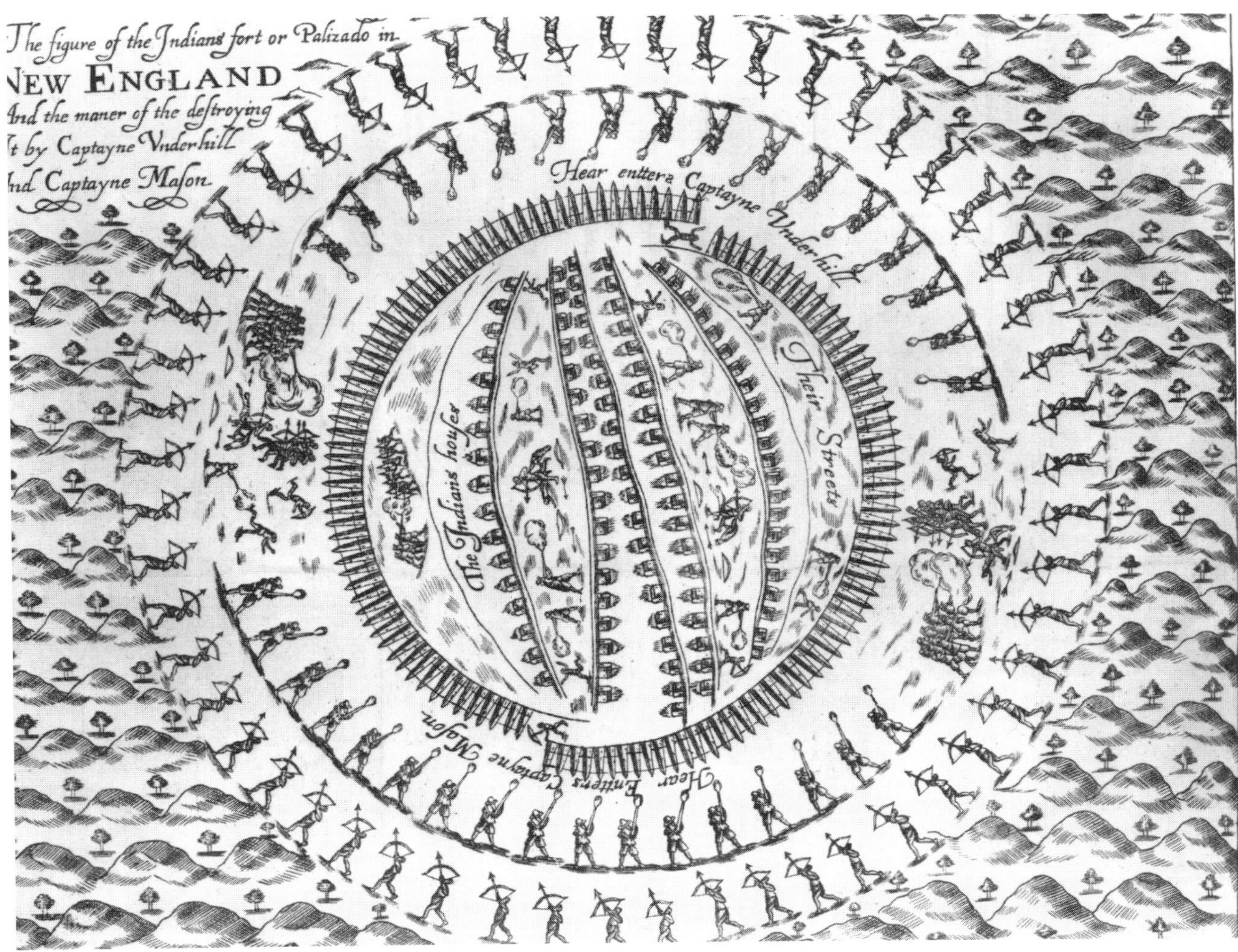

"The figure of the Indians' fort or palizado in New England and the manner of the destroying it by Captain Underhill and Captain Mason." (Library of Congress)

Spurred on by Uncas, the scheming Mohegan sachem, Bay Colony leaders in 1636 pressed their demands for Pequot tribute payments and for the surrender of the murderers of Captain John Stone and his crew. When yet another English trader was found murdered on his vessel near Block Island, Massachusetts, the Bay Colony launched a punitive raid against the Pequots (who were, in fact, innocent of the crime). Unable to draw their enemy into battle, 90 Massachusetts men under Captain John Endecott burned the Pequot villages on Block Island (22 August 1636). The scenario was repeated at Connecticut's Thames River, where undefended villages belonging to the Pequot and their Western Niantic allies were destroyed.

The Pequots retaliated by assaulting the English outposts at Wethersfield and Saybrook, Connecticut. The war quickly escalated. The Pequots and Western Niantics soon faced a combined force of Massachusetts men, Narragansetts, and Eastern Niantics on one front and Connecticut men and their Mohegan allies on another. In a major offensive (26 May 1637), Captain John Mason led 77 Connecticut militia and hundreds of Mohegans and Narragansetts against the Pequot fort at Mystic, Connecticut. They surrounded and burned the fort, killing 600–700 inhabitants, many of them noncombatants—a fact not lost on the Indian allies of the English, who protested the ferocity of the English attacks. The English suffered only two fatalities.

Pequot warriors at nearby Weinshauks arrived too late to save their kin. Their attempt to exact vengeance on the departing English and Indian forces resulted in the deaths of more than 100 additional Pequots. The Mystic massacre and subsequent defeat caused the remaining Pequots to abandon their villages and seek refuge with neighboring tribes. A 120-man force from Massachusetts led by Israel Stoughton engaged a much smaller Pequot force in a swamp known as

"Owl's Nest," killing or capturing approximately 40 Pequots (June 1637). Captive warriors were executed, and Pequot women and children were sold into slavery.

Connecticut troops then joined Massachusetts militia to battle the remaining Pequots. The English encircled their enemy in a swamp near New Haven where, following the surrender of 180 women and children, Pequot warriors battled until dawn (14 July 1637). Sassacus, the Pequot leader, and others managed to escape but were subsequently killed by Mohawks with whom they sought refuge.

The victorious English and their Indian allies treated surviving Pequots as spoils of war, dividing them and selling some into slavery. The English denied the Pequots the use of their tribal name and refused to allow them to rebuild their devastated villages. The Mohegans and Narragansetts agreed to execute any Pequot warriors still at large. In effect, the English asserted their hegemony and set an example for all American Indians by doing everything in their power to eradicate the Pequots socially, politically—and physically.

John J. Navin

References and further reading:

Cave, Alfred. *The Pequot War.* Amherst: University of Massachusetts Press, 1996.

Katz, Steven. "The Pequot War Reconsidered." *The New England Quarterly* 64 (1991).

Hauptman, Laurence, and James Wherry, eds. *The Pequots in Southern New England: The Fall and Rise of an Indian Nation.* Norman: University of Oklahoma Press, 1990.

Jennings, Francis. *The Invasion of America: Indians, Colonialism, and the Cant of Conquest.* Chapel Hill: University of North Carolina Press, 1975.

Salisbury, Neal. *Manitou and Providence: Indians, Europeans, and the Making of New England, 1500–1643.* New York: Oxford University Press, 1982.

Pericles (495–429 B.C.E.)

An incorruptible aristocrat with masterful speaking skills and clear military strategies who consolidated Athenian control over the Aegean. Pericles succeeded Cimon after the Spartan people rebuffed Athenian assistance in 462 B.C.E. Pushing his aggressive policy of spreading Athenian forces from Cyprus to Phoenicia to Egypt during the war with Persia, Pericles earned a reputation as a radical politician with strong imperialistic tendencies. From 450 through 429 B.C.E., he remained the preeminent leader of the Athenian city-state.

Reelected annually as the leader of the Board of 10 Generals, Pericles dictated foreign policy, concentrating resources on the naval fleet and thereby guaranteeing the supply of food and availability of strategic materials. In 437 B.C.E., he sailed into the Black Sea region to unseat the tyrant at Sniope and signed a treaty with the Bosporan king to provide Russian wheat. He also established a colony at Amphipolis to secure access to Macedonia. Known for the massive building program on the Acropolis, Pericles was also instrumental in the building of the 4-mile-long walls that connected the fortified city to the port of Piraeus.

From 456 through 446 B.C.E., the Athenians remained at peace with both the Persians and the Spartans. During this time, Pericles strengthened Athenian control over the region, alienating other city-states in the process. He banned Megarian traders from Aegean markets and interfered with local political disputes and customs. Sparta finally consented to lead an expedition against Athens. From 431 to 421 B.C.E., the Athenians and Spartans fought the Second Peloponnesian War. Pericles embarked on a policy of wearing the enemy down through naval raids around the Peloponnese, while the Spartan army attacked Attica but failed to take Athens. The inhabitants of the countryside took refuge in the city, where an epidemic broke out. It killed tens of thousands of Athenians, including Pericles, who died in 429 B.C.E.

Cynthia Clark Northrup

See also: Peloponnesian Wars

References and further reading:

Mattingly, Harold B. *The Athenian Empire Restored: Epigraphic and Historical Studies.* Ann Arbor: University of Michigan Press, 1996.

Pershing, John J. (1860–1948)

Commander of the American Expeditionary Force in World War I. Born on 11 September 1860 in Missouri. Pershing entered the U.S. Military Academy at West Point at the age of 22. Upon graduation, Jack, as he was then known, entered the cavalry and served in the West. From 1891 to 1894, he was a professor of military science at the University of Nebraska. During these years, he took a law degree and was admitted to the bar. After a brief term as an instructor at West Point, Pershing served with the 10th (Colored) U.S. Cavalry in Cuba during the Spanish-American War. His coolness under fire earned him distinction. He spent much of the next 13 years serving in the Philippines. In 1906, President Theodore Roosevelt promoted Pershing to the rank of brigadier general over 862 senior officers. From 1913 to 1916, he served with the U.S. Army's Southern Department. From March 1916 through February 1917, Pershing commanded the punitive expedition into northern Mexico in pursuit of the revolutionary bandit, Pancho Villa.

As the only American military officer to have held a large command in a foreign country, Pershing was a natural selection to command the American Expeditionary Forces after the declaration of war against Germany in April 1917. Secretary of War Newton Baker allowed Pershing wide leeway in establishing military policy. Pershing demanded and received greatly enlarged American divisions, the size of a European corps, as well as training based on marksmanship, emphasizing rifles over machine guns. In France, he fought to consolidate all American units under his own tactical control, as opposed to assigning U.S. soldiers to Allied units as replacements. Pershing threw his untested troops into battle in the spring of 1918 when the German offensive threatened Paris. In the fall, Pershing launched a major offensive against the Germans in the Meuse-Argonne region, still the single greatest battle in American history. An advocate of unconditional surrender, he counseled against the armistice of 11 November 1918.

Pershing returned to the United States a hero. Congress commissioned him general of the armies, the first officer to hold that title since General Ulysses S. Grant. From 1921 to 1924, Pershing served as U.S. Army chief of staff. He was considered a father figure to a younger generation of officers, including Dwight D Eisenhower, George Marshall, and George Patton. He died in New York City on 15 July 1948.

Gregory Dehler

See also: Baker, Newton D.; Chateau Thierry/Belleau Wood; March, Peyton; Meuse-Argonne; Mexico, U.S. Punitive Expedition in; St. Mihiel; World War I

References and further reading:

Pershing, John J. *My Experiences in the First World War.* New York: Da Capo, 1995.

Smythe, Donald. *Guerrilla Warrior: The Early Life of John J. Pershing.* New York: Charles Scribner's Sons, 1973.

Vandiver, Frank. *Black Jack: The Life and Times of John J. Pershing.* 2 vols. College Station: Texas A & M University Press, 1977.

Persian Civil Wars (1725–1794)

A near century of conflict and invasion that marked Persia's transition from the Middle Ages to the modern era. The Safavid dynasty had ruled Persia since 1514. Their shahs had been patrons of a great cultural renaissance, fixed the boundaries of modern Iran, and imposed Twelver Shiite Islam on the Persian people. But in 1718, a variety of ethnic minorities, autonomy-minded nomads, restive towns, and Sunni Muslims opposed to Shiism had begun to challenge a weakening Safavid regime. These disturbances inspired Mahmud, emir of the Ghilzai Afghans, to invade Persia in 1722. At the Battle of Gulnabad, he sliced up the larger Safavid army, captured the capital of Esfahan, and forced the shah to crown him as successor. Mahmud, however, lacked the force or support to exercise any kind of real power beyond the range of his tribal forces. As other Safavid princes, towns, and tribes joined the insurrection, both Russia and the Ottoman Empire sent expeditions against Iran's borders.

Declaring himself champion of the Safavids, Nadir Khan Afshar rallied much of the army. He drove the Ottomans back to Baghdad in 1733, persuaded Russia to evacuate the north, and retook the capital. In 1736, Nadir deposed the infant Safavid prince and made himself shah. To control the Persian Gulf, he launched an invasion of the sultanate of Oman. In 1739, campaigning against the Afghans, he noted the weakness of the Mogul state of India and plunged into the Ganges Valley. Nadir plundered Delhi and carried off the famous Peacock Throne. He then ranged over much of Uzbek territory, making vassals of Bukhara, Herat, and Khiva. In 1747, Nadir Shah's Qizilbash allies, fearful of his growing megalomania, murdered him.

Nadir's tribal units broke up into separate contingents, and Iran fell back into another decade of anarchy. Eventually, Karim Khan Zand made himself dominant, moving his capital to Shiraz. Recognizing the exhaustion of his people, he tried to avoid war (although he did occupy Basra in Iraq). Instead, he concentrated on repairing the state, keeping harmony among the key tribes like the Bakhtiyari and the Qajars, and patronizing Twelver Shiite Islam. Sadly, his death in 1779 set off another wave of anarchy between towns, tribes, and princes. Agha Muhammad Khan of the Qajar tribe finally succeeded in crushing or co-opting his rivals by 1796. His Qajar dynasty would rule Iran until the end of World War I.

Weston F. Cook Jr.

See also: Nadir Shah

References and further reading:

Avery, Peter, ed. *The Cambridge History of Islam.* Vol. 7. Cambridge, UK: Cambridge University Press, 1991.

Morgan, David. *Medieval Persia 1040–1797.* London: Longman's Press, 1988.

Persian Empire (550 B.C.E.–642 C.E.)

An empire encompassing Iran and at various times parts of Armenia, Asia Minor, and most of the Middle East. It was established by an Iranian people, the Persians, in two eras, the Achaemenid and the Parthian.

The Achaemenid Era

The Achaemenid era of the Persian empire (550–330 B.C.E.) began when Cyrus II Achaemenid of Fars/Persia defeated Astyages of Media in 559, capturing Ecbatana in 550 B.C.E. In 546 B.C.E., Cyrus defeated Croesus of Lydia and occupied

Babylon in 538 B.C.E. Appreciating logistics, Cyrus commissioned the Royal Road, a military highway allowing the Persian army to travel from Susa to Sardis in Lydia (Asia Minor) in three months. Cyrus was killed during a campaign against the Massagetae in 530 B.C.E. His son, Cambyses II, conquered Egypt in 525 B.C.E.

After Cambyses's death, Cyrus's son-in-law, Darius I (r. 522–486 B.C.E.), consolidated and expanded the Persian empire to an area of 2 million square miles with a population of 10 million people, encompassed by the rivers Indus, Danube, Jaxartes, and Nile. Darius divided the empire into 20 satrapies and devised an efficient message relay system by establishing outposts at distances of one horse-travel day apart.

Further improving logistics, Darius commissioned a canal from the Nile to the Red Sea, wide enough for two galleys to pass each other under oar. In 512 B.C.E., Thrace and Macedonia were conquered. The Ionian revolt (500–494 B.C.E.) prompted a Persian army to land in Attica on the plains of Marathon in 490 B.C.E. The numerically superior Persian force was defeated by the 10,000 hoplites of Athens and Plataea.

Xerxes I (r. 486–465 B.C.E.) launched a second campaign against Greece from Sardis in 480 B.C.E. with an army of 100,000. He commissioned a canal dug through the peninsula of Athos and a bridge over the Hellespont River. The Persian army was to march through Thrace, while the fleet sailed alongside to protect and provision. Persian forces marched into Attica and sacked Athens, marking the high point of Persian expansion to the West. The Persian fleet was subsequently defeated by Themistocles in the narrow strait of Salamis, using the maneuverable Greek triremes. Xerxes and the remaining Persian fleet retreated, and the Persian army under Mardonius was defeated in 479 B.C.E. at Plataea.

Achaemenid rule ended after Darius III Condomannus (r. 336–330 B.C.E.) was defeated by Alexander of Macedon, who employed the oblique battle form at Granicus in 334, Issus in 333, and Gaugamela in 331 B.C.E. Alexander occupied the Persian empire from 331 to 323 B.C.E.

The Parthian Era

The Parthian era of the Persian empire (247 B.C.E.–228 C.E.) began when Arsaces II established the independence of Parthia from the Seleucids, who were Alexander's successors. Parthia grew to become a counterweight to Rome. The resurrected Persian empire of Mithradates II (124–88 B.C.E.) stretched from Armenia to India. In 53 B.C.E., a Roman army of 40,000 under Marcus Licinius Crassus was annihilated by the Persian forces of Orodes I.

During the continued Roman-Persian struggle, the approximate border between the two empires was the Euphrates River. Major Roman campaigns were undertaken in the years 116, 161, 195, 217, and 232 C.E. The Parthian dynasty ended when Ardashir Sassan I of Fars defeated the Parthian army of Artabanus at Hormizdagh in 226. Ardashir proclaimed himself an Achaemenid heir, beginning the Sassanid dynasty of the Persian empire, which ruled until the Islamic conquest of Persia in 642 C.E.

Neville G. Panthaki

See also: Alexander the Great; Alexander's Wars of Conquest; Cyrus II the Great; Gaugamela, Battle of; Greek-Persian Wars; Issus, Battle of; Marathon, Battle of; Parthian Empire; Plataea, Battle of; Sassanid Empire; Shapur I; Shapur II; Xerxes I

References and further reading:

Cook, John Manuel. *The Persian Empire.* New York: Schocken Books, 1983.

Dandamaev, Mikhail. *A Political History of the Achaemenid Empire.* New York: E. J. Brill, 1989.

Debevoise, Neilson Carel. *A Political History of Parthia.* New York: Greenwood Press, 1968.

Vogelsang, W. J. *The Rise and Organization of the Achaemenid Empire.* New York: Brill, 1992.

Persian Wars of Expansion (559–509 B.C.E.)

Dramatic rise of a minor Asian kingdom into the world's most powerful empire. At the beginning of the sixth century B.C.E., Media was a tributary state of Assyria. King Astyages of Media married his daughter, Mandane, to Cambyses, king of Anshan. Cambyses governed Fars (Persia), a region about 300 miles in diameter on the northeastern shore of the Persian Gulf. His son Cyrus succeeded him as king of Anshan in 559 and immediately began intrigues against Media, inducing the Median general Harpagus to defect.

Cyrus was ready when Astyages attacked Persia in 550 B.C.E. He counterattacked, occupied the Median capital, Ecbatana, overthrew his grandfather, and ascended the joint throne of Media and Persia. This event is regarded as the founding of the Persian Empire, sometimes called the Achaemenid Empire, after the clan of Cyrus.

After incorporating Media, Cyrus marched northwest, around the Babylonian Empire, taking Armenia and Cappadocia. By defeating King Croesus at Pteria in 546 B.C.E., Cyrus gained Lydia and its tributary state of Ionia and thus controlled all of Asiatic Turkey. Between 545 and 540 B.C.E., he moved northeast into Central Asia nearly as far as modern Tashkent.

The biblical books 1 and 2 Kings, the Prophets, and Daniel show the impact of Persia on the ancient Hebrews. The 10 northern tribes were dispersed when their kingdom, Israel, fell to Assyria in 721 B.C.E. and further when Assyria fell to Babylon in 612 B.C.E. The two southern tribes were taken into captivity when Babylon defeated their kingdom, Judah, in 587 B.C.E., but after Persia conquered Babylon in 539 B.C.E., Cyrus released the Hebrew exiles by edict in 538 B.C.E., enabling a remnant to return home and found the religion of Judaism. When he died in battle against the Massagetes in 529 B.C.E., he was known as "Cyrus the Great" as much for his merciful and intelligent administration as for his military triumphs.

Cyrus's son Cambyses II came to power by murdering his brother, Cyrus's heir, Smerdis, in 529 B.C.E. Smerdis's death was kept secret. Cambyses led his army west, defeated Pharaoh Psamtik III at Pelusium in 525 B.C.E., and thus added Egypt to the empire. He died under mysterious circumstances in Syria in 522 B.C.E., possibly a suicide, probably insane.

Darius, husband of Cyrus's daughter Atossa, murdered Gaumata, who had been masquerading as Smerdis in Cambyses's absence, in 522 B.C.E. The Persian nobles acclaimed him king the next year. In 518 B.C.E., he expanded Cambyses's Egyptian conquests into Libya. By 513 B.C.E., he had gained all the land in India west of the Indus River. The same year, he pushed into Thrace. After suffering a major setback against the Scythians in the Danube Valley in 512 B.C.E., Darius returned to his capitals at Persepolis and Sardis and spent most of the period from 509 B.C.E. until his invasion of Greece in 492 B.C.E. consolidating his power.

By 518 B.C.E., the Persian Empire included 20 numbered provinces, or satrapies: Media, Susiana, Babylonia, Arabia, Assyria, Egypt, Armenia, Cappadocia, Lydia, Ionia, Cilicia, Sagartia, Parthia, Ariana, Bactria, Sogdiana, Arachosia, India, Gandhara, and Gedrosia. The boundaries, administrations, loyalties, and names of these satrapies frequently changed. At its greatest extent in 492 B.C.E., just after Darius conquered Macedonia, the Persian Empire stretched from Libya to the Indus River and from the Persian Gulf to the Aral Sea. It lasted until Alexander the Great conquered the empire at the Battle of Gaugamela in 331 B.C.E.

Eric v. d. Luft

See also: Alexander the Great; Assyria; Babylonian Empire; Croesus; Cyrus II the Great; Greek-Persian Wars; Persian Empire; Scythians

References and further reading:

Collins, Robert J. *The Medes and Persians: Conquerors and Diplomats.* New York: McGraw-Hill, 1972.

Culican, William. *The Medes and Persians.* New York: Praeger, 1965.

Curtis, John. *Ancient Persia.* Cambridge, MA: Harvard University Press, 1990.

Rogers, Robert William. *A History of Ancient Persia from Its Earliest Beginnings to the Death of Alexander the Great.* Freeport, NY: Books for Libraries Press, 1971.

Persian-Afghan Wars (1726–1857)

No less than three major wars between Persia and rebel Afghans in a 131-year period. These wars were intertwined with events in Mogul India, the Ottoman Empire, and czarist Russia but centered on the rise of Afghan, British, and French power in southern and southwestern Asia.

The war of 1726–1738 saw the Persians under Nadir Shah regain control of Afghanistan and invade Mogul India. Nadir developed a disciplined army slowly, never taking on battle unless he could win and turning rival Afghan tribes against each other rather than against Persia. He first targeted the fabled border fortress of Herat. There, he defeated the Abdali Afghans, who became his allies. He then turned on the Ghilzai Afghans and defeated them in pitched battle at Mihmandust in 1729 and Zhargan in 1730. Nadir now had command of more than 100,000 Afghanis plus his Persian troops, and after fighting the Turko-Persian War of 1730–1736, he stabilized Persia. In 1737, he besieged the fortified city of Kandahar with its 30-foot-thick walls and took it by deceit, partially burning it. This action opened the way for the Persian invasion of Mogul India two months later.

The war of 1836–1838 followed years of European meddling in Persian, Afghan, and Indian affairs. Shah Muhammed of Persia sought Russia's help to retake Herat from the Afghans, who were backed by the British. A Persian siege from November 1837 to September 1838 was repulsed with Persian losses as high as 1,700 men in one frontal assault. However, the Afghan ruler Dost Muhammed then sought to launch a second war against the Sikhs in India. This led to 12 years of British-Afghan hostilities.

The war of 1855–1857 involved yet another siege of Herat by the Persians. The Afghans, who had signed a peace treaty with the British in India, received British aid and repelled the last great effort by the Persians to break through into India again, as they had done under Nadir Shah.

Christopher Howell

See also: Panipat, Battles of; Mogul-Persian Wars; Persian Empire

References and further reading:

Adamec, Ludwig. *Dictionary of Afghan Wars, Revolutions, and Insurgencies.* Lanham, MD: Scarecrow Press, 1996.

Ladjevardian, Reza. *From Ancient Persia to Contemporary Iran.* Slage Press, 1999.

Peru-Bolivia Confederation, War of the (1836–1839)

Conflict caused by the brief unification of Peru and Bolivia under the leadership of Bolivian general Andrés Santa Cruz in 1836. Chile objected to the creation of the new state, which had the potential to threaten Chilean security. When Bolivia reneged on a treaty provision for tax exemptions on Chilean imports and Peru imposed a tariff on imports from

Valparaiso, tensions mounted. Chilean anger was further aroused by the use of a Peruvian port by dissident general Ramón Freire to launch a coup attempt on the government. Chile's president, Diego Portales, responded by ordering a naval attack on the Peruvian port of Callo, resulting in the seizure of three Peruvian ships. Santa Cruz responded by arresting a Chilean diplomat, an incident that infuriated Portales, who demanded that the confederation be dissolved. This along with other Chilean demands caused Santa Cruz to declare war.

Chile's initial invasion of Peru met with defeat and the capture of nearly the entire army. Santa Cruz offered to release the army in exchange for Chilean recognition of the confederation and the return of the three captured vessels. Chile agreed, and the army returned. Chile then renounced the agreement and launched another invasion. General Manuel Bulnes led Chile to victory at the Battle of Bunin and followed it up with a decisive triumph at Yungay on 20 January 1839. After his defeat at Yungay, Santa Cruz went into exile in Ecuador, and the Peru-Bolivia Confederation fell.

George M. Lauderbaugh

References and further reading:

Burr, Robert K. *By Reason or Force: Chile and the Balancing of Power in South America, 1830–1905.* Berkeley: University of California Press, 1965.

Peru-Ecuador Conflict (1941–1999)

One of the most persistent South American boundary disputes. Since their establishment as independent republics, Peru and Ecuador have disputed a triangular area on the upper Amazon of approximately 120,000 square miles, bounded on the south by the Mara and Amazon Rivers and on the north and east by the Putumayo River. The remoteness and topography of the region, the imprecision of Spanish colonial boundaries, the chaotic conditions that existed in the aftermath of the collapse of the Spanish Empire, and domestic politics explain why the dispute has been so long-lasting and so difficult to resolve. Numerous attempts to negotiate a settlement between 1830 and 1941 met with failure.

In July 1941, Peru invaded Ecuador's littoral province of El Oro and threatened the port of Guayaquil. Peru's army of more than 10,000 was supported by an air force of 25 planes and soon overwhelmed Ecuadorian defenses. Ecuador's ill-trained and poorly equipped armed forces, numbering less than 1,600, lacked air support. As Peruvian troops advanced on Guayaquil, Ecuador sought a negotiated settlement. The war resulted in 150 Ecuadorian and 400 Peruvian casualties. In January 1942, Ecuador and Peru signed the Rio Protocol, which provided for the withdrawal of Peruvian troops, the cession of some 80,000 square miles of the territory to Peru, and the creation of a boundary commission to delineate the border.

The discovery of the Cenapa River in 1951 complicated the demarcation process and provided Ecuador with an opportunity to continue to press for sovereign access to the Mara River. In 1960 Jose Maria Velasco Ibarra, Ecuador's stridently nationalist president, renounced the 1942 protocol. Hostilities began anew on 28 January 1981 in the disputed Cordillera del Condor region. In a week of fighting, Peruvian commandos and warplanes attacked three Ecuadorian outposts and forced their abandonment. The incident resulted in nearly 200 casualties.

After the 1981 conflict, Ecuador made a concerted effort to upgrade its armed forces in preparation for a renewed conflict in the Cordillera del Condor sector. Ecuador obtained Kifir fighter aircraft from Israel and purchased modern shoulder-fired surface-to-air missiles. In January 1995, Peru attempted to dislodge Ecuadorian troops from fortified positions in the disputed zone. The Ecuadorian modernization program paid off as surface-to-air missiles and Ecuadorian fighters shot down two Sukhoi SU-22 fighter bombers, one A-37, one Canberra bomber, and five helicopters and held its fortified outposts. Peru suffered 300 casualties, whereas Ecuadorian loses were placed at less than 50.

Negotiations intensified after the 1995 clash because both sides had each spent $250 million on the military operation, and both had little enough to show for it. In October 1998, Peru and Ecuador signed a final agreement that was soon ratified by both governments. Peru retained most of the territory gained in the 1941 war, while Ecuador was granted private property rights on the Mara River.

George Lauderbaugh

References and further reading:

Wood, Bryce. *Aggression and History: The Case of Ecuador and Peru.* Ann Arbor, MI: University Microfilms International, 1978.

Zook, David H., Jr. *Zarumilla Maranón: The Ecuador-Peru Dispute.* New York: Bookman Associates, 1964.

Peruvian Guerrilla War (1980–2000)

A Marxist uprising that did little to change conditions in Peru. In 1980, 12 years of military rule in Peru came to an end when Fernando Belaunde Terry became president for the second time. This was not the only aspect of the 1960s life to return to Peru in the 1980s. On the eve of the 1980 election, the guerrilla group Sendero Luminoso (Shining Path) commenced their "people's war" by burning ballot boxes in the Ayacucho region. Guerrilla activity had taken place in the 1960s, but this new activity by Sendero Luminoso heralded a bloody new phase of Peruvian history.

Sendero Luminoso had been born of a split within the pro-Soviet Communist Party in 1970. Its believers followed the ideas of the Peruvian Marxist Mariategui and Maoism. Their tactics were brutal, and they perceived violence as the fundamental mechanism for political change. They saw anybody involved with the government as legitimate targets, including those simply participating in elections. They reintroduced the Inca practice of displaying a dead dog before attacking a village and intimidated people into joining them. In July 1992, they detonated a car bomb in the Lima suburb of Miraflores, which killed 21 people and brought the war to the middle classes.

In 1982, a second guerrilla group was founded: Movimiento Revolucionario Tupac Amaru (MRTA). This group consisted of more middle-class members and avoided the indiscriminate and widespread violence of the Sendero Luminoso. It received a reputation for "flashy" operations and in July 1990 freed 60 prisoners from Lima's high-security Canto Grande prison.

Belaunde was succeeded as president by Alan Garcia in 1985, but guerrilla activity worsened. By 1990, half the country was under a state of emergency. In 1990, the unknown candidate Alberto Fujimori became president. Although he stood on a ticket of not increasing austerity measures, two months into office he introduced "Fujishock," which was much harsher than anything seen before. He also gave the army carte blanche in dealing with the guerrillas and ignored human rights abuses.

"Fujishock" appeared to be working, when in 1992 MRTA leader Victor Polay and Sendero Luminoso leader Abimael Guzman were arrested. During 1994–1995, many guerrillas gave themselves up under the Law of Repentance. It appeared Fujimori had defeated the guerrillas.

This perception quickly changed on 17 December 1996, when 14 MRTA members took more than 600 hostages at a reception at the Japanese Embassy in Lima. The hostages included 19 ambassadors and Fujimori's own brother. Although many were released, a standoff continued until 22 April 1997, when security forces attacked the embassy, freeing all the prisoners and managing to kill all the guerrillas.

Human rights abuses continued, provoking international protests of the treatment of four Chilean members of MRTA and the American Lori Berenson. (Her sentence was reduced in August 2000.)

The violent nature of Peruvian life continued, with mass demonstrations during Fujimori's much-debated third election in 2000. Although he won, he was forced to resign in November because of bribery scandals and was succeeded by Valentin Paniagua. The basic economic, political, and social causes of Peru's unrest and violence remained unaddressed.

M. J. Bain

See also: Nicaraguan Civil War (1979); Panama Incursion; Salvadorian Civil War

References and further reading:

Black, J. N. *Latin America: Its Problems and Its Promise.* Boulder, CO: Westview Press, 1998.

Latin American Regional Reports Andean Group Report. London: Latin America Newsletters, 1998–2000.

Loveman, B., and T. M. Davies Jr. *Che Guevara Guerrilla Warfare.* 3d ed. Wilmington: Scholarly Resources Inc, 1997.

Skidmore, T. E., and P. H. Smith. *Modern Latin America.* New York: Oxford University Press, 1997.

Pétain, Henri-Philippe (1856–1951)

French Army marshal and political figure. Born at Cauchy-à-la Tour, near Arras, on 24 April 1856, Pétain graduated from St. Cyr in 1878. Had he not fought in World War I, he would have retired as a colonel. Pétain held that new weapons gave the defense superiority. When World War I began, he saw that it would be a struggle of attrition, and he argued for

Portrait of Henri-Philippe Pétain. (Library of Congress)

wearing out the Germans along the entire front and only then mounting a "decisive effort."

At the start of the war, Pétain was temporarily commanding a brigade. He then commanded a division (September) and an army corps (November). By June 1915, he was a full general commanding the Second Army. When the Germans mounted their offensive at Verdun in February 1916, he was placed in charge of its defense, reorganizing its defenses and transforming logistics so that supplies ran smoothly to the front. His leadership at Verdun made him a national hero.

Following the disastrous April–May 1917 Nivelle Offensive, Pétain was called on to deal with widespread mutinies in the French army. Made commander of the French army in May, he improved conditions and morale and promised the men that he would not waste their lives needlessly.

In December 1918, there was general public satisfaction with Pétain's promotion to marshal of France, and he led the victory parade down the Champs Elysées on 14 July 1919. He retained command of the French army until 1931. Pétain supported the construction of the Maginot Line and served as war minister (1934). Appointed ambassador to Spain (1939), he was recalled to be the last premier of the Third Republic (June 1940).

Following the armistice with the Germans and the granting of emergency powers, Pétain set up an authoritarian government in southern, unoccupied France at Vichy that accepted collaboration with Nazi Germany. Tried as a war criminal after the war, he was convicted and sentenced to death, which was commuted to life in prison. Removed to the Isle d'Yeu, he died there on 23 July 1951.

Spencer C. Tucker

See also: Foch, Ferdinand; French Army; Joffre, Joseph Jacques Césaire; Verdun

References and further reading:

Griffiths, Richard. *Marshal Pétain.* London: Constable, 1970.

Lottman, Herbert R. *Pétain, Hero or Traitor.* New York: William Morrow, 1985.

Ryan, Stephen. *Pétain the Soldier.* New York: A. S. Barnes, 1969.

Peter I, Romanov, Czar of Russia ("The Great") (1672–1725)

Recognized as the first "modern" ruler of Russia who increased the pace of modernization in a military and administrative perspective, bringing Russia into the community of European great powers. Peter was born in Moscow on 9 June 1672. After the death of his half-brother Feodor, Peter and his half-brother Ivan became co-czars in April 1682, under the regency of Peter's half-sister Sophia, an impossible arrangement. In August 1689, Peter was acclaimed sole czar, following an unsuccessful coup by Sophia. However, possessing a curiosity for all things technical and military, Peter left governing to his mother, Natalia Naryshkin, until her death in 1694.

Peter's first military venture, to capture the fortress of Azov in June–October 1695, failed because of Russia's lack of naval power. After supervising the construction of 1,400 barges and 29 galleys at Voronezh, Peter made a second attempt in May–July 1696, which succeeded.

Peter is credited as being the father of the Russian navy, sending Russians abroad to learn craftsmanship. During his Grand Embassy through Europe from March 1697 to September 1698, Peter met Sir Isaac Newton, apprenticed in a Dutch shipyard, worked as a laborer at the Royal Navy shipyard in Greenwich, and recruited foreign labor to work in Russia, among other things. In 1701, Peter established the Admiralty and commissioned Kronstadt Naval Base at a cost of 6.25 million rubles. From 1701 to 1721, Russia's naval expenditure grew from 81,000 to 1.2 million rubles. By 1725, Russia possessed 48 ships of the line and 787 auxiliary craft, serviced by 28,000 men.

After the Swedes defeated the Russians at Narva on 30 November 1700, Peter embarked on a series of reforms to strengthen the military. Conscription was instituted in 1705, and training manuals and the order of battle were revised. After the feudal noble *strelt'sy* (musketeers) revolted in 1698, Peter patterned their replacements on the Preobrezhensky and Semonovsky regiments, which he had created for childhood war games; they were cultivated into elite, well-equipped formations known as the Guards Regiments in 1708.

A program to increase the amount and effectiveness of artillery quadrupled Russian pig iron production between 1700 and 1720. Government expenditure on the army and navy was 66 percent of the total in 1701, 80 percent in 1710, and 66 percent in 1724. By 1725, Russia possessed a regular army of 210,000 troops and 100,000 Cossacks.

Peter likewise instituted educational reforms, creating the Artillery Academy in 1701, the Engineering Academy in 1712, the Naval Academy in 1715, a Mining Institute in 1716, 40 basic schools for math and literacy in the provinces in 1722, and the Academy of Sciences in 1724.

By 1720, Russia was divided into 12 provinces and military districts, which made the military in each region responsible for its own conscription and boarding of recruits and allowed for direct expropriation of taxes. In 1722, the creation of the Table of Ranks, a grade scale of 14 positions in both the military and state bureaucracies, instituted a merit system.

Russia emerged victorious against the Swedes at the conclusion of the Great Northern War in 1721, with a victory on land at Poltava in 8 July 1709 and at sea during the Battle of Cape Hanko in 1714.

On 8 February 1725, Peter died in St. Petersburg, the city he had founded in 1703. He personified Russia's conflicting orientations through subsequent years: to the West and cities like St. Petersburg for modernization and development; to the East and the villages and countryside, away from "decadent" Western influences, to be renewed in the authority and orthodoxy of pure "Holy Mother Russia."

Neville G. Panthaki

See also: Charles XII; Northern War, Great; Poltava; Russo-Turkish Wars

References and further reading:

Anderson, Matthew Smith. *Peter the Great.* New York: Longman, 1995.

Kliuchevskii, Vasilii Osipovich. *Peter the Great.* London: Macmillan, 1958.

Raeff, Marc. *Peter the Great, Reformer or Revolutionary?* Boston: Heath, 1963.

Sumner, Benedict Humphrey. *Peter the Great and the Emergence of Russia.* London: English Universities Press, 1964.

Petersburg, Siege of (June 1864–April 1865)

The last major obstacle to the Union's seizure of Richmond. In June 1864, after the clash at Cold Harbor, Ulysses S. Grant settled into a siege at Petersburg, an important city about 20 miles south of Richmond. Once Grant realized that he could not take the Confederate defenses (which had begun two years earlier during George McClellan's Peninsula campaign), he decided to keep extending his line to his left to cut the roads and railroads supplying Petersburg and hence Richmond. Once he cut the last link, he knew that Robert E. Lee would have to abandon his defenses, come out into the open, and most likely be defeated by the large and well-supplied Army of the Potomac.

There were several major battles during the long siege, including Globe Tavern (18–21 August), Ream's Station (25 August), Peebles Farm (29 September), and Boydton Plank–Burgess's Mill (27 October).

Lee recognized that once winter ended, Grant would continue his plan to isolate Petersburg in the spring. Lee therefore had General John Gordon attack at Fort Stedman on 25 March 1865; Gordon's troops were led by soldiers with axes seeking to cut through the strong wooden defenses. Gordon's assault really was to cover Lee's effort to retreat to North Carolina, meet up with Joseph Johnston, defeat William Sherman's army, and then turn to face Grant—a fantastic, indeed, desperate conception. Grant was always cool when attacked and recognized that to secure a local superiority—mass—at the point of attack, Lee must have engaged in economy of force elsewhere. Grant ordered a general attack all along the siege lines.

Thus Lee felt he had no alternative but to order the evacuation of Petersburg and Richmond. Thereafter he tried to retreat south, was cut off by superior Union cavalry, and moved mostly westward to his fate at Appomattox Court House.

Charles M. Dobbs

See also: American Civil War; Grant, Ulysses Simpson; Lee, Robert Edward

References and further reading:

Hendrickson, Robert. *The Road to Appomattox.* New York: John Wiley, 1998.

Horn, John. *The Petersburg Campaign: June 1864–April 1865.* Conshohocken, PA: Combined Books, 1993.

Trudeau, Noah Andre. *The Last Citadel: Petersburg, Virginia, June 1864–April 1865.* Boston: Little, Brown, 1993.

Pharsalus, Battle of (48 B.C.E.)

A pivotal battle of the Roman civil wars in which Julius Caesar defeated Pompey and contributed to the demise of the Roman Republic. Fought on 9 August 48 B.C.E., the engagement occurred at an undetermined locale in the plains a few miles north of Pharsalus (Fársala, Greece), a Thessalian city near the Enipeus River.

After abortive assaults on Pompey's entrenchments at Dyrrachium (Durres, Albania) in early 48 B.C.E., Caesar retreated southeast into the interior of Greece, seeking provisions and drawing Pompey away from his supply fleet. By early August, both armies encamped near Pharsalus. Pompey's forces totaled between 36,000 and 47,000 infantry in 11 legions and almost 7,000 cavalry, and Caesar commanded approximately 24,000 infantry in eight understrength legions and 1,000 cavalry. Confident of victory through attrition, Pompey hesitated to attack. However, 200 senators accompanying him agitated for a decisive confrontation, and on 9 August he deployed while Caesar was breaking camp.

Both commanders employed traditional Roman tactics, each arraying their soldiers in three main lines of battle. Pompey hoped to flank Caesar's right with a massive cavalry assault, followed by close support from several thousand archers and slingers. Caesar brilliantly countered with a fourth line of six infantry cohorts, who charged with devastating effect into the horsemen as they passed. After obliterating Pompey's cavalry, slingers, and archers, this force maneuvered around his left, attacking the main lines from behind. Simultaneously, Caesar ordered his third line into action, relieving his first two lines. Their opponents, caught in this dire pincer, quickly became disorganized and fled, suffering losses of 6,000 dead and 24,000 captured. After his defeat, Pompey escaped to Pelusium (Tell el-Farama, Egypt), where henchmen of King Ptolemy XIII assassinated him. Caesar subdued the remaining Pompeians the following year.

Ian Janssen

See also: Caesar, Julius; Pompey the Great; Roman Civil Wars (88–30 B.C.E.)

References and further reading:
Greenhalgh, Peter. *Pompey: The Republican Prince.* Columbia: University of Missouri Press, 1982.
Jiménez, Ramon. *Caesar against Rome: The Great Roman Civil War.* Westport, CT: Praeger, 2000.

Philip, King (Metacomet)(1639–1676)

Instigator of proportionally the bloodiest war in American history. King Philip Metacomet, sachem of the Wampanoags, was the son of Massasoit, who had become allied with Plymouth colony during the Pequot War, and the younger brother of Alexander Wamsutta. Becoming leader of the tribe in 1662, Philip found that the situation in which his father had maintained the peace had significantly changed. Missionaries recruited "praying Indians," who enjoyed better status than non-Christians under the laws of the colonies, while Philip increasingly had to sell titles to land through the colonial courts in order to have his authority validated and to raise cash for European goods. At the same time, he was constantly accused of planning to wage war against the Plymouth or Massachusetts colonies. Many of these charges came from John Sassamon, a Christianized Indian who was a former secretary of Philip's. When Sassamon was murdered and three Wampanoags were hanged for the crime after a questionable trial, it seemed to Philip that not only had the colony forfeited its claim to his loyalty but that he had to strike quickly. Wampanoags attacked Swansea in June 1675, killing settlers, and drew other tribes to his cause after a total lunar eclipse occurred on 26 June, seemingly a portent of victory.

The settlers were enraged at the destruction of a series of towns, including Middlebury and Dartmouth, and infuriated by the "skulking" way of war used by the Indians, whose better marksmanship, stealth, and use of fire to obliterate settlements stymied their forts and defensive lines. While other tribes, including the Nipmuks, continued the war, Philip traveled to New York in the fall of 1675 to seek an alliance with the Mohawks but was defeated badly when Governor Edmund Andros incited the Mohawks against him. Philip was forced to return to Massachusetts, where he faced the problem that although the war had united the disparate and usually feuding colonies against all Indians, even those who fought alongside them, the war had done nothing to solidify the tribes, who acted independently. Philip was increasingly harried by Captain Benjamin Harris of Plymouth and then betrayed by an irate subordinate, who sought revenge after Philip ordered his brother executed for arguing in favor of surrender. Philip was killed in Harris's raid, but in the fury of the colonists, his body was dragged from the bog in which it had fallen and dismembered and his head was displayed in Plymouth for 25 years.

Full-length engraved portrait of Philip, alias Metacomet of Pokanoket. (Library of Congress)

Although the instigator of the war, King Philip played a minor role in the conflict, which continued in the hands of other Indian leaders until 1678. (Oddly, a U.S. Navy gunboat was named in honor of Metacomet in the mid–nineteenth century.)

Margaret Sankey

See also: King Philip's War

References and further reading:
Drake, James D. *King Philip's War: Civil War in New England 1675–6.* Amherst: University of Massachusetts Press, 1999.
Lepore, Jill. *The Name of War: King Philip's War and the Origins of American Identity.* New York: Alfred A. Knopf, 1998.
Schultz, Eric B., and Michael J. Tougais. *King Philip's War.* Woodstock, VT: Countryman Press, 1999.

Philip II Augustus (1165–1223)

Victor of the first Hundred Years War, between the Capetians and the Plantagenets. Philip was the son of King Louis VII. Crowned co-king in 1179, he ruled France a year later at the age of 16, after his father's death. He inherited the confrontation between the Capetians and the Plantagenets. The latter were kings of England but also vassals of the kings of France for Normandy, Anjou, and Guyenne.

Plantagenet power was a constant threat to Capetian monarchy. Philip's territorial policy was to extend royal domain by whatever means possible: marriage, bribe, felony, or war. In 1189, he supported the rebellion of Henry II's sons against their father and received Vermandois and Artois as a reward. He took advantage of the captivity of Richard I the Lionhearted to take Normandy but was defeated when Richard returned (at Fréteval in 1194 and at Courcelles in 1198). The French monarchy was saved by Richard's death in 1199.

The war with King John, Richard's successor, continued until 1216. John had refused to take an oath of allegiance to Philip. According to feudal law, John was a "felon" and had lost all rights to his French fiefs. Philip took Normandy (1202–1204) and Brittany (1205).

With the election of a new Holy Roman Emperor in 1213, a European alliance formed against Philip: John of England, Otto IV of Brunswick, and Ferrando of Portugal. In 1214, France was invaded from the south by John's army, soundly defeated by Philip's son on 12 July, at La Roche aux Moines, but the main threat was the emperor's coalition coming from the northern border. The Battle of Bouvines (27 July 1214) was a crushing victory for Philip. The emperor lost his crown to the French-supported Frederick II Hohenstaufen.

The end of Philip's reign saw expansion south. He accepted allegiance from Simon de Montfort for confiscated Toulouse County. He allowed his heir, Louis, to command a crusade (1217–1219) against the Albigencian heretics, resulting in a bridgehead for the French monarchy in southern France. When Philip died, he enjoyed an authority that was recognized far more widely than that of any previous French king. His nickname "Augustus" recalls the first Roman emperor, an important reformer. Philip first established bailiffs as an institution and also organized a royal central administration, the Curia Regis (king's court).

Gilles Boué

See also: Henry II, King of England; Richard I

References and further reading:
Baldwin, John W. *The Government of Philip Augustus: Foundations of French Royal Power in the Middle Ages.* Berkeley: University of California Press, 1986.
Bautier Robert, ed. *La France de Philippe Auguste.* Paris: CNRS, 1980.
Nicolle, David. *French Medieval Armies 1000–1300.* London: Osprey Publishing, 1991.

Philip II of Macedon (c. 382–336 B.C.E.)

Ruler who used innovations and organizational restructuring to turn the Macedonian army into a competent fighting force, laying the foundation for his domination of Greece and Alexander the Great's domination of Asia.

In 359 B.C.E., Philip's father, King Amyntas III, died in battle with the Illyrians. Using guile and force and notwithstanding the opposition of several pretenders, the young Philip managed to secure the throne of Macedon. He gathered up what army he could muster. Using a combination of bribery and force, he solidified his hold on the country. Having quickly reorganized and trained the army, he marched off to defeat the Illyrians.

Macedonia was an agrarian state with little in the way of an urban population. Mounted noblemen, the "Companions," were the backbone of the military. They fought as shock troops, requiring considerably more organization than Greek cavalry skirmishers. Philip furthered the effectiveness of the cavalry by the introduction of the *sarissa,* a long spear similar to the Napoleonic lance in size and weight.

In contrast, infantry peasant levies served only as an auxiliary arm fighting en masse with no tactical organization and would certainly have been unable to stand up to Greek hoplites in battle. Philip's other innovation, therefore, was the Macedonian phalanx. He borrowed heavily from the Theban phalanx, but where the typical Greek phalanx was between eight and 12 men deep, Philip's was 16. Although this took away from the width of the line, the cavalry was there to protect the flanks. More men meant a stronger push, all-important in shock warfare.

Philip's was an integrated army that represented a fusion of the mobile warfare of the Persians and the infantry shock tactics of the Greeks. It was the last step in the military revolution that produced the army of Alexander the Great and perhaps the pinnacle of Greek military might.

James Corbin

See also: Alexander the Great; Cavalry; Granicus, Battle of the
References and further reading:
Cawkwell, George. *Philip of Macedon.* London: Faber & Faber, 1978.
Delbruck, Hans. *Warfare in Antiquity.* Lincoln: University of Nebraska Press, 1975.
Prichett, W. Kendrick. *The Greek State at War.* Vol. 1. Berkeley: University of California Press, 1971.

Philippi, Battle of (42 B.C.E.)

Decisive battle in which Mark Antony and Octavian defeated the assassins of Julius Caesar, Brutus, and Cassius. After the murder of Julius Caesar, the consul Mark Antony, along with the designated heir Octavian and proconsul Aemilius Lepidus, formed an alliance known as the "Second Triumvirate." It was directed against Caesar's leading assassins, Brutus and Cassius, known as the "Liberators."

Leaving Lepidus to control Italy, Antony and Octavian moved to northern Greece. The army of the Liberators was positioned astride the Via Egnatia, to the west of Philippi, in a position partly protected by a marsh. Both armies contained 19 legions, but the army of the Liberators was superior in cavalry. Both sides entrenched, building stone dikes, palisades, and towers. Antony attempted an outflanking movement by cutting through the marsh. After a 10-day effort, Antony's troops finally attacked Cassius's camp and crushed its army. Cassius, not knowing that Brutus's forces had successfully assaulted Octavian's camp, committed suicide.

During the next three weeks, Antony and Octavian continued to alter their angles of attack in an attempt to outflank Brutus's remaining forces, as Brutus extended his lines eastward in response. In the end, Brutus, against his better judgment, agreed to a battle in which his army was routed. Desperate, he too took his own life.

Ioannis Georganas

See also: Cassius
References and further reading:
Gabba, Emilio. *Republican Rome: The Army and the Allies.* Oxford, UK: Blackwell, 1976.
Keppie, Lawrence. "The Roman Army of the Later Republic." In *Warfare in the Ancient World,* ed. John Hackett, 169–191. London: Sidgwick & Jackson, 1989.

Philippine Insurrection (1899–1902)

First major jungle war fought by the United States. The Philippine Insurrection stemmed from the Spanish-American War of 1898, in which the United States decisively defeated Spain and acquired an overseas empire that included the Philippine Islands. More specifically, U.S. involvement in the Philippines dated from the Battle of Manila Bay on 1 May 1898, when a U.S. naval squadron commanded by George Dewey destroyed a Spanish fleet. News of the victory prompted Filipino forces commanded by General Emilio Aguinaldo to declare independence from Spain and form a national government, but Spanish forces ignored them and surrendered to the United States instead. Their action left the question of independence in the hands of the Americans, who decided to annex the Philippines for economic and military reasons in February 1899.

In the same month, fighting broke out between U.S. occupation forces under the command of Elwell S. Otis and frustrated Filipino troops who believed they were trading their former Spanish masters for newer ones from the United States. The fighting, largely provoked by the Americans, quickly spread from Manila into the countryside. It remained conventional until 1900, with Filipino forces suffering enormous casualties at the hands of better-equipped U.S. troops. These losses forced Aguinaldo to switch to guerrilla tactics, causing serious American casualties and extending the war into remote villages where atrocities on both sides became commonplace. U.S. forces herded villagers into concentration camps in an effort to isolate guerrilla bands and suffered at the hands of Filipino foes who knew the terrain, climate, and vegetation far better than they did.

U.S. forces under Frederick Funston finally captured Aguinaldo in 1901, and fighting gradually diminished until the end of the war in 1902. One of the keys to the eventual American success was the creation of the Philippine Scouts in 1899. Organized into companies of Filipino collaborators commanded by U.S. enlisted men holding local commissions, the scouts proved far superior to American forces in conquering the climate, terrain, and enormous linguistic hurdles inherent in an archipelago containing several thousand dialects and languages. The scouts garrisoned remote areas, allowing U.S. troops to concentrate near Manila, and later served valiantly in the war against Japan. The guerrillas' cause was also hurt by the United States extending the promise of commonwealth status and, eventually, complete independence on a definite date, 4 July 1946. The U.S. Army also busied itself in a widespread program of what later would be called "civic action," building farm-to-market roads, artesian wells, docks, telegraph lines, and, most important to the Filipinos, schools.

The other critical U.S. action during the Philippine Insurrection came in July 1901, when William Howard Taft succeeded General Arthur MacArthur (U.S. military commander and father of Douglas MacArthur) as governor of the Philippines. Taft created a Philippine Constabulary of American officers and Filipino enlisted soldiers to garrison pacified regions. Constabulary forces became the national police force of the Philippines, formed the nucleus of the Philippine Army in 1936, and contributed an entire division to the Bataan campaign during World War II, the only sizable indigenous force to fight with their colonial masters in World War II in the Pacific. Both the Constabulary and the elite Philippine Scouts allowed U.S. forces under General Adna Chaffee (who succeeded MacArthur when Taft became governor) to rule through local intermediaries and gradually assume the daily task of enforcing law and order throughout the islands.

More than 4,000 U.S. soldiers and at least 20,000 Filipino guerrillas died before the insurrection ended in 1902, and the number of civilian deaths will never be known. The loss of life dampened American enthusiasm for empire in the early 1900s and foreshadowed the difficulty Americans would have fighting a jungle war in Vietnam during the 1960s. Most historians, in the strongly anti-imperialist climate from the 1960s on, viewed the Philippine Insurrection as a tragic mistake of American imperialism, one that delayed Philippine independence and needlessly cost the lives of thousands of Filipinos and Americans. Ironically, both sides fought together against the Japanese less than 40 years after the insurrection ended.

Lance Janda

See also: Aguinaldo, Emilio; MacArthur, Arthur, Jr.; Spanish-American War

References and further reading:

Langellier, J. Phillip. *Uncle Sam's Little Wars: The Spanish American War, Philippine Insurrection, and Boxer Rebellion, 1898–1902.* Greenhill Books, 1999.

Linn, Brian McAllister. *The Philippine War, 1899–1902.* Lawrence: University Press of Kansas, 2000.

Miller, Stuart Creighton. *Benevolent Assimilation: The American Conquest of the Philippines, 1899–1903.* New Haven, CT: Yale University Press, 1984.

Philippines, U.S. Loss of (7 December 1941–9 June 1942)

The worst defeat in American military history. Oddly, neither the Japanese army nor the government had any particular interest in the Philippines, an American possession in the western Pacific scheduled to receive its independence in 1946. But the imperial Japanese navy, supposedly the least aggressive of the Japanese military services, insisted that the U.S. air and submarine forces on the islands menaced the lines of communication to the "southern resources area," the Dutch East Indies, the highest priority on the list of Japanese conquests.

Japan's attack concentrated on the large northern island of Luzon, site of the capital, Manila, and where American military power was concentrated. On 8 December 1941, Japanese fighters and bombers, flying from Formosa, struck Luzon. General Douglas MacArthur, supreme commander of American and Filipino forces, and his staff knew of the attack on Pearl Harbor and had approximately 10 hours to prepare, yet the Japanese air strikes destroyed much of Major General Lewis Brereton's Far East Air Force, including 18 B-17 "Flying Fortresses" and 53 P-40 fighters on the ground at Clark and Iba Fields. MacArthur, Brereton, and Major General Richard Sutherland, MacArthur's chief of staff, offered conflicting postwar explanations for the catastrophe. In the following days (9–13 December), continuing Japanese raids further decimated American airpower and severely damaged Cavite Naval Base in Manila Bay. With the Japanese enjoying near-complete air superiority, Admiral Thomas Hart's Asiatic Fleet, save a few small vessels and patrol bombers, sailed south (14 December) to join the British and Dutch for an anticipated defense of the East Indies, while the battered remnants of the Far East Air Force redeployed (17 December) to Australia.

American air and naval power having been crippled, Japanese ground forces made a series of small landings between 8 December and 24 December at Batan Island, Camiguin Island, Appari (northern Luzon), Vigan (northwestern Luzon), Legaspi (southeastern Luzon), Davao (southeastern Mindanao), and Jolo Island, procuring airfields from which short-range fighters could support the main landings, establishing a stranglehold on strategically significant San Bernardino Strait, and securing bases for the upcoming invasion of the East Indies. The main landings, carried out by Lieutenant General Masaharu Homma's Fourteenth Army, followed on 22 and 24 December; the 48th Infantry Division came ashore at Lingayen Gulf, northwest of Manila, and a regiment of the 16th Infantry Division landed at Lamon Bay, southeast of the capital.

In accordance with a plan worked out by MacArthur, Filipino and American forces on Luzon, divided among Major General Jonathan Wainwright's North Luzon Force, Major General George Parker's South Luzon Force, and a reserve force, attempted to defeat the Lingayen landings on the beaches. Homma's forces brushed aside resistance offered primarily by ill-trained, poorly equipped Filipino units and drove inland.

Quickly recognizing his strategy's bankruptcy, MacArthur, on 23 December, ordered a phased withdrawal into the Bataan Peninsula, intending to hold out there until relief arrived from the United States. Beginning on 24 December,

American and Filipino forces executed MacArthur's order with consummate skill. Wainwright's North Luzon Force retreated south from Lingayen, holding in sequence a series of five defensive lines, while the South Luzon Force withdrew across central Luzon via Manila to reach Bataan. Japanese air commanders and General Homma unwittingly contributed to the success of the withdrawal; the former failed to bomb the crowded roads leading into the peninsula, and the latter hesitated to push his ground forces forward rapidly. The combination of American and Filipino skill and Japanese failures and hesitancy allowed somewhere between 65,000 and 80,000 American and Filipino soldiers and 26,000 civilians to reach the peninsula by 6 January 1942. U.S. artillery, often mounted on half-tracks, proved particularly effective in the retreat to Bataan.

From his headquarters on the island fortress of Corregidor at the mouth of Manila Bay, MacArthur established a defensive line near the center of the peninsula running from Mauban on the west coast to Mabatang on the east. Wainwright's forces, redesignated I Corps, assumed responsibility for the defense of the western sector (from Mauban to Mount Natib), and Parker's, redesignated II Corps, defended the eastern sector (from Mount Natib to Mabatang). Though determined, Bataan's defenders and civilians confronted a precarious situation, owing to grossly insufficient supplies of food, medicine, ammunition, gasoline, and other necessities. MacArthur's strategy of defending Luzon at the beaches had necessitated the moving to forward areas of vital supplies originally earmarked for Bataan. The bulk of these supplies had been abandoned during the retreat to the peninsula. Consequently, by the first week of January, the American and Filipino defenders of Bataan were on half-rations of 2,000 calories per day, a situation that worsened as the battle for the peninsula unfolded.

While MacArthur's forces retreated into Bataan, Manila fell to the Japanese. There Homma learned of the imminent redeployment of the 48th Infantry for the upcoming invasion of the East Indies—the timetable for which had been pushed forward in light of the spectacular successes won by Japanese forces throughout the Pacific—and its replacement by the quantitatively and qualitatively inferior 65th Brigade. Though losing the 48th cost him his best troops and left him outnumbered 3 to 1, a confident Homma anticipated a quick mop-up of Bataan's defenders.

Beginning on 9 January, the Japanese undertook a series of frontal attacks along the length of the Mauban-Mabatang line, forcing Parker's II Corps to give ground and breaching the enemy position in the center near Mount Natib. Fearing the Japanese might achieve a complete breakthrough, MacArthur ordered a withdrawal on 22 January to a new defensive position, the Bagac-Orion Line, located 8 miles to the

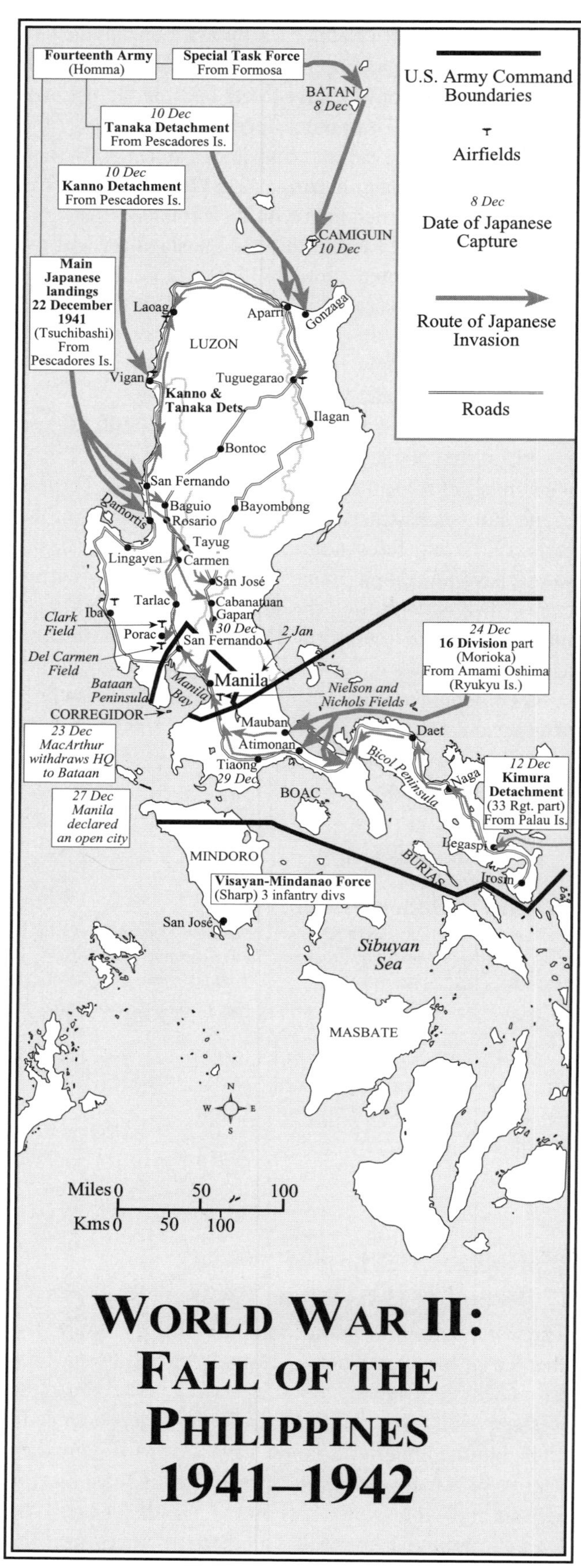

rear—a maneuver Wainwright and Parker completed by 26 January—and informed his superiors in Washington that the Japanese advance would be halted there. Homma, however, had other ideas, launching three small amphibious operations (23 January–1 February) against the "points" (located in southwestern Luzon) to outflank the American position. These assaults were contained and then repulsed, and Wainwright's forces simultaneously crushed a Japanese regiment that managed to penetrate his lines.

On 8 February, his forces decimated by heavy casualties, physical exhaustion, and disease, Homma halted offensive operations, withdrawing to more secure positions and requesting reinforcement. A lull of nearly two months ensued. The Japanese strengthened themselves with the addition of infantry reinforcements from the 21st and 4th Divisions, while the Americans and Filipinos grew weaker from malnourishment and disease. In the meantime, General George Marshall, chief of staff of the U.S. Army, ordered MacArthur, now a hero in the United States, to Australia on 22 January to assume command of the Southwest Pacific Theater. Reluctantly, MacArthur, accompanied by family, staff, and Philippine president Manuel Quezon, departed on 12 March.

His forces having recuperated, Homma commenced a new offensive on 3 April, for which the starving, disease-ridden defenders of the Bagac-Orion Line had no answer. In the opening 48 hours, the Japanese collapsed the American center and right, defended by Parker's II Corps, and forced I Corps on the left to retreat. Though MacArthur, who still considered himself responsible for the Philippines' defense, ordered a counteroffensive, Major General Edward King, now in command of the defense of Luzon, recognized the situation's hopelessness and surrendered on 9 April. Of the nearly 80,000 defenders in Bataan, approximately 2,000 escaped to Corregidor. The remaining 70,000-plus fell into Japanese captivity and had to endure an excruciating 65-mile trek north to San Fernando, where stifling boxcars awaited to carry them to prisoner-of-war camps. During the journey—subsequently labeled the "Bataan Death March"—Japanese soldiers acted with great brutality, beating and even executing those diseased and malnourished captives who could not continue; some 7,000 died before reaching the railhead.

During the two months that followed the fall of Bataan, the Japanese brought the Philippine campaign to a victorious conclusion. In early May, Homma's forces, having subjected the island fortress to a 27-day siege accompanied by continuous bombardment from artillery and aircraft, assaulted Corregidor, where General Wainwright—whom the War Department had formally entrusted with command in the Philippines—a small garrison of 11,000, and civilian refugees prepared for the worst. Although Wainwright's men fought gallantly and inflicted serious casualties on the attackers, the Japanese successfully established a foothold and moved toward the center of U.S. resistance, Malinta Tunnel. Recognizing further resistance as futile, Wainwright surrendered unconditionally on 6 May, reluctantly agreeing to broadcast an order of surrender to other American forces in the Philippines. During the next several weeks, American and Filipino forces in the central and southern island capitulated piecemeal, and formal resistance finally ended on 9 June 1942.

From the start, the Philippine Islands, close enough to Japan to provoke that aggressive nation but too far from the United States for effective relief, were doomed and all the geopolitical arguments for colonial possessions shown to be utterly false. Although the capitulation was unprecedented in U.S. military history, the Filipino-American defenders could take at least a measure of satisfaction in the realization that they had put up a much better fight against the Japanese onslaught than had any other colonial forces.

Bruce J. DeHart

See also: Bataan Death March; Corregidor; MacArthur, Douglas; Philippines, U.S. Retaking of; Wainwright, Jonathan Mayhew, IV

References and further reading:

Beck, John J. *MacArthur and Wainwright: The Sacrifice of the Philippines.* Albuquerque: University of New Mexico, 1974.

Connaughton, Richard M. *MacArthur and Defeat in the Philippines.* New York: Overlook Press, 1992.

Morton, Louis. *The Fall of the Philippines.* Washington, DC: Office of the Chief of Military History, Department of the Army, 1953.

Whitman, John W. *Bataan, Our Last Ditch: The Bataan Campaign, 1942.* New York: Hippocrene, 1990.

Philippines, U.S. Retaking of (20 October 1944–2 September 1945)

Major World War II battle on land and sea for control of the Philippine Islands, which were important to the United States both symbolically and strategically. Because the islands were a former American colony (and after that a commonwealth) and one of the first targets of the Japanese advance against the United States in late 1941 and early 1942, many Americans (not the least of whom was General Douglas MacArthur himself) felt a moral obligation to retake them. They were also a possible stepping-stone to the invasion of Japan.

In the continuing debate in Washington about the direction of the American Pacific offensive, General Douglas MacArthur, U.S. commander in the Southwest Pacific Theater, argued persistently for the retaking of the Philippine Is-

General Douglas MacArthur and aides wading ashore on Leyte, Philippine Islands, 1944. (Library of Congress)

lands. In the summer of 1944, the Joint Chiefs of Staff approved the invasion plans, with the island of Leyte as the initial target and the main island of Luzon as the final goal. The Japanese army command chose to contest the invasion of Leyte, and the struggle for control of that island developed into the major land battle for the Philippines.

The Battle of Leyte Gulf, the massive naval struggle between the American and Japanese fleets, raged concurrently with the fighting on land. The Japanese, underestimating as always the strength of the Americans, hoped to engage the U.S. Navy in a decisive confrontation. When the Battle of Leyte Gulf, the greatest naval battle in history, concluded, Japan had lost no less than four aircraft carriers, three battleships, six cruisers, 11 destroyers, and 500 planes and was a spent force.

After the relatively unopposed landings on Leyte Island, General Walter Krueger's Sixth Army made steady progress toward Ormoc, the major Japanese base on the western side of the island. General Suzuki's defensive fortifications, combined with typhoon rains, slowed but could not stop the American advance. Although Leyte was largely under American control by December 1944, fighting continued in that area through May 1945.

On 9 January 1945, the Americans landed on Luzon Island, where General Tomoyuki Yamashita (Tiger of Malaya) had withdrawn into the mountains, but a Japanese naval-marine rear guard put up a last-ditch defense of Manila, committing many atrocities against Filipino civilians and destroying most of the city. Despite the American victory, sporadic fighting continued on various islands until the end of the war and General Yamashita's surrender on 2 September.

The retaking of the Philippines produced two unforgettable images for U.S. wartime memory, one of Japanese fanaticism and the other of American dominance. During the Battle of Leyte Gulf, the Japanese resorted to suicide air attacks by bomb-laden warplanes, or kamikazes (divine wind), strengthening the belief in the United States that Japan would never surrender. Equally significant was the photo of General MacArthur wading ashore on Leyte on 20 October 1944 and announcing to the world, "People of the Philippines, I have returned!"

Harold J. Goldberg

See also: MacArthur, Douglas; Philippines, U.S. Loss of

References and further reading:

Cannon, M. Hamlin. *Leyte: The Return to the Philippines.* Washington, DC: Center of Military History, U.S. Army, 1987.

Krueger, Walter. *From Down Under to Nippon: The Story of the Sixth Army in World War II.* Washington, DC: Combat Forces Press, 1953.

MacArthur, Douglas. *Reminiscences.* New York: McGraw-Hill, 1964.

Spector, Ronald H. *Eagle against the Sun.* New York: Free Press, 1985.

Pickett, George Edward (1825–1875)

Confederate general in the American Civil War who is forever linked with one of the most gallant and heartbreaking moments in military history. Pickett was born on 25 January 1875 in Richmond, Virginia, to an upper-class family. After graduating last in the class of 1846 at the U.S. Military Academy at West Point, he was promoted to the rank of brevet first lieutenant for his service at Contreras and Churubusco in the Mexican-American War. He was then assigned to various posts, promoted to the rank of captain, and was later involved in the "Pig War," a dispute over San Juan Island with the British.

On 25 June 1861, Pickett resigned from the army and was ushered into the Confederacy as a colonel less than a month later. He was stationed on the Rappahannock River in the Department of Virginia and was later transferred to the Department of Northern Virginia, promoted to the rank of brigadier general, and given command of a brigade under General James Longstreet. He led his men in the Battles of Williamsburg, Seven Pines, and Gaine's Mill. In the last battle, he was wounded. After having recovered, he was promoted to major general and given a command of a division. He then served in the Fredericksburg and Tidewater campaigns.

On the third day at Gettysburg, Pickett's division was given the daunting task of charging straight into the center of the Union line at Cemetery Ridge, breaking through, and rolling the enemy up. His men were cut to ribbons by the Union guns, sustaining losses of 2,655 men wounded, killed, or captured. Pickett would remain bitter toward Robert E. Lee for the rest of his life. Afterward, he was sent to North Carolina, rejoined Lee at Cold Harbor, and was involved in the Richmond campaign. Lee relieved him of command because of the substantial losses he suffered at Five Forks, one day before peace was signed at Appomattox Court House.

T. Jason Soderstrum

See also: American Civil War; Gettysburg; Lee, Robert Edward; Longstreet, James

References and further reading:

Georg, Kathleen R. *Nothing but Glory: Pickett's Division at Gettysburg.* Gettysburg, PA: Thomas Publications, 1993.

Gordon, Lesley. *General George E. Pickett in Life and Legend.* Chapel Hill: University of North Carolina Press, 1998.

Longacre, Edward G. *Pickett, Leader of the Charge: A Biography of General George E. Pickett, C.S.A.* Shippensburg, PA: White Man Publishing, 1995.

Pilsudski, Józef Klemens (1867–1935)

Polish military commander and dictator. Born at Zulow in Russian-occupied Poland (in present-day Lithuania) on 5 December 1867, Pilsudski studied medicine at the University of Kharkov for one year before being arrested for an alleged conspiracy to assassinate Czar Alexander III. Pilsudski was sentenced to five years in Siberia and did not return to Poland until 1892. Following his return, Pilsudski became a leader of the Polish Socialist Party and published a clandestine newspaper, *Robotnik* (The Worker). After being forced to flee to Austrian-occupied Poland, he founded the Polish Riflemen's Association, with which he hoped to train an army of Poles to fight for Polish independence. Upon the outbreak of World War I, the Polish Riflemen's Association became the Polish Legion of the Austro-Hungarian army, which fought against imperial Russia. In 1916, the Central Powers proclaimed an independent Polish kingdom with Pilsudski as a member of the Polish Council of State. Refusing to fight under German command, however, he was imprisoned at Magdeburg and the Polish Legion was disbanded.

Released from Germany following the Armistice in November 1918, Pilsudski returned to Warsaw and proclaimed an independent Polish republic. As head of state and commander in chief of the Polish army, he sought to restore all the territories that had belonged to Poland at the time of the First Partition in 1772. These policies brought Poland into immediate conflict with the Bolshevik regime in the Soviet Union. During the Russo-Polish War (1919–1921), Pilsudski defeated the vastly superior Soviet armies at the Battle of Warsaw (1920) and thereby secured Polish independence. After resigning as chief of state in December 1922, he planned to live in quiet retirement, but on 12 May 1926 he led a coup d'état that overthrew the weak and inefficient parliamentary government and installed a regime under his control. From then until his death, Pilsudski was the virtual

Portrait of Józef Klemens Pilsudski. (Library of Congress)

dictator of Poland, though he retained only the positions of minister of war and commander in chief of the army. He died in Warsaw on 12 May 1935 and was buried among Poland's kings in the crypt of Wawel Cathedral in Cracow.

Alexander M. Bielakowski

See also: Russo-Polish War

References and further reading:

Garlicki, Andrzej. *Józef Pilsudski, 1867–1935.* London: Scholar Press, 1995.

Pilsudski, Józef. *Memories of a Polish Revolutionary and Soldier.* New York: AMS Press, 1971.

Pinkie (10 September 1547)

The last battle between English and Scottish national armies. The battle was fought in a war that erupted from England's attempt to secure a lasting arrangement with Scotland: England's persuasive efforts involved the sword, fire, and looting. After one English raiding column was annihilated at Ancrum Moor in February 1547, an English army advanced on Edinburgh with 18,000 infantry and 6,000 cavalry. It mustered 800 musketeers and 15 cannon and had naval support.

The Scottish army of 20,000 men occupied a strong position on the west bank of the Esk River, between sea and marsh. The English attempt to secure the only bridge over the Esk, which had been left unguarded, provoked the Scots to abandon their positions to move to the east bank. There they were attacked by English cavalry, but the Scots troops' rudimentary squares formation defeated these attacks. The cost to the Scots, however, was in time: the English were able to bring archers, cannon, and warships into action against massed but trapped Scottish pikemen. Subjected to murderous cross fire, the Scots tried to retreat, with inevitable consequences: panic and flight. The English cavalry rode down those fleeing the battlefield. Scottish dead numbered an incredible 10,000.

The aftermath was curious. In the short term, the Scots simply refused to treat, and English holdings were progressively reduced, with Edinburgh abandoned in 1550. But Scottish fear of French intentions, the growing strength of Protestantism in the country, and the English withdrawal from southern Scotland provided the basis for a rapprochement. In 1560, the Scots and the English combined to force the surrender and evacuation of the French garrison at Leith.

H. P. Willmott

See also: Anglo-Scots Wars

References and further reading:

Paterson, Raymond Campbell. *My Wound Is Deep. A History of the Later Anglo-Scots Wars, 1380–1560.* Edinburgh: John Donald, 1997.

Pitt, William, the Elder (1708–1778)

The architect of British victory in the Seven Years' War. William Pitt was born in 1708, grandson of Governor Thomas Pitt, founder of the family's fortune, who used profits from his place in the East India Company to buy Old Sarum, the family's rotten borough. After an education at Eton and Oxford University, Pitt was unsure of his professional future and accepted a cornetcy in Cobham's Horse before embarking on a grand tour of Europe in 1733 and returning in 1735 to take a seat in Parliament, representing Old Sarum. Quickly, Pitt made a reputation for crossing Robert Walpole and annoying George II, especially after goading the government into war with Spain in 1739. In 1746, he was named paymaster general and ostentatiously made a show of publicly accounting for all the army funds rather than personally profiting.

In 1756, Pitt pushed for an alliance with Prussia under Frederick the Great and, after the disasters of that year (Byng's naval failure at Minorca and Braddock's catastrophic defeat and death in western Virginia), was named one of the secretaries of state. Pitt's strategy in the Seven Years' War was simple: British force was concentrated on North America and the colonies, while subsidized Prussia carried Europe. It resulted in the victories of Robert Clive in India at Dakar and James Wolfe's capture of Quebec, as well as the naval battle at Quiberon Bay, which destroyed the French fleet. By 1761, however, Pitt's arrogance and inability to work with Prime Minister Lord Bute caused him to resign, crying "Frederick Betrayed!" about the peace treaty. In 1766, he was back in the ministry after protesting the Stamp Act and Declaratory Act but suffered a physical collapse and left again in1768. In his later years, Pitt advocated reform in India, reconciliation with the American colonies, and agricultural improvements. He died after an impassioned but incoherent speech on American liberties in April 1778.

Margaret Sankey

See also: Clive, Robert; Montcalm-Gozon, Louis-Joseph de, Marquis de Montcalm de Saint-Véran; Seven Years' War; Wolfe, James

References and further reading:

Black, Jeremy. *Pitt the Elder.* Cambridge, UK: Cambridge University Press, 1992.

Hotblack, Kate. *Chatham's Colonial Policy.* London: George Routledge and Sons, 1917.

Pizarro, Francisco (c. 1478–1541)

Spanish conquistador who subdued the Inca Empire in Peru. In 1502, Pizarro left Spain for the Caribbean island of Hispaniola in search of fame and fortune. He apprenticed for a number of years and in 1513 was one of Vasco Nunez de Balboa's lieutenants in the exploration of Panama. In Panama, Pizarro initiated plans for the exploration and conquest of lands on the west coast of South America. His first exploratory probe in 1524 met with failure, but a second expedition in 1527 revealed gold ornamentation among the indigenous populations. Pizarro organized a force of 180 men and 27 horses and landed in present-day Ecuador in 1531. After reconnoitering the coastal areas of Ecuador by land and sea, he landed at Tumbes and gathered important intelligence about internal strife in the Inca Empire. Surmising that the empire was on the brink of collapse, Pizarro boldly marched inland through narrow mountain defiles and arrived at the highland city of Cajamarca on 16 November 1532. There he encountered the Inca ruler, Atahualpa, backed by an army of 30,000. When Atahualpa rejected entreaties to convert to Christianity, Pizarro ordered his tiny band to attack. The ensuing battle resulted in the deaths of thousands of Indians and the capture of Atahualpa without the loss of one Spaniard. Pizarro held Atahualpa hostage and extracted a large ransom of gold, silver, and precious stones before ordering his execution. Pizarro next led a successful campaign against Cuzco, the capital of the Inca Empire, in 1533. In 1535 he founded the city of Lima and was the undisputed master of Peru. Explanations for the amazing success of the conquest of the well-organized and highly militarized empire that stretched nearly 2,000 miles from southern Colombia to Chile include the civil war of rival brothers for the throne, the decimating impact of smallpox on the vitality of

Half-length portrait of Francisco Pizarro wearing armor. (Library of Congress)

the population, the superior weapons of the conquerors, especially the use of horses and steel, and the audacious leadership of Pizarro. Pizarro was murdered in 1541 by members of a rival faction discontented with his governance of Peru.

George M. Lauderbaugh

See also: Cortez, Hernando

References and further reading:

Hemming, John. *The Conquest of the Incas.* New York: Harcourt Brace Jovanovich, 1973.

Lockhart, James. *The Men of Cajamarca: A Social and Biographical Study of the First Conquerors of Peru.* Austin: University of Texas Press, 1972.

Prescott, William Hickling. *History of the Conquest of Peru.* New York: New American Library, 1961.

Plains of Abraham (13 September 1759)

Battle that ended French power in North America. Having taken Louisbourg and Fort Duquesne in the Seven Years' War (called the French and Indian War in North America), the British the next year turned their attention to Quebec. Brigadier General James Wolfe left England in mid-February 1758, reaching Halifax in late April and Louisbourg in mid-May. When Wolfe embarked to attack Quebec, he had about 9,000 regular troops and several hundred American Rangers.

By late June, the large invasion force reached Ile d'Orleans without incident and was only 5 miles from Quebec. But the citadel's defenses were formidable, perched on a 200-foot bluff over the St. Lawrence River. Defended on two sides by rivers and steep bluffs, the city had constructed a wall on the west side and placed cannon to prevent attackers from scaling the wall.

Wolfe considered his choices. Louis-Joseph de Montcalm-Gozon, the Marquis de Montcalm de Saint-Véran, assumed that the British would attack from the north and had strengthened defenses accordingly; he also assumed British ships could not sail past Quebec to land troops to the more vulnerable western approach. Several times, the French tried to launch fire boats at the British fleet, but they were unsuccessful, and several times Wolfe sought to attack the city from the north and east and failed.

Finally, Wolfe accepted a plan from his subordinates to land west of Quebec, cutting off the city from its supplies further upriver. Meanwhile, Montcalm tried to stall matters, for by October, weather and the freezing of waterways would force a British retreat. Finally, the British secretly moved under cover of darkness and used a path to climb up to the plains west of town. Although the French received notice from pickets stationed there, they did not make good use of the information.

Montcalm decided to attack the British before they could begin siege operations and thus delay their plans. He gathered his men and attacked in the late morning of 13 September; the British held their fire and then decimated the French attackers. Both Montcalm and Wolfe were wounded several times, and both died.

The British, having cut supplies from upriver, began siege operations. The French defenders, short of food and low on morale, surrendered on 17 September, basically ending the French Empire in North America. Few battles have had such far-reaching consequences as that of the Plains of Abraham.

Charles M. Dobbs

See also: Louisbourg, Expedition against; Montcalm-Gozon, Louis-Joseph de, Marquis de Montcalm de Saint-Véran

References and further reading:

Casgrain, Abbé Henri Raymond. *Wolfe and Montcalm.* London: Oxford University Press, 1926.

Donaldson, Gordon. *Battle for a Continent: Quebec, 1759.* Toronto: Doubleday, 1973.

Stacy, C. P. *Quebec, 1759: The Siege and the Battle.* New York: St. Martin's Press, 1959.

Plassey, Battle of (23 June 1757)

The battle that gave control of Bengal to the British. In the eighteenth century, India saw a struggle for colonial supremacy between France and England. European nations fought each other through conflicts in these remote areas. The British East India Company had the delegated power of a sovereign state and its own private army and was continuously at war with the French or with French puppet Indian rulers.

In 1756, Suraja Dowla, nabob of Bengal (supported by the French), captured Calcutta and committed atrocities against British prisoners. The East India Company sent its army under Robert Clive to take control of Bengal and punish Suraja. Clive's troops consisted of less than 3,000 men with eight guns, facing an overwhelming force of more than 50,000 soldiers, mainly Indian warriors, with 53 guns manned by French artillerymen. The nabob's army was commanded by Mir Madan, but many Indians (including left-wing commander Mir Jafar) were plotting against Suraja, a fact Clive knew. The East India Company army pursued Suraja's army and found him entrenched near the village of Plassey. Clive massed his tiny force in a mango grove and found himself besieged by a large semicircle of Indians. The weather proved to be the decisive factor: a sudden monsoon rainstorm wet Suraja's powder at the very time the British covered their artillery. The battle commenced with inconclusive cavalry charges that were easily repulsed by Clive's guns. In the afternoon, Clive went over to the offensive and deployed to cannonade the nabob's camp at short range. After repulsing an Indian sortie, Clive assaulted Suraja's entrenchments, counting rightly on the disaffection of part of the Indian army. The Indian army disintegrated as Mir Jafar's soldiers changed side and began to flee without fighting. The French gunners continued fighting to the last, but by 5 P.M., the battle was over. Clive's casualties were incredibly low—18 killed and 45 wounded—to 500 Indians killed. Suraja was assassinated shortly afterward, and Mir Jafar became nabob, but with his power limited by the East India Company. The skirmish at Plassey proved to be the very foundation stone for the mighty British Empire in India.

Gilles Boué

See also: Carnatic Wars; Clive, Robert; Seven Years' War

References and further reading:

Edwardes, Michael. *The Battle of Plassey and the Conquest of Bengal.* London: Batsford, 1963.

Harrington, Peter. *Plassey 1757.* London: Osprey Publishing, 1994.

Plataea, Battle of (479 B.C.E.)

Ten years after the Battle of Marathon, Greek hoplites and Persian mixed troops clashed near the city of Plataea in 479 B.C.E. in the largest land battle of the Persian Wars. Perhaps based on the Persian experience at Marathon, Xerxes had persuaded a number of Greek cities to contribute heavy infantry to complement the Persian light infantry and cavalry.

The two forces met about 25 miles northwest of Athens. The Spartans, led by their king Pausanius, had joined forces with the Athenians and other Greek cities to bring their combined force up to 40,000 hoplites and auxiliary light troops. The Persians, commanded by Mardonius, had about the same number of men (50,000), but he had an overall superiority in cavalry and infantry archers. He found it difficult to use the latter to advantage against the Greek forces, and he did not have enough heavy infantry to confidently envelop the Greeks, who had taken up their position on a hill behind the stream Asopos. There the two sides faced off for several days. Persian cavalry constantly harried the Greeks and attacked their water and forage parties. The Greeks, confident in their ability to prevail in a shock action battle, attempted unsuccessfully to draw the main Persian army into an assault. Finally, Pausanius decided to withdraw and move his force closer to Plataea. He planned a nighttime withdrawal to confuse the Persians. By daybreak, only half of his force had successfully moved back toward the city. The Athenians and Spartans had only started their retreat in the morning.

The Persians, noticing the disorder of the Greeks, rushed forward to engage. The Persians relied on arrows to attack the hoplites. Unfortunately for Mardonius, his soldiers approached too closely to the Greeks, whereupon the Greeks charged the Persian line. Forced to drop their bows and defend themselves against bronze spears with their wicker armor, the Persians soon gave way and eventually collapsed. The Greek counterattack and pursuit killed Mardonius along with his elite guard and effectively destroyed the Persian field army.

This land victory, combined with the threat of an Athenian-led naval expedition against the Persians' lines of communications, unhinged Xerxes' military plans to conquer Greece and forced the Persians to withdraw back to Asia Minor.

Bryan R. Gibby

See also: Marathon, Battle of; Persian Empire; Persian Wars of Expansion; Thermopylae, Battle of

References and further reading:

Delbruck, Hans. *Warfare in Antiquity.* Trans. Walter J. Renfroe Jr. Lincoln: University of Nebraska Press, 1990.

Jones, Archer. *The Art of War in the Western World.* Chicago: University of Illinois Press, 1987.

Plattsburgh Movement (1915–1918)

A grassroots military preparedness campaign that began prior to the entry of the United States into World War I. The Plattsburgh Movement was an effort by private citizens to prepare for possible military action. It was led by old-stock, Ivy League–educated, eastern blue bloods and supported by General Leonard Wood. The first camp, held in Plattsburgh, New York, in the summer of 1915, trained middle-aged businessmen in military procedures. The National Defense Act of 1916 brought the War Department and these private organizations closer by permitting the federal government to pay for these training facilities, uniforms, food, and transportation. Throughout 1916 and 1917, Plattsburgh Movement training camps proliferated throughout the United States. After U.S. entry into the war in April 1917 and the enactment of conscription, the Plattsburgh camps became training centers for officer candidates recruited from civilian life.

In addition to training men for war, the groups that made up the Plattsburgh movement lobbied to improve camp conditions, organized liberty bond rallies, spoke at schools and other organizations, and produced training films. Following the Armistice, the Plattsburgh Movement advocated greater peacetime military preparedness, including universal military training.

Gregory Dehler

See also: Wood, Leonard; World War I

References and further reading:
Clifford, John Garry. *The Citizen Soldiers: The Plattsburgh Training Camp Movement, 1913–1920.* Louisville: University Press of Kentucky, 1972.
Sullivan, Mark. *Our Times.* Vol. 5. New York: Charles Scribner's Sons, 1933.
Seaton-Watson, Hugh. *The Decline of Imperial Russia.* London: Methuen, 1966.

Pleven/Plevna, Siege of (20 July–10 December 1877)

The crucial four-phase battle by the Russians to overcome Turkish forces defending Pleven/Plevna during the Russo-Turkish War (1877–1878). Russian (and Romanian, after August) forces participating in this battle numbered 130,000, against the Turkish force of 67,000.

War was declared on 24 April 1877, and a Russian army of 190,000 commanded by Grand Duke Nicholas crossed the Danube River on 27 June. They captured the Shipka Pass, situated in Turkish-occupied Bulgaria, on 19 July.

The Turkish forces of Osman Nuri Pasha marched from Vidin and reached Pleven/Plevna, where they held the Russian advance on 20 July. This action constituted the first phase of the battle.

Two subsequent Russian attempts to capture Pleven via a frontal assault failed. These second and third phases of the battle occurred on 30 July and 11–12 September. The Russian and Romanian forces lost 15,700 men.

Nicholas's decision to have the army retreat across the Danube River was overruled. Colonel Count E. I. von Todleben was placed in charge of the next assault of Pleven, and his engineers were employed to besiege the city.

Turkish forces on the perimeter of the city were not employed to aid Osman Pasha, who mounted a failed attempt to break out on 9–10 December. The Russians then launched their fourth and final, successful assault of this battle, and Pleven surrendered on 10 December 1877. The victory permitted Russian forces to continue unimpeded, entering Sofia on 4 January 1878 and Adrianople/Edirne on 20 January after the Battle of Plovdiv. The Siege of Pleven was instrumental to the defeat of Turkish forces in Bulgaria and the conclusion of the Russo-Turkish Wars on 3 March 1878 by the Treaty of San Stefano.

Neville G. Panthaki

See also: Balkan War, First; Kars, Battle of; Russo-Turkish Wars

References and further reading:
Anderson, M. S. *The Eastern Question.* London: Macmillan, 1970.
Menning, Bruce. *Bayonets before Bullets: The Imperial Russian Army, 1861–1914.* Bloomington: Indiana University Press, 1992.
Rupp, George. *A Wavering Friendship: Russia and Austria, 1876–1878.* Philadelphia: Porcupine Press, 1976.

Poitiers, Battle of (18 September 1356)

French defeat in the Hundred Years War. With the resumption of war, the main English effort in 1356 took the form of a *chevauchée* (armored, mounted raiding parties) from Bordeaux that reached Tours. The French, crossing the Loire River at Blois and moving faster than an enemy army laden with booty, managed to get astride the English line of retreat at Poitiers.

The English army, perhaps 12,000-men strong, took up a defensive position with one flank secured by a stream. The other flank consisted of the wagon park. Sunken lanes and hedges were manned by some 3,000 archers, with dismounted cavalry serving as supporting infantry. The French, numbering perhaps 30,000 men, were formed into four echelons. The French made no attempt to use their cavalry to turn the English position and used their armored knights as infantry.

The first French attack was easily defeated by English longbowmen, with few French reaching the English positions. A second attack was denied a breakthrough only by deployment of the rear English division into the front line, leaving the English without a reserve. The failure of this attack caused the flight of the third French force before it came into range. The fourth French force, exhausted by its approach march, was caught by English light infantry and cavalry. The French king and many of the highest nobles in the land were surrounded and captured. The French lost about 2,500 killed, with a similar numbered captured. English casualties numbered about 2,000. After the battle, the English resumed their withdrawal to Bordeaux.

H. P. Willmott

See also: Crécy, Battle of; Hundred Years War

References and further reading:
Hooper, Nicholas, and Matthew Bennett. *The Cambridge Illustrated Atlas of Warfare. The Middle Ages, 768–1487.* Cambridge, UK: Cambridge University Press, 1996.
Seward, Desmond. *The Hundred Years' War. The English in France, 1347–1453.* London: Constable, 1996.

Polish Campaign of 1939

Opening campaign of World War II. The German invasion of Poland in September 1939 was the first example of a new theory of armored warfare, which the Germans referred to as "blitzkrieg" (literally, lightning war). Poland historically suffered from a great geographic disadvantage—the central portion of Poland was flat with no natural boundaries. In addition, the Polish border with Germany extended for approximately 3,500 miles in 1939. When war broke out, Polish forces numbered about 1,000,000 men, but they were technologically outdated, especially in aircraft and tanks, and a great many of the troops were poorly trained reservists. At the same time, German forces numbered about 1,500,000 men, the most important part of which were 12 armored, mechanized, and motorized divisions. These divisions, in conjunction with the German Air Force (Luftwaffe), would be the deciding factor during the campaign.

On 1 September 1939, when Germany attacked, Poland's forces were thinly spread in a rough semicircle from the border with East Prussia in the north to the German surrogate state of Slovakia in the south. In the northwest, approximately a third of Poland's forces were concentrated in or near the Polish Corridor, where they were exposed to both East Prussia and Germany proper. About half of Poland's forces were in central Poland, either facing the main axis of the German advance or massed in reserve in the center of the country. The remainder of Poland's forces were even more thinly spread in southern and eastern Poland. Rather than deploying Polish forces behind natural and prepared defenses, which would have meant the loss of strategic industrial and resource centers in western Poland, the decision was made for them to be forward deployed. Unfortunately, this decision made it almost impossible to fight delaying actions against the German invaders because the German mechanized forces could easily overwhelm the slower Polish infantry forces.

The German forces quickly split the Polish army into disjointed fragments, some of which retreated, while others continued to fight hopeless battles. By 10 September, the Polish commander in chief, Marshal Edward Rydz-Smigly, ordered a general retreat toward the southeast. The situation was already desperate for the Poles when, on 17 September, the Soviet Union invaded eastern Poland in accordance with the Molotov-Ribbentrop Agreement. The next day, the Polish government crossed into exile in Romania. The Warsaw garrison resisted until September 28, and the last major force of the Polish army surrendered on October 6. Poland was then partitioned between Germany and the Soviet Union along the Bug River.

Despite its "lightning" victory, the Germans made many mistakes in deployment and tactics in their Polish campaign. But the remaining Allies, Great Britain and France, gave their enemy ample time to correct these deficiencies during the so-called Phony War, a time of near-immobility on the western front from September 1939 to May 1940. Though guerrilla warfare would continue (first against the Germans and then against the Soviets) until after the formal end of the war in May 1945, the Polish nation had ceased to exist.

Alexander M. Bielakowski

See also: Guderian, Heinz; World War II

References and further reading:

Bethell, Nicholas W. *The War Hitler Won: The Fall of Poland, September 1939.* New York: Holt, Rinehart and Winston, 1973.

Kennedy, Robert M. *German Campaign in Poland, 1939.* Washington, DC: Department of the Army, 1956.

Zaloga, Steven, and Victor Madej. *The Polish Campaign, 1939.* New York: Hippocrene Books, 1985.

Polish Wars of Expansion (1386–1498)

A series of wars fought sporadically between Poland and its neighbors from 1386 to 1498. By the end of the reign of Casimir III (1333–1370), the Polish monarchy had, under the Piast Dynasty, successfully unified the Kingdom of Poland and created a bureaucratic apparatus to govern the country. After the death of Casimir III in 1370 and his nephew Louis in 1382, Poland would begin a series of wars and dynastic marriages calculated to extend Polish control over neighboring territories. Some of these efforts began at the behest of the royal family; others were undertaken at the connivance of a group of powerful oligarchs close to the royal court, the so-called Cracow nobles. As a result, by the end of the expansion in 1498, the Polish royal family governed approximately one-third of mainland Europe.

In 1386, the Cracow nobles completed the first step toward the expansion of the Kingdom of Poland. At the insistence of the oligarchs, Jadwiga married the grand duke of Lithuania, Jagiello (later Wladyslaw II). As a result of this marriage, the two nations were linked through a common set of monarchs, although both remained technically independent nations.

A combined Polish and Lithuanian army was able to evict Hungarian garrisons from Ruthenia, thus advancing Polish territorial interests, and to extend Lithuanian influence along the Baltic Sea coast to the north of the grand duchy and among the Rus to the east. Combined Polish and Lithuanian forces were also able to compel the princes of Moldavia and Walachia to render homage to the Polish kingdom.

In 1409 and 1410, hostilities between Lithuania and the Teutonic Order led to the "Great War," which ended with the defeat of the order by a Polish and Lithuanian army commanded by Wladyslaw II and Vytautas (Witold) in the Battle of Tannenberg/Grunwald in 1410. Although the power of the order was considerably reduced, it received generous peace terms and was compelled only to recognize the right of the Lithuanians to govern some disputed territories along the

Baltic Sea. A second war with the order in 1422 forced the complete abandonment of its claims to Lithuanian territory.

The outbreak of the Hussite Wars in 1419 afforded a further opportunity for the aggrandizement of the Jagellonian dynasty. Hussite elements in Bohemia offered the kingdom to Wladyslaw II, which would have united a third country under his rule. Wladyslaw refused but allowed his cousin Vytautas to accept the offer.

Upon the death of Vytautas in 1430, Wladyslaw appointed his brother, Swidrigiello, as viceroy of Lithuania. Swidrigiello rebelled, abetted by the Teutonic Order, Sigismund of Luxembourg, and dissatisfied elements in Lithuania. Not until the death of Wladyslaw II in 1434 was the rebellion suppressed by his son, Wladyslaw III.

The death of Sigismund of Luxembourg at about the same time allowed the Jagellonian family another opportunity to acquire the Bohemian throne; the Polish court, in an effort to secure Bohemia, adopted a pro-Hussite policy. This in turn led to a pro-Hussite peasant rebellion in Poland, aimed at the church and noble hierarchy. The peasant revolt was defeated by the Cracow nobles at the Battle of Grotniki in 1439; noble dissatisfaction with the royal court enabled the Cracow nobles to compel the Jagellonians to defer further efforts to seize the Bohemian throne.

In 1440, Wladyslaw III appointed his brother Casimir viceroy of Lithuania. The Lithuanian nobles, true to form, rebelled and proclaimed Casimir as the independent grand duke of Lithuania. Wladyslaw was in no position to take action against his brother, for upon the death of Albert of Habsburg, also in 1440, he had been offered the kingdom of Hungary. As king of Hungary, Wladyslaw was drawn into the anti-Turkish crusade then being organized by the papacy in an effort to rescue Constantinople and Serbia from Turkish conquest.

After winning some initial victories in 1443, Wladyslaw negotiated an advantageous settlement with the Turks. Under papal pressure, this agreement was repudiated, and a second crusade was launched in 1444. This second crusade, the so-called Varna crusade, was poorly planned and led to the utter defeat of the crusading forces by the Turks at the Battle of Varna. Wladyslaw III was killed.

In 1454, Poland and Lithuania began the Thirteen Years' War with the Teutonic Order. This conflict led to the final defeat of the order and the Treaty of Thorn, which, although harsh, failed to eliminate completely the order as a force. The order surrendered more than half its remaining territory, and its grand master also agreed to become a vassal of the king of Poland and to accept Polish suzerainty over the remainder of the land held by the order.

Casimir IV's great object of policy was to obtain the reversion of the Kingdoms of Bohemia and Hungary for his sons. This goal was realized, and the descendants of Jagiello were able to gain by diplomacy that which would have been utterly unattainable by conquest. But in 1485, Casimir IV began a series of campaigns in Moldavia against the Crimean Tartars on behalf of the prince of Moldavia, Stefan cel Mare. Stefan became a Polish vassal, and Polish-Tartar warfare continued until the death of Stefan in 1501.

Thus, immediately before the death of Casimir IV in 1492, the Jagiellonian dynasty controlled the Kingdom of Poland and the Grand Duchy of Lithuania through the kingship of Casimir IV and the Kingdoms of Bohemia and Hungary through the kingship of Wladyslaw, Casimir's eldest son. Moldavia and the Teutonic Order had been reduced to dependent vassal states. This unity was, however, more apparent than real, as none of the kingdoms or lands had been formally merged, and all retained some tradition of electing rulers rather than recognizing hereditary succession.

The death of Casimir IV in 1492 led to the unraveling of the Jagiellonian holdings. The decline of Tartar power made possible a Turkish-Muscovite alliance in 1498, which precluded further Polish or Lithuanian efforts at expansion in those directions. The careful efforts of the Jagiellonians thus benefited the Kingdom of Poland and the Grand Duchy of Lithuania very little in the long term.

Joseph M. Isenberg

See also: Tannenberg, Battle of; Teutonic Knights

References and further reading:

Gieysztor, Aleksander, et al. *History of Poland.* Warsaw: PWN, 1979.

Zamoyski, Adam. *The Polish Way.* London: John Murray, 1987.

Poltava (8 July 1709)

The triumph of Peter I's military reforms, enabling the Russian army to rout the Swedish force of Charles XII. Poltava marked the decline of Sweden and the ascendancy of Russia as a European great power.

After defeating the Russians at Narva, Charles diverted his attack to Poland. The Swedish attack against Russia recommenced in January 1708 as 50,000 Swedes crossed the Berezina River. Charles paused at Mogilev, awaiting a Swedish auxiliary force of 15,000 men and supplies traveling from Livonia and led by General Adam Ludwig Lewenhaupt. On 9 October 1708, Russian forces led by Peter and General Prince Aleksandr Danilovich Menshikov engaged and defeated Lewenhaupt at Lesnaia. Lewenhaupt reached Charles with 6,000 men but no artillery or supplies.

In an effort to sequester resources, Charles diverted his attack into the Ukraine. He also believed that the Cossack Hetman Ivan Mazepa would provide an auxiliary 100,000

Russian and Swedish armies meet at the Battle of Poltava on 8 July 1709. (Library of Congress)

troops against Peter, yet Mazepa delivered fewer than 2,000 Cossacks to the Swedish side.

Charles and 22,000–28,000 Swedish troops were forced to winter in the Ukraine. In May 1709, the Swedes laid siege to Poltava. On 8 July 1709, 40,000 Russian troops with superior artillery engaged and defeated the Swedish force. The Russians set up entrenchments within a few hundred yards of the Swedish siege lines, prompting the Swedes to attack. Charles's plan was to mount a charge past the entrenchments and assault the main Russian force, but being injured, he left command to Field Marshal Karl Gustav Rhensköld.

The latter quarreled with his subordinates, and the unclear issuing of orders contributed to the Swedish defeat. Individual Swedish generals surrendered, either on the field or several days later while trying to cross the Dnieper River. Mazepa, Charles, and 1,500 Swedish troops escaped to Turkey. Lewenhaupt had been ordered to escape with a part of the Swedish army to Crimea and later to meet Charles in Turkey. However, Lewenhaupt and his army had capitulated in Perevolotina.

Neville G. Panthaki

See also: Charles XII; Northern War, Great; Peter I, Romanov, Czar of Russia; Russo-Turkish Wars

References and further reading:

Anderson, Matthew Smith. *Peter the Great.* New York: Longman, 1995.

Kliuchevskii, Vasilii Osipovich. *Peter the Great.* London: Macmillan, 1958.

Lisk, Jill. *The Struggle for Supremacy in the Baltic, 1600–1725.* New York: Funk and Wagnalls, 1968.

Sumner, Benedict Humphrey. *Peter the Great and the Emergence of Russia.* London: English Universities Press, 1964.

Pompey the Great (Gnaeus Pompeius Magnus) (106–48 B.C.E.)

Roman general, statesman, and member of the First Triumvirate with Julius Caesar and Marcus Licinius Crassus. Romans referred to Pompey, a member of a senatorial family, as Magnus, meaning "the Great," after he led a successful campaign in North Africa in 81 B.C.E. Prior to that, Pompey had fought on the side of Sulla against Gaius Marius during the Social War. After ending the Servile War led by Spartacus in 71 B.C.E., Pompey waged a five-year campaign against Sertorius in Spain. In 70 B.C.E., Pompey became consul, cleared the Mediterranean of pirates, and defeated Mithradates VI Eupator of Pontus. He also conquered the kingdoms of Armenia, Syria, and Jerusalem. Disputes with the Senate resulted in the formation of an alliance between Pompey and Julius Caesar. In 60 B.C.E., the two men, joined by Crassus, formed the First Triumvirate. Caesar left the administration of Rome to Pompey and Crassus in 59 B.C.E. and for the next 10 years focused on the conquest of Gaul. Pompey's marriage to Caesar's daughter Julia ensured friendly relations between the two men, but after her death a rivalry developed. In 53 B.C.E., Crassus died in Syria, and Pompey turned to the Senate in an effort to curb Caesar's growing power. The Senate demanded that Caesar resign his office and return to Rome. Instead, Caesar crossed the Rubicon River in 49 B.C.E. and attacked Italy with his forces. Pompey fled across the Adriatic and was defeated by Caesar at Pharsalus in 48 B.C.E. He then fled to Egypt, where he was treacherously killed.

Cynthia Clark Northrup

See also: Caesar, Julius; Marius, Gaius; Roman Civil Wars (88–30 B.C.E.); Sulla, Lucius Cornelius

References and further reading:

Greenhalgh, Peter. *Pompey, the Roman Alexander.* Columbia: University of Missouri Press, 1981.

Leach, John. *Pompey the Great.* Totowa, NJ: Rowman and Littlefield, 1978.

The death of Pontiac 1769. (Library of Congress)

Pontiac's Rebellion (1763–1766)

A widespread Indian uprising against British power in North America. At the close of the French and Indian War (called the Seven Years' War in Europe), English settlers began to move into western Pennsylvania and New York, confident that Indian power was broken with the French defeat. France had ceded Canada to England, and the American Indians found themselves without French arms. British troops took over former French posts and established garrisons at Fort Pitt, Detroit, Venango, Erie, and other sites. For several decades, the various woodland tribes became dependent on European firearms for hunting and survival. To secure their help in defeating the French, the British had made several treaties with the Indians ensuring that they would have their own land, English troops would leave, and supplies of ammunition would continue. Many Indians then helped the English, including some of the Iroquois. The Delaware, a people conquered by the Iroquois, were forced to go along with the agreement.

In the years following the conflict, however, the British Crown was unable to restrict white settlement west of the Appalachians. Crown forces also kept small garrisons in the western Indian lands and began to curtail the trade of firearms and ammunition. Cut off from these supplies, many Ottawa, Potawatomi, and Chippewa faced starvation. Moreover, the Delaware, eager to be free of Iroquois rule, were also growing restless. In the summer of 1763, the western Indians organized under the leadership of a charismatic Ottawa named Pontiac. They were joined in an uprising by the Seneca, Shawnee, and Delaware.

Indian raiders overran English forts in the Ohio territory, and only two held out: Fort Detroit and Fort Pitt. From New York to Virginia, settlers fled the frontier in terror. Colonel Henry Bouquet organized a 400-man force to relieve Fort Pitt. At Bushy Run, the Delaware and Shawnee ambushed Bouquet. He was driven back and took up position on a hill that evening. The next day, the Indians resumed their attacks, having surrounded the English force as was done with

Edward Braddock in 1755. Bouquet had some of his companies feint a retreat and then struck the Indians in their flank, driving them off. He reached Fort Pitt and the next year advanced to the Muskingum River in Ohio, where the Indians sued for peace.

Another force went to relieve Fort Detroit. British Indian agent William Johnson's diplomacy was as valuable as the military victories, convincing the Iroquois to put pressure on the Delaware, Shawnee, and Seneca to end the war. By late 1764, the Seneca fell into line with their Iroquoian brethren in siding with the English, and the united tribes launched raids on the Delaware and Shawnee. In 1766, Pontiac accepted a peace treaty with Johnson at Oswego, New York. With the power of the Indians broken, western Pennsylvania and Ohio were open to settlement. To prevent further outbreaks of violence, the English government did continue restricting white settlement beyond the mountains. This restriction became a major cause of anger for colonists in the years prior to the outbreak of the revolution, in that many had been promised land for service in the French and Indian War.

Robert Dunkerly

See also: French and Indian War

References and further reading:

Anderson, Fred. *Crucible of War.* New York: Alfred A. Knopf, 2000.
Jennings, Francis. *Empire of Fortune.* New York: W. W. Norton, 1988.
Wallace, Paul A. *Indians in Pennsylvania.* Harrisburg: Pennsylvania Historical and Museum Commission, 1961.

Pope, John (1822–1892)

Union general in the American Civil War, loser at Second Bull Run, and a failure as a field commander. Pope was born in Louisville, Kentucky, on 16 March 1822. After graduating from the U.S. Military Academy at West Point in 1842, he was assigned to the topographical engineers. He excelled in combat in the Mexican-American War under Zachary Taylor, being brevetted first lieutenant at Monterrey and captain at Buena Vista. From 1849 to 1861, he was an army engineer and railroad surveyor in the American West.

Commissioned brigadier general of volunteers under John C. Frémont in Missouri on 14 June 1861, Pope quickly mobilized and achieved significant gains. He soundly defeated Sterling Price at Blackwater, Missouri, on 18 December; captured New Madrid, Missouri, on 14 March 1862; was promoted to major general on 21 March; and won an amphibious battle for Island no. 10 near New Madrid in the Mississippi River on 7 April. He marched with Henry W. Halleck toward Corinth, Mississippi, in May and June.

Impressed by Pope's performance, President Abraham Lincoln called him east to take over the new Army of Virginia from George B. McClellan. Pope assumed command on 26 June and immediately alienated his men with his arrogance and insults. He also inadvertently raised Confederate morale with his harsh proposals for dealing with southern civilians. Hated by North and South alike, he soon rendered himself incapable of effective leadership.

Stonewall Jackson defeated Pope at Cedar Mountain, Virginia, on 9 August. Jeb Stuart raided his headquarters at Catlett's Station, Virginia, on 22 August and stole his uniform, dispatches, and notebook, thus providing the valuable information that Robert E. Lee needed to crush him at Second Bull Run. Jackson hampered his retreat toward Washington, D.C., at Chantilly, Virginia, on 1 September.

Lincoln relieved Pope of command on 2 September and reassigned him to the Northwest. He spent most of the rest of his career fighting the Sioux, until he retired in 1886. He died in Sandusky, Ohio, on 23 September 1892. John Pope is a prime example of an officer who does very well in school, is excellent at staff work, but finds himself out of his depth on the battlefield or in overall command.

Eric v. d. Luft

See also: American Civil War; Buena Vista; Bull Run, Second/Manassas Junction; Halleck, Henry Wager; Jackson, Thomas "Stonewall"; Lee, Robert Edward; Lincoln, Abraham; McClellan, George Brinton; Mexican-American War; Monterrey; Sioux Wars; Stuart, James Ewell Brown; Taylor, Zachary

References and further reading:

Cozzens, Peter. *General John Pope: A Life for the Nation.* Urbana: University of Illinois Press, 2000.
Jones, Robert Huhn. *The Civil War in the Northwest: Nebraska, Wisconsin, Iowa, Minnesota, and the Dakotas.* Norman: University of Oklahoma Press, 1960.
Pope, John. *The Military Memoirs of General John Pope.* Ed. Peter Cozzens and Robert I. Girardi. Chapel Hill: University of North Carolina Press, 1998.
Schutz, Wallace J., and Walter N. Trenerry. *Abandoned by Lincoln: A Military Biography of General John Pope.* Urbana: University of Illinois Press, 1990.

Porkchop Hill (16–18 April 1953)

Scene of heavy fighting amid Korean War armistice negotiations. In an effort to gain leverage in the negotiations, the Communist Chinese launched a major attack on the thinly defended and otherwise worthless position. The weight of the attack fell on E Company of the 31st Infantry Regiment,

7th U.S. Infantry Division. By the early morning hours of 17 April, the Chinese had captured the hill, along with several men from E Company. At this point K Company, under Lieutenant Joe Clemons, was given the task of recapturing the hill. After a tough all-night fight, severely depleted K Company held shaky positions on the hill.

As a fresh Chinese attack began, the question of whether or not to reinforce Porkchop now became political. The whole matter boiled down to this question: Were American commanders willing to expend more lives over a worthless hill in Korea in order to demonstrate U.S. resolve in the negotiations? After much hemming and hawing among senior officers, Porkchop was eventually reinforced and held, but at great cost, and then a few months later finally abandoned. The battle was memorialized in the 1959 film *Pork Chop Hill,* starring Gregory Peck.

John C. McManus

See also: Korean War

References and further reading:

Hermes, Walter G. *Truce Tent and Fighting Front: U.S. Army in the Korean War.* Reprint, Washington, DC: U.S. Army Office of the Chief of Military History, 1969.

Marshall, S. L. A. *Pork Chop Hill.* New York: Berkley Publishing Group, 2000.

Sandler, Stanley. *The Korean War: No Victors, No Vanquished.* Lexington: University of Kentucky Press, 1999.

Port Arthur, Siege of (May 1904–January 1905)

The first major phase of the Russo-Japanese War. The conflict opened with a Japanese naval attack on Russian warships in Port Arthur, before any declaration of war by Japan. The siege of Port Arthur began in May 1904 with Japanese landings on the Liaodong Peninsula in China and the movement of Japanese troops northward through Korea and ended in early January 1905 with the capitulation of the weakened Russian garrison. For the Japanese, capture of the port would deny the Russian navy a warm water anchorage and thereby help secure the sea-lanes between the Japanese islands and the northeast Asian mainland.

Russian land defenses included a series of trench works around the town, a series of linked concrete forts about 4,000 yards outside the line of trenches, and then some outer works—fortified hills and other positions—beyond the forts. These defenses should have presented a formidable problem to the Japanese, but it did not seem that the Russians made the position as difficult as they could have.

The Japanese made a series of costly assaults. On 25 May 1904, General Oku Yasukata's frontal assault was thrown back with heavy losses, but an effort to turn the Russian left succeeded. The Russians abandoned Nashan Hill and thereby conceded the port of Dairen to the Japanese. Throughout June, the Japanese prepared for the attack, and an indecisive Russian naval sortie failed. The Japanese army probed defenses in July and then in August and September made three unsuccessful efforts to penetrate defenses with heavy casualties.

In early October, the Japanese brought siege artillery that complemented efforts to mine Russian positions. In November, the Japanese concentrated on the weakened eastern defenses, and in early December they broke through at 203 Meter Hill, moved in artillery, and destroyed the Russian warships in Port Arthur harbor. Throughout December, the Japanese continued their attacks on northern defenses, and finally, on 1 January 1905, the hungry and weakened Russian garrison surrendered.

The Japanese suffered three times as many casualties as the Russians in the long, costly siege. Japanese commanders had favored mass attacks, in dense formations, at night. Such mass attacks actually demonstrated the defensive power of properly placed machine guns and supporting artillery, foreshadowing the carnage of World War I.

Charles M. Dobbs

See also: Russo-Japanese War

References and further reading:

Okamoto, Shumpei. *The Japanese Oligarchy and the Russo-Japanese War.* New York: Columbia University Press, 1970.

Warner, Denis, and Peggy Warner. *The Tide at Sunrise: A History of the Russo-Japanese War, 1904–1905.* London: Frank Cass, 1974.

Westwood, J. N. *Russia against Japan, 1904–1905: A New Look at the Russo-Japanese War.* Albany: State University of New York Press, 1986.

Portuguese-Castilian War (1369–1385)

War of Portuguese independence. Portugal grew out of Spain, and even when Portugal had emerged as a separate realm, its ruling houses still maintained close Spanish contacts and were very much involved in Spanish politics. Despite these connections, political changes led increasingly to an assertion of Portuguese nationhood totally separate from that of Spain. Two key events played a vital role in this process. One was the coming of the Black Death to Portugal in 1348 (with many subsequent outbreaks), initiating an era of agrarian crisis that undermined and then destroyed the old feudal landed order and turned Portugal into the largely commercial and maritime nation that it has been since. The second was the Portuguese-Castilian War of 1369 to 1385, actually a series of separate wars, which ultimately decided the issue of Portugal's independence from Spain to Portugal's advantage.

The war had its origins in a dispute over succession to the throne of Castile. Claimants to the throne included the Portuguese king, D. Fernando I (r. 1367–1383), and Enrique de Trastámara (later Enrique II of Castile, r. 1369–1379), both descended from Sancho IV (r. 1284–1295) of Castile. To advance his cause, Fernando allied himself with Aragon, Castile's hereditary enemy, and with the Muslim king of Granada. Although most of Portugal was not directly affected by the first war (1369–1371), because Portugal remained the aggressor for the most part, it was nonetheless disastrous for the Portuguese. The peace, however, was not overly severe.

With few of the outstanding issues of the first war resolved, a second (1372–1373) and then a third (1381–1382) followed quickly. Although both were Portuguese wars with Castile, both were also part of the Hundred Years War. Fernando had renounced his claim to the Castilian throne in favor of John of Gaunt, son of the English king Edward III. John was married to an illegitimate daughter of the old Castilian king, who had been assassinated by Enrique in 1369. Enrique allied himself with France. Aragon vacillated between the sides.

This time Portugal was not spared, and central Portugal, as well as the extreme northwest, suffered major Castilian invasions by land and sea. During the second war, much of Lisbon was destroyed by Enrique because the city had outgrown its walls and a large part of it now lay exposed to attack. Fernando's English allies were nearly as destructive as the Castilians. During the third war, the Portuguese launched a naval counterattack, but the Portuguese fleet was nearly destroyed, and the Spanish returned again by sea to attack Lisbon.

One result of repeated Portuguese disaster was the growing unpopularity of the monarch, D. Fernando, and his consort Leonor Teles de Meneses, who identified closely with Portugal's great landholders. When D. Fernando died, his legal successor was his daughter D. Beatriz, married to Juan I (r. 1379–1390), king of Castile. The hated Leonor became the regent, and Juan, anxious to assert his claim to Portugal, invaded.

The result was a revolution. The master of Avis, the later João I (r. 1385–1433), representing maritime and commercial Portugal, took the lead in the war despite the fact that much of the interior of the country and its landed interests still remained loyal to D. Beatriz. The fortunes of the war varied, but Portugal won a number of important victories, including the Battle of Aljubarrota (1385), on the site now occupied by the Portuguese national cathedral at Batalha, and ultimately forced the Spanish to withdraw. Although the final peace was not signed until 1432 and there were skirmishes as late as 1396–1397, the separateness of Portugal had been established.

Paul D. Buell

References and further reading:

Albuquerque, Luís de. *Introdução à História dos Descobrimentos Portugueses.* 3d rev. ed. Mira Sintra: Publicações Europa-America, n.d.

Marques, A. H. de Oliveira. *História de Portugal.* 12th edition, 3 vols. Lisbon: Palas Editores, 1985.

Russell, Peter E. *The English Intervention in Spain and Portugal in the Time of Edward III and Richard II.* Oxford, UK: Oxford University Press, 1965.

Potemkin, Prince Grigory Aleksandrovich (1739–1791)

Russian general, statesman, and lover of Empress Catherine the Great (r. 1762–1796). Born September 1739 in Smolensk Province, Potemkin joined the horse guards in the mid-1750s. Promoted to junior lieutenant in 1762, his initial command, in the Izmailovsky Regiment, followed in 1766. Potemkin distinguished himself during the Russo-Turkish War of 1768–1774. After spending the first year of the conflict on the staff of Field Marshal Aleksandr M. Golitsyn and as an aide-de-camp to Field Marshal Peter A. Rumiantsev, he received a field command in 1770. Potemkin proceeded to participate in many of the Russian army's most important victories on the Danubian front, proving himself Russia's most effective cavalry commander and winning a promotion to lieutenant general.

Returning to St. Petersburg in March 1774, Potemkin spent two years as Catherine's favorite, a position bringing rewards and responsibilities, including the war college's vice presidency. Replaced as official favorite in 1776, he remained the empress's most trusted adviser while devoting himself to administrative work, serving as governor-general of New Russia, president of the war college, and head of the Black Sea Admiralty. Under his leadership, the war college sponsored reforms ranging from alterations in army uniforms to adjustments in the composition of large-scale commands, and the Black Sea Admiralty strengthened Russia's naval power in the south.

Following the outbreak of a new war against the Turks (1787–1791), Catherine appointed Potemkin, now a field marshal, supreme commander of Russian forces. Although Russia achieved victory and Potemkin's performance earned substantial gifts and rewards from the empress, Potemkin was outshone by General Aleksandr Vasilyevich Suvorov, who won several critical victories. Potemkin died suddenly, in October 1791, en route to the Jassy peace conference.

Bruce J. DeHart

See also: Russo-Turkish Wars; Suvorov, Aleksandr Vasilyevich

References and further reading:

De Madariaga, Isabel. *Russia in the Age of Catherine the Great.* New Haven, CT: Yale University Press, 1980.

Soloveytchik, George. *Potemkin.* New York: W. W. Norton, 1947.

Powell, Colin L. (1937–)

U.S. Army commander and first African American to hold the positions of national security adviser, chairman of the Joint Chiefs of Staff, and secretary of state. Powell was born on 5 April 1937 in Brooklyn, New York, to Jamaican immigrants. He found his future career path while attending City College of New York, when he enrolled in the Reserve Officers Training Command, where he eventually held the highest student leadership position of cadet-colonel. In 1958 Powell received his commission as a second lieutenant in the U.S. Army.

In 1963, Powell served his first of two tours in Vietnam as an adviser to the Republic of Vietnam's 3d Infantry Regiment. As an adviser, he came under fire for the first time during Operation GRASSHOPPER in the A Shau Valley. In 1965, Powell was promoted to major two years ahead of schedule. He returned to Vietnam in 1968 as the plans officer for the Americal Division. After earning his M.B.A. at George Washington University, Powell was given command of the 32d Infantry Battalion in South Korea. In 1974, he was sent to the National War College and later served a brief tour as brigade commander in the 101st Airborne Division. In a rare step, Powell was promoted to brigadier general from lieutenant colonel on 1 January 1979.

During this time, Powell served in a variety of political-military positions for two administrations. Powell came to the public's attention in 1987 when he was nominated as President Ronald Reagan's national security adviser at a time when the National Security Council was reeling from the Iran-contra scandal. Powell was rewarded with a fourth star after the Reagan administration ended, and he briefly took command of U.S. Army Forces Command (FORSCOM) before President George Bush nominated him to be chairman of the Joint Chiefs of Staff. It was as chairman that Powell led the armed forces and captivated a nation with his presence and style during Operation JUST CAUSE in Panama and the Gulf War. He retired from the military in 1993, and in 2000 he was nominated by President-elect George W. Bush as secretary of state and was quickly confirmed.

Powell has been criticized for applying the "lessons learned" of Vietnam too rigidly, allowing Saddam Hussein to remain in power after his brutal invasion of Kuwait had been reversed, all in the name of avoiding a Vietnam-type "quagmire." Nonetheless, for perhaps most Americans of the time, he represented all that was right with the country, and he was so appealing that only his adamant refusal to run for office ended the "Powell for President" movement in 1996.

Michael Mulligan

See also: Gulf War; Vietnam Conflict; Somalia, U.S. Military Operations in

References and further reading:

Means, Howard. *Colin Powell: Soldier/Statesman–Statesman/Soldier.* New York: Donald I. Fine, 1992.

Powell, Colin. *My American Journey.* New York: Random House, 1995.

Woodward, Bob. *The Commanders.* New York: Pocket Star Books. 1992.

Powhatan War (1622, 1644)

A decade-long war against American Indian tribes in the Virginia colony that resulted in the first Indian reservation in North America. The English settlement of Tidewater Virginia brought people from two aggressive societies into contact in the early seventeenth century. With hopes of finding precious minerals and in expanding their empire, an English expedition founded Jamestown in 1607, constructing a wooden fort. At the same time, eastern Virginia was controlled by a confederacy of American Indians, numbering perhaps 10,000, under Powhatan. With initial contact, each side hoped to use the newcomers against traditional enemies, the English against the Spanish and the Powhatan Indians against rival tribes. A brisk trade developed: the English needed food, and the Powhatans wanted metal tools and weapons.

In the decade leading up to 1620, English settlements branched out up and down the James River. The colony's population was largely single and male and died young. Disease and starvation took a high toll on early settlers. Desperate for food, namely corn, the English were willing to take it forcibly if unable to trade for it with the Powhatans. By the 1620s, a tobacco boom swept Virginia, and this soil-depleting crop drove the British further inland in search of new land to cultivate. This period saw an aggressive expansion of English settlements as far west as present-day Richmond.

Powhatan died in 1618, just a few years after his daughter Pocahontas married an Englishman and left for London.

Powhatan's brother Opechancanough took over as head *werowance* (chief) and began to consolidate his control over various tribes such as the Mattaponi, Pamunkey, Appamatuck, and Chickahominey.

Realizing that the British demand for corn and land was insatiable, Opechancanough organized a strike to take the English out with one blow. The Indians planned a coordinated attack for the morning of 22 March 1622. Some settlements were forewarned, but others were entirely unprepared. Although successful in destroying some communities, the Powhatans could not fight a sustained war, and the English retaliated with raids on Indian towns and cornfields. Intermittent warfare continued for the next few years, punctuated by a few brief truces that never lasted.

English soldiers fought with matchlock muskets, accurate at ranges up to 30 yards. Musketeers were supported by troops armed with swords and pikes. The bow and arrows used by the American Indians had greater range and accuracy than the muskets, yet matchlocks became a highly prized item among them. Steel swords, shields, and weapons were also stolen from the English. After a decade of exhausting warfare, both sides agreed to a peace treaty in 1632.

English settlement expanded, and families increased the colony's population to 8,000 by 1640. Again hoping to eradicate the British swiftly, Opechancanough orchestrated another assault on 18 April 1644. Powhatan strength had never recovered from disease, warfare, and the poor crops of the previous decades. Brutal English counterattacks again destroyed villages and cornfields. In 1646, the Powhatans agreed to another peace treaty, establishing the first Indian reservations in what would become the United States. With the Indians crushed, colonial Virginia was free to expand to the west. The descendants of those who fought in the Powhatan wars still reside on these two reservations in Tidewater Virginia.

Robert Dunkerley

References and further reading:

Rountree, Helen C. *Pocahontas' People.* Norman: University of Oklahoma Press, 1990.

Steele, Ian K. *Warpaths.* Oxford, UK: Oxford University Press, 1999.

Prague, Siege of (1420)

Victory of Ján Žižka over Emperor Sigismund. The conflict in Bohemia between Catholics and the followers of the executed reformer, Ján Hus, became a civil war after the death of King Wenceslas IV, when his brother, Holy Roman Emperor Sigismund, claimed the throne over the objections of the Hussites. Supported by a papal bull denouncing his opponents as heretics, Sigismund entered Bohemia in May 1420, with a crusading army of 80,000, mostly Germans. He quickly captured Hradec Kralove (Königgrätz) and Kutná Hora and then marched toward Prague.

Responding to the entreaties of the Hussites in the city, the town of Tabor sent several thousand men under Hus's commander, Ján Žižka, to the capital. They defeated an army sent to block them. Under Žižka's direction, the Hussites strengthened the city's fortifications, built a watchtower on Vitkov hill, and put up barricades against Hradčany and Vyšehrad castles, which had fallen into Sigismund's hands. Unwilling to risk a direct assault on the city, Sigismund moved to blockade Prague. After capturing several surrounding towns, the crusaders crossed the Vltava River and approached Vitkov from the northeast on 14 July. Initially caught off-guard, Žižka led a counterattack up the south slope of the hill, surprising the crusaders in turn and driving them off the heights.

Though the losses to Sigismund's army were light, the Hussites' determination discouraged his hopes for a quick settlement of the war. After having himself crowned king at Hradčany, he abandoned the siege of Prague and sent the crusaders home. The victory at Vitkov saved the most important center of the Hussite movement and raised Žižka to prominence as the leading Hussite commander.

Brian Hodson

See also: Hussite Wars; Žižka, Ján

References and further reading:

Heymann, Frederick. *John Žižka and the Hussite Revolution.* Princeton: Princeton University Press, 1955.

Preston (17 August 1648)

The decisive battle of the Second English Civil War, ending Charles I's hopes. Following the collapse in spring 1658 of negotiations between crown and Parliament, it emerged that Charles had reached a settlement with the Solemn League and Covenant that controlled Scotland. This revelation led to a resurgence of royalism and scattered risings in England and Wales. Accordingly, on 8 July 1648, a Scottish army of 3,000 horse and 6,000 foot under the command of James, the Duke of Hamilton, crossed the English frontier and marched to Carlisle, where they were soon joined by 3,000 English royalists. This force was the basis of the army that marched south, attempting to gather further support as they went. At the same time, Parliament's officers marshaled their forces and moved to intercept Hamilton.

By 16 August, Hamilton had 20,000 troops, primarily Scots, and neared Preston on the west coast of England, but his men were tired, and their supplies were limited. With poor intelligence, Hamilton was unprepared for any serious opposition, and his men were strung out along the muddy roads into Preston. Skirmishing soon began as Oliver Cromwell's parliamentarians approached from the east (less than 9,000 men but primarily veterans). On the 17th, as rain poured down, Cromwell launched an attack against the disorganized Scots. Smashing through their lines, he forced Hamilton to withdraw. In the chaos, Cromwell's troops took the town, capturing much of the Scottish baggage train, taking 4,000 prisoners, and killing another 1,000. As night fell, although the fighting continued, so did the rain, and in the confusion the demoralized Scottish army retreated, having already abandoned most of its powder.

For all intents and purposes, this battle marked the end for Charles I's cause. Following this defeat, the beleaguered Scots were unable to provide any real assistance to the English royalists, and on 25 August Hamilton surrendered, with most of the remaining royalist strongholds in England quick to follow. What few forces remained in the field were quickly dispersed because after the disaster at Preston, it was difficult to find any who thought that Charles I's cause could continue.

Daniel German

See also: Cromwell, Oliver; English Civil War (1642–1649); Marston Moor

References and further reading:

Woolrych, Austin. *Battles of the English Civil War.* London: Weidenfeld & Nicolson, 1989.

Kenyon, John. *The Civil Wars of England.* London: Phoenix Press, 1989.

Princeton, Battle of (3 January 1777)

A minor battle of the American Revolution, but one that appreciably raised American morale.

In the aftermath of the surprise attack on the Hessians (German mercenary troops allied with the British) at Trenton, New Jersey, on 26 December 1776, Sir Charles Cornwallis moved from winter quarters to attack General George

George Washington on horseback during the Battle of Princeton. (Library of Congress)

Washington. He first moved to Princeton, gathered some 8,000 men, and left several regiments there as a rear guard.

Washington faced a difficult situation, for he was chronically short of food and supplies, and the enlistments of many of his men would expire at the New Year. Retreat across the Delaware to Pennsylvania was not possible. Rather, Washington and the Americans continued on the offensive and once again surprised their enemy. Leaving behind 400 men who kept campfires burning, made noise, and acted as if the entire army were in place, Washington and the bulk of American forces silently slipped around the enemy and then moved north-northeast from Trenton and advanced on Princeton. Fortunately for the Americans, Cornwallis chose to wait until the morning of 3 January to attack, disregarding advice from subordinates to attack immediately on January 2.

On 3 January, the Americans attacked a British regiment that was marching to join Cornwallis; initially, it was a confused fight, and the British more than held their own. After the main American contingent and Washington arrived, the Americans won, but fearing dispersion and Cornwallis's pursuit, they seized what supplies they could and broke off the attack.

Thereafter, Cornwallis withdrew British forces to New Brunswick, New Jersey, while Washington and the Americans went into winter quarters in Morristown. This brilliant campaign of maneuver, beginning at Trenton, helped renew confidence in the American cause and in Washington as commander of the American army.

Charles M. Dobbs

See also: American Revolution; Cornwallis, Sir Charles; Washington, George

References and further reading:

Bill, Alfred H. *The Campaign for Princeton, 1776–1777.* Princeton, NJ: Princeton University Press, 1948.

Smith, Samuel Steele. *The Battle of Princeton.* Monmouth Beach, NJ: Philip Freneau Press, 1967.

Prisoners of War

Persons captured either during military operations or as a consequence of military occupation. Technically, the term *prisoner of war* (POW) is of rather recent origin and has little in common with the people captured during or as a result of belligerent activities in earlier times. This is because the definition of POW relies on the principle of differentiation between combatants and noncombatants, which did not exist prior to the late nineteenth century.

In earlier times and especially antiquity, wars were mostly waged because of two reasons: to conquer new territories and their resources or only to rob these resources without permanently occupying the territory. The resources mainly were human ones, which means that the workforce was the single goal of the belligerent operation. Thus any persons captured during the operation, be they male or female, old or young, were regarded as having exclusively economic value and treated as slaves. Their lives were but part of the booty obtained in course of the operation. The Greek philosopher Plato stated that all those captured alive should be left to the victor's sole discretion as a "gift." That captivity was a very frequent fate in the ancient world is demonstrated by the Roman philosopher Seneca, who differentiated people not as slaves and free but as slaves and "not-yet-slaves." For the enslaved people, it was irrelevant if they were captured as soldiers or as simple inhabitants of the invaded city or territory. The only distinction made concerned the inhabitants of a fiercely defended town, who frequently were massacred as a deterrent for other cities.

This way of treating captured persons was not limited to the Greek and Roman cultures but merely mirrored a universal principle followed in ancient Egypt as well as medieval China, tribal Africa, and the pre-Columbian Americas. However, in certain cultures, it was also common to sacrifice the captured enemies on the altars of their gods.

Significant change was introduced by the Catholic Church in the Middle Ages, when in 1179 the Third Lateran Council prohibited the selling of Christians as slaves. From that time on, capturing people for the sole purpose of enslaving them was no longer acceptable. Instead, captives were released after their relatives had paid a certain ransom. This practice especially affected knights and later officers of noble ancestry, whose families could afford the large sums. As a consequence, the possibility of ransom payments offered a certain protection to the captured. However, those persons considered not profitable enough (footmen, members of the rural population) were either released or killed. Yet under the auspices of the church, many medieval treaties declared it inadmissible to kill women, children, peasants, and people of the church.

However, an entirely different attitude was held toward non-Christian enemies. Thus, it was still common either to kill or enslave non-Christian prisoners. During the Crusades, most Muslim soldiers were killed after having been captured by the Christian knights. Not until many knights themselves had fallen into the hands of their enemies did the system of sparing lives in favor of ransom payments also apply to Muslims.

The end of the Middle Ages brought important changes

in the way war was being waged: fighting became highly professionalized, with trained soldiers, officers, and mercenaries battling with each other, while the rest of the population left behind only bore the task of supplying the armies in the field. A differentiation between captured soldiers and "civilians" slowly became common. Only soldiers were specially treated as prisoners. However, this change did not cause an improvement in the situation of the ordinary soldier, who had no ransom to offer for his life or release. Therefore, it still was common to kill prisoners, but sometimes captors would hold back to ensure that the enemy would not kill those it had captured. Sources published in the famous seventeenth-century collection of military statutes, the *Corpus Iuris Militaris,* suggested, however, that it was the generals' Christian obligation to treat their prisoners with mercy and kindness. The exchange of prisoners between the belligerents according to a certain mathematical ratio (for example: one lieutenant equaled six soldiers, and one general equaled 3,000 soldiers) became more frequent during the following centuries and was very much consonant with Enlightenment rationality and precision.

In the nineteenth century, the Industrial Revolution and the French Revolution concept of mass citizen armies combined to cause many more soldiers to be captured in wartime. These prisoners were not exchanged but detained until the end of the hostilities to ensure that they would not fight again. The American Civil War and the Franco-Prussian War (1870–1871) are the most important examples of this new phenomenon. Suddenly, it became necessary to keep tens of thousands of prisoners in camps until the end of the war, which in the case of the American Civil War could be as long as four years. The countries' local infrastructures were often overwhelmed by the situation, and consequently a large percentage of prisoners died from starvation or lack of medical treatment.

But the nineteenth century was also a time of rising humanitarian sentiment, and the midcentury decades saw the first efforts to regulate the treatment of prisoners by international legal instruments. Although the 1864 Geneva Convention applied only to sick and wounded soldier personnel falling into the hands of the enemy and refrained from calling these persons "prisoners," the well-known "Lieber Code" issued by the U.S. Army in 1863 introduced the term *prisoners of war* and framed it by a legal definition. Articles 56 and 76 of the code prohibited their mistreatment and imposed the obligation to supply them with food. Yet this was an internal statute of the United States and by no means an internationally binding treaty.

Such an international instrument was not ratified until 1899, when the Hague Peace Conference adopted the Hague Convention (II) Respecting the Laws and Customs of War on Land. In its annex, Articles 4 to 20 dealt with the treatment of prisoners of war, taking as an example the regulations of the Lieber Code and the 1874 Brussels declaration (which also had not had the status of a treaty).

The experiences of World War I clearly demonstrated the shortcomings of the Hague Convention's provisions on prisoners. Initiated by the International Committee of the Red Cross, a new Geneva Convention was adopted by the community of states in 1929. This treaty supplemented rather than replaced the articles laid down in the Hague Conventions and proved invaluable for countless thousands of prisoners during World War II. However, the massive mistreatment of prisoners of war in Germany, Japan, and the Soviet Union clearly revealed even this convention's limits. In particular, the range of persons qualifying as POWs was too narrow to cover adequately the reality of twentieth-century war.

As part of a large-scale revision of the laws of warfare, the 1949 Geneva Convention greatly enlarges its predecessors but again proved to be far from perfect. Both the Korean War and the Vietnam conflict resulted in legal problems regarding the repatriation of prisoners against their will at the conclusion of hostilities. Additionally, guerrilla warfare brought forward new definitions of combatants that were different from the traditional ones tailored to the uniformed soldier operating in organized units. To entitle these belligerents to the protected status of prisoners of war, the 1977 Geneva Protocol I supplemented the 1949 convention but remains highly controversial.

Marcus Hanke

See also: Ancient Warfare; Guerrilla/Partisan/Irregular Warfare; Laws of War; Red Cross

References and further reading:

Hesseltine, William B. *Civil War Prisons.* New York: F. Ungar, 1964.

Keen, Maurice, ed. *Medieval Warfare.* Oxford, UK: Oxford University Press, 1999.

Levie, Howard S. *Prisoners of War in International Armed Conflict.* Newport, RI: U.S. Naval War College Press, 1977.

Propellants

Compounds used to move a projectile from the firing device to the target. Originally, gunpowder was used for this purpose. The cannon was a smoothbore, muzzle-loading weapon, firing solid round shot. Manufacturing techniques were extremely simple, and the explosive force of gunpowder is limited, which meant that until the late eighteenth century, gunners (and musketeers) were faced with problems of accuracy and consistency. One of the biggest problems was "windage," caused by gaps between barrel and projectile as the projectile traveled along the barrel after firing. These problems were partially solved with the invention of rifling and driving bands.

Gun propellants are mostly manufactured in powder form. They are low explosives, providing a developing thrust for the projectile as it travels along the barrel. In the early days of gunpowder, the consistency of the mixture of saltpeter, charcoal, and sulfur was difficult to control, but with the advent of nitrocellulose and similar powders, manufacturers were able to increase quality.

The problem with any propellant is to make it burn completely. Cannon would often produce a large muzzle flash, which was propellant burning after the projectile had left the bore. Modern rifles and guns still exhibit this problem, but to a lesser extent. The invention of smokeless powder also made the firing task easier, especially in an enclosed turret.

To ensure that the maximum propellant is burned out while the projectile is still in the barrel and therefore subject to the pressure caused by the propellant burning, powders are now manufactured in specific forms, with numerous holes pierced through each piece of propellant. These holes allow burning to proceed equally inside the powder grain as well as on the surface.

Manufacturers now produce single-base gun propellants from nitrocellulose with the addition of stabilizers and flash reducers. The powder is pressed into cylindrical or other shapes with the burning holes scientifically calculated to ensure maximum efficiency. These charges are assembled in varying weights for small-, medium-, and large-caliber guns.

Multibase propellants such as ballistite are used to make mortar increments. Just as guns do, mortars vary their range partly by changing the elevation of the gun or mortar barrel and partly by the amount of propellant charge used. Mortar increments are added externally to the mortar bomb and are fired by the basic charge, which is fitted to every mortar bomb. Some large-caliber weapons also use ballistite, which is prepared in grains, sticks, and multiperforated kerfed stick. Spherical powders in both single- and double-base (of nitrocellulose-nitroglycerine) are produced for small- and medium-caliber weapons, and some mortar increments are also made this way.

Until the late twentieth century, it was normal for a projectile to be propelled by a charge loaded into the weapon inside a cartridge case. Smaller-caliber ammunition was prepared as fixed ammunition, with bullet/projectile and propellant united in manufacture. Larger weapons, or those that fired more than one type of projectile (high-explosive alternating with smoke, illuminating shell, and solid shot, for instance), loaded the projectile first and then the cartridge case containing the required amount of propellant. Nowadays, caseless propellant is coming into general use, something that has been normal as bagged charge in naval guns since the mid–nineteenth century. These prepared propellant charges are designed to be totally self-consuming, leaving no empty shell case to be ejected.

Artillerymen have always been inventive by nature and have always tried for ever-longer ranges. The concept of rocketry appealed to them, and they adapted the idea of rocket propulsion by producing the base-bleed shell. These projectiles have a small rocket-type motor at their base, which is ignited on or after firing. Fueled by powder, the rocket-assisted shell has increased ranges quite significantly.

Rockets are fueled with either solid or liquid fuel. The solid fuel rocket has a warhead, a powder chamber and some means of igniting the propellant charge, and a shaped exhaust system to allow concentration of the expanding gases at the rear of the rocket. Early solid fuel rockets included the antitank rockets of World War II, fired from rails underneath aircraft wings. Aiming these rockets was done by eye, and they were essentially fire-and-forget weapons, having no internal guidance system or course correction mechanism. Modern solid fuel rockets are far more sophisticated, however, and have onboard guidance systems as well as sensor systems to aid target identification and even target selection.

Liquid-propelled rockets came of age with the German V-2 rocket. The previous venture, the V-1, was merely a pulse-jet-propelled semiaircraft, but the V-2 was a fully fledged ballistic missile. It was fueled by a mixture of liquid hydrogen and alcohol and achieved a range of more than 200 miles. It was a free-flight rocket, having no course correction capability.

Modern free-flight rockets have their ancestors in the weapons of the German and Russian armies during World War II. The German *Minenwerfer* and the Russian "Stalin Organ" were very simple solid fuel rockets with short ranges, but their effect was devastating because of the concentration of fire they could achieve. Area weapons such as these are now represented by the Multiple Launch Rocket System, which had such a destructive effect during the Gulf War.

Solid fuel rockets are preferable to liquid fuel rockets because of the high volatility of liquid propellants and because handling the concentrated acids used for some ballistic missiles is extremely hazardous. The main reason to use liquid fuel is that such rockets can be easily fueled when needed, for solid powder propellants have a habit of settling over time and deteriorating in performance.

David Westwood

See also: Artillery; Mortars; Rifles and Rifling

References and further reading:

Hogg, Ian V. *The Illustrated Encyclopaedia of Artillery.* London: Stanley Paul, 1987.

Ryan, J. W. *Guns, Mortars and Rockets.* Oxford, UK: Brassey, 1982.
The SNPE Explosives and Propellants Handbook. Paris: SNPE, 2000.

Psychological Operations

The use of psychology and propaganda by military units to persuade target audiences to adopt at least some of their views and possibly modify their behavior. The term *psychological operations* has been preferred since the Korean War in that target audiences might not be actually enemy personnel.

The employment of psychological operations goes at least back to biblical times, as when the Hebrew commander Gideon stampeded a numerically superior Midianite force by the sudden midnight display of torches accompanied by shouting, which gave the impression of a much larger force. In more recent times, American rebels were able to garner thousands of British and Hessian defectors by the use of leaflets promising free land in the New World. These leaflets were almost a textbook case of the basic principles of effective psychological operations: (1) know your target audience, (2) make believable promises, (3) do not mock or caricature your targets, (4) keep it simple but official-appearing, and most important, (5) do not lie. The Americans knew that for the British the very term *land-owning class* meant the rich, and it was obvious that the Americans had plenty of land, if nothing else. The leaflets decried the conditions in the British army, did not denounce the enemy, and were brief and to the point, sometimes bearing the name of George Washington; and defectors were indeed given land.

Nonetheless, such eighteenth-century efforts were isolated and limited. But the coming of the Industrial Revolution, with its railroads, telegraphs, cheap paper, and fast, powered printing presses, made large-scale psychological operations possible for the first time by World War I.

Here, the Allies conducted much more effective operations against the morale of the German army than vice-versa. Allied leaflets depicted the German soldier as a decent fellow who would be promptly returned to a better Germany at the end of the war, whereas the Germans' propaganda emphasized the "We Shall Crush You" theme, more effective to the already converted on the German home front than to enemy soldiers. One of the most effective American leaflets simply listed the weekly rations of the U.S. doughboy. The German target soldier needed but to compare such bounty with his own diet of mostly *kommisbrodt* (a rough army field loaf). No mention of the kaiser, "Huns," or the "Rape of Belgium," just a simple "Are You Hungry?" theme. Many German prisoners asserted that this one leaflet was primarily responsible for pushing a disgruntled, hungry soldier over the line to the actual act of wartime desertion. Another U.S. Army leaflet used the "Brave German Soldier, Your Government Has Lied to You" theme, counting up the actual 1 million or so U.S. troops already in France, compared to the minuscule number that the German High Command had publicly insisted would ever make their way through the U-boat-infested Atlantic. The German High Command first stupidly forbade their troops to read the leaflets, which simply whetted the soldiers' curiosity; then offered to pay for each "lying" leaflet turned in; and then simply gave up in despair. After the war, both the chief of staff of the German army and Adolf Hitler himself praised Allied propaganda.

World War II was in many ways a repetition of World War I on the propaganda front, except on a much larger and broader scale, but with the Germans and the Japanese still greatly inferior in their use of psychological weapons. Both Axis powers denigrated the Allied soldier as cowardly, weak, and misled. Their use of stilted, archaic language undermined any remaining validity of their leaflets. ("The fraud Rousevelt, hanging the President Election under his nose and from his policy ambition worked not only poor NIMITT but also MACCASIR like a robot, like this, WHAT IS PITY!!") A Japanese "sex" leaflet somewhat spoiled the effect with its last line: "Then, under the beautiful tropical moon, only DEATH awaits you, bullet hole in your guts . . . organizing death!" Actually, such "sex" leaflets were very popular with Allied troops, but for their explicit graphics, certainly not for their clumsy "political" messages, and they generated a brisk souvenir trade. German leaflets used less egregiously mangled syntax and language ("Well, what about the blisters *at* your feet?") but still could not refrain from clumsy, "un-American" phraseology ("Judeo-Bolshevik war-mongers"). That said, it should be pointed out that Axis radio propaganda was quite professional, if for no other reason than that its originators had the wit somehow to obtain the latest in popular American music, thus ensuring that "Tokyo Rose" and "Axis Sally" were widely listened to, if not taken seriously.

The garnering of prisoners of war is not the main intent of psychological operations; the goal is rather the weakening of morale. But Allied psywarriors did interview tens of thousands of German and Japanese troops for their reactions to their products. Few enemy soldiers admitted that Allied leaflets talked them into surrender, but many did say that they did adversely affect their morale. Whatever the value of the opinions of troops in the hands of their enemies, it is difficult to argue against the opinions of the Third Reich's hierarchy. Almost without exception, top Nazi and military officials took Allied psywar very seriously and (privately) gave it high praise. German propaganda minister Joseph Goebbels fulminated publicly against the "printed filth" composed by the "hireling Jewish scribes of Churchill and Roosevelt." At least one Nazi publication, *The Secret Weapon of the Enemy Is at Work,* warned all Germans to turn in any of the enemy's "lying filth" (presumably after it had been carefully read).

In the Pacific, the United States bungled badly at the start of the conflict. One leaflet displayed the words in Japanese and English, "I surrender." Wondering why this leaflet seemed to have no effect on the enemy, American psywarriors contacted Japanese Americans (in their internment camps) and got their answer. Japanese soldiers do not surrender; it is considered a fate literally worse than death. But "I Cease Resistance" or "I Take the Honorable Course" might have done better. Still, far fewer Japanese troops surrendered than did Germans (and many of the "Japanese" defectors were actually Koreans or Taiwanese), but those who did "cease resistance" proved invaluable. Being "dead men" as far as their homeland and families were concerned, they were willing to point out their former comrades' strongholds, give over information to Allied intelligence personnel, and generally cooperate in any way they could. But, again, the morale of the enemy was more important a target than actual surrendered troops, and Allied leaflets emphasized the Japanese army's indifference to its wounded ("Grenade Medicine") and the horrific casualties suffered by Japanese troops in the Philippines and in Burma and held out hope for a better life for Japan after the war. (This attitude was in distinct contrast, of course, to civilian propaganda on the American home front, which depicted the Japanese as bats, slugs, or myopic morons and emphasized America's duty to "Slap the Jap from the Map!")

The Korean War was the first "ideological" war for the United States, a battle between communism and democracy. On the battlefields, the United Nations (UN) Command rarely denounced communism or glorified capitalism or freedom but rather focused on the individual Communist-led soldier and his problems. Some leaflets cleverly played upon the differences between the Chinese and the Russians, with one map graphically contrasting China's vast expanse of old with the lands lost more recently through the notorious "unequal treaties"—lost to the Russians, not to "imperialist" Americans.

Once again, enemy propaganda to American and allied troops was nearly ludicrous in its language barbarisms and political tangles. But some showed commendable wit: "Use Your Head Soldier—If You Don't Want to Lose It!" (e.g., get out of the war); "Old Soldiers Never Die—But Young Ones Do"; "You Risk Your Life—Big Business Rakes in the Dough"; and (the best of the lot) "Leave Korea to the Koreans!" But the greatest Communist propaganda coup was their dissemination of the myth of the "brainwashing" of certain American POWs to favor communism and even to commit treason and of "collaboration" in the camps by a majority of those prisoners. Over the years, the documented rebuttals have never caught up with the unsupported assertions.

The great propaganda coup for the West in the Korean War was the refusal of some 22,000 Communist prisoners of the UN to return to their homelands. But here, again, the mere 22 U.S. captives of the Communists who refused repatriation seemed to receive the most publicity, particularly in the United States. (The fact that all of these defectors eventually returned to their capitalist hells was very rarely noted.)

In the Vietnam conflict a decade later, the Communist side directed its psychological operations as much at its enemies' home fronts as against its troops in the field. Propaganda directed to the Republic of Vietnam (South Vietnam) emphasized that the communist Vietcong was really a group of anti-imperialist freedom fighters who wanted nothing more than an independent and united Vietnam. The same theme played to receptive audiences in the United States, along with the theme that Americans were committing industrial-scale atrocities.

But in the field, it was a different story, as sophisticated and culturally aware American and South Vietnamese psyops garnered some 100,000 lower-level Vietcong cadre over 10 years in the Chieu Hoi (Open Arms) program. Once again, U.S. psyops concentrated on the enemy soldier, on his miseries in the field, his longing for his home village, and the horrors of modern warfare. A particularly clever leaflet illustrated President Richard M. Nixon's and Chairman Mao Zedong toasting each other during the former's unprecedented trip to Communist China. "The Mad Bomber of Hanoi" being feted by the "Elder Brother" of Asian communism! ("So now what are you fighting for?") No matter; the successful Communist strategic propaganda to the American home front and to the outside world is what is remembered to this day.

In the Gulf War (1990–1991), the coalition forces ranged against Saddam Hussein brought psychological operations to a fine art. Thousands of copies of the video entitled "Nations of the World Take a Stand" were distributed throughout the Middle East and in Baghdad itself. The message: "Your wicked leader, Saddam, is leading your beloved nation to ruin. We have no quarrel with the Iraqi people." At the strategic level, the Iraqi command was fooled by a well-orchestrated campaign of "disinformation" in the coalition media that emphasized the likelihood that the anti-Saddam forces would attack from the sea. They thus fell victim to the coalition's left-hook, cross-desert offensive. The "Arab Feast" leaflet, drawn up by the king of Saudi Arabia's personal illustrator so as to avoid any "alien" look, showed "brother Arab" troops inviting surrendering Iraqi soldiers to a sit-down feast—complete with bananas, unobtainable because of the coalition blockade. More ominous was the "B-52" leaflet that warned Iraqi soldiers: "You Cannot See This Bomber, You Cannot Hear It, but You Will Know When It Comes." The next such leaflet was addressed "To the Survivors of the Iraqi ——th Division: How Many Times Must You be Bombed Before You Get the Message?" Loudspeaker teams talked terrified Iraqi soldiers out of their bunkers and directed displaced civilians to the nearest shelter.

The dissemination of leaflets, always a weakness in earlier conflicts (leaflets "shoveled out" of an airplane tended to fly all over the cabin, fouling control cables and distracting the fight crew), were replaced by pinpoint drops using "hundred-mile-an-hour tape," and the leaflets themselves were carefully cut so that they could autorotate into a confined area. Helicopter-mounted loudspeakers replaced the nearly unintelligible aircraft-mounted speakers of previous conflicts, and Arabic-language tapes could be made in professional studio conditions and then broadcast in the field with good fidelity. The vast numbers of surrendering Iraqi troops waving safe-conduct passes gave vivid testimony to the effectiveness of coalition psyops.

In the former Yugoslavia, North Atlantic Treaty Organization (NATO) psychological operators faced a different challenge, civilian target audiences. American psyopers came in early with AM radio facilities, only to be confronted with FM local stations fully as developed as anything in the United States. NATO peacekeepers had to adapt to an audience that was as aware of Michael Jackson as of Slobodan Milosevic. Thus, instead of simple "Be Careful of Unexploded Mines" leaflets or radio and television messages, American psyopers contracted in the United States for a Superman comic book that much more vividly illustrated the dangers of unexploded ordnance to young people, eventually saving lives and limbs by the hundreds. Messages on soccer balls, pens, buttons, and newspapers drove home similar messages. But whether such effective psyops had any lasting ameliorative effect on historic Balkan ethnic hatreds is questionable.

As a result of the success of psychological operations in the former Yugoslavia and in the Gulf War, psychological operations are becoming an increasingly valued part of the armies of the developed world. But the principles of successful psywar have changed little, if at all, since the time of Midian or George Washington.

Stanley Sandler

References and further reading:

American Institutes for Research. *The Art and Science of Psychological Operations: Case Studies in Military Application.* 2 vols. Washington, DC: Department of the Army, 1976.

Daugherty, William E., with Morris Janowitz. *A Psychological Warfare Casebook.* Baltimore, MD: Operations Research Office, Johns Hopkins University, 1958.

Gilmore, Alison. *You Can't Fight Tanks with Bayonets: Psychological Warfare against the Japanese Army in the Southwest Pacific.* Lincoln: University of Nebraska Press, 1998.

Laurie, Clayton D. *The Propaganda Warriors: America's War against Nazi Germany.* Lawrence: University Press of Kansas, 1996.

Sandler, Stanley. *Cease Resistance; It's Good for You: A History of U.S. Army Combat Psychological Operations.* 2d ed. Fort Bragg, NC: U.S. Army Civil Affairs and Psychological Operations Command, 1999.

Ptolemy I Soter (c. 367–283 B.C.E.)

Alexander's general, king of Egypt, and founder of the Ptolemaic dynasty. Born in Macedonia in c. 367 B.C.E., Ptolemy achieved the rank of general under the leadership of Alexander the Great. After Alexander died in 323 B.C.E., his empire fragmented, with Ptolemy ruling Egypt and Libya. Legitimizing his position as successor by kidnapping the body of Alexander and erecting a lavish tomb in Alexandria, Ptolemy then successfully defended his territory against other Macedonian rulers and in the process gained control over Cyprus, Cyrenaica, and Judea.

While Ptolemy I solidified his position, three of Alexander's generals fought for control of the whole empire. Antigonus I attacked Seleukos I, the ruler of Babylon, but was defeated at Gaza in 312 B.C.E. Antigonus's son, Demetrius I, defeated Ptolemy I off the coast of Cyprus before laying siege to Rhodes in 304 B.C.E. Although Ptolemy lost Cyprus, Demetrius failed to capture Rhodes with 30,000 troops and the use of siege towers. In celebration of the victory, Ptolemy ordered the construction of the Colossus of Rhodes from materials abandoned by Demetrius after the siege. That same year, Ptolemy declared himself king of Egypt, establishing the Ptolemaic dynasty that lasted until Egypt became a Roman province upon the death of Cleopatra VII in 30 B.C.E.

In 301 B.C.E., Antigonus died in battle fighting against Selesuc I and Lysimachus. Ptolemy and Lysimachus joined forced against Demetrius, who had conquered Macedonia and ruled Greece. Two years after Demetrius's defeat in 285 B.C.E., Ptolemy abdicated the throne to Ptolemy II, his son by Berneike. He died in his sleep in 283 B.C.E. During his lifetime, he succeeded in creating a thriving capital at Alexandria, building and expanding the collection of ancient manuscripts of the renowned library of Alexandria, and constructing the lighthouse of Alexandria, one of the seven wonders of the ancient world.

Cynthia Clark Northrup

See also: Alexander the Great

References and further reading:

Ellis, Walter M. *Ptolemy of Egypt.* New York: Routledge, 1994.

Pugachev's Revolt (1773–1774)

Largest popular rebellion in Russian history before the twentieth century. Named for its instigator, Emelian Pugachev (1726–1775), the revolt erupted from tension between the Russian government and the Yaik Cossacks. Living along the Yaik River in the plain between the Ural Mountains and the Caspian Sea, the Yaik Cossacks were a frontier people who lived by fishing, herding, and salt production. Since the 1500s, they had fought a losing battle to preserve their independence against the encroachment of the Russian state.

During the eighteenth century, especially the opening decade of Catherine the Great's reign (1762–1796), the state's infringement upon Yaik independence produced resentment within the Yaik community. By the early 1770s, the Yaik Cossacks were ready to explode.

Discontent became open rebellion when Pugachev, a Don Cossack by birth and deserter from the Russian army, arrived in August 1773. Claiming to be the emperor Peter III (1762), who had been deposed and murdered 11 years earlier, Pugachev invited the Cossacks to help him reclaim power. Promising freedom and a special place in the Russian state, the "Pretender" quickly won the Cossacks' support. On 17 September, Pugachev and his followers attacked Yaitsk, capital of the Cossack community, initiating what became the largest popular rebellion Russia had yet experienced.

Once under way, the revolt spread rapidly, engulfing western Siberia, the Ural Mountains, and the Middle Volga River valley, as it attracted support from a variety of disaffected social groups, including the non-Russian Bashkirs, ascribed peasants, Old Believers, and private serfs. Each of these groups held specific grievances against the existing political and socioeconomic order and saw in Pugachev their liberator.

Undisciplined and poorly armed, Pugachev's motley armies proved no match for Russian army regulars, who arrived in force in December 1773 and January 1774. Winning major victories at Tatishchev (22 March), Ufa (23–24 March), Kazan (12–13 July), and Tsaritsyn (25 August), government troops crushed the rebellion and forced Pugachev and 300 of his followers to flee.

On route to Yaitsk, a small group of Cossacks, to save themselves, seized the "Pretender" and handed him over to government forces on 15 September. Transferred to Moscow, Pugachev was tried by a special court, which found him guilty of several crimes and sentenced him to death. Public execution followed on 10 January 1775. To wipe away the memory of the revolt, Catherine renamed the Yaik Cossacks, the Yaik River, and the city of Yaitsk the Ural Cossacks, the Ural River, and Uralsk. These measures could not, however, erase the memories of Russia's rulers, who—at least until the mid-nineteenth century—lived in fear of another Pugachev revolt.

Bruce J. DeHart

References and further reading:

Alexander, John. *Emperor of the Cossacks: Pugachev and the Frontier Jacquerie of 1773–1774.* Lawrence: University Press of Kansas, 1973.

Avrich, Paul. "Pugachev, 1773–1774." In *Russian Rebels, 1600–1800.* New York: W. W. Norton, 1972.

Raeff, Marc. "Pugachev's Rebellion." In *Preconditions of Revolution in Early Modern Europe,* ed. Robert Forster and Jack P. Greene. Baltimore, MD: Johns Hopkins Press, 1970.

Pulaski, Count Kazimierz (1747–1779)

Polish revolutionary who fought in the American Revolution. Born on 4 March 1747, in Podolia, Poland (in present-day Ukraine), Pulaski became a leader of the Confederation of Bar, a revolt against Russian control of Poland. Following the failure of the revolt, he traveled to France, where in December 1776 in Paris, he met Benjamin Franklin, the American ambassador, who convinced him to join the American colonists in their fight against Great Britain. In 1777, he was commissioned a colonel in the Continental army, and as a result of his distinguished service at the Battle of the Brandywine (where he served as Washington's aide-de-camp), he was appointed chief of cavalry and promoted to the rank of brigadier general. In 1778, with the permission of the Continental Congress, Pulaski organized an independent combined-arms unit of cavalry, infantry, and artillery, known as the Pulaski Legion. In 1779, Pulaski and his legion were ordered to South Carolina to support Major General Benjamin Lincoln. After helping to defend Charleston, South Carolina, against a British attack in May 1779, Pulaski and his legion joined with Lincoln and a French force, who were planning to besiege Savannah, Georgia. In an attack on 9 October 1779, he was mortally wounded and died two days later aboard the *Wasp* en route to Charleston. He was buried at sea.

Alexander M. Bielakowski

See also: American Revolution; Brandywine; Washington, George

References and further reading:

Szymanski, Leszek. *Casimir Pulaski: A Hero of the American Revolution.* New York: Hippocrene Books, 1993.

Punic Wars (264–146 B.C.E.)

In 264 B.C.E., the first of three wars broke out between the Roman Republic and the North African sea power Carthage.

An epic struggle for control of the western Mediterranean ensued.

The First Punic War (264–241 B.C.E.)

Messana (Messina), Sicily, threatened by the Greeks of Syracuse, appealed for help first to the Carthaginians, who garrisoned the city, and then to the Romans, who in turn expelled the Carthaginians. The Carthaginians besieged Messana but withdrew to Syracuse in the face of a Roman army. The Romans besieged Syracuse, and the city switched sides. Sicily was divided into Roman (the eastern part) and Carthaginian (the western part) possessions.

After two seasons of campaigning, the Romans realized they could not defeat the Carthaginians without challenging them at sea. In the winter of 261–260 B.C.E., the Romans finally built a fleet, arming the ships with marines and boarding devices rather than a ram. In 260 B.C.E., at Mylae, the new technology proved itself, and the Carthaginians, relying on intricate ramming techniques, were badly beaten.

The war in Sicily remained undecided, and the Romans invaded Africa. A Carthaginian fleet was defeated at Ecnomus in 256 B.C.E. The Roman campaign in Africa was successful for a time, but under the leadership of the Spartan Xanthippus, the Roman army in Africa was destroyed by the Carthaginians. The fleet evacuating the survivors was destroyed by a gale in 255 B.C.E.

Notwithstanding Carthaginian control of coastal waters, the Romans remained successful in Sicily. They captured Panormus (Palermo), and in 251 B.C.E., a Carthaginian force was decisively defeated, leaving the Carthaginians without a field army in Sicily. However, the remaining Carthaginian strongholds could not be taken. In 249 B.C.E., the Romans were severely defeated near the city of Drepana, and another fleet was lost on the south coast of Sicily.

In 247 B.C.E., Hamilcar Barca was sent to Sicily to take command of the fleet. He landed near Panormus and, from the nearby coastal height of Heircte, initiated a guerrilla war on land. He raided the coasts of southern Italy to pin down enemy forces and incite rebellion against Rome. When this strategy was ineffective, Hamilcar captured Eryxin in the vicinity of Drepana under cover of darkness (244 B.C.E.). From there, he continued his guerrilla war. However, in 241 B.C.E. the Romans defeated the Carthaginians at sea near the Aegeates Islands. Forced into a peace treaty, Carthage had to give up Sicily.

Rome had wrested the island of Sardinia from Carthaginian hands (238 B.C.E.), taking advantage of a mercenary revolt and subsequent war in Carthage (247–231 B.C.E.). To compensate for their loss, the Carthaginians started to extend their Spanish possessions. Initially under the command of Hamilcar and afterward under his son-in-law Hasdrubal, the Carthaginians conquered a large part of the Iberian Peninsula. In 220 B.C.E., Hamilcar's son Hannibal was chosen by the army to be its commander. Initially, he set out to subjugate the northern tribes of Iberia, but soon he would turn his eyes upon Rome.

The Second Punic War (218–202 B.C.E.)

In 219 B.C.E., Hannibal besieged Saguntum (Sagunto) in Spain, which turned for help to Rome. The Romans accused Carthage of breaking previous agreements, and although Rome did nothing to save Saguntum from capture (218 B.C.E.), Rome declared war.

In 218 B.C.E., Hannibal marched over the Pyrenees, and having evaded Publius Cornelius Scipio's army near the Rhone River, he marched over the Alps into the Po Valley, where he defeated the Romans near the river Trebia (218 B.C.E.). In 217 B.C.E., he destroyed a Roman army at Lake Trasimene in Etruria (Tuscany) and then won his most brilliant victory (216 B.C.E.) at Cannae in Apulia, completely wiping out two consular armies in one stroke. In reaction, Rome's age-old ally Capua (near Naples) switched sides, as others in Italy did later. Following the advice of Fabius Maximus Verrucosus, the Romans dogged Hannibal's footsteps, recapturing the towns he had taken, harassing his lines of supply, but never facing him in a decisive battle.

After Scipio failed to intercept Hannibal at the Rhone River, he sent his army to Spain under the leadership of his brother Gnaeus Scipio. Rejoining it after the Battle of the Trebia, he attacked the Carthaginians in northern Spain. In 215 B.C.E., the Scipios defeated the Carthaginians at Ibera (215 B.C.E.). By 211 B.C.E., the Carthaginians were pushed back far beyond the Ebro River, and the Scipios decided to attack their basis of power in southwestern Spain. However, attacked by three armies, both Scipios were defeated and killed.

In 214 B.C.E., Syracuse had broken its alliance with Rome and went over to the Carthaginians. Under the command of Marcus Claudius Marcellus, the Romans stormed the city (213 B.C.E.). The defenders were assisted by the machinery of the scientist Archimedes. A lengthy siege ensued, combined with campaigning against Carthaginian troops and numerous hostile towns. In 211 B.C.E., Syracuse was taken, and by 210 B.C.E., Sicily was entirely under Roman control. Besides the overseas expeditions to Sicily and Spain, the Romans also campaigned in Sardinia and Illyria (Albania).

After the secession of Capua, the war in Italy had been mainly fought in Campania. Continuing their delaying strategy, the Romans kept in the vicinity of Hannibal's army, avoiding direct battle. In 213 B.C.E., the Romans besieged Capua. The citizens held out for years, but Hannibal could not relieve the city. As a last resort, he marched to Rome but eventually retreated into Apulia. Capua surrendered in 211 B.C.E., and with Campania secured, the Romans followed Hannibal and continued the war in southern Italy.

In 210 B.C.E., Publius Cornelius Scipio Africanus Major, the son of Publius Cornelius Scipio, who had died the year before, was sent to take command in Spain. In 209 B.C.E., he captured Cartagena, Carthage's most important city in the peninsula, and the next year, he defeated Hannibal's brother Hasdrubal at Baecula (Bailen). Hasdrubal escaped with part of his army and marched to Italy to reinforce his brother. The Romans assembled a large force, intercepting and defeating Hasdrubal at Metaurus Valley (207 B.C.E.). Hannibal retreated into Calabria and remained there until his return to Africa (202 B.C.E.).

Scipio continued the war in Spain successfully, defeating the Carthaginians at Ilipa (206 B.C.E.) and forcing them to evacuate Spain. In 205 B.C.E., Scipio landed in North Africa and defeated the Carthaginians at the Great Plains (203 B.C.E.), whereupon Hannibal was recalled from Italy. At Zama (202 B.C.E.), Hannibal was finally defeated, and Carthage surrendered. As a result, Carthage lost all its overseas possessions and most of its African empire. Its fleet was limited to 10 ships, it was not allowed to make war without Rome's consent, and it was tributary to Rome.

The Third Punic War (149–146 B.C.E.)

From about 170 B.C.E., Massinissa, king of the neighboring Numidians, encroached upon Carthaginian possessions. Because he had been an important ally of Rome during the last stages of the Second Punic War—and possibly because of resentment, fear, and envy of Carthage's riches—Rome permitted Massinissa's encroachment. In 150 B.C.E., the Carthaginians assembled an army, marched to meet the Numidian king, and were defeated.

By attacking the Numidians, the Carthaginians had broken their treaty with Rome, and the Romans sent an army to Carthage. The city surrendered but resisted Roman demands that the population move inland and that the city be destroyed. The Romans besieged the city unsuccessfully because of incompetent command.

In 147 B.C.E., Publius Cornelius Scipio Aemilianus, the adopted grandson of Scipio Africanus Major, was chosen as consul and sent to Africa. Scipio invested the city completely by sea and by land, and in 146 B.C.E. the city was taken after fierce fighting. Carthage was pillaged and razed, and the surviving citizens were sold as slaves.

M. R. van der Werf

See also: Cannae, Battle of; Fabius Maximus Verrucosus "Cunctator"; Hamilcar Barca; Hannibal Barca; Lake Trasimene, Battle of; Marcellus, Marcus Claudius; Scipio Africanus Major, Publius Cornelius; Trebia, Battle of the; Zama, Battle of

References and further reading:

Bagnall, Nigel. *The Punic Wars: Rome, Carthage and the Struggle for the Mediterranean.* London: Pimlico, 1999.

Caven, B. *The Punic Wars.* London: Weidenfeld and Nicolson, 1980.

Lazenby, J. F. *Hannibal's War: A Military History of the Second Punic War.* Warminster: Aris & Phillips, 1978.

———. *The First Punic War: A Military History.* London: UCL Press, 1996.

Pusan Perimeter (August–September 1950)

United Nations Command final defensive lines along the Naktong River and the farthest advance of the North Korean invasion. By early August 1950, General Walton Walker was arranging for the defense of the most vital port of Pusan in southeastern Korea, essential to the support of the large-scale introduction of U.S. armed forces onto the peninsula. The U.S. 24th Division had sought to delay the North Korean advance down the western plain, while Republic of Korea (ROK) units fought a series of delaying actions in the more mountainous east side of the peninsula. Meanwhile, other units arranged for the defense around Pusan.

Initially, the Pusan perimeter was the Naktong River on the west and a northern line stretching eastward from Yongdok. Walker waged a flexible and aggressive defense. He used interior lines of defense to shift forces around and the U.S. 24th Division as a reserve to blunt North Korean attacks and to maintain the perimeter. He engaged in spoiling attacks and was able to blunt the initial greater armored strength of the enemy. Meanwhile, the North Koreans may have weakened their attack by assaulting too many objectives (including taking all of the southwestern plain while they were still assaulting Pusan), considering their limited forces.

From about 27 August through 10 September, the North Koreans attacked the perimeter. They had little success in maintaining bridgeheads across the Naktong River in the American sector of defense; they were able to push the ROK defenses about 10 miles south, but the South Koreans did not break, and the defense line held. Walker had maintained this defense, while General Douglas MacArthur diverted forces coming from the United States and the Pacific and even removed some battalions from Pusan to put together the two-division assault force for the Inchon invasion.

The North Koreans had their difficulties. Allied air power had quickly destroyed the small North Korean air force and then turned to Communist armor, truck traffic, and the road and rail communications from North Korea to the south, mostly on the western side of the peninsula. North Korean units besieging Pusan depended on a long supply line. The Soviets provided virtually no resupply (the reasons for which are still the subject of argument today). And to fill out decimated units, North Koreans press-ganged South Korean civilians and prisoners of war, but these conscripts were unwilling, little trained, and inexperienced—they certainly did not approach the quality of the initial invasion forces. Meanwhile, U.S. naval gunfire and allied airpower helped strengthen the defense of the perimeter until sufficient numbers of men, tanks, and artillery could be shipped to Korea.

Then, on 15 September 1950, MacArthur launched the Inchon invasion, while Walker scheduled a breakout from the Pusan perimeter for the next day. Led by the U.S. 1st Cavalry Division, which covered the final 100 miles in 11 hours, the Pusan defenders linked up with the Inchon invaders on 26 September near Osan, and it appeared the days of desperate defense were over. Eight North Korean divisions were cut off in the southwest, and virtually all of the North Korean units had to leave their tanks, heavy weapons, and supplies as they raced to the 38th parallel to avoid the rapidly advancing UN forces.

Charles M. Dobbs

See also: Korean War; MacArthur, Douglas; Walker, Walton

References and further reading:

Hoyt, Edwin P. *The Pusan Perimeter.* New York: Stein & Day, 1983.

James, D. Clayton, with Anne Sharp Wells. *Refighting the Last War: Command and Crisis in Korea, 1950–1953.* New York: Free Press, 1993.

Sandler, Stanley. *The Korean War: No Victors, No Vanquished.* London: Routledge; Lexington: University of Kentucky Press, 1999.

Pyramids (21 July 1798)

A battle between French forces of the Army of Egypt, 25,000 strong, commanded by Napoleon, and Egyptian and Mamluk forces 18,000–21,000 strong, commanded by Murad and Ibrahim Bey, on the west bank of the Nile River near Cairo. Although it was called the "Battle of the Pyramids," the pyramid complex at Giza is about 15 miles away from the site of the battle, and the pyramids played no role in the engagement; the name is something of a misnomer.

Since landing in Egypt on 1 July 1798, Bonaparte had sought to bring the Mamluk forces, commanded by Murad and Ibrahim Bey, to a decisive battle. Although several sharp actions were fought as the Mamluks retreated down the Nile, the French were unable to complete the destruction of their foe.

When the Mamluk forces arrived near Cairo, the commanders divided their force. The bulk of the forces, perhaps 100,000 strong, crossed the Nile River under the command of Ibrahim Bey and remained in Cairo. These troops played no part in the subsequent battle. A small force of about 6,000 cavalry and 12,000 or more unreliable infantry occupied the village of Embabeh, under the command of Murad Bey.

The French, arriving at 2 P.M. on the 21st, deployed in five large, division-sized squares, with noncombatants, wagons, and cavalry sheltered in the middle. The French deployed their available artillery at the corners of the squares.

At 3:30 P.M., the Mamluks opened the battle with a vigorous cavalry charge against the westernmost of the French squares, posted on the open flank of the French army. These squares, commanded by Jean Louis Reynier and Louis Charles Antoine Dessaix, had not quite fully deployed and were almost taken by surprise by the charge. Nevertheless, the French managed to form and to fend off the cavalry attack. While the Mamluk cavalry sought to overwhelm the French right, the French left, with its flank protected by the Nile, attacked the village of Embabeh and evicted the reluctant, conscripted peasants who formed Murad's infantry.

By 4:30 P.M., the Mamluks withdrew from the field. Two thousand heavily armored Mamluk cavalry were cut off from the retreat and attempted to swim the Nile under fire from the French. Few survived the attempt. Murad and 3,000 more cavalry were able to flee south toward Giza. The surviving infantry simply dispersed. The Mamluks lost 2,000 cavalry and an unknown number of infantry, and the French lost 29 killed and 260 wounded.

As a result of the battle, Bonaparte was able to occupy Cairo, which had been abandoned by Ibrahim Bey, and to undertake the government of Egypt. The practical benefits of the victory, however, were very largely negated by the destruction of the French fleet at Aboukir Bay on 2 August, which cut off communications between France and the Army of Egypt.

Joseph M. Isenberg

See also: Aboukir; Alexandria; French Revolutionary Wars; Kléber, Jean-Baptiste; Murat, Joachim, Grand Duke of Cleves-Berg, King of Naples; Napoleon I

References and further reading:

Chandler, David G. *Campaigns of Napoleon.* New York: Scribner, 1966.

Connelley, Owen. *Blundering to Glory.* Wilmington, DE: Scholarly Resources, 1999.

Pyrrhus (319–272 B.C.E.)

King of Epirus (in northwestern Greece) and inspiration for the term *Pyrrhic victory.* Supposedly descended from

Achilles and related to Alexander, Pyrrhus became king of Epirus at age 12 in 307 B.C.E. Losing the throne in a revolt, he earned a reputation as a fierce warrior, fighting along Demetrius Poliorcetes of Macedon at Ipsus (301 B.C.E.). As a royal hostage in Egypt, Pyrrhus allied with Ptolemy I, who helped him regain control of Epirus with Neoptolemus II (297 B.C.E.). Pyrrhus assassinated his co-ruler in 296 B.C.E., becoming the sole monarch. He engaged in a series of campaigns against Macedon, then ruled by Demetrius. In 281 B.C.E., the Tarentines (Italian Greeks) asked Pyrrhus for military assistance against Rome. Pyrrhus led an army, including elephants, to Italy and forced the Romans to retreat in a costly battle at Herculea in 280 B.C.E. He is said to have remarked, "One more such victory and I am lost," thus the term *Pyrrhic victory.* Pyrrhus, impressed by his foe, sued for peace. When the Romans declined, he withdrew to southern Italy. After another hard-fought battle at Asculum (279 B.C.E.), Pyrrhus left Italy for a mostly successful campaign in Sicily against the Carthaginians. He ruled much of Greek Sicily until his dictatorial manner inspired an uprising. Pyrrhus returned to Italy, badly losing the Battle of Beneventum to a Roman army. Pyrrhus returned to Epirus, conquered Macedonia in 274 B.C.E., and failed in an attempt to restore Cleonymus in Sparta in 272 B.C.E. He was killed in street fighting during a civil war in Argos. Perhaps the most famous general of his time, Pyrrhus was not a statesman and did not follow through on successes. He wrote several lost works on military strategy.

Harold Wise

See also: Ptolemy I Soter

References and further reading:

Cross, G. N. *Epirus.* Cambridge: Cambridge University Press, 1932.

Garouphalias, Petros. *Pyrrhus, King of Epirus.* London: Stacy International, 1979.

———. *Plutarch's Lives.* 2 vols. New York: Random House, 2001.

Q

Qianlong (Ch'ien-lung) (1711–1799)

Last great emperor of Qing dynasty (1644–1912). The Qianlong emperor was the grandson of the Kangxi emperor (1662–1722) and, after taking the throne in 1736, reigned for nearly 60 years. He abdicated in 1795 in favor of his son, the Zhia Qing emperor, so as not to rule longer than his beloved grandfather. He retained effective power until his death in 1799.

The Qianlong emperor expanded Qing boundaries to their greatest extent, gaining control over Tibet in 1751. In the next 10 years, Chinese armies secured Chinese Turkistan, what is now Xinjiang in extreme western China. Although China was not as successful in expanding its southern and southwestern boundaries, local rulers in what is now Vietnam and Burma accepted Chinese suzerainty.

The Qianlong emperor continued systems of control put into place by his predecessors. To preserve Manchu power in a sea of Chinese, he carefully apportioned key administrative posts between Chinese and Manchu appointees and continued the banner system, dividing both military forces and military leadership among Chinese, Manchus, and Mongols. He continued the examination system for entry into the bureaucracy.

Despite Qing successes against peoples on its immediate borders, the Qianlong emperor did not widen relations with the emerging West. Prohibitions against Christian missionaries remained, and Qing authorities sought to limit trade with Western nations to the distant port of Guangzhou, or Canton. Thus the Qianlong emperor would leave his successors a larger territory to protect and a bigger population to feed but also the greater corruption in government that marred his later years and thus less capacity to deal with the more confident and more powerful West.

Charles M. Dobbs

See also: French Colonial Wars; Manchu Expansion, Wars of; Yangzhou, Siege of

References and further reading:

Elvin, Mark. *The Pattern of the Chinese Past.* Stanford, CA: Stanford University Press, 1973.

Kahn, Harold L. *Monarchy in the Emperor's Eyes: Image and Reality in the Ch'ien-lung Reign.* Cambridge, MA: Harvard University Press, 1971.

Singer, Aubrey. *The Lion and the Dragon: The Story of the First British Embassy to the Court of the Emperor Qianlong in Peking.* London: Barrie & Jenkins, 1992.

Qin Shi Huangdi (Ch'in Shih-huang-ti) (259–210 B.C.E.)

The reign name of the first documented emperor of a unified China. Zhao Zheng was the son of the king of the state of Qin, one of seven contending states in China during the several-centuries-long Warring States Period. The state of Qin was located to the west, in the famous "bend of the Yellow River," where its rulers could have a protected rear as they fought the other warring states. Qin was also one of the first states to move from bronze to iron weapons. With a solid agricultural foundation based on irrigated sorghum and millet fields, it could afford to arm its peasantry and thus fielded larger armies than its opponents. The rules of chivalry that had characterized earlier fighting had long since been discarded, and Qin had the men, weaponry, organizational structure, and economic power to prevail in the final stages of the fighting.

Zhao became king at age 13 and assumed real power at age 21. In 230 B.C.E., Qin conquered the weakest of the six states, Han. By 221 B.C.E., it had united China, and King Zheng became the first Qin emperor, or Qin Shi Huangdi.

As emperor, he divided the country into districts, seeking to end the former feudal boundaries and loyalties; established uniform weights and measures, including axle lengths on carts; and constructed roads to improve communication and control within his vast empire. He is best known in the West for connecting many existing walls into the first of many Great Walls, delineating the settled agriculture of China from the nomadic agriculture north of the wall.

Zhao constructed a remarkable tomb—Mount Li—which is still unexcavated and is protected by a vast life-size army of more than 6,000 terracotta soldiers and horses. The find in 1974 of one division of this army has provided invaluable insights into Qin army organization and the role of various ethnic Chinese peoples in the army.

Zhao died, probably from mercury ingested as part of an alchemically inspired elixir of longevity, and his son was unable to continue the dynasty, which soon collapsed.

Charles M. Dobbs

See also: Chinese Imperial Wars; Great Wall of China; Han Wudi

References and further reading:

Bodde, Derk. *China's First Unifier: A Study of the Ch'in Dynasty as Seen in the Life of Li Ssu, 280–208 B.C.E.* London: Oxford University Press, 1967.

Chang, K. C. *Eastern Zhou and Qin Civilizations.* New Haven, CT: Yale University Press, 1985.

Cotterell, Arthur. *The First Emperor of China.* New York: Holt, Rinehart, and Winston, 1981.

Quadruple Alliance, War of the (1717–1719)

Conflict in which Spain, attempting to revise the settlement of the War of the Spanish Succession, fought the Holy Roman Empire, Britain, France, the Netherlands, and the House of Savoy. The end of the War of the Spanish Succession in 1714 and the death of Louis XIV (1638–1715) the next year left Europe a mine about to explode, a point fully grasped by the most energetic and able politician in Europe in the first half of the eighteenth century, Queen Elizabeth Farnese of Spain. Of the victors, the governments in France and Britain were considered illegitimate by a large portion of their subjects, and Duke Victor Amadeus of Savoy and Piedmont, now also king of Italy, and the Holy Roman Emperor Charles VI (1685–1740), now in direct control of Spain's former northern Italian imperial fiefs and the island of Sardinia, were utterly exposed to a resurgent Spanish navy.

In 1716, Elizabeth Farnese's husband, Philip V, uncle to the minor king of France, launched a conspiracy with sidelined members of the regency council; while at sea, her rapidly rebuilt navy initiated war by landing troops in Sardinia and Sicily. The emperor, despite losing Sardinia, was not at first disposed to intervene. He had grievances against France and Britain over the settlement of the previous war, and another segment of the European power train, Turkey, had just launched a revanchist war against Venice. The Venetians folded rapidly, compelling the emperor to intervene in eastern Europe. Thus, it was left to France to take the lead, drawing in Britain, already smarting from the effects of Spanish-supported internal subversion.

The Turks were defeated in 1717, freeing Habsburg forces, and the Holy Roman Empire was brought into the war. The emperor secured a reversion of Sicily for Sardinia (confirmed in the 1720 Treaty of London) and offered troops for expeditions to Sicily that reduced the Spanish garrisons there in 1717–1719, while a British fleet under George Byng, Earl of Torrington (1663–1733), destroyed the Spanish at Cape Passaro and subsequently in Messina harbor, and James Fitzjames, the Duke of Berwick (in French service), invaded Spain, burning the shipyards at Pasajes to check the buildup of the Spanish fleet in 1719.

Berwick's campaign was efficiently conducted, and at the time much attention attached to the imperial army's model campaign of sieges in Sicily, but the main interest of the War of the Quadruple Alliance in military history remains the naval battle of Cape Passaro.

Erik A. Lund

See also: Spanish Succession, War of the

References and further reading:

Armstrong, Edward. *Elisabeth Farnese: The Termagant of Spain.* London: Longman, Green, 1892.

K.k. Abtheilung für Kriegsgeschichte des k.k. Kriegsarchiv. *Feldzüge des Prinzen Eugen.* 21 vols. Vienna: K.k. Generalstabes, 1876–1891.

Lindsey, J. O. "International Relations." In *The New Cambridge Modern History,* vol. 7, 195–198. Cambridge, UK: Cambridge University Press, 1957.

Quatre Bras and Ligny (16 June 1815)

Simultaneous battles in the Hundred Days, just before Waterloo. Returned from Elba and rapidly remobilizing, Napoleon learned that the Congress of Vienna planned to gather a multinational army in Belgium to invade France. Napoleon decided to make a preemptive strike into Belgium to destroy the allied force before it could gain sufficient strength. His plan was to drive his 124,000-man army as a wedge between Gebhard Leberecht von Blücher's 116,000 Prussians and the 93,000 British and Dutch troops of Arthur Wellesley, the Duke of Wellington and then defeat each foe separately.

Marching north toward Brussels and crossing the frontier

on 15 June, Napoleon divided his forces, with Michel Ney commanding the left and Emmanuel de Grouchy the right. With his vanguard solidly between Blücher and Wellington, he ordered Ney's 53,000 to attack the Duke of Weimar's garrison of about 4,000 at Quatre Bras, a strategic crossroads about 18 miles south of Brussels, while he himself simultaneously led Grouchy's 71,000 against Blücher's 83,000 at Ligny, about 5 miles southeast of Quatre Bras. Ney inexplicably hesitated, which ruined the coordination of Napoleon's two-pronged attack and allowed Wellington to reinforce Weimar. When Ney finally attacked with 20,000 in midafternoon, the allied force had grown to about 21,000. Because of a miscommunication, the 30,000 men of the French I Corps never saw action in either battle. Wellington counterattacked after about four hours of fighting.

In the indecisive encounter at Quatre Bras, Ney lost 4,300 men and about 2 miles' worth of ground, and Wellington lost 4,700 men, including the Duke of Brunswick. Because Ney prevented Wellington from reinforcing Blücher, Napoleon won at Ligny, inflicting 16,000 casualties, losing only 11,500, and forcing Blücher to retreat away from Wellington. It was Napoleon's last victory. Heavy rain on 17 June stopped his pursuit of the Prussians.

Eric v. d. Luft

See also: Blücher, Gebhard Leberecht von; Brunswick, Frederick William, Duke of; Gneisenau, August Neidhart von; Napoleon I; Napoleonic Wars; Ney, Michel, duc d'Elchingen, Prince de La Moskova; Soult, Nicolas-Jean de Dieu; Waterloo; Wellington, Arthur Wellesley, Duke of

References and further reading:

Caldwell, George, and Robert Cooper. *Rifle Green at Waterloo: An Account of the 95th Foot in the Netherlands Campaign of 1813–14, at Quatre Bras and Waterloo 16th–18th June 1815, and the Occupation of Paris, with a Full Medal and Casualty Roll for the Fourteen Companies at Waterloo and Details of Weapons, Clothes, and Equipment Used in the Campaign.* Loughborough, UK: Bugle Horn, 1990.

Hofschroer, Peter. *1815: The Waterloo Campaign: Ligny and Quatre Bras.* London: Greenhill, 1998.

Uffindell, Andrew. *The Eagle's Last Triumph: Napoleon's Victory at Ligny, June 1815.* London: Greenhill, 1994.

Quebec, Battle of (31 December 1775)

The unsuccessful American assault on the seat of British power in Canada. During the early months of the American Revolution, many in the Continental Congress felt that Canada might join in the rebellion against England. The addition of Canada would also deny the British an invasion route into New England. A two-pronged invasion got under way in the fall of 1775. Few gave consideration to the fact that Canada's predominantly French Catholic population was mostly reconciled with English rule and suspicious of American intentions.

Colonel Benedict Arnold led a militia column through present-day Maine, traversing 300 miles through a wilderness devoid of roads or supplies. The group ran out of food and nearly starved to death, losing half its numbers en route. Outside Quebec, Arnold met General Richard Montgomery's force, which had come up through New York and had taken Montreal. The English garrison inside the walled city consisted of British regulars and Canadian militia under Sir Guy Carleton. The besieging Americans were outnumbered 1,800 to 1,000.

Knowing that in the spring British reinforcements would arrive, Arnold and Montgomery decided to assault the city on 31 December. A blizzard dumped snow on the attackers, and barricades impeded their progress. Montgomery and Arnold each struck different sectors of the city. Montgomery was killed at the head of his column, and his survivors retreated. Arnold's force entered the city itself but was unable to push on. Arnold was wounded, and rifleman leader Daniel Morgan was captured. The assault cost 372 casualties. Arnold was forced to retreat with the survivors, ending American hopes of annexing a "fourteenth colony." In the spring, British reinforcements did arrive, and Canada became a base for invasion for the remainder of the war and eventually an independent nation on its own.

Charles M. Dobbs

See also: American Revolution; Arnold, Benedict

References and further reading:

Bird, Harrison. *Attack on Quebec: The American Invasion of Canada, 1775.* New York: Oxford University Press, 1968.

Hatch, Robert M. *Thrust for Canada: The American Attempt on Quebec in 1775–1776.* Boston: Houghton Mifflin, 1979.

Shelton, Hal T. *General Robert Montgomery and the American Revolution.* New York: New York University Press, 1994.

Queen Anne's War (1702–1713)

War between Britain, France, and Spain in North America during the War of the Spanish Succession (1701–1714). Compared to the huge battles and large-scale sieges on the theaters of operation in Europe, the fighting in North America was relatively small-scale. The main reason was probably that New York and the Iroquois, who declared their neutrality in 1701, stayed out of this conflict. Warfare was limited to several raids against French or British villages or strongholds. The most famous example of the frontier campaigns was the Deerfield raid of 1704. Hertel de Rouville, a French Canadian, led 48 militia and around 200 Indians (Abkenaki,

Caughnawagas, and Hurons) 300 miles across the Green Mountains in the depths of winter to attack the town of Deerfield (in present-day Massachusetts) on 29 February. The small force killed 30 to 50 inhabitants, devastated the place, and carried off 100 prisoners on their return.

The New Englanders retaliated in 1704. A force of 550 men from Massachusetts attacked Castine. But as in King William's War (1689–1697), the main objective of the English colonists was Port Royal, the leading French base in Acadia. Two expeditions against this valuable port were launched in June and August 1707. Both failed because of the heavy resistance of the defenders under their new governor, Auger de Subercase. The fiasco called for the use of regulars, and a third attack proved to be successful. Francis Nicholson took the town at the head of 3,000 regular and militia troops in October 1710. By that point, Auger de Subercase commanded only 156 men. Port Royal, renamed Annapolis Royal, remained in English possession and the peninsula of Acadia became British Nova Scotia.

In 1711, the British decided to take New France in what could be called a complex combined military operation. This large expedition was designed to improve Britain's position in negotiations with France. A seaborne force under the command of Rear Admiral Sir Hovenden Walker and Brigadier General John Hill was to sail up the St. Lawrence River to attack Quebec, while Francis Nicholson led an army of 2,300 men from Albany to raid Montreal. Walker's invasion fleet of 31 transports escorted by 14 ships of the line sailed from Boston on 30 July. On board the vessels were 7,500 troops. But on 23–24 August, stormy weather and poor nighttime piloting caused eight transport ships to founder in the mouth of the St. Lawrence. Nearly 900 British sailors, soldiers, and accompanying women drowned near the Ile aux Oeufs. This led not only to the withdrawal of the fleet but also to the abandonment of Nicholson's landward advance on Canada. However, the Peace of Utrecht (1713) left Britain with Nova Scotia, Newfoundland, and Hudson's Bay. These gains strengthened the British position in an expected decisive struggle for the colonies and weakened the defenses of New France.

In the South, some 500 Carolina volunteers and 300 Yamasee under Governor James Moore of Carolina invaded Florida, but the garrison of St. Augustine successfully repulsed the attack. At the head of a large American Indian army, Moore returned in 1704, raiding western Florida and attacking Spanish missions near Tallahassee. Franco-Spanish privateers took revenge in 1706, when they attacked Charleston. This again resulted in British pressure on Florida: raids on Pensacola in 1706 and 1707 and an advance of a small force as far as Mobile in 1709. Although the British took the initiative in the following years, they did not gain any land in Florida from Spain in the Peace of Utrecht. The global contest for supremacy would continue for more than a century.

Juergen Luh

See also: Spanish Succession, War of the

References and further reading:

Black, Jeremy. *Britain as a Military Power, 1688–1815.* London: UCL Press, 1999.

Lynn, John A. *The Wars of Louis XIV, 1667–1714.* London: Longman, 1999.

Queenston Heights (13 October 1812)

One of several American setbacks along the Canadian border during the first year of the War of 1812. Major General Stephen Van Rensselaer, commanding American troops along the Niagara front, hoped to revive American plans to seize Canada following General William Hull's surrender of Detroit (August 1812) by attacking Queenston Heights. The Americans initially gained the advantage by attacking the British rear, but General Alexander Smyth, a regular army officer, refused to take orders from Van Rensselaer, a militia officer, and never moved against Fort George to prevent British general Isaac Brock from sending reinforcements to Queenston Heights. Brock overwhelmed the Americans, nearly forcing them off the precipice before being killed. A subsequent British-Iroquois attack cut the Americans to pieces. The presence of Indians, the sight of Americans returning wounded in battle, and dislike of Van Rensselaer caused the New York militia to refuse to cross the river to join the fight. The Americans lost approximately 90 killed, 100 wounded, and 800 captured at Queenston Heights. This defeat, coupled with failed campaigns against Fort Erie and Montreal in late 1812, contributed to the disintegration of the American army on the Niagara front and demonstrated the difficulty of relying on militia to fight the war, exposing the "War Hawk" Henry Clay's boast that the invasion of Canada would be a "mere matter of marching" by the militia for the ignorant bombast it truly was.

Dean Fafoutis

See also: U.S., Militia; War of 1812

References and further reading:

Compton, Smith C. *The Battle of Queenston Heights, U.C., October 1812: A Collection of Documents and Records Together with Factual Reports Dealing with the Events of the Day.* Toronto: McGraw Hill, 1968.

Hitsman, J. Mackay. *The Incredible War of 1812: A Military History.* Updated by Donald E. Graves. Toronto: Robin Brass Studio, 1999.

Whitfield, Carol. "The Battle of Queenston Heights." *Canadian Historic Sites* 11 (1974).